BRITISH RAILWAYS

LOCOMOTIVES & COACHING STOCK

2024

The Complete Guide to all
Locomotives & Coaching Stock which
operate on the National Rail network and
Eurotunnel

Robert Pritchard

PLATFORM
5

Published by Platform 5 Publishing Ltd,
52 Broadfield Road, Sheffield, S8 0XJ, England.

Printed in England by The Lavenham Press, Lavenham, Suffolk.

ISBN 978 1 915984 18 0

W0007125

CONTENTS

SECTION 1 – LOCOMOTIVES

SECTION 2 – LOCO-HAULED COACHING STOCK

SECTION 3 – DIESEL MULTIPLE UNITS

CONTENTS

SECTION 4 – ELECTRIC MULTIPLE UNITS

SECTION 5 – ON-TRACK MACHINES

SECTION 6 – CODES

COVER PHOTOGRAPHS

Front Cover: BR revised blue-liveried 37418 "An Comunn Gaidhealach" passes Dawlish on 18/07/23 with a 5Z01 14.48 Bristol Temple Meads–Penzance (operated by Loram) hauling Inspection Saloon 975025. **Stephen Ginn**

Back Cover: New Merseyrail unit 777009 leaves Kirkdale with the 12.31 Liverpool Central–Ormskirk on 11/11/23. **Robert Pritchard**

BRITAIN'S RAILWAY SYSTEM

The structure of Britain's railway system has changed significantly during recent years, following the ongoing Covid-19 pandemic and subsequent drop in passenger numbers. Although passengers have since been returning in numbers, that drop during 2020 meant that franchises were no longer profitable and the Government was forced to step in and provide financial support to operators. Initially in March 2020 the Transport Secretary suspended rail franchising and operators transitioned to "Emergency Measures Agreements". These EMAs suspended the normal financial agreements, instead transferring all revenue and cost risk to the Government. Operators in England all accepted these new arrangements and continued to operate trains (initially with reduced service frequencies) for a small management fee. Similar arrangements were put in place by the Scottish and Welsh Governments for ScotRail, Caledonian Sleeper and Transport for Wales.

The EMAs initially lasted for six months from which time longer "Emergency Recovery Management Agreements" (ERMAs) were put in place. These were similar management contracts which continued to see operators run services for a management fee. Since then operators have been transitioning to new National Rail Contracts (NRCs). During an NRC operators are paid a fixed management fee of around 1.5% for operating services and additional small performance fees if agreed targets are achieved.

In the longer term a new body called Great British Railways is planned to take over the running of the railways and specifically take over Network Rail's responsibilities as well as some functions currently carried out by the Department for Transport and Rail Delivery Group. The franchise model is likely to be changed to one of concessions, although this will take some years to fully implement.

In London and on Merseyside concessions are already in place. These see the operator paid a fee to run the service, within tightly specified guidelines. Operators running a concession would not normally take commercial risks, although there are usually penalties and rewards in the contract.

Britain's national railway infrastructure is owned by a "not for dividend" company, Network Rail. In 2014 Network Rail was reclassified as a public sector company, being described by the Government as a "public sector arm's-length body of the Department for Transport".

Most stations and maintenance depots are leased to and operated by the Train Operating Companies (TOCs), but some larger stations are controlled by Network Rail. The only exception is the infrastructure on the Isle of Wight: The Island Line franchise uniquely included maintenance of the infrastructure as well as the operation of passenger services. Both the infrastructure and trains are operated by South Western Railway.

Trains are operated by TOCs over Network Rail tracks (termed the National Network), regulated by access agreements between the parties involved. In general, TOCs are responsible for the provision and maintenance of the trains and staff necessary for the direct operation of services, whilst

Network Rail is responsible for the provision and maintenance of the infrastructure and also for staff to regulate the operation of services.

The Department for Transport (DfT) is the authority for the national network. Transport Scotland has operated ScotRail since April 2022 and is also responsible for the Caledonian Sleeper franchises. In February 2021 the Welsh Government took over the operation of the Wales & Borders franchise (Transport for Wales) from KeolisAmey.

Each franchise was set up with the right to run specified services within a specified area for a period of time, in return for the right to charge fares and, where appropriate, to receive financial support from the Government. Subsidy was payable in respect of socially necessary services. Service standards are monitored by the DfT throughout the duration of the franchise. Franchisees earned revenue primarily from fares and from subsidy. They generally leased stations from Network Rail and earned rental income by sub-letting parts of them, for example to retailers.

TOC's and open access operator's main costs are the track access charges they pay to Network Rail, the costs of leasing stations and rolling stock and of employing staff. Franchisees may do light maintenance work on rolling stock or contract it out to other companies. Heavy maintenance is normally carried out by the Rolling Stock Leasing Companies, according to contracts.

DOMESTIC PASSENGER TRAIN OPERATORS

The majority of passenger trains are operated by Train Operating Companies, now supported by the Government through National Rail Contracts. For reference the date of the expiry of the original franchise is also given here (if later than the current NRC expiry date).

Name of franchise	Operator	Trading Name
Caledonian Sleeper	Scottish Government	**Caledonian Sleeper**

The original Sleeper franchise started in April 2015 when operation of the ScotRail and ScotRail Sleeper franchises was separated. Abellio won the ScotRail franchise and Serco the Caledonian Sleeper franchise. The Scottish Government took over the operation of the Sleeper from Abellio in 2023. Caledonian Sleeper operates four trains nightly between London Euston and Scotland using locomotives hired from GBRf. New CAF Mark 5 rolling stock was introduced during 2019.

Chiltern	Arriva (Deutsche Bahn)	**Chiltern Railways**

NRC until 1 April 2025 with the option to extend to December 2027

Chiltern Railways operates a frequent service between London Marylebone, Oxford, Banbury and Birmingham Snow Hill, with some peak trains extending to Kidderminster. There are also regular services from Marylebone to Stratford-upon-Avon and to Aylesbury Vale Parkway via Amersham (along the London Underground Metropolitan Line). The fleet consists of DMUs of Classes 165, and 168 plus a number of locomotive-hauled rakes used on some of the Birmingham route trains, worked by Class 68s hired from DRS.

Cross Country   Arriva (Deutsche Bahn)   **CrossCountry**
NRC until 15 October 2027 with the option to extend to October 2031

CrossCountry operates a network of long distance services between Scotland, the North-East of England and Manchester to the South-West of England, Reading, Southampton, Bournemouth and Guildford, centred on Birmingham New Street. These trains are formed of diesel Class 220/221 Voyagers. Inter-urban services also link Nottingham, Leicester and Stansted Airport with Birmingham and Cardiff. These trains use Class 170 DMUs.

Crossrail   MTR   **Elizabeth Line**
Concession until 25 May 2025

This concession started in May 2015. Initially Crossrail took over the Liverpool Street–Shenfield stopping service from Greater Anglia, using a fleet of Class 315 EMUs, with the service branded "TfL Rail". The core Crossrail railway in central London started operating in May 2022 and since then the operation has been branded the "Elizabeth Line". Class 345 EMUs are now used on all services running from Reading/Heathrow Airport to Shenfield/Abbey Wood.

East Coast   DfT   **London North Eastern Railway**
Operated by DfT's "Operator of Last Resort" until at least June 2025

LNER operates frequent long distance trains on the East Coast Main Line between London King's Cross, Leeds, Lincoln, Harrogate, York, Newcastle-upon-Tyne and Edinburgh, with less frequent services to Bradford, Skipton, Hull, Middlesbrough, Glasgow, Stirling, Aberdeen and Inverness. A fleet of 65 Hitachi Class 800 and 801 "Azuma" trains (a mix of bi-mode and electric, 5- and 9-car units) operate the majority of services. A small number of Class 91+Mark 4 sets have been retained and are mainly used on Leeds and some York services.

East Midlands   Transport UK Group   **East Midlands Railway**
NRC until 17 October 2026 with the option to extend to October 2030

EMR operates a mix of long distance high speed services on the Midland Main Line (MML), from London St Pancras to Sheffield, Nottingham (plus peak-hour trains to Lincoln) and Corby, and local and regional services ranging from the long distance Norwich–Liverpool route to Nottingham–Skegness, Nottingham–Mansfield–Worksop, Derby–Matlock and Newark Castle–Crewe. It also operates local services across Lincolnshire. Trains on the MML are worked by a fleet of Class 222 DMUs, whilst the local and regional fleet consists of DMU Classes 158 and 170. Class 360 EMUs operate services on the St Pancras–Corby route.

East Anglia   Transport UK Group (60%)/Mitsui Group (40%)   **Greater Anglia**
NRC until 19 September 2024 with option for a 2 year extension; original franchise was until 11 October 2025

Greater Anglia operates main line trains between London Liverpool Street, Ipswich and Norwich and local trains into Norfolk, Suffolk and parts of Cambridgeshire. It also runs local and commuter services into Liverpool Street from the Great Eastern (including Southend, Braintree and Clacton) and West Anglia (including Ely/Cambridge and Stansted Airport) routes. In 2019–20 a new fleet of Stadler EMUs and bi-mode units (Classes 745 and 755) was introduced on the GEML and in East Anglia, replacing older DMUs and loco-hauled trains. A large fleet of 133 new 5-car Class 720 Aventras now operates all other services out of Liverpool Street.

Essex Thameside   Trenitalia   **c2c**
NRC until 25 July 2025; original franchise was until 10 November 2029

c2c operates an intensive, principally commuter, service from London Fenchurch Street to Southend and Shoeburyness, via both Upminster and Tilbury. The fleet consists of 74 Class 357 EMUs and a fleet of 12 new 5-car Class 720 Aventras.

Great Western   First Group   **Great Western Railway**
NRC until 21 June 2025 with the option to extend to June 2028

Great Western Railway operates long distance trains from London Paddington to South Wales, the West Country and Worcester and Hereford. In addition, there are frequent trains along the Thames Valley corridor to Newbury/Bedwyn and Oxford, plus local and regional trains throughout the South-West including the Cornish, Devon and Thames Valley branches, the Reading–Gatwick North Downs Line and Cardiff–Portsmouth Harbour and Bristol–Weymouth regional routes. Long distance services are in the hands of a fleet of Class 800/802 bi-mode InterCity Express Trains. DMUs of Classes 165 and 166 are used on the Thames Valley branches and North Downs routes as well as on local services around Bristol and Exeter and across to Cardiff. Class 387 EMUs are used between Paddington, Reading, Didcot Parkway and Newbury. Classes 150, 158, 165 and 166 and a small fleet of short 4-car HSTs are used on local and regional trains in the South-West. A small fleet of Class 57s is maintained to work the overnight "Cornish Riviera" Sleeper service between London Paddington and Penzance formed of Mark 3 coaches.

London Rail   Arriva (Deutsche Bahn)   **London Overground**
Concession until 3 May 2026

London Overground operates services on the Richmond–Stratford North London Line and the Willesden Junction–Clapham Junction West London Line, plus the East London Line from Highbury & Islington to New Cross and New Cross Gate, with extensions to Clapham Junction (via Denmark Hill), Crystal Palace and West Croydon. It also runs services from London Euston to Watford Junction. All these use Class 378 EMUs, with Class 710s also used on the Watford Junction route. Class 710s operate services on the Gospel Oak–Barking Riverside line. London Overground also operates some suburban services from London Liverpool Street – to Chingford, Enfield Town and Cheshunt. These services mainly use Class 710/1s, with one of these units additionally used on the Romford–Upminster shuttle.

Merseyrail Electrics   Serco (50%)/Transport UK Group (50%)   **Merseyrail**
Concession until 22 July 2028. Under the control of Merseytravel PTE instead of the DfT
Due to be reviewed every five years to fit in with the Merseyside Local Transport Plan

Merseyrail operates services between Liverpool and Southport, Ormskirk, Headbolt Lane (Kirkby), Hunts Cross, New Brighton, West Kirby, Chester and Ellesmere Port. A new fleet of Class 777 EMUs are currently replacing the Class 507 and 508 EMUs.

Northern   DfT   **Northern**
Operated by DfT's "Operator of Last Resort" until further notice

Northern operates a range of inter-urban, commuter and rural services throughout the North of England, including those around the cities of Leeds, Manchester, Sheffield, Liverpool and Newcastle. The network extends from Chathill in the north to Nottingham in the south, and Cleethorpes in the east to St Bees in the west. Long distance services include Leeds–Carlisle, Morpeth–Carlisle and York–Blackpool North. The operator uses a large fleet of DMUs of Classes 150, 155, 156, 158, 170 and 195 plus EMU Classes 323, 331 and 333. New fleets of DMUs (Class 195) and EMUs (Class 331) are used on a number of routes, and were followed by Class 769 bi-mode diesel electric units (converted from Class 319s) in 2021.

ScotRail   Scottish Government   **ScotRail**
Operated by the Scottish Government from April 2022, having taken over ScotRail from Abellio

ScotRail provides almost all passenger services within Scotland and also trains from Glasgow to Carlisle via Dumfries. The company operates a large fleet of DMUs of Classes 156, 158 and 170 and EMU Classes 318, 320, 334, 380 and 385. A fleet of 25 refurbished HSTs have been introduced onto InterCity services between Edinburgh/Glasgow and Aberdeen and Inverness and also between Inverness and Aberdeen. In 2021 five Class 153s were also introduced on the West Highland Line (mainly the Oban line) to provide more capacity and space for bikes and other luggage.

South Eastern   DfT   **Southeastern**
Operated by DfT's "Operator of Last Resort" until further notice.

Southeastern operates all services in the south-east London suburbs, the whole of Kent and part of Sussex, which are primarily commuter services to London. It also operates domestic High Speed trains on HS1 from London St Pancras to Ashford, Ramsgate, Dover and Faversham with additional peak services on other routes. EMUs of Classes 375, 376, 377, 465, 466 and 707 are used, along with Class 395s on the High Speed trains.

South Western   First Group (70%)/MTR (30%)   **South Western Railway**
NRC until 25 May 2025

South Western Railway operates trains from London Waterloo to destinations across the South and South-West including Woking, Basingstoke, Southampton, Portsmouth, Salisbury, Exeter, Reading and Weymouth, as well as suburban services from Waterloo. SWR also runs services between Ryde and Shanklin on the Isle of Wight, from November 2021 using a fleet of five third rail Vivarail Class 484 units (converted former LU D78 stock). The rest of the fleet consists of DMU Classes 158 and 159 and EMU Classes 444, 450, 455, 458 and 701. The new fleet of Bombardier Class 701s are being delivered will enter service during 2024–25.

Thameslink, Southern &   Govia (Go-Ahead/Keolis)   **Govia Thameslink Railway**
Great Northern (TSGN)
NRC until 1 April 2025 with the option to extend to April 2028

TSGN is the largest operator in Great Britain (the former Southern franchise was combined with Thameslink/Great Northern in 2015). GTR uses four brands: "Thameslink" for trains between Cambridge North, Peterborough, Bedford and Rainham, Sevenoaks, East Grinstead, Brighton, Littlehampton and Horsham via central London and also on the Sutton/Wimbledon loop using Class 700 EMUs. "Great Northern" comprises services from London King's Cross and Moorgate to Welwyn Garden City, Hertford North, Peterborough, Cambridge and King's Lynn using Class 387 and 717 EMUs. "Southern" operates predominantly commuter services between London, Surrey and Sussex and "metro" services in South London, as well as services along the south Coast between Southampton, Brighton, Hastings and Ashford, plus the cross-London service from South Croydon to Milton Keynes. Class 171 DMUs are used on Ashford–Eastbourne and London Bridge–Uckfield services, whilst all other services are in the hands of Class 377 and 700 EMUs. Finally, Gatwick Express operates semi-fast trains between London Victoria, Gatwick Airport and Brighton using Class 387/2 EMUs.

Trans-Pennine Express   DfT   **TransPennine Express**
Operated by DfT's "Operator of Last Resort" until further notice.

TransPennine Express operates predominantly long distance inter-urban services linking major cities across the North of England, along with Edinburgh and Glasgow in Scotland. The main services are Manchester Airport–Saltburn, Manchester Piccadilly–Hull, Manchester Piccadilly–York–Scarborough and Liverpool–Newcastle/Edinburgh along the North Trans-Pennine route via Huddersfield, Leeds and York, and Liverpool–Manchester Piccadilly–Cleethorpes along the South Trans-Pennine route via Sheffield. TPE also operates Manchester Airport–Edinburgh/Glasgow and Liverpool–Glasgow services. The fleet consists of Class 185

DMUs, plus Class 397s used on Manchester Airport/Liverpool–Scotland and Class 802 bi-mode units used mainly on Liverpool–Newcastle/Edinburgh.

Wales & Borders   Welsh Government   Transport for Wales

From February 2021 the Welsh Government took direct control of rail service operation. Infrastructure management continues to be managed by KeolisAmey.

Transport for Wales was procured by the Welsh Government and operates a mix of long distance, regional and local services throughout Wales, including the Valley Lines network of lines around Cardiff, and also through services to the English border counties and to Manchester and Birmingham. The fleet consists of DMUs of Classes 150, 153, 158, 197 and 231 and locomotive-hauled Mark 4 sets hauled by Class 67s. Rebuilt Class 230 diesel-battery units are used on some services on the Wrexham–Bidston line and new Stadler fleets (Classes 398/756) will be introduced in South Wales by 2025, with Class 197s rolled out elsewhere.

West Coast Partnership   First Group (70%)/Trenitalia (30%)   Avanti West Coast

NRC until 18 October 2026 with the option to extend to 17 October 2032

Avanti West Coast operates long distance services along the West Coast Main Line from London Euston to Birmingham/Wolverhampton, Manchester, Liverpool, Blackpool North and Glasgow/Edinburgh using Class 390 Pendolino EMUs. It also operates Class 221 Voyagers on the Euston–Chester–Holyhead route and a small number of trains from Wolverhampton to Shrewsbury and to Wrexham. New Hitachi Class 805 and 807 units are due into service from 2024.

West Midlands Trains   Transport UK Group (70%)/JR East (15%)/West Midlands Railway/ Mitsui (15%)   London Northwestern

NRC until 19 September 2024 with option to extend to September 2026; original franchise ran until 31 March 2026

West Midlands Trains operates services under two brand names. West Midlands Railway trains are local and regional services around Birmingham, including to Stratford-upon-Avon, Worcester, Hereford, Redditch, Rugeley and Shrewsbury. WMR is managed by a consortium of 16 councils and the Department for Transport. London Northwestern is the brand used for long distance and regional services from London Euston to Northampton and Birmingham/ Crewe and also between Birmingham and Liverpool, Bedford–Bletchley and Watford Junction–St Albans Abbey. The fleet consists of DMU Classes 139, 150, 172 and 196 and EMU Classes 323, 350 and 730. New fleets of CAF Class 196 DMUs and Alstom Class 730 EMUs are being introduced across a number of routes.

NON-FRANCHISED SERVICES

The following operators run non-franchised, or "open access" services
(* special seasonal services):

Operator	Trading Name	Route
Heathrow Airport Holdings	Heathrow Express	London Paddington–Heathrow Airport

Heathrow Express is a frequent express passenger service between London
Paddington and Heathrow Airport using a sub-fleet of Great Western
Railway Class 387 EMUs (operated jointly with GWR).

Hull Trains (part of First)	Hull Trains	London King's Cross–Hull

Hull Trains operates seven trains a day on weekdays from Hull to London
King's Cross via the East Coast Main Line. Bi-mode Class 802s were
introduced in 2019–20. Two trains in each direction start back from and
extend to Beverley.

Grand Central (part of Arriva)	Grand Central	London King's Cross–Sunderland/ Bradford Interchange

Grand Central operates five trains a day from Sunderland and four from
Bradford Interchange to London King's Cross using Class 180 or 221 DMUs.

Locomotive Services (TOC)	Locomotive Services	

Locomotive Services runs various excursions across the network using
diesel, electric and steam locomotives operating under the brands Saphos
Trains (principally steam-hauled trips), Statesman Rail (diesel-locomotive
hauled trips and land cruises), Rail Charter Services, Midland Pullman (HST
tours using the luxury HST set) and Intercity (mainly electric locomotive-
hauled tours).

First East Coast	Lumo	London King's Cross–Edinburgh

Lumo started operating services from London to Edinburgh via the East
Coast Main Line in October 2021 and now operates five trains per day using
new electric Class 803 units.

North Yorkshire Moors Railway Enterprises	North Yorkshire Moors Railway	Pickering–Grosmont–Whitby/ Battersby, Sheringham–Cromer*

The North Yorkshire Moors Railway operates services on the national
network between Grosmont and Whitby as an extension of its Pickering–
Grosmont services and also operates services between Sheringham and
Cromer on behalf of the North Norfolk Railway.

South Yorkshire Supertram	Stagecoach Supertram	Meadowhall South–Rotherham Parkgate

South Yorkshire Supertram holds a passenger licence to allow the operation
of the pilot tram-train service linking Sheffield city centre with Rotherham
Central and Rotherham Parkgate.

| Tyne & Wear PTE | Tyne & Wear Metro | Pelaw–Sunderland |

Tyne & Wear Passenger Transport Executive holds a passenger license to allow the operation of its Metro service over Network Rail tracks between Pelaw and Sunderland.

| Vintage Trains | Vintage Trains | Birmingham Snow Hill–Stratford-upon-Avon* |

Vintage Trains operates steam-hauled services on a seasonal basis.

| West Coast Railway Company | West Coast Railway Company | Fort William–Mallaig*
York–Settle–Carlisle*
Carnforth–York–Scarborough* |

WCRC operates steam-hauled services on these routes on a seasonal basis and a range of other excursions across the network, including the Northern Belle luxury train.

INTERNATIONAL PASSENGER OPERATORS

Eurostar International operates passenger services between London St Pancras and mainland Europe. The company, established in 2010, is jointly owned by SNCF (the national operator of France): 55%, SNCB (the national operator of Belgium): 5% and Patina Rail: 40%. Patina Rail is made up of Canadian-based Caisse de dépôt et placement du Québec (CDPG) and UK-based Hermes Infrastructure (owning 30% and 10% respectively). This 40% was previously owned by the UK Government until it was sold in 2015.

In addition, a service for the conveyance of accompanied road vehicles through the Channel Tunnel is provided by the tunnel operating company, Eurotunnel. All Eurotunnel services are operated in top-and-tail mode by the powerful Class 9 Bo-Bo-Bo locomotives.

FREIGHT TRAIN OPERATORS

The following operators operate freight services or empty passenger stock workings under "Open Access" arrangements:

Colas Rail: Colas Rail operates a number of On-Track Machines and also supplies infrastructure monitoring trains for Network Rail. It also operates a number of different freight flows, including oil and timber. Colas Rail has a small but varied fleet consisting of Class 37s, 56s, 66s and 70s. It also uses HST power cars (Class 43) on some Network Rail test trains.

DB Cargo (UK): The biggest freight operator in the country, DBC (EWS until bought by Deutsche Bahn, when it was initially called DB Schenker) provides a large number of infrastructure trains to Network Rail and also operates biomass, steel, intermodal and aggregate trains nationwide. The core fleet is Class 66s. Of the original 250 ordered, 69 are currently working with DB's French and Polish operations, although some of the French locos do return to the UK when major maintenance is required and others have returned to the UK permanently. The small pool of remaining Class 60s are due to be withdrawn in 2024.

DBC's fleet of Class 67s are used on passenger or standby duties for Transport for Wales and LNER and also on excursions or special trains. The Class 90s have all now been stored and the Class 92s are mainly used on a limited number of overnight freights on High Speed 1.

DBC also operates the Class 325 EMUs for Royal Mail.

Devon & Cornwall Railways (part of Cappagh Construction Contractors (London)): DCRail specialises in short-term freight haulage contracts, using Class 56s or four Class 60s acquired from DB Cargo. It has also purchased a number of other Class 60s, some of which will be returned to service.

Direct Rail Services: DRS has built on its original nuclear flask traffic to operate a number of different services. The main flows are intermodal plus the provision of crews and locomotives to Network Rail for autumn RailHead Treatment Trains and also infrastructure trains. DRS has a varied fleet of locomotives, with Class 37s, 57s and 66s working alongside the more modern Class 68s and diesel-electric Class 88s. Class 68s are hired to Chiltern Railways for passenger work.

Freightliner: Freightliner (owned by Genesee & Wyoming) operates container trains from the main Ports at Southampton, Felixstowe, Tilbury and London Gateway to major cities including London, Manchester, Leeds and Birmingham. It also operates trains of coal, cement, infrastructure and aggregates. Most services are worked by Class 66s, with Class 70s mainly used on some of the heavier intermodal trains and cement trains from the Peak District. A fleet of Class 90 electrics are used on intermodal trains on the Great Eastern and West Coast Main Lines, this includes 13 locomotives previously operated by Greater Anglia.

The six Class 59/2s were purchased from DB Cargo and are used alongside the Mendip Rail 59/0s and 59/1s on stone traffic from the Mendip quarries and around the South-East.

GB Railfreight: GBRf (owned by Infracapital) operates a mixture of traffic types, mainly using Class 66s together with a small fleet of Class 73s on infrastructure duties and test trains in the South-East and ten Class 60s acquired from Colas Rail in 2018. The company has also now purchased a number of Class 56s and owns a single Class 59, 59003. Most of the Class 56s are being rebuilt as Class 69s with a new GM engine. A fleet of Class 92s is also used on some intermodal flows to and from Dollands Moor or through the Channel Tunnel to Calais. Traffic includes coal, intermodal, biomass, aggregates and gypsum as well as infrastructure services for Network Rail and London Underground. GBRf also supplies various locomotives, including Classes 66, 73/9 and 92 to work the Caledonian Sleeper and owns the three former Colas Rail Class 47s as well as leasing some Class 57/3s from Porterbrook.

GBRf operates some excursion trains, including those using the preserved Class 201 "Hastings" DEMU.

LORAM (UK): LORAM has a freight license and operates a limited number of trains, most hauling On-Track Machines on inspections saloons using hired-in locomotives operating on behalf of Network Rail.

Rail Adventure: This German based company now has a UK license and has rebuilt some former Grand Central/East Midlands HST power cars for stock movements. In 2022 the company took over Birmingham based train operating company SLC Operations which operates a number of contracts for Network Rail.

Rail Operations Group: This company mainly facilitates rolling stock movements by providing drivers or using locomotives hired from other companies or by using Class 37s hired from Europhoenix. It has also operated trails using Class 319 and 768 bi-mode units on parcels logistics services under its **Orion** subsidiary. The company plans to introduce its new Class 93 locomotives in 2024.

Varamis Rail: This new operator obtained an operating license in 2022 and has been operating Class 321 units converted to carry parcels. A new service started linking Birmingham with Glasgow in 2022.

West Coast Railway Company: WCRC has a freight licence but doesn't operate any freight as such – only empty stock movements. Its fleet of Class 47s, supplemented by steam locomotives and a smaller number of Class 33s, 37s and 57s, is used on excursion work nationwide.

In addition, Amey, Balfour Beatty Rail, Harsco Rail, Swietelsky Babcock Rail (SB Rail) and VolkerRail operate trains formed of On-Track Machines.

PROVISION OF INFORMATION

This book has been compiled with care to be as accurate as possible, but some information is not easily available and the publisher cannot be held responsible for any errors or omissions. We would like to thank the companies and individuals who have been helpful in supplying information to us. The author is always pleased to receive notification of any inaccuracies that may be found, to enhance future editions. Please send comments to:

Robert Pritchard, Platform 5 Publishing Ltd, 52 Broadfield Road, Sheffield, S8 0XJ, England.

e-mail: robert.pritchard@platform5.com   **Tel:** 0114 255 2625.

UPDATES

This book is updated to the start of January 2024. The Platform 5 railway magazine "**Today's Railways UK**" publishes Stock Changes every month to update this book. The magazine also contains news and rolling stock information on the railways of Great Britain and is normally published on the second Monday of every month. For further details of **Today's Railways UK**, please contact Platform 5 Publishing Ltd or visit our website **www.platform5.com**.

1. LOCOMOTIVES

INTRODUCTION

This section contains details of all locomotives which can run on Britain's national railway network, plus those of Eurotunnel.

Locomotives currently approved for use on the national railway network fall into four broad types: passenger, freight, mixed traffic and shunting.

Passenger
The number of dedicated passenger locomotives has not changed significantly in recent years. Classes 43 (HST) and 91 and some members of Classes 57, 67, 68, 73/9 and 92 are dedicated to franchised and Open Access passenger operations. Excursion trains have a few dedicated locomotives but mainly use locomotives that are best described as mixed traffic.

Freight
By far the most numerous locomotives are those used solely for bulk commodity and intermodal freight. Since 1998 a large number of new Class 66 locomotives have replaced many former BR designs and in more recent years smaller numbers of Class 70s have also been introduced. There are however a significant number of BR era Class 20, 37, 47, 50, 56, 60, 73/1, 90 and 92 locomotives still in use; their number has increased slightly as some locomotives have been reinstated to cope with demand. In addition, there is a small fleet of Class 59s acquired privately in the 1980s and 1990s and a number of re-engined Class 57s in use.

Mixed Traffic
In addition to their use on passenger and commodity freight workings these locomotives are used for stock movements and specialist infrastructure and test trains. The majority, but not all, are fitted with Electric Train Supply. Locomotives from Classes 20, 33, 37, 47, 57, 67, 68, 73/9, 88 and 90 fall into this category. Also included under this heading are preserved locomotives permitted to operate on the national railway network. Although these have in the past solely operated excursion trains they are increasingly seeing occasional use on other types of trains. Some, such as Class 50s with GB Railfreight, are frequently used by the main freight companies.

Shunting
Very few shunting locomotives are now permitted to operate freely on the National Railway network. The small number that are have to be fitted with a plethora of safety equipment in order to have engineering acceptance. They are mainly used for local workings such as trips between yards or stock movements between depots and stations. Otherwise, shunting locomotives are not permitted to venture from depots or yards onto the National Railway network other than into defined limits within interface infrastructure. Remotely-controlled driverless shunters are not included in this book. However, all ex-BR shunting locomotives are listed under Section 1.1 "Diesel Shunting Locomotives".

Locomotives which are owned by, for example, DB Cargo or Freightliner, which have been withdrawn from service and are awaiting disposal are listed in the main part of the book. Locomotives which are awaiting disposal at scrapyards are listed in the "Locomotives Awaiting Disposal" section.

Only preserved locomotives which are currently passed for operation on the National Railway network are included. Others, which may still be Network Rail registered but not at present certified for use, are not included, but can be found in the Platform 5 book, "Preserved Locomotives of British Railways".

LAYOUT OF INFORMATION

Locomotive classes are listed in numerical order of class. Principal details and dimensions are quoted for each class in metric and/or imperial units as considered appropriate bearing in mind common UK usage.

The heading "Total" indicates how many of that particular class are listed in this book.

Where numbers actually carried are different from those officially allocated, these are noted in class headings where appropriate. Where locomotives have been recently renumbered, the most immediate previous number is shown in parentheses. Each entry is laid out as in the following example:

No.	Detail	Livery	Owner	Pool		Allocn.	Name
60055 +	**DC**	DC	DCRO		TO		Thomas Barnado

Detail Differences. Only detail differences which currently affect the areas and types of train which locomotives may work are shown. Where such differences occur within a class or part class, they are shown in the "Detail" column alongside the individual locomotive number.

Codes: Codes are used to denote the livery, owner, pool and depot of each locomotive. Details of these will be found in section 6 of this book.

The owner is the responsible custodian of the locomotive and this may not always be the legal owner. Actual ownership can be very complicated. Some vehicles are owned by finance/leasing companies. Others are owned by subsidiary companies of a holding company or by an associate company of the responsible custodian or operator.

Depot allocation codes for all locomotives are shown in this book (apart from shunting locomotives where the actual location of each is shown). It should be noted that today much locomotive maintenance is undertaken away from these depots. This may be undertaken at fuelling points, berthing sidings or similar, or by mobile maintenance teams. Therefore locomotives in particular may not return to their "home" depots as often as in the past.

(S) denotes that the locomotive is stored (the actual location is shown).

Names: Only names carried with official sanction are listed. Names are shown in UPPER/lower case characters as actually shown on the name carried on the locomotive.

Builders: These are shown in the class headings. More details and a full list of builders can be found in section 6.7.

GENERAL INFORMATION

CLASSIFICATION AND NUMBERING

All locomotives are classified and allocated numbers under the TOPS numbering system, introduced in 1972. This comprises a two-digit class number followed by a three-digit serial number.

For diesel locomotives, class numbers offer an indication of engine horsepower as shown in the table below.

Class No. Range	Engine hp
01–14	0–799
15–20	800–1000
21–31	1001–1499
32–39	1500–1999
40–54, 57	2000–2999
55–56, 58–70	3000+

For electric locomotives class numbers are allocated in ascending numerical order under the following scheme:

Class 71–80   Direct current and DC/diesel dual system locomotives.
Class 81 onwards   Alternating current and AC/DC dual system locomotives.

Numbers in the 89101–89999 series are allocated to locomotives which have been deregistered but subsequently re-registered for use on the national railway network and whose original number has already been reused. These numbers are normally only carried inside locomotive cabs and are not carried externally in normal circumstances.

WHEEL ARRANGEMENT

For main line locomotives the number of driven axles on a bogie or frame is denoted by a letter (A = 1, B = 2, C = 3) and the number of non-powered axles is denoted by a number. The use of the letter "o" after a letter indicates each axle is individually powered, whilst the "+" symbol indicates bogies are inter-coupled.

For shunting locomotives, the Whyte notation is used. In this notation the number of leading wheels are given, followed by the number of driving wheels and then the trailing wheels.

UNITS OF MEASUREMENT

All dimensions and weights are quoted for locomotives in an "as new" condition with all necessary supplies (eg oil, water and sand) on board. Dimensions are quoted in the order length x width. Lengths quoted are over buffers or couplers as appropriate. All widths quoted are maxima. Where two different wheel diameter dimensions are shown, the first refers to powered wheels and the second refers to non-powered wheels. All weights are shown as metric tonnes (t = tonnes).

HAULAGE CAPABILITY OF DIESEL LOCOMOTIVES

The haulage capability of a diesel locomotive depends upon three basic factors:

1. Adhesive weight. The greater the weight on the driving wheels, the greater the adhesion and more tractive power can be applied before wheelslip occurs.

2. The characteristics of its transmission. To start a train the locomotive has to exert a pull at standstill. A direct drive diesel engine cannot do this, hence the need for transmission. This may be mechanical, hydraulic or electric. The present British Standard for locomotives is electric transmission. Here the diesel engine drives a generator or alternator and the current produced is fed to the traction motors. The force produced by each driven wheel depends on the current in its traction motor. In other words, the larger the current, the harder it pulls. As the locomotive speed increases, the current in the traction motor falls, hence the *Maximum Tractive Effort* is the maximum force at its wheels the locomotive can exert at a standstill. The electrical equipment cannot take such high currents for long without overheating. Hence the *Continuous Tractive Effort* is quoted which represents the current which the equipment can take continuously.

3. The power of its engine. Not all power reaches the rail, as electrical machines are approximately 90% efficient. As the electrical energy passes through two such machines (the generator or alternator and the traction motors), the *Power at Rail* is approximately 81% (90% of 90%) of the engine power, less a further amount used for auxiliary equipment such as radiator fans, traction motor blowers, air compressors, battery charging, cab heating, Electric Train Supply (ETS) etc. The power of the locomotive is proportional to the tractive effort times the speed. Hence when on full power there is a speed corresponding to the continuous tractive effort.

HAULAGE CAPABILITY OF ELECTRIC LOCOMOTIVES

Unlike a diesel locomotive, an electric locomotive does not develop its power on board and its performance is determined only by two factors, namely its weight and the characteristics of its electrical equipment. Whereas a diesel locomotive tends to be a constant power machine, the power of an electric locomotive varies considerably. Up to a certain speed it can produce virtually a constant tractive effort. Hence power rises with speed according to the formula given in section three above, until a maximum speed is reached at which tractive effort falls, such that the power also falls. Hence the power at the speed corresponding to the maximum tractive effort is lower than the maximum speed.

BRAKE FORCE

Brake Force (also known as brake power) is a measure of the braking power of a locomotive. The Brake Force available is dependant on the adhesion between the rail and the wheels being braked and the normal reaction of the rail on the wheels being braked (and hence on the weight per braked wheel). A locomotive's Brake Force is shown on its data panels so operating staff can ensure sufficient brake power is available for specific trains.

ELECTRIC TRAIN SUPPLY (ETS)

A number of locomotives are equipped to provide a supply of electricity to the train being hauled to power auxiliaries such as heating, cooling fans, air conditioning and kitchen equipment. ETS is provided from the locomotive by means of a separate alternator (except Class 33 locomotives, which have a DC generator). The ETS index of a locomotive is a measure of the electrical power available for train supply. Class 55 locomotives provide an ETS directly from one of their traction generators into the train supply.

Similarly, most locomotive-hauled carriages also have an ETS index, which in this case is a measure of the power required to operate equipment mounted in the carriage. The sum of the ETS indices of all the hauled vehicles in a train must not exceed the ETS index of the locomotive.

ETS is commonly (but incorrectly) known as ETH (Electric Train Heating), which is a throwback to the days before locomotive-hauled carriages were equipped with electrically powered auxiliary equipment other than for train heating.

ROUTE AVAILABILITY (RA)

This is a measure of a railway vehicle's axle load. The higher the axle load of a vehicle, the higher the RA number on a scale from 1 to 10. Each Network Rail route has a RA number and in general no vehicle with a higher RA number may travel on that route without special clearance.

MULTIPLE WORKING

Multiple working between vehicles (ie two or more powered vehicles being driven from one cab) is facilitated by jumper cables connecting the vehicles. However, not all types of locomotive are compatible with each other, and a number of different systems are in use. Some are compatible with others, some are not. BR used "multiple working codes" to designate which locomotives were compatible. The list below shows which classes of locomotives are compatible with each other – the former BR multiple working code being shown in brackets. It should be noted that some locomotives have had the equipment removed or made inoperable.

With other classes:
Classes 20, 25, 31, 33, 37 40 & 73/1*. (Blue Star)
Classes 56 & 58. (Red Diamond)
Classes 59, 66, 67, 68, 70, 73/9 & 88.
* DRS adapted the systems so its Classes 20/3, 37 & 57 could work with each other only.

With other members of same class only:
Class 43, Class 47 (Green Circle), Class 50 (Orange Square), Class 60.

PUSH-PULL OPERATION

Some locomotives are modified to operate passenger and service (formed of laboratory, test and inspection carriages) trains in "push-pull" mode – which allows the train to be driven from either end – either with locomotives at each end (both under power) or with a driving brake van at one end and a locomotive at the other. Various different systems are now in use. Electric locomotive Classes 86, 87, 90 & 91 use a time-division multiplex (TDM) system for push-pull working which utilises the existing Railway Clearing House (RCH) jumper cables fitted to carriages. Previously these cables had only been used to control train lighting and public address systems.

More recently locomotives of Classes 67 and 68 have used the Association of American Railroads (AAR) system.

ABBREVIATIONS

Standard abbreviations used in this book are:

a   Train air brake equipment only.
b   Drophead buckeye couplers.
c   Scharfenberg couplers.
d   Fitted with retractable Dellner couplers.
e   European Railway Traffic Management System (ERTMS) signalling equipment fitted.
k   Fitted with Swinghead Automatic "buckeye" combination couplers.
p   Train air, vacuum and electro-pneumatic brakes.
r   Radio Electric Token Block signalling equipment fitted.
s   Slow Speed Control equipment.
v   Train vacuum brake only.
x   Train air and vacuum brakes ("Dual brakes").
+   Additional fuel tank capacity.

In all cases use of the above abbreviations indicates the equipment in question is normally operable. The definition of non-standard abbreviations and symbols is detailed in individual class headings.

1.1. DIESEL SHUNTING LOCOMOTIVES

All BR design shunting locomotives still in existence, apart from those considered to be preserved, are listed together in this section. Preserved shunting locomotives are listed in the Platform 5 publication "Preserved Locomotives of British Railways" (a small number are listed in both that book and in this publication).

Few shunting locomotives have engineering acceptance and are equipped to operate on Network Rail infrastructure (beyond interface infrastructure), but those that are known to be permitted are indicated here.

For shunting locomotives, instead of the two-letter depot code, actual locations at the time of publication are given. Pool codes for shunting locomotives are not shown.

CLASS 03   BR/GARDNER   0-6-0

Built: 1958–62 by BR at Swindon or Doncaster Works.
Engine: Gardner 8L3 of 152 kW (204 hp) at 1200 rpm.
Transmission: Mechanical. Fluidrive type 23 hydraulic coupling to Wilson-Drewry CA5R7 gearbox with SCG type RF11 final drive.
Maximum Tractive Effort: 68 kN (15300 lbf).
Continuous Tractive Effort: 68 kN (15300 lbf) at 3.75 mph.
Train Brakes: Air & vacuum.
Brake Force: 13 t.   **Dimensions:** 7.93 x 2.59 m.
Weight: 31.3 t.   **Wheel Diameter:** 1092 mm.
Design Speed: 28.5 mph.   **Maximum Speed:** 28.5 mph.
Fuel Capacity: 1364 litres.   **Route Availability:** 1.
Train Supply: Not equipped.   **Total:** 2.

Number Notes Livery Owner Location

Number	Notes	Livery	Owner	Location
03084		G	WC	West Coast Railway Company, Carnforth Depot
D2381	v	G	WC	West Coast Railway Company, Carnforth Depot (S)

CLASS 07   BR/RUSTON & HORNSBY   0-6-0

Built: 1962 by Ruston & Hornsby, Lincoln.
Engine: Paxman 6RPHL Mk III of 205 kW (275 hp) at 1360 rpm.
Transmission: Electric. One AEI RTB 6652 traction motor.
Maximum Tractive Effort: 126 kN (28240 lbf).
Continuous Tractive Effort: 71 kN (15950 lbf) at 4.38 mph.
Train Brakes: Vacuum.
Brake Force:
Weight: 43.6 t.   **Dimensions:** 8.17 x 2.59 m.
Design Speed: 20 mph.   **Wheel Diameter:** 1067 mm.
Fuel Capacity: 1400 litres.   **Maximum Speed:** 20 mph.
Total: 1.   **Train Supply:** Not equipped.

Number	Notes	Livery	Owner	Location
07007	v	B	AF	Arlington Fleet Services, Eastleigh Works, Hants

Other number or name carried: 2991 Bruce

CLASS 08   BR/ENGLISH ELECTRIC   0-6-0

Built: 1955–62 by BR at Crewe, Darlington, Derby Locomotive, Doncaster or Horwich Works.
Engine: English Electric 6KT of 298 kW (400 hp) at 680 rpm.
Main Generator: English Electric 801.
Traction Motors: Two English Electric 506.
Maximum Tractive Effort: 156 kN (35000 lbf). § 200 kN (45 000 lbf).
Continuous Tractive Effort: 49 kN (11100 lbf) at 8.8 mph.

Power at Rail: 194 kW (260 hp).	**Train Brakes:** Air & vacuum.
Brake Force: 19 t.	**Dimensions:** 8.92 x 2.59 m.
Weight: 49.6–50.4 t.	**Wheel Diameter:** 1372 mm.
Design Speed: 20 mph.	**Maximum Speed:** 15 mph.
Fuel Capacity: 3037 litres.	**Route Availability:** 5.
Train Supply: Not equipped.	**Total:** 172.

* Locomotives with engineering acceptance to operate on Network Rail infrastructure. 08850 has acceptance for use between Grosmont and Whitby only, for rescue purposes.

§ 08308 has been converted into a battery powered prototype by Positive Traction as part of the "08e" project with battery packs providing 331 kW (450 hp).

† – Fitted with remote control equipment.

Non-standard liveries:

08308   Green & silver "08e".
08401   Dark green.
08442   Dark grey lower bodyside & light grey upper bodyside.
08445   Yellow, blue & green.
08447   Lilac.
08502   Mid blue.
08568   Dark grey lower bodyside & light grey upper bodyside. Red solebar stripe.
08598   Yellow.
08600   Red with a light grey roof.
08630   Black with red cabsides and solebar stripe.
08645   All over black with a white cross.
08682   Multi-coloured.
08730   ABP Ports blue
08774   Red with a light grey roof.
08899   Crimson lake.
08956   Serco Railtest dark green.

Number	Notes	Livery	Owner	Location
08220	v	**B**	EE	Nottingham Transport Heritage Centre, Ruddington
08308	§ a	**O**	PT	Barrow Hill Roundhouse, Chesterfield, Derbys
08331		**K**	20	Midland Railway-Butterley, Derbyshire
08375	a	**RL**	RL	Victoria Group, Port of Boston, Boston
08389	a†	**E**	HN	Celsa Steel UK, Tremorfa Steelworks, Cardiff
08401	a	**O**	ED	Hunslet Engine Company, Barton-under-Needwood, Staffs
08405	a†	**E**	RS	Northern, Neville Hill Depot, Leeds

08410	* a	GW	AD	AV Dawson, Ayrton Rail Terminal, Middlesbrough
08411	a	B	RS	RSS, Rye Farm, Wishaw, Sutton Coldfield (S)
08417	* a	Y	HN	West Midlands Trains, Tyseley Depot, Birmingham
08418	a	E	WC	West Coast Railway Company, Carnforth Depot (S)
08423	a	RL	RL	Weardale Railway, Wolsingham, County Durham
08428	ak	E	HN	Barrow Hill Roundhouse, Chesterfield, Derbys (S)
08441	* a	RS	RS	Greater Anglia, Crown Point Depot, Norwich
08442	a	0	WM	Nemesis Rail, Burton-on-Trent, Staffordshire (S)
08445	a	0	ED	Daventry International Railfreight Terminal, Crick
08447	a	0	RU	Assenta Rail, Hamilton, Glasgow (S)
08451	*	B	AM	Alstom, Polmadie Depot, Glasgow
08454		B	AM	Alstom, Widnes Technology Centre, Cheshire
08460	a	RS	RS	GB Railfreight, Bescot Yard
08472	* a	WA	ED	Reid Freight, Longton, Stoke-on-Trent (S)
08473		B	WM	Nemesis Rail, Burton-on-Trent, Staffordshire (S)
08480	* a	RS	RS	Hitachi, Craigentinny Depot, Edinburgh
08483	* a	K	LS	L&NWR Heritage Company, Crewe Diesel Depot
08484		RS	RS	Greater Anglia, Crown Point Depot, Norwich
08485	a	B	WC	West Coast Railway Company, Carnforth Depot
08495		B	WM	Nemesis Rail, Burton-on-Trent, Staffordshire (S)
08499	a	B	TW	Transport for Wales, Canton Depot, Cardiff
08500		E	HN	HNRC, Worksop Depot, Nottinghamshire (S)
08502		0	HN	HNRC, Worksop Depot, Nottinghamshire (S)
08507	a	RB	RS	GB Railfreight, Whitemoor Yard, March, Cambs
08511	a	RS	RS	GB Railfreight, Eastleigh East Yard
08516	a	AW	RS	Arriva TrainCare, Bristol Barton Hill Depot
08523	*	B	RL	EMD, Longport Works, Stoke-on-Trent
08525		ST	EM	Northern, Neville Hill Depot, Leeds (S)
08527		FA	HN	Barrow Hill Roundhouse, Chesterfield, Derbys (S)
08530	*	FL	FL	Hunslet Engine Company, Barton-under-Needwood, Staffs (S)
08531	* a	FH	FL	Nemesis Rail, Burton-on-Trent, Staffordshire
08536		B	RS	RSS, Rye Farm, Wishaw, Sutton Coldfield (S)
08567		AG	AF	Arlington Fleet Services, Eastleigh Works
08568		0	RS	RSS, Rye Farm, Wishaw, Sutton Coldfield (S)
08571	* a	WA	ED	Barrow Hill Roundhouse, Chesterfield, Derbys (S)
08573		K	RL	Weardale Railway, Wolsingham, County Durham
08575		FL	FL	Nemesis Rail, Burton-on-Trent, Staffordshire (S)
08578		E	HN	HNRC, Worksop Depot, Nottinghamshire (S)
08580	*	RS	RS	RSS, Rye Farm, Wishaw, Sutton Coldfield
08585	*	FG	FL	Freightliner, Trafford Park FLT
08588		RL	RL	Alstom, Ilford Works, London
08593		E	RS	RSS, Rye Farm, Wishaw, Sutton Coldfield (S)
08596	* a†	WA	ED	Reid Freight, Longton, Stoke-on-Trent (S)
08598		0	AD	AV Dawson, Ayrton Rail Terminal, Middlesbrough
08600	a	0	AD	AV Dawson, Ayrton Rail Terminal, Middlesbrough
08605	†	IC	RS	Willesden Euroterminal Stone Terminal, London
08611	*	B	AM	Alstom, Wembley Depot, London
08613		RL	RL	PD Ports, Teesport, Grangetown, Middlesbrough
08615	*	HU	ED	Hunslet Engine Company, Barton-under-Needwood, Staffs
08616		LM	WM	West Midlands Trains, Tyseley Depot, Birmingham
08617	*	B	AM	Alstom, Oxley Depot, Wolverhampton

08622		K	RL	Heidelberg Materials, Ketton Cement Works, nr Stamford
08623		DB	HN	HNRC, Worksop Depot, Nottinghamshire (S)
08624	*	FG	FL	Freightliner, Felixstowe FLT
08629		RS	RS	Daventry International Railfreight Terminal, Crick
08630	†	O	HN	Celsa Steel UK, Tremorfa Steelworks, Cardiff
08631		B	LS	L&NWR Heritage Company, Crewe Diesel Depot
08632	†	RS	RS	GB Railfreight, Peterborough Depot
08641	*	B	GW	Great Western Railway, Laira Depot, Plymouth
08643		B	ED	Aggregate Industries, Merehead Rail Terminal
08644	*	B	GW	Great Western Railway, Laira Depot, Plymouth
08645	*	O	GW	Great Western Railway, Long Rock Depot, Penzance
08648	*	K	RL	ScotRail, Inverness Depot
08649		KB	ME	Gemini Rail Group, Wolverton Works, Milton Keynes (S)
08650		B	MR	Heidelberg Materials, Whatley Quarry, near Frome
08652		B	RS	RSS, Rye Farm, Wishaw, Sutton Coldfield (S)
08653		E	HN	Shackerstone, Battlefield Line (S)
08663	* a	B	HH	Hitachi, Newton Aycliffe, Co Durham
08669	* a	WA	ED	Wabtec Rail, Doncaster Works
08670	* a	RS	RS	GB Railfreight, Bescot Yard
08676		E	HN	East Kent Light Railway, Shepherdswell, Kent (S)
08678	a	WC	WC	West Coast Railway Company, Carnforth Depot
08682		O	HN	Shackerstone, Battlefield Line (S)
08683	*	RS	RS	GB Railfreight, Eastleigh East Yard
08685		E	HN	Barrow Hill Roundhouse, Chesterfield, Derbys (S)
08690		ST	EM	Northern, Neville Hill Depot, Leeds (S)
08691	*	FG	FL	Freightliner, Ipswich Depot
08696	* a	B	AM	Alstom, Wembley Depot, London
08700		B	RL	HNRC, Worksop Depot, Nottinghamshire
08701	a	RX	HN	Shackerstone, Battlefield Line (S)
08703	a	GB	RS	RSS, Rye Farm, Wishaw, Sutton Coldfield
08704		RB	RV	DB Cargo UK, Knottingley Depot
08706	†	E	RS	Colne Valley Railway
08709		E	RS	RSS, Rye Farm, Wishaw, Sutton Coldfield (S)
08711	k	RX	HN	Nemesis Rail, Burton-on-Trent, Staffordshire (S)
08714		E	HN	HNRC, Worksop Depot, Nottinghamshire (S)
08721	*	B	AM	Alstom, Widnes Technology Centre, Cheshire
08724	*	WA	ED	Wabtec Rail, Doncaster Works
08730		O	RS	European Metal Recycling, Kingsbury, nr Tamworth
08735	†	AW	AV	Arriva TrainCare, Eastleigh Depot
08737		G	LS	L&NWR Heritage Company, Southall Depot
08738		RS	RS	Freightliner, Felixstowe FLT
08742	†	RX	HN	Barrow Hill Roundhouse, Chesterfield, Derbys (S)
08743		B	SU	SembCorp Utilities UK, Wilton, Middlesbrough
08752	†	RS	RS	Imerys Minerals, Goonbarrow
08754	*	RL	RL	Eastern Rail Services, Great Yarmouth, Norfolk
08756		RL	RL	Loram, Derby
08757		RG	PO	Telford Steam Railway
08762		RL	RL	Alstom, Ilford Works, London
08764	*	B	AM	Alstom, Polmadie Depot, Glasgow
08765		HN	HN	Barrow Hill Roundhouse, Chesterfield, Derbys (S)
08774	a	O	AD	AV Dawson, Ayrton Rail Terminal, Middlesbrough

08780		G	LS	L&NWR Heritage Company, Crewe Diesel Depot
08782	a†	CU	HN	Barrow Hill Roundhouse, Chesterfield, Derbys (S)
08783		E	RS	RSS, Rye Farm, Wishaw, Sutton Coldfield
08784		DG	PO	Nottingham Heritage Railway, Ruddington
08785	* a	FG	FL	Freightliner, Southampton Maritime FLT
08786	a	DG	HN	Barrow Hill Roundhouse, Chesterfield, Derbys (S)
08787		B	MR	Hunslet Engine Company, Barton-under-Needwood, Staffs (S)
08788	*	RL	RL	PD Ports, Teesport, Grangetown, Middlesbrough
08790	*	B	AM	Alstom, Longsight Depot, Manchester
08795		K	LL	Chrysalis Rail, Landore Depot, Swansea
08798		E	HN	Barrow Hill Roundhouse, Chesterfield, Derbys (S)
08799	a	HN	HN	HNRC, Worksop Depot, Nottinghamshire
08804	†	E	HN	Shackerstone, Battlefield Line (S)
08805		FO	WM	Nemesis Rail, Burton-on-Trent, Staffordshire (S)
08809		RL	RL	Heidelberg Materials, Ketton Cement Works, nr Stamford
08810	a	LW	AV	Arriva TrainCare, Eastleigh Depot, Hampshire
08818		GB	HN	HNRC, Worksop Depot, Nottinghamshire
08822	*	IC	GW	Great Western Railway, St Philip's Marsh Depot, Bristol
08823	a	HU	ED	Tata Steel, Shotton Works, Deeside
08824	ak	K	HN	Barrow Hill Roundhouse, Chesterfield, Derbys (S)
08825		N	PO	Chinnor & Princes Risborough Railway
08834		HN	HN	Northern, Allerton Depot, Liverpool
08836	*	GW	GW	Great Western Railway, Laira Depot, Plymouth
08846		B	RS	West Midlands Trains, Tyseley Depot, Birmingham
08847	*	CD	RL	PD Ports, Teesport, Grangetown, Middlesbrough
08850	*	B	NY	North Yorkshire Moors Railway, Grosmont Depot
08853	* a	WA	ED	Wabtec Rail, Doncaster Works
08865		E	HN	HNRC, Worksop Depot, Nottinghamshire
08868		AW	HN	Arriva TrainCare, Crewe Depot, Cheshire
08870		IC	ER	Eastern Rail Services, Great Yarmouth, Norfolk
08871		CD	RL	Loram, Derby
08872		E	EY	European Metal Recycling, Attercliffe, Sheffield (S)
08874	*	SL	RL	Weardale Railway, Wolsingham, County Durham
08877		DG	HN	HNRC, Worksop Depot, Nottinghamshire
08879		E	HN	Breedon, Hope Cement Works, Derbys (S)
08885		B	RL	Weardale Railway, Wolsingham, County Durham (S)
08887	* a	B	AM	Alstom, Longsight Depot, Manchester
08891	*	FG	FL	Freightliner, Ipswich Depot
08892		DR	HN	HNRC, Worksop Depot, Nottinghamshire
08899		O	RS	RSS, Rye Farm, Wishaw, Sutton Coldfield
08903		B	SU	SembCorp Utilities UK, Wilton, Middlesbrough
08904	d	E	HN	HNRC, Worksop Depot, Nottinghamshire
08905		E	HN	Shackerstone, Battlefield Line (S)
08908		ST	EM	Northern, Neville Hill Depot, Leeds (S)
08912		B	AD	AV Dawson, Ayrton Rail Terminal, Middlesbrough (S)
08918		DG	HN	Nemesis Rail, Burton-on-Trent, Staffordshire (S)
08921		E	RS	RSS, Rye Farm, Wishaw, Sutton Coldfield (S)
08922		DG	PO	Spa Valley Railway
08924	†	GB	HN	Celsa Steel UK, Tremorfa Steelworks, Cardiff
08925		G	GB	HNRC, Worksop Depot, Nottinghamshire (S)
08927		G	RS	Avon Valley Railway

08933		**B**	MR	Hunslet Engine Company, Barton-under-Needwood, Staffs
08934	a	**G**	GB	HNRC, Worksop Depot, Nottinghamshire
08936		**B**	RL	Weardale Railway, Wolsingham, County Durham
08937		**G**	BD	Dartmoor Railway, Meldon Quarry, nr Okehampton
08939		**ECR**	RS	Garston Car Terminal, Liverpool
08943		**HN**	HN	Alstom, Central Rivers Depot, Barton-under-Needwood
08947		**B**	MR	Heidelberg Materials, Whatley Quarry, near Frome
08948	c	**EP**	EU	Eurostar, Temple Mills Depot, London
08950		**ST**	EM	Northern, Neville Hill Depot, Leeds
08954	*	**B**	AM	Alstom, Polmadie Depot, Glasgow
08956		**O**	LO	Barrow Hill Roundhouse, Chesterfield, Derbys (S)

Other numbers or names carried:

08423	"LOCO 2" / "14"	08743	Bryan Turner
08442	"0042"	08754	"H041"
08451	Loopy Lou	08757	EAGLE C.U.R.C.
08460	SPIRIT OF THE OAK	08762	"H067"
08483	Bungle	08774	ARTHUR VERNON DAWSON
08484	CAPTAIN NATHANIEL DARELL	08780	Zippy / D3948
08499	REDLIGHT	08787	"08296"
08525	DUNCAN BEDFORD	08790	LONGSIGHT TMD
08567	John Atkinson Stevens	08799	Ian Goddard 1938–2016
	20th May 1925–19th July 1984	08805	Robin Jones
08568	St. Rollox		40 YEARS SERVICE
08585	Vicky	08809	"24"
08588	"H047"	08810	RICHARD J. WENHAM
08605	"WIGAN 2"		EASTLEIGH DEPOT
08613	"H064"		DECEMBER 1989 – JULY 1999
08615	UNCLE DAI	08818	MOLLY / "4"
08616	TYSELEY 100 / Bam Bam / 3783	08822	Dave Mills
08617	Steve Purser	08823	KEVLA
08622	"H028" / "19"	08824	"IEMD 01"
08624	Rambo PAUL RAMSEY	08846	"003"
08630	"CELSA 3"	08847	"LOCO 1"
08641	Pride of Laira	08865	GILLY
08644	Laira Diesel Depot	08871	"H074"
	50 Years 1962–2012	08885	"H042" / "18"
08645	St. Piran	08899	Midland Counties Railway
08649	Bradwell		175 1839–2014
08669	Bob Machin	08903	John W Antill
08678	"555"	08924	"CELSA 2"
08690	DAVID THIRKILL	08927	D4157
08691	Terri	08934	D4164
08703	Steve Blick (Concrete Bob)	08937	D4167
	ShunterSpot	08950	DAVID LIGHTFOOT
08735	Geoff Hobbs 42		
08737	D3905		

CLASS 09   BR/ENGLISH ELECTRIC   0-6-0

Built: 1959–62 by BR at Darlington or Horwich Works.
Engine: English Electric 6KT of 298 kW (400 hp) at 680 rpm.
Main Generator: English Electric 801.
Traction Motors: English Electric 506.
Maximum Tractive Effort: 111 kN (25000 lbf).
Continuous Tractive Effort: 39 kN (8800 lbf) at 11.6 mph.

Power at Rail: 201 kW (269 hp).	**Train Brakes:** Air & vacuum.
Brake Force: 19 t.	**Dimensions:** 8.92 x 2.59 m.
Weight: 49 t.	**Wheel Diameter:** 1372 mm.
Design Speed: 27 mph.	**Maximum Speed:** 27 mph.
Fuel Capacity: 3037 litres.	**Route Availability:** 5.
Train Supply: Not equipped.	**Total:** 10.

Class 09/0. Built as Class 09.

09002	**G**	GB	Barrow Hill Roundhouse, Chesterfield, Derbys (S)
09006	**E**	HN	Nemesis Rail, Burton-on-Trent, Staffordshire (S)
09007	**G**	LN	London Overground, Willesden Depot, London
09009	**G**	GB	Gemini Rail Group, Wolverton Works, Milton Keynes
09014	**DG**	HN	Nemesis Rail, Burton-on-Trent, Staffordshire (S)
09022	**B**	VG	Victoria Group, Port of Boston, Boston
09023	**E**	EY	European Metal Recycling, Attercliffe, Sheffield (S)

Class 09/1. Converted from Class 08 1992–93 by RFS Industries, Kilnhurst.
110 V electrical equipment.

09106	**HN**	HN	Celsa Steel UK, Tremorfa Steelworks, Cardiff

Class 09/2. Converted from Class 08 1992 by RFS Industries, Kilnhurst.
90 V electrical equipment.

09201	**DG**	HN	HNRC, Worksop Depot, Nottinghamshire (S)
09204	**AW**	AV	Arriva TrainCare, Crewe Depot, Cheshire

Other numbers or names carried:

09007	D3671		09106	"6"
09022	PB144			

CLASS 18   CLAYTON HYBRID+   Bo-Bo

Beacon Rail ordered 15 Class 18 Bo-Bo diesel-battery hybrid shunters (Type CBD90) from Clayton Equipment as potential replacements for Classes 08/09. Although GB Railfreight hired 18001 for shunting at Whitemoor Yard at March for assessment purposes no other customers have yet been found for these locomotives which are stored awaiting developments at Wolverton.
Built: 2021–23 by Clayton Equipment Company, Burton-on-Trent.
Batteries/Engine: 524 kWh battery + JCB Dieselmax 430 of 55 kW (74 hp).
Main Generator:
Traction Motors:
Maximum Tractive Effort: 303 kN (68000 lbf).

Continuous Tractive Effort:
Power at Rail: 416 kW (558 hp).
Brake Force:
Weight: 90 t.
Design Speed: 12 mph.
Fuel Capacity:
Train Supply: Not equipped.

Train Brakes: Air.
Dimensions: 13.64 x ?? m.
Wheel Diameter:
Maximum Speed: 12 mph.
Route Availability:
Total: 15.

18001	**BN**	BN	Gemini Rail Group, Wolverton Works (S)
18002	**BN**	BN	Gemini Rail Group, Wolverton Works (S)
18003	**BN**	BN	Gemini Rail Group, Wolverton Works (S)
18004	**BN**	BN	Gemini Rail Group, Wolverton Works (S)
18005	**BN**	BN	Gemini Rail Group, Wolverton Works (S)
18006	**BN**	BN	Gemini Rail Group, Wolverton Works (S)
18007	**BN**	BN	Gemini Rail Group, Wolverton Works (S)
18008	**BN**	BN	Gemini Rail Group, Wolverton Works (S)
18009	**BN**	BN	Gemini Rail Group, Wolverton Works (S)
18010	**BN**	BN	Gemini Rail Group, Wolverton Works (S)
18011	**BN**	BN	Gemini Rail Group, Wolverton Works (S)
18012	**BN**	BN	Gemini Rail Group, Wolverton Works (S)
18013	**BN**	BN	Gemini Rail Group, Wolverton Works (S)
18014	**BN**	BN	Gemini Rail Group, Wolverton Works (S)
18015	**BN**	BN	Gemini Rail Group, Wolverton Works (S)

1.2. MAIN LINE DIESEL LOCOMOTIVES

CLASS 20   ENGLISH ELECTRIC   Bo-Bo

Built: 1957–68 by English Electric at Vulcan Foundry, Newton-le-Willows or by Robert Stephenson & Hawthorns at Darlington.
Engine: English Electric 8SVT Mk II of 746 kW (1000 hp) at 850 rpm.
Main Generator: English Electric 819/3C.
Traction Motors: English Electric 526/5D or 526/8D.
Maximum Tractive Effort: 187 kN (42000 lbf).
Continuous Tractive Effort: 111 kN (25000 lbf) at 11 mph.
Power at Rail: 574 kW (770 hp).
Brake Force: 35 t.
Weight: 73.4–73.5 t.
Design Speed: 75 mph.
Fuel Capacity: 1727 litres.
Train Supply: Not equipped.

Train Brakes: Air & vacuum.
Dimensions: 14.25 x 2.67 m.
Wheel Diameter: 1092 mm.
Maximum Speed: 75 mph.
Route Availability: 5.
Total: 27.

Non-standard liveries/numbering:

20056   Yellow with grey cabsides and red solebar. Carries No. "81".
20066   Dark blue with yellow stripes. Carries No. "82".
20096   Carries original number D8096.
20107   Carries original number D8107.
20110   Carries original number D8110.
20142   LUL Maroon.

20168   Breedon Aggregates. Carries No. "2".
20227   LUL Maroon.
20906   White. Carries No. "3".

Class 20/0. Standard Design.

20007	**G**	EE	MOLO	SK	
20056	**0**	HN	HNRL	SC (S)	
20066	**0**	HN	HNRL	BH (S)	
20096	**G**	LS	LSLO	CL	
20107	**G**	LS	LSLO	CL	Jocelyn Feilding 1940–2020
20118	**F0**	LS	LSLO	CL	Saltburn-by-the-Sea
20132	**F0**	LS	LSLO	CL	
20142	**0**	20	MOLO	SK	SIR JOHN BETJEMAN
20168	**0**	HN	HNRL	HO	SIR GEORGE EARLE
20189	**B**	20	MOLO	SK	
20205	**B**	2L	MOLO	SK	
20227	**0**	2L	MOLO	SK	SHERLOCK HOLMES

Class 20/3. Locomotives refurbished by Direct Rail Services in the 1990s.
Details as Class 20/0 except:

Refurbished: 15 locomotives were refurbished 1995–96 by Brush Traction at Loughborough (20301–305) or 1997–98 by RFS(E) at Doncaster (20306–315). Disc indicators or headcode panels removed.

Train Brakes: Air.	**Maximum Speed:** 60 mph (+ 75 mph).	
Weight: 73 t (+ 76 t).	**Fuel Capacity:** 2909 (+ 4909) litres.	
Brake Force: 35 t (+ 31 t).	**RA:** 5 (+ 6).	

20301	(20047)	r	**DS**	HN HNRS	WS (S)
20302	(20084)	r	**DS**	HN HNRS	BH (S)
20303	(20127)	r	**DS**	HN HNRS	WS (S)
20304	(20120)	r	**DS**	HN HNRS	WS (S)
20305	(20095)	r	**DS**	HN HNRS	WS (S)
20308	(20187)	r+	**DS**	HN HNRS	WS (S)
20309	(20075)	r+	**DS**	HN HNRS	HO
20311	(20102)	r+	**HN**	HN HNRL	BH (S)
20312	(20042)	r+	**DS**	HN HNRS	WS (S)
20314	(20117)	r+	**HN**	HN HNRL	WS (S)

Class 20/9. Harry Needle Railroad Company (former Hunslet-Barclay/DRS) locomotives. Details as Class 20/0 except:

Refurbished: 1989 by Hunslet-Barclay at Kilmarnock.

Train Brakes: Air.	**Fuel Capacity:** 1727 (+ 4727) litres.
RA: 5 (+ 6).	

20901	(20101)		**GB**	HN HNRL	BH
20903	(20083)	+	**DR**	HN HNRS	BU (S)
20904	(20041)		**DR**	HN HNRS	BU (S)
20905	(20225)	+	**GB**	HN HNRL	BH
20906	(20219)		**0**	HN HNRL	HO

CLASS 25   BR/BEYER PEACOCK/SULZER   Bo-Bo

Built: 1965 by Beyer Peacock at Gorton.
Engine: Sulzer 6LDA28-B of 930 kW (1250 hp) at 750 rpm.
Main Generator: AEI RTB15656.   **Traction Motors:** AEI 253AY.
Maximum Tractive Effort: 200 kN (45000 lbf).
Continuous Tractive Effort: 93 kN (20800 lbf) at 17.1 mph.

Power at Rail: 708 kW (949 hp).	**Train Brakes:** Air & vacuum.
Brake Force: 38 t.	**Dimensions:** 15.39 x 2.73 m.
Weight: 71.5 t.	**Wheel Diameter:** 1143 mm.
Design Speed: 90 mph.	**Maximum Speed:** 60 mph.
Fuel Capacity: 2270 litres.	**Route Availability:** 5.
Train Supply: Not equipped.	**Total:** 1.

Carries original number D7628.

Only certified for use on Network Rail tracks between Whitby and Grosmont, as an extension of North Yorkshire Moors Railway services.

25278	**GG**	NY	MBDL	NY	SYBILLA

CLASS 31   BRUSH/ENGLISH ELECTRIC   A1A-A1A

Built: 1958–62 by Brush Traction at Loughborough.
Engine: English Electric 12SVT of 1100 kW (1470 hp) at 850 rpm.
Main Generator: Brush TG160-48.   **Traction Motors:** Brush TM73-68.
Maximum Tractive Effort: 160 kN (35900 lbf).
Continuous Tractive Effort: 83 kN (18700 lbf) at 23.5 mph.

Power at Rail: 872 kW (1170 hp).	**Train Brakes:** Air & vacuum.
Brake Force: 49 t.	**Dimensions:** 17.30 x 2.67 m.
Weight: 106.7–111 t.	**Wheel Diameter:** 1092/1003 mm.
Design Speed: 90 mph.	**Maximum Speed:** 90 mph.
Fuel Capacity: 2409 litres.	**Route Availability:** 5.
Train Supply: Not equipped.	**Total:** 3.

Non-standard livery: 31452 All over dark green.

31106	**B**	X		EMR Kingsbury (S)	
31128	**B**	NS	NRLO	BU	CHARYBDIS
31452	**0**	ER	ERSL	YA	

CLASS 33   BRCW/SULZER   Bo-Bo

Built: 1959–62 by the Birmingham Railway Carriage & Wagon Company at Smethwick.
Engine: Sulzer 8LDA28 of 1160 kW (1550 hp) at 750 rpm.
Main Generator: Crompton Parkinson CG391B1.
Traction Motors: Crompton Parkinson C171C2.
Maximum Tractive Effort: 200 kN (45000 lbf).
Continuous Tractive Effort: 116 kN (26000 lbf) at 17.5 mph.

Power at Rail: 906 kW (1215 hp).	**Train Brakes:** Air & vacuum.
Brake Force: 35 t.	**Dimensions:** 15.47 x 2.82 (2.64 m 33/2).

Weight: 76-78 t.   **Wheel Diameter:** 1092 mm.
Design Speed: 85 mph.   **Maximum Speed:** 85 mph.
Fuel Capacity: 3410 litres.   **Route Availability:** 6.
Train Supply: Electric, index 48 (750 V DC only).
Total: 5.

Non-standard numbering: 33012 Carries original number D6515.

Class 33/0. Standard Design.

33012	**G**	71	MBDL	SW	Lt Jenny Lewis RN
33025	**WC**	WC	AWCA	CS	
33029	**WC**	WC	AWCA	CS	
33030	**DR**	WC	AWCX	CS (S)	

Class 33/2. Built to former Loading Gauge of Tonbridge–Battle Line.
Equipped with slow speed control.

33207	**WC**	WC	AWCA	CS	Jim Martin

CLASS 37   ENGLISH ELECTRIC   Co-Co

Built: 1960–66 by English Electric at Vulcan Foundry, Newton-le-Willows or
by Robert Stephenson & Hawthorns at Darlington.
Engine: English Electric 12CSVT of 1300 kW (1750 hp) at 850 rpm.
Main Generator: English Electric 822/10G.
Traction Motors: English Electric 538/A.
Maximum Tractive Effort: 247 kN (55500 lbf).
Continuous Tractive Effort: 156 kN (35000 lbf) at 13.6 mph.
Power at Rail: 932 kW (1250 hp).   **Train Brakes:** Air & vacuum.
Brake Force: 50 t.   **Dimensions:** 18.75 x 2.74 m.
Weight: 102.8–108.4 t.   **Wheel Diameter:** 1092 mm.
Design Speed: 90 mph.   **Maximum Speed:** 80 mph.
Fuel Capacity: 4046 (+ 7683) litres. **Route Availability:** 5.
Train Supply: Not equipped.   **Total:** 62.

Non-standard liveries and numbering:

37424 Also carries the number 37558.
37508 Previously numbered 37606.
37521 Carries original number D6817.
37667 Carries original number D6851.
37688 Two-tone trainload freight grey with Construction decals.
37703 Carries the number 37067.
37905 Also carries original number D6836.

Class 37/0. Standard Design.

37025	**BL**	37	COTS	BO (S)	Inverness TMD
37038 a	**DI**	HN	HNRS	WS (S)	
37057	**CS**	CS	COTS	CW	Barbara Arbon
37059 ar+	**DI**	HN	HNRL	BQ (S)	
37069 ar+	**DI**	EP	EPUK	LR (S)	
37099	**CS**	CS	COTS	CW	MERL EVANS 1947–2016
37116 +	**CS**	CS	COTS	CW	

37175 a	**CS**	CS	COTS	CW	
37190	**B**	LS	MBDL	MG (S)	
37207	**B**	EP	EPUK	GCR (S)	
37218 ar+	**DR**	EP	EPUK	LR (S)	
37219	**CS**	CS	COTS	CW	Jonty Jarvis 8-12-1998 to 18-3-2005
37240	**F**	VT	MBDL	TM	
37254	**CS**	CS	COTS	CW	Cardiff Canton
37259 ar	**DS**	HN	HNRS	WS (S)	

Class 37/4. Refurbished with electric train supply equipment. Main generator replaced by alternator. Regeared (CP7) bogies. Details as Class 37/0 except:
Main Alternator: Brush BA1005A.   **Power At Rail:** 935 kW (1254 hp).
Traction Motors: English Electric 538/5A.
Maximum Tractive Effort: 256 kN (57440 lbf).
Continuous Tractive Effort: 184 kN (41250 lbf) at 11.4 mph.
Weight: 107 t.   **Design Speed:** 80 mph.
Fuel Capacity: 7683 litres.
Train Supply: Electric, index 30.

37401 ar	**BL**	LS	LSLO	CL	
37402 a	**BL**	AN	MBDL	CL (S)	
37403	**BL**	SP	RAJV	NY	Isle of Mull
37405 av	**HN**	HN	COFS	BH	
37407	**BL**	DR	XHSO	KM	Blackpool Tower
37409 ar	**IS**	LS	LSLO	CL	Loch Awe
37418	**BL**	SB	LRLO	ZA	An Comunn Gaidhealach
37419 ar	**IC**	DR	XHSO	KM	Driver Tony Kay 1974–2019
37421	**CS**	CS	COTS	CW	
37422 ar	**DR**	DR	XHSO	KM	Victorious
37423 ar	**DR**	EP	EPUK	LR (S)	
37424	**BL**	DR	XSDP	KM (S)	Avro Vulcan XH558
37425 ar	**RR**	DR	XHSO	KM	Sir Robert McAlpine/Concrete Bob

Class 37/5. Refurbished without train supply equipment. Main generator replaced by alternator. Regeared (CP7) bogies. Details as Class 37/4 except:
Power At Rail: 932 kW (1250 hp).
Maximum Tractive Effort: 248 kN (55590 lbf).
Weight: 106.1–110.0 t.
Train Supply: Not equipped.

37508	**FO**	SB	LRLO	BU (S)	
37510 a	**EX**	EP	GROG	LR	Orion
37516 s	**WC**	WC	AWCA	CS	Loch Laidon
37517 as	**LH**	WC	AWCX	CS (S)	
37518 ar	**WC**	WC	AWCA	CS	Fort William/An Gearasdan
37521	**G**	LS	LSLO	CL	

Class 37/6. Originally refurbished for Nightstar services. Main generator replaced by alternator. UIC jumpers. Details as Class 37/5 except:
Maximum Speed: 90 mph.   **Train Brake:** Air.
Train Supply: Not equipped, but electric through wired.

| 37601 ad | **EX** | EP | GROG | LR | Perseus |

37602	ar	**DS**	HN	HNRS	BH (S)	
37603	a	**DS**	HN	HNRL	WS (S)	
37604	a	**DS**	HN	HNRL	WS (S)	
37607	ar	**HN**	HN	COTS	BH	
37608	ard	**EX**	EP	GROG	LR	Andromeda
37609	a	**DI**	HN	HNRL	WS (S)	
37610	ar	**BL**	HN	COTS	BH	
37611	ad	**RO**	EP	GROG	LR	Denise
37612	a	**DR**	HN	COTS	BH	

Class 37/5 continued.

37667	ars	**G**	LS	LSLO	CL	FLOPSIE
37668	e	**WC**	WC	AWCA	CS	
37669	e	**WC**	WC	AWCA	CS	
37676	a	**WC**	WC	AWCA	CS	Loch Rannoch
37685	a	**WC**	WC	AWCA	CS	Loch Arkaig
37688		**O**	D0	MBDL	CL	Great Rocks

Class 37/7. Refurbished locomotives. Main generator replaced by alternator. Regeared (CP7) bogies. Ballast weights added. Details as Class 37/5 except:
Main Alternator: GEC G564AZ (37800) Brush BA1005A (others).
Maximum Tractive Effort: 276 kN (62000 lbf).
Weight: 120 t.   **Route Availability:** 7.

37706		**WC**	WC	AWCA	CS	
37712	a	**WC**	WC	AWCX	CS (S)	
37716		**DI**	DR	XHSO	KM	
37800	d	**RO**	EP	GROG	LR	Cassiopeia
37884	d	**EX**	EP	GROG	LR	Cepheus

Class 37/9. Refurbished locomotives. New power unit. Main generator replaced by alternator. Ballast weights added. Details as Class 37/4 except:
Engine: * Mirrlees 6MB275T of 1340 kW (1800 hp) or † Ruston 6RK270T of 1340 kW (1800 hp) at 900 rpm.
Main Alternator: Brush BA15005A.
Maximum Tractive Effort: 279 kN (62680 lbf).
Weight: 120 t.   **Route Availability:** 7.
Train Supply: Not equipped.

37901	*	**EX**	EP	EPUK	LR	Mirrlees Pioneer
37905	†	**G**	UR	UKRM	LR (S)	
37906	†	**FO**	UR	UKRM	BL (S)	

Class 97/3. Class 37s refurbished for use on the Cambrian Lines which are signalled by ERTMS. Details as Class 37/0.

97301	(37100)	e	**Y**	NR	QETS	RO (S)	
97302	(37170)	e	**Y**	NR	QETS	ZA	Ffestiniog & Welsh Highland Railways/Rheilffyrdd Ffestiniog ac Eryri
97303	(37178)	e	**Y**	NR	QETS	ZA	Dave Berry
97304	(37217)	e	**Y**	NR	QETS	ZA	John Tiley

CLASS 40   ENGLISH ELECTRIC   1Co-Co1

Built: 1961 by English Electric at Vulcan Foundry, Newton-le-Willows.
Engine: English Electric 16SVT Mk2 of 1492 kW (2000 hp) at 850 rpm.
Main Generator: English Electric 822/4C.
Traction Motors: English Electric 526/5D or EE526/7D.
Maximum Tractive Effort: 231 kN (52000 lbf).
Continuous Tractive Effort: 137 kN (30900 lbf) at 18.8 mph.
Power at Rail: 1160 kW (1550 hp).   **Train Brakes:** Air & vacuum.
Brake Force: 51 t.   **Dimensions:** 21.18 x 2.78 m.
Weight: 132 t.   **Wheel Diameter:** 914/1143 mm.
Design Speed: 90 mph.   **Maximum Speed:** 90 mph.
Fuel Capacity: 3250 litres.   **Route Availability:** 6.
Train Supply: Steam heating.   **Total:** 2.

40013 Carries original number D213.
40145 Carries original number 345.

40013	**G**	ST	LSLO	CL	Andania
40145	**G**	40	CFSL	CS	

CLASS 43   BREL/PAXMAN   Bo-Bo

Built: 1975–82 by BREL at Crewe Works.
Engine: MTU 16V4000R41R of 1680kW (2250 hp) at 1500 rpm.
(* Paxman 12VP185 of 1680 kW (2250 hp) at 1500 rpm.)
Main Alternator: Brush BA1001B.
Traction Motors: Brush TMH68–46 or GEC G417AZ (43124–152); frame mounted.
Maximum Tractive Effort: 80 kN (17980 lbf).
Continuous Tractive Effort: 46 kN (10340 lbf) at 64.5 mph.
Power at Rail: 1320 kW (1770 hp).   **Train Brakes:** Air.
Brake Force: 35 t.   **Dimensions:** 17.79 x 2.74 m.
Weight: 70.25–75.0 t.   **Wheel Diameter:** 1020 mm.
Design Speed: 125 mph.   **Maximum Speed:** 125 mph.
Fuel Capacity: 4500 litres.   **Route Availability:** 5.
Train Supply: Three-phase electric.   **Total:** 148.

† Buffer fitted.
§ Modified GWR power cars that can operate with power door fitted short sets.

43013, 43014 & 43062 are fitted with measuring apparatus & front-end cameras.

Non-standard liveries:

43206 Original HST blue & yellow. Carries the number 43006
43238 All-over red
43312 Original HST blue & yellow. Carries the number 43112

43003		**SI**	A	HAPC	HA
43004 §		**GW**	A	EFPC	LA	Caerphilly Castle
43007		**O**	A	SCXL	YA (S)
43012		**SI**	A	HAPC	HA
43013 †		**Y**	P	QCAR	ZA	Mark Carne CBE
43014 †		**Y**	P	QCAR	ZA
43015		**SI**	A	HAPC	HA
43017		**FB**	A	SCEL	EP (S)
43020		**FB**	A	SCEL	EP (S)	MTU Power. Passion. Partnership
43021		**SI**	A	HAPC	HA
43023		**FB**	A	SCEL	EP (S)
43024		**FB**	A	SCEL	EP (S)
43025		**FB**	125	ICHP	RD (S)
43026		**SI**	A	HAPC	HA
43027 §		**GW**	GW	EFPC	LA (S)	Acton Castle
43028		**SI**	A	HAPC	HA
43029 §		**GW**	GW	EFPC	LA (S)	Caldicot Castle
43030		**SI**	A	HAPC	ZK (S)
43031		**SI**	A	HAPC	HA
43032		**SI**	A	HAPC	HA
43033		**SI**	A	HAPC	HA
43034		**SI**	A	HAPC	HA
43035		**SI**	A	HAPC	HA
43036		**SI**	A	HAPC	HA
43037		**SI**	A	HAPC	HA
43042 §		**GW**	A	EFPC	LA	Tregenna Castle
43044 *		**IE**	125	ICHP	RD	Edward Paxman
43046 *		**MP**	LS	LSLO	CL	Geoff Drury 1930–1999 Steam Preservation and Computerised Track Recording Pioneer
43047 *		**MP**	LS	LSLO	CL
43048 *		**ST**	125	ICHP	SK
43049 *		**MP**	LS	LSLO	CL	Neville Hill
43050 *		**ST**	P	SBXL	LB
43054 *		**ST**	DA	MBDL	LB
43055 *		**MP**	LS	LSLO	CL
43058 *		**RC**	LS	LSLO	CL
43059 *		**MP**	LS	LSLO	CL
43062		**Y**	P	QCAR	ZA	John Armitt
43063		**FB**	GW	SBXL	LA (S)
43066 *		**ST**	DA	MBDL	LB
43076 *		**ST**	DA	MBDL	LB
43083 *		**ST**	LS	LSLO	ZG (S)
43088 §		**GW**	FG	EFPC	LA (S)
43089 *		**ST**	125	ICHP	SK
43091		**FB**	GW	SBXL	LA (S)

43092 §	**GW**	FG	EFPC	LA	Cromwell's Castle
43093 §	**GW**	FG	EFPC	LA	Berkeley Castle
43094 §	**GW**	FG	EFPC	LA (S)	St Mawes Castle
43097 §	**GW**	FG	EFPC	LA	Castle Drogo
43098 §	**GW**	FG	EFPC	LA (S)	Walton Castle
43122 §	**GW**	FG	EFPC	LA (S)	Dunster Castle
43124	**SI**	A	HAPC	HA	
43125	**SI**	A	HAPC	HA	
43126	**SI**	A	HAPC	HA	
43127	**SI**	A	HAPC	HA	
43128	**SI**	A	HAPC	HA	
43129	**SI**	A	HAPC	HA	
43130	**SI**	A	HAPC	HA	
43131	**SI**	A	HAPC	HA	
43132	**SI**	A	HAPC	HA	
43133	**SI**	A	HAPC	HA	
43134	**SI**	A	HAPC	HA	Gordon Aikman BEM MND Campaigner 1985–2017
43135	**SI**	A	HAPC	HA	
43136	**SI**	A	HAPC	HA	
43137	**SI**	A	HAPC	HA	
43138	**SI**	A	HAPC	HA	
43139	**SI**	A	HAPC	HA	
43141	**SI**	A	HAPC	HA	
43142	**SI**	A	HAPC	HA	
43143	**SI**	A	HAPC	HA	
43144	**SI**	A	HAPC	HA	
43145	**SI**	A	HAPC	HA	
43146	**SI**	A	HAPC	HA	
43147	**SI**	A	HAPC	HA	
43148	**SI**	A	HAPC	HA	
43149	**SI**	A	HAPC	HA	
43150	**SI**	A	HAPC	HA	
43151	**SI**	A	HAPC	HA	
43152	**SI**	A	HAPC	HA	
43153 §	**GW**	FG	EFPC	LA (S)	Chûn Castle
43154 §	**GW**	FG	EFPC	LA (S)	Compton Castle
43155 §	**GW**	FG	EFPC	LA (S)	Rougemont Castle
43156 §	**GW**	FG	EFPC	LA	Maen Castle
43159	**FB**	125	ICHP	SK	Rio Warrior
43160 §	**GW**	FG	EFPC	LA (S)	
43161	**FB**	GW	SBXL	LA (S)	
43162 §	**GW**	FG	EFPC	LA (S)	Caerhays Castle
43163	**SI**	A	HAPC	HA	
43164	**SI**	A	HAPC	HA	
43165	**FB**	A	SCEL	EP (S)	
43168	**SI**	A	HAPC	HA	
43169	**SI**	A	HAPC	HA	
43174	**FB**	A	SCEL	EP (S)	
43175	**SI**	A	HAPC	HA	
43176	**SI**	A	HAPC	HA	

43177	**SI**	A	HAPC	HA	
43179	**SI**	A	HAPC	HA	
43181	**SI**	A	HAPC	HA	
43182	**SI**	A	HAPC	HA	
43183	**SI**	A	HAPC	HA	
43185	**IC**	A	SCEL	ZK (S)	
43186 §	**GW**	A	EFPC	LA	Taunton Castle
43187 §	**GW**	A	EFPC	LA	Cardiff Castle
43188 §	**GW**	A	EFPC	LA	Newport Castle
43189 §	**GW**	A	EFPC	LA	Launceston Castle
43190	**FB**	A	SCEL	EP (S)	
43191	**FB**	A	SCEL	EP (S)	
43194 §	**GW**	FG	EFPC	LA (S)	Okehampton Castle
43198 §	**GW**	FG	EFPC	LA	Driver Stan Martin 25 June 1950 – 6 November 2004/Driver Brian Cooper 15 June 1947 – 5 October 1999

Class 43/2. Rebuilt CrossCountry and former LNER, East Midlands Railway or Grand Central power cars. Power cars were renumbered by adding 200 to their original number or 400 to their original number (former Grand Central), except 43123 which became 43423.

43206 (43006)	**0**	A	IECP	EP (S)	
43238 (43038)	**0**	A	SCEL	EP (S)	
43251 (43051)	**VE**	P	COTS	ZA	
43257 (43057)	**VE**	P	COTS	ZA	
43272 (43072)	**VE**	P	COTS	ZA	
43274 (43074)	**ER**	P	COTS	ZA	
43277 (43077)	**CT**	P	COTS	ZA	Safety Task Force
43285 (43085)	**XC**	P	COTS	ZA	
43290 (43090)	**VE**	P	COTS	ZA	
43295 (43095)	**VE**	A	SCEL	EP (S)	
43296 (43096)	**VE**	RA	HHPC	ZG (S)	
43299 (43099)	**VE**	P	COTS	ZA	
43300 (43100)	**VE**	P	IECP	Reid's, Stoke (S)	
43301 (43101)	**XC**	P	COTS	ZA	
43303 (43103)	**XC**	P	COTS	ZA	
43305 (43105)	**VE**	A	SCEL	EP (S)	
43306 (43106)	**VE**	A	SCEL	NC (S)	
43307 (43107)	**VE**	A	SCEL	NC (S)	
43308 (43108)	**VE**	RA	HHPC	ZG (S)	
43309 (43109)	**VE**	A	SCEL	EP (S)	
43310 (43110)	**VE**	A	SCEL	EP (S)	
43311 (43111)	**VE**	A	SCEL	EP (S)	
43312 (43112)	**0**	A	SCEL	EP (S)	
43314 (43114)	**VE**	A	SCEL	EP (S)	
43315 (43115)	**VE**	A	SCEL	EP (S)	
43316 (43116)	**VE**	A	SCEL	NC (S)	
43317 (43117)	**VE**	A	SCEL	EP (S)	
43318 (43118)	**VE**	A	SCEL	EP (S)	
43319 (43119)	**VE**	A	SCEL	EP (S)	
43320 (43120)	**VE**	A	SCEL	NC (S)	

43321	(43121)		**XC**	P	COTS	ZA
43357	(43157)		**XC**	P	COTS	ZA
43367	(43167)		**VE**	A	SCEL	EP (S)
43378	(43178)		**XC**	A	SCXL	YA (S)
43423	(43123)	†	**EA**	RA	HHPC	ZG (S)
43465	(43065)	†	**RA**	RA	HHPC	KI
43467	(43067)	†	**EA**	RA	HHPC	ZG (S)
43468	(43068)	†	**RA**	RA	HHPC	KI
43480	(43080)	†	**RA**	RA	HHPC	KI
43484	(43084)	†	**RA**	RA	HHPC	KI

CLASS 45   BR/SULZER   1Co-Co1

Built: 1963 by BR at Derby Locomotive Works.
Engine: Sulzer 12LDA28B of 1860 kW (2500 hp) at 750 rpm.
Main Generator: Crompton-Parkinson CG426 A1.
Traction Motors: Crompton-Parkinson C172 A1.
Maximum Tractive Effort: 245 kN (55000 lbf).
Continuous Tractive Effort: 134 kN (31600 lbf) at 22.3 mph.

Power at Rail: 1491 kW (2000 hp).	**Train Brakes:** Air & vacuum.
Brake Force: 63 t.	**Dimensions:** 20.70 x 2.78 m.
Weight: 135 t.	**Wheel Diameter:** 914/1143 mm.
Design Speed: 90 mph.	**Maximum Speed:** 90 mph.
Fuel Capacity: 3591 litres.	**Route Availability:** 6.
Train Supply: Electric, index 66.	**Total:** 1.

45118	**B**	LS	LSLS	BH	THE ROYAL ARTILLERYMAN

CLASS 47   BR/BRUSH/SULZER   Co-Co

Built: 1963–67 by Brush Traction, at Loughborough or by BR at Crewe Works.
Engine: Sulzer 12LDA28C of 1920 kW (2580 hp) at 750 rpm.
Main Generator: Brush TG160-60 Mk4 or TM172-50 Mk1.
Traction Motors: Brush TM64-68 Mk1 or Mk1A.
Maximum Tractive Effort: 267 kN (60000 lbf).
Continuous Tractive Effort: 133 kN (30000 lbf) at 26 mph.
Power at Rail: 1550 kW (2080 hp).   **Train Brakes:** Air.
Brake Force: 61 t.   **Dimensions:** 19.38 x 2.79 m.
Weight: 111.5–120.6 t.   **Wheel Diameter:** 1143 mm.
Design Speed: 95 mph.   **Maximum Speed:** 95 mph.
Fuel Capacity: 3273 (+ 5887) litres.   **Route Availability:** 6 or 7.
Train Supply: Not equipped.   **Total:** 44.

Class 47s exported for use abroad are listed in section 1.6 of this book.

Non-standard liveries/numbering:

47270   Also carries original number 1971.
47501   Carries original number D1944.
47739   GBRf dark blue.
47773   Also carries original number D1755.
47798   Royal Train claret with Rail Express Systems markings.
47805   Carries original number D1935.
47810   Carries original number D1924.
47830   Also carries original number D1645.

Recent renumberings:

47593 was renumbered from 47790 in 2019.
47614 was renumbered from 47853 in 2019.

Class 47/0. Standard Design. Built with train air and vacuum brakes.

47237 x+	**WC**	WC	AWCA	CS	
47245 x+	**WC**	WC	AWCA	CS	V.E. Day 75th Anniversary
47270 +	**B**	WC	AWCA	CS	

Class 47/3. Built with train air and vacuum brakes. Details as Class 47/0 except: **Weight:** 113.7 t.

47355 a+	**K**	WC	AWCX	CS (S)	

Class 47/4. Electric Train Supply equipment.
Details as Class 47/0 except:

Weight: 120.4–125.1 t.   **Fuel Capacity:** 3273 (+ 5537) litres.
Train Supply: Electric, index 66.   **Route Availability:** 7.

47501 x+	**GG**	LS	LSLO	CL	CRAFTSMAN
47526 x	**BL**	WC	AWCX	CS (S)	
47580 x	**BL**	47	MBDL	TM	County of Essex
47593	**BL**	LS	LSLO	CL	Galloway Princess
47614 +	**B**	LS	LSLO	CL	

Class 47/7. Previously fitted with an older form of TDM.
Details as Class 47/4 except:

Weight: 118.7 t.   **Fuel Capacity:** 5887 litres.
Maximum Speed: 100 mph.

47703	**FR**	HN	HNRL	ZB	
47712	**IS**	CD	LSLO	CL	Lady Diana Spencer
47714	**AR**	HN	HNRL	ZB	
47715	**N**	HN	HNRL	WS	

Class 47/7. Former Railnet dedicated locomotives.
Details as Class 47/0 except:

Fuel Capacity: 5887 litres.

47727	**CA**	GB	GBDF	LR	Edinburgh Castle/
					Caisteal Dhùn Èideann
47739	**O**	GB	GBDF	LR	
47746 x	**WC**	WC	AWCA	CS	Chris Fudge 29.7.70 – 22.6.10
47749 d	**B**	GB	GBDF	LR	CITY OF TRURO
47760 x	**WC**	WC	AWCA	CS	
47768	**RX**	WC	AWCX	CS (S)	
47772 x	**WC**	WC	AWCA	CS	Carnforth TMD
47773 x	**GG**	70	MBDL	TM	
47776 x	**RX**	WC	AWCX	CS (S)	
47786	**WC**	WC	AWCA	CS	Roy Castle OBE
47787	**WC**	WC	AWCX	CS (S)	

Class 47/4 continued. Route Availability: 6.

47798 x	**O**	NM	MBDL	YK	Prince William
47802 +	**WC**	WC	AWCA	CS	
47804	**WC**	WC	AWCA	CS	
47805 +	**GG**	LS	LSLO	CL	Roger Hosking MA 1925–2013
47810 +	**GG**	LS	LSLO	CL	Crewe Diesel Depot
47812 +	**WC**	WC	AWCA	CS	
47813 +	**RO**	WC	AWCA	CS	
47815 +	**GG**	WC	AWCA	CS	Great Western
47816 +	**GL**	LS	DHLT	CL (S)	
47818 +	**DS**	AF	MBDL	ZG (S)	
47826 +	**WC**	WC	AWCA	CS	
47828 +	**IC**	D0	LSLO	CL	
47830 +	**GG**	FL	DFLH	CB	BEECHING'S LEGACY
47832 +	**WC**	WC	AWCA	CS	
47841 +	**IC**	LS	LSLS	MG (S)	The Institution of Mechanical
					Engineers
47843 +	**RB**	HN	SROG	WS (S)	
47847 +	**BL**	HN	SROG	WS (S)	
47848 +	**WC**	WC	AWCA	CS	
47851 +	**WC**	WC	AWCA	CS	
47854 +	**WC**	WC	AWCA	CS	Diamond Jubilee

CLASS 50　　　ENGLISH ELECTRIC　　　Co-Co

Built: 1967–68 by English Electric at Vulcan Foundry, Newton-le-Willows.
Engine: English Electric 16CVST of 2010 kW (2700 hp) at 850 rpm.
Main Generator: English Electric 840/4B.
Traction Motors: English Electric 538/5A.
Maximum Tractive Effort: 216 kN (48500 lbf).
Continuous Tractive Effort: 147 kN (33000 lbf) at 23.5 mph.
Power at Rail: 1540 kW (2070 hp).　　**Train Brakes:** Air & vacuum.
Brake Force: 59 t.　　　　　　　　　　**Dimensions:** 20.88 x 2.78 m.
Weight: 116.9 t.　　　　　　　　　　　**Wheel Diameter:** 1092 mm.
Design Speed: 105 mph.　　　　　　　**Maximum Speed:** 90 mph.
Fuel Capacity: 4796 litres.　　　　　　**Route Availability:** 6.
Train Supply: Electric, index 61.　　　**Total:** 5.

Non-standard numbering:

50007　Running with the number 50014 and "Warspite" name on one side.
50050　Also carries original number D400.

50007	**GB**	50	CFOL	KR	Hercules
50008	**HH**	HH	HVAC	BH	Thunderer
50044	**B**	50	CFOL	KR	Exeter
50049	**GB**	50	CFOL	KR	Defiance
50050	**B**	NB	COFS	CW	Fearless

CLASS 52　　　BR/MAYBACH　　　C-C

Built: 1961–64 by BR at Swindon Works.
Engine: Two Maybach MD655 of 1007 kW (1350 hp) each at 1500 rpm.
Transmission: Hydraulic. Voith L630rV.
Maximum Tractive Effort: 297 kN (66700 lbf).
Continuous Tractive Effort: 201 kN (45200 lbf) at 14.5 mph.
Power at Rail: 1490 kW (2000 hp).　　**Train Brakes:** Air & vacuum.
Brake Force: 83 t.　　　　　　　　　　**Dimensions:** 20.70 m x 2.78 m.
Weight: 110 t.　　　　　　　　　　　　**Wheel Diameter:** 1092 mm.
Design Speed: 90 mph.　　　　　　　　**Maximum Speed:** 90 mph.
Fuel Capacity: 3900 litres.　　　　　　**Route Availability:** 6.
Train Supply: Steam heating.　　　　　**Total:** 1.

Never allocated a number in the 1972 number series.

D1015	**B**	DT	MBDL	KR	WESTERN CHAMPION

CLASS 55   ENGLISH ELECTRIC   Co-Co

Built: 1961 by English Electric at Vulcan Foundry, Newton-le-Willows.
Engine: Two Napier-Deltic D18-25 of 1230 kW (1650 hp) each at 1500 rpm.
Main Generators: Two English Electric 829/1A.
Traction Motors: English Electric 538/A.
Maximum Tractive Effort: 222 kN (50000 lbf).
Continuous Tractive Effort: 136 kN (30500 lbf) at 32.5 mph.

Power at Rail: 1969 kW (2640 hp).	**Train Brakes:** Air & vacuum.
Brake Force: 51 t.	**Dimensions:** 21.18 x 2.68 m.
Weight: 100 t.	**Wheel Diameter:** 1092 mm.
Design Speed: 105 mph.	**Maximum Speed:** 100 mph.
Fuel Capacity: 3755 litres.	**Route Availability:** 5.
Train Supply: Electric, index 66.	**Total:** 4.

Non-standard numbering:

55002	Carries original number D9002.
55009	Carries original number D9009.
55016	Carries original number D9016.

55002	GG	NM	MBDL	YK	THE KING'S OWN YORKSHIRE LIGHT INFANTRY
55009	B	DP	MBDL	BH	ALYCIDON
55016	GG	LS	MBDL	MG (S)	GORDON HIGHLANDER
55022	B	LS	LSLO	CL	ROYAL SCOTS GREY

CLASS 56   BRUSH/BR/RUSTON   Co-Co

Built: 1976–84 by Electroputere at Craiova, Romania (as sub-contractors for Brush) or BREL at Doncaster or Crewe Works.
Engine: Ruston Paxman 16RK3CT of 2460 kW (3250 hp) at 900 rpm.
Main Alternator: Brush BA1101A.
Traction Motors: Brush TM73-62.
Maximum Tractive Effort: 275 kN (61800 lbf).
Continuous Tractive Effort: 240 kN (53950 lbf) at 16.8 mph.

Power at Rail: 1790 kW (2400 hp).	**Train Brakes:** Air.
Brake Force: 60 t.	**Dimensions:** 19.36 x 2.79 m.
Weight: 126 t.	**Wheel Diameter:** 1143 mm.
Design Speed: 80 mph.	**Maximum Speed:** 80 mph.
Fuel Capacity: 5228 litres.	**Route Availability:** 7.
Train Supply: Not equipped.	**Total:** 21.

All equipped with Slow Speed Control.

Class 56s exported for use abroad are listed in section 1.6 of this book.

Most of the locomotives at Longport are being rebuilt as Class 69s.

Non-standard liveries:

56009 All over blue.
56303 All over dark green.

56009	**O**	EO	UKRS	LT (S)	
56049	**CS**	CS	COFS	CW	Robin of Templecombe 1938–2013
56051	**CS**	CS	COFS	CW	Survival
56077	**LH**	GB	UKRS	LT (S)	
56078	**CS**	CS	COFS	CW	
56081	**B**	GB	GBGD	LR	
56087	**CS**	BN	COFS	CW	
56090	**CS**	BN	COFS	CW	
56091	**DC**	DC	DCRO	LR	Driver Wayne Gaskell
					The Godfather
56094	**CS**	CS	COFS	CW	
56096	**CS**	BN	COFS	CW	
56097	**F**	EO		LT (S)	
56098	**BL**	GB	GBGD	LR	
56103	**DC**	DC	DCRS	LR (S)	
56104	**FO**	GB	UKRL	LT (S)	
56105	**CS**	BN	COFS	CW	
56113	**CS**	BN	COFS	CW	
56301	(56045)	**FA**	56	UKRL	LR	
56302	(56124)	**CS**	CS	COFS	CW	PECO The Railway Modeller
						2016 70 Years
56303	(56125)	**O**	GB	HTLX	Willesden F Sdgs (S)	
56312	(56003)	**DC**	GB	GBGD	LT (S)	

CLASS 57   BRUSH/GM   Co-Co

Built: 1964–65 by Brush Traction at Loughborough or BR at Crewe Works as
Class 47. Rebuilt 1997–2004 by Brush Traction at Loughborough.
Engine: General Motors 12 645 E3 of 1860 kW (2500 hp) at 904 rpm.
Main Alternator: Brush BA1101D (recovered from Class 56).
Traction Motors: Brush TM64-68 Mark 1 or Mark 1A.
Maximum Tractive Effort: 244.5 kN (55000 lbf).
Continuous Tractive Effort: 140 kN (31500 lbf) at ?? mph.

Power at Rail: 1507 kW (2025 hp).	**Train Brakes:** Air.
Brake Force: 80 t.	**Dimensions:** 19.38 x 2.79 m.
Weight: 120.6 t.	**Wheel Diameter:** 1143 mm.
Design Speed: 75 mph.	**Maximum Speed:** 75 mph.
Fuel Capacity: 5550 litres.	**Route Availability:** 6
Train Supply: Not equipped.	**Total:** 32.

Non-standard liveries:

57311   LNWR lined black
57604   Original Great Western Railway green.

Class 57/0. No Train Supply Equipment. Rebuilt 1997–2000.

57001	(47356)	**WC**	WC	AWCA	CS (S)
57002	(47322)	**DI**	DR	LSLO	WS (S)	RAIL EXPRESS
57003	(47317)	**DR**	LS	LSLO	CL
57005	(47350)	**AZ**	WC	AWCX	CS (S)
57006	(47187)	**WC**	WC	AWCA	CS
57007	(47332)	**DI**	LS	LSLO	CL (S)
57008	(47060)	**DS**	WC	AWCA	CS (S)
57009	(47079)	**GG**	WC	AWCA	CS	G. J. CHURCHWARD
57010	(47231)	**WC**	WC	AWCA	CS
57011	(47329)	**DS**	WC	AWCA	CS (S)
57012	(47204)	**WC**	WC	AWCA	CS

Class 57/3. Electric Train Supply Equipment. Former Virgin Trains locomotives fitted with retractable Dellner couplers. Rebuilt 2002–04. Details as Class 57/0 except:

Engine: General Motors 12645F3B of 2050 kW (2750 hp) at 954 rpm.
Main Alternator: Brush BA1101F (recovered from Class 56) or Brush BA1101G.
Fuel Capacity: 5887 litres.   **Train Supply:** Electric, index 100.
Design Speed: 95 mph.   **Maximum Speed:** 95 mph.
Brake Force: 60 t.   **Weight:** 117 t.

57301	(47845)	d	**DR**	P	XSDP	ZA (S)
57302	(47827)	d	**DS**	LS	LSLO	ZG (S)	Chad Varah
57303	(47705)	d	**DR**	P	XSDP	CR (S)
57304	(47807)	d	**DI**	DR	XHVT	KM	Pride of Cheshire
57305	(47822)	d	**DR**	P	GBBS	LR
57306	(47814)	d	**DI**	P	GBBS	LR	Her Majesty's Railway Inspectorate 175
57307	(47225)	d	**DI**	DR	XHVT	KM	LADY PENELOPE
57308	(47846)	d	**DI**	DR	XHVT	KM	Jamie Ferguson
57309	(47806)	d	**DI**	DR	XHVT	KM	Pride of Crewe
57310	(47831)	d	**DR**	P	GBBS	LR	Pride of Cumbria
57311	(47817)	d	**O**	LS	LSLO	CL
57312	(47330)	d	**RO**	P	EFOO	PZ
57313	(47371)		**PC**	WC	AWCA	CS	Scarborough Castle
57314	(47372)		**WC**	WC	AWCA	CS	Conwy Castle
57315	(47234)		**PC**	WC	AWCA	CS
57316	(47290)		**WC**	WC	AWCA	CS	Alnwick Castle

Class 57/6. Electric Train Supply Equipment. Prototype ETS loco. Rebuilt 2001. Details as Class 57/0 except:

Main Alternator: Brush BA1101E.   **Fuel Capacity:** 3273 litres.
Train Supply: Electric, index 95.   **Weight:** 113t.
Design Speed: 95 mph.   **Maximum Speed:** 95 mph.
Brake Force: 60 t.

57601	(47825)		**PC**	WC	AWCA	CS	Windsor Castle

Class 57/6. Electric Train Supply Equipment. Great Western Railway locomotives. Rebuilt 2004. Details as Class 57/3.

57602 (47337)	**GW** P	EFOO	PZ	Restormel Castle
57603 (47349)	**GW** P	EFOO	PZ	Tintagel Castle
57604 (47209)	**0** P	EFOO	PZ	PENDENNIS CASTLE
57605 (47206)	**GW** P	EFOO	PZ	Totnes Castle

CLASS 58   BREL/RUSTON   Co-Co

Built: 1983–87 by BREL at Doncaster Works.
Engine: Ruston Paxman 12RK3ACT of 2460 kW (3300 hp) at 1000 rpm.
Main Alternator: Brush BA1101B.
Traction Motors: Brush TM73-62.
Maximum Tractive Effort: 275 kN (61800 lbf).
Continuous Tractive Effort: 240 kN (53950 lbf) at 17.4 mph.

Power at Rail: 1780 kW (2387 hp).	**Train Brakes:** Air.
Brake Force: 60 t.	**Dimensions:** 19.13 x 2.72 m.
Weight: 130 t.	**Wheel Diameter:** 1120 mm.
Design Speed: 80 mph.	**Maximum Speed:** 80 mph.
Fuel Capacity: 4214 litres.	**Route Availability:** 7.
Train Supply: Not equipped.	**Total:** 2.

All equipped with Slow Speed Control.

Class 58s exported for use abroad are listed in section 1.6 of this book.

58012	**F**	PO	BL (S)	
58016	**ML**	PO	LR (S)	
58023	**ML**	PO	LR (S)	

CLASS 59   GENERAL MOTORS   Co-Co

Built: 1985 (59001–004) or 1989 (59005) by General Motors, La Grange, Illinois, USA or 1990 (59101–104), 1994 (59201) and 1995 (59202–206) by General Motors, London, Ontario, Canada.
Engine: General Motors 16-645E3C two stroke of 2460 kW (3300 hp) at 904 rpm.
Main Alternator: General Motors AR11 MLD-D14A.
Traction Motors: General Motors D77B.
Maximum Tractive Effort: 506 kN (113550 lbf).
Continuous Tractive Effort: 291 kN (65300 lbf) at 14.3 mph.

Power at Rail: 1889 kW (2533 hp).	**Train Brakes:** Air.
Brake Force: 69 t.	**Dimensions:** 21.35 x 2.65 m.
Weight: 121 t.	**Wheel Diameter:** 1067 mm.
Design Speed: 60 (* 75) mph.	**Maximum Speed:** 60 (* 75) mph.
Fuel Capacity: 4546 litres.	**Route Availability:** 7.
Train Supply: Not equipped.	**Total:** 15.

Class 59/0. Owned by Freightliner and GB Railfreight.

59001	**AI**	FL	DFHG	MD	YEOMAN ENDEAVOUR
59002	**AI**	FL	DHLT	LD (S)	ALAN J DAY
59003	**GB**	GB	GBYH	RR	YEOMAN HIGHLANDER
59004	**AI**	FL	DFHG	MD	PAUL A HAMMOND
59005	**AI**	FL	DFHG	MD	KENNETH J PAINTER

Class 59/1. Owned by Freightliner.

59101	**HM**	FL	DFHG	MD	Village of Whatley
59102	**HA**	FL	DFHG	MD	Village of Chantry
59103	**HA**	FL	DFHG	MD	Village of Mells
59104	**HA**	FL	DFHG	MD	Village of Great Elm

Class 59/2. Owned by Freightliner.

59201	*	**FG**	FL	DFHG	MD	
59202	*	**FG**	FL	DFHG	MD	Pride of Ferrybridge
59203	*	**FG**	FL	DFHG	MD	
59204	*	**FG**	FL	DFHG	MD	
59205	*b	**FG**	FL	DFHG	MD	
59206	*b	**FG**	FL	DFHG	MD	John F. Yeoman Rail Pioneer

CLASS 60   BRUSH/MIRRLEES   Co-Co

Built: 1989–93 by Brush Traction at Loughborough.
Engine: Mirrlees 8MB275T of 2310 kW (3100 hp) at 1000 rpm.
Main Alternator: Brush BA1006A.
Traction Motors: Brush TM2161A.
Maximum Tractive Effort: 500 kN (106500 lbf).
Continuous Tractive Effort: 336 kN (71570 lbf) at 17.4 mph.
Power at Rail: 1800 kW (2415 hp). **Train Brakes:** Air.
Brake Force: 74 t (+ 62 t). **Dimensions:** 21.34 x 2.64 m.
Weight: 129 t (+ 131 t). **Wheel Diameter:** 1118 mm.
Design Speed: 62 mph. **Maximum Speed:** 60 mph.
Fuel Capacity: 4546 (+ 5225) litres. **Route Availability:** 8.
Train Supply: Not equipped. **Total:** 97.

All equipped with Slow Speed Control.

* Refurbished locomotives.

60034 carries its name on one side only.

60500 originally carried the number 60016.

Non-standard and Advertising liveries:

60028 Cappagh (blue).
60062 Steel on steel (various colours).
60066 Powering Drax (silver).
60074 Puma Energy (grey).
60081 Original Great Western Railway green.
60099 Tata Steel (silver).

60001	*	**DB**	DB	WQBA	TO (S)
60002	+*	**GB**	BN	GBTG	TO	GRAHAM FARISH 50TH ANNIVERSARY 1970–2020
60003	+	**E**	DB	WQCA	TO (S)	FREIGHT TRANSPORT ASSOCIATION
60004	+	**E**	GB	WQCA	TO (S)
60005	+	**E**	DB	WQCA	TO (S)
60007	+*	**DB**	DB	WQBA	TO (S)	The Spirit of Tom Kendell
60008		**E**	DC	DCRS	LB (S)
60009	+	**E**	DC	DCRS	LB (S)
60010	+*	**DB**	DB	WQBA	TO (S)
60011		**DB**	DB	WQBA	TO (S)
60012	+	**E**	DB	WQDA	TO (S)
60013		**EG**	DC	DCRS	LB (S)
60014		**EG**	GB	WQCA	TO (S)
60015	+*	**DB**	DB	WQBA	TO (S)
60017	+*	**DB**	DB	WQBA	TO (S)
60018		**E**	GB	WQCA	TO (S)
60019	*	**DB**	DB	WQBA	TO (S)	Port of Grimsby & Immingham
60020	+*	**DB**	DB	WQBA	TO (S)	The Willows
60021	+*	**GB**	BN	GBTG	TO	PENYGHENT
60022	+	**E**	DC	DCRS	LB (S)
60023	+	**E**	DB	WQCA	TO (S)
60024	*	**DB**	DB	WCAT	TO	Clitheroe Castle
60025	+	**E**	DB	WQCA	TO (S)
60026	+*	**BN**	BN	GBTG	TO	HELVELLYN
60027	+	**E**	DB	WQCA	TO (S)
60028	+	**O**	DC	DCRO	LB
60029		**DC**	DC	DCRO	LB	Ben Nevis
60030	+	**E**	DB	WQCA	TO (S)
60031		**E**	DB	WQCA	TO (S)
60032		**F**	DB	WQDA	TO (S)
60033	+	**CU**	DB	WQCA	TO (S)	Tees Steel Express
60034		**EG**	DB	WQCA	TO (S)	Carnedd Llewelyn
60035		**E**	DB	WQCA	TO (S)
60036		**E**	DB	WQBA	TO (S)	GEFCO
60037	+	**E**	DB	WQDA	TO (S)
60038	+	**E**	DC	DCRS	LB (S)
60039	*	**DB**	DB	WQBA	TO (S)	Dove Holes
60040	*	**DB**	DB	WQBA	TO (S)	The Territorial Army Centenary
60041	+	**E**	DB	WQCA	TO (S)
60042		**E**	DB	WQCA	TO (S)
60043		**E**	DB	WQCA	TO (S)
60044	*	**DB**	DB	WQBA	TO (S)	Dowlow
60045		**E**	DB	WQCA	TO (S)	The Permanent Way Institution
60046	+	**DC**	DC	DCRO	LB	William Wilberforce
60047	*	**CS**	BN	GBTG	TO
60048		**E**	DB	WQCA	TO (S)
60049		**E**	DB	WQCA	TO (S)
60051	+	**E**	DB	WQCA	TO (S)
60052	+	**E**	DB	WQDA	TO (S)	Glofa Twr – The last deep mine in Wales – Tower Colliery

60053	E	DB	WQCA	TO (S)	
60054 +*	DB	DB	WQBA	TO (S)	
60055 +	DC	DC	DCRO	LB	Thomas Barnardo
60056 +*	CS	BN	GBTG	TO	
60057	EG	DC	DCRS	LB (S)	
60058 +	E	DB	WQCA	TO (S)	
60059 +*	DB	DB	WQBA	TO (S)	Swinden Dalesman
60060	EG	DC	DCRS	LR (S)	
60061	F	DC	DCRS	LB (S)	
60062 *	0	DB	WCAT	TO	Sonia
60063 *	DB	DB	WQBA	TO (S)	
60064 +	EG	DC	DCRS	LB (S)	
60065	E	DB	WQBA	TO (S)	Spirit of JAGUAR
60066 *	AL	DB	WQBA	TO (S)	
60067	EG	DB	WQCA	TO (S)	
60068	EG	DB	WQDA	TO (S)	
60069	E	DB	WQCA	TO (S)	Slioch
60070 +	F	DC	DCRS	LB (S)	
60071 +	E	DB	WQCA	TO (S)	Ribblehead Viaduct
60072	EG	DB	WQCA	TO (S)	
60073	EG	DB	WQCA	TO (S)	
60074 *	AL	DB	WCAT	TO	Luke
60075	E	DC	DCRS	LB (S)	
60076 *	CS	BN	GBTG	TO	Dunbar
60077 +	EG	DB	WQDA	TO (S)	
60078	ML	DB	WQDA	TO (S)	
60079 *	DB	DB	WQBA	TO (S)	
60080 +	E	DC	DCRS	LB (S)	
60081 +	0	LS	WQDA	TO (S)	
60082	EG	DB	WQCA	CE (S)	
60083	E	DB	WQCA	TO (S)	
60084	EG	DB	WQDA	TO (S)	
60085 *	GB	BN	GBTG	TO	
60087 *	GB	BN	GBTG	TO	
60088	F	DB	WQCA	TO (S)	
60089 +	E	DB	WQDA	TO (S)	
60090 +	EG	DC	DCRS	LB (S)	
60091 +*	DB	DB	WQBA	TO (S)	Barry Needham
60092 +*	DB	DB	WQBA	TO (S)	
60093	E	DB	WQDA	TO (S)	
60094	E	DB	WQCA	TO (S)	Rugby Flyer
60095 *	GB	BN	GBTG	TO	
60096 +*	CS	BN	GBTG	TO	
60097 +	E	DB	WQCA	TO (S)	
60098 +	E	DC	DCRS	LB (S)	
60099	AL	DC	DCRS	LR (S)	
60100 *	DB	DB	WCAT	TO	Midland Railway - Butterley
60500	E	DB	WQCA	TO (S)	

CLASS 66   GENERAL MOTORS/EMD   Co-Co

Built: 1998–2008 by General Motors/EMD, London, Ontario, Canada (Model JT42CWR (low emission locomotives Model JT42CWRM)) or 2013–16 by EMD/Progress Rail, Muncie, Indiana (66752–779).
Engine: General Motors 12N-710G3B-EC two stroke of 2385 kW (3200 hp) at 904 rpm. 66752–779 GM 12N-710G3B-T2.
Main Alternator: General Motors AR8/CA6.
Traction Motors: General Motors D43TR.
Maximum Tractive Effort: 409 kN (92000 lbf).
Continuous Tractive Effort: 260 kN (58390 lbf) at 15.9 mph.

Power at Rail: 1850 kW (2480 hp).	**Train Brakes:** Air.
Brake Force: 68 t.	**Dimensions:** 21.35 x 2.64 m.
Weight: 127 t.	**Wheel Diameter:** 1120 mm.
Design Speed: 87.5 mph.	**Maximum Speed:** 75 mph.
Fuel Capacity: 6550 litres.	**Route Availability:** 7.
Train Supply: Not equipped.	**Total:** 415.

All equipped with Slow Speed Control.

Class 66s previously used in the UK but now in use abroad are listed in section 1.6 of this book. Some of the DBC 66s moved to France return to Great Britain from time to time for maintenance or operational requirements.

66422 carries its name on one side only.

Class 66 delivery dates. The Class 66 design and delivery evolved over an 18-year period, with more than 400 locomotives delivered. For clarity the delivery dates (by year) for each batch of locomotives is as follows:

66001–250	EWS (now DB Cargo). 1998–2000 (some now in use in France or Poland, ten sold to GB Railfreight and five on long-term hire to DRS).
66301–305	Fastline. 2008. Later transferred to DRS and then in 2022 to GB Railfreight.
66306–316	GB Railfreight. Number series reserved for additional locomotives being imported from mainland Europe in 2023–24.
66401–410	DRS. 2003. Now in use with GB Railfreight or Colas Rail and renumbered 66733–737 and 66742–746 (66734[i] since scrapped).
66411–420	DRS. 2006. Now leased by Freightliner (66411/412/417 exported to Poland).
66421–430	DRS. 2007
66431–434	DRS. 2008
66501–505	Freightliner. 1999
66506–520	Freightliner. 2000
66521–525	Freightliner. 2000 (66521 since scrapped).
66526–531	Freightliner. 2001
66532–537	Freightliner. 2001
66538–543	Freightliner. 2001
66544–553	Freightliner. 2001
66554	Freightliner. 2002 (replacement for 66521).
66555–566	Freightliner. 2002

66567–574	Freightliner. 2003. 66573–574 now used by Colas Rail and renumbered 66846–847.
66575–577	Freightliner. 2004. Now used by Colas Rail and renumbered 66848–850.
66578–581	Freightliner. 2005. Now used by GBRf and renumbered 66738–741.
66582–594	Freightliner. 2007 (66582/583/584/586 exported to Poland).
66595–599	Freightliner. 2008 (66595 exported to Poland).
66601–606	Freightliner. 2000
66607–612	Freightliner. 2002 (66607/609/611/612 exported to Poland)
66613–618	Freightliner. 2003
66619–622	Freightliner. 2005
66623–625	Freightliner. 2007 (66624/625 exported to Poland).
66701–707	GB Railfreight. 2001
66708–712	GB Railfreight. 2002
66713–717	GB Railfreight. 2003
66718–722	GB Railfreight. 2006
66723–727	GB Railfreight. 2006
66728–732	GB Railfreight. 2008
66734[11]	GB Railfreight. Imported from mainland Europe in 2021.
66747–749	Built in 2008 as 20078968-004/006/007 (DE 6313/15/16) for Crossrail AG in the Netherlands but never used. Sold to GB Railfreight in 2012.
66750–751	Built in 2003 as 20038513-01/04 and have worked in the Netherlands, Germany and Poland. GBRf secured these two locomotives on lease in 2013.
66752–772	GB Railfreight. 2014
66773–779	GB Railfreight. 2016
66780–789	GB Railfreight. 1998–2000. Former DBC locomotives acquired in 2017 that have been renumbered in the GBRf number series.
66790–792	Built in 2002 as 20018352-3/4/5 (T66403–405) for CargoNet, Norway. Sold to Beacon Rail and leased to GBRf from 2019.
66793–799	Second-hand locos imported from mainland Europe in 2020–21 for GB Railfreight.
66951–952	Freightliner. 2004
66953–957	Freightliner. 2008 (66954 exported to Poland).

Advertising and non-standard liveries:

66004	I am a Climate Hero (green).
66023	Celebrating the King's Coronation (blue).
66109	PD Ports (dark blue).
66587	Ocean Network Express (pink with white stripes).
66708	**GB** livery with the addition of a large Ukraine flag.
66709	MSC – blue with images of a container ship.
66718	London Underground 150 (black).
66720	Wascosa blue with orange cabsides.
66721	London Underground 150 (white with tube map images). Also carries the numbers 1933 and 2013.
66723	Also carries the number ZA723.
66731	Thank you NHS (blue with orange cabsides).
66734	Platinum Jubilee (purple).
66747	Newell & Wright (blue, white & red).

66769	Prostate Cancer UK (black with blue lettering).
66775	Also carries the number F231.
66779	BR dark green.
66780	Cemex (grey, blue & red).
66783	Biffa (red & orange).
66793	Two-tone trainload freight grey with Construction decals.
66794	Two-tone trainload freight grey with Petroleum decals.
66796	It's Cleaner by Rail (green & blue).
66797	Beacon Rail (all-over blue with yellow solebar stripe and large yellow circle logo).

Class 66/0. DB Cargo-operated locomotives.

All fitted with Swinghead Automatic "Buckeye" Combination Couplers except 66001 and 66002.

66031, 66091, 66108, 66122 and 66126 are on long-term hire to DRS.

† Fitted with additional lights and drawgear for Lickey banking duties.

t Fitted with tripcocks for working over London Underground tracks between Harrow-on-the-Hill and Amersham.

66001 t	**DB**	DB	WBAE	TO	
66002	**E**	DB	WBAE	TO	
66003	**E**	DB	WBAE	TO	
66004	**AL**	DB	WBAR	TO	
66005	**MT**	DB	WBAE	TO	Maritime Intermodal One
66006	**E**	DB	WBAT	TO	
66007	**DB**	DB	WBAT	TO	
66009	**DB**	DB	WBAE	TO	
66010	**DB**	DB	WBAT	TO	
66011	**E**	DB	WBAE	TO	
66012	**DB**	DB	WBAE	TO	
66013	**E**	DB	WBAE	TO	
66014	**DB**	DB	WBAT	TO	
66015	**E**	DB	WBAE	TO	
66017 t	**DB**	DB	WBAT	TO	
66018	**DB**	DB	WQBA	TO (S)	
66019 t	**DB**	DB	WBAT	TO	
66020	**DB**	DB	WBAE	TO	
66021	**DB**	DB	WBAT	TO	
66023	**0**	DB	WBAT	TO	
66024	**E**	DB	WBAE	TO	
66025	**DB**	DB	WBAT	TO	
66026	**DB**	DB	WBAI	TO	
66027	**DB**	DB	WBAE	TO	
66028	**E**	DB	WBAE	TO	
66030	**E**	DB	WBAT	TO	
66031	**DR**	DB	XHIM	KM	
66032	**DB**	DB	WBAE	TO	
66034	**DB**	DB	WBAE	TO	
66035	**DB**	DB	WBAE	TO	Resourceful
66037	**E**	DB	WQBA	TO (S)	

66039		**DB**	DB	WBET	TO	
66040		**E**	DB	WBAT	TO	
66041		**DB**	DB	WBAT	TO	
66043		**E**	DB	WQBA	TO (S)	
66044		**DB**	DB	WBAT	TO	
66047		**MT**	DB	WBAE	TO	Maritime Intermodal Two
66050		**DB**	DB	WBAE	TO	
66051		**MT**	DB	WBAT	TO	Maritime Intermodal Four
66053		**E**	DB	WBAE	TO	
66054		**DB**	DB	WBAT	TO	
66055	†	**DB**	DB	WBLE	TO	Alain Thauvette
66056	†	**DB**	DB	WBLE	TO	
66057	†	**E**	DB	WBLE	TO	
66059	†	**E**	DB	WBLE	TO	
66060		**E**	DB	WBAT	TO	
66061		**DB**	DB	WBAE	TO	
66063		**E**	DB	WBAE	TO	
66065		**DB**	DB	WBAT	TO	
66066		**DB**	DB	WBAT	TO	Geoff Spencer
66067		**DB**	DB	WBAT	TO	
66068		**E**	DB	WBAT	TO	
66069		**DB**	DB	WBAT	TO	
66070		**DB**	DB	WBAT	TO	
66073		**DB**	DB	WBAE	TO	
66074		**DB**	DB	WBAE	TO	
66075		**E**	DB	WBAE	TO	
66076		**E**	DB	WBAE	TO	
66077		**DB**	DB	WBAT	TO	Benjamin Gimbert G.C.
66078		**DB**	DB	WBAE	TO	
66079		**DB**	DB	WBAT	TO	James Nightall G.C.
66080		**E**	DB	WBAE	TO	
66082		**DB**	DB	WBAE	TO	
66083		**E**	DB	WBAT	TO	
66084		**DB**	DB	WBAT	TO	
66085		**DB**	DB	WBAT	TO	
66086		**DB**	DB	WBAE	TO	
66087		**E**	DB	WBAE	TO	
66088		**DB**	DB	WBAT	TO	
66089		**E**	DB	WBAT	TO	
66090		**MT**	DB	WBAE	TO	Maritime Intermodal Six
66091		**DR**	DB	XHIM	KM	
66092		**E**	DB	WBAT	TO	
66093		**DB**	DB	WBAE	TO	
66094		**DB**	DB	WBAE	TO	
66095		**E**	DB	WBAE	TO	
66096		**E**	DB	WBAT	TO	
66097		**DB**	DB	WBAT	TO	
66098		**E**	DB	WBAE	TO	
66099	r	**DB**	DB	WBBE	TO	
66100	r	**DB**	DB	WBBE	TO	Armistice 100 1918–2018
66101	r	**DB**	DB	WBBE	TO	

66102 r	**DB**	DB	WBBE	TO	
66103 r	**E**	DB	WBBE	TO	
66104 r	**DB**	DB	WBBT	TO	
66105 r	**DB**	DB	WBBE	TO	
66106 r	**E**	DB	WBBE	TO	
66107 r	**DB**	DB	WBBT	TO	
66108 r	**DR**	DB	XHIM	KM	
66109	**AL**	DB	WBAT	TO	Teesport Express
66110 r	**DB**	DB	WBBE	TO	
66111 r	**E**	DB	WBBE	TO	
66112 r	**E**	DB	WBBE	TO	
66113 r	**DB**	DB	WBBT	TO	
66114 r	**DB**	DB	WBBE	TO	
66115	**DB**	DB	WBAE	TO	
66116	**E**	DB	WBAE	TO	
66117	**DB**	DB	WBAE	TO	
66118	**DB**	DB	WBAE	TO	
66119	**E**	DB	WBAE	TO	
66120	**E**	DB	WBAE	TO	
66121	**E**	DB	WBAE	TO	
66122	**DR**	DB	XHIM	KM	
66124	**DB**	DB	WBAT	TO	
66125	**DB**	DB	WBAE	TO	
66126	**DR**	DB	XHIM	KM	
66127	**E**	DB	WBAE	TO	
66128	**DB**	DB	WBAE	TO	
66129	**E**	DB	WBAT	TO	
66130	**DB**	DB	WBAT	TO	
66131	**DB**	DB	WBAE	TO	
66133	**E**	DB	WBAE	TO	
66134	**DB**	DB	WBAE	TO	
66135	**DB**	DB	WBAE	TO	
66136	**DB**	DB	WBAE	TO	
66137	**DB**	DB	WBAE	TO	
66138	**E**	DB	WQBA	TO (S)	
66139	**DB**	DB	WBAE	TO	
66140	**E**	DB	WBAE	TO	
66142	**MT**	DB	WBAT	TO	Maritime Intermodal Three
66143	**DB**	DB	WBAE	TO	
66144	**DB**	DB	WBAT	TO	
66145	**E**	DB	WQBA	TO (S)	
66147	**DB**	DB	WBAE	TO	
66148	**MT**	DB	WBAE	TO	Maritime Intermodal Seven
66149	**DB**	DB	WBHT	TO	
66150	**DB**	DB	WBAE	TO	
66151	**E**	DB	WBAE	TO	
66152	**DB**	DB	WBAE	TO	Derek Holmes Railway Operator
66154	**DB**	DB	WBAT	TO	
66155	**E**	DB	WBAT	TO	
66156	**DB**	DB	WBHT	TO	
66158	**E**	DB	WBAE	TO	

66160	**E**	DB	WBAT	TO	
66161	**E**	DB	WBHT	TO	
66162	**MT**	DB	WBAT	TO	Maritime Intermodal Five
66164	**E**	DB	WBAE	TO	
66165	**DB**	DB	WBAT	TO	
66167	**DB**	DB	WBHT	TO	
66168	**DB**	DB	WBAT	TO	
66169	**E**	DB	WBAT	TO	
66170	**E**	DB	WBAE	TO	
66171	**E**	DB	WBHT	TO	
66172	**E**	DB	WBAE	TO	PAUL MELLENEY
66174	**E**	DB	WBHT	TO	
66175	**DB**	DB	WBAE	TO	Rail Riders Express
66176	**E**	DB	WBAT	TO	
66177	**E**	DB	WBAE	TO	
66179	**E**	DB	WBAT	TO	
66181	**E**	DB	WBHT	TO	
66182	**DB**	DB	WBAE	TO	
66183	**E**	DB	WBHT	TO	
66185	**DB**	DB	WBAT	TO	DP WORLD London Gateway
66186	**E**	DB	WBAT	TO	
66187	**E**	DB	WBAE	TO	
66188	**E**	DB	WBAT	TO	
66190	**DB**	DB	WBAE	TO	Martin House Children's Hospice
66192	**DB**	DB	WBAT	TO	
66194	**E**	DB	WBHT	TO	
66197	**DB**	DB	WBAE	TO	
66198	**E**	DB	WBAT	TO	
66199	**E**	DB	WBAE	TO	
66200	**E**	DB	WBVT	TO	
66205	**DB**	DB	WBAI	TO	
66206	**DB**	DB	WBVT	TO	
66207	**E**	DB	WBAE	TO	
66221	**E**	DB	WBHT	TO	
66224	**E**	DB	WBAI	TO (S)	
66230	**DB**	DB	WQCA	TO (S)	
66244	**DB**	DB	WBAE	TO	

Class 66/3. Former Fastline and DRS-operated locomotives now operated by GB Railfreight. Low emission. Details as Class 66/0 except:

Engine: EMD 12N-710G3B-T2 two stroke of 2420 kW (3245 hp) at 904 rpm.
Traction Motors: General Motors D43TRC.
Fuel Capacity: 5150 litres.

66301	r	**DR**	BN	GBLT	RR
66302	r	**DR**	BN	GBLT	RR
66303	r	**DR**	BN	GBLT	RR
66304	r	**DR**	BN	GBLT	RR
66305	r	**DR**	BN	GBLT	RR

Class 66/3. Number series reserved for further locomotives being sourced from mainland Europe for GB Railfreight. Locomotives are being delivered during 2023–24.

66306 (CB1001)	**GB**	AK	GBSD	RR	SCS Logistics
66307 (77502)	**GB**	AK	GBSD	RR	IPSWICH TOWN
66308 (77503)	**GB**	AK	GBSD	RR	
66309 (77501)	**GB**	AK	GBSD	RR	
66310 (77507)		AK		LB	
66311 (77504)		AK		LB	
66312 (266107)		AK		LB	
66313 (CB1000)		AK		LB	
66314 (77505)		AK			
66315 (77506)		AK			
66316 (29003)		AK			

Class 66/4. Low emission. Akiem-owned. Details as Class 66/3.

66413	**FG**	AK	DFIN	LD	
66414	**FH**	AK	DFIN	LD	
66415	**FG**	AK	DFIN	LD	You Are Never Alone
66416	**FH**	AK	DFIN	LD	
66418	**FH**	AK	DFIN	LD	PATRIOT – IN MEMORY OF FALLEN RAILWAY EMPLOYEES
66419	**FG**	AK	DFIN	LD	Lionesses' Roar
66420	**FH**	AK	DFIN	LD	
66421	**DR**	AK	XHIM	KM	Gresty Bridge TMD
66422	**DR**	AK	XHIM	KM	Max Joule 1958–1999
66423	**DR**	AK	XHIM	KM	
66424	**DR**	AK	XHIM	KM	Driver Paul Scrivens 1969–2021
66425	**DR**	AK	XHIM	KM	Nigel J Kirchstein 1957–2021
66426	**DR**	AK	XHIM	KM	
66427	**DR**	AK	XHIM	KM	
66428	**DR**	AK	XHIM	KM	Carlisle Eden Mind
66429	**DR**	AK	XHIM	KM	
66430	**DR**	AK	XHIM	KM	
66431	**DR**	AK	XHIM	KM	
66432	**DR**	AK	XHIM	KM	
66433	**DR**	AK	XHIM	KM	Carlisle Power Signal Box 50th Anniversary 1973–2023
66434	**DR**	AK	XHIM	KM	

Class 66/5. Standard design. Freightliner-operated locomotives. Details as Class 66/0.

66501	**FL**	P	DHLT	LD (S)	Japan 2001
66502	**FG**	P	DFIM	LD	Basford Hall Centenary 2001
66503	**FG**	P	DFIM	LD	The RAILWAY MAGAZINE Celebrating 125 years 1897–2022
66504	**FH**	P	DFIM	LD	
66505	**FL**	P	DFIM	LD	
66506	**FL**	E	DFIM	LD	Crewe Regeneration
66507	**FL**	E	DFIM	LD	
66508	**FG**	E	DFIM	LD	City of Doncaster

66509	**FG**	E	DFIM	LD	Josiah's Wish
66510	**FL**	E	DFIM	LD	
66511	**FL**	E	DFIM	LD	
66512	**FL**	E	DFIM	LD	
66513	**FL**	E	DFIM	LD	
66514	**FL**	E	DFIM	LD	
66515	**FL**	E	DFIM	LD	
66516	**FL**	E	DFIM	LD	
66517	**FL**	E	DFIM	LD	
66518	**FL**	E	DFIM	LD	
66519	**FL**	E	DFIM	LD	
66520	**FL**	E	DFIM	LD	
66522	**FL**	E	DFIM	LD	
66523	**FL**	E	DFIM	LD	
66524	**FL**	E	DFIM	LD	
66525	**FL**	E	DFIM	LD	
66528	**FH**	P	DFIM	LD	Madge Elliot MBE Borders Railway Opening 2015
66531	**FL**	P	DFIM	LD	
66532	**FL**	P	DFIM	LD	P&O Nedlloyd Atlas
66533	**FL**	P	DFIM	LD	Hanjin Express/Senator Express
66534	**FL**	P	DFIM	LD	OOCL Express
66536	**FL**	P	DFIM	LD	
66537	**FL**	P	DFIM	LD	
66538	**FL**	E	DFIM	LD	
66539	**FL**	E	DFIM	LD	
66540	**FL**	E	DFIM	LD	Ruby
66541	**FL**	E	DFIM	LD	
66542	**FL**	E	DFIM	LD	
66543	**FL**	E	DFIM	LD	
66544	**FL**	P	DFIM	LD	
66545	**FL**	P	DFIM	LD	
66546	**FL**	P	DFIM	LD	
66547	**FL**	P	DFIM	LD	
66548	**FL**	P	DFIM	LD	
66549	**FL**	P	DFIM	LD	
66550	**FL**	P	DFIM	LD	
66551	**FL**	P	DFIM	LD	
66552	**FL**	P	DHLT	LD (S)	Maltby Raider
66553	**FL**	P	DFIM	LD	
66554	**FL**	E	DFIM	LD	
66555	**FL**	E	DFIM	LD	
66556	**FL**	E	DFIM	LD	
66557	**FL**	E	DFIM	LD	
66558	**FL**	E	DFIM	LD	
66559	**FL**	E	DFIM	LD	
66560	**FL**	E	DFIM	LD	
66561	**FL**	E	DFIM	LD	
66562	**FL**	E	DFIM	LD	
66563	**FL**	E	DFIM	LD	
66564	**FL**	E	DFIM	LD	

66565	FL	E	DFIM	LD
66566	FL	E	DFIM	LD
66567	FL	E	DFIM	LD
66568	FL	E	DFIM	LD
66569	FL	E	DFIM	LD
66570	FL	E	DFIM	LD
66571	FL	E	DFIM	LD
66572	FL	E	DFIM	LD

Class 66/5. Freightliner-operated low emission locomotives. Details as Class 66/3.

66585	FL	HX	DFIN	LD	
66587	AL	HX	DFIN	LD	AS ONE, WE CAN
66588	FL	HX	DFIN	LD	
66589	FL	HX	DFIN	LD	
66590	FL	HX	DFIN	LD	
66591	FL	HX	DFIN	LD	
66592	FL	HX	DFIN	LD	Johnson Stevens Agencies
66593	FL	HX	DFIN	LD	3MG MERSEY MULTIMODAL GATEWAY
66594	FL	HX	DFIN	LD	NYK Spirit of Kyoto
66596	FL	BN	DFIN	LD	
66597	FL	BN	DFIN	LD	Viridor
66598	FL	BN	DFIN	LD	
66599	FL	BN	DHLT	LD (S)	

Class 66/6. Freightliner-operated locomotives with modified gear ratios.
Details as Class 66/0 except:
Maximum Tractive Effort: 467 kN (105080 lbf).
Continuous Tractive Effort: 296 kN (66630 lbf) at 14.0 mph.
Design Speed: 65 mph.   **Maximum Speed**: 65 mph.

66601	FL	P	DFHH	LD	The Hope Valley
66602	FL	P	DFHH	LD	
66603	FL	P	DFHH	LD	
66604	FL	P	DFHH	LD	
66605	FG	P	DFHH	LD	
66606	FL	P	DFHH	LD	
66607	FL	P	DFHH	LD	
66610	FL	P	DFHH	LD	
66613	FL	E	DFHH	LD	
66614	FL	E	DFHH	LD	1916 POPPY 2016
66615	FL	E	DFHH	LD	
66616	FL	E	DFHH	LD	
66617	FL	E	DFHH	LD	
66618	FL	E	DFHH	LD	Railways Illustrated Annual Photographic Awards Alan Barnes
66619	FL	E	DFHH	LD	Derek W. Johnson MBE
66620	FL	E	DFHH	LD	
66621	FL	E	DFHH	LD	
66622	FL	E	DFHH	LD	

Class 66/6. Freightliner-operated low emission locomotive with modified gear ratios. Details as Class 66/6 except:

Fuel Capacity: 5150 litres.

66623	**FG**	AK	DFHH	LD	Lest We Forget

Class 66/7. Standard design. GB Railfreight-operated locomotives. Details as Class 66/0 except 66793–796 which are as Class 66/6.

66701	**GB**	E	GBBT	RR	
66702	**GB**	E	GBBT	RR	Blue Lightning
66703	**GB**	E	GBBT	RR	Doncaster PSB 1981–2002
66704	**GB**	E	GBBT	RR	Colchester Power Signalbox
66705	**GB**	E	GBBT	RR	Golden Jubilee
66706	**GB**	E	GBBT	RR	Nene Valley
66707	**GB**	E	GBBT	RR	Sir Sam Fay GREAT CENTRAL RAILWAY
66708	**0**	E	GBBT	RR	Слава УКраïнi/Glory to Ukraine
66709	**AL**	E	GBBT	RR	Sorrento
66710	**GB**	E	GBBT	RR	Phil Packer BRIT
66711	**AI**	E	GBBT	RR	Sence
66712	**GB**	E	GBBT	RR	Peterborough Power Signalbox
66713	**GB**	E	GBBT	RR	Forest City
66714	**GB**	E	GBBT	RR	Cromer Lifeboat
66715	**GB**	E	GBBT	RR	VALOUR – IN MEMORY OF ALL RAILWAY EMPLOYEES WHO GAVE THEIR LIVES FOR THEIR COUNTRY
66716	**GB**	E	GBBT	RR	LOCOMOTIVE & CARRIAGE INSTITUTION CENTENARY 1911–2011
66717	**GB**	E	GBBT	RR	Good Old Boy

66718–751. GB Railfreight locomotives.

Details as Class 66/0 except 66718–732/747–749 as below:

Engine: EMD 12N-710G3B-T2 two stroke of 2420 kW (3245 hp) at 904 rpm.
Traction Motors: General Motors D43TRC.
Fuel Capacity: 5546 litres (66718–722) or 5150 litres (66723–732/747–749).

66747–749 were originally built for Crossrail AG in the Netherlands.

66750/751 were originally built for mainland Europe in 2003.

66718	**AL**	E	GBLT	RR	Peter, Lord Hendy of Richmond Hill of Imber in the County of Wiltshire
66719	**GB**	E	GBLT	RR	METRO-LAND
66720	**0**	E	GBLT	RR	wascosa
66721	**AL**	E	GBLT	RR	Harry Beck
66722	**GB**	E	GBLT	RR	Sir Edward Watkin
66723	**GB**	E	GBLT	RR	Chinook
66724	**GB**	E	GBLT	RR	Drax Power Station
66725	**GB**	E	GBLT	RR	SUNDERLAND
66726	**GB**	E	GBLT	RR	SHEFFIELD WEDNESDAY
66727	**MT**	E	GBLT	RR	Maritime One
66728	**GB**	P	GBLT	RR	Institution of Railway Operators
66729	**GB**	P	GBLT	RR	DERBY COUNTY

66730	**GB**	P	GBLT		RR	Whitemoor
66731	**AL**	P	GBLT		RR	Capt. Tom Moore
						A True British Inspiration
66732	**GB**	P	GBLT		RR	GBRf The First Decade 1999–2009
						John Smith – MD
66733 (66401) r	**GB**	P	GBFM		RR	Cambridge PSB
66734[1](PB04)	**O**	BN	GBEB		RR	PLATINUM JUBILEE
66735 (66403)	**GB**	P	GBBT		RR	PETERBOROUGH UNITED
66736 (66404) r	**GB**	P	GBFM		RR	WOLVERHAMPTON WANDERERS
66737 (66405) r	**GB**	P	GBFM		RR	Lesia
66738 (66578)	**GB**	BN	GBBT		RR	HUDDERSFIELD TOWN
66739 (66579) r	**GB**	BN	GBFM		RR	Bluebell Railway
66740 (66580) r	**GB**	BN	GBFM		RR	Sarah
66741 (66581)	**GB**	BN	GBBT		RR	Swanage Railway
66742 (66406, 66841)	**GB**	BN	GBBT		RR	ABP Port of Immingham
						Centenary 1912–2012
66743 (66407, 66842) r	**M**	BN	GBFM		RR	
66744 (66408, 66843)	**GB**	BN	GBBT		RR	Crossrail
66745 (66409, 66844)	**GB**	BN	GBRT		RR	
66746 (66410, 66845) r	**M**	BN	GBFM		RR	
66747 (20078968-007)	**AL**	BN	GBEB		RR	Made in Sheffield
66748 (20078968-004)	**GB**	BN	GBEB		RR	West Burton 50
66749 (20078968-006)	**GB**	BN	GBEB		RR	Christopher Hopcroft MBE
						60 Years Railway Service
66750 (20038513-01)	**GB**	BN	GBEB		RR	Bristol Panel Signal Box
66751 (20038513-04) c	**GB**	BN	GBEB		RR	Inspiration Delivered
						Hitachi Rail Europe

66752–779. Low emission, new build GB Railfreight locomotives. Details as Class 66/3.

66752	**GB**	GB	GBEL	RR	The Hoosier State
66753	**GB**	GB	GBEL	RR	EMD Roberts Road
66754	**GB**	GB	GBEL	RR	Northampton Saints
66755	**GB**	GB	GBEL	RR	Tony Berkeley OBE
					RFG Chairman 1997–2018
66756	**GB**	GB	GBEL	RR	Royal Corps of Signals
66757	**GB**	GB	GBEL	RR	West Somerset Railway
66758	**GB**	GB	GBEL	RR	The Pavior
66759	**GB**	GB	GBEL	RR	Chippy
66760	**GB**	GB	GBEL	RR	David Gordon Harris
66761	**GB**	GB	GBEL	RR	Wensleydale Railway Association
					25 Years 1990–2015
66762	**GB**	GB	GBEL	RR	
66763	**GB**	GB	GBEL	RR	Severn Valley Railway
66764	**GB**	GB	GBEL	RR	Major John Poyntz Engineer &
					Railwayman
66765	**GB**	GB	GBEL	RR	Julia Garn
66766	**GB**	GB	GBEL	RR	Gail Richardson
66767	**GB**	GB	GBEL	RR	King's Cross PSB 1971–2021

66768	**GB**	GB	GBEL	RR	
66769	**AL**	GB	GBEL	RR	LMA LEAGUE MANAGERS ASSOCIATION/ Paul Taylor Our Inspiration
66770	**GB**	GB	GBEL	RR	
66771	**GB**	GB	GBEL	RR	Amanda
66772	**GB**	GB	GBEL	RR	Maria
66773	**GB**	GB	GBNB	RR	Pride of GB Railfreight
66774	**GB**	GB	GBNB	RR	
66775	**GB**	GB	GBNB	RR	HMS Argyll
66776	**GB**	GB	GBNB	RR	Joanne
66777	**GB**	GB	GBNB	RR	Annette
66778	**GB**	GB	GBNB	RR	Cambois Depot 25 Years
66779	**0**	GB	GBEL	RR	EVENING STAR

66780–789. Standard design. Former DB Cargo locomotives acquired by GB Railfreight in 2017. Details as Class 66/0. Fitted with Swinghead Automatic "Buckeye" Combination Couplers.

† Fitted with additional lights and drawgear formerly used for Lickey banking duties.

66780	(66008)	**AL**	GB	GBOB	RR	The Cemex Express
66781	(66016)	**GB**	GB	GBOB	RR	Darius Cheskin
66782	(66046)	**GB**	GB	GBOB	RR	
66783	(66058) †	**AL**	GB	GBOB	RR	The Flying Dustman
66784	(66081)	**GB**	GB	GBOB	RR	Keighley & Worth Valley Railway 50th Anniversary 1968–2018
66785	(66132)	**GB**	GB	GBOB	RR	John Ellis
66786	(66141)	**GB**	GB	GBOB	RR	Cambridge University Railway Club Founded by Junior Members in 1911
66787	(66184)	**GB**	GB	GBOB	RR	Three Bridges ASC
66788	(66238)	**GB**	GB	GBOB	RR	LOCOMOTION 15
66789	(66250)	**BL**	GB	GBOB	RR	British Rail 1948–1997

66790–799. Locomotives sourced from mainland Europe.

66790	(T66403)	**GB**	BN	GBBT	RR	Louise
66791	(T66404)	**BN**	BN	GBBT	RR	
66792	(T66405)	**GB**	BN	GBBT	RR	Collaboration
66793	(29004)	**0**	BN	GBHH	RR	
66794	(29005)	**0**	BN	GBHH	RR	Steve Hannam
66795	(561-05)	**GB**	BN	GBHH	RR	Bescot LDC
66796	(561-01)	**AL**	BN	GBHH	RR	The Green Progressor
66797	(513-09)	**0**	BN	GBEB	RR	
66798	(561-03)	**GB**	BN	GBEB	RR	Justine
66799	(6602)	**GB**	BN	GBEB	RR	Modern Railways Diamond Jubilee

Class 66/8. Standard design. Colas Rail locomotives. Details as Class 66/0.

66846	(66573)	**CS**	BN	COLO	HJ	
66847	(66574)	**CS**	BN	COLO	HJ	Terry Baker
66848	(66575)	**CS**	BN	COLO	HJ	
66849	(66576)	**CS**	BN	COLO	HJ	Wylam Dilly
66850	(66577)	**CS**	BN	COLO	HJ	David Maidment OBE

Class 66/9. Freightliner locomotives. Low emission "demonstrator" locomotives. Details as Class 66/3. * **Fuel Capacity:** 5905 litres.

66951	*	**FL**	E	DFIN	LD
66952		**FL**	E	DFIN	LD

Class 66/5. Freightliner-operated low emission locomotives. Owing to the 665xx number range being full, subsequent deliveries of 66/5s were numbered from 66953 onwards. Details as Class 66/5 (low emission).

66953	**FL**	BN	DFIN	LD	
66955	**FL**	BN	DHLT	LD (S)	
66956	**FL**	BN	DHLT	LD (S)	
66957	**FL**	BN	DFIN	LD	Stephenson Locomotive Society 1909–2009

CLASS 67   ALSTOM/GENERAL MOTORS   Bo-Bo

Built: 1999–2000 by Alstom at Valencia, Spain, as sub-contractors for General Motors (General Motors model JT42 HW-HS).
Engine: GM 12N-710G3B-EC two stroke of 2385 kW (3200 hp) at 904 rpm.
Main Alternator: General Motors AR9A/HEP7/CA6C.
Traction Motors: General Motors D43FM.
Maximum Tractive Effort: 141 kN (31770 lbf).
Continuous Tractive Effort: 90 kN (20200 lbf) at 46.5 mph.

Power at Rail: 1860 kW.	**Train Brakes:** Air.
Brake Force: 78 t.	**Dimensions:** 19.74 x 2.72 m.
Weight: 90 t.	**Wheel Diameter:** 965 mm.
Design Speed: 125 mph.	**Maximum Speed:** 125 mph.
Fuel Capacity: 4927 litres.	**Route Availability:** 8.
Train Supply: Electric, index 66.	**Total:** 30.

All equipped with Slow Speed Control and Swinghead Automatic "Buckeye" Combination Couplers.

The following locomotives have been modified to operate with Transport for Wales Mark 4 stock: 67008, 67010, 67012, 67013, 67014, 67015, 67017, 67020, 67022, 67025, 67029.

Non-standard liveries:

67007 Platinum Jubille (purple).
67026 Diamond Jubilee (silver).
67029 All over silver with DB logos.

67001		**AB**	DB	WQDA	CE (S)
67002		**DB**	DB	WEAC	CE
67003		**AB**	DB	WQDA	TO (S)
67004	r	**DB**	DB	WQDA	TO (S)
67005		**RZ**	DB	WAAC	CE	Queen's Messenger
67006		**RZ**	DB	WAAC	CE	Royal Sovereign
67007	r	**0**	DB	WABC	CE
67008		**TW**	DB	WAWC	CE
67009	r	**E**	DB	WQDA	CE (S)
67010		**DB**	DB	WAWC	CE

▲ RMS Locotec-liveried 08754 shunts Transport for Wales DMU 197 102 into Wolverton Works on 19/06/23. **Mark Beal**

▼ Brand new Beacon Rail-liveried 18012 and 18011 are seen stored at Wolverton Works on 26/05/23. **Mark Beal**

▲ LUL maroon-liveried 20142 and BR green 20007 pass Saxilby with 6Z35 13.05 Doncaster–Derby RTC wagon movement on 04/02/22. **Robert Pritchard**

▼ BR blue-liveried 31128 shunts stock at Pickering on the North Yorkshire Moors Railway on 09/06/23. **Andy Chard**

▲ West Coast Railway Company-liveried 33029 and 33025 clear the summit at Whiteball with a Burton-on-Trent–Paignton railtour on 29/05/23. **Stephen Ginn**

▼ Colas Rail-liveried 37099 hauls 1Q50 13.43 Derby RTC–Doncaster test train through Barnetby on 29/06/23. **Jonathan Longbottom**

▲ Europhoenix-liveried 37608 and 37510 top-and-tail London Overground EMU 710374 through Sheffield on a 5Q99 Derby–Derby turning movement on 03/10/22.
Robert Pritchard

▲ BR green-liveried 40145 is seen at Crewe on 12/11/22. **Stuart Hood**

▼ ScotRail InterCity-liveried 43168 and 43003 pass Bishopbriggs shortly after departure from Glasgow Queen Street with the 08.41 to Aberdeen on 09/06/23. **Robert Pritchard**

▲ Rail Adventure-liveried HST power cars 43484 and 43465 pass Clay Cross on 20/03/23 hauling Railvac 3 as 6X43 10.03 Tyne Yard–Butterley. **Robert Pritchard**

▼ BR blue-liveried 47749 approaches Eastleigh hauling South Western Railway EMU 701055 from Derby to Eastleigh depot on 10/08/23.　　　**Steve Stubbs**

20

▲ GB Railfreight-liveried 50007 is seen on display at Long Marston on 22/06/23.　　**Ian Beardsley**

▼ BR blue-liveried 55009 approaches Sheffield with the 06.57 Willington–London King's Cross "Capital Deltic Reprise" railtour on 29/07/23.　　**Robert Pritchard**

▲ Colas Rail-liveried 56096 is seen at Nottingham with 0Z41 12.08 Doncaster–Nottingham Eastcroft depot light engine move on 12/06/23. **Robert Pritchard**

▼ Pullman Car Company-liveried 57313 is seen at Powderham, between Dawlish and Exeter, with the 17.30 Paignton–Birmingham International Northern Belle on 22/08/23. **Robin Ralston**

▲ Hanson Quarry Products-liveried 59104 and Freightliner-liveried 66589 pass Langley with 7A09 07.18 Merehead–Acton on 18/10/22. **Robert Pritchard**

▼ Cappagh-liveried 60028 is seen at Dove Holes quarry on 27/07/23. **Steve Stubbs**

▲ In retro 1980s style two-tone trainload freight grey with Petroleum logos, GB Railfreight 66794 passes Ashford (Surrey) with 6Y26 10.51 Newhaven Marine–Woking loaded sand. **Robert Pritchard**

▲ Transport for Wales-liveried 67008 leaves Crewe with the 12.30 Manchester Piccadilly–Cardiff Central on 16/06/23. **Andy Chard**

▼ DRS (Class 68 style)-liveried 68001 and 68018 top-and-tail 6Z95 15.51 Winfrith–Crewe at Dorchester South on 20/04/23. **Stephen Ginn**

▲ GB Railfreight-liveried 69001 is seen near Feltham with 6Y42 14.05 Hoo Junction–Eastleigh on 16/08/23. **Tom McAtee**

▼ Freightliner-liveried 70001 passes Slindon, Staffordshire with 4M58 Southampton–Garston intermodal on 03/04/23. **Brad Joyce**

▲ BR Civil Engineers-liveried 73119 and Southern-liveried 73202 pass Maidstone East with the 10.55 Tonbridge–Nottingham Branch Line Society railtour on 11/06/23.   **Robert Pritchard**

▼ BR InterCity-liveried 86101 hauls a 5Z91 London Euston–Crewe stock movement past Slindon, Staffordshire on 14/05/23.   **Brad Joyce**

▲ New DRS-liveried 88002 passes Wandel with 4Z27 08.40 Mossend–Daventry intermodal on 08/10/22. **Robin Ralston**

▲ New Freightliner-liveried 90008 and 90013 pass Castlethorpe, near Milton Keynes, with 4M87 11.13 Felixstowe–Trafford Park intermodal on 19/04/23.
Mark Beal

▼ LNER oxblood-liveried 91114 leaves Newark North Gate with the 14.03 London King's Cross–Leeds on 07/05/23. **Ian Beardsley**

▲ Caledonian Sleeper-liveried 92038 is seen at London Euston after arrival with the Lowland Sleeper from Scotland on 17/06/23. **Robert Pritchard**

▼ Eurotunnel Class 9/7 freight shuttle locomotive 9701 leaves the Cheriton Eurotunnel terminus (Folkestone) with another lorry shuttle for Coquelles (Calais) on 08/04/23. **Robert Pritchard**

67011 r	**E**	DB	WQDA	CE (S)	
67012	**CM**	DB	WAWC	CE	
67013	**DB**	DB	WAWC	CE	
67014	**TW**	DB	WAWC	CE	
67015	**DB**	DB	WAWC	CE	
67016	**E**	DB	WQAA	CE (S)	
67017	**TW**	DB	WAWC	CE	
67018	**DB**	DB	WQDA	CE (S)	Keith Heller
67019	**E**	DB	WQDA	TO (S)	
67020	**TB**	DB	WAWC	CE	
67021	**PC**	DB	WAAC	CE	
67022	**TB**	DB	WAWE	CE	
67023	**CS**	BN	COTS	RU	Stella
67024	**PC**	DB	WAAC	CE	
67025	**TW**	DB	WAWC	CE	
67026	**O**	DB	WQDA	CE (S)	Diamond Jubilee
67027	**GB**	BN	COTS	RU	
67028	**DB**	DB	WQBA	CE (S)	
67029	**O**	DB	WAWC	CE	Royal Diamond
67030 r	**E**	DB	WQDA	TO (S)	

CLASS 68   VOSSLOH/STADLER   Bo-Bo

New Vossloh/Stadler mixed-traffic locomotives operated by DRS.

Built: 2012–16 by Vossloh/Stadler, Valencia, Spain.
Engine: Caterpillar C175-16 of 2800 kW (3750 hp) at 1740 rpm.
Main Alternator: ABB WGX560.
Traction Motors: 4 x AMXL400 AC frame mounted ABB 4FRA6063.
Maximum Tractive Effort: 317 kN (71260 lbf).
Continuous Tractive Effort: 258 kN (58000 lbf) at 20.5 mph.

Power at Rail:	**Train Brakes:** Air & rheostatic.
Brake Force: 73 t.	**Dimensions:** 20.50 x 2.69 m.
Weight: 85 t.	**Wheel Diameter:** 1100 mm.
Design Speed: 100 mph.	**Maximum Speed:** 100 mph.
Fuel Capacity: 5600 litres.	**Route Availability:** 7.
Train Supply: Electric, index 96.	**Total:** 34.

68008–015 have been modified to operate in push-pull mode on the Chiltern Railways locomotive-hauled Mark 3 sets.

68019–034 were modified to operate in push-pull mode with the TransPennine Express Mark 5A stock but this has now been stored.

Non-standard and advertising liveries:

68006 Powering a greener Britain (dark & light green).
68014 On Track to a Greener Future (green & white).

68001	**DI**	BN	XHVE	CR	Evolution
68002	**DI**	BN	XHVE	CR	Intrepid
68003	**DI**	BN	XHVE	CR	Astute
68004	**DI**	BN	XHVE	CR	Rapid

68005	**DI**	BN	XHVE	CR	Defiant
68006	**O**	BN	XHVE	CR	Pride of the North
68007	**DR**	BN	XHVE	CR	Valiant
68008	**DI**	BN	XHCS	CR	Avenger
68009	**DI**	BN	XHCS	CR	Titan
68010	**CM**	BN	XHCE	CR	Oxford Flyer
68011	**CM**	BN	XHCE	CR	
68012	**CM**	BN	XHCE	CR	
68013	**CM**	BN	XHCE	CR	Peter Wreford-Bush
68014	**AL**	BN	XHCE	CR	
68015	**CM**	BN	XHCE	CR	Kev Helmer
68016	**DI**	BN	XHVE	CR	Fearless
68017	**DI**	BN	XHVE	CR	Hornet
68018	**DI**	BN	XHVE	CR	Vigilant
68019	**TP**	BN	XHTP	CR	Brutus
68020	**TP**	BN	XHTP	CR	Reliance
68021	**TP**	BN	TPEX	CR	Tireless
68022	**TP**	BN	XHTP	CR	Resolution
68023	**TP**	BN	TPEX	CR	Achilles
68024	**TP**	BN	TPEX	CR	Centaur
68025	**TP**	BN	TPEX	CR	Superb
68026	**TP**	BN	TPEX	CR	Enterprise
68027	**TP**	BN	TPEX	CR	Splendid
68028	**TP**	BN	TPEX	CR	Lord President
68029	**TP**	BN	TPEX	CR	Courageous
68030	**TP**	BN	TPEX	CR	Black Douglas
68031	**TP**	BN	XHTP	CR	Felix
68032	**TP**	BN	TPEX	CR	Destroyer
68033	**DI**	DR	XHTP	CR	The Poppy
68034	**DI**	DR	XHTP	CR	Rail Riders 2020

CLASS 69   BRUSH/BR/RUSTON/EMD   Co-Co

These locomotives are heavy rebuilds of Class 56s for GB Railfreight, with new General Motors engines, the same type as used in the Class 66s. The first rebuild were completed and entered service in 2021 and 16 locomotives will be rebuilt. Donor locomotives shown for 69011–017 are provisional.

Built: 1976–84 by Electroputere at Craiova, Romania (as sub-contractors for Brush) or BREL at Doncaster or Crewe Works. Rebuilt 2019–24 by ElectroMotive Diesel Services, Longport.
Engine: General Motors 12N-710G3B-T2 two stroke of 2385 kW (3200 hp) at 904 rpm.
Main Traction Alternator: General Motors EMD AR10/CA6.
Traction Motors: Brush TM73-62.
Maximum Tractive Effort: 280 kN (62900 lbf).
Continuous Tractive Effort: 240 kN (54000lbf).

Power at Rail: 2080 kW.	**Train Brakes:** Air.
Brake Force: 60 tonnes.	**Dimensions:** 19.36 x 2.79 m.
Weight: 125 tonnes.	**Wheel Diameter:** 1143 mm.
Design Speed: 80 mph.	**Maximum Speed:** 80 mph.

Fuel Capacity: 5200 litres.   **Route Availability:** 7.
Train Supply: Not equipped.   **Total:** 16.

Non-standard livery: 69004 British Rail Railway Technical Centre (red & dark blue).

69001	(56031)	**GB**	PG	GBRG	RR	Mayflower
69002	(56311)	**BL**	PG	GBRG	RR	Bob Tiller CM&EE
69003	(56018)	**GB**	PG	GBRG	RR	The Railway Observer
69004	(56069)	**O**	PG	GBRG	RR	
69005	(56007)	**G**	PG	GBRG	RR	Eastleigh
69006	(56128)	**GB**	PG	GBRG	RR	Pathfinder Railtours Peter Watts 50 years service 1973–2023
69007	(56037)	**B**	PG	GBRG	RR	Richard Trevithick
69008	(56038)	**GB**	PG	GBRG	RR	
69009	(56060)	**U**	PG	GBRG	RR	
69010	(56065)	**U**	PG	GBRG	RR	
69011	(56032)		PG			
69012	(56077)		PG			
69013	(56312)		PG			
69014	(56104)		PG			
69015	(56009)		PG			
69016	(56097)		PG			

CLASS 70   GENERAL ELECTRIC   Co-Co

GE "PowerHaul" locomotives. 70012 was badly damaged whilst being unloaded in 2011 and was returned to Pennsylvania.

70801 (built as 70099) is a Turkish-built demonstrator that arrived in Britain in 2012. Colas Rail leased this locomotive and then in 2013 ordered a further nine locomotives (70802–810) that were delivered in 2014. 70811–817 followed in 2017.

Built: 2009–17 by General Electric, Erie, Pennsylvania, USA or by TÜLOMSAS, Eskişehir, Turkey (70801).
Engine: General Electric PowerHaul P616LDA1 of 2848 kW (3820 hp) at 1500 rpm.
Main Alternator: General Electric GTA series.
Traction Motors: AC-GE 5GEB30.
Maximum Tractive Effort: 544 kN (122000 lbf).
Continuous Tractive Effort: 427 kN (96000 lbf) at 11 mph.

Power at Rail:	**Train Brakes:** Air.
Brake Force: 96.7 t.	**Dimensions:** 21.71 x 2.64 m.
Weight: 129 t.	**Wheel Diameter:** 1066 mm.
Design Speed: 75 mph.	**Maximum Speed:** 75 mph.
Fuel Capacity: 6000 litres.	**Route Availability:** 7.
Train Supply: Not equipped.	**Total:** 36.

Class 70/0. Freightliner locomotives.

70001	**FH**	AK	DFGI	LD	PowerHaul
70002	**FH**	AK	DFGI	LD	
70003	**FH**	AK	DFGI	LD	
70004	**FH**	AK	DFGI	LD	The Coal Industry Society
70005	**FH**	AK	DFGI	LD	
70006	**FH**	AK	DFGI	LD	
70007	**FH**	AK	DFGI	LD	
70008	**FH**	AK	DFGI	LD	
70009	**FH**	AK	COLO	CF	
70010	**FH**	AK	DFGI	LD	
70011	**FH**	AK	DHLT	LD (S)	
70013	**FH**	AK	DHLT	LD (S)	
70014	**FH**	AK	DFGI	LD	
70015	**FH**	AK	DFGI	LD	
70016	**FH**	AK	DFGI	LD	
70017	**FH**	AK	DFGI	LD	
70018	**FH**	AK	DHLT	LD (S)	
70019	**FH**	AK	DHLT	LD (S)	
70020	**FH**	AK	DFGI	LD	

Class 70/8. Colas Rail locomotives.

70801	**CS**	LF	COLO	CF
70802	**CS**	LF	COLO	CF
70803	**CS**	LF	COLO	CF
70804	**CS**	LF	COLO	CF
70805	**CS**	LF	COLO	CF
70806	**CS**	LF	COLO	CF
70807	**CS**	LF	COLO	CF
70808	**CS**	LF	COLO	CF
70809	**CS**	LF	COLO	CF
70810	**CS**	LF	COLO	CF
70811	**CS**	BN	COLO	CF
70812	**CS**	BN	COLO	CF
70813	**CS**	BN	COLO	CF
70814	**CS**	BN	COLO	CF
70815	**CS**	BN	COLO	CF
70816	**CS**	BN	COLO	CF
70817	**CS**	BN	COLO	CF

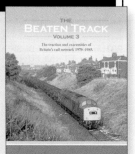

1.3. ELECTRO-DIESEL & ELECTRIC LOCOMOTIVES

CLASS 73/1   BR/ENGLISH ELECTRIC   Bo-Bo

Electro-diesel locomotives which can operate either from a DC supply or using power from a diesel engine.

Built: 1965–67 by English Electric Co. at Vulcan Foundry, Newton-le-Willows.
Engine: English Electric 4SRKT of 447 kW (600 hp) at 850 rpm.
Main Generator: English Electric 824/5D.
Electric Supply System: 750 V DC from third rail.
Traction Motors: English Electric 546/1B.
Maximum Tractive Effort (Electric): 179 kN (40000 lbf).
Maximum Tractive Effort (Diesel): 160 kN (36000 lbf).
Continuous Rating (Electric): 1060 kW (1420 hp) giving a tractive effort of 35 kN (7800 lbf) at 68 mph.
Continuous Tractive Effort (Diesel): 60 kN (13600 lbf) at 11.5 mph.
Maximum Rail Power (Electric): 2350 kW (3150 hp) at 42 mph.
Train Brakes: Air, vacuum & electro-pneumatic († Air & electro-pneumatic).
Brake Force: 31 t.   **Dimensions:** 16.36 x 2.64 m.
Weight: 77 t.   **Wheel Diameter:** 1016 mm.
Design Speed: 90 mph.   **Maximum Speed:** 90 mph.
Fuel Capacity: 1409 litres.   **Route Availability:** 6.
Train Supply: Electric, index 66 (on electric power only). **Total:** 15.

Formerly numbered E6007–E6020/E6022–E6026/E6028–E6049 (not in order).

Locomotives numbered in the 732xx series are classed as 73/2 and were originally dedicated to Gatwick Express services.

There have been two separate Class 73 rebuild projects. For GBRf 11 locomotives were rebuilt at Brush, Loughborough with a 1600 hp MTU engine (renumbered 73961–971). For Network Rail 73104/211 were rebuilt at RVEL Derby (now LORAM) with 2 x QSK19 750 hp engines (73951/952).

Non-standard liveries and numbering:

73110   Carries original number E6016.
73139   Light blue & light grey.
73235   Plain dark blue.

73101	PC	GB	GBZZ	ZG (S)	
73107	GB	GB	GBED	SE	Tracy
73109	GB	GB	GBED	SE	Battle of Britain 80th Anniversary
73110	B	GB	GBZZ	ZG (S)	
73119	CE	GB	GBED	SE	Paul Taylor
73128	GB	GB	GBED	SE	O.V.S. BULLEID C.B.E.
73136	GB	GB	GBED	SE	Mhairi
73138	Y	GB	QADD	LB (S)	
73139	O	GB	GBZZ	ZG (S)	

73141	**GB**	GB	GBED	SE	SPA VALLEY RAILWAY
					25 YEAR ANNIVERSARY
73201 †	**B**	GB	GBED	SE	Broadlands
73202 †	**SN**	GB	GBED	SE	
73212 †	**GB**	GB	GBED	SE	Stephen Eaves
73213 †	**GB**	GB	GBED	SE	Rhodalyn
73235 †	**0**	P	HYWD	BM	

CLASS 73/9 (RVEL)   BR/RVEL   Bo-Bo

The 7395x number series was used for rebuilt Network Rail locomotives.

Rebuilt: Re-engineered by RVEL Derby 2013–15.
Engine: 2 x QSK19 of 560 kW (750 hp) at 1800 rpm (total 1120 kw (1500 hp)).
Main Alternator: 2 x Marathon Magnaplus.
Electric Supply System: 750 V DC from third rail.
Traction Motors: English Electric 546/1B.
Maximum Tractive Effort (Electric): 179 kN (40000 lbf).
Maximum Tractive Effort (Diesel): 179 kN (40000 lbf).
Continuous Rating (Electric): 1060 kW (1420 hp) giving a tractive effort of 35 kN (7800 lbf) at 68 mph.
Continuous Tractive Effort (Diesel): 990 kW (1328 hp) giving a tractive effort of 33 kN (7420 lbf) at 68 mph.
Maximum Rail Power (Electric): 2350 kW (3150 hp) at 42 mph.

Train Brakes: Air.	**Brake Force:** 31 t.
Weight: 77 t.	**Dimensions:** 16.36 x 2.64 m.
Maximum Speed: 90 mph.	**Wheel Diameter:** 1016 mm.
Fuel Capacity: 2260 litres.	**Route Availability:** 6.
Train Supply: Not equipped.	**Total:** 2.

| 73951 | (73104) | **Y** | HN | QADD | KR (S) Malcolm Brinded |
| 73952 | (73211) | **Y** | HN | QADD | KR (S) Janis Kong |

CLASS 73/9 (GBRf)   BR/BRUSH   Bo-Bo

GBRf Class 73s rebuilt at Brush Loughborough. 73961–965 are normally used on Network Rail contracts and 73966–971 are used by Caledonian Sleeper.

Rebuilt: Re-engineered by Brush, Loughborough 2014–16.
Engine: MTU 8V4000 R43L of 1195 kW (1600 hp) at 1800 rpm.
Main Alternator: Lechmotoren SDV 87.53-12.
Electric Supply System: 750 V DC from third rail (73961–965 only).
Traction Motors: English Electric 546/1B.
Maximum Tractive Effort (Electric): 179 kN (40000 lbf).
Maximum Tractive Effort (Diesel): 179 kN (40000 lbf).
Continuous Rating (Electric): 1060 kW (1420 hp) giving a tractive effort of 35 kN (7800 lbf) at 68 mph.
Continuous Tractive Effort (Diesel):
Maximum Rail Power (Electric): 2350 kW (3150 hp) at 42 mph.

Train Brakes: Air.	**Brake Force:** 31 t.
Weight: 77 t.	**Dimensions:** 16.36 x 2.64 m.
Maximum Speed: 90 mph.	**Wheel Diameter:** 1016 mm.

Fuel Capacity: 1409 litres.   **Route Availability:** 6.
Train Supply: Electric, index 38 (electric & diesel). **Total:** 11.

73961	(73209)	**GB** GB	GBNR	SE	Alison
73962	(73204)	**GB** GB	GBNR	SE	Dick Mabbutt
73963	(73206)	**GB** GB	GBNR	SE	Janice
73964	(73205)	**GB** GB	GBNR	SE	Jeanette
73965	(73208)	**GB** GB	GBNR	SE	Des O' Brien

73966–971 have been rebuilt for Caledonian Sleeper but their third rail
electric capability has been retained. They have a higher Train Supply index
and a slightly higher fuel capacity. Details as 73961–965 except:
Fuel Capacity: 1509 litres.   **Train Supply:** Electric, index 96.

73005 and 73006 were originally assembled at Eastleigh Works.

73966	(73005)	d	**CA** GB	GBCS	EC
73967	(73006)	d	**CA** GB	GBCS	EC
73968	(73117)	d	**CA** GB	GBCS	EC
73969	(73105)	d	**CA** GB	GBCS	EC
73970	(73103)	d	**CA** GB	GBCS	EC
73971	(73207)	d	**CA** GB	GBCS	EC

CLASS 86   BR/ENGLISH ELECTRIC   Bo-Bo

Built: 1965–66 by English Electric Co at Vulcan Foundry, Newton-le-Willows
or by BR at Doncaster Works.
Electric Supply System: 25 kV AC 50 Hz overhead.
Traction Motors: AEI 282BZ axle hung.
Maximum Tractive Effort: 207 kN (46500 lbf).
Continuous Rating: 3010 kW (4040 hp) giving a tractive effort of 85 kN
(19200 lbf) at 77.5 mph.
Maximum Rail Power: 4550 kW (6100 hp) at 49.5 mph.
Train Brakes: Air.   **Brake Force:** 40 t.
Dimensions: 17.83 x 2.65 m.   **Weight:** 83–86.8 t.
Wheel Diameter: 1156 mm.   **Train Supply:** Electric, index 74.
Design Speed: 110–125 mph.   **Maximum Speed:** 100 mph.
Route Availability: 6.   **Total:** 3.

Formerly numbered E3101–E3200 (not in order).

Class 86s exported for use abroad are listed in section 1.6 of this book.

Class 86/1. Class 87-type bogies & motors. Details as above except:

Traction Motors: GEC 412AZ frame mounted.
Maximum Tractive Effort: 258 kN (58000 lbf).
Continuous Rating: 3730 kW (5000 hp) giving a tractive effort of 95 kN
(21300 lbf) at 87 mph.
Maximum Rail Power: 5860 kW (7860 hp) at 50.8 mph.
Wheel Diameter: 1150 mm.
Design Speed: 110 mph.   **Maximum Speed:** 110 mph.

86101	**IC** LS	LSLO	CL	Sir William A Stanier FRS

Class 86/2. Standard design rebuilt with resilient wheels & Flexicoil suspension. Details as in main class heading.

Non-standard livery: BR "Electric blue". Also carries number E3137.

86259 x   **0**   PP   MBEL   RU   Les Ross/Peter Pan

Class 86/4. Details as Class 86/2 except:

Traction Motors: AEI 282AZ axle hung.
Maximum Tractive Effort: 258 kN (58000 lbf).
Continuous Rating: 2680 kW (3600 hp) giving a tractive effort of 89 kN (20000 lbf) at 67 mph.
Maximum Rail Power: 4400 kW (5900 hp) at 38 mph.
Weight: 83–83.9 t.
Design Speed: 100 mph.   **Maximum Speed:** 100 mph.

86401   **CA** WC AWCA   CS   Mons Meg

CLASS 87   BREL/GEC   Bo-Bo

Built: 1973–75 by BREL at Crewe Works.
Electric Supply System: 25 kV AC 50 Hz overhead.
Traction Motors: GEC G412AZ frame mounted.
Maximum Tractive Effort: 258 kN (58000 lbf).
Continuous Rating: 3730 kW (5000 hp) giving a tractive effort of 95 kN (21300 lbf) at 87 mph.
Maximum Rail Power: 5860 kW (7860 hp) at 50.8 mph.
Train Brakes: Air.   **Brake Force:** 40 t.
Dimensions: 17.83 x 2.65 m.   **Weight:** 83.3 t.
Wheel Diameter: 1150 mm.   **Train Supply:** Electric, index 95.
Design Speed: 110 mph.   **Maximum Speed:** 110 mph.
Route Availability: 6.   **Total:** 1.

Class 87s exported for use abroad are listed in section 1.6 of this book.

87002   **IC** LS LSLO   CL   Royal Sovereign

CLASS 88   VOSSLOH/STADLER   Bo-Bo

Vossloh/Stadler bi-mode DRS locomotives.

Built: 2015–16 by Vossloh/Stadler, Valencia, Spain.
Electric Supply System: 25 kV AC 50 Hz overhead.
Engine: Caterpillar C27 12-cylinder of 708 kW (950 hp) at 1750 rpm.
Main Alternator: ABB AMXL400.
Traction Motors: ABB AMXL400.
Maximum Tractive Effort (Electric): 317 kN (71260 lbf).
Maximum Tractive Effort (Diesel): 317 kN (71260 lbf).
Continuous Rating: 4000kW (5360hp) giving a tractive effort of 258 kN (58000 lbf) at 28 mph (electric).
Maximum Rail Power:

Train Brakes: Air, regenerative & rheostatic.
Brake Force: 73 t.   **Dimensions:** 20.50 x 2.69 m.
Weight: 85 t.   **Wheel Diameter:** 1100 mm.
Fuel Capacity: 1800 litres.   **Train Supply:** Electric, index 96.
Design Speed: 100 mph.   **Maximum Speed:** 100 mph.
Route Availability: 7.   **Total:** 10.

Non-standard livery: 88010 Refrigerated rail COOL move (blue & white).

88001	DI	BN	XHVE	KM	Revolution
88002	DI	BN	XHVE	KM	Prometheus
88003	DI	BN	XHVE	KM	Genesis
88004	DI	BN	XHVE	KM	Pandora
88005	DI	BN	XHVE	KM	Minerva
88006	DI	BN	XHVE	KM	Juno
88007	DI	BN	XHVE	KM	Electra
88008	DI	BN	XHVE	KM	Ariadne
88009	DI	BN	XHVE	KM	Diana
88010	O	BN	XHVE	KM	Aurora

CLASS 90   GEC   Bo-Bo

Built: 1987–90 by BREL at Crewe Works (as sub-contractors for GEC).
Electric Supply System: 25 kV AC 50 Hz overhead.
Traction Motors: GEC G412CY frame mounted.
Maximum Tractive Effort: 258 kN (58000 lbf).
Continuous Rating: 3730 kW (5000 hp) giving a tractive effort of 95 kN (21300 lbf) at 87 mph.
Maximum Rail Power: 5860 kW (7860 hp) at 68.3 mph.
Train Brakes: Air.   **Dimensions:** 18.80 x 2.74 m.
Brake Force: 40 t.   **Wheel Diameter:** 1150 mm.
Weight: 84.5 t.   **Maximum Speed:** 110 mph.
Design Speed: 110 mph.   **Route Availability:** 7.
Train Supply: Electric, index 95.   **Total:** 50.

Advertising liveries:

90021   Malcolm Group – 100 Years (blue & black).
90024   Malcolm Logistics (blue).
90039   I am the backbone of the economy (black).

90001	b	IC	LS	LSLO	CL	Royal Scot
90002	b	IC	LS	LSLO	CL	Wolf of Badenoch
90003		FG	FL	DFLC	CB	
90004		FG	FL	DFLC	CB	
90005		FG	FL	DFLC	CB	
90006		FG	FL	DFLC	CB	Modern Railways Magazine/ Roger Ford
90007		FG	FL	DFLC	CB	
90008		FG	FL	DFLC	CB	
90009		FG	FL	DFLC	CB	
90010		FG	FL	DFLC	CB	

90011	**FG**	FL	DFLC	CB	
90012	**FG**	FL	DFLC	CB	
90013	**FG**	FL	DFLC	CB	
90014	**FG**	FL	DFLC	CB	Over the Rainbow
90015	**FG**	FL	DFLC	CB	
90016	**FG**	FL	DFLC	CB	
90017	**E**	DB	WQDA	CE (S)	
90018	**DB**	DB	WQDA	CE (S)	The Pride of Bellshill
90019	**DB**	DB	WQDA	CE (S)	Multimodal
90020	**GC**	DB	WQDA	CE (S)	
90021	**AL**	DB	WQDA	CE (S)	Donald Malcolm
90022	**EG**	DB	WQDA	CE (S)	Freightconnection
90023	**E**	DB	WQDA	CE (S)	
90024	**AL**	DB	WQDA	CE (S)	
90025	**F**	DB	WQDA	CE (S)	
90026	**GC**	DB	WQDA	CE (S)	
90027	**F**	DB	WQDA	CE (S)	Allerton T&RS Depot
90028	**DB**	DB	WQDA	CE (S)	Sir William McAlpine
90029	**GC**	DB	WQDA	CE (S)	
90030	**E**	DB	WQDA	CE (S)	
90031	**E**	DB	WQDA	CE (S)	The Railway Children Partnership Working For Street Children Worldwide
90032	**E**	DB	WQDA	CE (S)	
90033	**FE**	DB	WQDA	CE (S)	
90034	**DR**	DB	WQDA	CE (S)	
90035	**DB**	DB	WQDA	CE (S)	
90036	**DB**	DB	WQDA	CE (S)	Driver Jack Mills
90037	**DB**	DB	WQDA	CE (S)	Christine
90038	**FE**	DB	WQDA	CE (S)	
90039	**AL**	DB	WQDA	CE (S)	The Chartered Institute of Logistics and Transport
90040	**DB**	DB	WQDA	CE (S)	
90041	**FG**	FL	DFLC	CB	
90042	**FH**	FL	DFLC	CB	
90043	**FH**	FL	DFLC	CB	
90044	**FG**	FL	DFLC	CB	
90045	**FH**	FL	DFLC	CB	
90046	**FL**	FL	DFLC	CB	
90047	**FG**	FL	DFLC	CB	
90048	**FG**	FL	DFLC	CB	
90049	**FH**	FL	DFLC	CB	
90050	**FF**	AV	DHLT	CQ (S)	

CLASS 91   GEC   Bo-Bo

Built: 1988–91 by BREL at Crewe Works (as sub-contractors for GEC).
Electric Supply System: 25 kV AC 50 Hz overhead.
Traction Motors: GEC G426AZ.
Maximum Tractive Effort: 190 kN (43 000 lbf).
Continuous Rating: 4540 kW (6090 hp) giving a tractive effort of 170 kN at 96 mph.
Maximum Rail Power: 4700 kW (6300 hp) at ?? mph.

Train Brakes: Air.	**Dimensions:** 19.41 x 2.74 m.
Brake Force: 45 t.	**Wheel Diameter:** 1000 mm.
Weight: 84 t.	**Maximum Speed:** 125 mph.
Design Speed: 140 mph.	**Route Availability:** 7.
Train Supply: Electric, index 95.	**Total:** 14.

Locomotives were originally numbered in the 910xx series, but were renumbered upon completion of overhauls at Bombardier, Doncaster by the addition of 100 to their original number.

In early 2024 91105 was temporarily carrying the number "91000".

Advertising liveries:

91110 Battle of Britain (black and grey).
91111 For the fallen (various with poppy and Union Jack vinyls).

91101	**LC**	E	IECA	NL	FLYING SCOTSMAN
91105	**LC**	E	IECA	NL	
91106	**LC**	E	IECA	NL	
91107	**LC**	E	IECA	NL	SKYFALL
91109	**LC**	E	IECA	NL	Sir Bobby Robson
91110	**AL**	E	IECA	NL	BATTLE OF BRITAIN MEMORIAL FLIGHT
91111	**AL**	E	IECA	NL	For the Fallen
91114	**LC**	E	IECA	NL	Durham Cathedral
91117	**EX**	EP	EPUK	BH (S)	
91119	**IC**	E	IECA	NL	Bounds Green INTERCITY Depot 1977–2017
91120	**IC**	EP	EPUK	CQ	
91124	**LC**	E	IECA	NL	
91127	**LC**	E	IECA	NL	Neville Hill
91130	**LC**	E	IECA	NL	Lord Mayor of Newcastle

CLASS 92   BRUSH   Co-Co

Built: 1993–96 by Brush Traction at Loughborough.
Electric Supply System: 25 kV AC 50 Hz overhead or 750 V DC third rail.
Traction Motors: Asea Brown Boveri design. Model 6FRA 7059B (Asynchronous 3-phase induction motors).
Maximum Tractive Effort: 400 kN (90 000 lbf).
Continuous Rating: 5040 kW (6760 hp) on AC, 4000 kW (5360 hp) on DC.

Maximum Rail Power:	**Train Brakes:** Air.
Brake Force: 63 t.	**Dimensions:** 21.34 x 2.67 m.
Weight: 126 t.	**Wheel Diameter:** 1070 mm.

Design Speed: 140 km/h (87 mph).   **Maximum Speed:** 140 km/h (87 mph).
Train Supply: Electric, index 180 (AC), 108 (DC).
Route Availability: 7.   **Total:** 33.

* Fitted with TVM430 signalling equipment to operate on High Speed 1.

Class 92s exported for use abroad are listed in section 1.6 of this book.

Advertising livery: 92017 Stobart Rail (two-tone blue & white).

92004	**EG**	DB	WQCA	CE (S)	Jane Austen
92006	d **CA**	GB	GBSL	WB	
92007	**EG**	DB	WQBA	CE (S)	Schubert
92008	**EG**	DB	WQCA	CE (S)	Jules Verne
92009	* **DB**	DB	WFAC	CE	Marco Polo
92010	*d **CA**	GB	GBST	WB	
92011	* **EG**	DB	WFBC	CE	Handel
92013	**EG**	DB	WQBA	CE (S)	Puccini
92014	d **CA**	GB	GBSL	WB	
92015	* **DB**	DB	WFBC	CE	
92016	* **DB**	DB	WQCA	CE (S)	
92017	**AL**	DB	WQCA	CE (S)	Bart the Engine
92018	*d **CA**	GB	GBST	WB	
92019	* **EG**	DB	WFBC	CE	Wagner
92020	d **GB**	GB	GBSL	WB	BILLY STIRLING
92021	**EP**	GB	GBSD	LB (S)	Purcell
92023	*d **CA**	GB	GBSL	WB	
92028	d **GB**	GB	GBST	WB	
92029	**DB**	DB	WFBC	CE	
92031	* **DB**	DB	WQBA	CE (S)	
92032	*d **GB**	GB	GBCT	WB	IMechE Railway Division
92033	d **CA**	GB	GBSL	WB	Railway Heritage Trust
92035	**EG**	DB	WQCA	CE (S)	Mendelssohn
92036	* **EG**	DB	WFBC	CE	Bertolt Brecht
92037	**EG**	DB	WQCA	CE (S)	Sullivan
92038	*d **CA**	GB	GBST	WB	
92040	**EP**	GB	GBSD	LB (S)	Goethe
92041	* **EG**	DB	WFBC	CE	Vaughan Williams
92042	* **DB**	DB	WFBC	CE	
92043	*d **GB**	GB	GBST	WB	Andy Withers 50 YEARS SERVICE
92044	* **EP**	GB	GBCT	WB	Couperin
92045	**EP**	GB	GBSD	LB (S)	Chaucer
92046	**EP**	GB	GBSD	LB (S)	Sweelinck

CLASS 93   STADLER   Bo-Bo

In January 2021 Rail Operations Group placed a order with Stadler for a new design of mixed-traffic tri-mode locomotives, the Class 93. The framework order is for an initial 30 locomotives, to be confirmed in batches of ten.

The locomotive is a development of the DRS Class 88 and as well as having a more powerful CAT diesel engine and electric capability will be fitted with batteries and a higher maximum speed of 110 mph. The first locomotive was delivered in June 2023 and was due to start main line testing during early 2024.

Built: 2021–24 by Stadler, Valencia, Spain.
Electric Supply System: 25 kV AC 50 Hz overhead.
Engine: Caterpillar C32 12-cylinder of 900 kW (1205 hp) at   rpm.
Batteries: 2 x LTO battery packs providing 400 kW (535 hp).
Main Alternator:
Traction Motors:
Maximum Tractive Effort: 290 kN (65200 lbf).
Continuous Rating: 4660 kW (5360 hp).
Maximum Rail Power:
Train Brakes: Air, regenerative & electro-pneumatic.

Brake Force: 73 t.	**Dimensions:**	
Weight: 86 t.	**Wheel Diameter:**	
Fuel Capacity: 3600 litres.	**Train Supply:**	
Design Speed: 110 mph.	**Maximum Speed:** 110 mph.	
Route Availability: 7.	**Total:** 30.	

93001	**RG**	RO	GROG	WS
93002	**RG**	RO		
93003		RO		
93004		RO		
93005		RO		
93006		RO		
93007		RO		
93008		RO		
93009		RO		
93010		RO		
93011		RO		
93012		RO		
93013		RO		
93014		RO		
93015		RO		
93016		RO		
93017		RO		
93018		RO		
93019		RO		
93020		RO		
93021		RO		
93022		RO		
93023		RO		
93024		RO		
93025		RO		
93026		RO		
93027		RO		
93028		RO		
93029		RO		
93030		RO		

CLASS 99   STADLER EURODUAL   Co-Co

In April 2022 GB Railfreight placed a order with Stadler for 30 of a British version of Stadler's Eurodual design, to be designated Class 99.

The locomotive is principally designed for heavy freight duties and is bi-mode, operating off either 25 kV AC overhead electrification or an onboard diesel engine. 30 have been ordered with an option for a further 20. The first locomotives are due to enter service in 2025. Full details awaited.

Built: 2023– by Stadler, Valencia, Spain.
Electric Supply System: 25 kV AC 50 Hz overhead.
Engine: Cummins QSK50 of 1800 kW (2400 hp).
Main Alternator:
Traction Motors:
Maximum Tractive Effort (Electric): 500 kN (112 400 lbf).
Maximum Tractive Effort (Diesel):
Continuous Rating: 6250 kW (8380 hp).
Maximum Rail Power:
Train Brakes: Air, regenerative & electro-pneumatic.

Brake Force:	**Dimensions:**
Weight:	**Wheel Diameter:**
Fuel Capacity: 3000 litres.	**Train Supply:** Index 96.
Design Speed: 75 mph.	**Maximum Speed:** 75 mph.
Route Availability: 7.	**Total:** 30.

99001	BN
99002	BN
99003	BN
99004	BN
99005	BN
99006	BN
99007	BN
99008	BN
99009	BN
99010	BN
99011	BN
99012	BN
99013	BN
99014	BN
99015	BN
99016	BN
99017	BN
99018	BN
99019	BN
99020	BN
99021	BN
99022	BN
99023	BN
99024	BN
99025	BN
99026	BN

99027	BN
99028	BN
99029	BN
99030	BN

1.4. EUROTUNNEL LOCOMOTIVES

DIESEL LOCOMOTIVES

0001–10 are registered on TOPS as 21901–910.

0001–0005   Krupp MaK   Bo-Bo

Channel Tunnel maintenance and rescue train locomotives.
Built: 1991–92 by MaK at Kiel, Germany (Model DE 1004).
Engine: MTU 12V396 TC 13 of 950 kW (1275 hp) at 1800 rpm.
Main Alternator: ABB.   **Traction Motors:** ABB.
Maximum Tractive Effort: 305 kN (68600 lbf).
Continuous Tractive Effort: 140 kN (31500 lbf) at 20 mph.
Power At Rail: 750 kW (1012 hp).   **Dimensions:** 14.40 x ?? m.
Brake Force: 120 kN.   **Wheel Diameter:** 1000 mm.
Train Brakes: Air.   **Weight:** 90 t.
Maximum Speed: 100 km/h.   **Design Speed:** 120 km/h.
Fuel Capacity: 3500 litres.   **Multiple Working:** Within class.
Train Supply: Not equipped.   **Signalling System:** TVM430 cab signalling.

0001	**GY**	ET	CT		0004	**GY**	ET	CT
0002	**GY**	ET	CT		0005	**GY**	ET	CT
0003	**GY**	ET	CT					

0006–0010   Krupp MaK   Bo-Bo

Channel Tunnel maintenance and rescue locomotives. Rebuilt from
Netherlands Railways/DB Cargo Nederland Class 6400. 0006/07 were
added to the Eurotunnel fleet in 2011, and 0008–10 in 2016.

Built: 1990–91 by MaK at Kiel, Germany (Model DE 6400).
Engine: MTU 12V396 TC 13 of 1180 kW (1580 hp) at 1800 rpm.
Main Alternator: ABB.   **Traction Motors:** ABB.
Maximum Tractive Effort: 290 kN (65200 lbf).
Continuous Tractive Effort: 140 kN (31500 lbf) at 20 mph.
Power At Rail: 750 kW (1012 hp).   **Dimensions:** 14.40 x ?? m.
Brake Force: 120 kN.   **Wheel Diameter:** 1000 mm.
Train Brakes: Air.   **Weight:** 80 t.
Maximum Speed: 120 km/h.   **Design Speed:** 120 km/h.
Fuel Capacity: 2900 litres.   **Multiple Working:** Within class.
Train Supply: Not equipped.

Not fitted with TVM 430 cab signalling so have to operate with another locomotive when used on HS1. 0010 can only be used for shunting at Coquelles depot.

0006	(6456)	**GY**	ET	CT		0009	(6451)	**GY**	ET	CT
0007	(6457)	**GY**	ET	CT		0010	(6447)	**EB**	ET	CO
0008	(6450)	**GY**	ET	CT						

0031–0042   HUNSLET/SCHÖMA   0-4-0

Built: 1989–90 by Hunslet Engine Company at Leeds as 900 mm gauge.
Rebuilt: 1993–94 by Schöma in Germany to 1435 mm gauge as Type CFL 200 DCL-R.
Engine: Deutz F10L 413 FW of 170 kW (230 hp) at 2300 rpm.
Transmission: Mechanical Clark 5421-179 type.
Maximum Tractive Effort: 68 kN (15300 lbf).
Continuous Tractive Effort: 47 kN (10570 lbf) at 5 mph.
Power At Rail: 130.1 kW (175 hp).

Brake Force:	**Dimensions:** 7.87 (* 10.94) x 2.69 m.
Weight: 25 t. (* 28 t.)	**Wheel Diameter:** 1010 mm.
Maximum Speed: 48 km/h (* 75 km/h).	
Fuel Capacity: 450 litres.	**Train Brakes:** Air.
Train Supply: Not equipped.	**Multiple Working:** Not equipped.

* Rebuilt with inspection platforms to check overhead catenary (Type CS 200).

0031		**GY**	ET	CT	FRANCES
0032		**GY**	ET	CT	ELISABETH
0033		**GY**	ET	CT	SILKE
0034		**GY**	ET	CT	AMANDA
0035		**GY**	ET	CT	MARY
0036		**GY**	ET	CT	LAURENCE
0037		**GY**	ET	CT	LYDIE
0038		**GY**	ET	CT	JENNY
0039	*	**GY**	ET	CT	PACITA
0040		**GY**	ET	CT	JILL
0041	*	**GY**	ET	CT	KIM
0042		**GY**	ET	CT	NICOLE

ELECTRIC LOCOMOTIVES

9005–9840   BRUSH/ABB   Bo-Bo-Bo

Built: 1993–2002 by Brush Traction, Loughborough.
Electric Supply System: 25 kV AC 50 Hz overhead.
Traction Motors: Asea Brown Boveri design. Asynchronous 3-phase motors. Model 6FHA 7059 (as built). Model 6FHA 7059C (7000 kW rated locos).
Maximum Tractive Effort: 400kN (90 000 lbf).
Continuous Rating: Class 9/0: 5760 kW (7725 hp). Class 9/7 and 9/8: 7000 kW (9387 hp).

Maximum Rail Power:			**Multiple Working:** TDM system.	
Brake Force: 50 t.			**Dimensions:** 22.01 x 2.97 x 4.20 m.	
Weight: 136 t.			**Wheel Diameter:** 1250 mm.	
Maximum Speed: 140 km/h.			**Design Speed:** 140 km/h.	
Train Supply: Electric.			**Train Brakes:** Air.	

Class 9/0 Original build locos. Built 1993–94.

9005	**EB**	ET	CO	JESSYE NORMAN
9007	**EB**	ET	CO	
9011	**EB**	ET	CO	JOSÉ VAN DAM[1]
9013	**EB**	ET	CO	MARIA CALLAS[1]
9015	**EB**	ET	CO	LÖTSCHBERG 1913[1]
9018	**EB**	ET	CO	WILHELMENIA FERNANDEZ
9022	**EB**	ET	CO	DAME JANET BAKER
9024	**EB**	ET	CO	GOTTHARD 1882
9026	**EB**	ET	CO	
9029	**EB**	ET	CO	THOMAS ALLEN
9033	**EB**	ET	CO	MONTSERRAT CABALLE
9036	**EB**	ET	CO	ALAIN FONDARY[1]
9037	**EB**	ET	CO	

Class 9/7. Increased power freight shuttle locos. Built 2001–02 (9711–23 built 1998–2001 as 9101–13 and rebuilt as 9711–23 2010–12).

9701	**EB**	ET	CO	
9702	**EB**	ET	CO	
9703	**EB**	ET	CO	
9704	**EB**	ET	CO	
9705	**EB**	ET	CO	
9706	**EB**	ET	CO	
9707	**EB**	ET	CO	

9711	(9101)	**EB**	ET	CO	
9712	(9102)	**EB**	ET	CO	
9713	(9103)	**EB**	ET	CO	
9714	(9104)	**EB**	ET	CO	
9715	(9105)	**EB**	ET	CO	
9716	(9106)	**EB**	ET	CO	
9717	(9107)	**EB**	ET	CO	
9718	(9108)	**EB**	ET	CO	
9719	(9109)	**EB**	ET	CO	
9720	(9110)	**EB**	ET	CO	
9721	(9111)	**EB**	ET	CO	
9722	(9112)	**EB**	ET	CO	
9723	(9113)	**EB**	ET	CO	

Class 9/8 Locos rebuilt from Class 9/0 by adding 800 to the loco number. Uprated to 7000 kW.

90xx and 98xx locomotives have a cab in the blunt end for shunting, except 9840 which does not have this feature.

9801	**EB**	ET	CO	LESLEY GARRETT
9802	**EB**	ET	CO	STUART BURROWS

9803	**EB**	ET	CO	BENJAMIN LUXON[1]
9804	**EB**	ET	CO	
9806	**EB**	ET	CO	REGINE CRESPIN
9808	**EB**	ET	CO	ELISABETH SODERSTROM
9809	**EB**	ET	CO	
9810	**EB**	ET	CO	
9812	**EB**	ET	CO	LUCIANO PAVAROTTI[1]
9814	**EB**	ET	CO	LUCIA POPP
9816	**EB**	ET	CO	
9819	**EB**	ET	CO	MARIA EWING[1]
9820	**EB**	ET	CO	NICOLAI GHIAROV
9821	**EB**	ET	CO	
9823	**EB**	ET	CO	DAME ELISABETH LEGGE-SCHWARZKOPF
9825	**EB**	ET	CO	
9827	**EB**	ET	CO	BARBARA HENDRICKS
9828	**EB**	ET	CO	DAME KIRI TE KANAWA[1]
9831	**EB**	ET	CO	
9832	**EB**	ET	CO	RENATA TEBALDI[1]
9834	**EB**	ET	CO	MIRELLA FRENI
9835	**EB**	ET	CO	NICOLAI GEDDA
9838	**EB**	ET	CO	HILDEGARD BEHRENS
9840	**EB**	ET	CO	

[1] nameplates carried on one side only.

1.5. LOCOMOTIVES AWAITING DISPOSAL

Locomotives that are still extant but best classed as awaiting disposal are listed here.

66048   EMD, Longport Works

1.6. LOCOMOTIVES EXPORTED FOR USE ABROAD

This section details former British Railways (plus privatisation era) diesel and electric locomotives that have been exported from Great Britain for use in industrial locations or with a main line operator abroad. Not included are locos that are classed as "preserved" abroad. These can be found in the Platform 5 "Preserved Locomotives of British Railways" publication.

(S) denotes locomotives that are stored.

Number Other no./name   Operator/Location

Class 03

03156		Ferramenta Pugliese, Terlizzi, Bari, Italy

Class 43

43008		Nigeria
43009		Nigeria
43010		Nigeria
43016		Nigeria
43022		Ferrocarril del Istmo de Tehuantepec, Mexico
43040		Nigeria
43158		Ferrocarril del Istmo de Tehuantepec, Mexico
43170		Ferrocarril del Istmo de Tehuantepec, Mexico
43172		Nigeria
43184		Nigeria
43192		Nigeria
43239		Nigeria
43304		Nigeria
43366		Nigeria

Class 47

47375	92 70 00 47375-5	Komplex Rail, Hungary

Class 56

56101	92 55 0659 001-5	V-Híd, Hungary
56115	92 55 0659 002-3	V-Híd, Hungary
56117	92 55 0659 003-1	V-Híd, Hungary (S) Budapest Keleti

Class 58

58025		DB, Spain, (S) Albacete
58027	L52	DB, Spain, (S) Albacete
58041	L36	Transfesa, Spain, (S) Albacete
58044		DB, France, (S) Woippy, Metz
58050	L53	DB, Spain, (S) Albacete

Class 66

The second number shown is the running number for the locomotives operated by Freightliner in Poland.

66022	DBC, France	66203	DBC, Poland	66240	DBC, France
66029	DBC, France	66204	DBC, Poland	66241	DBC, France
66033	DBC, France	66208	DBC, France	66242	DBC, France
66036	DBC, France	66209	DBC, France	66243	DBC, France
66038	DBC, France	66210	DBC, France	66245	DBC, France
66042	DBC, France	66211	DBC, France	66246	DBC, France
66045	DBC, France	66212	DBC, France	66247	DBC, France
66049	DBC, France	66213	DBC, France	66248	DBC, Poland
66052	DBC, France	66214	DBC, France	66249	DBC, France
66062	DBC, France	66215	DBC, France	66411 66013	FL, Poland
66064	DBC, France	66216	DBC, France	66412 66015	FL, Poland
66071	DBC, France	66217	DBC, France	66417 66014	FL, Poland
66072	DBC, France	66218	DBC, France	66526	FL, Poland
66123	DBC, France	66219	DBC, France	66527 66016	FL, Poland
66146	DBC, Poland	66220	DBC, Poland	66529	FL, Poland
66153	DBC, Poland	66222	DBC, France	66530 66017	FL, Poland
66157	DBC, Poland	66223	DBC, France	66535 66018	FL, Poland
66159	DBC, Poland	66225	DBC, France	66582 66009	FL, Poland
66163	DBC, Poland	66226	DBC, France	66583 66010	FL, Poland
66166	DBC, Poland	66227	DBC, Poland	66584 66011	FL, Poland
66173	DBC, Poland	66228	DBC, France	66586 66008	FL, Poland
66178	DBC, Poland	66229	DBC, France	66595 66020	FL, Poland
66180	DBC, Poland	66231	DBC, France	66608 66603	FL, Poland
66189	DBC, Poland	66232	DBC, France	66609 66605	FL, Poland
66191	DBC, France	66233	DBC, France	66611 66604	FL, Poland
66193	DBC, France	66234	DBC, France	66612 66606	FL, Poland
66195	DBC, France	66235	DBC, France	66624 66602	FL, Poland
66196	DBC, Poland	66236	DBC, France	66625 66601	FL, Poland
66201	DBC, France	66237	DBC, Poland	66954 66019	FL, Poland
66202	DBC, France	66239	DBC, France		

Class 86

86213	91 52 00 87703-2	Lancashire Witch	Bulmarket, Bulgaria
86215	91 55 0450 005-8		V-Híd, Hungary
86217	91 55 0450 006-6		V-Híd, Hungary
86218	91 55 0450 004-1		V-Híd, Hungary
86228	91 55 0450 007-4		V-Híd, Hungary
86231	91 52 00 85005-4	Lady of the Lake	Bulmarket, Bulgaria
86232	91 55 0450 003-3		V-Híd, Hungary
86233			Bulmarket, Bulgaria (S) Obraztsov
86234			Bulmarket, Bulgaria
86235	91 52 00 85004-7	Novelty	Bulmarket, Bulgaria
86242	91 55 0450 008-2		V-Híd, Hungary
86248	91 55 0450 001-7		V-Híd, Hungary
86250	91 55 0450 002-5		V-Híd, Hungary
86424	91 55 0450 009-0		V-Híd, Hungary (S) Budapest
86604			Express Service, Obraztsov, Ruse
86605			Express Service, Obraztsov, Ruse
86607			Express Service, Obraztsov, Ruse
86608			Express Service, Obraztsov, Ruse
86609			Express Service, Obraztsov, Ruse

86610			Express Service, Obraztsov, Ruse
86612			Express Service, Obraztsov, Ruse
86613			Express Service, Obraztsov, Ruse
86614			Express Service, Obraztsov, Ruse
86622			Express Service, Obraztsov, Ruse
86627			Express Service, Obraztsov, Ruse
86628			Express Service, Obraztsov, Ruse
86632			Express Service, Obraztsov, Ruse
86637			Express Service, Obraztsov, Ruse
86638			Express Service, Obraztsov, Ruse
86639			Express Service, Obraztsov, Ruse
86701	91 52 00 87701-6	Orion	Bulmarket, Bulgaria
86702	91 52 00 87702-4	Cassiopeia	Bulmarket, Bulgaria

Class 87

87003	91 52 00 87003-7		BZK, Bulgaria
87004	91 52 00 87004-5	Britannia	BZK, Bulgaria
87006	91 52 00 87006-0		BZK, Bulgaria (S) Obraztsov, Ruse
87007	91 52 00 87007-8		BZK, Bulgaria
87008	87008-9		BZK, Bulgaria (S) Obraztsov, Ruse
87009	91 52 00 87009-4		Bulmarket, Bulgaria
87010	91 52 00 87010-2		BZK, Bulgaria (S) Obraztsov, Ruse
87012	91 52 00 87012-8		BZK, Bulgaria
87013	91 52 00 87013-6		BZK, Bulgaria
87014	87014-7		BZK, Bulgaria (S) Obraztsov, Ruse
87017	91 52 00 87017-7	Iron Duke	Bulmarket, Bulgaria
87019	91 52 00 87019-3		BZK, Bulgaria
87020	91 52 00 87020-1		BZK, Bulgaria
87022	91 52 00 87022-7		BZK, Bulgaria
87023	91 52 00 87023-5	Velocity	Bulmarket, Bulgaria
87025	91 52 00 87025-0		Bulmarket, Bulgaria
87026	91 52 00 87026-8		BZK, Bulgaria
87028	91 52 00 87028-4		BZK, Bulgaria
87029	91 52 00 87029-2		BZK, Bulgaria
87033	91 52 00 87033-4		BZK, Bulgaria
87034	91 52 00 87034-2		BZK, Bulgaria

Class 92

92001	91 53 0 472 002-1	Mircea Eliade	DB Cargo, Romania
92002	91 53 0 472 003-9	Lucian Blaga	Transagent Rail, Croatia
92003	91 53 0 472 007-0	Beethoven	DB Cargo, Romania
92005	91 53 0 472-005-4		Transagent Rail, Croatia
92012	91 53 0 472 001-3	Mihai Eminescu	Transagent Rail, Croatia
92022		Charles Dickens	DB Cargo, Bulgaria (S) Aurubis
92024	91 53 0 472 004-7	Marin Preda	Transagent Rail, Croatia
92025	91 52 1 688 025-1	Oscar Wilde	DB Cargo, Bulgaria
92026	91 53 0 472 008-8	Britten	DB Cargo, Romania
92027	91 52 1 688 027-7	George Eliot	DB Cargo, Bulgaria
92030	91 52 1 688 030-1	Ashford	DB Cargo, Bulgaria
92034	91 52 1 688 034-3	Kipling	DB Cargo, Bulgaria
92039	91 53 0 472 006-2	Eugen Ionescu	DB Cargo, Romania

2. LOCO-HAULED COACHING STOCK

INTRODUCTION

This section contains details of all locomotive-hauled or propelled coaching stock, often referred to as carriages, which can run on Britain's national railway network.

The number of locomotive-hauled or propelled carriages in use on the national railway network is much fewer than was once the case. Those that remain fall into two distinct groups.

Firstly, there are those used by franchised and open access operators for regular timetabled services. Today, most of these are formed in fixed or semi-fixed formations with either locomotives or a locomotive and Driving Brake Carriage at either end which allows for push-pull operation. There are also a small number of mainly overnight trains with variable formations which use conventional locomotive haulage.

Secondly, there are those used for what can best be described as excursion trains. These include a wide range of carriage types ranging from luxurious saloons to those more suited to the "bucket and spade" seaside type of excursion. These are formed into sets to suit the requirements of the day. From time to time some see limited use with franchised and open access operators to cover for stock shortages and times of exceptional demand such as major sporting events.

In addition, there remain a small number of carriages referred to as "Service Stock" which are used internally within the railway industry and are not used to convey passengers.

FRANCHISED & OPEN ACCESS OPERATORS

For each operator regularly using locomotive-hauled carriages brief details are given here of the sphere of operation. For details of operators using HSTs see Section 2.2.

Caledonian Sleeper
This franchise, operated by Serco until June 2023, started in 2015 when the Anglo-Scottish Sleeper operation was split from the ScotRail franchise. Caledonian Sleeper operates seating and sleeping car services between London Euston and Scotland using sets of new CAF Mark 5 Sleeping Cars and seated carriages.

GBRf is contracted to supply the motive power for the Sleepers. Class 92s are used between London Euston and Edinburgh/Glasgow Central and rebuilt Class 73/9s between Edinburgh and Inverness, Aberdeen and Fort William, with Class 66s assisting as required, usually on the Inverness or Fort William legs.

Chiltern Railways

Chiltern operates four sets of Mark 3 carriages hauled by DRS Class 68 locomotives on its Mainline services between London Marylebone and Birmingham Moor Street/Kidderminster. Trains operate as push-pull sets.

Great Western Railway

The "Night Riviera" seating and sleeping car service between London Paddington and Penzance uses sets of Mark 3 carriages hauled by Class 57/6 locomotives.

London North Eastern Railway

LNER has retained eight rakes of Mark 4 carriages and these are hauled by Class 91 locomotives in push-pull formation on a number of InterCity services mainly between London King's Cross and Leeds or York. All other services on the East Coast Main Line are in the hands of LNER's fleet of 65 "Azuma" bi-mode or electric units.

North Yorkshire Moors Railway

In addition to operating the North Yorkshire Moors Railway between Pickering and Grosmont the company operates through services to Whitby. A fleet of Mark 1 passenger carriages and Pullman Cars are used for these services. It also operates the "North Norfolkman" services on behalf of the North Norfolk Railway between Sheringham and Cromer.

TransPennine Express

TPE withdrew its 13 Mark 5A sets at the end of 2023.

Transport for Wales

TfW ceased using its Mark 3 rakes in March 2020. It took on lease three shortened rakes of ex-LNER Mark 4s and these were introduced in spring 2021 on the Cardiff–Holyhead route, in push-pull mode with Class 67s. TfW also purchased an additional five Mark 4 rakes (including four originally intended for use on Grand Central's Euston–Blackpool North open access service) that were introduced on the Manchester–Cardiff route from 2023, also using Class 67s. The sets initially operated in 4-car formation, but are currently being lengthened to five carriages.

West Coast Railway Company

WCRC operates two sets of Mark 1 or Mark 2 carriages on its regular steam-hauled "Jacobite" trains between Fort William and Mallaig. These trains normally operate between late March/early April and late October.

EXCURSION TRAIN OPERATORS

Usually, three types of companies will be involved in the operation of an excursion train. There will be the promoter, the rolling stock provider and the train operator. In many cases two or more of these roles may be undertaken by the same or associated companies. Only a small number of Train Operating Companies facilitate the operation of excursion trains. This takes various forms ranging from the complete package of providing and operating the train, through offering a "hook up and haul" service, to operating the train for a third-party rolling stock custodian.

DB Cargo UK
DBC offers a hook up and haul service and regularly operates the Royal Train and the Belmond British Pullman. Its own Company Train has been stored.

Direct Rail Services
DRS has offered a hook up and haul service for Riviera Trains and its client promoters but has sold its own fleet of carriages.

GB Railfreight
GBRf initially operated excursion trains using the preserved Class 201 "Hastings" DEMU. It now also operates a small number of company excursions using hired-in carriages. The company also offers a hook up and haul service operating the Royal Scotsman luxury train, as well as trains for Riviera Trains and its client promoters.

Locomotive Services
This vertically integrated company gained an operating license in 2017. From its base at Crewe, excursion trains are operated across the country using its increasingly varied fleet of steam, diesel and electric locomotives and Mark 1/2/3 carriages, and also using the "Midland Pullman" HST set.

Rail Operations Group
This company has operated a small number of excursion trains using hired in carriages. It also offers a hook up and haul service.

Vintage Trains
This vertically integrated company gained a licence in 2018. From its base at Tyseley it operates the "Shakespeare Express" steam service between Birmingham and Stratford-upon-Avon and also the "Polar Express" during the lead up to Christmas. It also operates excursions using its fleet of steam and diesel locomotives and Mark 1/2 carriages and Pullman cars.

West Coast Railway Company
This vertically integrated company has its own large fleet of steam and diesel locomotives as well as a full range of different carriage types. It operates its own regular trains, including the luxury Northern Belle, the "Jacobite" steam service between Fort William and Mallaig, the "Dalesman" steam and diesel services over the Settle & Carlisle route and numerous excursion trains for itself and client promoters. In addition, it offers a hook up and haul service operating trains for companies such as The Princess Royal Locomotive Trust and the Scottish Railway Preservation Society.

LAYOUT OF INFORMATION

Carriages are listed in numerical order of painted number in batches according to type.

Where a carriage has been renumbered, the former number is shown in parentheses. If a carriage has been renumbered more than once, the original number is shown first, followed by the most recent previous number.

Each carriage entry is laid out as in the following example (previous number(s) column may be omitted where not applicable):

No.	Prev. No.	Notes	Livery	Owner	Operator	Depot/Location
82301	(82117)	g	**CM**	AV	CR	AL

Codes: Codes are used to denote the livery, owner, operator and depot/location of each carriage. Details of codes used can be found in Section 6 of this book.

The owner is the responsible custodian of the carriage and this may not always be the legal owner. Actual ownership can be very complicated. Some vehicles are owned by finance/leasing companies. Others are owned by subsidiary companies of a holding company or by an associate company of the responsible custodian or operator.

The operator is the organisation which facilitates the use of the carriage and may not be the actual train operating company which runs the train. If no operator is shown the carriage is considered to be not in use.

The depot is the facility primarily responsible for the carriages maintenance. Light maintenance and heavy overhauls may also be carried out elsewhere.

The location is where carriages not in use are currently being kept or are stored.

GENERAL INFORMATION

CLASSIFICATION AND NUMBERING

Seven different numbering systems were in use on British Rail. These were the British Rail series, the four pre-nationalisation companies' series', the Pullman Car Company's series and the UIC (International Union of Railways) series. In this book BR number series carriages and former Pullman Car Company series are listed separately. There is also a separate listing of "Saloon" type carriages, that includes pre-nationalisation survivors, which are permitted to run on the national railway system, Locomotive Support Carriages and Service Stock. Please note the Mark 2 Pullman carriages were ordered after the Pullman Car Company had been nationalised and are therefore numbered in the British Rail series. The new CAF Mark 5/Mark 5A carriages have been allocated numbers in the British Rail series.

Also listed separately are the British Rail and Pullman Car Company number series carriages used on North Yorkshire Moors Railway and North Norfolk Railway services on very limited parts of the national railway network. This is due to their very restricted sphere of operation.

The BR number series grouped carriages of a particular type together in chronological order. Major modifications affecting type of accommodation resulted in renumbering into a more appropriate or new number series. Since privatisation such renumbering has not always taken place, resulting in renumbering which has been more haphazard and greater variations within numbering groups.

With the introduction of the TOPS numbering system, coaching stock (including multiple unit vehicles) retained their original BR number unless this conflicted with a locomotive number. Carriages can be one–five digits, although no one or two-digit examples remain in use on the national network. BR generally numbered "Service Stock" in a six-digit wagon number series.

UNITS OF MEASUREMENT

All dimensions and weights are quoted for carriages in an "as new" condition or after a major modification, such as fitting with new bogies etc. Dimensions are quoted in the order length x width. Lengths quoted are over buffers or couplers as appropriate. All widths quoted are maxima. All weights are shown as metric tonnes (t = tonnes).

DIMENSIONS

Carriage lengths are summarised as follows:

Mark 1: 19.35 m or 17.37 m.
Mark 2: 19.66 m.
Mark 3: 23.00 m.
Mark 3 HST: 23.00 m.

Mark 4: 23.00 m.
Mark 5: 22.20 m.
Mark 5A: 22.20–22.37 m.

DETAILED INFORMATION & CODES

Under each type heading, the following details are shown:

* "Mark" of carriage (see below).
* Descriptive text.
* Number of First Class seats, Standard Class seats, lavatory compartments and wheelchair spaces shown as F/S nT nW respectively. A number in brackets indicates tip-up seats (in addition to the regular seats).
* Bogie type (see below).
* Additional features.
* ETS Index.
* Weight: All weights are shown as metric tonnes.

BOGIE TYPES

Gresley. LNER design of bogie first used in the "Gresley" era. Used by BR on some Mark 1 catering carriages. Now used for some saloons.

BR Mark 1 (BR1). Double bolster leaf spring bogie. Generally 90 mph, but Mark 1 bogies may be permitted to run at 100 mph with special maintenance. Weight: 6.1 t.

BR Mark 2 (BR2). Single bolster leaf-spring bogie used on certain types of non-passenger stock and suburban stock (all now withdrawn). Weight: 5.3 t.

COMMONWEALTH (C). Heavy, cast steel coil spring bogie. 100 mph. Weight: 6.75 t.

B4. Coil spring fabricated bogie. Generally 100 mph, but B4 bogies may be permitted to run at 110 mph with special maintenance. Weight: 5.2 t.

B5. Heavy duty version of B4. 100 mph. Weight: 5.3 t.

B5 (SR). A bogie originally used on Southern Region EMUs, similar in design to B5. Now also used on locomotive-hauled carriages. 100 mph.

BT10. A fabricated bogie designed for 125 mph. Air suspension.

T4. A 125 mph bogie designed by BREL (now Bombardier Transportation).

BT41. Fitted to Mark 4 carriages, designed by SIG in Switzerland. At present limited to 125 mph, but designed for 140 mph.

CAF. Fitted to CAF Mark 5 and Mark 5A carriages.

BRAKES

Air braking is now standard on British main line trains. Carriages with other equipment are denoted:

b   Air braked, through vacuum pipe.
v   Vacuum braked.
x   Dual braked (air and vacuum).

HEATING & VENTILATION

Electric heating and ventilation is now standard on British main-line trains. Certain carriages for use on excursion services may also have steam heating facilities, or be steam heated only. All carriages used on North Yorkshire Moors Railway and North Norfolk Railway trains have steam heating.

NOTES ON ELECTRIC TRAIN SUPPLY

The sum of ETS indices in a train must not be more than the ETS index of the locomotive or generator van. The normal voltage on British trains is 1000 V. Suffix "X" denotes 600 amp wiring instead of 400 amp. Trains whose ETS index is higher than 66 must be formed completely of 600 amp wired stock. Class 33 and 73/1 locomotives cannot provide a suitable electric train supply for Mark 2D, Mark 2E, Mark 2F, Mark 3, Mark 3A, Mark 3B or Mark 4 carriages. Class 55 locomotives provide an ETS directly from one of their traction generators into the train line. Consequently, voltage fluctuations can result in motor-alternator flashover. Thus these locomotives are not suitable for use with Mark 2D, Mark 2E, Mark 2F, Mark 3, Mark 3A, Mark 3B or Mark 4 carriages unless modified motor-alternators are fitted. Such motor alternators were fitted to Mark 2D and 2F carriages used on the East Coast Main Line, but few remain fitted.

PUBLIC ADDRESS

It is assumed all carriages are now fitted with public address equipment, although certain stored carriages may not have this feature. In addition, it is assumed all carriages with a conductor's compartment have public address transmission facilities, as have catering carriages.

COOKING EQUIPMENT

It is assumed that Mark 1 catering carriages have gas powered cooking equipment, whilst Mark 2, 3 and 4 catering carriages have electric powered cooking equipment unless stated otherwise.

ADDITIONAL FEATURE CODES

(+4) Indicates tip-up seats in that carriage (in addition to the fixed seats).
d   Central Door Locking.
dg   Driver–Guard communication equipment.
f   Facelifted or fluorescent lighting.
h   "High density" seating
k   Composition brake blocks (instead of cast iron).
n   Day/night lighting.
pg   Public address transmission and driver-guard communication.
pt   Public address transmission facility.
q   Catering staff to shore telephone.
T   Toilet
TD   A universal access toilet suitable for use by person of reduced mobility.
w   Wheelchair space.

More modern Mark 4 and Mark 5 carriages were fitted with retention toilets as built and most Mark 3s were later retrofitted with them (as have all HST vehicles that are still in regular passenger service). Mark 1, 2 and 3 charter stock still used on the main line have mainly now been fitted with retention toilets.

BUILD DETAILS

Lot Numbers
Carriages ordered under the auspices of BR were allocated a lot (batch) number when ordered and these are quoted in class headings and sub-headings.

Builders
These are shown for each lot. More details and a full list of builders can be found in section 6.7.

Information on sub-contracting works which built parts of carriages eg the underframes etc is not shown.

In addition to the above, certain vintage Pullman cars were built or rebuilt at the following works:

Metropolitan Carriage & Wagon Company, Birmingham (later Alstom).
Midland Carriage & Wagon Company, Birmingham.
Pullman Car Company, Preston Park, Brighton.
Conversions have also been carried out at the Railway Technical Centre, Derby, LNWR Crewe and Blakes Fabrications, Edinburgh.

THE DEVELOPMENT OF BR STANDARD COACHES

Mark 1

The standard BR coach built from 1951 to 1963 was the Mark 1. This type features a separate underframe and body. The underframe is normally 64ft 6in long, but certain vehicles were built on shorter (57ft) frames. Tungsten lighting was standard and until 1961, BR Mark 1 bogies were generally provided. In 1959 Lot No. 30525 (Open Standard) appeared with fluorescent lighting and melamine interior panels, and from 1961 onwards Commonwealth bogies were fitted in an attempt to improve the quality of ride which became very poor when the tyre profiles on the wheels of the BR1 bogies became worn. Later batches of Open Standard and Open Brake Standard retained the features of Lot No. 30525, but compartment vehicles – whilst utilising melamine panelling in Standard Class – still retained tungsten lighting. Wooden interior finish was retained in First Class vehicles where the only change was to fluorescent lighting in open vehicles (except Lot No. 30648, which had tungsten lighting). In later years many Mark 1 coaches had BR 1 bogies replaced by B4. More recently a small number of carriages have had BR1 bogies replaced with Commonwealth bogies.

XP64

In 1964, a new prototype train was introduced. Known as "XP64", it featured new seat designs, pressure heating & ventilation, aluminium compartment doors and corridor partitions, foot pedal operated toilets and B4 bogies. The vehicles were built on standard Mark 1 underframes. Folding exterior doors were fitted, but these proved troublesome and were later replaced with hinged doors. All XP64 coaches have been withdrawn, but some have been preserved.

Mark 2

The prototype Mark 2 vehicle (W13252) was produced in 1963. This was a Corridor First of semi-integral construction and had pressure heating & ventilation, tungsten lighting, and was mounted on B4 bogies. This vehicle has now been preserved at the Mid Norfolk Railway. The production build was similar, but wider windows were used. The Open Standard vehicles used a new seat design similar to that in the XP64 and fluorescent lighting was provided. Interior finish reverted to wood. Mark 2 vehicles were built from 1964–66.

Mark 2A–2C

The Mark 2A design, built 1967–68, incorporated the remainder of the features first used in the XP64 coaches, ie foot pedal operated toilets (except Open Brake Standard), new First Class seat design, aluminium compartment doors and partitions together with fluorescent lighting in first class compartments. Folding gangway doors (lime green coloured) were used instead of the traditional one-piece variety.

Mark 2B coaches had wide wrap around doors at vehicle ends, no centre doors and a slightly longer body. In Standard Class there was one toilet at each end instead of two at one end as previously. The folding gangway doors were red.

Mark 2C coaches had a lowered ceiling with twin strips of fluorescent lighting and ducting for air conditioning, but air conditioning was never fitted.

Mark 2D–2F

These vehicles were fitted with air conditioning. They had no opening top-lights in saloon windows, which were shallower than previous ones.

Mark 2E vehicles had smaller toilets with luggage racks opposite. The folding gangway doors were fawn coloured.

Mark 2F vehicles had a modified air conditioning system, plastic interior panels and InterCity 70 type seats.

Mark 3

The Mark 3 design has BT10 bogies, is 75 ft (23 m) long and is of fully integral construction with InterCity 70 type seats. Gangway doors were yellow (red in Kitchen Buffet First) when new, although these were changed on refurbishment. Locomotive-hauled coaches are classified Mark 3A, Mark 3 being reserved for HST trailers. A new batch of Open First and Open Brake First, classified Mark 3B, was built in 1985 with Advanced Passenger Train-style seating and revised lighting. The last vehicles in the Mark 3 series were the driving brake vans ("Driving Van Trailers") built for West Coast Main Line services but now mostly withdrawn.

A number of Mark 3 vehicles were converted for use as HST trailers with CrossCountry, Grand Central and Great Western Railway.

Mark 4

The Mark 4 design was built by Metro-Cammell for use on the East Coast Main Line after electrification and featured a body profile suitable for tilting trains, although tilt is not fitted, and is not intended to be. This design is suitable for 140 mph running, although is restricted to 125 mph because the signalling system on the route is not suitable for the higher speed. The bogies for these coaches were built by SIG in Switzerland and are designated BT41. Power operated sliding plug exterior doors are standard. All Mark 4s were rebuilt with completely new interiors in 2003–05 for GNER and referred to as "Mallard" stock. These rakes generally run in fixed formations: eight are still operated by London North Eastern Railway and eight shorter sets by Transport for Wales.

New CAF carriages were introduced by Caledonian Sleeper and TransPennine Express. CAF has designated them "Mark 5" and "Mark 5A" but it should be emphasised that these are not a development of the BR standard coach. The TransPennine Express coaches have since been stored.

2.1. BRITISH RAILWAYS NUMBER SERIES COACHING STOCK

KITCHEN FIRST

Mark 1. Spent most of its life as a Royal Train vehicle and was numbered 2907 for a time. 24/–. B5 bogies. ETS 2.

Lot No. 30633 Swindon 1961. 41 t.

| 325 | **VN** | WC | *WC* | CS | DUART |

PULLMAN KITCHEN

Mark 2. Pressure Ventilated. Built with First Class seating but this has been replaced with a servery area. Gas cooking. 2T. B5 bogies. ETS 6.

Lot No. 30755 Derby 1966. 40 t.

| 504 | **PC** | WC | *WC* | CS | ULLSWATER |
| 506 | **PC** | WC | *WC* | CS | WINDERMERE |

PULLMAN OPEN FIRST

Mark 2. Pressure Ventilated. 36/– 2T. B4 bogies. ETS 5.

Lot No. 30754 Derby 1966. 35 t.

Non-standard livery: 546 Maroon & beige.

546	**O**	WC		CS	CITY OF MANCHESTER
548	**PC**	WC	*WC*	CS	GRASMERE
549	**PC**	WC	*WC*	CS	BASSENTHWAITE
550	**PC**	WC	*WC*	CS	RYDAL WATER
551	**PC**	WC	*WC*	CS	BUTTERMERE
552	**PC**	WC	*WC*	CS	ENNERDALE WATER
553	**PC**	WC	*WC*	CS	CRUMMOCK WATER

PULLMAN OPEN BRAKE FIRST

Mark 2. Pressure Ventilated. 30/– 2T. B4 bogies. ETS 4.

Lot No. 30753 Derby 1966. 35 t.

| 586 | **PC** | WC | *WC* | CS | DERWENTWATER |

BUFFET FIRST

Mark 2F. Air conditioned. Converted 1988–89/91 at BREL, Derby from Mark 2F Open Firsts. 1200/03/11/20/21 have Stones equipment, others have Temperature Ltd. 25/– 1T 1W. B4 bogies. d. ETS 6X.

1200/03/11/20. Lot No. 30845 Derby 1973. 33 t.
1207/10/12/21. Lot No. 30859 Derby 1973–74. 33 t.

1200	(3287, 6459)	**BG**	RV	*RV*	BU	
1203	(3291)	**CC**	LS	*LS*	CL	
1207	(3328, 6422)	**V**	WC		CS	
1210	(3405, 6462)	**FS**	ER		YA	
1211	(3305)	**PC**	LS	*LS*	CL	SNAEFELL
1212	(3427, 6453)	**BG**	RV	*RV*	BU	
1220	(3315, 6432)	**FS**	ER		WO	
1221	(3371)	**IC**	WC		CS	

KITCHEN WITH BAR

Mark 1. Built with no seats but three Pullman-style seats now fitted in bar area. B5 bogies. ETS 1.

Lot No. 30624 Cravens 1960–61. 41 t.

1566	**VN**	WC	*WC*	CS	CAERDYDD

KITCHEN BUFFET UNCLASSIFIED

Mark 1. Built with 23 loose chairs. All remaining vehicles were refurbished with 23 fixed polypropylene chairs and fluorescent lighting. 1683/91 were further refurbished with 21 chairs, wheelchair space and carpets. ETS 2 (* 2X).

Now used on excursion trains with the seating area adapted to various uses including servery and food preparation areas, with some or all seating removed.

1651–91. Lot No. 30628 Pressed Steel 1960–61. Commonwealth bogies. 39 t.
1730. Lot No. 30512 BRCW 1960–61. B5 bogies. 37 t.

1651		**CH**	RV	*RV*	BU		1683		**RB**	RV		BU
1657		**BG**	RV	*RV*	BU		1691		**BG**	RV	*RV*	BU
1666	x	**M**	LS	*LS*	CL		1730	x	**CC**	SP	*SP*	BO
1671	x*	**BG**	RV	*RV*	BU							

BUFFET STANDARD

Mark 1. These carriages are basically an open standard with two full window spaces removed to accommodate a buffet counter, and four seats removed to allow for a stock cupboard. All remaining vehicles now have fluorescent lighting. –/44 2T. Commonwealth bogies. ETS 3.

1861 has had its toilets replaced with store cupboards.

1813–32. Lot No. 30520 Wolverton 1960. 38 t.
1840. Lot No. 30507 Wolverton 1960. 37 t.
1859–63. Lot No. 30670 Wolverton 1961–62. 38 t.
1882. Lot No. 30702 Wolverton 1962. 38 t.

1813	x	**CH**	RV	*RV*	BU	1860	x	**M**	WC	*WC*	CS
1832	x	**CH**	RV		BU	1861	x	**M**	WC	*WC*	CS
1840	v	**M**	WC	*WC*	CS	1863	x	**CC**	LS	*LS*	CL
1859	x	**M**	SP	*SP*	BO	1882	x	**M**	WC	*WC*	CS

KITCHEN UNCLASSIFIED

Mark 1. These carriages were built as Unclassified Restaurants. They were rebuilt with buffet counters and 23 fixed polypropylene chairs, then further refurbished by fitting fluorescent lighting. Further modified for use as servery vehicle with seating removed and kitchen extended. ETS 2X.

1953. Lot No. 30575 Swindon 1960. B4/B5 bogies. 36.5 t.
1961. Lot No. 30632 Swindon 1961. Commonwealth bogies. 39 t.

1953		**VN**	WC	*WC*	CS	1961	x	**M**	WC	*WC*	CS

Name: 1953   CAERDYDD

HM THE QUEEN'S SALOON

Mark 3. Converted from an Open First built 1972. Consists of a lounge, bedroom and bathroom for HM The Queen, and a combined bedroom and bathroom for the Queen's dresser. One entrance vestibule has double doors. Air conditioned. BT10 bogies. ETS 9X.

Lot No. 30886 Wolverton 1977. 36 t.

2903	(11001)	**RP**	NR	*RT*		ZN

HRH THE DUKE OF EDINBURGH'S SALOON

Mark 3. Converted from an Open Standard built 1972. Consists of a combined lounge/dining room, a bedroom and a shower room for the Duke, a kitchen and a valet's bedroom and bathroom. Air conditioned. BT10 bogies. ETS 15X.

Lot No. 30887 Wolverton 1977. 36 t.

2904	(12001)	**RP**	NR	*RT*		ZN

ROYAL HOUSEHOLD SLEEPING CAR

Mark 3A. Built to similar specification as Sleeping Cars 10647–729. 12 sleeping compartments for use of Royal Household with a fixed lower berth and a hinged upper berth. 2T plus shower room. Air conditioned. BT10 bogies. ETS 11X.

Lot No. 31002 Derby/Wolverton 1985. 44 t.

| 2915 | | RP | NR | | *RT* | | ZN |

HRH THE PRINCE OF WALES'S DINING CAR

Mark 3. Converted from HST TRUK (kitchen car) built 1976. Large kitchen retained, but dining area modified for Royal use seating up to 14 at central table(s). Air conditioned. BT10 bogies. ETS 13X.

Lot No. 31059 Wolverton 1988. 43 t.

| 2916 | (40512) | RP | NR | | *RT* | | ZN |

ROYAL KITCHEN/HOUSEHOLD DINING CAR

Mark 3. Converted from HST TRUK built 1977. Large kitchen retained and dining area slightly modified with seating for 22 Royal Household members. Air conditioned. BT10 bogies. ETS 13X.

Lot No. 31084 Wolverton 1990. 43 t.

| 2917 | (40514) | RP | NR | | *RT* | | ZN |

ROYAL HOUSEHOLD CARS

Mark 3. Converted from HST TRUKs built 1976/77. Air conditioned. BT10 bogies. ETS 10X.

Lot Nos. 31083 (* 31085) Wolverton 1989. 41.05 t.

| 2918 | (40515) | | RP | NR | | ZN |
| 2919 | (40518) * | | RP | NR | | ZN |

ROYAL HOUSEHOLD COUCHETTES

Mark 2B. Converted from Corridor Brake First built 1969. Consists of luggage accommodation, guard's compartment, workshop area, 350 kW diesel generator and staff sleeping accommodation. B5 bogies. ETS 2X (when generator not in use). ETS index ?? (when generator in use).

Lot No. 31044 Wolverton 1986. 48 t.

| 2920 | (14109, 17109) | RP | NR | | *RT* | | ZN |

Mark 2B. Converted from Corridor Brake First built 1969. Consists of luggage accommodation, kitchen, brake control equipment and staff accommodation. B5 bogies. ETS 7X.

Lot No. 31086 Wolverton 1990. 41.5 t.

2921   (14107, 17107)   **RP**   NR   *RT*   ZN

HRH THE PRINCE OF WALES'S SLEEPING CAR

Mark 3B. Air conditioned. BT10 bogies. ETS 7X.

Lot No. 31035 Derby/Wolverton 1987.

2922   **RP**   NR   *RT*   ZN

ROYAL SALOON

Mark 3B. Air conditioned. BT10 bogies. ETS 6X.

Lot No. 31036 Derby/Wolverton 1987.

2923   **RP**   NR   *RT*   ZN

OPEN FIRST

Mark 1. 42/– 2T. ETS 3. Many now fitted with table lamps.

3058 was numbered DB 975313 and 3093 was numbered DB 977594 for a time when in departmental service for BR.

3045. Lot No. 30091 Doncaster 1954. B4 bogies. 33 t.
3058. Lot No. 30169 Doncaster 1955. Commonwealth bogies 35 t.
3091/93. Lot No. 30472 BRCW 1959. B4 bogies. 33 t.
3096–3100. Lot No. 30576 BRCW 1959. B4 bogies. 33 t.

3045	x **CC**	LS	*LS*	CL	3096	x **M**	SP *SP*	BO
3058	x **M**	WC *WC*	CS	3097	**CH**	WC	CS
3091	x **CH**	LS		ZG	3098	x **M**	WC *WC*	CS
3093	x **M**	WC *WC*	CS	3100	x **CC**	LS *LS*	CL

Names:

3058	FLORENCE	3093	FLORENCE
3091	MARGUERITE		

Later design with fluorescent lighting, aluminium window frames and Commonwealth bogies.

3128/36/41/43/46/47/48 were renumbered 1058/60/63/65/68/69/70 when reclassified Restaurant Open First, then 3600/05/08/09/06/04/10 when declassified to Open Standard, but have since regained their original numbers. 3136 was numbered DB 977970 for a time when in use with Serco Railtest as a Brake Force Runner.

3105 has had its luggage racks removed and has tungsten lighting.

3105–28. Lot No. 30697 Swindon 1962–63. 36 t.
3130–50. Lot No. 30717 Swindon 1963. 36 t.

3105	x	M	WC	*WC*	CS		3125	x	CC	LS	*LS*	CL
3106	x	M	WC	*WC*	CS		3128	x	M	WC	*WC*	CS
3107	x	CC	LS	*LS*	CL		3130	x	M	WC	*WC*	CS
3110	x	CH	RV	*RV*	BU		3136	x	M	WC	*WC*	CS
3112	x	CH	SP		BO		3140	x	CC	LS	*LS*	CL
3113	x	M	WC	*WC*	CS		3141		CH	WC	*WC*	CS
3115	x	M	SP	*SP*	BO		3143	x	M	WC	*WC*	CS
3117	x	M	WC	*WC*	BO		3146		CH	WC		CS
3119	x	CH	WC		CS		3147		CH	WC		CS
3120		M	WC	*WC*	CS		3148		CC	LS	*LS*	CL
3121		CH	WC	*WC*	CS		3149		CH	WC	*WC*	CS
3122	x	CC	LS	*LS*	CL		3150		CC	SP	*SP*	BO
3123		CH	WC		CS							

Names:

3105	JULIA		3128	VICTORIA
3106	ALEXANDRA		3130	PAMELA
3113	JESSICA		3136	DIANA
3117	CHRISTINA		3143	PATRICIA

OPEN FIRST

Mark 2D. Air conditioned. Stones equipment. 42/– 2T. B4 bogies. ETS 5.

† Interior modified to Pullman Car standards with new seating, new panelling, tungsten lighting and table lights.

Lot No. 30821 Derby 1971–72. 34 t.

3174	†	VN	WC	*WC*	CS	GLAMIS
3182	†	VN	WC		CS	WARWICK
3188		PC	LS	*LS*	CL	CADAIR IDRIS

OPEN FIRST

Mark 2E. Air conditioned. Stones equipment. 42/– 2T (* 36/– 2T). B4 bogies. ETS 5.

r Refurbished with new seats.
† Interior modified to Pullman Car standards with new seating, new panelling, tungsten lighting and table lights.

Lot No. 30843 Derby 1972–73. 32.5 t. († 35.8 t).

3229		PC	LS	*LS*	CL	SNOWDON
3231	*	PC	LS	*LS*	CL	LOCHNAGAR
3232	dr	BG	WC		CS	
3247	†	VN	WC	*WC*	CS	CHATSWORTH
3267	†	VN	WC	*WC*	CS	BELVOIR
3273	†	VN	WC	*WC*	CS	ALNWICK
3275	†	VN	WC	*WC*	CS	HARLECH

OPEN FIRST

Mark 2F. Air conditioned. 3278–3314/3359–79 have Stones equipment, others have Temperature Ltd. All refurbished in the 1980s with power-operated vestibule doors, new panels and new seat trim. 42/– 2T. B4 bogies. d. ETS 5X.

r Further refurbished with table lamps and modified seats with burgundy seat trim.

3278–3314. Lot No. 30845 Derby 1973. 33.5 t.
3325–3426. Lot No. 30859 Derby 1973–74. 33.5 t.
3431–3438. Lot No. 30873 Derby 1974–75. 33.5 t.

3278	r	**BG**	RV	*RV*	BU	3356	r	**BG**	RV	*RV*	BU
3304	r	**BG**	RV	*RV*	BU	3359	r	**M**	WC	*WC*	CS
3312		**PC**	LS	*LS*	CL	3360	r	**PC**	WC	*WC*	CS
3313	r	**M**	WC	*WC*	CS	3362	r	**PC**	WC	*WC*	CS
3314	r	**BG**	RV	*RV*	BU	3364	r	**BG**	RV	*RV*	BU
3325	r	**BG**	RV	*RV*	BU	3384	r	**PC**	LS	*LS*	CL
3326	r	**M**	WC	*WC*	CS	3386	r	**BG**	RV	*RV*	BU
3330	r	**CC**	LS	*LS*	CL	3390	r	**BG**	RV	*RV*	BU
3333	r	**BG**	RV	*RV*	BU	3392	r	**M**	WC	*WC*	CS
3340	r	**BG**	RV	*RV*	BU	3395	r	**M**	WC	*WC*	CS
3344	r	**PC**	LS	*LS*	CL	3397	r	**BG**	RV	*RV*	BU
3345	r	**BG**	RV	*RV*	BU	3426	r	**PC**	LS	*LS*	CL
3348	r	**PC**	LS	*LS*	CL	3431	r	**M**	WC	*WC*	CS
3350	r	**M**	WC	*WC*	CS	3438	r	**PC**	LS	*LS*	CL
3352	r	**M**	WC	*WC*	CS						

Names:

3312	HELVELLYN		3384	PEN-Y-GHENT
3344	BEN CRUACHAN		3426	BEN NEVIS
3348	INGLEBOROUGH		3438	BEN LOMOND

OPEN STANDARD

Mark 1. –/64 2T. ETS 4.

4831–36. Lot No. 30506 Wolverton 1959. Commonwealth bogies. 37 t.
4854/56. Lot No. 30525 Wolverton 1959–60. B4 bogies. 33 t.

4831	x	**M**	SP	*SP*	BO	4854	x	**M**	WC	*WC*	CS
4832	x	**M**	SP	*SP*	BO	4856	x	**M**	SP	*SP*	BO
4836	x	**M**	SP	*SP*	BO						

OPEN STANDARD

Mark 1. Commonwealth bogies. –/64 2T. ETS 4.

4905. Lot No. 30646 Wolverton 1961. 36 t.
4927–5044. Lot No. 30690 Wolverton 1961–62. 37 t.

4905	x	**M**	WC	*WC*	CS	4984	x	**M**	WC *WC*	CS
4927	x	**CC**	RV	*RV*	BU	4991		**CH**	WC	CS
4931	v	**M**	WC	*WC*	CS	4994	x	**M**	WC *WC*	CS
4940	x	**M**	WC	*WC*	CS	4998		**CH**	WC	CS
4946	x	**CH**	RV	*RV*	BU	5009	x	**CH**	WC	CS
4949	x	**CH**	RV	*RV*	BU	5028	x	**M**	SP *SP*	BO
4951	x	**M**	WC	*WC*	CS	5032	x	**M**	WC *WC*	CS
4954	v	**M**	WC	*WC*	CS	5033	x	**M**	WC *WC*	CS
4959		**CH**	WC		CS	5035	x	**M**	WC *WC*	CS
4960	x	**M**	WC	*WC*	CS	5044	x	**M**	WC *WC*	CS
4973	x	**M**	WC	*WC*	CS					

OPEN STANDARD

Mark 2. Pressure ventilated. –/64 2T. B4 bogies. ETS 4.

Lot No. 30751 Derby 1965–67. 32 t.

5157	v	**CH**	VT	*VT*	TM	5200	v	**M**	WC *WC*	CS
5171	v	**M**	WC	*WC*	CS	5212	v	**CH**	VT *VT*	TM
5177	v	**CH**	VT	*VT*	TM	5216	v	**M**	WC *WC*	CS
5191	v	**CH**	VT	*VT*	TM	5222	v	**M**	WC *WC*	CS
5198	v	**CH**	VT	*VT*	TM					

OPEN STANDARD

Mark 2. Pressure ventilated. –/48 2T. B4 bogies. ETS 4.

Lot No. 30752 Derby 1966. 32 t.

5229		**M**	WC	*WC*	CS	5239		**M**	WC *WC*	CS
5236	v	**M**	WC	*WC*	CS	5249	v	**M**	WC *WC*	CS
5237	v	**M**	WC	*WC*	CS					

Name: 5239 LEIGH

OPEN STANDARD

Mark 2A. Pressure ventilated. –/64 2T (w –/62 2T). B4 bogies. ETS 4.

f Facelifted vehicles.

5278–92. Lot No. 30776 Derby 1967–68. 32 t.
5366–5419. Lot No. 30787 Derby 1968. 32 t.

5278		**M**	WC	*WC*	CS	5366	f	**CC**	LS *LS*	CL
5292	f	**CC**	RV		BU	5419	w	**M**	WC *WC*	CS

OPEN STANDARD

Mark 2B. Pressure ventilated. –/62. B4 bogies. ETS 4.

Lot No. 30791 Derby 1969. 32 t.

5453		**M**	WC	*WC*	CS		5487		**M**	WC	*WC*	CS

OPEN STANDARD

Mark 2E. Air conditioned. Stones equipment. Refurbished with new interior panelling. –/64 2T. B4 bogies. d. ETS 5.

s   Modified design of seat headrest and centre luggage stack. –/60 2T.

5787. Lot No. 30837 Derby 1972. 33.5 t.
5810. Lot No. 30844 Derby 1972–73. 33.5 t.

5787	s	**DS**	ER		YA		5810		**DR**	ER		YA

OPEN STANDARD

Mark 2F. Air conditioned. Temperature Ltd equipment. InterCity 70 seats. All were refurbished in the 1980s with power-operated vestibule doors, new panels and seat trim. They have subsequently undergone a second refurbishment with carpets and new seat trim. Carriages used as Network Rail Service Stock can be found in the Service Stock section. –/64 2T. B4 bogies. d. ETS 5X.

q   Fitted with two wheelchair spaces. –/60 2T 2W.
s   Fitted with centre luggage stack. –/60 2T.
t   Fitted with centre luggage stack and wheelchair space. –/58 2T 1W.

5912–55. Lot No. 30846 Derby 1973. 33 t.
5961–6158. Lot No. 30860 Derby 1973–74. 33 t.
6173–83. Lot No. 30874 Derby 1974–75. 33 t.

5912		**PC**	LS	*LS*	CL		5998		**BG**	RV	*RV*	BU
5919	pt	**DR**	ER		ZG		6000	t	**M**	WC	*WC*	CS
5921		**AR**	RV	*RV*	BU		6008	s	**DS**	NR		CF
5929		**BG**	RV	*RV*	BU		6012		**M**	WC	*WC*	CS
5937		**DS**	ER		YA		6021		**PC**	WC	*WC*	CS
5945		**SR**	RV		BU		6022	s	**M**	WC	*WC*	CS
5950		**AR**	RV	*RV*	BU		6024		**BG**	RV	*RV*	BU
5952		**BG**	RV	*RV*	BU		6027	q	**SR**	RV		BU
5955		**SR**	RV		BU		6042		**AR**	RV	*RV*	BU
5961	pt	**BG**	RV	*RV*	BU		6046		**DR**	ER		ZG
5964		**AR**	RV	*RV*	BU		6051		**BG**	RV	*RV*	BU
5965	t	**SR**	RV		BU		6054		**BG**	RV	*RV*	BU
5976	t	**SR**	RV		BU		6064		**DS**	ER		YA
5985		**AR**	RV	*RV*	BU		6067	pt	**BG**	RV	*RV*	BU
5987		**SR**	RV		BU		6103		**M**	WC	*WC*	CS
5991		**CC**	LS	*LS*	CL		6115	s	**M**	WC	*WC*	CS

6137	s pt	**SR**	RV		BU	6176	t	**BG**	RV	*RV*	BU
6158		**BG**	RV	*RV*	BU	6177	s	**SR**	RV		BU
6173		**DS**	ER		ZG	6183	s	**SR**	RV		BU

BRAKE GENERATOR VAN

Mark 1. Renumbered 1989 from BR departmental series. Converted from Gangwayed Brake Van in 1973 to three-phase supply brake generator van for use with HST trailers. Modified 1999 for use with locomotive-hauled stock. B5 bogies. ETS index ??.

Lot No. 30400 Pressed Steel 1958.

6310	(81448, 975325)	**CH**	RV	*RV*		BU

GENERATOR VAN

Mark 1. Converted from Gangwayed Brake Vans in 1992. B4 (* B5) bogies. ETS index 75.

6311. Lot No. 30162 Pressed Steel 1958. 37.25 t.
6312. Lot No. 30224 Cravens 1956. 37.25 t.
6313. Lot No. 30484 Pressed Steel 1958. 37.25 t.

6311	(80903, 92911)		**CC**	LS	*LS*	CL
6312	(81023, 92925)		**M**	WC	*WC*	CS
6313	(81553, 92167)	*	**PC**	BE	*BP*	SL

BUFFET STANDARD

Mark 2C. Converted from Open Standard by removal of one seating bay and replacing this with a counter with a space for a trolley, now replaced with a more substantial buffet. Adjacent toilet removed and converted to steward's washing area/store. Pressure ventilated. –/55 1T. B4 bogies. ETS 4.

Lot No. 30795 Derby 1969–70. 32.5 t.

6528	(5592)		**M**	WC	*WC*	CS

SLEEPER RECEPTION CAR

Mark 2F. Converted from Open First. These vehicles consist of pantry, microwave cooking facilities, seating area for passengers (with loose chairs, staff toilet plus two bars). Later refurbished again with new "sofa" seating as well as the loose chairs. Converted at RTC, Derby (6700), Ilford (6701–05) and Derby (6706–08). Air conditioned.

6700/01/03/05–08 have Stones equipment and 6702/04 have Temperature Ltd equipment. The number of seats per coach can vary but typically is 25/– 1T (12 seats as "sofa" seating and 13 loose chairs). B4 bogies. d. ETS 5X.

6705 and 6706 have been rebuilt as private saloons. Full details awaited.

6708 also carries the branding "THE HIPPOCRENE BAR".

6700–02/04/08. Lot No. 30859 Derby 1973–74. 33.5 t.
6703/05–07. Lot No. 30845 Derby 1973. 33.5 t.

6700	(3347)	**CA**	ER		YA
6701	(3346)	**CA**	BR		ZK
6702	(3421)	**FS**	ER		YA
6703	(3308)	**CA**	ER		WO
6704	(3341)	**FS**	ER		YA
6705	(3310, 6430)	**CC**	LS	*LS*	CL	ARDNAMURCHAN
6706	(3283, 6421)	**CC**	LS	*LS*	CL	MOUNT MGAHINGA
6707	(3276, 6418)	**FS**	ER		YA
6708	(3370)	**CC**	LS	*LS*	CL	MOUNT HELICON

BUFFET FIRST

Mark 2D. Converted from Buffet Standard by the removal of another seating bay and fitting a more substantial buffet counter with boiler and microwave oven. Now converted to First Class with new seating and end luggage stacks. Air conditioned. Stones equipment. 30/– 1T. B4 bogies. d. ETS 5. Lot No. 30822 Derby 1971. 33 t.

6723	(5641, 6662)	**M**	WC		CS
6724	(5721, 6665)	**M**	WC	*WC*	CS

OPEN BRAKE STANDARD WITH TROLLEY SPACE

Mark 2. This vehicle uses the same bodyshell as Mark 2 Corridor Brake Firsts and has First Class seat spacing and wider tables. Converted from Open Brake Standard by removal of one seating bay and replacing this with a counter with a space for a trolley. Adjacent toilet removed and converted to a steward's washing area/store. –/23. B4 bogies. ETS 4.

Lot No. 30757 Derby 1966. 31 t.

9101	(9398)	v	**CH**	VT	*VT*	TM

OPEN BRAKE STANDARD

Mark 2. These vehicles use the same bodyshell as Mark 2 Corridor Brake Firsts and have First Class seat spacing and wider tables. Pressure ventilated. –/31 1T. B4 bogies. ETS 4.

9104 was originally numbered 9401. It was renumbered when converted to Open Brake Standard with trolley space. Now returned to original layout.

Lot No. 30757 Derby 1966. 31.5 t.

9104	v	**M**	WC	*WC*	CS	9392	v	**M**	WC	*WC*	CS
9391		**M**	WC	*WC*	CS						

OPEN BRAKE STANDARD

Mark 2D. Air conditioned. Stones Equipment. B4 bogies. d. pg. ETS 5.

r Refurbished with new interior panelling –/31 1T.
s Refurbished with new seating –/22 1TD.

Lot No. 30824 Derby 1971. 33 t.

9479	r	**PC**	LS	*LS*	CL	9493	s	**M**	WC	*WC*	CS
9488	s	**SR**	DR		ML						

OPEN BRAKE STANDARD

Mark 2E. Air conditioned. Stones Equipment. Refurbished with new interior panelling. –/32 1T (* –/30 1T 1W). B4 bogies. d. pg. ETS 5.

Lot No. 30838 Derby 1972. 33 t.

Non-standard livery: 9502 Pullman umber & cream.

s Modified design of seat headrest.

9497		**CA**	ER		WO	9507	s	**BG**	RV	*RV*	BU
9502	s	**O**	BE	*BP*	SL	9509	s	**AV**	RV		BU
9504	s*	**BG**	RV	*RV*	BU						

OPEN BRAKE STANDARD

Mark 2F. Air conditioned. Temperature Ltd equipment. All were refurbished in the 1980s with power-operated vestibule doors, new panels and seat trim. All now further refurbished with carpets. –/32 1T (w –/30 1T 1W). B4 bogies. d. pg. ETS 5X.

9537 has had all its seats removed for the purpose of carrying luggage.

Lot No. 30861 Derby 1974. 34 t.

9513		**IC**	ER		ZG	9526	n	**BG**	RV	*RV*	BU
9520	nw	**AR**	RV	*RV*	BU	9527	n	**SR**	RV		BU
9521		**DS**	RV		BU	9537	n	**V**	RV		BU
9525		**DR**	LO		CN	9539		**SR**	RV		BU

DRIVING OPEN BRAKE STANDARD

Mark 2F. Air conditioned. Temperature Ltd equipment. Push & pull (tdm system). Converted from Open Brake Standard, these vehicles originally had half cabs at the brake end. They have since been refurbished and have had their cabs widened and the cab-end gangways removed. Five vehicles (9701–03/08/14) have been converted for use in Network Rail test trains and can be found in the Service Stock section of this book. –/30(+1) 1W. B4 bogies. d. pg. Cowcatchers. ETS 5X.

Lot No. 30861 Derby 1974. Converted Glasgow 1979. Disc brakes. 34 t.

9704	(9512)	**DS**	LS	CL		9709	(9515)	**DS**	ER	YA
9705	(9519)	**DS**	ER	YA		9710	(9518)	**DS**	ER	YA
9707	(9511)	**IS**	LS	CL					

OPEN BRAKE UNCLASSIFIED

Mark 2E. Converted from Open Standard with new seating by Railcare, Wolverton. Air conditioned. Stones equipment. Five vehicles (9801/03/06/08/10) are currently used in Network Rail test trains and can be found in the Service Stock section of this book. –/31 2T. B4 bogies. d. ETS 4X.

9800/02. Lot No. 30837 Derby 1972. 33.5 t.
9804–09. Lot No. 30844 Derby 1972–73. 33.5 t.

9800	(5751)	**CA**	ER	WO		9805	(5833)	**FS**	ER	YA
9802	(5772)	**CA**	ER	YA		9807	(5851)	**FS**	ER	YA
9804	(5826)	**FS**	LS	CL		9809	(5890)	**FS**	ER	YA

KITCHEN BUFFET FIRST

Mark 3A. Air conditioned. Converted from HST catering vehicles and Mark 3 Open Firsts. 18/– plus two seats for staff use (* 24/–, † 35/– 1T, t 23/– 1T 1W). BT10 bogies. d. ETS 14X.

† Refurbished Great Western Railway Sleeper coaches fitted with new Transcal seating.

Non-standard liveries:

10211 EWS dark maroon.
10241 Livery trials.

10211. Lot No. 30884 Derby 1977. 39.8 t.
10212–229. Lot No. 30878 Derby 1975–76. 39.8 t.
10237–259. Lot No. 30890 Derby 1979. 39.8 t.

10211	(40510)		**0**	DB		TO		10229	(11059)	*	**GA**	ER	RO	YA
10212	(11049)		**VT**	ER		YA		10237	(10022)	*	**B**	NS		BU
10217	(11051)	†	**GW**	P	GW	PZ		10241	(10009)	*	**0**	P		IL
10219	(11047)	†	**GW**	P	GW	PZ		10249	(10012)	t	**AW**	ER		YA
10225	(11014)	†	**GW**	P	GW	PZ		10259	(10025)	t	**AW**	ER		YA

KITCHEN BUFFET FIRST

Mark 3A. Air conditioned. Rebuilt 2011–12 and fitted with sliding plug doors. Interiors originally refurbished for Wrexham & Shropshire with Primarius seating, a new kitchen area and universal-access toilet. Retention toilets. 30/– 1TD 1W. BT10 bogies. ETS 14X.

10271/273/274. Lot No. 30890 Derby 1979. 41.3 t.
10272. Lot No. 30884 Derby 1977. 41.3 t.

10271 (10018, 10236)	**CM**	AV	*CR*	AL
10272 (40517, 10208)	**CM**	AV	*CR*	AL
10273 (10021, 10230)	**CM**	AV	*CR*	AL
10274 (10010, 10255)	**CM**	AV	*CR*	AL

KITCHEN BUFFET STANDARD

Mark 4. Air conditioned. Rebuilt from First to Standard Class with bar adjacent to seating area instead of adjacent to end of coach. Retention toilets. –/30 1T. BT41 bogies. ETS 6X.

Lot No. 31045 Metro-Cammell 1989–92. 43.2 t.

10300	**LC**	E	*LN*	NL	10315	**LC**	E	*LN*	NL
10301	**TB**	TW	*TW*	CP	10318	**TB**	TW	*TW*	CP
10305	**VE**	TW		BK	10321	**TB**	TW	*TW*	CP
10306	**LC**	E	*LN*	NL	10324	**LC**	E	*LN*	NL
10309	**LC**	E	*LN*	NL	10325	**VE**	TW	*TW*	CP
10311	**LC**	E	*LN*	NL	10328	**VE**	TW	*TW*	CP
10312	**VE**	TW	*TW*	CP	10330	**TB**	TW	*TW*	CP
10313	**LC**	E	*LN*	NL	10333	**LC**	E	*LN*	NL

BUFFET STANDARD or FIRST

Mark 3A. Air conditioned. Converted from Mark 3 Open Standard at Derby 2006. –/54 * now fitted with First Class seating. 32/–. d. ETS 13X.

Lot No. 30877 Derby 1975–77. 37.8 t.

10404 (12068) *	**IS**	LS	*LS*	CL
10406 (12020)	**GA**	HH	*HH*	DC

BUFFET STANDARD

Mark 3A. Air conditioned. Converted from Mark 3 Kitchen Buffet First 2015–16. –/54. BT10 bogies. d. ETS 13X.

10411. Lot No. 30884 Derby 1977. 37.8 t.
10413/416. Lot No. 30878 Derby 1975–76. 37.8 t.
10417. Lot No. 30890 Derby 1979. 37.8 t.

10411	(40519, 10200)	**IC**	LS	*LS*	CL
10413	(11034, 10214)	**GA**	ER	*RO*	YA
10416	(11035, 10228)	**IC**	LS	*LS*	CL

SLEEPING CAR WITH PANTRY

Mark 3A. Air conditioned. Retention toilets. 12 compartments with a fixed lower berth and a hinged upper berth, plus an attendant's compartment (* 11 compartments with a fixed lower berth and a hinged upper berth + one compartment for a disabled person. 1TD). 2T. BT10 bogies. d. ETS 7X.

Non-standard livery: 10546 EWS dark maroon.

Lot No. 30960 Derby 1981–83. 41 t.

10501	**FS**	ER		YA		10584		**GW**	P	*GW*	PZ
10502	**FS**	ER		YA		10589		**GW**	P	*GW*	PZ
10504	**FS**	LS		KR		10590		**GW**	P	*GW*	PZ
10513	**FS**	LS		KR		10594		**GW**	P	*GW*	PZ
10519	**CC**	LS	*LS*	CL		10596		**GW**	P	*GW*	PZ
10520	**CC**	LS	*LS*	CL		10600		**FS**	ER		YA
10532	**GW**	P	*GW*	PZ		10601	*	**GW**	P	*GW*	PZ
10534	**GW**	P	*GW*	PZ		10610		**FS**	WC		CS
10546	**O**	DB		TO		10612	*	**GW**	P	*GW*	PZ
10551	**FS**	P		LA		10614		**FS**	WC		CS
10553	**FS**	P		LA		10616	*	**GW**	P	*GW*	PZ
10563	**GW**	P	*GW*	PZ							

SLEEPING CAR

Mark 3A. Air conditioned. Retention toilets. 13 compartments with a fixed lower berth and a hinged upper berth (* 11 compartments with a fixed lower berth and a hinged upper berth + one compartment for a disabled person. 1TD). 2T. BT10 bogies. ETS 6X.

10734 was originally 2914 and used as a Royal Train staff sleeping car. It has 12 berths and a shower room and is ETS 11X.

10648–729. Lot No. 30961 Derby 1980–84. 43.5 t.
10734. Lot No. 31002 Derby/Wolverton 1985. 42.5 t.

10648	d*	**FS**	LS		KR		10703	d	**VN**	WC	*WC*	CS
10650	d*	**FS**	LS		KR		10714	d*	**FS**	PO		CS
10675	d	**FS**	LS		KR		10718	d*	**FS**	WC		CS
10683	d	**FS**	LS		KR		10719	d*	**FS**	PO		CS
10688	d	**PC**	LS	*LS*	CL		10729		**VN**	WC	*WC*	CS
10699	d*	**FS**	ER		YA		10734		**VN**	WC	*WC*	CS

Names:

| 10729 | CREWE | | 10734 | BALMORAL |

OPEN FIRST

Mark 3A. Air conditioned. All refurbished with table lamps and new seat cushions and trim. 48/– 2T. BT10 bogies. d. ETS 6X.

Non-standard livery: 11039 EWS dark maroon.

Lot No. 30878 Derby 1975–76. 34.3 t.

11018	**VT**	ER		YA	11048	**VT**	ER	YA
11039	**0**	DB		TO				

OPEN FIRST

Mark 3B. Air conditioned. InterCity 80 seats. All refurbished with table lamps and new seat cushions and trim. Retention toilets. 48/– 1T. BT10 bogies. d. ETS 6X.

† Fitted with disabled toilet and reduced seating, including three Compin Pegasus seats. 37/– 1TD 2W.

Non-standard livery: 11074 Original HST prototype grey & BR blue.

Lot No. 30982 Derby 1985. 36.5 t.

11066	**IS**	LS	*LS*	CL	11087 †	**IC**	LS	*LS*	CL
11068	**IC**	LS	*LS*	CL	11090 †	**GA**	ER		YA
11070	**IC**	LS	*LS*	CL	11091	**IC**	LS	*LS*	CL
11074	**0**	ER		YA	11092 †	**GA**	HH	*HH*	DC
11075	**IC**	LS	*LS*	CL	11093 †	**GA**	HH	*HH*	DC
11076	**IC**	LS	*LS*	CL	11095 †	**GA**	ER	*RO*	YA
11077	**IC**	LS	*LS*	CL	11098 †	**IC**	LS	*LS*	CL
11078 †	**GA**	ER	*RO*	YA	11099 †	**GA**	HH	*HH*	DC
11082	**IS**	LS	*LS*	CL	11101 †	**GA**	HH	*HH*	DC

OPEN FIRST

Mark 4. Air conditioned. Rebuilt with new interior by Bombardier Wakefield 2003–05 (some converted from Standard Class vehicles). Retention toilets. 41/– 1T (plus 2 seats for staff use). BT41 bogies. ETS 6X.

11229. Lot No. 31046 Metro-Cammell 1989–92. 41.3 t.
11279–295. Lot No. 31049 Metro-Cammell 1989–92. 41.3 t.

11229		**LC**	E	*LN*	NL	11286 (12482)	**LC**	E	*LN*	NL
11279 (12521)	**LC**	E	*LN*	NL	11288 (12517)	**LC**	E	*LN*	NL
11284 (12487)	**LC**	E	*LN*	NL	11295 (12475)	**LC**	E	*LN*	NL
11285 (12537)	**LC**	E	*LN*	NL					

OPEN FIRST (DISABLED)

Mark 4. Air conditioned. Rebuilt from Open First by Bombardier Wakefield 2003–05. Retention toilets. 42/– 1TD 1W. BT41 bogies. ETS 6X.

Lot No. 31046 Metro-Cammell 1989–92. 40.7 t.

11306	(11276)	**LC**	E	*LN*	NL	11319	(11247)	**TB**	TW *TW* CP
11308	(11263)	**LC**	E	*LN*	NL	11320	(11255)	**TB**	TW *TW* CP
11312	(11225)	**LC**	E	*LN*	NL	11321	(11245)	**TB**	TW *TW* CP
11313	(11210)	**LC**	E	*LN*	NL	11322	(11228)	**TB**	TW *TW* CP
11315	(11238)	**LC**	E	*LN*	NL	11323	(11235)	**VE**	TW *TW* CP
11316	(11227)	**VE**	TW		BK	11324	(11253)	**VE**	TW *TW* CP
11317	(11223)	**LC**	E	*LN*	NL	11325	(11231)	**VE**	TW *TW* CP
11318	(11251)	**LC**	E	*LN*	NL	11326	(11206)	**LC**	E *LN* NL

OPEN FIRST

Mark 4. Air conditioned. Rebuilt from Open First by Bombardier Wakefield 2003–05. Separate area for 7 smokers, although smoking is no longer allowed. Retention toilets. 46/– 1TD 1W. BT41 bogies. ETS 6X.

Lot No. 31046 Metro-Cammell 1989–92. 42.1 t.

11406	(11205)	**LC**	E	*LN*	NL	11416	(11254)	**LC**	E *LN* NL
11408	(11218)	**LC**	E	*LN*	NL	11417	(11226)	**LC**	E *LN* NL
11412	(11209)	**LC**	E	*LN*	NL	11418	(11222)	**LC**	E *LN* NL
11413	(11212)	**LC**	E	*LN*	NL	11426	(11252)	**LC**	E *LN* NL
11415	(11208)	**LC**	E	*LN*	NL				

OPEN FIRST

CAF Mark 5A. Air conditioned. Former TransPennine Express coaches. Retention toilets. 30/– 1TD 2W. CAF bogies. ETS XX.

CAF Beasain 2017–18. 32.7 t.

11501	**TP**	BN	ZN	11508	**TP**	BN	CY
11502	**TP**	BN	GA	11509	**TP**	BN	CY
11503	**TP**	BN	LM	11510	**TP**	BN	CY
11504	**TP**	BN	LM	11511	**TP**	BN	MA
11505	**TP**	BN	MA	11512	**TP**	BN	MA
11506	**TP**	BN	MA	11513	**TP**	BN	CY
11507	**TP**	BN	CY				

OPEN STANDARD

Mark 3A. Air conditioned. All refurbished with modified seat backs and new layout and further refurbished with new seat trim. –/76 2T († –/70 2T 1W, z –/70 1TD 1T 2W). BT10 bogies. d. ETS 6X.

* Further refurbished with more unidirectional seating and one toilet removed. Retention toilets. –/80 1T (t –/64 1T).
s Refurbished Sleeper day coaches fitted with new Transcal seating to a 2+2 layout and a universal access toilet. Retention toilets. –/65 1TD 1W.

12171 was converted from Open Composite 11910, formerly Open First 11010.

Non-standard livery: 12092 Original HST prototype grey & BR blue.

12021–167. Lot No. 30877 Derby 1975–77. 34.3 t.
12171. Lot No. 30878 Derby 1975–76. 34.3 t.

12021	*	**GA**	ER	*RO*	YA	12100	s	**GW**	P	*GW*	PZ
12032	*	**GA**	ER		YA	12111	*t	**IS**	LS	*LS*	CL
12036	†	**CM**	ER		YA	12122	z	**VT**	ER		YA
12043	†	**CM**	ER		YA	12125	*	**GA**	HH	*HH*	DC
12061	*	**GA**	NS		BU	12133		**VT**	ER		YA
12064	*	**GA**	ER		YA	12137	*	**GA**	NS		BU
12078		**VT**	ER		YA	12138		**VT**	ER		YA
12079	*	**GA**	NS		BU	12142	s	**GW**	P	*GW*	PZ
12090	*	**GA**	NS		BU	12146	*	**GA**	NS		BU
12091	*	**GA**	ER	*RO*	YA	12154	*	**GA**	HH	*HH*	DC
12092		**O**	ER		YA	12161	s	**GW**	P	*GW*	PZ
12094		**CM**	ER		YA	12164	*	**GA**	NS		BU
12097	*	**GA**	ER		YA	12167	*	**GA**	NS		BU
12098	*	**GA**	ER		YA	12171	*t	**IS**	LS	*LS*	CL

OPEN STANDARD

Mark 3A (†) or Mark 3B. Air conditioned. Converted from Mark 3A or 3B Open First. Fitted with Grammer seating. –/70 2T 1W. BT10 bogies. d. ETS 6X.

12176/180. Mark 3B. Lot No. 30982 Derby 1985. 38.5 t.
12182. Mark 3A. Lot No. 30878 Derby 1975–76. 38.5 t.

12176	(11064)		**AW**	ER		YA
12180	(11084)		**AW**	ER		YA
12182	(11013)	†	**AW**	ER		YA

OPEN STANDARD (END)

Mark 4. Air conditioned. Rebuilt with new interior by Bombardier Wakefield 2003–05. Separate area for 26 smokers, although smoking is no longer allowed. Retention toilets. –/76 1T. BT41 bogies. ETS 6X.

Lot No. 31047 Metro-Cammell 1989–91. 39.5 t.

12205	**LC**	E	*LN*	NL		12219	**VE**	TW	*TW*	CP
12208	**LC**	E	*LN*	NL		12220	**LC**	E	*LN*	NL
12210	**TB**	TW	*TW*	CP		12222	**TB**	TW	*TW*	CP
12211	**TB**	TW	*TW*	CP		12223	**LC**	E	*LN*	NL
12212	**LC**	E	*LN*	NL		12224	**TB**	TW	*TW*	CP
12213	**LC**	E	*LN*	NL		12225	**VE**	TW	*TW*	CP
12214	**LC**	E	*LN*	NL		12226	**LC**	E	*LN*	NL
12215	**VE**	TW		LE		12228	**LC**	E	*LN*	NL
12217	**VE**	TW	*TW*	CP						

OPEN STANDARD (DISABLED)

Mark 4. Air conditioned. Rebuilt with new interior by Bombardier Wakefield 2003–05. Retention toilets. –/68 2W 1TD. BT41 bogies. ETS 6X.

Lot No. 31048 Metro-Cammell 1989–91. 39.4 t.

12303	**LC**	E	*LN*	NL		12315	**VE**	TW	*TW*	CP
12304	**VE**	TW	*TW*	CP		12316	**TB**	TW	*TW*	CP
12308	**VE**	TW		BK		12323	**TB**	TW	*TW*	CP
12309	**LC**	E	*LN*	NL		12324	**VE**	TW	*TW*	CP
12310	**TB**	TW	*TW*	CP		12325	**LC**	E	*LN*	NL
12311	**LC**	E	*LN*	NL		12326	**TB**	TW	*TW*	CP
12312	**LC**	E	*LN*	NL		12328	**LC**	E	*LN*	NL
12313	**LC**	E	*LN*	NL		12330	**LC**	E	*LN*	NL

OPEN STANDARD

Mark 4. Air conditioned. Rebuilt with new interior by Bombardier Wakefield 2003–05. Retention toilets. –/76 1T. BT41 bogies. ETS 6X.

Lot No. 31049 Metro-Cammell 1989–92. 40.8 t.

12404	**LC**	E	*LN*	NL		12420	**LC**	E	*LN*	NL
12406	**LC**	E	*LN*	NL		12422	**LC**	E	*LN*	NL
12407	**LC**	E	*LN*	NL		12424	**LC**	E	*LN*	NL
12409	**LC**	E	*LN*	NL		12426	**LC**	E	*LN*	NL

12427	**LC**	E	*LN*		NL	12452	**GC**	TW		LE
12428	**LC**	E	*LN*		NL	12454	**VE**	TW	*TW*	CP
12429	**LC**	E	*LN*		NL	12461	**GC**	TW		LE
12430	**LC**	E	*LN*		NL	12465	**LC**	E	*LN*	NL
12431	**LC**	E	*LN*		NL	12467	**LC**	E	*LN*	NL
12432	**LC**	E	*LN*		NL	12469	**LC**	E	*LN*	NL
12433	**LC**	E	*LN*		NL	12474	**LC**	E	*LN*	NL
12434	**GC**	TW			LE	12477	**GC**	TW		CP
12442	**LC**	E	*LN*		NL	12481	**LC**	E	*LN*	NL
12444	**LC**	E	*LN*		NL	12485	**LC**	E	*LN*	NL
12446	**VE**	TW	*TW*		CP	12515	**LC**	E	*LN*	NL
12447	**VE**	TW	*TW*		CP	12526	**VE**	TW		BK

OPEN STANDARD

Mark 3A. Air conditioned. Rebuilt 2011–13 and fitted with sliding plug doors. Original InterCity 70 seating retained but mainly arranged around tables. Retention toilets. –/72(+6) or * –/69(+4) 1T. BT10 bogies. ETS 6X.

12602–609/614–616/618/620. Lot No. 30877 Derby 1975–77. 36.2 t (* 37.1 t).
12601/613/617–619/621/623/625/627. Lot No. 30878 Derby 1975–76. 36.2 t (* 37.1 t).

12602	(12072)		**CM**	AV	*CR*	AL
12603	(12053)	*	**CM**	AV	*CR*	AL
12604	(12131)		**CM**	AV	*CR*	AL
12605	(11040)	*	**CM**	AV	*CR*	AL
12606	(12048)		**CM**	AV	*CR*	AL
12607	(12038)	*	**CM**	AV	*CR*	AL
12608	(12069)		**CM**	AV	*CR*	AL
12609	(12014)	*	**CM**	AV	*CR*	AL
12610	(12117)		**CM**	AV	*CR*	AL
12613	(11042, 12173)	*	**CM**	AV	*CR*	AL
12614	(12145)		**CM**	AV	*CR*	AL
12615	(12059)	*	**CM**	AV	*CR*	AL
12616	(12127)		**CM**	AV	*CR*	AL
12617	(11052, 12174)	*	**CM**	AV	*CR*	AL
12618	(11008, 12169)		**CM**	AV	*CR*	AL
12619	(11058, 12175)	*	**CM**	AV	*CR*	AL
12620	(12124)		**CM**	AV	*CR*	AL
12621	(11046)	*	**CM**	AV	*CR*	AL
12623	(11019)	*	**CM**	AV	*CR*	AL
12625	(11030)	*	**CM**	AV	*CR*	AL
12627	(11054)	*	**CM**	AV	*CR*	AL

OPEN STANDARD

CAF Mark 5A. Air conditioned. Former TransPennine Express coaches. Retention toilets. –/69 1T (* –/59(+6) 1T + bike spaces). CAF bogies. ETS XX.

CAF Beasain 2017–18. 31.8 t (* 31.6 t).

12701		**TP**	BN	ZN	12721 *	**TP**	BN	CY
12702		**TP**	BN	ZN	12722	**TP**	BN	CY
12703	*	**TP**	BN	ZN	12723	**TP**	BN	CY
12704		**TP**	BN	GA	12724 *	**TP**	BN	CY
12705		**TP**	BN	GA	12725	**TP**	BN	CY
12706	*	**TP**	BN	GA	12726	**TP**	BN	CY
12707		**TP**	BN	LM	12727 *	**TP**	BN	CY
12708		**TP**	BN	LM	12728	**TP**	BN	CY
12709	*	**TP**	BN	LM	12729	**TP**	BN	CY
12710		**TP**	BN	LM	12730 *	**TP**	BN	CY
12711		**TP**	BN	LM	12731	**TP**	BN	MA
12712	*	**TP**	BN	LM	12732	**TP**	BN	MA
12713		**TP**	BN	MA	12733 *	**TP**	BN	MA
12714		**TP**	BN	MA	12734	**TP**	BN	MA
12715	*	**TP**	BN	MA	12735	**TP**	BN	MA
12716		**TP**	BN	MA	12736 *	**TP**	BN	MA
12717		**TP**	BN	MA	12737	**TP**	BN	CY
12718	*	**TP**	BN	MA	12738	**TP**	BN	CY
12719		**TP**	BN	CY	12739 *	**TP**	BN	CY
12720		**TP**	BN	CY				

DRIVING OPEN BRAKE STANDARD

CAF Mark 5A. Air conditioned. Former TransPennine Express coaches. –/64. CAF bogies. ETS XX.

CAF Irun 2017–18. 32.9 t.

12801	**TP**	BN	ZN	12808	**TP**	BN	CY
12802	**TP**	BN	Newport	12809	**TP**	BN	CY
12803	**TP**	BN	LM	12810	**TP**	BN	CY
12804	**TP**	BN	LM	12811	**TP**	BN	MA
12805	**TP**	BN	MA	12812	**TP**	BN	MA
12806	**TP**	BN	MA	12813	**TP**	BN	CY
12807	**TP**	BN	CY	12814	**TP**	BN	GA

CORRIDOR FIRST

Mark 1. Seven compartments. 42/– 2T. B4 bogies. ETS 3.

Lot No. 30381 Swindon 1959. 33 t.
Lot No. 30667 Swindon 1962. Commonwealth bogies. 36 t.

13227	x	**CC**	LS	*LS*	CL	13230	xk	**M**	SP	*SP*	BO
13229	xk	**M**	SP	*SP*	BO	13306	x	**M**	WC	*WC*	CS

Name: 13306   JOANNA

OPEN FIRST

Mark 1 converted from Corridor First in 2013–14. 42/– 2T. Commonwealth bogies. ETS 3.

Lot No. 30667 Swindon 1962. 35 t.

13320 x **M** WC *WC* CS ANNA

CORRIDOR FIRST

Mark 2A. Seven compartments. Pressure ventilated. 42/– 2T. B4 bogies. ETS 4.

Lot No. 30774 Derby 1968. 33 t.

13440 v **M** WC *WC* CS

SLEEPER SEATED CARRIAGE WITH BRAKE

CAF Mark 5. Air conditioned. Retention toilets. –/31 1TD 1W. CAF bogies. ETS XX.

CAF Irun 2016–18. 32.5 t.

15001	**CA**	LF	*CA*	PO	15007	**CA**	LF	*CA*	PO
15002	**CA**	LF	*CA*	PO	15008	**CA**	LF	*CA*	PO
15003	**CA**	LF	*CA*	PO	15009	**CA**	LF	*CA*	PO
15004	**CA**	LF	*CA*	PO	15010	**CA**	LF	*CA*	PO
15005	**CA**	LF	*CA*	PO	15011	**CA**	LF	*CA*	PO
15006	**CA**	LF	*CA*	PO					

SLEEPER LOUNGE CAR

CAF Mark 5. Air conditioned. –/30 or –/28 1W. CAF bogies. ETS XX.

CAF Beasain 2016–18. 35.5 t.

15101	**CA**	LF	*CA*	PO	15106	**CA**	LF	*CA*	PO
15102	**CA**	LF	*CA*	PO	15107	**CA**	LF	*CA*	PO
15103	**CA**	LF	*CA*	PO	15108	**CA**	LF	*CA*	PO
15104	**CA**	LF	*CA*	PO	15109	**CA**	LF	*CA*	PO
15105	**CA**	LF	*CA*	PO	15110	**CA**	LF	*CA*	PO

SLEEPING CAR (FULLY ACCESSIBLE)

CAF Mark 5. Air conditioned. Retention toilets. Two fully accessible berths (one with double bed, one with foldable upper bed), two berths with double beds and en-suite toilets and showers, two berths with foldable upper beds. 2TD 2T, plus two showers. CAF bogies. ETS XX.

CAF Castejon/Irun 2016–18. 35.5 t.

15201	**CA**	LF	*CA*	PO	15208	**CA**	LF	*CA*	PO
15202	**CA**	LF	*CA*	PO	15209	**CA**	LF	*CA*	PO
15203	**CA**	LF	*CA*	PO	15210	**CA**	LF	*CA*	PO
15204	**CA**	LF	*CA*	PO	15211	**CA**	LF	*CA*	PO
15205	**CA**	LF	*CA*	PO	15212	**CA**	LF	*CA*	PO
15206	**CA**	LF	*CA*	PO	15213	**CA**	LF	*CA*	PO
15207	**CA**	LF	*CA*	PO	15214	**CA**	LF	*CA*	PO

SLEEPING CAR

CAF Mark 5. Air conditioned. Retention toilets. 6 en-suite toilet/shower and 4 non en-suite compartments with a fixed lower berth and hinged upper berth. 7T. CAF bogies. ETS XX.

CAF Beasain 2016–18. 38.0 t.

15301	**CA**	LF	*CA*	PO	15321	**CA**	LF	*CA*	PO
15302	**CA**	LF	*CA*	PO	15322	**CA**	LF	*CA*	PO
15303	**CA**	LF	*CA*	PO	15323	**CA**	LF	*CA*	PO
15304	**CA**	LF	*CA*	PO	15324	**CA**	LF	*CA*	PO
15305	**CA**	LF	*CA*	PO	15325	**CA**	LF	*CA*	PO
15306	**CA**	LF	*CA*	PO	15326	**CA**	LF	*CA*	PO
15307	**CA**	LF	*CA*	PO	15327	**CA**	LF	*CA*	PO
15308	**CA**	LF	*CA*	PO	15328	**CA**	LF	*CA*	PO
15309	**CA**	LF	*CA*	PO	15329	**CA**	LF	*CA*	PO
15310	**CA**	LF	*CA*	PO	15330	**CA**	LF	*CA*	PO
15311	**CA**	LF	*CA*	PO	15331	**CA**	LF	*CA*	PO
15312	**CA**	LF	*CA*	PO	15332	**CA**	LF	*CA*	PO
15313	**CA**	LF	*CA*	PO	15333	**CA**	LF	*CA*	PO
15314	**CA**	LF	*CA*	PO	15334	**CA**	LF	*CA*	PO
15315	**CA**	LF	*CA*	PO	15335	**CA**	LF	*CA*	PO
15316	**CA**	LF	*CA*	PO	15336	**CA**	LF	*CA*	PO
15317	**CA**	LF	*CA*	PO	15337	**CA**	LF	*CA*	PO
15318	**CA**	LF	*CA*	PO	15338	**CA**	LF	*CA*	PO
15319	**CA**	LF	*CA*	PO	15339	**CA**	LF	*CA*	PO
15320	**CA**	LF	*CA*	PO	15340	**CA**	LF	*CA*	PO

CORRIDOR BRAKE FIRST

Mark 1. Four compartments. 24/– 1T. Commonwealth bogies. ETS 2.

Lot No. 30668 Swindon 1961. 36 t.

17013 (14013)		**CC**	LS	*LS*	CL	
17018 (14018)	v	**CH**	VT		TM	BOTAURUS

CORRIDOR BRAKE FIRST

Mark 2A. Four compartments. Pressure ventilated. 24/– 1T. B4 bogies. ETS 4.

17090 was numbered 35503 for a time when declassified.

17056. Lot No. 30775 Derby 1967–68. 32 t.
17090/102. Lot No. 30786 Derby 1968. 32 t.

17056 (14056)		**PC**	LS	*LS*	CL
17090 (14090)	v	**CH**	VT		TM
17102 (14102)		**M**	WC	*WC*	CS

COUCHETTE/GENERATOR COACH

Mark 2B. Formerly part of Royal Train. Converted from Corridor Brake First built 1969. Consists of luggage accommodation, guard's compartment, 350 kW diesel generator and staff sleeping accommodation. Pressure ventilated. B5 bogies. ETS 5X (when generator not in use). ETS index ?? (when generator in use).

Lot No. 30888 Wolverton 1977. 46 t.

17105 (14105, 2905)	**BG**	RV	*RV*	BU

CORRIDOR BRAKE FIRST

Mark 2D. Four compartments. Air conditioned. Stones equipment. 24/– 1T. B4 Bogies. ETS 5.

Lot No. 30823 Derby 1971–72. 33.5 t.

17159 (14159)	d	**CC**	LS	*LS*	CL	
17167 (14167)		**VN**	WC	*WC*	CS	MOW COP

OPEN BRAKE UNCLASSIFIED

Mark 3B. Air conditioned. Fitted with hydraulic handbrake. Used as Sleeper day coaches. Refurbished with new Transcal seating 2018. 55/– 1T. BT10 bogies. pg. d. ETS 6X.

Lot No. 30990 Derby 1986. 35.8 t.

17173	**GW**	P	*GW*	PZ		17175	**GW**	P	*GW*	PZ
17174	**GW**	P	*GW*	PZ					

CORRIDOR STANDARD

Mark 1. –/48 2T. Eight Compartments. Commonwealth bogies. ETS 4.

Currently in use as part of the Harry Potter World exhibition at Leavesden, near Watford.

Lot No. 30685 Derby 1961–62. 36 t.

18756 (25756)	x	**M**	WC		Warner Bros, Leavesden

CORRIDOR BRAKE COMPOSITE

Mark 1. There are two variants depending upon whether the Standard Class compartments have armrests. Each vehicle has two First Class and three Standard Class compartments. 12/18 2T (* 12/24 2T). Commonwealth bogies. ETS 2.

21241. Lot No. 30669 Swindon 1961–62. 36 t.
21256. Lot No. 30731 Derby 1963. 37 t.
21266/269. Lot No. 30732 Derby 1964. 37 t.

21241	x	**M**	SP	*SP*	BO	21266	x*	**M**	WC	*WC*	CS
21256	x	**M**	WC	*WC*	CS	21269	*	**CC**	RV		BU

CORRIDOR BRAKE STANDARD

Mark 1. Four compartments. –/24 1T. ETS 2.

35185. Lot No. 30427 Wolverton 1959. B4 bogies. 33 t.
35459/465. Lot No. 30721 Wolverton 1963. Commonwealth bogies. 37 t.

35185	x	**M**	SP	*SP*	BO
35459	x	**M**	WC	*WC*	CS
35465	x	**CC**	LS	*LS*	CL

CORRIDOR BRAKE GENERATOR STANDARD

Mark 1. Four compartments. –/24 1T. Fitted with an ETS generator in the former luggage compartment. ETS 2 (when generator not in use). ETS index ?? (when generator in use).

Lot No. 30721 Wolverton 1963. Commonwealth bogies. 37 t.

35469	x	**CH**	RV	*RV*	BU

BRAKE/POWER KITCHEN

Mark 2C. Pressure ventilated. Converted from Corridor Brake First (declassified to Corridor Brake Standard) built 1970. Converted by West Coast Railway Company 2000–01. Consists of 60 kVA generator, guard's compartment and electric kitchen. B5 bogies. ETS ? (when generator not in use). ETS index ?? (when generator in use).

Non-standard livery: Brown.

Lot No. 30796 Derby 1969–70. 32.5 t.

35511 (14130, 17130)	**0**	LS		CL

KITCHEN CAR

Mark 1. Converted 1989/2006/2017–19 from Kitchen Buffet Unclassified. 80041/020 had buffet and seating area replaced with additional kitchen and food preparation area. 80043 had a full length kitchen fitted. Fluorescent lighting. Commonwealth or (†) B5 bogies. ETS 2X.

Lot No. 30628 Pressed Steel 1960–61. 39 t (* 36.4 t).

80041 (1690)	x	**M**	RV		BU
80042 (1646)		**CH**	RV	*RV*	BU
80043 (1680)	*	**PC**	LS	*LS*	CL
80044 (1659)	†	**CC**	LS	*LS*	CL

DRIVING BRAKE VAN (110 mph)

Mark 3B. Air conditioned. T4 bogies. dg. ETS 5X.

Non-standard livery: 82146 All over silver with DB logos.

Lot No. 31042 Derby 1988. 45.2 t.

82115	**B**	NS		BU	82139	**IC**	LS	*LS*	CL
82127	**IC**	LS	*LS*	CL	82146	**0**	DB		TO
82136	**GA**	NS		BU					

Name: 82139 My Lovely Horse

DRIVING BRAKE VAN (140 mph)

Mark 4. Air conditioned. Swiss-built (SIG) bogies. dg. ETS 6X.

Advertising liveries:

82200 Lest we Forget (light blue).
82216 Tŷ Gobaith (Hope House) Children's Hospice (white).
82226 Alzheimer's Society Cymru (blue).
82229 Royal National Lifeboat Institution (black).

Lot No. 31043 Metro-Cammell 1988. 43.5 t.

82200	**AL**	TW	*TW*	CP		82216	**AL**	TW	*TW*	CP
82201	**TB**	TW	*TW*	CP		82218	**VE**	HN		WS
82204	**VE**	TW		LE		82220	**VE**	TW		LE
82205	**LC**	E	*LN*	NL		82222	**LC**	E	*LN*	NL
82208	**LC**	E	*LN*	NL		82223	**LC**	E	*LN*	NL
82210	**VE**	HN		WS		82225	**LC**	E	*LN*	NL
82211	**LC**	E	*LN*	NL		82226	**AL**	TW	*TW*	CP
82212	**LC**	E	*LN*	NL		82227	**TB**	TW	*TW*	CP
82213	**LC**	E	*LN*	NL		82229	**AL**	TW	*TW*	CP
82214	**LC**	E	*LN*	NL		82230	**TB**	TW	*TW*	CP

DRIVING BRAKE VAN (100 mph)

Mark 3B. Air conditioned. T4 bogies. dg. ETS 6X.

82301–305 converted 2008. 82306 converted 2011–12. 82309 converted 2013.

g Fitted with a diesel generator for use while stabled in terminal stations or at depots. 48.5 t.

Lot No. 31042 Derby 1988. 45.2 t.

82301	(82117)	g	**CM**	AV	*CR*	AL
82302	(82151)	g	**CM**	AV	*CR*	AL
82303	(82135)	g	**CM**	AV	*CR*	AL
82304	(82130)	g	**CM**	AV	*CR*	AL
82305	(82134)	g	**CM**	AV	*CR*	AL
82306	(82144)		**AW**	NS		BU
82309	(82104)	g	**CM**	AV	*CR*	AL

GANGWAYED BRAKE VAN (100 mph)

Mark 1. Short frame (57 ft). Load 10 t. Adapted 199? for use as Brake Luggage Van. Guard's compartment retained and former baggage area adapted for secure stowage of passengers' luggage. B4 bogies. 100 mph. ETS 1X.

Lot No. 30162 Pressed Steel 1956–57. 30.5 t.

92904	(80867, 99554)	**VN**	WC	*WC*	CS

HIGH SECURITY GENERAL UTILITY VAN

Mark 1. Short frame (57 ft). Load 14 t. Modified with new floors, three roller shutter doors per side and the end doors removed. Commonwealth bogies. ETS 0X.

Lot No. 30616 Pressed Steel 1959–60. 32 t.

94225	(86849, 93849)	**M**	WC	*WC*	CS

GENERAL UTILITY VAN (100 mph)

Mark 1. Short frame (57 ft). Load 14 t. Screw couplers. Adapted 2013/2010 for use as a water carrier with 3000 gallon capacity. ETS 0.

Non-standard livery: 96100 GWR Brown.

96100. Lot No. 30565 Pressed Steel 1959. 30 t. B5 bogies.
96175. Lot No. 30403 York/Glasgow 1958–60. 32 t. Commonwealth bogies.

96100	(86734, 93734)	x	**0**	VT	*VT*	TM
96175	(86628, 93628)	x	**M**	WC	*WC*	CS

KITCHEN CAR

Mark 1 converted from Corridor First in 2008 with staff accommodation. Commonwealth bogies. ETS 3.

Lot No. 30667 Swindon 1961. 35 t.

99316	(13321)	x	**M**	WC	*WC*	CS

BUFFET STANDARD

Mark 1 converted from Open Standard in 2013 by the removal of two seating bays and fitting of a buffet. –/48 2T. Commonwealth bogies. ETS 4.

Lot No. 30646 Wolverton 1961. 36 t.

99318	(4912)	x	**M**	WC	*WC*	CS

KITCHEN CAR

Mark 1 converted from Corridor Standard in 2011 with staff accommodation. Commonwealth bogies. ETS 3.

Lot No. 30685 Derby 1961–62. 34 t.

99712	(18893)	x	**M**	WC	*WC*	CS

OPEN STANDARD

Mark 1 Corridor Standard rebuilt in 1997 as Open Standard using components from 4936. –/64 2T. Commonwealth bogies. ETS 4.

Lot No. 30685 Derby 1961–62. 36 t.

99722	(25806, 18806)	x	**M**	WC	*WC*	CS

LUL 4 TC USED AS HAULED STOCK

The Class 438 4 TC sets were unpowered units designed to work in push-pull mode with Class 430 (4 Rep) tractor units and Class 33/1, 73 and 74 locomotives. They were converted from locomotive-hauled coaching stock built 1952–57.

The vehicles listed are owned by London Underground and used on both special services on the LU Metropolitan Line and on occasional specials on the National Rail network, top-and-tailed by locomotives.

Mark 1. Trailer Brake Second side corridor with Lavatory (TBSK). Lot No. 30229. Metro-Cammell 1957. 35.5 t.

70823 (34970) **M**   LU   *WC*   RS

Mark 1. Trailer First side corridor with Lavatory (TFK). Lot No. 30019. Swindon 1954. 33.5 t.

71163 (13097) **M**   LU   *WC*   RS

Mark 1. Driving Trailer Second Open (DTSO).

76297. Lot No. 30086. Eastleigh 1955. 32.0 t.
76324. Lot No. 30149. Swindon 1956. 32.0 t.

76297 (3938)   **M**   LU   *WC*   RS
76324 (4009)   **M**   LU   *WC*   RS

NNR REGISTERED CARRIAGES

These carriages are permitted to operate on the national railway network only between Sheringham and Cromer as an extension of North Norfolk Railway (NNR) "North Norfolkman" services. Only NNR coaches currently registered for use on the national railway network are listed.

KITCHEN BUFFET STANDARD

Mark 1. Built as Unclassified Restaurant. Rebuilt with Buffet Counter and seating reduced. –/23. Commonwealth bogies. Lot No. 30632 Swindon 1960–61. 39 t.

1969   v   **CC**   NN   *NY*   NO

OPEN FIRST

Mark 1. 42/–. Commonwealth bogies. Lot No. 30697 Swindon 1962–63. 36 t.

3116   v   **CC**   NN   *NY*   NO

OPEN STANDARD

Mark 1. –/48 2T. BR Mark 1 bogies. Lot No. 30121 Eastleigh 1953–55. 32 t.

4372   v   **CC**   NN   *NY*   NO

CORRIDOR BRAKE COMPOSITE

Mark 1. Also carried the number DB977580 when in departmental service. 12/18 2T. B4 bogies. Lot No. 30425 Metro-Cammell 1959. 36 t.

21224 v   **CC**   NN   *NY*   NO

GANGWAYED BRAKE VAN

Mark 1. Short frame (57 ft). Now fitted with a kitchen. BR Mark 1 bogies. Lot No. 30224 Cravens 1955–56. 31.5 t.

81033 v   **CC**   NN   *NY*   NO

▲ BR chocolate & cream-liveried Mark 1 Kitchen Buffet Unclassified 1651 is seen at Banbury on 29/10/22. **Mark Beal**

▼ BR blue & grey-liveried Mark 1 Kitchen Buffet Unclassified 1657 is seen at Paddock Wood on 11/06/23. **Robert Pritchard**

▲ Royal Train-liveried Mark 2B Royal Household Couchette 2920 is seen near Milton Keynes on 08/06/23. **Mark Beal**

▼ BR carmine & cream-liveried Mark 1 Open First 3045 is seen at Girvan on 21/09/22. **Andy Chard**

▲ BR maroon-liveried Mark 2F Open First 3326 is seen at Wandel on 14.06.23.
Robin Ralston

▼ BR blue & grey-liveried Mark 2F Open First 3397 is seen at Maidstone East on 11/06/23.
Robert Pritchard

▲ Pullman Car Company-liveried Mark 2F Open First 3426 "Ben Nevis" is seen at Penzance on 05/08/23. **Ian Beardsley**

▼ BR carmine & cream-liveried Mark 1 Open Standard 4927 is seen at Banbury on 29/10/22. **Mark Beal**

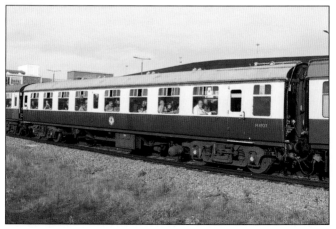

▲ BR chocolate & cream-liveried Mark 2 Open Standard 5191 is seen at Totnes on 24/08/22. **Robin Ralston**

▼ Pullman Car Company-liveried VSOE Generator Van 6313 is seen at Crofton Park on 09/04/23. **Robert Pritchard**

▲ BR carmine & cream-liveried former Sleeper Reception Car 6705 has been rebuilt as a private saloon for Locomotive Services. It is seen at Woofferton (near Ludlow) on 07/04/23. **Dave Gommersall**

▼ ScotRail InterCity-liveried Driving Open Brake Standard 9707 is seen near Linlithgow with the 09.02 Edinburgh–Glasgow Queen Street railtour on 25/02/23, being propelled by 47712. **Richard Birse**

▲ Still in Greater Anglia livery, with "The Real Charter Train Co." branding, is Mark 3B Open First 11099, seen near Mexborough on 19/03/23.**Robert Pritchard**

▼ New LNER oxblood-liveried Mark 4 Open First (Disabled) 11318 is seen at London King's Cross on 12/08/23.   **Ian Beardsley**

▲ ScotRail InterCity-liveried Mark 3A Open Standard 12171 is seen at Keighley on the Keighley & Worth Valley Railway on 25/05/23. **Robert Pritchard**

▼ Transport for Wales black-liveried Mark 4 Open Standard (End) 12211 (previously in Grand Central livery) is seen at Cardiff Central on 14/04/23.
Robert Pritchard

▲ Chiltern Railways Mainline-liveried Mark 3A Open Standard 12615 is seen at Beaconsfield on 09/04/22. **Robert Pritchard**

▼ TransPennine Express-liveried Mark 5A Driving Open Brake Standard 12814 leads the 09.26 Cleethorpes–Manchester Airport away from Sheffield on 09/12/22. **Robert Pritchard**

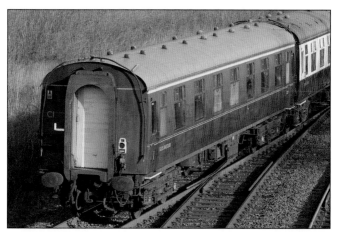

▲ BR maroon-liveried Mark 1 Open First 13230 is seen at Inverkeithing East Junction on 01/02/23.　　**Robin Ralston**

▼ Caledonian Sleeper-liveried Sleeper Seated Carriage with brake 15005 is seen at Ravenstruther on 30/12/22.　　**Robin Ralston**

▲ BR blue & grey-liveried Mark 2B Couchette/Generator Coach 17105 is seen at Paddock Wood on 11/06/23. **Robert Pritchard**

▼ BR maroon-liveried Mark 1 Corridor Brake Standard support carriage 35486 is seen at London King's Cross on 16/10/22. **Robert Pritchard**

▲ BR InterCity-liveried Mark 3B Driving Brake Van 82139 leads the 14.29 Crewe–London Euston away from Crewe on 19/08/21. **Cliff Beeton**

▼ In a special livery for the Alzheimer's Society Cymru, Transport for Wales Mark 4 Driving Brake Van 82226 brings up the rear of the 06.27 Manchester Piccadilly–Cardiff Central at Newport on 19/06/23. **Robert Pritchard**

▲ Midland Pullman-liveried HST Trailer Kitchen Buffet First 40802 is seen near Drem on 03/04/23.
Robin Ralston

▼ ScotRail InterCity-liveried HST Trailer Standard 42300 is seen at Bishopbriggs on 09/06/23.
Robert Pritchard

▲ Great Western Railway-liveried HST Trailer Guard's Standard 49109 is seen at Par on 06/06/23. **Robert Pritchard**

▼ Royal Scotsman State Car No. 4 (Saloon 99964) is seen near Breich on the Shotts line on 27/03/23. **Robin Ralston**

▲ BR carmine & cream-liveried Club Car 99993 is seen at Woofferton (near Ludlow) on 07/04/23.   **Dave Gommersall**

▼ Pullman Car Company-liveried VSOE Pullman Kitchen First 284 "VERA" is seen at Crofton Park on 09/04/23.   **Robert Pritchard**

▲ Network Rail yellow-liveried Mark 2B Test Train Staff Coach 977969 is seen near Saxilby on 12/11/22.   **Robert Pritchard**

▼ Network Rail yellow-liveried New Measurement Train Staff Coach 977984 is seen at Mexborough on 19/03/23.   **Robert Pritchard**

NYMR REGISTERED CARRIAGES

These carriages are permitted to operate on the national railway network but may only be used to convey fare-paying passengers between Middlesbrough and Whitby on the Esk Valley branch as an extension of North Yorkshire Moors Railway services between Pickering and Grosmont. Only NYMR coaches currently registered for use on the national railway network are listed.

f Converted to a "fuss free" universal access carriage with new universal access toilet and two wheelchair spaces.

RESTAURANT FIRST

Mark 1. 24/–. Commonwealth bogies. Lot No. 30633 Swindon 1961. 42.5 t.

324	x	**PC**	NY	*NY*	NY	JOS de CRAU

BUFFET STANDARD

Mark 1. –/44 2T. Commonwealth bogies.

1823. Lot No. 30520 Wolverton 1960. 38 t.
1878. Lot No. 30702 Wolverton 1962. 38 t.

1823	v	**M**	NY	*NY*	NY		1878	v	**CC**	NY	*NY*	NY

OPEN STANDARD

Mark 1. –/64 2T (* –/60 2W 2T, † –/60 3W 1T, f –/48 1TD 2W). BR Mark 1 bogies.

3798–3805. Lot No. 30079 York 1953. 33 t.
3860/72. Lot No. 30080 York 1954. 33 t.
3948. Lot No. 30086 Eastleigh 1954–55. 33 t.
4198/4252. Lot No. 30172 York 1956. 33 t.
4286/90. Lot No. 30207 BRCW 1956. 33 t.
4455. Lot No. 30226 BRCW 1957. 33 t.
4597. Lot No. 30243 York 1957. 33 t.

3798	v	**M**	NY	*NY*	NY		4198	v	**M**	NY	*NY*	NY
3801	v	**CC**	NY	*NY*	NY		4252	v*	**CC**	NY	*NY*	NY
3805	fv	**M**	NY	*NY*	NY		4286	v	**CC**	NY	*NY*	NY
3860	v*	**M**	NY	*NY*	NY		4290	v	**M**	NY	*NY*	NY
3872	v†	**M**	NY	*NY*	NY		4455	v	**CC**	NY	*NY*	NY
3948	v	**CC**	NY	*NY*	NY		4597	fv	**CC**	NY	*NY*	NY

OPEN STANDARD

Mark 1. –/48 2T. BR Mark 1 bogies.

4786. Lot No. 30376 York 1957. 33 t.
4817. Lot No. 30473 BRCW 1959. 33 t.

| 4786 | v | **CH** | NY | *NY* | NY | | 4817 | v | **M** | NY | *NY* | NY |

OPEN STANDARD

Mark 1. Later vehicles built with Commonwealth bogies. –/64 2T (f –/48 1TD 2W).

Lot No. 30690 Wolverton 1961–62. Aluminium window frames. 37 t.

4921	v	**M**	NY	*NY*	NY		5001	fv	**M**	NY	*NY*	NY
4990	v	**M**	NY	*NY*	NY		5029	v	**M**	NY	*NY*	NY
5000	v	**M**	NY	*NY*	NY							

OPEN BRAKE STANDARD

Mark 1. –/39 1T. BR Mark 1 bogies.

Lot No. 30170 Doncaster 1956. 34 t.

| 9225 | v | **M** | NY | *NY* | NY | | 9274 | v | **M** | NY | *NY* | NY |
| 9235 | v | **M** | NY | *NY* | NY | | | | | | | |

CORRIDOR COMPOSITE

Mark 1. 24/18 1T. BR Mark 1 bogies.

15745. Lot No. 30179 Metro Cammell 1956. 36 t.
16156/191. Lot No. 30665 Derby 1961. 36 t.

| 15745 | v | **M** | NY | *NY* | NY | | 16191 | v | **M** | NY | *NY* | NY |
| 16156 | v | **CC** | NY | *NY* | NY | | | | | | | |

CORRIDOR BRAKE COMPOSITE

Mark 1. Two First Class and three Standard Class compartments. 12/18 2T. BR Mark 1 bogies.

Lot No. 30185 Metro Cammell 1956. 36 t.

| 21100 | v | **CC** | NY | *NY* | NY |

CORRIDOR BRAKE STANDARD

Mark 1. –/24 1T. BR Mark 1 bogies.

Lot No. 30233 Gloucester 1957. 35 t.

35089 v   **CC**   NY   *NY*   NY

PULLMAN BRAKE THIRD

Built 1928 by Metropolitan Carriage & Wagon Company. –/30. Gresley bogies. 37.5 t.

232   v   **PC**   NY   *NY*   NY   CAR No. 79

PULLMAN KITCHEN FIRST

Built by Metro-Cammell 1960–61 for East Coast Main Line services. 20/– 2T. Commonwealth bogies. 41.2 t.

318   x   **PC**   NY   *NY*   NY   ROBIN

PULLMAN PARLOUR FIRST

Built by Metro-Cammell 1960–61 for East Coast Main Line services. 29/– 2T. Commonwealth bogies. 38.5 t.

328   x   **PC**   NY   *NY*   NY   OPAL

2.2. HIGH SPEED TRAIN TRAILER CARS

HSTs traditionally consist of a number of trailer cars (usually between four and nine) with a power car at each end. All trailers are classified Mark 3 and have BT10 bogies with disc brakes and central door locking. Heating is by a 415V three-phase supply and vehicles have air conditioning. Maximum speed is 125 mph.

The trailer cars have one standard 23 m bodyshell for both First and Standard Class, thus facilitating easy conversion from one class to the other.

All vehicles underwent a mid-life refurbishment in the 1980s with Standard Class seating layouts revised to incorporate unidirectional seating In addition to facing. A further refurbishment programme was completed in November 2000, with each company having a different scheme as follows:

Great Western Trains (later First Great Western). Green seat covers and extra partitions between seat bays.

Great North Eastern Railway. New lighting panels and brown seat covers.

Virgin CrossCountry. Green seat covers. Standard Class vehicles had four seats in the centre of each carriage replaced with a luggage stack.

Midland Mainline. Grey seat covers, redesigned seat squabs, side carpeting and two seats in the centre of each Standard Class carriage and one in First Class carriages replaced with a luggage stack.

Since then there were many separate, and very different, projects:

Midland Mainline was first to refurbish its vehicles a second time in 2003–04. This involved fitting new fluorescent and halogen ceiling lighting, although the original seats were retained, but with blue upholstery.

East Midlands Trains embarked on another, less radical, refurbishment in 2009–10 which included retention of the original seats but with red upholstery in Standard Class and blue in First. Subsequent operator East Midlands Railway used some former LNER rakes for a time before replacing all of its HSTs in 2021.

First Great Western (now **Great Western Railway**) started a major rebuild of its HST sets in 2006, with the programme completed in 2008. The new interiors featured new lighting and seating. In First Class Primarius seats were used with high-back Grammer seats in Standard Class. A number of sets operated without a full buffet or kitchen car, instead using one of 19 TS vehicles converted to include a "mini buffet" counter for use on shorter distance services. During 2012 15 402xx and 407xx buffet vehicles were converted to Trailer Standards to make the rakes formed as 7-cars up to 8-cars.

Most of the former GWR vehicles have now been scrapped, but GWR has retained a small number of short 4-car sets for local and regional services, although these are expected to be replaced soon. Trailers have been fitted with power doors and renumbered in the 48xxx and 49xxx series'.

Having increased its sets to 9-car sets in 2004, at the end of 2006 **GNER** embarked on a major rebuild of its HSTs. All vehicles have similar interiors to the Mark 4 "Mallard" fleet, with new Primarius seating. The refurbishment of the 13 sets was completed by **National Express East Coast** in late 2009, these trains were later operated by **Virgin Trains East Coast** and then **London North Eastern Railway**. VTEC refurbished its sets in 2015–16, with the same seats retained but with new upholstery, and leather in First Class, but all sets were taken out of traffic with LNER by the end of 2019.

Open access operator **Grand Central** started operation in December 2007 with a new service from Sunderland to London King's Cross. This operator had three sets mostly using stock converted from loco-hauled Mark 3s. The seats in Standard Class have First Class spacing and in most vehicles are all facing. These sets were withdrawn in December 2017 and transferred to East Midlands Trains (then EMR). They were refurbished in 2018–19, with ex-GWR buffet cars used instead of the original Grand Central buffet cars.

CrossCountry reintroduced HSTs to the Cross-Country network from 2008. Five sets were refurbished at Wabtec, Doncaster principally for use on the Plymouth–Edinburgh route. Three of these sets use stock mostly converted from loco-hauled Mark 3s and two are sets ex-Midland Mainline. The interiors are similar to refurbished East Coast sets, although the seating layout is different and one toilet per carriage has been removed in favour of a luggage stack. These sets were later fitted with sliding power doors but were withdrawn in 2023.

ScotRail started operating HSTs from October 2018. The operator has a fleet of 25 sets, of which five are 5-cars and the rest are 4-cars, but it is planned to make more up to five carriages. They have been fitted with sliding power doors for use between Glasgow/Edinburgh and Aberdeen/Inverness, and on the Aberdeen–Inverness route.

Crewe-based **Locomotive Services** has acquired a number of former GWR and EMR HST vehicles and power cars. It uses its premium "Midland Pullman" set in a striking blue livery on luxury trips and also formed a second rake in 2021 for Rail Charter Services in green/silver livery, but this has now been disbanded. The **125 Group** also plans to return its rake of trailers and its power cars to the main line. The future for many of the other remaining vehicles appears to be export – with one HST set shipped to Mexico in summer 2023 and others set to follow.

Operator Codes

Operator codes are shown in the heading before each set of vehicles. The first letter is always "T" for HST carriages, denoting a Trailer vehicle. The second letter denotes the passenger accommodation in that vehicle, for example "F" for First. "GS" denotes Guards accommodation and Standard Class seating. This is followed by catering provision, with "B" for buffet, and "K" for a kitchen and buffet:

TC	Trailer Composite	TGFB	Trailer Guard's Buffet First
TCK	Trailer Composite Kitchen	TSB	Trailer Buffet Standard
TF	Trailer First	TS	Trailer Standard
TFB	Trailer Buffet First	TGF	Trailer Guard's First
TFKB	Trailer Kitchen Buffet First	TGS	Trailer Guard's Standard

Power doors: All HSTs now operated by Great Western Railway and ScotRail (and also those withdrawn by CrossCountry in 2023) have been fitted with power sliding doors and retention toilets. Vehicles so fitted are shown with a "p" in the Notes column.

TRAILER BUFFET STANDARD   TSB

19 vehicles (40101–119) were converted at Laira 2009–10 from HST TSs for First Great Western. All other vehicles now scrapped. Grammer seating.

40106. Lot No. 30897 Derby 1977–79. –/70 1T. 35.5 t.

40106 (42162)   **FD**   LS   KR

TRAILER BUFFET FIRST   TFB

Converted from TSB by fitting First Class seats. Renumbered from 404xx series by subtracting 200. Refurbished by First Great Western and fitted with Primarius leather seating. 23/–.

Lot No. 30883 Derby 1976–77. 36.12 t.

40221   **EA** LS   CL

TRAILER GUARD'S MINIATURE BUFFET FIRST   TGFB

Refurbished 2018–21 for ScotRail. Former Great Western Railway vehicles. Primarius seating. Fitted with a new corner buffet counter and kitchen. 32/– 1T.

40601–626. For Lot No. details see TF. 39.1 t.

40601	(41032) p	**SI**	A	*SR*	IS	40614	(41010) p	**SI**	A	*SR*	IS
40602	(41038) p	**SI**	A		ZB	40615	(41022) p	**SI**	A	*SR*	IS
40603	(41006) p	**SI**	A	*SR*	IS	40616	(41142) p	**SI**	A	*SR*	IS
40604	(41024) p	**SI**	A	*SR*	IS	40617	(41144) p	**SI**	A	*SR*	IS
40605	(41094) p	**SI**	A	*SR*	IS	40618	(41016) p	**SI**	A	*SR*	IS
40606	(41104) p	**SI**	A	*SR*	IS	40619	(41124) p	**SI**	A	*SR*	IS
40607	(41136) p	**SI**	A	*SR*	IS	40620	(41158) p	**SI**	A	*SR*	IS
40608	(41122) p	**SI**	A		ZN	40621	(41146) p	**SI**	A	*SR*	IS
40609	(41020) p	**SI**	A	*SR*	IS	40623	(41180) p	**SI**	A		ZB
40610	(41103) p	**SI**	A	*SR*	IS	40624	(41116) p	**SI**	A	*SR*	IS
40611	(41130) p	**SI**	A	*SR*	IS	40625	(41137) p	**SI**	A	*SR*	IS
40612	(41134) p	**SI**	A	*SR*	IS	40626	(41012) p	**SI**	A	*SR*	IS
40613	(41135) p	**SI**	A	*SR*	IS						

TRAILER KITCHEN BUFFET FIRST   TFKB

These vehicles have larger kitchens than the 402xx and 404xx series vehicles, and are used in trains where a full meal service is required. They were renumbered from the 403xx series (in which the seats were unclassified) by adding 400 to the previous number. 17/–.

*   Refurbished former GWR vehicles. Primarius leather seating.
m Refurbished former LNER vehicles with Primarius leather seating.

40715. Lot No. 30921 Derby 1978–79. 38.16 t.
40728–734. Lot No. 30940 Derby 1979–80. 38.16 t.
40741/750. Lot No. 30948 Derby 1980–81. 38.16 t.
40755. Lot No. 30966 Derby 1982. 38.16 t.

40715 *	**GW**	A		EP	40741	**ST**	125	*RA*	SK
40728	**ST**	NS		BU	40750 m	**VE**	A		YA
40730	**ST**	125		SK	40755 *	**GW**	A		ZG
40734 *	**FD**	A		EP					

TRAILER KITCHEN BUFFET FIRST   TFKB

These vehicles have been converted from TSBs in the 404xx series to be similar to the 407xx series vehicles. 17/–. Primarius leather seating.

40802 and 40804 were numbered 40212 and 40232 for a time when fitted with 23 First Class seats.

40801/802/808. Lot No. 30883 Derby 1976–77. 38.16 t.
40804. Lot No. 30899 Derby 1978–79. 38.16 t.

40801 (40027, 40427)	**MP**	LS	*LS*	CL
40802 (40012, 40412)	**MP**	LS	*LS*	CL
40804 (40032, 40432)	**RC**	LS	*LS*	CL
40808 (40015, 40415)	**FD**	LS		ZG

TRAILER BUFFET FIRST   TFB

Converted from TSB by First Great Western. Refurbished with Primarius leather seating. 23/–.

Lot No. 30883 Derby 1976–77. 36.12 t.

40902 (40023, 40423)	**FD**	FG		YA

TRAILER FIRST   TF

As built and m 48/– 2T (m† 48/– 1T – one toilet removed for trolley space).
*   Refurbished former GWR vehicles. Primarius leather seating.
m Refurbished former LNER vehicles with Primarius leather seating.
px Refurbished former CrossCountry vehicles with power doors,
    Primarius seating and one toilet removed. 39/– 1TD 1W.
s   Fitted with centre luggage stack, disabled toilet and wheelchair space.
    46/– 1TD 1T 1W.
w Wheelchair space. 47/– 2T 1W.

41026/035. Lot No. 30881 Derby 1976–77. 33.66 t.
41057–117. Lot No. 30896 Derby 1977–78. 33.66 t.
41149–166. Lot No. 30947 Derby 1980. 33.66 t.
41167/169. Lot No. 30963 Derby 1982. 33.66 t.
41176. Lot No. 30897 Derby 1977. 33.66 t.
41182/183. Lot No. 30939 Derby 1979–80. 33.66 t.
41187. Lot No. 30969 Derby 1982. 33.66 t.
41193/194. Lot No. 30878 Derby 1975–76. 34.3 t. Converted from Mark 3A Open First.
41208. Lot No. 30877 Derby 1975–77. Converted from Mark 3A Open Standard.

41026 px	**XC**	A		YA	41059 *w	**MP**	LS	*LS*	CL
41035 px	**XC**	A		YA	41063	**ST**	LS	*LS*	CL
41057	**ST**	125	*RA*	SK	41067 s	**ST**	125		SK

41087	m†	**VE**	A		YA	41160	*w	**RC**	LS	*LS*	CL
41106	*w	**FD**	A		ZG	41162	*w	**MP**	LS	*LS*	CL
41108	*w	**MP**	LS	*LS*	CL	41166	*w	**RC**	LS	*LS*	CL
41117		**ST**	LS	*LS*	CL	41167	*w	**FD**	LS		ZG
41149	*w	**MP**	LS	*LS*	CL	41169	*w	**MP**	LS	*LS*	CL

41176	(42142, 42352)	*w	**MP**	LS *LS*	CL
41182	(42278)	*w	**MP**	LS *LS*	CL
41183	(42274)	*w	**MP**	LS *LS*	CL
41187	(42311)	*w	**RC**	LS *LS*	CL

The following carriages were converted from loco-hauled Mark 3 vehicles.

41193	(11060)	px	**XC**	P	YA
41194	(11016)	px	**XC**	P	LM
41208	(12112, 42406)	w	**EA**	LS	ZG

TRAILER STANDARD   TS

Standard seating and m –/76 2T.
* Refurbished former Great Western Railway vehicles. Grammer seating. –/80 2T (unless h – high density).
h "High density" former Great Western Railway vehicles. –/84 2T.
k "High density" former Great Western Railway refurbished vehicle with disabled persons toilet and 5, 6 or 7 tip-up seats. –/72 1T 1TD 2W.
m Refurbished former LNER vehicles with Primarius seating.
pr Refurbished ScotRail vehicles with power doors and Grammer seating. –/68(+6).
ps Refurbished ScotRail vehicles with power doors and Grammer seating. –/74 1T.
p* Refurbished ScotRail vehicles with power doors, Grammer seating and universal access toilet. –/58 1TD 2W.
px Refurbished former CrossCountry vehicles with power doors and Primarius seating. –/80 1T.
pt Refurbished former CrossCountry vehicles with power doors, Primarius seating and universal access toilet. –/64 1TD 2W.
u Centre luggage stack (EMR) –/74 2T.
w Centre luggage stack and wheelchair space (EMR) –72 2T 1W.
† Disabled persons toilet (LNER) –/62 1T 1TD 1W.

42004–078. Lot No. 30882 Derby 1976–77. 33.6 t.
42096–250. Lot No. 30897 Derby 1977–79. 33.6 t.
42252–301. Lot No. 30939 Derby 1979–80. 33.6 t.
42319. Lot No. 30969 Derby 1982. 33.6 t.
42325–337. Lot No. 30983 Derby 1984–85. 33.6 t.
42342/360. Lot No. 30949 Derby 1982. 33.47 t. Converted from TGS.
42343/345. Lot No. 30970 Derby 1982. 33.47 t. Converted from TGS.
42347/350/351/379/380/551–562. Lot No. 30881 Derby 1976–77. 33.66 t. Converted from TF.
42363/567–569. Lot No. 30896 Derby 1977–78. 33.66 t. Converted from TF.

42366–378/404/408. Lot No. 30877 Derby 1975–77. 34.3 t. Converted from Mark 3A Open Standard.
42506. Lot No. 30940 Derby 1979–80. 34.8 t. Converted from TFKB.
42571–579. Lot No. 30938 Derby 1979–80. 33.66 t. Converted from TF.
42581/583. Lot No. 30947 Derby 1980. 33.66 t. Converted from TF.
42584/585. Lot No. 30878 Derby 1975–76. Converted from Mark 3A Open First.

42004	p*	**SI**	A	*SR*	IS	42184	ps	**SI**	A	*SR*	IS
42009	ps	**SI**	A	*SR*	IS	42185	ps	**SI**	A	*SR*	IS
42010	ps	**SI**	A	*SR*	IS	42200	p*	**SI**	A	*SR*	IS
42012	p*	**SI**	A	*SR*	IS	42206	p*	**SI**	A	*SR*	IS
42013	ps	**SI**	A	*SR*	IS	42207	p*	**SI**	A	*SR*	IS
42014	ps	**SI**	A	*SR*	IS	42208	ps	**SI**	A	*SR*	IS
42019	ps	**SI**	A		ZN	42209	ps	**SI**	A	*SR*	IS
42021	p*	**SI**	A	*SR*	IS	42213	ps	**SI**	A	*SR*	IS
42023	ps	**SI**	A	*SR*	IS	42220	w	**ST**	LS	*LS*	CL
42024	*k	**FD**	A		EP	42234	px	**XC**	P		YA
42029	ps	**SI**	A	*SR*	IS	42245	pr	**SI**	A	*SR*	IS
42030	p*	**SI**	A	*SR*	IS	42250	ps	**SI**	A	*SR*	IS
42032	ps	**SI**	A	*SR*	IS	42252	ps	**SI**	A	*SR*	IS
42033	ps	**SI**	A	*SR*	IS	42253	p*	**SI**	A	*SR*	IS
42034	pr	**SI**	A	*SR*	IS	42255	p*	**SI**	A	*SR*	IS
42035	ps	**SI**	A	*SR*	IS	42256	ps	**SI**	A	*SR*	IS
42036	px	**XC**	A		EP	42257	ps	**SI**	A	*SR*	IS
42037	px	**XC**	A		YA	42259	p*	**SI**	A	*SR*	IS
42038	px	**XC**	A		YA	42265	p*	**SI**	A	*SR*	IS
42045	ps	**SI**	A		ZB	42267	p*	**SI**	A	*SR*	IS
42046	ps	**SI**	A	*SR*	IS	42268	p*	**SI**	A	*SR*	IS
42047	ps	**SI**	A	*SR*	IS	42269	ps	**SI**	A	*SR*	IS
42051	px	**XC**	A		YA	42275	p*	**SI**	A		ZB
42052	px	**XC**	A		YA	42276	ps	**SI**	A		ZB
42053	px	**XC**	A		YA	42277	ps	**SI**	A	*SR*	IS
42054	ps	**SI**	A	*SR*	IS	42279	p*	**SI**	A	*SR*	IS
42055	p*	**SI**	A		ZN	42280	pr	**SI**	A	*SR*	IS
42056	ps	**SI**	A	*SR*	IS	42281	p*	**SI**	A	*SR*	IS
42072	pr	**SI**	A	*SR*	IS	42288	ps	**SI**	A	*SR*	IS
42075	ps	**SI**	A	*SR*	IS	42290	px	**XC**	P		YA
42077	ps	**SI**	A	*SR*	IS	42291	p*	**SI**	A	*SR*	IS
42078	ps	**SI**	A	*SR*	IS	42292	p*	**SI**	A		ZB
42096	ps	**SI**	A	*SR*	IS	42293	ps	**SI**	A	*SR*	IS
42097	px	**XC**	A		YA	42295	p*	**SI**	A	*SR*	IS
42100	u	**ST**	LS	*LS*	CL	42296	ps	**SI**	A	*SR*	IS
42107	pr	**SI**	A	*SR*	IS	42297	p*	**SI**	A	*SR*	IS
42110	m	**VE**	NS		BU	42299	ps	**SI**	A	*SR*	IS
42111	u	**ST**	125	*RA*	SK	42300	pr	**SI**	A	*SR*	IS
42119	u	**ST**	125	*RA*	SK	42301	ps	**SI**	A	*SR*	IS
42120	u	**ST**	125	*RA*	SK	42319	*h	**GW**	LS		KR
42129	ps	**SI**	A	*SR*	IS	42325	pr	**SI**	A	*SR*	IS
42143	ps	**SI**	A	*SR*	IS	42333	ps	**SI**	A	*SR*	IS
42144	ps	**SI**	A	*SR*	IS	42337	w	**ST**	125	*RA*	SK
42183	p*	**SI**	A	*SR*	IS						

42342	(44082)	px	**XC**	A		YA
42343	(44095)	ps	**SI**	A	*SR*	IS
42345	(44096)	p*	**SI**	A	*SR*	IS
42347	(41054)	*k	**FD**	A		EP
42350	(41047)	ps	**SI**	A	*SR*	IS
42351	(41048)	ps	**SI**	A	*SR*	IS
42360	(44084, 45084)	p*	**SI**	A	*SR*	IS

42366–378 were converted from loco-hauled Mark 3 vehicles for CrossCountry.

42366	(12007)	pt	**XC**	P		YA
42368	(12028)	px	**XC**	P		YA
42369	(12050)	px	**XC**	P		YA
42370	(12086)	px	**XC**	P		LM
42371	(12052)	pt	**XC**	P		YA
42372	(12055)	px	**XC**	P		YA
42373	(12071)	px	**XC**	P		YA
42375	(12113)	px	**XC**	P		Reid's, Stoke
42376	(12085)	pt	**XC**	P		YA
42377	(12102)	px	**XC**	P		LM
42378	(12123)	px	**XC**	P		YA
42379	(41036)	pt	**XC**	A		YA
42380	(41025)	pt	**XC**	A		YA

These carriages were converted from loco-hauled Mark 3 vehicles for Grand Central. They have a lower density seating layout (most seats arranged around tables). –/62 2T.

42404	(12152)	**EA**	A		EP
42408	(12121)	**EA**	A		EP

Converted from TFKB or TSB buffet cars to TS vehicles in 2011–12 at Wabtec Kilmarnock for FGW. Refurbished with Grammer seating. –/84 1T. 34.8 t.

42506	(40324, 40724)	**FD**	A		EP

These carriages were converted from TF to TS vehicles in 2014 at Wabtec Kilmarnock for FGW. Refurbished with Grammer seating. –/80 1T (pr –/68(+6). 35.5 t.

42551	(41003)	pr	**SI**	A	*SR*	IS
42553	(41009)	pr	**SI**	A	*SR*	IS
42555	(41015)	pr	**SI**	A	*SR*	IS
42557	(41019)	pr	**SI**	A	*SR*	IS
42558	(41021)	pr	**SI**	A	*SR*	IS
42559	(41023)	pr	**SI**	A	*SR*	IS
42561	(41031)	pr	**SI**	A	*SR*	IS
42562	(41037)	pr	**SI**	A		ZB
42567	(41093)	pr	**SI**	A	*SR*	IS
42568	(41101)	pr	**SI**	A	*SR*	IS
42569	(41105)		**FD**	A		EP
42571	(41121)	pr	**SI**	A		ZN
42574	(41129)	pr	**SI**	A	*SR*	IS
42575	(41131)	pr	**SI**	A	*SR*	IS

42576	(41133)	pr	**SI**	A		ZB
42577	(41141)	pr	**SI**	A	*SR*	IS
42578	(41143)	pr	**SI**	A	*SR*	IS
42579	(41145)	pr	**SI**	A	*SR*	IS
42581	(41157)	pr	**SI**	A	*SR*	IS
42583	(41153, 42385)		**GW**	LS		KR

These carriages were converted from loco-hauled carriages for Grand Central, before being converted to TS for East Midlands Railway. –/62 2T.

42584	(11045, 41201)	**EA**	A	EP
42585	(11017, 41202)	**EA**	A	YA

TRAILER GUARD'S STANDARD/FIRST   TGS/TGF

As built and m –/65 1T.
* Refurbished Great Western Railway vehicles. Grammer seating and toilet removed for trolley store. –/67 (unless h).
† Converted to Trailer Guard's First (TGF) with Primarius seating. 36/–.
p Refurbished former CrossCountry vehicles with power doors and Primarius seating. –/67.
h "High density" Great Western Railway vehicles. –/71.
s Fitted with centre luggage stack (EMR) –/63 1T.

44000. Lot No. 30953 Derby 1980. 33.47 t.
44012–081. Lot No. 30949 Derby 1980–82. 33.47 t.

44000	*h	**GW**	125		RD		44052	p	**XC**	P		YA
44012	p	**XC**	A		YA		44072	p	**XC**	P		YA
44017	p	**XC**	A		EP		44078	†	**MP**	LS	*LS*	CL
44021	p	**XC**	P		LM		44081	†	**MP**	LS	*LS*	CL
44047	s	**ST**	LS	*LS*	CL							

TRAILER COMPOSITE KITCHEN   TCK

Converted from Mark 3A Open Standard. Refurbished former CrossCountry vehicles with Primarius seating. Small kitchen for the preparation of hot food and stowage space for two trolleys between First and Standard Class. One toilet removed. 30/8 1T.

45001–005. Lot No. 30877 Derby 1975–77. 34.3 t.

45001	(12004)	p	**XC**	P	YA
45002	(12106)	p	**XC**	P	YA
45003	(12076)	p	**XC**	P	YA
45004	(12077)	p	**XC**	P	YA
45005	(12080)	p	**XC**	P	YA

TRAILER COMPOSITE   TC

Converted from TF for First Great Western 2014–15. Refurbished with Grammer seating. 24/39 1T.

46006. Lot No. 30896 Derby 1977–78. 35.6 t. Converted from TF.
46012. Lot No. 30938 Derby 1979–80. 35.6 t. Converted from TF.
46014. Lot No. 30963 Derby 1982. 35.6 t. Converted from TF.

46006	(41081)	**FD**	LS		ZG
46012	(41147)	**FD**	LS		KR
46014	(41168)	**CC**	LS	*LS*	CL	MOIDART

TRAILER STANDARD   TS

Refurbished for Great Western Railway 2017–21 and fitted with power doors and retention toilets. Used in 4-car sets on local and regional services across the South-West. –/84 1T († –/62 + 5 tip-ups 1TD 2W).

48102–137/140–150. For Lot No. details see TS. 36.3 t.

48102	(42218)	p†	**GW**	FG *GW*	LA
48104	(41107, 42365)	p	**GW**	FG *GW*	LA
48105	(42266)	p†	**GW**	FG *GW*	LA
48106	(42258)	p	**GW**	FG *GW*	LA
48107	(42101)	p	**GW**	FG *GW*	LA
48108	(42174)	p†	**GW**	FG *GW*	LA
48109	(42085)	p	**GW**	FG *GW*	LA
48110	(42315)	p	**GW**	FG	LA
48111	(42224)	p†	**GW**	FG	LA
48112	(42222)	p	**GW**	FG	LA
48114	(42317)	p†	**GW**	FG *GW*	LA
48117	(42271)	p†	**GW**	A *GW*	LA
48118	(42073)	p	**GW**	A *GW*	LA
48119	(42204)	p	**GW**	A *GW*	LA
48120	(42201)	p†	**GW**	A *GW*	LA
48121	(42027)	p	**GW**	A *GW*	LA
48122	(42214)	p	**GW**	A *GW*	LA
48123	(42211)	p†	**GW**	A *GW*	LA
48124	(42212)	p	**GW**	A *GW*	LA
48126	(42138)	p†	**GW**	A *GW*	LA
48127	(42349)	p	**GW**	A	EP
48128	(42044)	p	**GW**	A	EP
48129	(42008)	p†	**GW**	A	EP
48130	(42102, 48131)	p	**GW**	FG *GW*	LA
48136	(41114, 42570)	p	**GW**	FG *GW*	LA
48137	(41163, 42582)	p	**GW**	FG *GW*	LA
48140	(42005)	p	**GW**	GW	YA
48141	(42015)	p†	**GW**	GW	YA
48142	(42016)	p	**GW**	GW	YA
48143	(42050)	p	**GW**	GW	EP

48144	(42066)	p†	**GW**	GW		EP
48145	(42048)	p	**GW**	GW		EP
48146	(42074)	p	**GW**	GW		EP
48147	(42081)	p†	**GW**	GW		EP
48148	(42071)	p	**GW**	GW		EP
48149	(42087)	p	**GW**	GW	*GW*	LA
48150	(42580)	p	**GW**	GW	*GW*	LA

TRAILER GUARD'S STANDARD   TGS

Refurbished for Great Western Railway 2017–21 and fitted with power doors. –/71.

49102–117. For Lot No. details see TGS. 35.7 t.

49102	(44083)	p	**GW**	FG	*GW*	LA
49103	(44097)	p	**GW**	FG	*GW*	LA
49104	(44101)	p	**GW**	FG		LA
49105	(44090)	p	**GW**	FG	*GW*	LA
49106	(44033)	p	**GW**	A	*GW*	LA
49108	(44067)	p	**GW**	A	*GW*	LA
49109	(44003)	p	**GW**	A	*GW*	LA
49110	(44014)	p	**GW**	A		EP
49112	(44079)	p	**GW**	FG		LA
49114	(44005)	p	**GW**	GW		YA
49115	(44016)	p	**GW**	GW		EP
49116	(44002)	p	**GW**	GW		EP
49117	(44042)	p	**GW**	GW	*GW*	LA

2.3. HST SET FORMATIONS

GREAT WESTERN RAILWAY

GWR has been reducing its number of short 4-car HST sets since 2022 – from 16 sets down to seven at the time of writing. These trains are now used mainly on local services between Plymouth and Penzance.

Number of sets: 7.   **Usual number of daily diagrams:** 3.
Formations: 4-cars.   **Allocation:** Laira (Plymouth).
Other maintenance and servicing depots: Long Rock (Penzance), St Philip's Marsh (Bristol).
Operation: Plymouth–Penzance plus one service to Exeter.

Set	D	C	B	A
GW02	48106	48105	48104	49102
GW03	48109	48108	48107	49103
GW05	48130	48114	48102	49105
GW06	48118	48117	48136	49106
GW07	48121	48120	48119	49108
GW08	48124	48123	48122	49117
GW09	48137	48126	48150	49109

Spare:

LA:	48149

SCOTRAIL

ScotRail has introduced refurbished HSTs onto its Edinburgh/Glasgow–Aberdeen/Inverness services – branded INTER-7-CITY as they serve Scotland's seven cities. It is ultimately planned that there will be 17 5-car and eight 4-car sets (HA22 was written off in the 2020 Carmont accident). The first 5-car sets were introduced in 2021 and further 4-cars sets will be lengthened to 5-cars as passenger demand dictates. Sets HA02, HA08 and HA23 are currently not in service.

Number of sets: 25.
Usual number of daily diagrams: 15.
Formations: 4-cars or 5-cars.
Allocation: Power cars: Haymarket (Edinburgh), Trailers: Inverness.
Operation: Edinburgh/Glasgow–Aberdeen, Edinburgh/Glasgow–Inverness, Aberdeen–Inverness.

Set	A	B	C	D	E	
HA01	40601	42004	42561	42046		
HA02	40602	42292	42562	42045		*(stored at Wabtec, Doncaster)*
HA03	40603	42021	42557	42143		
HA04	40604	42183	42559	42343		
HA05	40605	42345	42034	42184	42029	
HA06	40606	42206	42581	42208	42033	
HA07	40607	42207	42574	42288	42056	
HA08	40608	42055	42571	42019		*(stored at Gemini, Wolverton)*
HA09	40609	42253	42107	42257		
HA10	40610	42360	42551	42252	42351	
HA11	40611	42267	42325	42301	42023	
HA12	40612	42275	42576	42276		
HA13	40613	42279	42280	42296		
HA14	40614	42012	42245	42013		
HA15	40615	42030	42559	42010		
HA16	40616	42291	42577	42075		
HA17	40617	42295	42558	42250		
HA18	40618	42297	42555	42014		
HA19	40619	42255	42568	42256		
HA20	40620	42200	42575	42129		
HA21	40621	42299	42300	42277		
HA23	40623	42268	42567	42269		*(stored at Wabtec, Doncaster)*
HA24	40624	42265	42553	42293		
HA25	40625	42259	42578	42333		
HA26	40626	42281	42072	42350		

Extra coaches that have been refurbished to make further sets up to 5-car rakes:

42009 42032 42035 42047 42054 42077 42078 42096 42144
42185 42209 42213

2.4. SALOONS

Several specialist passenger carrying carriages, normally referred to as
saloons are permitted to run on the national railway system. Many of these
are to pre-nationalisation designs.

WCJS FIRST CLASS SALOON

Built 1892 by LNWR, Wolverton. Originally dining saloon mounted on six-
wheel bogies. Rebuilt with new underframe with four-wheel bogies in 1927.
Rebuilt 1960 as observation saloon with DMU end. Gangwayed at other
end. The interior has a saloon, kitchen, guards vestibule and observation
lounge. 19/– 1T. Gresley bogies. 28.5 t. 75 mph. ETS x.

41   (484, 45018) x   **M**   WC *WC*   CS

LNWR DINING SALOON

Built 1890 by LNWR, Wolverton. Mounted on the underframe of LMS
General Utility Van 37908 in the 1980s. Contains kitchen and dining area
seating 12 at tables for two. 12/–. Gresley bogies. 75 mph. 25.4 t. ETS x.

159   (5159)   x   **M**   WC *WC*   CS

GNR FIRST CLASS SALOON

Built 1912 by GNR, Doncaster. Contains entrance vestibule, lavatory, two
separate saloons, library and luggage space. 19/– 1T. Gresley bogies.
75 mph. 29.4 t. ETS x.

Non-standard livery: Teak.

807   (4807)   x   **0**   WC *WC*   CS

LNER GENERAL MANAGERS SALOON

Built 1945 by LNER, York. Gangwayed at one end with a veranda at the
other. The interior has a dining saloon seating 12, kitchen, toilet, office and
nine seat lounge. 21/– 1T. B4 bogies. 75 mph. 35.7 t. ETS 3.

1999   (902260)   **M**   WC   CS   DINING CAR No. 2

GENERAL MANAGER'S SALOON

Renumbered 1989 from London Midland Region departmental series. Formerly the LMR General Manager's saloon. Rebuilt from LMS period 1 Corridor Brake First M5033M to dia 1654 and mounted on the underframe of BR suburban Brake Standard M43232. Screw couplings have been removed. B4 bogies. 100 mph. ETS 2X.

LMS Lot No. 326 Derby 1927. 27.5 t.

6320   (5033, DM 395707)   x   **M**   PR   *PR*   SK

SUPPORT CAR

Converted 199? from Courier vehicle converted from Mark 1 Corridor Brake Standard 1986–87. Toilet retained and former compartment area replaced with train manager's office, crew locker room, linen store and dry goods store. The former luggage area has been adapted for use as an engineers' compartment and workshop. B5 bogies. 100 mph. ETS 2.

Lot No. 30721 Wolverton 1963. 35.5 t.

99545   (35466, 80207)   **PC**   BE   *BP*   SL   BAGGAGE CAR No. 11

SERVICE CAR

Converted from BR Mark 1 Corridor Brake Standard. Commonwealth bogies. 100 mph. ETS 2.

Lot No. 30721 Wolverton 1963.

99886   (35407)   x   **M**   WC   *WC*   CS   86   SERVICE CAR No. 1

ROYAL SCOTSMAN SALOONS

Built 1960 by Metro-Cammell as Pullman Kitchen Second for East Coast Main Line Services. Rebuilt 2016 as a Spa Car with two large bedrooms with bathroom/spa areas. Commonwealth bogies. xx t. ETS ?.

99337   (CAR No. 337)   **M**   BE   *RS*   HN   STATE SPA CAR

Built 1960 by Metro-Cammell as Pullman Kitchen First for East Coast Main Line services. Rebuilt 2013 as dining car. Commonwealth bogies. 38.5 t. ETS ?.

99960   (321 SWIFT)   **M**   BE   *RS*   HN   DINING CAR No. 2

Built 1960 by Metro-Cammell as Pullman Parlour First (§ Pullman Kitchen First) for East Coast Main Line services. Rebuilt 1990 as sleeping cars with four twin sleeping rooms (*§ three twin sleeping rooms and two single sleeping rooms at each end). Commonwealth bogies. 38.5 t. ETS ?.

99961	(324 AMBER) *	**M**	BE	*RS*	HN	STATE CAR No. 1
99962	(329 PEARL)	**M**	BE	*RS*	HN	STATE CAR No. 2
99963	(331 TOPAZ)	**M**	BE	*RS*	HN	STATE CAR No. 3
99964	(313 FINCH) §	**M**	BE	*RS*	HN	STATE CAR No. 4

Built 1960 by Metro-Cammell as Pullman Kitchen First for East Coast Main Line services. Rebuilt 1990 as observation car with open verandah seating 32. B4 bogies. 36.95 t. ETS ?.

| 99965 | (319 SNIPE) | **M** | BE | *RS* | HN | OBSERVATION CAR |

Built 1960 by Metro-Cammell as Pullman Kitchen First for East Coast Main Line services. Rebuilt 1993 as dining car. Commonwealth bogies. 38.5 t. ETS ?.

| 99967 | (317 RAVEN) | **M** | BE | *RS* | HN | DINING CAR No. 1 |

Mark 3A. Converted 1997 from a Sleeping Car at Carnforth Railway Restoration & Engineering Services. BT10 bogies. Attendant's and adjacent two sleeping compartments converted to generator room containing a 160 kW Volvo unit. In 99968 four sleeping compartments remain for staff use with another converted for use as a staff shower and toilet. The remaining five sleeping compartments have been replaced by two passenger cabins. In 99969 seven sleeping compartments remain for staff use. A further sleeping compartment, along with one toilet, have been converted to store rooms. The other two sleeping compartments have been combined to form a crew mess. 41.5 t. 99968 ETS index ?. 99969 ETS 7X (when generator not in use). ETS index ?? (when generator in use).

Lot No. 30960 Derby 1981–83.

| 99968 | (10541) | **M** | BE | *RS* | HN | STATE CAR No. 5 |
| 99969 | (10556) | **M** | BE | *RS* | HN | SERVICE CAR |

"CLUB CAR"

Converted from BR Mark 1 Open Standard at Carnforth Railway Restoration & Engineering Services in 1994. Contains kitchen, pantry and two dining saloons. 20/– 1T. Commonwealth bogies. 100 mph. ETS 4.

Lot No. 30724 York 1963. 37 t.

| 99993 | (5067) | x | **CC** | LS | *LS* | CL | CLUB CAR |

BR INSPECTION SALOON

Mark 1. Short frames. Non-gangwayed. Observation windows at each end. The interior layout consists of two saloons interspersed by a central lavatory/kitchen/guards/luggage section. 90 mph. ETS x.

BR Wagon Lot No. 3095 Swindon 1957. B4 bogies. 30.5 t.

| 999506 | | **M** | WC | *WC* | CS | |

2.5. PULLMAN CAR COMPANY SERIES

Pullman cars have never generally been numbered as such, although many have carried numbers, instead they have carried titles. However, a scheme of schedule numbers exists which generally lists cars in chronological order. In this section those numbers are shown followed by the car's title. Cars described as "kitchen" contain a kitchen in addition to passenger accommodation and have gas cooking unless otherwise stated. Cars described as "parlour" consist entirely of passenger accommodation. Cars described as "brake" contain a compartment for the use of the guard and a luggage compartment in addition to passenger accommodation.

PULLMAN PARLOUR FIRST

Built 1927 by Midland Carriage & Wagon Company. 26/– 2T. Gresley bogies. 41 t. ETS 2.

| 213 | MINERVA | **PC** | BE | *BP* | SL |

PULLMAN KITCHEN FIRST

Built 1928 by Metropolitan Carriage & Wagon Company. 20/– 1T. Gresley bogies. 42 t. ETS 4.

| 238 | PHYLISS | **PC** | BE | | SL |

PULLMAN PARLOUR FIRST

Built 1928 by Metropolitan Carriage & Wagon Company. 24/– 2T. Gresley bogies. 40 t. ETS 4.

| 239 | AGATHA | **PC** | BE | | SL |
| 243 | LUCILLE | **PC** | BE | *BP* | SL |

PULLMAN KITCHEN FIRST

Built 1925 by BRCW. Rebuilt by Midland Carriage & Wagon Company in 1928. 20/– 1T. Gresley bogies. 41 t. ETS 4.

| 245 | IBIS | **PC** | BE | *BP* | SL |

PULLMAN PARLOUR FIRST

Built 1928 by Metropolitan Carriage & Wagon Company. 24/– 2T. Gresley bogies. ETS 4.

| 254 | ZENA | **PC** | BE | *BP* | SL |

PULLMAN KITCHEN FIRST

Built 1928 by Metropolitan Carriage & Wagon Company. 20/– 1T. Gresley bogies. 42 t. ETS 4.

| 255 | IONE | **PC** | BE | *BP* | SL |

PULLMAN KITCHEN COMPOSITE

Built 1932 by Metropolitan Carriage & Wagon Company. Originally included in 6-Pul EMU. Electric cooking. 12/16 1T. EMU bogies. ETS x.

264	RUTH		**PC**	BE		SL

PULLMAN KITCHEN FIRST

Built 1932 by Metropolitan Carriage & Wagon Company. Originally included in "Brighton Belle" EMUs but now used as hauled stock. Electric cooking. 20/– 1T. B5 (SR) bogies (§ EMU bogies). 44 t. ETS 2.

280	AUDREY		**PC**	BE	*BP*	SL
281	GWEN		**PC**	BE	*BP*	SL
283	MONA	§	**PC**	BE		SL
284	VERA		**PC**	BE	*BP*	SL

PULLMAN PARLOUR THIRD

Built 1932 by Metropolitan Carriage & Wagon Company. Originally included in "Brighton Belle" EMUs. –/56 2T. EMU bogies. ETS x.

Non-standard livery: BR Revised Pullman (blue & white lined out in white).

286	CAR No. 86	**0**	BE	SL

PULLMAN BRAKE THIRD

Built 1932 by Metropolitan Carriage & Wagon Company. Originally driving motor cars in "Brighton Belle" EMUs. Traction and control equipment removed for use as hauled stock. –/48 1T. EMU bogies. ETS x.

292	CAR No. 92	**PC**	BE	SL
293	CAR No. 93	**PC**	BE	SL

PULLMAN PARLOUR FIRST

Built 1951 by Birmingham Railway Carriage & Wagon Company. 32/– 2T. Gresley bogies. 39 t. ETS 3.

301	PERSEUS	**PC**	BE	*BP*	SL

Built 1952 by Pullman Car Company, Preston Park using underframe and bogies from 176 RAINBOW, the body of which had been destroyed by fire. 26/– 2T. Gresley bogies. 38 t. ETS 4.

302	PHOENIX	**PC**	BE	*BP*	SL

PULLMAN PARLOUR FIRST

Built 1951 by Birmingham Railway Carriage & Wagon Company. 32/– 2T. Gresley bogies. 39 t. ETS 3.

308	CYGNUS	**PC**	BE	*BP*	SL

PULLMAN BAR FIRST

Built 1951 by Birmingham Railway Carriage & Wagon Company. Rebuilt 1999 by Blake Fabrications, Edinburgh with original timber-framed body replaced by a new fabricated steel body. Contains kitchen, bar, dining saloon and coupé. Electric cooking. 14/– 1T. Gresley bogies. ETS 3.

310   PEGASUS   x **PC** LS *LS* CL

Also carries "THE TRIANON BAR" branding.

PULLMAN KITCHEN FIRST

Built 1960 by Birmingham Railway Carriage & Wagon Company. Originally part of the National Collection. Rebuilt by Vintage Trains and returned to service 2021. Electric cooking. 26/– 1T. Commonwealth bogies. ETS x.

311   EAGLE   x **PC** VT *VT* TM

PULLMAN PARLOUR FIRST

Built 1960–61 by Metro-Cammell for East Coast Main Line services. –/36 2T. Commonwealth bogies. 38.5 t. ETS x.

| 325 | AMBER | x | **PC** | WC | *WC* | CS |
| 326 | EMERALD | x | **PC** | WC | *WC* | CS |

PULLMAN KITCHEN SECOND

Built 1960–61 by Metro-Cammell for East Coast Main Line services. Commonwealth bogies. –/30 1T. 40 t. ETS x.

335   CAR No. 335   x **PC** VT *VT* TM

PULLMAN PARLOUR SECOND

Built 1960–61 by Metro-Cammell for East Coast Main Line services. 347 is used as an Open First. –/42 2T. Commonwealth bogies. 38.5 t. ETS x.

347	DIAMOND	x	**PC**	WC	*WC*	CS
348	TOPAZ	x	**PC**	WC	*WC*	CS
349	CAR No. 349	x	**PC**	VT	*VT*	TM
350	TANZANITE	x	**PC**	WC	*WC*	CS
351	SAPPHIRE	x	**PC**	WC	*WC*	CS
352	AMETHYST	x	**PC**	WC	*WC*	CS
353	CAR No. 353	x	**PC**	VT		TM

PULLMAN SECOND BAR

Built 1960–61 by Metro-Cammell for East Coast Main Line services. –/24+17 bar seats. Commonwealth bogies. 38.5 t. ETS x.

354   THE HADRIAN BAR   x **PC** WC *WC* CS

2.6. LOCOMOTIVE SUPPORT CARRIAGES

These carriages have been adapted from Mark 1s and Mark 2s for use as support carriages for heritage steam and diesel locomotives. Some seating is retained for the use of personnel supporting the locomotives operation with the remainder of the carriage adapted for storage, workshop, dormitory and catering purposes. These carriages can spend considerable periods of time off the national railway system when the locomotives they support are not being used on that system. No owner or operator details are included in this section. After the depot code, the locomotive(s) each carriage is usually used to support is given.

CORRIDOR BRAKE FIRST

Mark 1. Commonwealth bogies. ETS 2.

14007. Lot No. 30382 Swindon 1959. 35 t.
17025. Lot No. 30718 Swindon 1963. Metal window frames. 36 t.

14007	(14007, 17007)	x	**M**	Chasewater Rly	LNER 61264
17025	(14025)	v	**M**	CS	LMS 45690

CORRIDOR BRAKE FIRST

Mark 2A. Pressure ventilated. B4 bogies. ETS 4.

14060. Lot No. 30775 Derby 1967–68. 32 t.
17096. Lot No. 30786 Derby 1968. 32 t.

14060	(14060, 17060)	v	**M**	TM	LMS 45596	
17096	(14096)		**PC**	SL	SR 35028	MERCATOR

CORRIDOR BRAKE COMPOSITE

Mark 1. ETS 2.

21096. Lot No. 30185 Metro-Cammell 1956. BR Mark 1 bogies. 32.5 t.
21232. Lot No. 30574 GRCW 1960. B4 bogies. 34 t.
21249. Lot No. 30669 Swindon 1961–62. Commonwealth bogies. 36 t.

21096	x	**CC**	CL	LNER 60007
21232	x	**M**	SK	LMS 46201
21249	x	**M**	SL	New Build 60163

CORRIDOR BRAKE STANDARD

Mark 1. Metal window frames and melamine interior panelling. ETS 2.

35317/322. Lot No. 30699 Wolverton 1962–63. Commonwealth bogies. 37 t.
35451–486. Lot No. 30721 Wolverton 1963. Commonwealth bogies. 37 t.

35317	x	**CC**	CL	Locomotives Services Crewe-based locomotives
35322	x	**M**	CS	WCRC Carnforth-based locomotives
35451	x	**CC**	CL	Locomotives Services Crewe-based locomotives
35461	x	**CC**	CL	Locomotives Services Crewe-based locomotives
35463	v	**M**	CS	WCRC Carnforth-based locomotives
35468	x	**M**	YK	National Railway Museum locomotives
35470	v	**CH**	TM	Tyseley Locomotive Works-based locos
35476	x	**M**	SK	LMS 46233
35479	v	**M**	CL	LNER 61306/LNER 60007
35486	x	**M**	BQ	LNER 60103

CORRIDOR BRAKE FIRST

Mark 2C. Pressure ventilated. Renumbered when declassified. B4 bogies. ETS 4.

Lot No. 30796 Derby 1969–70. 32.5 t.

35508 (14128, 17128)		**M**	BQ	LMS 44871/45212/45407

CORRIDOR BRAKE FIRST

Mark 2A. Pressure ventilated. Renumbered when declassified. B4 bogies. ETS 4.

Lot No. 30786 Derby 1968. 32 t.

35517 (14088, 17088)	b	**M**	BQ	LMS 44871/45212/45407
35518 (14097, 17097)	b	**G**	CS	SR 34067

COURIER VEHICLE

Mark 1. Converted 1986–87 from Corridor Brake Standards. ETS 2.

80204/217. Lot No. 30699 Wolverton 1962. Commonwealth bogies. 37 t.
80220. Lot No. 30573 Gloucester 1960. B4 bogies. 33 t.

80204 (35297)	**M**	CS	WCRC Carnforth-based locomotives
80217 (35299)	**M**	CS	WCRC Carnforth-based locomotives
80220 (35276)	**M**	NY	LNER 62005

2.7. 95xxx & 99xxx RANGE NUMBER CONVERSION TABLE

The following table is presented to help readers identify carriages which may still carry numbers in the 95xxx and 99xxx number ranges of the former private owner number series, which is no longer in general use.

9xxxx	BR No.	9xxxx	BR No.	9xxxx	BR No.
95325	Pullman 325	99350	Pullman 350	99673	550
95402	Pullman 326	99351	Pullman 351	99674	551
95403	Pullman 311	99352	Pullman 352	99675	552
99040	21232	99353	Pullman 353	99676	553
99041	35476	99354	Pullman 354	99677	586
99052	Saloon 41	99361	Pullman 335	99678	504
99121	3105	99371	3128	99679	506
99122	3106	99405	35486	99680	17102
99125	3113	99530	Pullman 301	99716 *	18808
99127	3117	99531	Pullman 302	99721	18756
99128	3130	99532	Pullman 308	99723	35459
99131	Saloon 1999	99534	Pullman 245	99880	Saloon 159
99241	35449	99535	Pullman 213	99881	Saloon 807
99302	13323	99536	Pullman 254	99883	2108
99304	21256	99537	Pullman 280	99885	2110
99311	1882	99539	Pullman 255	99887	2127
99312	35463	99541	Pullman 243	99953	35468
99326	4954	99543	Pullman 284	99966	34525
99327	5044	99546	Pullman 281	99970	Pullman 232
99328	5033	99547	Pullman 292	99971	Pullman 311
99329	4931	99548	Pullman 293	99972	Pullman 318
99347	Pullman 347	99670	546	99973	324
99348	Pullman 348	99671	548	99974	Pullman 328
99349	Pullman 349	99672	549		

* The number 99716 has also been applied to 3416 for filming purposes.

2.8. SET FORMATIONS

LNER MARK 4 SET FORMATIONS

The LNER Mark 4 sets generally run in fixed formations. Class 91 locomotives are positioned next to Coach B. Most Mark 4 sets were withdrawn in 2019–20, leaving eight rakes still on lease to LNER.

Set	B	C	D	E	F	H	K	L	M	DVT
NL06	12208	12406	12420	12422	12313	10309	11279	11306	11406	82208
NL08	12205	12481	12485	12407	12328	10300	11229	11308	11408	82211
NL12	12212	12431	12404	12426	12330	10333	11284	11312	11412	82212
NL13	12228	12469	12430	12424	12311	10313	11285	11313	11413	82213
NL15	12226	12442	12409	12515	12309	10306	11286	11315	11415	82214
NL16	12213	12428	12433	12467	12312	10315	11418	11318	11416	82222
NL17	12223	12444	12427	12432	12303	10324	11288	11317	11417	82225
NL26	12220	12474	12465	12429	12325	10311	11295	11326	11426	82223
Spare	12214									82205

TfW MARK 4 SET FORMATIONS

In 2021 Transport for Wales returned three shortened four-coach Mark 4 sets to service to replace its Mark 3 sets. They are used on selected services on the Cardiff–Manchester route and also to Holyhead, hauled by Class 67s. The sets are currently being lengthened to five-coach rakes using the spare Open Standard (Disabled) coaches listed.

Transport for Wales also purchased the four sets previously planned to be operated by Grand Central, plus another to make an eighth set and these were introduced at the start of 2023, mainly on the Manchester route. They are also to be lengthened to five coaches.

Set					DVT
HD01	12225	12315	10325	11323	82226
HD02	12219	12304	10328	11324	82229
HD03	12217	12324	10312	11325	12446	82216

Extra coaches to augment the above sets:
12447 12454

Set					DVT
HD04	12211	12310	10318	11319	82201
HD05	12224	12326	10321	11320	82200
HD06	12222	12323	10330	11321	82227
HD07	12210	12316	10301	11322	82230
HD08	12215	12308	10305	11316	12526	82220 *(currently out of service)*

Extra coaches to augment the above sets:
12434 12452 12461 12477

Spare 82204

FORMER TPE MARK 5A SET FORMATIONS

The 13 TransPennine Express Mark 5A coaches were withdrawn at the end of 2023 after just over four years in service, with no new operator lined up for them at the time of writing. The sets were hauled by Class 68 locomotives in push-pull mode and the formations as they operated with TPE are shown below.

Set	E	D	C	B	A
TP01	11501	12701	12702	12703	12801
TP02	11502	12704	12705	12706	12814
TP03	11503	12707	12708	12709	12803
TP04	11504	12710	12711	12712	12804
TP05	11505	12713	12714	12715	12805
TP06	11506	12716	12717	12718	12806
TP07	11507	12719	12720	12721	12807
TP08	11508	12722	12723	12724	12808
TP09	11509	12725	12726	12727	12809
TP10	11510	12728	12729	12730	12810
TP11	11511	12731	12732	12733	12811
TP12	11512	12734	12735	12736	12812
TP13	11513	12737	12738	12739	12813
Spare					12802

2.9. SERVICE STOCK

Carriages in this section are used for internal purposes within the railway industry, ie they do not generate revenue from outside the industry. Most are numbered in the former BR departmental number series.

BARRIER, ESCORT & TRANSLATOR VEHICLES

These vehicles are used to move multiple units, HST and other vehicles around the national railway system.

Barrier Vehicles. Mark 1/2A. Renumbered from BR departmental series, or converted from various types. B4 bogies (* Commonwealth bogies).

6330. Mark 2A. Lot No. 30786 Derby 1968.
6336/38/44. Mark 1. Lot No. 30715 Gloucester 1962.
6340. Mark 1. Lot No. 30669 Swindon 1962.
6346. Mark 2A. Lot No. 30777 Derby 1967.
6348. Mark 1. Lot No. 30163 Pressed Steel 1957.

6330	(14084, 975629)		**RO**	A	*RO*	LR
6336	(81591, 92185)		**FB**	A	*GW*	LA
6338	(81581, 92180)		**FB**	A	*RO*	LR
6340	(21251, 975678)	*	**RO**	A	*RO*	LR
6344	(81263, 92080)		**RO**	A	*RO*	LR
6346	(9422)		**RO**	A	*RO*	LR
6348	(81233, 92963)		**FB**	A	*GW*	LA

Mark 4 Barrier Vehicles. Mark 2A. Converted from Corridor First. B4 bogies. Lot No. 30774 Derby 1968.

6352	(13465, 19465)	**HB**	E	WS
6353	(13478, 19478)	**HB**	E	WS

EMU Translator Vehicles. Mark 1. Converted 1980 from Restaurant Unclassified Opens. 6376/77 have Tightlock couplers and 6378/79 Dellner couplers. Commonwealth bogies.

Lot No. 30647 Wolverton 1959–61.

6376	(1021, 975973)	**PB**	P	*GB*	ZG	*(works with 6377)*
6377	(1042, 975975)	**PB**	P	*GB*	ZG	*(works with 6376)*
6378	(1054, 975971)	**RO**	RO	*RO*	LR	*(works with 6379)*
6379	(1059, 975972)	**RO**	RO	*RO*	LR	*(works with 6378)*

Brake Force Runners. Mark 1. Previously used as HST Barrier Vehicles. Converted from Gangwayed Brake Vans in 1994–95. B4 bogies.

6392. Lot No. 30715 Gloucester 1962.
6397. Lot No. 30716 Gloucester 1962.

6392	(81588, 92183)	**Y**	CS	*CS*	ZA
6397	(81600, 92190)	**Y**	CS	*CS*	ZA

HST Barrier Vehicles. Mark 1. Converted from Gangwayed Brake Vans in 1994–95. B4 bogies.

6393. Lot No. 30716 Gloucester 1962.
6394. Lot No. 30162 Pressed Steel 1956–57.
6398/99. Lot No. 30400 Pressed Steel 1957–58.

6393	(81609, 92196)	**PB**	P	*GB*	ZG
6394	(80878, 92906)	**PB**	P	*GB*	ZG
6398	(81471, 92126)	**PB**	EM	*EM*	NL
6399	(81367, 92994)	**PB**	EM	*EM*	NL

Escort Coaches. Converted from Mark 2A (* Mark 2E) Open Brake Standards. 9419/28 use the same bodyshell as the Mark 2A Corridor Brake First. B4 bogies.

9419. Lot No.30777 Derby 1970.
9428. Lot No.30820 Derby 1970.
9506/08. Lot No.30838 Derby 1972.

9419		**DS**	DR	*DR*	KM
9428		**DS**	DR	*DR*	KM
9506	*	**DS**	DR	*DR*	KM
9508	*	**DS**	DR	*DR*	KM

EMU Translator Vehicles. Converted from Class 508 driving cars.

64664. Lot No. 30979 York 1979–80.
64707. Lot No. 30981 York 1979–80.

64664	**AG**	A	*GB*	ZG	Liwet	*(works with 64707)*
64707	**AG**	A	*GB*	ZG	Labezerin	*(works with 64664)*

EMU Translator Vehicles. Converted from Class 489 DMLVs that had originally been Class 414/3 DMBSOs. Previously used as de-icing coaches.

Lot No. 30452 Ashford/Eastleigh 1959. Mk 4 bogies.

68501	(61281)	**AG**	AF	*RO*	LR
68504	(61286)	**AG**	AF	*RO*	LR

Generator Vans. Former Nightstar Generator Vans converted from Mark 3A Sleeping Cars that are now used as carriage pre-heaters. Gangways removed. Two Cummins diesel generator groups provide a 1500 V train supply.

Lot No. 30960 Derby 1981–83. BT10 bogies.

96371	(10545, 6371)	**CA**	ER	IS
96372	(10564, 6372)	**EP**	ER	YA
96373	(10568, 6373)	**EP**	ER	YA
96374	(10585, 6374)	**IC**	ER	YA
96375	(10587, 6375)	**EP**	ER	YA

Eurostar Barrier Vehicles. Mark 1. Converted from General Utility Vans with bodies removed. Fitted with B4 bogies for use as Eurostar barrier vehicles.

96380/381. Lot No. 30417 Pressed Steel 1958–59.
96383. Lot No. 30565 Pressed Steel 1959.
96384. Lot No. 30616 Pressed Steel 1959–60.

96380	(86386, 6380)	**B**	EU	*EU*	TI

96381	(86187, 6381)	**B**	EU	*EU*	TI	
96383	(86664, 6383)	**B**	EU	*EU*	TI	
96384	(86955, 6384)	**B**	EU	*EU*	TI	

Brake Force Runners or Universal Barrier Vehicles. Converted from Motorail vans built 1998–99 by Marcroft Engineering using underframe and running gear from Motorail General Utility Vans. Those operated by Colas Rail are often used in test trains and the Universal Barrier Vehicles have been fitted with Dellner couplers for use on multiple unit stock moves. B5 bogies.

Lot No. 30417 Pressed Steel 1958–59.

96602	(86097, 96150)	**MG**	MG	*RA*	KI	Henry
96603	(86334, 96155)	**MG**	MG	*RA*	KI	Oliver
96604	(86337, 96156)	**Y**	CS	*CS*	ZA	
96605	(86344, 96157)	**MG**	MG	*RA*	KI	Ernest
96606	(86324, 96213)	**Y**	CS	*CS*	ZA	
96607	(86351, 96215)	**MG**	MG	*RA*	KI	Philip
96608	(86385, 96216)	**Y**	CS	*CS*	ZA	
96609	(86327, 96217)	**Y**	CS	*CS*	ZA	

EMU Translator Vehicles. Converted from various Mark 1s.

975864. Lot No. 30054 Eastleigh 1951–54. Commonwealth bogies.
975867. Lot No. 30014 York 1950–51. Commonwealth bogies.
975974/978. Lot No. 30647 Wolverton 1959–61. B4 bogies.

975864	(3849)	**HB**	E		BU		*(works with 975867)*
975867	(1006)	**HB**	E		BU		*(works with 975864)*
975974	(1030)	**AG**	A	*GB*	ZG	Paschar	*(works with 975978)*
975978	(1025)	**AG**	A	*GB*	ZG	Perpetiel	*(works with 975974)*

LABORATORY, TESTING & INSPECTION COACHES

These coaches are used for research, testing and inspection on the national railway system. Many are fitted with sophisticated technical equipment.

Plain Line Pattern Recognition or Staff Accommodation Coaches. Converted from BR Mark 2F Buffet First (*) or Open Standard. B4 bogies.

1256. Lot No. 30845 Derby 1973.
5971/81. Lot No. 30860 Derby 1973–74.

1256	(3296)	*	**Y**	NR	*CS*	ZA
5971			**Y**	NR	*CS*	ZA
5981			**Y**	NR	*CS*	ZA

Brake Force Runners or Staff Accommodation Coaches. Converted from BR Mark 2F Open Standard. B4 bogies.

Lot No. 30860 Derby 1973–74.

5995	**Y**	NR	*CS*	ZA
6001	**Y**	NR	*CS*	ZA
6117	**Y**	NR	*CS*	ZA
6122	**Y**	NR	*CS*	ZA

Generator Vans. Mark 1. Converted from BR Mark 1 Gangwayed Brake Vans. B5 bogies.

6260. Lot No. 30400 Pressed Steel 1957–58.
6261. Lot No. 30323 Pressed Steel 1957.
6262. Lot No. 30228 Metro-Cammell 1957–58.
6263. Lot No. 30163 Pressed Steel 1957.
6264. Lot No. 30173 York 1956.

6260	(81450, 92116)	**Y**	NR	*CS*	ZA
6261	(81284, 92988)	**Y**	NR	*CS*	ZA
6262	(81064, 92928)	**Y**	NR	*CS*	ZA
6263	(81231, 92961)	**Y**	NR	*CS*	ZA
6264	(80971, 92923)	**Y**	NR	*CS*	ZA

Staff Coach. Mark 2D. Converted from BR Mark 2D Open Brake Standard. Lot No. 30824 Derby 1971. B4 bogies.

9481	**Y**	NR	*CS*	ZA

Test Train Brake Force Runners. Mark 2F. Converted from BR Mark 2F Open Brake Standard. Lot No. 30861 Derby 1974. B4 bogies.

9516	**Y**	NR	*CS*	ZA	*(works with 72616)*
9523	**Y**	NR	*CS*	ZA	

Driving Trailer Coaches. Converted 2008 at Serco, Derby from Mark 2F Driving Open Brake Standards. Fitted with generator. Disc brakes. B4 bogies.

9701–08. Lot No. 30861 Derby 1974. Converted to Driving Open Brake Standard Glasgow 1974.
9714. Lot No. 30861 Derby 1974. Converted to Driving Open Brake Standard Glasgow 1986.

9701	(9528)	**Y**	NR	*CS*	ZA
9702	(9510)	**Y**	NR	*CS*	ZA
9703	(9517)	**Y**	NR	*CS*	ZA
9708	(9530)	**Y**	NR	*CS*	ZA
9714	(9536)	**Y**	NR	*CS*	ZA

Test Train Brake Coaches. Former Caledonian Sleeper coaches now used for staff accommodation in test trains. Fitted with toilets with retention tanks. Converted from Mark 2E Open Standard with new seating by Railcare Wolverton. B4 bogies.

9801/03. Lot No. 30837 Derby 1972.
9806–10. Lot No. 30844 Derby 1972–73.

9801	(5760)	**FB**	ER	*CS*	ZA
9803	(5799)	**FB**	ER	*CS*	ZA
9806	(5840)	**FB**	ER	*CS*	ZA
9808	(5871)	**FB**	ER	*CS*	ZA
9810	(5892)	**FB**	ER	*CS*	ZA

Ultrasonic Test Coach. Converted from Class 421 EMU MBSO.

62287. Lot No. 30808. York 1970. SR Mark 6 bogies.
62384. Lot No. 30816. York 1970. SR Mark 6 bogies.

62287	**Y**	NR	*CS*	ZA
62384	**Y**	NR	*CS*	ZA

Test Train Brake Force Runners. Converted from Mark 2F Open Standard converted to Class 488/3 EMU TSOLH. These vehicles are included in test trains to provide brake force and are not used for any other purposes. Lot No. 30860 Derby 1973–74. B4 bogies.

72612	(6156)	**Y**	NR	*CS*	ZA
72616	(6007)	**Y**	NR	*CS*	ZA *(works with 9516)*

Structure Gauging Train Coach. Converted from Mark 2F Open Standard converted to Class 488/3 EMU TSOLH. Lot No. 30860 Derby 1973–74. B4 bogies.

72630	(6094)	**Y**	NR	*CS*	ZA *(works with 99666)*

Plain Line Pattern Recognition Coaches. Converted from BR Mark 2F Open Standard converted to Class 488/3 EMU TSOLH. Lot No. 30860 Derby 1973–74. B4 bogies.

72631	(6096)	**Y**	NR	*CS*	ZA
72639	(6070)	**Y**	NR	*CS*	ZA

Structure Gauging Train Coach. Converted from BR Mark 2E Open First then converted to exhibition van. Lot No. 30843 Derby 1972–73. B4 bogies.

99666	(3250)	**Y**	NR	*CS*	ZA *(works with 72630)*

Inspection Saloon. Converted from Class 202 DEMU TRB at Stewarts Lane for use as a BR Southern Region General Manager's Saloon. Overhauled at FM Rail, Derby 2004–05 for use as a New Trains Project Saloon. Can be used in push-pull mode with suitably equipped locomotives. Eastleigh 1958. SR Mark 4 bogies.

975025	(60755)	**G**	NR	*CS*	ZA	CAROLINE

Overhead Line Equipment Test Coach ("MENTOR"). Converted from BR Mark 1 Corridor Brake Standard. Lot No. 30142 Gloucester 1954–55. Fitted with pantograph.

975091 (34615)	Y	NR	*CS*	ZA

New Measurement Train Conference Coach. Converted from prototype HST TF Lot No. 30848 Derby 1972. BT10 bogies.

975814 (11000, 41000)	Y	NR	*CS*	ZA

New Measurement Train Lecture Coach. Converted from prototype HST catering vehicle. Lot No. 30849 Derby 1972–73. BT10 bogies.

975984 (10000, 40000)	Y	NR	*CS*	ZA

Radio Survey Coach. Converted from BR Mark 2E Open Standard. Lot No. 30844 Derby 1972–73. B4 bogies.

977868 (5846)	Y	NR	*CS*	ZA

Staff Coach. Converted from Royal Household couchette Lot No. 30889, which in turn had been converted from BR Mark 2B Corridor Brake First. Lot No. 30790 Derby 1969. B5 bogies.

977969 (14112, 2906)	Y	NR	*CS*	ZA

Track Inspection Train Coach. Converted from BR Mark 2E Open Standard. Lot No. 30844 Derby 1972–73. B4 bogies.

977974 (5854)	Y	NR	*CS*	ZA

Electrification Measurement Coach. Converted from BR Mark 2F Open First converted to Class 488/2 EMU TFOH. Lot No. 30859 Derby 1973–74. B4 bogies.

977983 (3407, 72503)	Y	NR	*CS*	ZA

New Measurement Train Staff Coach. Converted from HST catering vehicle. Lot No. 30884 Derby 1976–77. BT10 bogies.

977984 (40501)	Y	P	*CS*	ZA

Structure Gauging Train Coaches. Converted from Mark 2F Open Standard converted to Class 488/3 EMU TSOLH or from BR Mark 2D Open First subsequently declassified to Open Standard and then converted to exhibition van. B4 bogies.

977985. Lot No. 30860 Derby 1973–74.
977986. Lot No. 30821 Derby 1971.

977985 (6019, 72715)	Y	NR	*CS*	ZA *(works with 977986)*
977986 (3189, 99664)	Y	NR	*CS*	ZA *(works with 977985)*

New Measurement Train Test Coach. Converted from HST TGS. Lot No. 30949 Derby 1982. BT10 bogies.

977993 (44053)	Y	P	*CS*	ZA

New Measurement Train Track Recording Coach. Converted from HST TGS. Lot No. 30949 Derby 1982. BT10 bogies.

977994 (44087)	Y	P	*CS*	ZA

New Measurement Train Coach. Converted from HST catering vehicle. Lot No. 30921 Derby 1978–79. Fitted with generator. BT10 bogies.

977995	(40719, 40619)	Y	P	*CS*	ZA

Radio Survey Coach. Converted from Mark 2F Open Standard converted to Class 488/3 EMU TSOLH. Lot No. 30860 Derby 1973–74. B4 bogies.

977997	(72613, 6126)	Y	NR	*CS*	ZA

Track Recording Coach. Purpose built Mark 2. BR Wagon Lot No. 3830 Derby 1976. B4 bogies.

999550		Y	NR	*CS*	ZA

Ultrasonic Test Coaches. Converted from Class 421 EMU MBSO and Class 432 EMU MSO.

999602/605. Lot No. 30862 York 1974. SR Mk 6 bogies.
999606. Lot No. 30816. York 1970. SR Mk 6 bogies.

999602	(62483)	Y	NR	*CS*	ZA
999605	(62482)	Y	NR	*CS*	ZA
999606	(62356)	Y	NR	*CS*	ZA

BREAKDOWN TRAIN COACHES

These coaches are formed in trains used for the recovery of derailed railway vehicles and were converted from BR Mark 1 Corridor Brake Standard and General Utility Van. The current use of each vehicle is given.

971001/003/004. Lot No. 30403 York/Glasgow 1958–60. Commonwealth bogies.
971002. Lot No. 30417 Pressed Steel 1958–59. Commonwealth bogies.
975087. Lot No. 30032 Wolverton 1951–52. BR Mark 1 bogies.
975464. Lot No. 30386 Charles Roberts 1956–58. Commonwealth bogies.
975471. Lot No. 30095 Wolverton 1953–55. Commonwealth bogies.
975477. Lot No. 30233 GRCW 1955–57. BR Mark 1 bogies.
975486. Lot No. 30025 Wolverton 1950–52. Commonwealth bogies.

971001	(86560, 94150)	Y	NR	*DB*	SP	Tool & Generator Van
971002	(86624, 94190)	Y	NR	*DB*	SP	Tool Van
971003	(86596, 94191)	Y	NR	*DB*	SP	Tool Van
971004	(86194, 94168)	Y	NR	*DB*	SP	Tool Van
975087	(34289)	Y	NR	*DB*	SP	Tool & Generator Van
975464	(35171)	Y	NR	*DB*	SP	Staff Coach
975471	(34543)	Y	NR	*DB*	SP	Staff Coach
975477	(35108)	Y	NR	*DB*	SP	Staff Coach
975486	(34100)	Y	NR	*DB*	SP	Tool & Generator Van

INFRASTRUCTURE MAINTENANCE COACH

Winterisation Train Coach. Converted from BR Mark 2E Open Standard. Lot No. 30844 Derby 1972–73. B4 bogies.

977869	(5858)	Y	NR	*DR*	Perth CS

INTERNAL USER VEHICLES

These vehicles are confined to yards and depots or do not normally move.
Details are given of the internal user number (if allocated), type, former identity,
current use and location. Many no longer see regular use. * = Grounded body.

041989*	BR SPV 975423	Stores Van	Toton Depot
061202*	BR GUV 93498	Stores Van	Laira Depot, Plymouth
–	BR NKA 94199	Stores Van	EG Steels, Hamilton
083602	BR CCT 94494	Stores van	Three Bridges Station
083637	BR NW 99203	Stores van	Stewarts Lane Depot
083644	BR Ferry Van 889201	Stores van	Eastleigh Depot
083664	BR Ferry Van 889203	Stores van	Eastleigh Depot
–	BR Open Standard 5636	Instruction Coach	St Philip's Marsh Depot
–	BR BV 6396	Stores van	Longsight Depot (Manchester)
–	BR RFKB 10256	Instruction Coach	Yoker Depot
–	BR RFKB 10260	Instruction Coach	Yoker Depot
–	BR Open Standard (End) 12230	Training Coach	Network Rail York Rail Operating Centre
–	BR Open Standard 12415	Training Coach	Fire Service Training College, Moreton-in-Marsh
–	BR Open Standard 12417	Training Coach	Fire Service Training College, Moreton-in-Marsh
–	BR Open Standard 12443	Training Coach	Fire Service Training College, Moreton-in-Marsh
–	BR Open Standard 12468	Training Coach	Network Rail York Rail Operating Centre
–	BR SPV 88045*	Stores Van	Thames Haven Yard
–	BR NL 94003	Stores van	Burton-on-Trent Depot
–	BR NK 94121	Stores van	Toton Depot
–	BR NB 94438	Stores van	Toton Depot
–	BR CCT 94663*	Stores van	Mossend Up Yard
–	BR GUV 96139	Stores van	Longsight Depot, Manchester
–	BR Ferry Van 889200	Stores van	Stewarts Lane Depot
–	BR Ferry Van 889202	Stores van	Stewarts Lane Depot
–	SR PMV 977045*	Stores Van	EMD, Longport Works
–	SR CCT 2516*	Stores Van	Eastleigh Depot

Abbreviations:

BV =	Barrier Vehicle
CCT =	Covered Carriage Truck (a 4-wheeled van similar to a GUV)
GUV =	General Utility Van (bogied van with side and end doors)
NB =	High Security Brake Van (converted from Gangwayed Brake Van, gangways removed)
NK =	High Security General Utility Van (end doors removed)
NKA =	High Security Mail Van
NL =	Newspaper Van (converted from a GUV)
NW =	Bullion Van (converted from a Corridor Brake Standard)
PMV =	Parcels & Miscellaneous Van (a 4-wheeled van similar to a CCT but without end doors)
RFKB =	Kitchen Buffet First
SPV =	Special Parcels Van (a 4-wheeled van converted from a Fish Van)

2.10. COACHING STOCK AWAITING DISPOSAL

This list shows the locations of carriages awaiting disposal. The definition of which vehicles are awaiting disposal is somewhat vague, but often these are vehicles of types not now in normal service, those not expected to see further use or that have originated from preservationists as a source of spares or possible future use or carriages which have been damaged by fire, vandalism or collision. * = grounded body.

1201	TM	4849	CS	6179	CS	94101	CS
1252	SH	4932	CS	6324	CP	94106	BU
1253	SH	5179	TM	6351	BU	94116	BU
1658	CL	5183	TM	6360	NL	94153	WE
1679	RO	5186	TM	6361	NL	94166	BL
1696	YA	5194	TM	6364	CF	94170	CL
1800	RO	5238	CS	6365	CF	94176	BU
1883	CL	5331	FA	6412	CL	94195	BU
1954	CL	5386	FA	6720	FA	94196	CS
2131	CS	5420	TM	7204	CL	94197	BU
2833	CS	5478	CS	7931	BU	94214	CS
2909	CS	5631	BU	9440	SH	94222	CS
3051	YA	5657	BU	9489	CS	94227	HM
3060	CL	5710	CS	9490	BU	94229	CL
3241	CS	5777	BU	9496	DE	94303	CS
3255	FA	5797	RO	9529	YA	94304	MH
3277	RO	5815	SH	9531	WO	94308	CS
3279	BU	5876	SH	10222	BU	94310	WE
3292	BU	5888	SH	10242	BU	94311	WE
3295	RO	5922	ZG	10257	BU	94313	WE
3309	TM	5924	ZG	10530	ZN	94322*	CS
3318	BU	5925	SH	10578	ZN	94333	HL
3331	BU	5928	TM	10588	ZN	94335	CL
3334	KY	5954	BU	10656	ZN	94336	CL
3336	KY	5958	SH	11006	BU	94337	WE
3351	TM	5959	ZG	11097	BU	94338	WE
3358	BU	5978	SH	12096	ZN	94401	CS
3368	FA	6009	SH	13508	RO	94410	WE
3379	KY	6029	SH	17013	ZG	94420	CS
3388	FA	6036	ZG	18808	SH	94423	BU
3399	FA	6041	CS	35333	ZG	94427	WE
3400	BU	6045	SH	35467	CL	94429	HM
3408	CS	6073	SH	68505	ZG	94431	CS
3416	TM	6110	BU	80374	BL	94434	CL
3417	KY	6134	SH	80403	CS	94445	WE
3424	BU	6139	BU	80404	CS	94450	WE
4362	BU	6151	SH	80414	SL	94451	WE
4796	BU	6152	ZG	92114	ZA	94482	CS
4799	BU	6154	SH	94058	BU	94488	BU

94490	BU	94546	HL	99019	CS	975920 Portobello
94492	WE	94547	CS	99884	YA	977085 BU
94495	HL	94548*	CS	975081	BU	977169 BU
94504	HL	95410	CS	975280	BU	977241 BU
94515	ZG	95727	WE	975484	CS	977450 BL
94517	BU	95754	CS	975490	BU	083439 BU
94520	BU	95761	WE	975639	CS	
94522	CL	95763	BL	975681	CS	DS70220 Western
94531	BU	96132	CS	975682	CS	Trading Estate
94538	CL	96164	CS	975685	CS	Siding, North Acton
94539	CS	96170	CS	975686	CS	
94540	TJ	96178	CS	975687	CS	Pullman 315 CS
94545	HM	96191	CS	975688	CS	Pullman 316 HN

3. DIESEL MULTIPLE UNITS

INTRODUCTION

This section contains details of all Diesel Multiple Units, usually referred to as DMUs, which can run on Britain's national railway network.

Since the 1980s DMUs have replaced more traditional locomotive-hauled trains on many routes. DMUs today work a wide variety of services, from long distance Intercity to inter-urban and suburban duties.

LAYOUT OF INFORMATION

DMUs are listed in numerical order of set – using current numbers as allocated by the Rolling Stock Library. Individual "loose" vehicles are listed in numerical order after vehicles formed into fixed formations. Where sets or vehicles have been renumbered in recent years, former numbering detail is shown in parentheses. Each entry is laid out as in the following example:

RSL Set No.	Detail	Livery	Owner	Operator	Depot	Formation	
156 505	w	**SR**	A	*SR*	CK	52505	57505

Codes: Codes are used to denote the livery, owner, operator and depot allocation of each Diesel Multiple Unit. Details of these can be found in section 6 of this book. Where a unit or spare car is off-lease, the operator column is left blank.

Detail Differences: Detail differences which currently affect the areas and types of train which vehicles may work are shown, plus differences in interior layout. Where such differences occur within a class, these are shown either in the heading information or alongside the individual set or vehicle number. The following standard abbreviations are used:

e   European Railway Traffic Management System (ERTMS) signalling
    equipment fitted.
r   Radio Electric Token Block signalling equipment fitted.

Use of the above abbreviations indicates the equipment fitted is normally operable. Meaning of non-standard abbreviations is detailed in individual class headings.

Set Formations: Regular set formations are shown where these are normally maintained. Readers should note set formations might be temporarily varied from time to time to suit maintenance and/or operational requirements. Vehicles shown as "Spare" are not formed in any regular set formation.

Names: Only names carried with official sanction are listed. Names are shown in UPPER/lower case characters as actually shown on the name carried on the vehicle(s). Unless otherwise shown, complete units are regarded as named rather than just the individual car(s) which carry the name.

GENERAL INFORMATION

CLASSIFICATION AND NUMBERING

DMU Classes are listed in class number order.

First generation ("Heritage") DMUs were classified in the series 100–139.
Parry People Movers (not technically DMUs) are classified in the series 139.
Second generation DMUs are classified in the series 140–199.
Diesel Electric Multiple Units are classified in the series 200–249.
Service units are classified in the series 930–999.

First and second generation individual cars are numbered in the series 50000–59999 and 79000–79999.

Parry People Mover cars are numbered in the 39000 series.

DEMU individual cars are numbered in the series 60000–60999, except for a few former EMU vehicles which retain their EMU numbers.

For all new vehicles allocated by the Rolling Stock Library since 2014 6-digit vehicle numbers are being used. The Class 230 D-Train DEMU or battery unit individual cars are numbered in the 300xxx series.

WHEEL ARRANGEMENT

A system whereby the number of powered axles on a bogie or frame is denoted by a letter (A = 1, B = 2, C= 3 etc) and the number of unpowered axles is denoted by a number is used in this publication. The letter "o" after a letter indicates that each axle is individually powered.

UNITS OF MEASUREMENT

Principal details and dimensions are quoted for each class in metric and/or imperial units as considered appropriate bearing in mind common UK usage.

All dimensions and weights are quoted for vehicles in an "as new" condition with all necessary supplies (eg oil, water, sand) on board. Dimensions are quoted in the order Length – Width. All lengths quoted are over buffers or couplers as appropriate. Where two lengths are quoted, the first refers to outer vehicles in a set and the second to inner vehicles. All width dimensions quoted are maxima. All weights are shown as metric tonnes (t = tonnes).

OPERATING CODES

These codes are used by railway operating staff to describe the various different types of vehicles and normally appear on data panels on the inner (ie non driving) ends of vehicles.

The first part of the code describes whether the car has a motor or a driving cab as follows:

DM Driving motor   DT Driving trailer   M Motor   T Trailer

The next letter is a "B" for cars with a brake compartment.
This is followed by the saloon details:

F   First   L   denotes a vehicle with a toilet.
S   Standard   W   denotes a Wheelchair space.
C   Composite

Finally vehicles with a buffet or kitchen area are suffixed RB or RMB for a miniature buffet counter.

Where two vehicles of the same type are formed within the same unit, the above codes may be suffixed by (A) and (B) to differentiate between the vehicles.

A composite is a vehicle containing both First and Standard Class accommodation, whilst a brake vehicle is a vehicle containing separate specific accommodation for the conductor.

Where vehicles have been declassified, the correct operating code which describes the actual vehicle layout is quoted in this publication.

BUILD DETAILS

Lot Numbers

Vehicles ordered under the auspices of BR were allocated a Lot (batch) number when ordered and these are quoted in class headings and sub-headings. Vehicles ordered since 1995 have no Lot Numbers, but the manufacturer and location that they were built is given.

ACCOMMODATION

The information given in class headings and sub-headings is in the form F/S nT (or TD) nW. For example, 12/54 1T 1W denotes 12 First Class and 54 Standard Class seats, one toilet and one space for a wheelchair. A number in brackets (ie (+2)) denotes tip-up seats (in addition to the fixed seats). The seating layout of open saloons is indicated as 2+1, 2+2 or 3+2. Where units have First Class accommodation as well as Standard Class and the layout is different for each class then these are shown separately prefixed by "1:" and "2:".

TD denotes a universal access toilet suitable for use by people with disabilities. By law all trains should have been fitted with such facilities by the start of 2020. All serviceable DMUs have now been fitted with a universal access toilet apart from a handful of Transport for Wales Class 153/9s which should operate with a PRM compliant unit and have had their toilets locked out of use.

3.1. DIESEL MECHANICAL & DIESEL HYDRAULIC UNITS

3.1.1. FIRST GENERATION UNIT

CLASS 117   PRESSED STEEL SUBURBAN

First generation 3-car unit registered for use on the Swanage Railway services into Wareham station only. No set number is carried.
Construction: Steel.
Engines: Two Leyland 680/1 of 112 kW (150 hp) at 1800 rpm.
Transmission: Mechanical. Cardan shaft and freewheel to a four-speed epicyclic gearbox and final drive.
Bogies: DD10 (motor) and DT9 (trailer).
Brakes: Vacuum.
Couplers: Screw.
Dimensions: 20.45 x 2.82 m.
Gangways: Within unit.
Doors: Manually-operated slam.
Maximum Speed: 70 mph.
Seating Layout: 3+2 facing.
Multiple Working: "Blue Square" coupling code. First Generation vehicles cannot be coupled to Second Generation units.

DMBS. Lot No. 30546 1959–60. –/65. 36.5 t.
TCL: Lot No. 30547 1959–60. 22/48 2T. 30.5 t.
DMS: Lot No. 30548 1959–60. –/89. 36.5 t.

–		**G**	SG	*SG*	SW	51356	59486	51388

CLASS 121   PRESSED STEEL SUBURBAN

First generation units.
Construction: Steel.
Engines: Two Leyland 1595 of 112 kW (150 hp) at 1800 rpm.
Transmission: Mechanical. Cardan shaft and freewheel to a four-speed epicyclic gearbox and final drive.
Bogies: DD10.
Brakes: Vacuum.
Couplers: Screw.
Dimensions: 20.45 x 2.82 m.
Gangways: Non gangwayed single cars with cabs at each end.
Wheel arrangement: 1-A + A-1.
Doors: Manually-operated slam.
Maximum Speed: 70 mph.
Seating Layout: 3+2 facing (121 022 has a heavily modified interior).

Multiple Working: "Blue Square" coupling code. First Generation vehicles cannot be coupled to Second Generation units.

121 022 was formerly in departmental use as 977873. Refurbished in 2023 as a Locomotive Services executive vehicle.

121 028 was formerly registered in departmental use as 977860. Now registered for use on the Swanage Railway services into Wareham station only.

121 034 was formerly in departmental use as 977828 and then used by Chiltern Railways until 2017. Currently on loan to the Ecclesbourne Valley Railway. Fitted with central door locking.

DMBS. Lot No. 30518 1960. –/65. 38.0 t.

121 022	**CC** LS	*LS*	CL	55022	FLORA
121 028	**G** SG	*SG*	SW	55028	
121 034	**G** LS	*LS*	CL	55034	

3.1.2. PARRY PEOPLE MOVERS

CLASS 139   PPM-60

Gas/flywheel hybrid drive Railcars used on the Stourbridge Junction–Stourbridge Town branch.
Body construction: Stainless steel framework.
Chassis construction: Welded mild steel box section.
Primary Drive: Ford MVH420 2.3 litre 64 kW (86 hp) LPG fuel engine driving through Newage marine gearbox, Tandler bevel box and 4 "V" belt driver to flywheel.
Flywheel Energy Store: 500 kg, 1 m diameter, normal operational speed range 1000–1500 rpm.
Final transmission: 4 "V" belt driver from flywheel to Tandler bevel box, Linde hydrostatic transmission and spiral bevel gearbox at No. 2 end axle.
Braking: Normal service braking by regeneration to flywheel (1 m/s/s); emergency/parking braking by sprung-on, air-off disc brakes (3 m/s/s).
Maximum Speed: 45 mph.   **Dimensions:** 8.7 x 2.4 m.
Doors: Deans powered doors, double-leaf folding (one per side).
Seating Layout: 1+1 unidirectional/facing.
Multiple Working: Not applicable.

39001–002. DMS. Main Road Sheet Metal, Leyland 2007–08. –/17(+4) 1W. 12.5 t.

139 001	**WM** P	*WM*	SJ	39001
139 002	**WM** P	*WM*	SJ	39002

3.1.3. SECOND GENERATION UNITS

All units in this section have air brakes and are equipped with public address, with transmission equipment on driving vehicles and flexible diaphragm gangways. Except where otherwise stated, transmission is Voith 211r hydraulic with a cardan shaft to a Gmeinder GM190 final drive.

CLASS 142   PACER   BREL DERBY/LEYLAND

DMS–DMSL. The remaining Class 142s were withdrawn from normal passenger service at the end of 2020 and most have now been disposed of, either for scrap or preservation. Some can be found in the DMUs in Industrial Service section (Section 3.3).

Construction: Steel underframe, rivetted steel body and roof. Built from Leyland National bus parts on Leyland Bus four-wheeled underframes.
Engines: One Cummins LT10-R of 165 kW (225 hp) at 1950 rpm.
Couplers: BSI at outer ends, bar within unit.
Dimensions: 15.55 x 2.80 m.
Gangways: Within unit only.   **Wheel Arrangement:** 1-A + A-1.
Doors: Twin-leaf inward pivoting.   **Maximum Speed:** 75 mph.
Seating Layout: 3+2 mainly unidirectional bus/bench style unless stated.
Multiple Working: Within class and with Classes 143, 144, 150, 153, 155, 156, 158 and 159.

Non-standard liveries:

142 003 Original Greater Manchester PTE (orange & brown).
142 013 Revised Greater Manchester PTE (light grey/dark grey with red & white stripes).

t   Former First North Western facelifted units – DMS fitted with a luggage/bicycle rack and wheelchair space.

55544–588. DMS. Lot No. 31003 1985–86. –/62 (t –/53 or 55 1W). 24.5 t.
55594–638. DMSL. Lot No. 31004 1985–86. –/59 1T. 25.0 t.

142 003		**0**	LS	*LS*	CL	55544	55594	
142 007	t	**0**	LS	*LS*	CL	55548	55598	
142 014	t	**N0**	LS		ZG	55555	55605	
Spare		**N0**	A		GA	55588		(ex-142 047)

CLASS 144   PACER   ALEXANDER/BREL DERBY

DMS–DMSL or DMS–MS–DMSL. As Class 143, but underframes built by BREL. Class 144s finished in service with Northern in 2020. Many have since been preserved or can be found in DMUs in Industrial Service (Section 3.3).

Construction: Steel underframe, aluminium alloy body and roof. Alexander bus bodywork on four-wheeled underframes.
Engines: One Cummins LT10-R of 165 kW (225 hp) at 1950 rpm.
Couplers: BSI at outer ends, bar within unit.
Dimensions: 15.45/15.43 x 2.80 m.

Gangways: Within unit only. **Wheel Arrangement:** 1-A + A-1.
Doors: Twin-leaf inward pivoting. **Maximum Speed:** 75 mph.
Seating Layout: 2+2 high-back Richmond seating, mainly unidirectional.
Multiple Working: Within class and with Classes 142, 143, 150, 153, 155, 156, 158 and 159.

DMS. Lot No. 31015 BREL Derby 1986–87. –/45(+3) 1W 24.0 t.
MS. Lot No. 31037 BREL Derby 1987. –/58. 23.5 t.
DMSL. Lot No. 31016 BREL Derby 1986–87. –/41(+3) 1T. 24.5 t.

144 005	**NO**	LO	WS	55805		55828	
144 019	**NO**	VT	TM	55819	55855	55842	
Spare	**NO**	VT	TM	55850			(ex-144 014)
Spare	**NO**	VT	TM	55859	55846		(ex-144 023)

CLASS 150/0   PROTOTYPE SPRINTER BREL YORK

DMSL–MS–DMS. Prototype Sprinter.

Construction: Steel.
Engines: One Cummins NT855R5 of 213 kW (285 hp) at 2100 rpm.
Bogies: BX8P (powered), BX8T (non-powered).
Couplers: BSI at outer end of driving vehicles, bar non-driving ends.
Dimensions: 19.93/19.92 x 2.73 m.
Gangways: Within unit only. **Wheel Arrangement:** 2-B + 2-B + B-2.
Doors: Twin-leaf sliding. **Maximum Speed:** 75 mph.
Seating Layout: 3+2 (mainly unidirectional).
Multiple Working: Within class and with Classes 142, 143, 144, 153, 155, 156, 158, 159, 170 and 172.

DMSL. Lot No. 30984 1984. –/58(+3) 1TD 2W. 35.4 t.
MS. Lot No. 30986 1984. –/91. 38.2 t.
DMS. Lot No. 30985 1984. –/69(+6). 36.1 t.

150 001	**NR**	A	*NO*	NL	55200	55400	55300
150 002	**NR**	A	*NO*	NL	55201	55401	55301

CLASS 150/0   SPRINTER   BREL YORK

DMSL–DMS–DMS (150005 DMSL–DMSL–DMS). In 2021 Northern reformed 150003–006 as new 3-car units using a 150/1 unit with a 150/2 vehicle inserted as a centre car.

Construction: Steel.
Engines: One Cummins NT855R5 of 213 kW (285 hp) at 2100 rpm.
Bogies: BP38 (powered), BT38 (non-powered).
Couplers: BSI. **Dimensions:** 19.74 x 2.82 m.
Gangways: Within unit only.
Wheel Arrangement: 2-B + 2-B/B-2 + B-2.
Doors: Twin-leaf sliding. **Maximum Speed:** 75 mph.

Seating Layout: 3+2 facing/unidirectional.
Multiple Working: Within class and with Classes 142, 143, 144, 153, 155, 156, 158, 159, 170 and 172.

DMSL. Lot No. 31011 1985–86. † –/56(+3) 1TD 2W, * –/55(+3) 1TD 2W. 38.3 t.
DMS. Lot No. 31018 1986–87. † –/70(+6), * –/58(+10). 36.5 t.
DMSL (52223). Lot No. 31017 1986–87. –/58(+3) 1TD 2W. 37.5 t.
DMS. Lot No. 31012 1985–86. † –/70(+6), * –/65. 38.1 t.

150 003	†	**NR**	A	*NO*	NL	52116	57209	57116
150 004	†	**NR**	A	*NO*	NL	52112	57212	57112
150 005	†	**NR**	A	*NO*	NL	52117	52223	57117
150 006	*	**NR**	A	*NO*	NL	52147	57223	57147

CLASS 150/1   SPRINTER   BREL YORK

DMSL–DMS.

Construction: Steel.
Engines: One Cummins NT855R5 of 213 kW (285 hp) at 2100 rpm.
Bogies: BP38 (powered), BT38 (non-powered).
Couplers: BSI.   **Dimensions:** 19.74 x 2.82 m.
Gangways: Within unit only.   **Wheel Arrangement:** 2-B + B-2.
Doors: Twin-leaf sliding.   **Maximum Speed:** 75 mph.
Seating Layout: 3+2 facing as built but units operated by Centro were reseated with mainly unidirectional seating.
Multiple Working: Within class and with Classes 142, 143, 144, 153, 155, 156, 158, 159, 170 and 172.

† Refurbished Northern units with original Ashbourne seating.
* Refurbished Northern or LNR units. Chapman seating.

DMSL. Lot No. 31011 1985–86. † –/56(+3) or 58(+3) 1TD 2W, * –/55(+3) 1TD 2W. 38.3 t.
DMS. Lot No. 31012 1985–86. † –/70(+6) or –/71(+6)), * –/65. 38.1 t.

150 101	†	**NR**	A	*NO*	NH	52101	57101
150 102	†	**NR**	A	*NO*	NH	52102	57102
150 103	†	**NR**	A	*NO*	NH	52103	57103
150 104	†	**NR**	A	*NO*	NH	52104	57104
150 105	†	**NR**	A	*NO*	NH	52105	57105
150 106	†	**NR**	A	*NO*	NH	52106	57106
150 107	†	**NR**	A	*NO*	NH	52107	57107
150 108	†	**NR**	A	*NO*	NH	52108	57108
150 109	†	**NR**	A	*NO*	NH	52109	57109
150 110	†	**NR**	A	*NO*	NH	52110	57110
150 111	†	**NR**	A	*NO*	NH	52111	57111
150 113	†	**NR**	A	*NO*	NH	52113	57113
150 114	†	**NR**	A	*NO*	NH	52114	57114
150 115	†	**NR**	A	*NO*	NH	52115	57115
150 118	†	**NR**	A	*NO*	NH	52118	57118
150 119	†	**NR**	A	*NO*	NH	52119	57119
150 120	†	**NR**	A	*NO*	NH	52120	57120

150 121	†	**NR**	A	*NO*	NH	52121	57121
150 122	†	**NR**	A	*NO*	NH	52122	57122
150 123	†	**NR**	A	*NO*	NH	52123	57123
150 124	†	**NR**	A	*NO*	NH	52124	57124
150 125	†	**NR**	A	*NO*	NH	52125	57125
150 126	†	**NR**	A	*NO*	NH	52126	57126
150 127	†	**NR**	A	*NO*	NH	52127	57127
150 128	†	**NR**	A	*NO*	NH	52128	57128
150 129	†	**NR**	A	*NO*	NH	52129	57129
150 130	†	**NR**	A	*NO*	NH	52130	57130
150 131	†	**NR**	A	*NO*	NH	52131	57131
150 132	†	**NR**	A	*NO*	NH	52132	57132
150 133	*	**NR**	A	*NO*	NH	52133	57133
150 134	*	**NR**	A	*NO*	NH	52134	57134
150 135	*	**NR**	A	*NO*	NH	52135	57135
150 136	*	**NR**	A	*NO*	NH	52136	57136
150 137	*	**LN**	A	*WM*	BY	52137	57137
150 138	*	**NR**	A	*NO*	NH	52138	57138
150 139	*	**LN**	A	*WM*	BY	52139	57139
150 140	*	**NR**	A	*NO*	NH	52140	57140
150 141	*	**LN**	A	*WM*	BY	52141	57141
150 142	*	**NR**	A	*NO*	NH	52142	57142
150 143	*	**NR**	A	*NO*	NH	52143	57143
150 144	*	**NR**	A	*NO*	NH	52144	57144
150 145	*	**NR**	A	*NO*	NH	52145	57145
150 146	*	**NR**	A	*NO*	NH	52146	57146
150 148	*	**NR**	A	*NO*	NH	52148	57148
150 149	*	**NR**	A	*NO*	NH	52149	57149
150 150	*	**NR**	A	*NO*	NH	52150	57150

CLASS 150/2   SPRINTER   BREL YORK

DMSL–DMS.

Construction: Steel.
Engines: One Cummins NT855R5 of 213 kW (285 hp) at 2100 rpm.
Bogies: BP38 (powered), BT38 (non-powered).
Couplers: BSI.   **Dimensions:** 19.74 x 2.82 m.
Gangways: Throughout.   **Wheel Arrangement:** 2-B + B-2.
Doors: Twin-leaf sliding.   **Maximum Speed:** 75 mph.
Seating Layout: 3+2 mainly unidirectional seating as built, but most units
have now been refurbished with new 2+2 seating.
Multiple Working: Within class and with Classes 142, 143, 144, 153, 155,
156, 158, 159, 170 and 172.

c Former First North Western units with 3+2 Chapman seating.
q Refurbished Great Western Railway units. Original Ashbourne seating.
   Full details awaited.
t Refurbished Transport for Wales units with 2+2 Chapman seating.
* Refurbished Great Western Railway units with 2+2 Chapman seating.
† Refurbished Northern units. 3+2 Chapman seating.

§ Refurbished Northern units. Original Ashbourne seating.

DMSL. Lot No. 31017 1986–87. * –/50(+4) 1TD 2W, † –/58(+3) 1TD 2W,
§ –/58(+3) 1TD 2W, c –/62 1TD, t –/50 1TD 2W. 37.5 t (* 35.8 t, † and § 38.1 t).
DMS. Lot No. 31018 1986–87. * –/58(+10), † –/70(+6), § –/72(+3), c –/70,
t –/58(+4). 36.5 t.

150 201	†	**NR**	A	*NO*	NL	52201 57201
150 202	q	**GW**	A	*GW*	EX	52202 57202
150 203	†	**NR**	A	*NO*	NL	52203 57203
150 204	†	**NR**	A	*NO*	NL	52204 57204
150 205	†	**NR**	A	*NO*	NL	52205 57205
150 206	†	**NR**	A	*NO*	NL	52206 57206
150 207	c	**GW**	A	*GW*	EX	52207 57207
150 208	t	**TW**	P	*TW*	CF	52208 57208
150 210	†	**NR**	A	*NO*	NL	52210 57210
150 211	†	**NR**	A	*NO*	NL	52211 57211
150 213	t	**TW**	P	*TW*	CF	52213 57213
150 214	§	**NR**	A	*NO*	NL	52214 57214
150 215	†	**NR**	A	*NO*	NL	52215 57215
150 216	q	**GW**	A	*GW*	EX	52216 57216
150 217	t	**TW**	P	*TW*	CF	52217 57217
150 218	†	**NR**	A	*NO*	NH	52218 57218
150 219	*	**FB**	P	*GW*	EX	52219 57219
150 220	§	**NR**	A	*NO*	NL	52220 57220
150 221	*	**GW**	P	*GW*	EX	52221 57221
150 222	†	**NR**	A	*NO*	NL	52222 57222
150 224	†	**NR**	A	*NO*	NH	52224 57224
150 225	†	**NR**	A	*NO*	NH	52225 57225
150 226	†	**NR**	A	*NO*	NH	52226 57226
150 227	t	**TW**	P	*TW*	CF	52227 57227
150 228	§	**NR**	P	*NO*	NL	52228 57228
150 229	t	**TW**	P	*TW*	CF	52229 57229
150 230	t	**TW**	P	*TW*	CF	52230 57230
150 231	t	**TW**	P	*TW*	CF	52231 57231
150 232	*	**GW**	P	*GW*	EX	52232 57232
150 233	*	**GW**	P	*GW*	EX	52233 57233
150 234	*	**GW**	P	*GW*	EX	52234 57234
150 235	t	**TW**	P	*TW*	CF	52235 57235
150 236	t	**TW**	P	*TW*	CF	52236 57236
150 237	t	**TW**	P	*TW*	CF	52237 57237
150 238	*	**FB**	P	*GW*	EX	52238 57238
150 239	*	**GW**	P	*GW*	EX	52239 57239
150 240	t	**TW**	P	*TW*	CF	52240 57240
150 241	t	**TW**	P	*TW*	CF	52241 57241
150 242	t	**TW**	P	*TW*	CF	52242 57242
150 243	*	**GW**	P	*GW*	EX	52243 57243
150 244	*	**GW**	P	*GW*	EX	52244 57244
150 245	t	**TW**	P	*TW*	CF	52245 57245
150 246	*	**GW**	P	*GW*	EX	52246 57246
150 247	*	**GW**	P	*GW*	EX	52247 57247

150 248	*	**GW**	P	*GW*	EX	52248	57248
150 249	*	**GW**	P	*GW*	EX	52249	57249
150 250	t	**TW**	P	*TW*	CF	52250	57250
150 251	t	**TW**	P	*TW*	CF	52251	57251
150 252	t	**TW**	P	*TW*	CF	52252	57252
150 253	t	**TW**	P	*TW*	CF	52253	57253
150 254	t	**TW**	P	*TW*	CF	52254	57254
150 255	t	**TW**	P	*TW*	CF	52255	57255
150 256	t	**TW**	P	*TW*	CF	52256	57256
150 257	t	**TW**	P	*TW*	CF	52257	57257
150 258	t	**TW**	P	*TW*	CF	52258	57258
150 259	t	**TW**	P	*TW*	CF	52259	57259
150 260	t	**TW**	P	*TW*	CF	52260	57260
150 261	*	**GW**	P	*GW*	EX	52261	57261
150 262	t	**TW**	P	*TW*	CF	52262	57262
150 263	*	**GW**	P	*GW*	EX	52263	57263
150 264	t	**TW**	P	*TW*	CF	52264	57264
150 265	*	**GW**	P	*GW*	EX	52265	57265
150 266	*	**GW**	P	*GW*	EX	52266	57266
150 267	t	**TW**	P	*TW*	CF	52267	57267
150 268	§	**NR**	P	*NO*	NL	52268	57268
150 269	§	**NR**	P	*NO*	NL	52269	57269
150 270	§	**NR**	P	*NO*	NL	52270	57270
150 271	§	**NR**	P	*NO*	NL	52271	57271
150 272	§	**NR**	P	*NO*	NL	52272	57272
150 273	§	**NR**	P	*NO*	NL	52273	57273
150 274	§	**NR**	P	*NO*	NL	52274	57274
150 275	§	**NR**	P	*NO*	NL	52275	57275
150 276	§	**NR**	P	*NO*	NL	52276	57276
150 277	§	**NR**	P	*NO*	NL	52277	57277
150 278	t	**TW**	P	*TW*	CF	52278	57278
150 279	t	**AW**	P	*TW*	CF	52279	57279
150 280	t	**TW**	P	*TW*	CF	52280	57280
150 281	t	**TW**	P	*TW*	CF	52281	57281
150 282	t	**TW**	P	*TW*	CF	52282	57282
150 283	t	**TW**	P	*TW*	CF	52283	57283
150 284	t	**TW**	P	*TW*	CF	52284	57284
150 285	t	**TW**	P	*TW*	CF	52285	57285

Names:

150 214	The Bentham Line A Dementia-Friendly Railway
150 233	Peter West OBE
150 275	The Yorkshire Regiment Yorkshire Warrior

CLASS 153   SUPER SPRINTER   LEYLAND BUS

DMSL. Converted by Hunslet-Barclay, Kilmarnock from Class 155 2-car units. The only Class 153s remaining in passenger service now are with Transport for Wales and ScotRail.

Construction: Steel underframe, rivetted steel body and roof. Built from Leyland National bus parts on Leyland Bus bogied underframes.
Engine: One Cummins NT855R5 of 213 kW (285 hp) at 2100 rpm.
Bogies: One P3-10 (powered) and one BT38 (non-powered).
Couplers: BSI.
Dimensions: 23.21 x 2.70 m.
Gangways: Throughout.   **Wheel Arrangement:** 2-B.
Doors: Single-leaf sliding plug.   **Maximum Speed:** 75 mph.
Seating Layout: 2+2 facing/unidirectional.
Multiple Working: Within class and with Classes 142, 143, 144, 150, 155, 156, 158, 159, 170 and 172.

Cars numbered in the 573xx series were renumbered by adding 50 to their original number so that the last two digits correspond with the set number.

c Chapman seating.
d Richmond seating.
† Refurbished Transport for Wales units with a new universal access toilet.

§ 153305/370/373/377/380 have been converted to "active travel" bicycle carrying vehicles by ScotRail for West Highland Line services. Richmond seating.
n These units now form part of the Network Rail infrastructure monitoring or testing fleet and have been fitted with additional equipment such as for switch & crossing monitoring.

Non-standard liveries:

153305/370/373/377/380 ScotRail active travel (**SR** livery with various graphics).
153317   Light grey
153376   Light blue

52301–52335. DMSL. Lot No. 31026 1987–88. Converted under Lot No. 31115 1991–92. –/72(+3) 1T 1W. (s –/72 1T 1W, t –/72(+2) 1T 1W), † –/56(+5) 1TD 2W, § –/24 1T + bike/luggage racks). 41.2 t.
57301–57335. DMSL. Lot No. 31027 1987–88. Converted under Lot No. 31115 1991–92. –/72(+3) 1T 1W (s –/72 1T 1W, † –/56(+5) 1TD 2W, § –/24 1T + bike/luggage racks). 41.2 t.

153 301	d	**NO**	A		EP	52301
153 303	†c	**TW**	TW	*TW*	CF	52303
153 304	ds	**NO**	A		EP	52304
153 305	§	**0**	A	*SR*	CK	52305
153 308	c	**EM**	A		GCR	52308
153 311	n	**EM**	P	*CS*	ZA	52311
153 312	†	**TW**	TW	*TW*	CF	52312
153 315	ds	**NO**	A		EP	52315
153 317	n	**0**	A		BQ	52317

153 318	d	TW	TW	*TW*	CF	52318	
153 319	c	EM	A		EP	52319	
153 320	tc	TW	P	*TW*	CF	52320	
153 323	tc	TW	P	*TW*	CF	52323	
153 325	tc	TW	P	*TW*	CF	52325	
153 327	tc	TW	TW	*TW*	CF	52327	
153 329	tc	TW	P	*TW*	CF	52329	
153 333	tc	TW	P	*TW*	CF	52333	
153 334	ct	LM	P		LM	52334	
153 351	d	NO	A		EP	57351	
153 353	tc	TW	TW	*TW*	CF	57353	
153 354	c	LM	P		LM	57354	
153 355	c	EM	A		EP	57355	
153 356	c	LM	P		LM	57356	
153 357	c	EM	A		EP	57357	
153 361	tc	TW	P	*TW*	CF	57361	
153 362	tc	TW	TW	*TW*	CF	57362	
153 365	c	LM	P		LM	57365	
153 367	tc	TW	P	*TW*	CF	57367	
153 369	tc	TW	P	*TW*	CF	57369	
153 370	§	0	A	*SR*	CK	57370	
153 371	c	LM	P		GCR	57371	
153 373	§	0	A	*SR*	CK	57373	
153 375	c	LM	P		LM	57375	
153 376	n	0	P	*CS*	ZA	57376	
153 377	§	0	A	*SR*	CK	57377	
153 378	d	NO	A		EP	57378	
153 379	n	EM	P	*CS*	ZA	57379	
153 380	§	0	A	*SR*	CK	57380	
153 381	c	EM	P		LM	57381	
153 382	d	TW	TW	*TW*	CF	57382	
153 383	c	EM	P		LM	57383	Ecclesbourne Valley Railway 150 Years
153 384	n	EM	P	*CS*	ZA	57384	
153 385	n	EM	P	*CS*	ZA	57385	

Class 153/5. Transport for Wales units being rebuilt or to be rebuilt as "active travel" units with additional space for bicycles. 153 568 and 153 572 will be renumbered from 153/9s. Full details awaited.

153 507	(153 307)	NO	TW	LE	52307
153 528	(153 328)	NO	TW	LE	52328
153 531	(153 331)	NO	TW	LE	52331
153 552	(153 352)	NO	TW	LE	57352
153 568	(153 968)				
153 572	(153 972)				

Class 153/9. Transport for Wales units that are not fully PRM compliant. Renumbered into the 1539xx series as they should operate with a PRM compliant unit. Toilets locked out of use.

153 906	(153 306)	c	**TW**	P	*TW*	CF	52306
153 909	(153 309)	c	**TW**	P	*TW*	CF	52309
153 910	(153 310)	c	**TW**	P	*TW*	CF	52310
153 913	(153 313)	cs	**TW**	P	*TW*	CF	52313
153 914	(153 314)	c	**TW**	P	*TW*	CF	52314
153 921	(153 321)	ct	**TW**	P	*TW*	CF	52321
153 922	(153 322)	c	**TW**	P	*TW*	CF	52322
153 926	(153 326)	c	**TW**	P	*TW*	CF	52326
153 935	(153 335)	c	**TW**	P	*TW*	CF	52335
153 968	(153 368)	d	**TW**	TW	*TW*	CF	57368
153 972	(153 372)	d	**TW**	TW	*TW*	CF	57372

CLASS 155   SUPER SPRINTER   LEYLAND BUS

DMSL–DMS. Fitted with a universal access toilet.

Construction: Steel underframe, rivetted steel body and roof. Built from Leyland National bus parts on Leyland Bus bogied underframes.
Engines: One Cummins NT855R5 of 213 kW (285 hp) at 2100 rpm.
Bogies: One P3-10 (powered) and one BT38 (non-powered).
Couplers: BSI.
Dimensions: 23.21 x 2.70 m.
Gangways: Throughout.   **Wheel Arrangement:** 2-B + B-2.
Doors: Single-leaf sliding plug.   **Maximum Speed:** 75 mph.
Seating Layout: 2+2 facing/unidirectional Chapman seating.
Multiple Working: Within class and with Classes 142, 143, 144, 150, 153, 156, 158, 159, 170 and 172.
DMSL. Lot No. 31057 1988. –/64 1TD 2W. 39.0 t.
DMS. Lot No. 31058 1988. –/76. 40.4 t.

155 341	**NR**	P	*NO*	NL	52341	57341
155 342	**NR**	P	*NO*	NL	52342	57342
155 343	**NR**	P	*NO*	NL	52343	57343
155 344	**NR**	P	*NO*	NL	52344	57344
155 345	**NR**	P	*NO*	NL	52345	57345
155 346	**NR**	P	*NO*	NL	52346	57346
155 347	**NR**	P	*NO*	NL	52347	57347

CLASS 156   SUPER SPRINTER   METRO-CAMMELL

DMSL–DMS.

Construction: Steel.
Engines: One Cummins NT855R5 of 213 kW (285 hp) at 2100 rpm.
Bogies: One P3-10 (powered) and one BT38 (non-powered).
Couplers: BSI.
Dimensions: 23.03 x 2.73 m.

Gangways: Throughout.	**Wheel Arrangement:** 2-B + B-2.
Doors: Single-leaf sliding.	**Maximum Speed:** 75 mph.

Seating Layout: 2+2 facing/unidirectional.
Multiple Working: Within class and with Classes 142, 143, 144, 150, 153, 155, 158, 159, 170 and 172.

† Former Greater Anglia units. Chapman seating.
* Angel-owned Northern units. Richmond seating.
§ Porterbrook-owned Northern units. Chapman seating.
b Refurbished by Brodies, Kilmarnock with Fainsa seating.
m Northern units (ex-East Midlands Railway). Chapman seating.
n Northern units refurbished with new Fainsa seating.
w ScotRail units refurbished with new Fainsa seating.

156 402/409/412/416–418/419/422 were renumbered 156 902/909/912/916–918/919/922 respectively for a time during 2019–22.

Northern promotional vinyls: 156 480 Royal Air Force (light blue & white)

DMSL. Lot No. 31028 1987–89. † –/62 1TD 2W, * –/64(+2) 1TD 2W, § –/62(+2) 1TD 2W, n –/66 1TD 2W, m –/62 (+2) 1TD 2W, u –/68, w –/66(+3) 1TD 2W. 38.6 t.
DMS. Lot No. 31029 1987–89. † and n –/74, *–/72(+4), u –/72, w –/76. 36.1 t.

156 401	m	**NR**	P	*NO*	NH	52401	57401
156 402	†	**NR**	P	*NO*	NH	52402	57402
156 403	m	**NR**	P	*NO*	NH	52403	57403
156 404	m	**NR**	P	*NO*	NH	52404	57404
156 405	m	**NR**	P	*NO*	NH	52405	57405
156 406	m	**NR**	P	*NO*	NH	52406	57406
156 408	m	**NR**	P	*NO*	NH	52408	57408
156 409	m	**NR**	P	*NO*	NH	52409	57409
156 410	m	**NR**	P	*NO*	NH	52410	57410
156 411	m	**NR**	P	*NO*	NH	52411	57411
156 412	†	**NR**	P	*NO*	NH	52412	57412
156 413	m	**NR**	P	*NO*	NH	52413	57413
156 414	m	**NR**	P	*NO*	NH	52414	57414
156 415	m	**NR**	P	*NO*	NH	52415	57415
156 416	†	**NR**	P	*NO*	HT	52416	57416
156 417	†	**NR**	P	*NO*	HT	52417	57417
156 418	†	**NR**	P	*NO*	NH	52418	57418
156 419	†	**NR**	P	*NO*	NH	52419	57419
156 420	§	**NR**	P	*NO*	NH	52420	57420
156 421	§	**NR**	P	*NO*	HT	52421	57421
156 422	†	**NR**	P	*NO*	NH	52422	57422

156 423	§	**NR**	P	*NO*	NH	52423	57423
156 424	§	**NR**	P	*NO*	NH	52424	57424
156 425	§	**NR**	P	*NO*	NH	52425	57425
156 426	§	**NR**	P	*NO*	NH	52426	57426
156 427	§	**NR**	P	*NO*	NH	52427	57427
156 428	§	**NR**	P	*NO*	NH	52428	57428
156 429	§	**NR**	P	*NO*	NH	52429	57429
156 430	w	**SR**	A	*SR*	CK	52430	57430
156 431	w	**SR**	A	*SR*	CK	52431	57431
156 432	w	**SR**	A	*SR*	CK	52432	57432
156 433	w	**SR**	A	*SR*	CK	52433	57433
156 434	w	**SR**	A	*SR*	CK	52434	57434
156 435	w	**SR**	A	*SR*	CK	52435	57435
156 436	w	**SR**	A	*SR*	CK	52436	57436
156 437	w	**SR**	A	*SR*	CK	52437	57437
156 438	*	**NR**	A	*NO*	HT	52438	57438
156 439	w	**SR**	A	*SR*	CK	52439	57439
156 440	§	**NR**	P	*NO*	HT	52440	57440
156 441	§	**NR**	P	*NO*	NH	52441	57441
156 442	w	**SR**	A	*SR*	CK	52442	57442
156 443	*	**NR**	A	*NO*	HT	52443	57443
156 444	*	**NR**	A	*NO*	HT	52444	57444
156 445	rw	**SR**	A	*SR*	CK	52445	57445
156 446	rw	**SR**	A	*SR*	CK	52446	57446
156 447	n	**NR**	A	*NO*	HT	52447	57447
156 448	*	**NR**	A	*NO*	HT	52448	57448
156 449	n	**NR**	A	*NO*	HT	52449	57449
156 450	rw	**SR**	A	*SR*	CK	52450	57450
156 451	*	**NR**	A	*NO*	HT	52451	57451
156 452	§	**NR**	P	*NO*	NH	52452	57452
156 453	rw	**SR**	A	*SR*	CK	52453	57453
156 454	*	**NR**	A	*NO*	HT	52454	57454
156 455	§	**NR**	P	*NO*	NH	52455	57455
156 456	rw	**SR**	A	*SR*	CK	52456	57456
156 457	rw	**SR**	A	*SR*	CK	52457	57457
156 458	rw	**SR**	A	*SR*	CK	52458	57458
156 459	§	**NR**	P	*NO*	NH	52459	57459
156 460	§	**NR**	P	*NO*	NH	52460	57460
156 461	§	**NR**	P	*NO*	NH	52461	57461
156 462	w	**SR**	A	*SR*	CK	52462	57462
156 463	*	**NR**	A	*NO*	HT	52463	57463
156 464	§	**NR**	P	*NO*	NH	52464	57464
156 465	n	**NR**	A	*NO*	HT	52465	57465
156 466	§	**NR**	P	*NO*	NH	52466	57466
156 467	w	**SR**	A	*SR*	CK	52467	57467
156 468	*	**NR**	A	*NO*	HT	52468	57468
156 469	*	**NR**	A	*NO*	HT	52469	57469
156 470	m	**EM**	A		EP	52470	57470
156 471	*	**NR**	A	*NO*	HT	52471	57471
156 472	*	**NR**	A	*NO*	HT	52472	57472

156 473	m	**EM**	A		EP	52473	57473
156 474	rw	**SR**	A	SR	CK	52474	57474
156 475	*	**NR**	A	NO	HT	52475	57475
156 476	rw	**SR**	A	SR	CK	52476	57476
156 477	rw	**SR**	A	SR	CK	52477	57477
156 478	rb	**SR**	BR		ZK	52478	57478
156 479	*	**NR**	A	NO	HT	52479	57479
156 480	*	**NR**	A	NO	HT	52480	57480
156 481	*	**NR**	A	NO	HT	52481	57481
156 482	*	**NR**	A	NO	HT	52482	57482
156 483	*	**NR**	A	NO	HT	52483	57483
156 484	*	**NR**	A	NO	HT	52484	57484
156 485	n	**NR**	A	NO	HT	52485	57485
156 486	*	**NR**	A	NO	HT	52486	57486
156 487	*	**NR**	A	NO	HT	52487	57487
156 488	*	**NR**	A	NO	HT	52488	57488
156 489	*	**NR**	A	NO	HT	52489	57489
156 490	*	**NR**	A	NO	HT	52490	57490
156 491	*	**NR**	A	NO	HT	52491	57491
156 492	rw	**SR**	A	SR	CK	52492	57492
156 493	rw	**SR**	A	SR	CK	52493	57493
156 494	w	**SR**	A	SR	CK	52494	57494
156 495	w	**SR**	A	SR	CK	52495	57495
156 496	n	**NR**	A	NO	HT	52496	57496
156 497	m	**EM**	A		EP	52497	57497
156 498	m	**EM**	A		EP	52498	57498
156 499	rt	**SR**	A	SR	CK	52499	57499
156 500	rw	**SR**	A	SR	CK	52500	57500
156 501	w	**SR**	A	SR	CK	52501	57501
156 502	w	**SR**	A	SR	CK	52502	57502
156 503	w	**SR**	A	SR	CK	52503	57503
156 504	w	**SR**	A	SR	CK	52504	57504
156 505	w	**SR**	A	SR	CK	52505	57505
156 506	w	**SR**	A	SR	CK	52506	57506
156 507	w	**SR**	A	SR	CK	52507	57507
156 508	w	**SR**	A	SR	CK	52508	57508
156 509	w	**SR**	A	SR	CK	52509	57509
156 510	w	**SR**	A	SR	CK	52510	57510
156 511	w	**SR**	A	SR	CK	52511	57511
156 512	w	**SR**	A	SR	CK	52512	57512
156 513	w	**SR**	A	SR	CK	52513	57513
156 514	w	**SR**	A	SR	CK	52514	57514

Names:

156 469	The Royal Northumberland Fusiliers (The Fighting Fifth)
156 480	Spirit of The Royal Air Force
156 483	William George 'Billy' Hardy 14/01/1903 – 10/03/1950

Class 156/9. Former Greater Anglia unit now in storage.

156 907	(156 407)	†	**EI**	P		LM	52407	57407

CLASS 158/0   BREL

DMSL(B)–DMSL(A) or DMCL–DMSL or DMSL–MSL–DMSL.

Construction: Welded aluminium.
Engines: 158 701–813/158 880–890/158 950–959: One Cummins NTA855R1
of 260 kW (350 hp) at 2100 rpm.
158 815–862: One Perkins 2006-TWH of 260 kW (350 hp) at 2100 rpm.
158 863–872: One Cummins NTA855R3 of 300 kW (400 hp) at 1900 rpm.
Bogies: One BREL P4 (powered) and one BREL T4 (non-powered) per car.
Couplers: BSI.   **Dimensions:** 22.57 x 2.70 m.
Gangways: Throughout.   **Wheel Arrangement:** 2-B + B-2.
Doors: Twin-leaf swing plug.   **Maximum Speed:** 90 mph.
Seating Layout: 2+2 facing/unidirectional.
Multiple Working: Within class and with Classes 142, 143, 144, 150, 153,
155, 156, 159, 170 and 172.

ScotRail 158s 158 701–736/738–741 are "fitted" for RETB. When a unit
arrives at Inverness the cab display unit is clipped on and plugged in.
Transport for Wales units have ETCS plugged in at Shrewsbury for working
the Cambrian Lines.

*   Refurbished ScotRail units fitted with Grammer seating, additional
        luggage racks and cycle stowage areas.
        ScotRail units 158 726–736/738–741 are fitted with Richmond seating.
†   Refurbished East Midlands Railway units with Grammer seating.
§   Northern 3-car units (original seating).
n   Refurbished Northern units with new Fainsa seating.
p   Refurbished ScotRail units with Richmond seating.
s   Refurbished Transport for Wales units with Grammer seating.
z   Refurbished Great Western Railway units. Units 158 745–749/751/762/
        767 (some formed into 3-car sets) have Richmond seating.

DMSL(B). Lot No. 31051 BREL Derby 1989–92. † 68(+3) 1TD 2W, § –/64(+3)
1TD 2W, n –/66 1TD 2W, s –/64(+4) 1TD 2W, z –/62 1TD 2W. 38.5 t.
MSL. Lot No. 31050 BREL Derby 1991. –/68 1T. 38.5 t.
DMSL(A). Lot No. 31052 BREL Derby 1989–92. –/70 1T († –/74, n –/72 1T, * & p
–/64(+2) 1T, z –/68) plus cycle stowage area. 38.5 t.

The above details refer to the "as built" condition. The following DMSL(B)
have now been converted to DMCL as follows:
52701–736/738–741 (ScotRail). 15/53 1TD 1W (* refurbished sets –/60(+6)
1TD 1W plus cycle stowage area).

158 701	*	**SR**	P	*SR*	IS	52701 57701
158 702	*	**SR**	P	*SR*	IS	52702 57702
158 703	*	**SR**	P	*SR*	IS	52703 57703
158 704	*	**SR**	P	*SR*	IS	52704 57704
158 705	*	**SR**	P	*SR*	IS	52705 57705
158 706	*	**SR**	P	*SR*	IS	52706 57706
158 707	*	**SR**	P	*SR*	IS	52707 57707
158 708	*	**SR**	P	*SR*	IS	52708 57708
158 709	*	**SR**	P	*SR*	IS	52709 57709

158 710	*	**SR**	P	*SR*	IS	52710	57710	
158 711	*	**SR**	P	*SR*	IS	52711	57711	
158 712	*	**SR**	P	*SR*	IS	52712	57712	
158 713	*	**SR**	P	*SR*	IS	52713	57713	
158 714	*	**SR**	P	*SR*	IS	52714	57714	
158 715	*	**SR**	P	*SR*	IS	52715	57715	
158 716	*	**SR**	P	*SR*	IS	52716	57716	
158 717	*	**SR**	P	*SR*	IS	52717	57717	
158 718	*	**SR**	P	*SR*	IS	52718	57718	
158 719	*	**SR**	P	*SR*	IS	52719	57719	
158 720	*	**SR**	P	*SR*	IS	52720	57720	
158 721	*	**SR**	P	*SR*	IS	52721	57721	
158 722	*	**SR**	P	*SR*	IS	52722	57722	
158 723	*	**SR**	P	*SR*	IS	52723	57723	
158 724	*	**SR**	P	*SR*	IS	52724	57724	
158 725	*	**SR**	P	*SR*	IS	52725	57725	
158 726	p	**SR**	P	*SR*	CK	52726	57726	
158 727	p	**SR**	P	*SR*	CK	52727	57727	
158 728	p	**SR**	P	*SR*	CK	52728	57728	
158 729	p	**SR**	P	*SR*	CK	52729	57729	
158 730	p	**SR**	P	*SR*	CK	52730	57730	
158 731	p	**SR**	P	*SR*	CK	52731	57731	
158 732	p	**SR**	P	*SR*	CK	52732	57732	
158 733	p	**SR**	P	*SR*	CK	52733	57733	
158 734	p	**SR**	P	*SR*	CK	52734	57734	
158 735	p	**SR**	P	*SR*	CK	52735	57735	
158 736	p	**SR**	P	*SR*	CK	52736	57736	
158 738	p	**SR**	P	*SR*	CK	52738	57738	
158 739	p	**SR**	P	*SR*	CK	52739	57739	
158 740	p	**SR**	P	*SR*	CK	52740	57740	
158 741	p	**SR**	P	*SR*	CK	52741	57741	
158 745	z	**GW**	P	*GW*	PM	52745	57745	
158 747	z	**GW**	P	*GW*	PM	52747	57747	
158 748	z	**GW**	P	*GW*	PM	52748	57748	
158 749	z	**GW**	P	*GW*	PM	52749	57749	
158 750	z	**GW**	P	*GW*	PM	52750	57750	
158 752	§	**NR**	P	*NO*	NL	52752	58716	57752
158 753	§	**NR**	P	*NO*	NL	52753	58710	57753
158 754	§	**NR**	P	*NO*	NL	52754	58708	57754
158 755	§	**NR**	P	*NO*	NL	52755	58702	57755
158 756	§	**NR**	P	*NO*	NL	52756	58712	57756
158 757	§	**NR**	P	*NO*	NL	52757	58706	57757
158 758	§	**NR**	P	*NO*	NL	52758	58714	57758
158 759	§	**NR**	P	*NO*	NL	52759	58713	57759
158 760	z	**GW**	P	*GW*	PM	52760	57760	
158 762	z	**GW**	P	*GW*	PM	52762	57762	
158 765	z	**GW**	P	*GW*	PM	52765	57765	
158 766	z	**GW**	P	*GW*	PM	52766	57766	
158 767	z	**GW**	P	*GW*	PM	52767	57767	
158 768	z	**GW**	P	*GW*	PM	52768	57768	
158 769	z	**GW**	P	*GW*	PM	52769	57769	

158 770	†	**ST**	P	*EM*	NM	52770	57770	
158 771	z	**GW**	P	*GW*	PM	52771	57771	
158 773	†	**EI**	P	*EM*	NM	52773	57773	
158 774	†	**EI**	P	*EM*	NM	52774	57774	
158 777	†	**ST**	P	*EM*	NM	52777	57777	
158 780	†	**ST**	A	*EM*	NM	52780	57780	
158 782	n	**NR**	A	*NO*	NL	52782	57782	
158 783	†	**ST**	A	*EM*	NM	52783	57783	
158 784	n	**NR**	A	*NO*	NL	52784	57784	
158 785	†	**ST**	A	*EM*	NM	52785	57785	
158 786	n	**NR**	A	*NO*	NL	52786	57786	
158 787	n	**NR**	A	*NO*	NL	52787	57787	
158 788	†	**ST**	A	*EM*	NM	52788	57788	
158 789	n	**NR**	A	*NO*	NL	52789	57789	
158 790	n	**NR**	A	*NO*	NL	52790	57790	
158 791	n	**NR**	A	*NO*	NL	52791	57791	
158 792	n	**NR**	A	*NO*	HT	52792	57792	
158 793	n	**NR**	A	*NO*	NL	52793	57793	
158 794	n	**NR**	A	*NO*	NL	52794	57794	
158 795	n	**NR**	A	*NO*	NL	52795	57795	
158 796	n	**NR**	A	*NO*	NL	52796	57796	
158 797	n	**NR**	A	*NO*	NL	52797	57797	
158 798	z	**GW**	P	*GW*	EX	52798	58715	57798
158 799	†	**ST**	P	*EM*	NM	52799	57799	
158 806	†	**ST**	P	*EM*	NM	52806	57806	
158 810	†	**ST**	P	*EM*	NM	52810	57810	
158 812	†	**ST**	P	*EM*	NM	52812	57812	
158 813	†	**ST**	P	*EM*	NM	52813	57813	
158 815	n	**NR**	A	*NO*	HT	52815	57815	
158 816	n	**NR**	A	*NO*	HT	52816	57816	
158 817	n	**NR**	A	*NO*	HT	52817	57817	
158 818	es	**TW**	A	*TW*	MN	52818	57818	
158 819	es	**TW**	A	*TW*	MN	52819	57819	
158 820	es	**TW**	A	*TW*	MN	52820	57820	
158 821	es	**TW**	A	*TW*	MN	52821	57821	
158 822	es	**TW**	A	*TW*	MN	52822	57822	
158 823	es	**TW**	A	*TW*	MN	52823	57823	
158 824	es	**TW**	A	*TW*	MN	52824	57824	
158 825	es	**TW**	A	*TW*	MN	52825	57825	
158 826	es	**TW**	A	*TW*	MN	52826	57826	
158 827	es	**TW**	A	*TW*	MN	52827	57827	
158 828	es	**TW**	A	*TW*	MN	52828	57828	
158 829	es	**TW**	A	*TW*	MN	52829	57829	
158 830	es	**TW**	A	*TW*	MN	52830	57830	
158 831	es	**TW**	A	*TW*	MN	52831	57831	
158 832	es	**TW**	A	*TW*	MN	52832	57832	
158 833	es	**TW**	A	*TW*	MN	52833	57833	
158 834	es	**TW**	A	*TW*	MN	52834	57834	
158 835	es	**TW**	A	*TW*	MN	52835	57835	
158 836	es	**TW**	A	*TW*	MN	52836	57836	
158 837	es	**TW**	A	*TW*	MN	52837	57837	

158 838	es	**TW**	A	*TW*	MN	52838	57838
158 839	es	**TW**	A	*TW*	MN	52839	57839
158 840	es	**TW**	A	*TW*	MN	52840	57840
158 841	es	**TW**	A	*TW*	MN	52841	57841
158 842	n	**NR**	A	*NO*	HT	52842	57842
158 843	n	**NR**	A	*NO*	HT	52843	57843
158 844	n	**NR**	A	*NO*	HT	52844	57844
158 845	n	**NR**	A	*NO*	HT	52845	57845
158 846	†	**ST**	A	*EM*	NM	52846	57846
158 847	†	**ST**	A	*EM*	NM	52847	57847
158 848	n	**NR**	A	*NO*	HT	52848	57848
158 849	n	**NR**	A	*NO*	HT	52849	57849
158 850	n	**NR**	A	*NO*	HT	52850	57850
158 851	n	**NR**	A	*NO*	HT	52851	57851
158 852	†	**ST**	A	*EM*	NM	52852	57852
158 853	n	**NR**	A	*NO*	HT	52853	57853
158 854	†	**ST**	A	*EM*	NM	52854	57854
158 855	n	**NR**	A	*NO*	HT	52855	57855
158 856	†	**ST**	A	*EM*	NM	52856	57856
158 857	†	**ST**	A	*EM*	NM	52857	57857
158 858	†	**ST**	A	*EM*	NM	52858	57858
158 859	n	**NR**	A	*NO*	HT	52859	57859
158 860	n	**NR**	A	*NO*	HT	52860	57860
158 861	n	**NR**	A	*NO*	HT	52861	57861
158 862	†	**ST**	A	*EM*	NM	52862	57862
158 863	†	**ST**	A	*EM*	NM	52863	57863
158 864	†	**ST**	A	*EM*	NM	52864	57864
158 865	†	**ST**	A	*EM*	NM	52865	57865
158 866	†	**ST**	A	*EM*	NM	52866	57866
158 867	n	**NR**	A	*NO*	NL	52867	57867
158 868	n	**NR**	A	*NO*	NL	52868	57868
158 869	n	**NR**	A	*NO*	NL	52869	57869
158 870	n	**NR**	A	*NO*	NL	52870	57870
158 871	n	**NR**	A	*NO*	NL	52871	57871
158 872	n	**NR**	A	*NO*	NL	52872	57872

Names:

158 847	Lincoln Castle Explorer
158 854	The Station Volunteer
158 864	ELR 50 VISIT LINCOLNSHIRE in 2020

Class 158/8. Refurbished South Western Railway and East Midlands Railway units. Converted from former TransPennine Express units at Wabtec, Doncaster in 2007. 2+1 seating in First Class.

Details as Class 158/0 except:

DMCL. Lot No. 31051 BREL Derby 1989–92. 13/40(+2) 1TD 1W. 38.5 t.
DMSL. Lot No. 31052 BREL Derby 1989–92. –/70 1T. 38.5 t.

158 880	(158 737)	**ST**	P	*SW*	SA	52737	57737
158 881	(158 742)	**ST**	P	*SW*	SA	52742	57742
158 882	(158 743)	**ST**	P	*SW*	SA	52743	57743

158 883	(158 744)	**ST**	P	*SW*	SA	52744	57744
158 884	(158 772)	**ST**	P	*SW*	SA	52772	57772
158 885	(158 775)	**ST**	P	*SW*	SA	52775	57775
158 886	(158 779)	**ST**	P	*SW*	SA	52779	57779
158 887	(158 781)	**SW**	P	*SW*	SA	52781	57781
158 888	(158 802)	**SW**	P	*SW*	SA	52802	57802
158 889	(158 808)	**ST**	P	*EM*	NM	52808	57808
158 890	(158 814)	**SW**	P	*SW*	SA	52814	57814

CLASS 158/9   BREL

DMSL–DMS. Units leased by West Yorkshire PTE but managed by Eversholt Rail. Refurbished with new Fainsa seating. Details as Class 158/0 except for seating and toilets.

DMSL. Lot No. 31051 BREL Derby 1990–92. –/66 1TD 2W. 38.5 t.
DMS. Lot No. 31052 BREL Derby 1990–92. –/72 and parcels area. 38.5 t.

158 901	**NR**	E	*NO*	NL	52901	57901
158 902	**NR**	E	*NO*	NL	52902	57902
158 903	**NR**	E	*NO*	NL	52903	57903
158 904	**NR**	E	*NO*	NL	52904	57904
158 905	**NR**	E	*NO*	NL	52905	57905
158 906	**NR**	E	*NO*	NL	52906	57906
158 907	**NR**	E	*NO*	NL	52907	57907
158 908	**NR**	E	*NO*	NL	52908	57908
158 909	**NR**	E	*NO*	NL	52909	57909
158 910	**NR**	E	*NO*	NL	52910	57910

CLASS 158/0   BREL

DMSL(A)–DMSL(B)–DMSL(A). Units reformed as 3-car hybrid sets for Great Western Railway. For vehicle details see above. Formations can be flexible depending on when unit exams become due.

158 950	**GW**	P	*GW*	EX	57751	52761	57761
158 951	**GW**	P	*GW*	EX	57251	52764	57764
158 958	**GW**	P	*GW*	EX	57746	52776	57776
158 959	**GW**	P	*GW*	EX	52746	52778	57778

CLASS 159/0   BREL

DMCL–MSL–DMSL. Built as Class 158. Converted before entering passenger service to Class 159 by Rosyth Dockyard.

Construction: Welded aluminium.
Engines: One Cummins NTA855R3 of 300 kW (400 hp) at 1900 rpm.
Bogies: One BREL P4 (powered) and one BREL T4 (non-powered) per car.

Couplers: BSI.	**Dimensions:** 22.57 x 2.70 m.
Gangways: Throughout.	**Wheel Arrangement:** 2-B + B-2 + B-2.
Doors: Twin-leaf swing plug.	**Maximum Speed:** 90 mph.

Seating Layout: 1: 2+1 facing, 2: 2+2 facing/unidirectional.
Multiple Working: Within class and with Classes 142, 143, 144, 150, 153, 155, 156, 158 and 170.

DMCL. Lot No. 31051 BREL Derby 1992–93. 23/24(+2) 1TD 2W. 38.5 t.
MSL. Lot No. 31050 BREL Derby 1992–93. –/70(+6) 1T. 38.5 t.
DMSL. Lot No. 31052 BREL Derby 1992–93. –/72 1T. 38.5 t.

159 001	**SW**	P	*SW*	SA	52873	58718	57873
159 002	**SW**	P	*SW*	SA	52874	58719	57874
159 003	**SW**	P	*SW*	SA	52875	58720	57875
159 004	**SW**	P	*SW*	SA	52876	58721	57876
159 005	**SW**	P	*SW*	SA	52877	58722	57877
159 006	**SW**	P	*SW*	SA	52878	58723	57878
159 007	**SW**	P	*SW*	SA	52879	58724	57879
159 008	**SW**	P	*SW*	SA	52880	58725	57880
159 009	**SW**	P	*SW*	SA	52881	58726	57881
159 010	**SW**	P	*SW*	SA	52882	58727	57882
159 011	**SW**	P	*SW*	SA	52883	58728	57883
159 012	**SW**	P	*SW*	SA	52884	58729	57884
159 013	**SW**	P	*SW*	SA	52885	58730	57885
159 014	**SW**	P	*SW*	SA	52886	58731	57886
159 015	**SW**	P	*SW*	SA	52887	58732	57887
159 016	**SW**	P	*SW*	SA	52888	58733	57888
159 017	**SW**	P	*SW*	SA	52889	58734	57889
159 018	**SW**	P	*SW*	SA	52890	58735	57890
159 019	**SW**	P	*SW*	SA	52891	58736	57891
159 020	**SW**	P	*SW*	SA	52892	58737	57892
159 021	**SW**	P	*SW*	SA	52893	58738	57893
159 022	**SW**	P	*SW*	SA	52894	58739	57894

CLASS 159/1   BREL

DMCL–MSL–DMSL. Units converted from Class 158s at Wabtec, Doncaster in 2006–07 for South West Trains.

Details as Class 158/0 except:
Seating Layout: 1: 2+1 facing, 2: 2+2 facing/unidirectional.

DMCL. Lot No. 31051 BREL Derby 1989–92. 24/24(+2) 1TD 2W. 38.5 t.
MSL. Lot No. 31050 BREL Derby 1989–92. –/70 1T. 38.5 t.
DMSL. Lot No. 31052 BREL Derby 1989–92. –/72 1T. 38.5 t.

159 101	(158 800)	**ST**	P	*SW*	SA	52800	58717	57800
159 103	(158 804)	**ST**	P	*SW*	SA	52804	58704	57804
159 104	(158 805)	**ST**	P	*SW*	SA	52805	58705	57805
159 105	(158 807)	**ST**	P	*SW*	SA	52807	58707	57807
159 106	(158 809)	**ST**	P	*SW*	SA	52809	58709	57809
159 107	(158 811)	**ST**	P	*SW*	SA	52811	58711	57811
159 108	(158 801)	**ST**	P	*SW*	SA	52801	58701	57801
Spare		**ST**	P		LM	52803		

CLASS 165/0   NETWORK TURBO   BREL

DMSL–DMS and DMSL–MS–DMS. Chiltern Railways units. Refurbished 2003–05 with First Class seats removed and air conditioning fitted.

Construction: Welded aluminium.
Engines: One Perkins 2006-TWH of 260 kW (350 hp) at 2100 rpm.
Bogies: BREL P3-17 (powered), BREL T3-17 (non-powered).
Couplers: BSI.
Dimensions: 23.50/23.25 x 2.81 m.
Gangways: Within unit only.   **Wheel Arrangement:** 2-B (+ B-2) + B-2.
Doors: Twin-leaf swing plug.   **Maximum Speed:** 75 mph.
Seating Layout: 2+2/3+2 facing/unidirectional.
Multiple Working: Within class and with Classes 166, 168, 170 and 172.

Fitted with tripcocks for working over London Underground tracks between Harrow-on-the-Hill and Amersham.

58801–822/58873–878. DMSL. Lot No. 31087 BREL York 1990. –/77(+7) 1TD 2W. 42.1 t.
58823–833. DMSL. Lot No. 31089 BREL York 1991–92. –/77(+7) 1TD 2W. 40.1 t.
MS. Lot No. 31090 BREL York 1991–92. –/106. 37.0 t.
DMS. Lot No. 31088 BREL York 1991–92. –/94. 41.5 t.

165 001	**CR**	A	*CR*	AL	58801	58834
165 002	**CR**	A	*CR*	AL	58802	58835
165 003	**CR**	A	*CR*	AL	58803	58836
165 004	**CR**	A	*CR*	AL	58804	58837
165 005	**CR**	A	*CR*	AL	58805	58838
165 006	**CR**	A	*CR*	AL	58806	58839
165 007	**CR**	A	*CR*	AL	58807	58840
165 008	**CR**	A	*CR*	AL	58808	58841
165 009	**CR**	A	*CR*	AL	58809	58842
165 010	**CR**	A	*CR*	AL	58810	58843
165 011	**CR**	A	*CR*	AL	58811	58844
165 012	**CR**	A	*CR*	AL	58812	58845
165 013	**CR**	A	*CR*	AL	58813	58846
165 014	**CR**	A	*CR*	AL	58814	58847
165 015	**CR**	A	*CR*	AL	58815	58848
165 016	**CR**	A	*CR*	AL	58816	58849
165 017	**CR**	A	*CR*	AL	58817	58850
165 018	**CR**	A	*CR*	AL	58818	58851
165 019	**CR**	A	*CR*	AL	58819	58852
165 020	**CR**	A	*CR*	AL	58820	58853
165 021	**CR**	A	*CR*	AL	58821	58854
165 022	**CR**	A	*CR*	AL	58822	58855
165 023	**CR**	A	*CR*	AL	58873	58867
165 024	**CR**	A	*CR*	AL	58874	58868
165 025	**CR**	A	*CR*	AL	58875	58869
165 026	**CR**	A	*CR*	AL	58876	58870
165 027	**CR**	A	*CR*	AL	58877	58871
165 028	**CR**	A	*CR*	AL	58878	58872

165 029	**CR**	A	*CR*	AL	58823	55404	58856
165 030	**CR**	A	*CR*	AL	58824	55405	58857
165 031	**CR**	A	*CR*	AL	58825	55406	58858
165 032	**CR**	A	*CR*	AL	58826	55407	58859
165 033	**CR**	A	*CR*	AL	58827	55408	58860
165 034	**CR**	A	*CR*	AL	58828	55409	58861
165 035	**CR**	A	*CR*	AL	58829	55410	58862
165 036	**CR**	A	*CR*	AL	58830	55411	58863
165 037	**CR**	A	*CR*	AL	58831	55412	58864
165 038	**CR**	A	*CR*	AL	58832	55413	58865
165 039	**CR**	A	*CR*	AL	58833	55414	58866

CLASS 165/1   NETWORK TURBO   BREL

Great Western Railway units. DMSL–MS–DMS or DMSL–DMS. In 2015 GWR removed First Class from all its Class 165s, it was later reinstated on the 3-car units. Air cooling equipment fitted.

Construction: Welded aluminium.
Engines: One Perkins 2006-TWH of 260 kW (350 hp) at 2100 rpm.
Bogies: BREL P3-17 (powered), BREL T3-17 (non-powered).
Couplers: BSI.
Dimensions: 23.50/23.25 x 2.81 m.
Gangways: Within unit only.   **Wheel Arrangement:** 2-B (+ B-2) + B-2.
Doors: Twin-leaf swing plug.   **Maximum Speed:** 90 mph.
Seating Layout: 3+2/2+2 facing/unidirectional.
Multiple Working: Within class and with Classes 166, 168, 170 and 172.

58953–969. DMSL. Lot No. 31098 BREL York 1992. 16/44 1TD 2W. 40.8 t.
58879–898. DMSL. Lot No. 31096 BREL York 1992. –/75 1TD 2W. 40.8 t.
MS. Lot No. 31099 BREL 1992. –/102. 38.1 t.
58916–932. DMS. Lot No. 31097 BREL 1992. –/98. 37.0 t.
58933–952. DMS. Lot No. 31097 BREL 1992. –/84. 37.0 t.

165 101	**GW**	A	*GW*	PM	58953	55415	58916
165 102	**GW**	A	*GW*	PM	58954	55416	58917
165 103	**GW**	A	*GW*	PM	58955	55417	58918
165 104	**GW**	A	*GW*	RG	58956	55418	58919
165 105	**GW**	A	*GW*	RG	58957	55419	58920
165 106	**GW**	A	*GW*	RG	58958	55420	58921
165 107	**GW**	A	*GW*	RG	58959	55421	58922
165 108	**GW**	A	*GW*	PM	58960	55422	58923
165 109	**GW**	A	*GW*	RG	58961	55423	58924
165 110	**GW**	A	*GW*	RG	58962	55424	58925
165 111	**GW**	A	*GW*	RG	58963	55425	58926
165 112	**GW**	A	*GW*	RG	58964	55426	58927
165 113	**GW**	A	*GW*	RG	58965	55427	58928
165 114	**GW**	A	*GW*	RG	58966	55428	58929
165 116	**GW**	A	*GW*	RG	58968	55430	58931
165 117	**GW**	A	*GW*	RG	58969	55431	58932
165 118	**GW**	A	*GW*	RG	58879		58933
165 119	**GW**	A	*GW*	RG	58880		58934

165 120	GW	A	GW	RG	58881	58935
165 121	GW	A	GW	RG	58882	58936
165 122	GW	A	GW	RG	58883	58937
165 123	GW	A	GW	RG	58884	58938
165 124	GW	A	GW	RG	58885	58939
165 125	GW	A	GW	RG	58886	58940
165 126	GW	A	GW	RG	58887	58941
165 127	GW	A	GW	RG	58888	58942
165 128	GW	A	GW	RG	58889	58943
165 129	GW	A	GW	PM	58890	58944
165 130	GW	A	GW	PM	58891	58945
165 131	GW	A	GW	PM	58892	58946
165 132	GW	A	GW	PM	58893	58947
165 133	GW	A	GW	PM	58894	58948
165 134	GW	A	GW	PM	58895	58949
165 135	GW	A	GW	PM	58896	58950
165 136	GW	A	GW	PM	58897	58951
165 137	GW	A	GW	PM	58898	58952

Names:

165 119   Norman Topsom MBE
165 120   Roger Watkins THE GWR MASTER TRAIN PLANNER

CLASS 166   NETWORK EXPRESS TURBO   ABB

DMCL–MS–DMSL. Great Western Railway units, built for Paddington–Oxford/Newbury services. Air conditioned and with additional luggage space compared to the Class 165s. The DMSL vehicles have had their 16 First Class seats declassified.

Construction: Welded aluminium.
Engines: One Perkins 2006-TWH of 260 kW (350 hp) at 2100 rpm.
Bogies: BREL P3-17 (powered), BREL T3-17 (non-powered).
Couplers: BSI.
Dimensions: 23.50 x 2.81 m.
Gangways: Within unit only.   **Wheel Arrangement:** 2-B + B-2 + B-2.
Doors: Twin-leaf swing plug.   **Maximum Speed:** 90 mph.
Seating Layout: 1: 2+2 facing, 2: 2+2/3+2 facing/unidirectional.
Multiple Working: Within class and with Classes 165, 168, 170 and 172.

DMCL. Lot No. 31116 ABB York 1992–93. 16/53 1TD 2W. 41.2 t.
MS. Lot No. 31117 ABB York 1992–93. –/91. 39.1 t.
DMSL. Lot No. 31116 ABB York 1992–93. –/84 1T. 39.6 t.

166 201	GW	A	GW	PM	58101	58601	58122
166 202	GW	A	GW	PM	58102	58602	58123
166 203	GW	A	GW	PM	58103	58603	58124
166 204	GW	A	GW	PM	58104	58604	58125
166 205	GW	A	GW	PM	58105	58605	58126
166 206	GW	A	GW	PM	58106	58606	58127
166 207	GW	A	GW	PM	58107	58607	58128
166 208	GW	A	GW	PM	58108	58608	58129
166 209	GW	A	GW	PM	58109	58609	58130

166 210	**GW**	A	*GW*	PM	58110	58610	58131
166 211	**GW**	A	*GW*	PM	58111	58611	58132
166 212	**GW**	A	*GW*	PM	58112	58612	58133
166 213	**GW**	A	*GW*	PM	58113	58613	58134
166 214	**GW**	A	*GW*	PM	58114	58614	58135
166 215	**GW**	A	*GW*	PM	58115	58615	58136
166 216	**GW**	A	*GW*	PM	58116	58616	58137
166 217	**GW**	A	*GW*	PM	58117	58617	58138
166 218	**GW**	A	*GW*	PM	58118	58618	58139
166 219	**GW**	A	*GW*	PM	58119	58619	58140
166 220	**GW**	A	*GW*	PM	58120	58620	58141
166 221	**GW**	A	*GW*	PM	58121	58621	58142

Names:

166 204	Norman Topsom MBE
166 220	Roger Watkins THE GWR MASTER TRAIN PLANNER

CLASS 168   CLUBMAN   ADTRANZ/BOMBARDIER

Air conditioned.

Construction: Welded aluminium bodies with bolt-on steel ends.
Engines: One MTU 6R183TD13H of 315 kW (422 hp) at 1900 rpm (*MTU 6H 1800 + MTU EnergyPack battery system for hybrid operation).
Transmission: Hydraulic. Voith T211rzze to ZF final drive.
Bogies: One Adtranz P3–23 and one BREL T3–23 per car.
Couplers: BSI at outer ends, bar within unit.
Dimensions: Class 168/0: 24.10/23.61 x 2.69 m. Others: 23.62/23.61 x 2.69 m.
Gangways: Within unit only.   **Wheel Arrangement:** 2-B (+ B-2 + B-2) + B-2.
Doors: Twin-leaf swing plug.   **Maximum Speed:** 100 mph.
Seating Layout: 2+2 facing/unidirectional.
Multiple Working: Within class and with Classes 165 and 166.

Fitted with tripcocks for working over London Underground tracks between Harrow-on-the-Hill and Amersham.

Non-standard livery: 168329 HybridFLEX (dark blue, green & grey).

Class 168/0. Original Design. DMSL(A)–MS–MSL–DMSL(B) or DMSL(A)–MSL–MS–DMSL(B).

58451–455 were numbered 58656–660 for a time when used in 168 106–110.

58151–155. DMSL(A). Adtranz Derby 1997–98. –/57 1TD 1W. 44.0 t.
58651–655. MSL. Adtranz Derby 1998. –/73 1T. 41.0 t.
58451–455. MS. Adtranz Derby 1998. –/77. 41.0 t.
58251–255. DMSL(B). Adtranz Derby 1998. –/68 1T. 43.6 t.

168 001	**CL**	P	*CR*	AL	58151	58651	58451	58251
168 002	**CL**	P	*CR*	AL	58152	58652	58452	58252
168 003	**CL**	P	*CR*	AL	58153	58453	58653	58253
168 004	**CL**	P	*CR*	AL	58154	58654	58454	58254
168 005	**CL**	P	*CR*	AL	58155	58655	58455	58255

Name: 168001   Adrian Shooter CBE

Class 168/1. These units are effectively Class 170s. DMSL(A)–MSL–MS–DMSL(B) or DMSL(A)–MS–DMSL(B).

58461–463 were renumbered from 58661–663.

58156–163. DMSL(A). Adtranz Derby 2000. –/57 1TD 2W. 45.2 t.
58456–460. MS. Bombardier Derby 2002. –/76. 41.8 t.
58756–757. MSL. Bombardier Derby 2002. –/73 1T. 42.9 t.
58461–463. MS. Adtranz Derby 2000. –/76. 42.4 t.
58256–263. DMSL(B). Adtranz Derby 2000. –/69 1T. 45.2 t.

168 106	**CL**	P	*CR*	AL	58156	58756	58456	58256
168 107	**CL**	P	*CR*	AL	58157	58757	58457	58257
168 108	**CL**	P	*CR*	AL	58158		58458	58258
168 109	**CL**	P	*CR*	AL	58159		58459	58259
168 110	**CL**	P	*CR*	AL	58160		58460	58260
168 111	**CL**	E	*CR*	AL	58161		58461	58261
168 112	**CL**	E	*CR*	AL	58162		58462	58262
168 113	**CL**	E	*CR*	AL	58163		58463	58263

Class 168/2. These units are effectively Class 170s. DMSL(A)–(MS)–MS–DMSL(B).

58164–169. DMSL(A). Bombardier Derby 2003–04. –/57 1TD 2W. 45.4 t.
58365–367. MS. Bombardier Derby 2006. –/76. 43.3 t.
58464/468/469. MS. Bombardier Derby 2003–04. –/76. 44.0 t.
58465–467. MS. Bombardier Derby 2006. –/76. 43.3 t.
58264–269. DMSL(B). Bombardier Derby 2003–04. –/69 1T. 45.5 t.

168 214	**CL**	P	*CR*	AL	58164		58464	58264
168 215	**CL**	P	*CR*	AL	58165	58365	58465	58265
168 216	**CL**	P	*CR*	AL	58166	58366	58466	58266
168 217	**CL**	P	*CR*	AL	58167	58367	58467	58267
168 218	**CL**	P	*CR*	AL	58168		58468	58268
168 219	**CL**	P	*CR*	AL	58169		58469	58269

Class 168/3. Former South West Trains/TransPennine Express Class 170s taken on by Chiltern Railways in 2015–16 and renumbered in the 168 3xx series. 170 309 was originally numbered 170 399. DMSL(A)–DMSL(B).

50301–308/399. DMCL. Adtranz Derby 2000–01. –/59 1TD 2W. 45.8 t.
79301–308/399. DMSL. Adtranz Derby 2000–01. –/69 1T. 45.8 t.

168 321	(170 301)		**CL**	P	*CR*	AL	50301	79301
168 322	(170 302)		**CL**	P	*CR*	AL	50302	79302
168 323	(170 303)		**CL**	P	*CR*	AL	50303	79303
168 324	(170 304)		**CL**	P	*CR*	AL	50304	79304
168 325	(170 305)		**CL**	P	*CR*	AL	50305	79305
168 326	(170 306)		**CL**	P	*CR*	AL	50306	79306
168 327	(170 307)		**CL**	P	*CR*	AL	50307	79307
168 328	(170 308)		**CL**	P	*CR*	AL	50308	79308
168 329	(170 309)	*	**CL**	P	*CR*	AL	50399	79399

▲ The Swanage Railway's Class 117 (51388/59486/51356) and Class 121 55028 are registered for use on the national network from Worgret Jn to Wareham. Here they arrive at Wareham with the 12.14 from Swanage on 05/09/23. **Tony Christie**

▼ BR carmine & cream-liveried 121 022 (55022) arrives at Glenfinnan with a Locomotive Services special to Arisaig on 28/09/23. **Mike Heath**

▲ West Midlands Railway-liveried Parry People Mover 139001 arrives at Stourbridge Junction with the 10.20 shuttle from Stourbridge Town on 13/06/21.
Jamie Squibbs

▼ Greater Manchester PTE-liveried 142003, owned by Locomotive Services, is seen at Llandudno after arrival with the "Saint Tudno Wanderer" railtour from Wilmslow on 27/09/23.
Paul Beardsley

▲ London Northwestern Railway-liveried 150137 passes Husborne Crawley, near Ridgmont, with the 09.45 Bletchley–Bedford crew training run prior to the resumption of services on the Marston Vale Line on 22/09/23. **Mark Beal**

▼ Converted to a Network Rail Inspection Train, light blue liveried 153376 passes Lower Hartburn with 2Q21 09.47 Doncaster–Doncaster on 17/08/23. **Alex Ayre**

▲ Northern-liveried 155344 is seen near Anlaby Road Junction (Hull) with the 09.45 York–Bridlington on 28/09/21. **Robin Ralston**

▼ ScotRail-liveried 156457 and 156431 leave Glasgow Central with the 16.47 to East Kilbride on 09/06/23. **Robert Pritchard**

▲ East Midlands Railway (interim)-liveried 158773 (with Pride stripes) leads Stagecoach-liveried 158799 on the 14.51 Liverpool Lime Street–Norwich away from Sheffield on 24/06/23. **Robert Pritchard**

▼ South Western Railway-liveried 159017 and 159014 pass Queenstown Road Battersea with the 17.53 London Waterloo–Yeovil Junction on 07/06/23. **Robert Pritchard**

▲ Chiltern Railways-liveried 165019 passes Neasden with the 17.17 London Marylebone–Oxford on 24/05/22. **Robert Pritchard**

▼ Great Western Railway-liveried 166214 runs along the sea wall at Dawlish with the 07.39 Paignton–Exmouth on 07/06/23. **Robert Pritchard**

▲ Chiltern Railways Mainline-liveried 168 323 and 168 108 leave Haddenham & Thame Parkway with the 08.00 London Marylebone–Birmingham Moor Street on 09/04/22. **Robert Pritchard**

▼ CrossCountry-liveried 170 103 is seen at Nottingham with the 15.07 to Cardiff Central on 12/06/23. **Robert Pritchard**

▲ Southern-liveried 171802 passes Redhill with an empty stock working on 18/07/23. **Alex Dasi-Sutton**

▼ West Midlands Railway-liveried 172214 and 172218 call at The Hawthorns with the 16.03 Dorridge–Worcester Foregate Street on 14/10/22. **Robert Pritchard**

▲ Grand Central-liveried 180 102 passes South Otterington on the East Coast Main Line with the 08.53 Sunderland–London King's Cross on 09/08/23. **Alex Ayre**

▼ TransPennine Express-liveried 185 116 and 185 123 head away from Sheffield with the 10.26 Cleethorpes–Manchester Piccadilly on 22/10/22. **Robert Pritchard**

▲ Northern-liveried 195 105 leaves Sheffield with the 17.14 to Manchester Piccadilly on 16/08/23. **Robert Pritchard**

▼ West Midlands Railway-liveried 196 110 leaves Shrewsbury with the 12.40 to Birmingham New Street on 10/12/22. **Robert Pritchard**

▲ Transport for Wales-liveried 197015 passes East Didsbury with the 12.53 Llandudno Junction–Manchester Airport on 29/05/23. **Robert Pritchard**

▼ Preserved "Hastings" DEMU 1001 is seen at London Bridge with a UK Railtours excursion that visited the 13 London termini on 15/04/23. **Ian Beardsley**

▲ CrossCountry-liveried 220031 and 221123 arrive at Chesterfield with the 12.03 Edinburgh–Plymouth on 16/08/23. **Robert Pritchard**

▼ Avanti West Coast Voyager-liveried 221108 and 221110 approach Gretna Green with the diverted 10.22 Glasgow Central–Carlisle on 08/03/23. **Robin Ralston**

▲ East Midlands Railway interim-liveried 222103 approaches Dronfield with the 15.02 London St Pancras–Sheffield on 17/08/23. **Robert Pritchard**

▼ Transport for Wales-liveried 230010 arrives at Gwerysllt with the 14.34 Bidston–Wrexham Central on 13/06/23. **Cliff Beeton**

▲ Transport for Wales-liveried 231 008 is seen at Cardiff Central with the 12.28 Ystrad Mynach–Penarth on 19/06/23. **Robert Pritchard**

▼ Swietelsky Babcock Rail Plasser & Theurer Dynamic Tamper DR 75012 approaches Wolverton with 6Q60 09.31 Bletchley–Bletchley via Croft on 20/02/23. **Mark Beal**

▲ VolkerRail Matisa B41 UE Tampers DR75401 and DR75402 pass Saxilby with 6J38 10.08 Doncaster–Peterborough on 04/11/22. **Robert Pritchard**

▼ Network Rail Mobile Maintenance Train DR97804/DR97604/DR97504 is seen stabled at Leicester on 14/01/23. **Ian Beardsley**

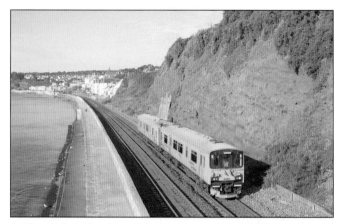

▲ Network Rail yellow-liveried Track Assessment Unit 950001 runs along the sea wall at Dawlish with 2Q08 03.39 Penzance–Exeter Riverside on 23/08/23.
Robin Ralston

▼ Network Rail Independent Snowploughs ADB965235 and ADB965223 pass Cogload Junction with 7Z21 11.22 Taunton Fairwater Yard–Weston-super-Mare–Taunton Fairwater Yard test run, powered by 37419 and 37601. **Tony Christie**

CLASS 170 TURBOSTAR ADTRANZ/BOMBARDIER

Various formations. Air conditioned.

Construction: Welded aluminium bodies with bolt-on steel ends.
Engines: One MTU 6R183TD13H of 315 kW (422 hp) at 1900 rpm.
Transmission: Hydraulic. Voith T211rzze to ZF final drive.
Bogies: One Adtranz P3–23 and one BREL T3–23 per car.
Couplers: BSI at outer ends (Dellner on 170/9), bar within later-build units.
Dimensions: 23.62/23.61 x 2.69 m.
Gangways: Within unit only.   **Wheel Arrangement:** 2-B (+ B-2) + B-2.
Doors: Twin-leaf sliding plug.   **Maximum Speed:** 100 mph.
Seating Layout: 1: 2+1 facing/unidirectional. 2: 2+2 unidirectional/facing.
Multiple Working: Within class and with Classes 150, 153, 155, 156, 158, 159 and 172.

Class 170/1. CrossCountry (former Midland Mainline) units. Lazareni seating. DMSL–MS–DMCL/DMSL–DMCL.

DMSL. Adtranz Derby 1998–99. –/59 1TD 2W. 45.0 t.
MS. Adtranz Derby 2001. –/80. 43.0 t.
DMCL. Adtranz Derby 1998–99. 9/52 1T. 44.8 t

170 101	**XC**	P	*XC*	TS	50101	55101	79101
170 102	**XC**	P	*XC*	TS	50102	55102	79102
170 103	**XC**	P	*XC*	TS	50103	55103	79103
170 104	**XC**	P	*XC*	TS	50104	55104	79104
170 105	**XC**	P	*XC*	TS	50105	55105	79105
170 106	**XC**	P	*XC*	TS	50106	55106	79106
170 107	**XC**	P	*XC*	TS	50107	55107	79107
170 108	**XC**	P	*XC*	TS	50108	55108	79108
170 109	**XC**	P	*XC*	TS	50109	55109	79109
170 110	**XC**	P	*XC*	TS	50110	55110	79110
170 111	**XC**	P	*XC*	TS	50111		79111
170 112	**XC**	P	*XC*	TS	50112		79112
170 113	**XC**	P	*XC*	TS	50113		79113
170 114	**XC**	P	*XC*	TS	50114		79114
170 115	**XC**	P	*XC*	TS	50115		79115
170 116	**XC**	P	*XC*	TS	50116		79116
170 117	**XC**	P	*XC*	TS	50117		79117

Class 170/2. East Midlands Railway and Transport for Wales 3-car units. Previously operated by Greater Anglia. 170 208 due to transfer to East Midlands Railway in early 2024. Chapman seating. DMCL–MSL–DMSL.

DMCL. Adtranz Derby 1999. 7/39 1TD 2W. 44.3 t.
MSL. Adtranz Derby 1999. –/74 1T. 42.8 t.
DMSL. Adtranz Derby 1999. –/66 1T. 44.8 t.

170 201	**ER**	P	*EM*	DY	50201	56201	79201
170 202	**ER**	P	*EM*	DY	50202	56202	79202
170 203	**ER**	P	*EM*	DY	50203	56203	79203
170 204	**ER**	P	*EM*	DY	50204	56204	79204
170 205	**ER**	P	*EM*	DY	50205	56205	79205

170 206	**GA**	P	*EM*	DY	50206	56206	79206
170 207	**GA**	P	*EM*	DY	50207	56207	79207
170 208	**GA**	P	*TW*	CF	50208	56208	79208

Class 170/2. East Midlands Railway 2-car units. Previously operated by Greater Anglia and Transport for Wales. Chapman seating. DMSL–DMCL.

DMSL. Bombardier Derby 2002. –/57 1TD 2W. 45.7 t.
DMCL. Bombardier Derby 2002. 9/53 1T. 45.7 t.

170 270	**ER**	P	*EM*	DY	50270	79270
170 271	**ER**	P	*EM*	DY	50271	79271
170 272	**ER**	P	*EM*	DY	50272	79272
170 273	**ER**	P	*EM*	DY	50273	79273

Class 170/3. Units built for Hull Trains, now used by ScotRail. Chapman seating. DMSL–MSL–DMSL.

DMSL(A). Bombardier Derby 2004. –/55 1TD 2W. 46.5 t.
MSL. Bombardier Derby 2004. –/71 1T. 44.7 t.
DMSL(B). Bombardier Derby 2004. –/67 1T. 47.0 t.

170 393	**SR**	P	*SR*	HA	50393	56393	79393
170 394	**SR**	P	*SR*	HA	50394	56394	79394
170 395	**SR**	P	*SR*	HA	50395	56395	79395
170 396	**SR**	P	*SR*	HA	50396	56396	79396

Class 170/3. CrossCountry units. Lazareni seating. DMSL–MS–DMCL.

DMSL. Bombardier Derby 2002. –/59 1TD 2W. 45.4 t.
MS. Bombardier Derby 2002. –/80. 43.0 t.
DMCL. Bombardier Derby 2002. 9/52 1T. 45.8 t.

| 170 397 | **XC** | P | *XC* | TS | 50397 | 56397 | 79397 |
| 170 398 | **XC** | P | *XC* | TS | 50398 | 56398 | 79398 |

Class 170/4. ScotRail and East Midlands Railway units. Chapman seating. DMCL–MS–DMCL.

170422–424 were numbered 170922–924 in 2022–23. Originally ex-Scotland and latterly ex-Southern 171 201/202 and 171 401/402.

Advertising livery: 170 407 BTP text number 61016 (blue).

DMCL(A). Adtranz Derby 1999–2001. 9/43 1TD 2W. 45.2 t.
MS. Adtranz Derby 1999–2001. –/76. 42.5 t.
DMCL(B). Adtranz Derby 1999–2001. 9/49 1T. 45.2 t.

170 401	**SR**	P	*SR*	HA	50401	56401	79401
170 402	**SR**	P	*SR*	HA	50402	56402	79402
170 403	**SR**	P	*SR*	HA	50403	56403	79403
170 404	**SR**	P	*SR*	HA	50404	56404	79404
170 405	**SR**	P	*SR*	HA	50405	56405	79405
170 406	**SR**	P	*SR*	HA	50406	56406	79406
170 407	**AL**	P	*SR*	HA	50407	56407	79407
170 408	**SR**	P	*SR*	HA	50408	56408	79408
170 409	**SR**	P	*SR*	HA	50409	56409	79409
170 410	**SR**	P	*SR*	HA	50410	56410	79410

170 411	**SR**	P	*SR*	HA	50411	56411	79411	
170 412	**SR**	P	*SR*	HA	50412	56412	79412	
170 413	**SR**	P	*SR*	HA	50413	56413	79413	
170 414	**SR**	P	*SR*	HA	50414	56414	79414	
170 415	**SR**	P	*SR*	HA	50415	56415	79415	
170 416	**ER**	E	*EM*	DY	50416	56416	79416	
170 417	**ER**	E	*EM*	DY	50417	56417	79417	The Key Worker
170 418	**ER**	E	*EM*	DY	50418	56418	79418	
170 419	**ER**	E	*EM*	DY	50419	56419	79419	
170 420	**ER**	E	*EM*	DY	50420	56420	79420	
170 422	**ER**	E	*EM*	DY	50422	56422	79422	
170 423	**ER**	E	*EM*	DY	50423	56423	79423	
170 424	**SN**	E	*EM*	DY	50424	56424	79424	

Class 170/4. ScotRail units. Chapman seating. DMCL–MS–DMCL.

DMCL. Bombardier Derby 2003–05. 9/43 1TD 2W. 46.8 t.
MS. Bombardier Derby 2003–05. –/76. 43.7 t.
DMCL. Bombardier Derby 2003–05. 9/49 1T. 46.5 t.

170 425	**SR**	P	*SR*	HA	50425	56425	79425
170 426	**SR**	P	*SR*	HA	50426	56426	79426
170 427	**SR**	P	*SR*	HA	50427	56427	79427
170 428	**SR**	P	*SR*	HA	50428	56428	79428
170 429	**SR**	P	*SR*	HA	50429	56429	79429
170 430	**SR**	P	*SR*	HA	50430	56430	79430
170 431	**SR**	P	*SR*	HA	50431	56431	79431
170 432	**SR**	P	*SR*	HA	50432	56432	79432
170 433	**SR**	P	*SR*	HA	50433	56433	79433
170 434	**SR**	P	*SR*	HA	50434	56434	79434

Class 170/4. ScotRail and Northern units. Originally built as Standard Class only. 170450–457 were retro-fitted with First Class but those used by Northern are now Standard Class only. Chapman seating. DMSL–MS–DMSL or † DMCL–MS–DMCL.

DMSL/DMCL. Bombardier Derby 2004–05. –/55 1TD 2W († 9/47 1TD 2W). 46.3 t.
MS. Bombardier Derby 2004–05. –/76. 43.4 t.
DMSL/DMCL. Bombardier Derby 2004–05. –/67 1T († 9/49 1T 1W). 46.4 t.

170 450		**SR**	P	*SR*	HA	50450	56450	79450
170 451	†	**SR**	P	*SR*	HA	50451	56451	79451
170 452	†	**SR**	P	*SR*	HA	50452	56452	79452
170 453	†	**NR**	P	*NO*	BG	50453	56453	79453
170 454	†	**NR**	P	*NO*	BG	50454	56454	79454
170 455	†	**NR**	P	*NO*	BG	50455	56455	79455
170 456	†	**NR**	P	*NO*	BG	50456	56456	79456
170 457	†	**NR**	P	*NO*	BG	50457	56457	79457
170 458		**NR**	P	*NO*	BG	50458	56458	79458
170 459		**NR**	P	*NO*	BG	50459	56459	79459
170 460		**NR**	P	*NO*	BG	50460	56460	79460
170 461		**NR**	P	*NO*	BG	50461	56461	79461

Class 170/4. ScotRail and Northern units. Standard Class only units. Chapman seating. DMSL–MS–DMSL.

50470–471. DMSL(A). Adtranz Derby 2001. –/55 1TD 2W. 45.1 t.
50472–478. DMSL(A). Bombardier Derby 2004–05. –/57 1TD 2W. 45.8 t.
56470–471. MS. Adtranz Derby 2001. –/76. 42.4 t.
56472–478. MS. Bombardier Derby 2004–05. –/76. 43.0 t.
79470–471. DMSL(B). Adtranz Derby 2001. –/67 1T. 45.1 t.
79472–478. DMSL(B). Bombardier Derby 2004–05. –/67 1T. 45.8 t.

170 470	**SR**	P	*SR*	HA	50470	56470	79470
170 471	**SR**	P	*SR*	HA	50471	56471	79471
170 472	**NR**	P	*NO*	BG	50472	56472	79472
170 473	**NR**	P	*NO*	BG	50473	56473	79473
170 474	**NR**	P	*NO*	BG	50474	56474	79474
170 475	**NR**	P	*NO*	BG	50475	56475	79475
170 476	**NR**	P	*NO*	BG	50476	56476	79476
170 477	**NR**	P	*NO*	BG	50477	56477	79477
170 478	**NR**	P	*NO*	BG	50478	56478	79478

Class 170/5. East Midlands Railway 2-car units. Lazareni seating. DMSL–DMSL.

170530–535 were reduced from 3-car units to 2-car units in 2020 prior to their transfer (along with 170501–517) to East Midlands Railway.

DMSL(A). Adtranz Derby 1999–2000. –/55 1TD 2W. 45.8 t.
DMSL(B). Adtranz Derby 1999–2000. –/67 1T. 45.9 t.

170 501	**ER**	P	*EM*	DY	50501	79501
170 502	**ER**	P	*EM*	DY	50502	79502
170 503	**ER**	P	*EM*	DY	50503	79503
170 504	**ER**	P	*EM*	DY	50504	79504
170 505	**ER**	P	*EM*	DY	50505	79505
170 506	**ER**	P	*EM*	DY	50506	79506
170 507	**ER**	P	*EM*	DY	50507	79507
170 508	**ER**	P	*EM*	DY	50508	79508
170 509	**ER**	P	*EM*	DY	50509	79509
170 510	**ER**	P	*EM*	DY	50510	79510
170 511	**ER**	P	*EM*	DY	50511	79511
170 512	**ER**	P	*EM*	DY	50512	79512
170 513	**ER**	P	*EM*	DY	50513	79513
170 514	**ER**	P	*EM*	DY	50514	79514
170 515	**ER**	P	*EM*	DY	50515	79515
170 516	**ER**	P	*EM*	DY	50516	79516
170 517	**ER**	P	*EM*	DY	50517	79517

170 530	(170 630)	**ER**	P	*EM*	DY	50630	79630
170 531	(170 631)	**ER**	P	*EM*	DY	50631	79631
170 532	(170 632)	**ER**	P	*EM*	DY	50632	79632
170 533	(170 633)	**ER**	P	*EM*	DY	50633	79633
170 534	(170 634)	**ER**	P	*EM*	DY	50634	79634
170 535	(170 635)	**ER**	P	*EM*	DY	50635	79635

Class 170/6. CrossCountry 3-car units. Lazareni seating. DMSL–MS–DMCL.

170 618–623 were augmented from 2-car to 3-car in 2020–21 using centre cars from 170 630–635, having been built as 2-car units 170 518–523.

DMSL. Adtranz Derby 2000. –/59 1TD 2W. 45.8 t.
MS. Adtranz Derby 2000. –/74. 42.5 t.
DMCL. Adtranz Derby 2000. 9/52 1T. 45.9 t.

170 618	(170 518)	**XC**	P	*XC*	TS	50518	56630	79518
170 619	(170 519)	**XC**	P	*XC*	TS	50519	56631	79519
170 620	(170 520)	**XC**	P	*XC*	TS	50520	56632	79520
170 621	(170 521)	**XC**	P	*XC*	TS	50521	56633	79521
170 622	(170 522)	**XC**	P	*XC*	TS	50522	56634	79522
170 623	(170 523)	**XC**	P	*XC*	TS	50523	56635	79523

170 636	**XC**	P	*XC*	TS	50636	56636	79636
170 637	**XC**	P	*XC*	TS	50637	56637	79637
170 638	**XC**	P	*XC*	TS	50638	56638	79638
170 639	**XC**	P	*XC*	TS	50639	56639	79639

Name (carried on MS): 170 622   PRIDE OF LEICESTER

CLASS 171   TURBOSTAR   BOMBARDIER

DMCL–DMSL or DMCL–MS–DMCL. Southern units. Air conditioned. Chapman seating.

Construction: Welded aluminium bodies with bolt-on steel ends.
Engines: One MTU 6R183TD13H of 315 kW (422 hp) at 1900 rpm.
Transmission: Hydraulic. Voith T211rzze to ZF final drive.
Bogies: One Adtranz P3–23 and one BREL T3–23 per car.
Couplers: Dellner 12 at outer ends, bar within unit (Class 171/8).
Dimensions: 23.62/23.61 x 2.69 m.
Gangways: Within unit only.   **Wheel Arrangement:** 2-B (+ B-2 + B-2) + B-2.
Doors: Twin-leaf swing plug.   **Maximum Speed:** 100 mph.
Seating Layout: 1: 2+1 facing/unidirectional. 2: 2+2 facing/unidirectional.
Multiple Working: Within class and with EMU Classes 375 and 377 in an emergency.

Class 171/2. 3-car unit rebuilt from ScotRail Class 170. DMCL–MS–DMCL. On hire from East Midlands Railway to Southern.

DMCL(A). Adtranz Derby 1999–2001. 9/43 1TD 2W. 45.2 t.
MS. Adtranz Derby 1999–2001. –/76. 42.5 t.
DMCL(B). Adtranz Derby 1999–2001. 9/49 1T. 45.2 t.

171 201	(170 421)	**SN**	P	*SN*	SU	50421	56421	79421

Class 171/7. 2-car units. DMCL–DMSL.

171 730 was formerly South West Trains unit 170 392, before transferring to Southern in 2007.

50727–729. DMCL. Bombardier Derby 2005. 9/43 1TD 2W. 46.3 t.
50392. DMCL. Bombardier Derby 2003. 9/43 1TD 2W. 46.6 t.

79727–729. DMSL. Bombardier Derby 2005. –/64 1T. 46.2 t.
79392. DMSL. Bombardier Derby 2003. –/64 1T. 46.5 t.

171 727	**SN**	P	*SN*	SU	50727	79727
171 728	**SN**	P	*SN*	SU	50728	79728
171 729	**SN**	P	*SN*	SU	50729	79729
171 730	**SN**	P	*SN*	SU	50392	79392

Class 171/8. Built as 4-car units but reduced to 3-car units in 2022.
DMCL(A)–MS–DMCL(B).

DMCL(A). Bombardier Derby 2004. 9/43 1TD 2W. 46.5 t.
MS. Bombardier Derby 2004. –/74. 43.7 t.
DMCL(B). Bombardier Derby 2004. 9/50 1T. 46.5 t.

171 801	**SN**	P	*SN*	SU	50801	54801	79801
171 802	**SN**	P	*SN*	SU	50802	54802	79802
171 803	**SN**	P	*SN*	SU	50803	54803	79803
171 804	**SN**	P	*SN*	SU	50804	54804	79804
171 805	**SN**	P	*SN*	SU	50805	54805	79805
171 806	**SN**	P	*SN*	SU	50806	54806	79806

Class 171/8. Former 2-car units extended to 3-car units in 2022 using MS vehicles from 171 801–806. DMCL–MS–DMSL.

DMCL. Bombardier Derby 2003. 9/43 1TD 2W. 47.6 t.
MS. Bombardier Derby 2004. –/74. 43.7 t.
DMSL. Bombardier Derby 2003. –/64 1T. 47.8 t.

171 807	(171 721)	**SN**	P	*SN*	SU	50721	56806	79721
171 808	(171 722)	**SN**	P	*SN*	SU	50722	56804	79722
171 809	(171 723)	**SN**	P	*SN*	SU	50723	56802	79723
171 810	(171 724)	**SN**	P	*SN*	SU	50724	56805	79724
171 811	(171 725)	**SN**	P	*SN*	SU	50725	56803	79725
171 812	(171 726)	**SN**	P	*SN*	SU	50726	56801	79726

CLASS 172   TURBOSTAR   BOMBARDIER

New generation West Midlands Trains Turbostars. Air conditioned.

Construction: Welded aluminium bodies with bolt-on steel ends.
Engines: One MTU 6H1800R83 of 360 kW (483 hp) at 1800 rpm.
Transmission: Mechanical. Supplied by ZF, Germany.
Bogies: B5006 type "lightweight" bogies.
Couplers: BSI at outer ends, bar within unit.
Dimensions: 23.62/23.00 x 2.69 m.
Gangways: 172/0 & 172/1: Within unit only. 172/2: Throughout.
Wheel Arrangement: 2-B (+ B-2) + B-2.
Doors: Twin-leaf sliding plug.
Maximum Speed: 100 mph.
Seating Layout: 2+2 facing/unidirectional.
Multiple Working: Within class and with Classes 150, 153, 155, 156, 158, 159, 165, 166 and 170.

Class 172/0. Formerly operated by London Overground. DMSL–DMS.

59311–318. DMSL. Bombardier Derby 2009–10. –/57(+4) 1TD 2W. 41.6 t.
59411–418. DMS. Bombardier Derby 2009–10. –/64(+12). 41.5 t.

172 001	**WM**	A	*WM*	TS	59311	59411
172 002	**WM**	A	*WM*	TS	59312	59412
172 003	**WM**	A	*WM*	TS	59313	59413
172 004	**WM**	A	*WM*	TS	59314	59414
172 005	**WM**	A	*WM*	TS	59315	59415
172 006	**WM**	A	*WM*	TS	59316	59416
172 007	**WM**	A	*WM*	TS	59317	59417
172 008	**WM**	A	*WM*	TS	59318	59418

Class 172/1. Formerly operated by Chiltern Railways. DMSL–DMS.

59111–114. DMSL. Bombardier Derby 2009–10. –/60(+5) 1TD 2W. 42.4 t.
59211–214. DMS. Bombardier Derby 2009–10. –/80. 41.8 t.

172 101	**WM**	A	*WM*	TS	59111	59211
172 102	**WM**	A	*WM*	TS	59112	59212
172 103	**WM**	A	*WM*	TS	59113	59213
172 104	**WM**	A	*WM*	TS	59114	59214

Class 172/2. 2-car units with end gangways. DMSL–DMS.

50211–222. DMSL. Bombardier Derby 2010–11. –/52(+11) 1TD 2W. 42.5 t.
79211–222. DMS. Bombardier Derby 2010–11. –/68(+8). 41.9 t.

172 211	**WM**	P	*WM*	TS	50211	79211
172 212	**WM**	P	*WM*	TS	50212	79212
172 213	**WM**	P	*WM*	TS	50213	79213
172 214	**WM**	P	*WM*	TS	50214	79214
172 215	**WM**	P	*WM*	TS	50215	79215
172 216	**WM**	P	*WM*	TS	50216	79216
172 217	**WM**	P	*WM*	TS	50217	79217
172 218	**WM**	P	*WM*	TS	50218	79218
172 219	**WM**	P	*WM*	TS	50219	79219
172 220	**WM**	P	*WM*	TS	50220	79220
172 221	**WM**	P	*WM*	TS	50221	79221
172 222	**WM**	P	*WM*	TS	50222	79222

Class 172/3. 3-car units with end gangways. DMSL–MS–DMS.

172 333/338 are running with misformed formations, as shown.

50331–345. DMSL. Bombardier Derby 2010–11. –/52(+11) 1TD 2W. 42.5 t.
56331–345. MS. Bombardier Derby 2010–11. –/72(+8). 38.8 t.
79331–345. DMS. Bombardier Derby 2010–11. –/68(+8). 41.9 t.

172 331	**WM**	P	*WM*	TS	50331	56331	79331
172 332	**WM**	P	*WM*	TS	50332	56332	79332
172 333	**WM**	P	*WM*	TS	50338	56333	79333
172 334	**WM**	P	*WM*	TS	50334	56334	79334
172 335	**WM**	P	*WM*	TS	50335	56335	79335
172 336	**WM**	P	*WM*	TS	50336	56336	79336
172 337	**WM**	P	*WM*	TS	50337	56337	79337

172 338	**WM**	P	*WM*	TS	50333	56338	79338	
172 339	**WM**	P	*WM*	TS	50339	56339	79339	
172 340	**WM**	P	*WM*	TS	50340	56340	79340	
172 341	**WM**	P	*WM*	TS	50341	56341	79341	
172 342	**WM**	P	*WM*	TS	50342	56342	79342	ROGER SUMNER
172 343	**WM**	P	*WM*	TS	50343	56343	79343	
172 344	**WM**	P	*WM*	TS	50344	56344	79344	
172 345	**WM**	P	*WM*	TS	50345	56345	79345	

CLASS 175   CORADIA 1000   ALSTOM

Air conditioned. All units were withdrawn from service with Transport for Wales during 2023.

Construction: Steel.
Engines: One Cummins N14 of 335 kW (450 hp).
Transmission: Hydraulic. Voith T211rzze to ZF Voith final drive.
Bogies: ACR (Alstom FBO) – LTB-MBS1, TB-MB1, MBS1-LTB.
Couplers: Scharfenberg outer ends and bar within unit (Class 175/1).
Dimensions: 23.70 x 2.73 m.
Gangways: Within unit only.   **Wheel Arrangement:** 2-B (+ B-2) + B-2.
Doors: Single-leaf swing plug.   **Maximum Speed:** 100 mph.
Seating Layout: 2+2 facing/unidirectional.
Multiple Working: Within class and with Class 180.

175 004/005/006/101/109/115 are in misformed formations, as shown.

Class 175/0. DMSL–DMSL. 2-car units.

DMSL(A). Alstom Birmingham 1999–2000. –/54 1TD 2W. 48.8 t.
DMSL(B). Alstom Birmingham 1999–2000. –/64 1T. 50.7 t.

175 001	**TW**	A	CH	50701	79701
175 002	**TW**	A	LE	50702	79702
175 003	**TW**	A	CH	50703	79703
175 004	**TW**	A	LE	50759	79759
175 005	**TW**	A	LE	50705	79751
175 006	**TW**	A	CY	50706	79765
175 007	**TW**	A	CY	50707	79707
175 008	**TW**	A	ZI	50708	79708
175 009	**TW**	A	ZI	50709	79709
175 010	**TW**	A	ZI	50710	79710
175 011	**TW**	A	CY	50711	79711

Class 175/1. DMSL–MSL–DMSL. 3-car units.

DMSL(A). Alstom Birmingham 1999–2001. –/54 1TD 2W. 50.7 t.
MSL. Alstom Birmingham 1999–2001. –/68 1T. 47.5 t.
DMSL(B). Alstom Birmingham 1999–2001. –/64 1T. 49.5 t.

| 175 101 | **TW** | A | CF | 50751 | 56751 | 79704 |
| 175 102 | **TW** | A | LE | 50752 | 56752 | 79752 |

175 103	**TW**	A		HD	50753	56753	79753
175 104	**TW**	A		HD	50754	56754	79754
175 105	**TW**	A		HD	50755	56755	79755
175 106	**TW**	A		HD	50756	56756	79756
175 107	**TW**	A		CY	50757	56757	79757
175 108	**TW**	A		ZI	50758	56758	79758
175 109	**TW**	A		CF	50704	56759	79705
175 110	**TW**	A		ZI	50760	56760	79760
175 111	**TW**	A		MA	50761	56761	79761
175 112	**TW**	A		HD	50762	56762	79762
175 113	**TW**	A		CH	50763	56763	79763
175 114	**TW**	A		CY	50764	56764	79764
175 115	**TW**	A		CH	50765	56765	79706
175 116	**TW**	A		CY	50766	56766	79766

CLASS 180   CORADIA 1000   ALSTOM

Air conditioned.

Construction: Steel.
Engines: One Cummins QSK19 of 560 kW (750 hp) at 2100 rpm.
Transmission: Hydraulic. Voith T312br to Voith final drive.
Bogies: ACR (Alstom FBO): LTB1-MBS2, TB1-MB2, TB1-MB2, TB2-MB2, MBS2-LTB1.
Couplers: Scharfenberg outer ends, bar within unit.
Dimensions: 23.71/23.03 x 2.73 m.
Gangways: Within unit only.
Wheel Arrangement: 2-B + B-2 + B-2 + B-2 + B-2.
Doors: Single-leaf swing plug.   **Maximum Speed:** 125 mph.
Seating Layout: 1: 2+1 facing/unidirectional, 2: 2+2 facing/unidirectional.
Multiple Working: Within class and with Class 175.

A number of Grand Central Class 180 sets are currently running with misformed formations, as shown.

DMSL(A). Alstom Birmingham 2000–01. –/46 2W 1TD. 51.7 t.
MFL. Alstom Birmingham 2000–01. 42/– 1T 1W + catering point. 49.6 t.
MSL. Alstom Birmingham 2000–01. –/68 1T. 49.5 t.
MSLRB. Alstom Birmingham 2000–01. –/56 1T. 50.3 t.
DMSL(B). Alstom Birmingham 2000–01. –/56 1T. 51.4 t.

180 101	**GC**	A	*GC*	HT	50901	54901	55901	56901	59905
180 102	**GC**	A	*GC*	HT	50902	54902	55902	56903	59902
180 103	**GC**	A	*GC*	HT	50903	54907	55906	56902	59903
180 104	**GC**	A	*GC*	HT	50904	54904	55904	56904	59904
180 105	**GC**	A	*GC*	HT	50905	54905	55905	56905	59901
180 106	**GC**	A	*GC*	HT	50906	54906	55903	56906	59906
180 107	**GC**	A	*GC*	HT	50907	54903	55907	56907	59907
180 108	**GC**	A	*GC*	HT	50908	54908	55908	56908	59908
180 109	**EI**	A		EP	50909	54909	55909	56909	59909
180 110	**EI**	A	*GC*	HT	50910	54910	55910	56910	59910
180 111	**EI**	A		EP	50911	54911	55911	56911	59911
180 112	**GC**	A	*GC*	HT	50912	54912	55912	56912	59912

| 180 113 | **EI** | A | | EP | 50913 54913 55913 56913 59913 |
| 180 114 | **GC** | A | *GC* | HT | 50914 54914 55914 56914 59914 |

Names (carried on DMSL(A):

180 105	THE YORKSHIRE ARTIST ASHLEY JACKSON
180 107	HART OF THE NORTH
180 108	WILLIAM SHAKESPEARE
180 112	JAMES HERRIOT
180 114	KIRKGATE CALLING

CLASS 185   DESIRO UK   SIEMENS

Air conditioned. Grammer seating in Standard Class and Fainsa in First Class.

Construction: Aluminium.
Engines: One Cummins QSK19 of 560 kW (750 hp) at 2100 rpm.
Transmission: Voith.   **Bogies:** Siemens.
Couplers: Dellner 12.   **Dimensions:** 23.76/23.75 x 2.66 m.
Gangways: Within unit only.   **Wheel Arrangement:** 2-B + 2-B + B-2.
Doors: Double-leaf sliding plug.   **Maximum Speed:** 100 mph.
Seating Layout: 1: 2+1 facing/unidirectional, 2: 2+2 facing/unidirectional.
Multiple Working: Within class only.

DMCL. Siemens Krefeld 2005–06. 15/18(+8) 2W 1TD + catering point. 55.4 t.
MSL. Siemens Krefeld 2005–06. –/72 1T. 52.7 t.
DMS. Siemens Krefeld 2005–06. –/64(+4). 54.9 t.

185 101	**TP**	E	*TP*	AK	51101	53101	54101
185 102	**TP**	E	*TP*	AK	51102	53102	54102
185 103	**TP**	E	*TP*	AK	51103	53103	54103
185 104	**TP**	E	*TP*	AK	51104	53104	54104
185 105	**TP**	E	*TP*	AK	51105	53105	54105
185 106	**TP**	E	*TP*	AK	51106	53106	54106
185 107	**TP**	E	*TP*	AK	51107	53107	54107
185 108	**TP**	E	*TP*	AK	51108	53108	54108
185 109	**TP**	E	*TP*	AK	51109	53109	54109
185 110	**TP**	E	*TP*	AK	51110	53110	54110
185 111	**TP**	E	*TP*	AK	51111	53111	54111
185 112	**TP**	E	*TP*	AK	51112	53112	54112
185 113	**TP**	E	*TP*	AK	51113	53113	54113
185 114	**TP**	E	*TP*	AK	51114	53114	54114
185 115	**TP**	E	*TP*	AK	51115	53115	54115
185 116	**TP**	E	*TP*	AK	51116	53116	54116
185 117	**TP**	E	*TP*	AK	51117	53117	54117
185 118	**TP**	E	*TP*	AK	51118	53118	54118
185 119	**TP**	E	*TP*	AK	51119	53119	54119
185 120	**TP**	E	*TP*	AK	51120	53120	54120
185 121	**TP**	E	*TP*	AK	51121	53121	54121
185 122	**TP**	E	*TP*	AK	51122	53122	54122
185 123	**TP**	E	*TP*	AK	51123	53123	54123
185 124	**TP**	E	*TP*	AK	51124	53124	54124
185 125	**TP**	E	*TP*	AK	51125	53125	54125

185 126	**TP**	E	*TP*	AK	51126	53126	54126
185 127	**TP**	E	*TP*	AK	51127	53127	54127
185 128	**TP**	E	*TP*	AK	51128	53128	54128
185 129	**TP**	E	*TP*	AK	51129	53129	54129
185 130	**TP**	E	*TP*	AK	51130	53130	54130
185 131	**TP**	E	*TP*	AK	51131	53131	54131
185 132	**TP**	E	*TP*	AK	51132	53132	54132
185 133	**TP**	E	*TP*	AK	51133	53133	54133
185 134	**TP**	E	*TP*	AK	51134	53134	54134
185 135	**TP**	E	*TP*	AK	51135	53135	54135
185 136	**TP**	E	*TP*	AK	51136	53136	54136
185 137	**TP**	E	*TP*	AK	51137	53137	54137
185 138	**TP**	E	*TP*	AK	51138	53138	54138
185 139	**TP**	E	*TP*	AK	51139	53139	54139
185 140	**TP**	E	*TP*	AK	51140	53140	54140
185 141	**TP**	E	*TP*	AK	51141	53141	54141
185 142	**TP**	E	*TP*	AK	51142	53142	54142
185 143	**TP**	E	*TP*	AK	51143	53143	54143
185 144	**TP**	E	*TP*	AK	51144	53144	54144
185 145	**TP**	E	*TP*	AK	51145	53145	54145
185 146	**TP**	E	*TP*	AK	51146	53146	54146
185 147	**TP**	E	*TP*	AK	51147	53147	54147
185 148	**TP**	E	*TP*	AK	51148	53148	54148
185 149	**TP**	E	*TP*	AK	51149	53149	54149
185 150	**TP**	E	*TP*	AK	51150	53150	54150
185 151	**TP**	E	*TP*	AK	51151	53151	54151

Name (carried on both driving cars):

185 113   Hull Paragon 175 YEARS

CLASS 195   CIVITY   CAF

DMS–DMS or DMS–MS–DMS. New Northern units. Air conditioned.

Construction: Aluminium.
Engines: One Rolls-Royce MTU 6H 1800 R85L of 390 kW (523 hp) per car.
Transmission: Mechanical, supplied by ZF, Germany.
Bogies: CAF.
Couplers: Dellner 12.   **Dimensions:** 24.03/23.35 x 2.71 m.
Gangways: Within unit only.   **Wheel Arrangement:**
Doors: Sliding plug.   **Maximum Speed:** 100 mph.
Seating Layout: 2+2 facing/unidirectional.
Multiple Working: Within class only.

Class 195/0. DMS–DMS. 2-car units.

DMS(A). CAF Zaragoza/Irun/Newport 2017–20. –/45(+8) 1TD 2W. 43.9 t.
DMS(B). CAF Zaragoza/Irun/Newport 2017–20. –/63(+7). 43.2 t.

195 001	**NR**	E	*NO*	NH	101001	103001
195 002	**NR**	E	*NO*	NH	101002	103002
195 003	**NR**	E	*NO*	NH	101003	103003
195 004	**NR**	E	*NO*	NH	101004	103004

195 005	**NR**	E	*NO*	NH	101005	103005
195 006	**NR**	E	*NO*	NH	101006	103006
195 007	**NR**	E	*NO*	NH	101007	103007
195 008	**NR**	E	*NO*	NH	101008	103008
195 009	**NR**	E	*NO*	NH	101009	103009
195 010	**NR**	E	*NO*	NH	101010	103010
195 011	**NR**	E	*NO*	NH	101011	103011
195 012	**NR**	E	*NO*	NH	101012	103012
195 013	**NR**	E	*NO*	NH	101013	103013
195 014	**NR**	E	*NO*	NH	101014	103014
195 015	**NR**	E	*NO*	NH	101015	103015
195 016	**NR**	E	*NO*	NH	101016	103016
195 017	**NR**	E	*NO*	NH	101017	103017
195 018	**NR**	E	*NO*	NH	101018	103018
195 019	**NR**	E	*NO*	NH	101019	103019
195 020	**NR**	E	*NO*	NH	101020	103020
195 021	**NR**	E	*NO*	NH	101021	103021
195 022	**NR**	E	*NO*	NH	101022	103022
195 023	**NR**	E	*NO*	NH	101023	103023
195 024	**NR**	E	*NO*	NH	101024	103024
195 025	**NR**	E	*NO*	NH	101025	103025

Class 195/1. DMS–MS–DMS. 3-car units.

DMS(A). CAF Zaragoza/Irun/Newport 2017–20. –/45(+8) 1TD 2W. 43.9 t.
MS. CAF Zaragoza/Irun/Newport 2017–20. –/76(+4).
DMS(B). CAF Zaragoza/Irun/Newport 2017–20. –/63(+7). 43.2 t.

195 101	**NR**	E	*NO*	NH	101101	102101	103101	
195 102	**NR**	E	*NO*	NH	101102	102102	103102	
195 103	**NR**	E	*NO*	NH	101103	102103	103103	
195 104	**NR**	E	*NO*	NH	101104	102104	103104	Deva Victrix
195 105	**NR**	E	*NO*	NH	101105	102105	103105	
195 106	**NR**	E	*NO*	NH	101106	102106	103106	
195 107	**NR**	E	*NO*	NH	101107	102107	103107	
195 108	**NR**	E	*NO*	NH	101108	102108	103108	
195 109	**NR**	E	*NO*	NH	101109	102109	103109	Pride of Cumbria
195 110	**NR**	E	*NO*	NH	101110	102110	103110	
195 111	**NR**	E	*NO*	NH	101111	102111	103111	Key Worker
195 112	**NR**	E	*NO*	NH	101112	102112	103112	
195 113	**NR**	E	*NO*	NH	101113	102113	103113	
195 114	**NR**	E	*NO*	NH	101114	102114	103114	
195 115	**NR**	E	*NO*	NH	101115	102115	103115	
195 116	**NR**	E	*NO*	NH	101116	102116	103116	Proud to be Northern
195 117	**NR**	E	*NO*	NH	101117	102117	103117	
195 118	**NR**	E	*NO*	NH	101118	102118	103118	
195 119	**NR**	E	*NO*	NH	101119	102119	103119	
195 120	**NR**	E	*NO*	NH	101120	102120	103120	
195 121	**NR**	E	*NO*	NH	101121	102121	103121	
195 122	**NR**	E	*NO*	NH	101122	102122	103122	
195 123	**NR**	E	*NO*	NH	101123	102123	103123	
195 124	**NR**	E	*NO*	NH	101124	102124	103124	

195 125	**NR**	E	*NO*	NH	101125	102125	103125	
195 126	**NR**	E	*NO*	NH	101126	102126	103126	
195 127	**NR**	E	*NO*	NH	101127	102127	103127	
195 128	**NR**	E	*NO*	NH	101128	102128	103128	Calder Champion
195 129	**NR**	E	*NO*	NH	101129	102129	103129	
195 130	**NR**	E	*NO*	NH	101130	102130	103130	
195 131	**NR**	E	*NO*	NH	101131	102131	103131	
195 132	**NR**	E	*NO*	NH	101132	102132	103132	
195 133	**NR**	E	*NO*	NH	101133	102133	103133	

CLASS 196   CIVITY   CAF

DMS–DMS or DMS–MS–MS–DMS. New West Midlands Trains used on local services between Birmingham and Shrewsbury and Hereford. Air conditioned.

Construction: Aluminium.
Engines: One Rolls-Royce MTU 6H 1800 R85L of 390 kW (523 hp) per car.
Transmission: Mechanical, supplied by ZF, Germany.
Bogies: CAF.
Couplers: Dellner 12.   **Dimensions:** 24.03/23.35 x 2.71 m.
Gangways: Throughout.   **Wheel Arrangement:**
Doors: Sliding plug.   **Maximum Speed:** 100 mph.
Seating Layout: 2+2 facing/unidirectional.
Multiple Working: Within class only.

Class 196/0. DMS–DMS. 2-car units.

DMS(A). CAF Zaragoza/Beasain/Newport 2019–21. –/58(+4) 1TD 2W.
DMS(B). CAF Zaragoza/Beasain/Newport 2019–21. –/76(+3).

196 001	**WM**	CO	*WM*	TS	121001	124001	GRAISELEY WOLVES
196 002	**WM**	CO	*WM*	TS	121002	124002	
196 003	**WM**	CO	*WM*	TS	121003	124003	
196 004	**WM**	CO	*WM*	TS	121004	124004	SIR EDWARD ELGAR
196 005	**WM**	CO	*WM*	TS	121005	124005	
196 006	**WM**	CO	*WM*	TS	121006	124006	
196 007	**WM**	CO	*WM*	TS	121007	124007	
196 008	**WM**	CO	*WM*	TS	121008	124008	
196 009	**WM**	CO	*WM*	TS	121009	124009	
196 010	**WM**	CO	*WM*	TS	121010	124010	
196 011	**WM**	CO	*WM*	TS	121011	124011	
196 012	**WM**	CO	*WM*	TS	121012	124012	

Class 196/1. DMS–MS–MS–DMS. 4-car units.

DMS(A). CAF Zaragoza/Irun/Newport 2019–21. –/58(+4) 1TD 2W. 41.4 t.
MS(A). CAF Zaragoza/Irun/Newport 2019–21. –/88. 39.8 t.
MS(B). CAF Zaragoza/Irun/Newport 2019–21. –/82 1T. 40.3 t.
DMS(B). CAF Zaragoza/Irun/Newport 2019–21. –/76(+3). 42.7 t.

196 101	**WM**	CO	*WM*	TS	121101	122101	123101	124101
196 102	**WM**	CO	*WM*	TS	121102	122102	123102	124102
196 103	**WM**	CO	*WM*	TS	121103	122103	123103	124103

196 104	**WM** CO	*WM* TS	121104	122104	123104	124104
196 105	**WM** CO	*WM* TS	121105	122105	123105	124105
196 106	**WM** CO	*WM* TS	121106	122106	123106	124106
196 107	**WM** CO	*WM* TS	121107	122107	123107	124107
196 108	**WM** CO	*WM* TS	121108	122108	123108	124108
196 109	**WM** CO	*WM* TS	121109	122109	123109	124109
196 110	**WM** CO	*WM* TS	121110	122110	123110	124110
196 111	**WM** CO	*WM* TS	121111	122111	123111	124111
196 112	**WM** CO	*WM* TS	121112	122112	123112	124112
196 113	**WM** CO		121113	122113	123113	124113
196 114	**WM** CO		121114	122114	123114	124114

Name (carried on end cars): 196 101   CHARLES DARWIN

CLASS 197   CIVITY   CAF

DMS–DMS or DMS–MS–DMS. New units currently entering service with Transport for Wales. Air conditioned.

21 2-car units will be fitted with ETCS signalling equipment for operating the Cambrian Lines (197 003/022–041) and 14 3-car units (195 113–116) have First Class seating.

Construction: Aluminium.
Engines: One Rolls-Royce MTU 6H 1800 R85L of 390 kW (523 hp) per car.
Transmission: Mechanical, supplied by ZF, Germany.
Bogies: CAF.
Couplers: Dellner 12.   **Dimensions:** 24.03/23.35 x 2.71 m.
Gangways: Throughout.   **Wheel Arrangement:**
Doors: Sliding plug.   **Maximum Speed:** 100 mph.
Seating Layout: 2+2 facing/unidirectional.
Multiple Working: Within class only.

Class 197/0. DMS–DMS. 2-car units.

DMS(A). CAF Beasain/Newport 2020–24. –/42(+6) 1TD 2W + catering area.
DMS(B). CAF Beasain/Newport 2020–24. –/74.

197 001	**TW** SM	*TW* CH	131001	133001	
197 002	**TW** SM	*TW* CH	131002	133002	
197 003	**TW** SM		131003	133003	
197 004	**TW** SM	*TW* CH	131004	133004	
197 005	**TW** SM	*TW* CH	131005	133005	
197 006	**TW** SM	*TW* CH	131006	133006	
197 007	**TW** SM	*TW* CH	131007	133007	Happy Valley
197 008	**TW** SM	*TW* CH	131008	133008	
197 009	**TW** SM	*TW* CH	131009	133009	
197 010	**TW** SM	*TW* CH	131010	133010	
197 011	**TW** SM	*TW* CH	131011	133011	
197 012	**TW** SM	*TW* CH	131012	133012	
197 013	**TW** SM	*TW* CH	131013	133013	
197 014	**TW** SM	*TW* CH	131014	133014	
197 015	**TW** SM	*TW* CH	131015	133015	
197 016	**TW** SM	*TW* CH	131016	133016	

197 017	**TW**	SM	*TW*	CH	131017	133017	
197 018	**TW**	SM	*TW*	CH	131018	133018	
197 019	**TW**	SM	*TW*	CH	131019	133019	
197 020	**TW**	SM	*TW*	CH	131020	133020	
197 021	**TW**	SM	*TW*	CH	131021	133021	
197 022	**TW**	SM			131022	133022	
197 023	**TW**	SM			131023	133023	
197 024	**TW**	SM			131024	133024	
197 025	**TW**	SM			131025	133025	
197 026	**TW**	SM			131026	133026	
197 027	**TW**	SM			131027	133027	
197 028	**TW**	SM			131028	133028	
197 029	**TW**	SM			131029	133029	
197 030	**TW**	SM			131030	133030	
197 031	**TW**	SM			131031	133031	
197 032	**TW**	SM			131032	133032	
197 033	**TW**	SM			131033	133033	
197 034	**TW**	SM			131034	133034	
197 035	**TW**	SM			131035	133035	
197 036	**TW**	SM			131036	133036	
197 037	**TW**	SM			131037	133037	
197 038	**TW**	SM			131038	133038	
197 039	**TW**	SM			131039	133039	
197 040	**TW**	SM			131040	133040	
197 041	**TW**	SM			131041	133041	
197 042	**TW**	SM	*TW*	CH	131042	133042	
197 043	**TW**	SM	*TW*	CH	131043	133043	
197 044	**TW**	SM	*TW*	CH	131044	133044	
197 045	**TW**	SM	*TW*	CH	131045	133045	
197 046	**TW**	SM	*TW*	CH	131046	133046	
197 047	**TW**	SM	*TW*	CH	131047	133047	
197 048	**TW**	SM	*TW*	CH	131048	133048	
197 049	**TW**	SM	*TW*	CH	131049	133049	Castell Caeriw Cyflym/ Carew Castle Express
197 050	**TW**	SM	*TW*	CH	131050	133050	
197 051	**TW**	SM	*TW*	CH	131051	133051	

Class 197/1. DMS–MS–DMS or DMS–MS–DMC. 3-car units.

DMS(A). CAF Beasain/Newport 2020–24. –/42(+6) 1TD 2W + catering area.
MS. CAF Beasain/Newport 2020–24. –/72(+3) 1T.
DMS(B). CAF Beasain/Newport 2020–24. –/74 (* DMC 16/42).

197 101	**TW**	SM	*TW*	CH	131101	132101	133101
197 102	**TW**	SM			131102	132102	133102
197 103	**TW**	SM			131103	132103	133103
197 104	**TW**	SM	*TW*	CH	131104	132104	133104
197 105	**TW**	SM	*TW*	CH	131105	132105	133105
197 106	**TW**	SM	*TW*	CH	131106	132106	133106
197 107	**TW**	SM	*TW*	CH	131107	132107	133107
197 108	**TW**	SM	*TW*	CH	131108	132108	133108
197 109	**TW**	SM	*TW*	CH	131109	132109	133109

197 110	**TW**	SM	*TW*	CH	131110	132110	133110
197 111	**TW**	SM	*TW*	CH	131111	132111	133111
197 112	**TW**	SM	*TW*	CH	131112	132112	133112
197 113	* **TW**	SM			131113	132113	133113
197 114	* **TW**	SM			131114	132114	133114
197 115	* **TW**	SM	*TW*	CH	131115	132115	133115
197 116	* **TW**	SM			131116	132116	133116
197 117	* **TW**	SM			131117	132117	133117
197 118	* **TW**	SM			131118	132118	133118
197 119	* **TW**	SM			131119	132119	133119
197 120	* **TW**	SM			131120	132120	133120
197 121	* **TW**	SM			131121	132121	133121
197 122	* **TW**	SM			131122	132122	133122
197 123	* **TW**	SM			131123	132123	133123
197 124	* **TW**	SM			131124	132124	133124
197 125	* **TW**	SM			131125	132125	133125
197 126	* **TW**	SM			131126	132126	133126

3.2. DIESEL ELECTRIC UNITS

CLASS 201/202   PRESERVED "HASTINGS" UNIT   BR

DMBS–TSL–TSL–TSRB–TSL–DMBS.

Preserved unit made up from various Class 201 short-frame cars and Class 202 long-frame cars. The "Hastings" units were made with narrow body-profiles for use on the section between Tonbridge and Battle which had tunnels of restricted loading gauge. These tunnels were converted to single track operation in the 1980s thus allowing standard loading gauge stock to be used. There are nine vehicles that are main line registered and the formation used can be flexible, but at the time of writing it was running in the 7-car formation shown. The set also contains a Class 411 EMU trailer (not Hastings line gauge) and a Class 422 EMU buffet car.

Construction: Steel.
Engine: One English Electric 4SRKT Mk. 2 of 450 kW (600 hp) at 850 rpm.
Main Generator: English Electric EE824.
Traction Motors: Two English Electric EE507 mounted on the inner bogie.
Bogies: SR Mk 4. (Former EMU TSL vehicles have Commonwealth bogies).
Couplers: Drophead buckeye.
Dimensions: 18.40 x 2.50 m (60000), 20.35 x 2.50 m (60116/118/119/528/529), 18.36 x 2.50 m (60501), 20.35 x 2.82 (69337), 20.30 x 2.82 (70262).
Gangways: Within unit only.   **Doors:** Manually operated slam.
Wheel arrangement: 2-Bo + 2-2 + 2-2 + 2-2- + 2-2- + Bo-2 + Bo-2.
Brakes: Electro-pneumatic and automatic air.
Maximum Speed: 75 mph.   **Seating Layout:** 2+2 facing.
Multiple Working: Other ex-BR Southern Region DEMU vehicles.

60000. DMBS. Lot No. 30329 Eastleigh 1957. –/22. 55.0 t.
60116. DMBS. Lot No. 30395 Eastleigh 1957. –/31. 56.0 t.

60118/119. DMBS. Lot No. 30395 Eastleigh 1957. –/30. 56.0 t.
60501. TSL. Lot No. 30331 Eastleigh 1957. –/52 2T. 29.5 t.
60528/529. TSL. Lot No. 30397 Eastleigh 1957. –/60 2T. 30.5 t.
69337. TSRB (ex-Class 422 EMU). Lot No. 30805 York 1970. –/40. 35.0 t.
70262. TSL (ex-Class 411/5 EMU). Lot No. 30455 Eastleigh 1958. –/64 2T. 31.5 t.

| 201 001 | **G** HD *HD* | SE | 60116 | 60529 | 70262 | 69337 | 60528 | 60118 | 60119 |
| Spares | **G** HD *HD* | SE | 60000 | 60501 | | | | | |

Names:

| 60000 | Hastings | 60118 | Tunbridge Wells |
| 60116 | Mountfield | | |

CLASS 220   VOYAGER   BOMBARDIER

DMS–MS–MS–DMF.

Construction: Steel.
Engine: Cummins QSK19 of 520 kW (700 hp) at 1800 rpm.
Transmission: Two Alstom Onix 800 three-phase traction motors of 275 kW.
Braking: Rheostatic and electro-pneumatic.
Bogies: Bombardier B5005.
Couplers: Dellner 12 at outer ends, bar within unit.
Dimensions: 23.85/23.00 x 2.73 m.
Gangways: Within unit only.
Wheel Arrangement: 1A-A1 + 1A-A1 + 1A-A1 + 1A-A1.
Doors: Single-leaf swing plug.
Maximum Speed: 125 m.p.h.
Seating Layout: 1: 2+1 facing/unidirectional, 2: 2+2 mainly unidirectional.
Multiple Working: Within class and with Classes 221 and 222 (in an emergency). Also can be controlled from Class 57/3 locomotives.

DMS. Bombardier Bruges/Wakefield 2000–01. –/42 1TD 1W. 51.1 t.
MS(A). Bombardier Bruges/Wakefield 2000–01. –/66. 45.9 t.
MS(B). Bombardier Bruges/Wakefield 2000–01. –/66 1TD. 46.7 t.
DMF. Bombardier Bruges/Wakefield 2000–01. 26/– 1TD 1W. 50.9 t.

220 001	**XC**	BN	*XC*	CZ	60301	60701	60201	60401
220 002	**XC**	BN	*XC*	CZ	60302	60702	60202	60402
220 003	**XC**	BN	*XC*	CZ	60303	60703	60203	60403
220 004	**XC**	BN	*XC*	CZ	60304	60704	60204	60404
220 005	**XC**	BN	*XC*	CZ	60305	60705	60205	60405
220 006	**XC**	BN	*XC*	CZ	60306	60706	60206	60406
220 007	**XC**	BN	*XC*	CZ	60307	60707	60207	60407
220 008	**XC**	BN	*XC*	CZ	60308	60708	60208	60408
220 009	**XC**	BN	*XC*	CZ	60309	60709	60209	60409
220 010	**XC**	BN	*XC*	CZ	60310	60710	60210	60410
220 011	**XC**	BN	*XC*	CZ	60311	60711	60211	60411
220 012	**XC**	BN	*XC*	CZ	60312	60712	60212	60412
220 013	**XC**	BN	*XC*	CZ	60313	60713	60213	60413
220 014	**XC**	BN	*XC*	CZ	60314	60714	60214	60414
220 015	**XC**	BN	*XC*	CZ	60315	60715	60215	60415
220 016	**XC**	BN	*XC*	CZ	60316	60716	60216	60416

220 017	**XC**	BN	*XC*	CZ	60317	60717	60217	60417
220 018	**XC**	BN	*XC*	CZ	60318	60718	60218	60418
220 019	**XC**	BN	*XC*	CZ	60319	60719	60219	60419
220 020	**XC**	BN	*XC*	CZ	60320	60720	60220	60420
220 021	**XC**	BN	*XC*	CZ	60321	60721	60221	60421
220 022	**XC**	BN	*XC*	CZ	60322	60722	60222	60422
220 023	**XC**	BN	*XC*	CZ	60323	60723	60223	60423
220 024	**XC**	BN	*XC*	CZ	60324	60724	60224	60424
220 025	**XC**	BN	*XC*	CZ	60325	60725	60225	60425
220 026	**XC**	BN	*XC*	CZ	60326	60726	60226	60426
220 027	**XC**	BN	*XC*	CZ	60327	60727	60227	60427
220 028	**XC**	BN	*XC*	CZ	60328	60728	60228	60428
220 029	**XC**	BN	*XC*	CZ	60329	60729	60229	60429
220 030	**XC**	BN	*XC*	CZ	60330	60730	60230	60430
220 031	**XC**	BN	*XC*	CZ	60331	60731	60231	60431
220 032	**XC**	BN	*XC*	CZ	60332	60732	60232	60432
220 033	**XC**	BN	*XC*	CZ	60333	60733	60233	60433
220 034	**XC**	BN	*XC*	CZ	60334	60734	60234	60434

Names:

220 009 Hixon January 6th 1968 | 220 016 VOYAGER20

CLASS 221   SUPER VOYAGER   BOMBARDIER

* DMS–MS–MS–MSRMB–DMF (Avanti West Coast or Grand Central units) or DMS–MS–(MS)–MS–DMF (CrossCountry units). Built as tilting units but tilt now isolated on CrossCountry sets.

Construction: Steel.
Engine: Cummins QSK19 of 520 kW (700 hp) at 1800 rpm.
Transmission: Two Alstom Onix 800 three-phase traction motors of 275 kW.
Braking: Rheostatic and electro-pneumatic.
Bogies: Bombardier HVP.
Couplers: Dellner 12 at outer ends, bar within unit.
Dimensions: 23.85/23.00 x 2.73 m.
Gangways: Within unit only.
Wheel Arrangement: 1A-A1 + 1A-A1 + 1A-A1 (+ 1A-A1) + 1A-A1.
Doors: Single-leaf swing plug.
Maximum Speed: 125 mph.
Seating Layout: 1: 2+1 facing/unidirectional, 2: 2+2 mainly unidirectional.
Multiple Working: Within class and with Classes 220 and 222 (in an emergency). Also can be controlled from Class 57/3 locomotives.

* Avanti West Coast or Grand Central units. MSRMB moved adjacent to the DMF. The seating in this vehicle (2+2 facing) can be used by First or Standard Class passengers depending on demand.

Non-standard livery: 221 142 and 221 143 **GC** livery on the driving cars only.

DMS. Bombardier Bruges/Wakefield 2001–02. –/42 1TD 1W. 58.5 t (* 58.9 t.)
60751–794 MS (* MSRMB). Bombardier Bruges/Wakefield 2001–02. –/66 (* –/52). 54.1 t (* 55.9 t.)

60951–994. MS. Bombardier Bruges/Wakefield 2001–02. –/66 1TD (* –/68 1TD). 54.8 t (* 54.3 t.)
60851–890. MS. Bombardier Bruges/Wakefield 2001–02. –/62 1TD (* –/68 1TD). 54.4 t (* 55.0 t.)
DMF. Bombardier Bruges/Wakefield 2001–02. 26/– 1TD 1W. 58.9 t (* 59.1 t.)

221 101	*	**VW**	BN	*AW*	CZ	60351	60951	60851	60751	60451
221 102	*	**AM**	BN	*AW*	CZ	60352	60952	60852	60752	60452
221 103	*	**AM**	BN	*AW*	CZ	60353	60953	60853	60753	60453
221 104	*	**AM**	BN	*AW*	CZ	60354	60954	60854	60754	60454
221 105	*	**AM**	BN	*AW*	CZ	60355	60955	60855	60755	60455
221 106	*	**AM**	BN	*AW*	CZ	60356	60956	60856	60756	60456
221 107	*	**AM**	BN	*AW*	CZ	60357	60957	60857	60757	60457
221 108	*	**AM**	BN	*AW*	CZ	60358	60958	60858	60758	60458
221 109	*	**AM**	BN	*AW*	CZ	60359	60959	60859	60759	60459
221 110	*	**AM**	BN	*AW*	CZ	60360	60960	60860	60760	60460
221 111	*	**AM**	BN	*AW*	CZ	60361	60961	60861	60761	60461
221 112	*	**AM**	BN	*AW*	CZ	60362	60962	60862	60762	60462
221 113	*	**AM**	BN	*AW*	CZ	60363	60963	60863	60763	60463
221 114	*	**AM**	BN	*AW*	CZ	60364	60964	60864	60764	60464
221 115	*	**AM**	BN	*AW*	CZ	60365	60965	60865	60765	60465
221 116	*	**AM**	BN	*AW*	CZ	60366	60966	60866	60766	60466
221 117	*	**AM**	BN	*AW*	CZ	60367	60967	60867	60767	60467
221 118	*	**AM**	BN	*AW*	CZ	60368	60968	60868	60768	60468
221 119		**XC**	BN	*XC*	CZ	60369	60769	60969	60869	60469
221 120		**XC**	BN	*XC*	CZ	60370	60770	60970	60870	60470
221 121		**XC**	BN	*XC*	CZ	60371	60771	60971	60871	60471
221 122		**XC**	BN	*XC*	CZ	60372	60772	60972	60872	60472
221 123		**XC**	BN	*XC*	CZ	60373	60773	60973	60873	60473
221 124		**XC**	BN	*XC*	CZ	60374	60774	60974	60874	60474
221 125		**XC**	BN	*XC*	CZ	60375	60775	60975	60875	60475
221 126		**XC**	BN	*XC*	CZ	60376	60776	60976	60876	60476
221 127		**XC**	BN	*XC*	CZ	60377	60777	60977	60877	60477
221 128		**XC**	BN	*XC*	CZ	60378	60778	60978	60878	60478
221 129		**XC**	BN	*XC*	CZ	60379	60779	60979	60879	60479
221 130		**XC**	BN	*XC*	CZ	60380	60780	60980	60880	60480
221 131		**XC**	BN	*XC*	CZ	60381	60781	60981	60881	60481
221 132		**XC**	BN	*XC*	CZ	60382	60782	60982	60882	60482
221 133		**XC**	BN	*XC*	CZ	60383	60783	60983	60883	60483
221 134		**XC**	BN	*XC*	CZ	60384	60784	60984	60884	60484
221 135		**XC**	BN	*XC*	CZ	60385	60785	60985	60885	60485
221 136		**XC**	BN	*XC*	CZ	60386	60786		60886	60486
221 137		**XC**	BN	*XC*	CZ	60387	60787	60987	60887	60487
221 138		**XC**	BN	*XC*	CZ	60388	60788	60988	60888	60488
221 139		**XC**	BN	*XC*	CZ	60389	60789	60989	60889	60489
221 140		**XC**	BN	*XC*	CZ	60390	60790		60890	60490
221 141		**XC**	BN	*XC*	CZ	60391	60791	60991		60491
221 142	*	**O**	BN	*GC*	XW	60392	60992	60986	60792	60492
221 143	*	**O**	BN	*GC*	XW	60393	60993	60994	60793	60493
221 144		**XC**	BN	*XC*	CZ	60394	60794	60990		60494

Names (carried on MS No. 609xx):

221 101   101 SQUADRON
221 114   ROYAL AIR FORCE CENTENARY 1918–2018
221 116   City of Bangor/Dinas Bangor *(alt. sides)*

CLASS 222   MERIDIAN   BOMBARDIER

Construction: Steel.
Engine: Cummins QSK19 of 560 kW (750 hp) at 1800 rpm.
Transmission: Two Alstom Onix 800 three-phase traction motors of 275 kW.
Braking: Rheostatic and electro-pneumatic.
Bogies: Bombardier B5005.   **Dimensions:** 23.85/23.00 x 2.73 m.
Couplers: Dellner at outer ends, bar within unit.
Gangways: Within unit only.   **Wheel Arrangement:** All cars 1A-A1.
Doors: Single-leaf swing plug.   **Maximum Speed:** 125 mph.
Seating Layout: 1: 2+1, 2: 2+2 facing/unidirectional.
Multiple Working: Within class and with Classes 220 and 221 (in an emergency).

222 001–004. 7-car units. DMF–MF–MF–MSRMB–MS–MS–DMS.

The 7-car units were built as 9-car units, before being reduced to 8-car sets and then later to 7-car sets to strengthen all 4-car units to 5-cars. 222 007 was built as a 9-car unit but later reduced to a 5-car unit. A further reforming programme planned in 2022 saw 7-cars 222 005/006 reduced to 5-cars to enable 222 101–104 to be augmented from 4-cars to 5-cars.

DMRF. Bombardier Bruges 2004–05. 22/– 1TD 1W. 52.8 t.
MF. Bombardier Bruges 2004–05. 42/– 1T. 46.8 t.
MSRMB. Bombardier Bruges 2004–05. –/62. 48.0 t.
MS. Bombardier Bruges 2004–05. –/68 1T. 47.0 t.
DMS. Bombardier Bruges 2004–05. –/38 1TD 1W. 49.4 t.

222 001	**EI**	E	*EM*	DY	60241	60445	60341	60621
					60561	60551	60161	
222 002	**EI**	E	*EM*	DY	60242	60346	60342	60622
					60562	60544	60162	
222 003	**EI**	E	*EM*	DY	60243	60446	60343	60623
					60563	60553	60163	
222 004	**EI**	E	*EM*	DY	60244	60345	60344	60624
					60564	60554	60164	

Names (carried on MSRMB):

222 001   THE ENTREPRENEUR EXPRESS
222 002   THE CUTLERS' COMPANY
222 004   CHILDREN'S HOSPITAL SHEFFIELD

222 005–023. 5-car units. DMF–MC–MSRMB–MS–DMS (or DMF–MF–MSRMB–MS–DMS).

DMRF. Bombardier Bruges 2003–04. 22/– 1TD 1W. 52.8 t.
MC. Bombardier Bruges 2003–04. 28/22 1T. 48.6 t.
MF. Bombardier Bruges 2004–05. 42/– 1T. 46.8 t.

MSRMB. Bombardier Bruges 2003–04. –/62. 49.6 t.
MS. Bombardier Bruges 2004–05. –/68 1T. 47.0 t.
DMS. Bombardier Bruges 2003–04. –/40 1TD 1W. 51.0 t.

222 005	**EI**	E	*EM*	DY	60245	60347	60625	60565	60165
222 006	**EI**	E	*EM*	DY	60246	60447	60626	60556	60166
222 007	**EI**	E	*EM*	DY	60247	60442	60627	60567	60167
222 008	**EI**	E	*EM*	DY	60248	60918	60628	60545	60168
222 009	**EI**	E	*EM*	DY	60249	60919	60629	60557	60169
222 010	**EI**	E	*EM*	DY	60250	60920	60630	60546	60170
222 011	**EI**	E	*EM*	DY	60251	60921	60631	60531	60171
222 012	**EI**	E	*EM*	DY	60252	60922	60632	60532	60172
222 013	**EI**	E	*EM*	DY	60253	60923	60633	60533	60173
222 014	**EI**	E	*EM*	DY	60254	60924	60634	60534	60174
222 015	**EI**	E	*EM*	DY	60255	60925	60635	60535	60175
222 016	**EI**	E	*EM*	DY	60256	60926	60636	60536	60176
222 017	**EI**	E	*EM*	DY	60257	60927	60637	60537	60177
222 018	**EI**	E	*EM*	DY	60258	60928	60638	60444	60178
222 019	**EI**	E	*EM*	DY	60259	60929	60639	60547	60179
222 020	**EI**	E	*EM*	DY	60260	60930	60640	60543	60180
222 021	**EI**	E	*EM*	DY	60261	60931	60641	60552	60181
222 022	**EI**	E	*EM*	DY	60262	60932	60642	60542	60182
222 023	**EI**	E	*EM*	DY	60263	60933	60643	60541	60183

Names (carried on MSRMB or DMS):

222 006 THE CARBON CUTTER
222 008 Derby Etches Park
222 015 175 YEARS OF DERBY'S RAILWAYS 1839–2014
222 022 INVEST IN NOTTINGHAM

222 101–104. 5-car former Hull Trains units. Extended from 4-cars to 5-cars in 2022. 222 101/102 DMF–MC–MSRMB–MS–DMS and 222 103/104 DMF–MF–MC–MSRMB–DMS.

DMRF. Bombardier Bruges 2005. 22/– 1TD 1W. 52.8 t.
MC 60571–574. Bombardier Bruges 2005. 11/46 1T. 47.1 t.
MF 60441/443. Bombardier Bruges 2004–05. 42/– 1T. 46.8 t.
MSRMB 60681–684. Bombardier Bruges 2005. –/62. 48.0 t.
MS 60555/566. Bombardier Bruges 2004–05. –/68 1T. 47.0 t.
DMS. Bombardier Bruges 2005. –/40 1TD 1W. 49.4 t.

222 101	**EI**	E	*EM*	DY	60271	60571	60681	60555	60191
222 102	**EI**	E	*EM*	DY	60272	60572	60682	60566	60192
222 103	**EI**	E	*EM*	DY	60273	60443	60573	60683	60193
222 104	**ER**	E	*EM*	DY	60274	60441	60574	60684	60194

CLASS 230 D-TRAIN METRO-CAMMELL/VIVARAIL

The Class 230 D-Train is a DEMU, diesel-battery or battery unit rebuilt from former London Underground D78 Stock by Vivarail. The original D-Train used the bodyshells, bogies and electric traction motors of D78 Stock. Instead of being powered by electricity the motors are instead powered by new underfloor-mounted diesel engines: two per driving car. Modern IGBT electronic controls replaced the previous mechanical camshaft controllers, incorporating automotive stop-start technology and dynamic braking.

230001 was a prototype unit and was followed by 230002, a prototype diesel-battery hybrid that has since been exported to the USA. West Midlands Trains ordered three diesel sets (230003–005) for use on the Bedford–Bletchley Marston Vale Line from spring 2019, but these were stored after Vivarail went into admnistration in 2022 and have since been acquired by Great Western Railway. This was followed by an order by Transport for Wales for five 3-car diesel-battery hybrid sets (230006–010) for the Wrexham–Bidston line.

In 2021 original prototype diesel unit 230001 was rebuilt as a fast-charge battery demonstrator unit and it is to be introduced onto the GWR West Ealing–Greenford shuttle in 2024.

South Western Railway also has five straight electric sets that it uses on the Isle of Wight (Class 484).

Construction: Aluminium.
Engines/batteries: 230001: 3 x 84kWh Hoppecke batteries in each driving car. 230003–005: 2 x Ford Duratorq 3.2 litre diesel engines of 150kW (200hp) per car. 230 006–010: 4 x Ford Duratorq 3.2 litre diesel engines in centre cars and 2 x 100kWh Hoppecke batteries in each driving car.
Traction motors: TSA TMW 32-43-4 AC motors of 135 kW.
Control System: IGBT Inverter.   **Braking:** Rheostatic & Dynamic.
Bogies: Bombardier FLEXX1000 flexible-frame.
Dimensions: 18.37/18.12 x 2.84 m.
Couplers: LUL automatic wedgelock. **Gangways:** Within unit only.
Wheel Arrangement: Bo-Bo + Bo-Bo or to be advised.
Doors: Sliding.   **Maximum Speed:** 60 mph.
Seating Layout: Longitudinal or 2+2 facing.
Multiple Working: Within class.

Rebuilt from former London Underground D78 Stock 2016–20. Original D78 numbers are shown alongside the new running numbers.

Class 230/0. Prototype fast-charge battery unit. Refitted with a low density seating layout for demonstration purposes.

DMS(A). Metro-Cammell Birmingham 1979–83. –/28. 38.8 t.
TS. Metro-Cammell Birmingham 1979–83. –/34(+5) 1TD 2W. 20.7 t.
DMS(B). Metro-Cammell Birmingham 1979–83. –/32. 38.8 t.

230 001   **GW** GW   LM   300001 (7058) 300201 (17058) 300101 (7511)

Name (carried on 300001): Viva Venturer

Class 230/0. Former West Midlands Trains diesel units. Following Vivarail entering administration in late 2022 these units were taken out of service.

DMS(A). Metro-Cammell Birmingham 1979–83. –/58(+2). 33.3 t.
DMS(B). Metro-Cammell Birmingham 1979–83. –/40(+7) 1TD 2W. 32.3 t.

230 003	**LN** GW	RG	300003 (7069)		300103 (7127)
230 004	**LN** GW	RG	300004 (7100)		300104 (7500)
230 005	**LN** GW	RG	300005 (7066)		300105 (7128)

Class 230/0. Transport for Wales diesel-battery units. Unit weight 99.75 t.

DMS(A). Metro-Cammell Birmingham 1979–83. –/46(+2).
MS. Metro-Cammell Birmingham 1979–83. –/50(+2).
DMS(B). Metro-Cammell Birmingham 1979–83. –/33(+6) 1TD 2W. 35.0 t.

230 006	**TW** TW *TW*	BD	300006 (7098)	300206 (17066)	300106 (7510)
230 007	**TW** TW *TW*	BD	300007 (7103)	300207 (17063)	300107 (7529)
230 008	**TW** TW *TW*	BD	300008 (7120)	300208 (17050)	300108 (7065)
230 009	**TW** TW *TW*	BD	300009 (7055)	300209 (17084)	300109 (7523)
230 010	**TW** TW *TW*	BD	300010 (7090)	300210 (17071)	300110 (7017)

CLASS 231   FLIRT DMU   STADLER

DMS–TS–PP–TS–DMS. New articulated Transport for Wales FLIRT DMUs for the Cheltenham–Maesteg and Cardiff–Ebbw Vale lines featuring a centre power pack housing diesel engines (with no passenger accommodation in this vehicle) similar to the Greater Anglia Class 755. Air conditioned. Initially in service on the Rhymney Valley line.

Construction: Aluminium.
Engines: Four Deutz V8 of 480 kW (645 hp).
Bogies: Stadler/Jacobs.
Couplers: Dellner 10.
Dimensions: 21.05/15.70/7.20 (PP) m x 2.72.2.82 (PP) m.
Gangways: Within unit.   **Wheel Arrangement:** Bo-2-2-2-2-Bo.
Doors: Sliding plug.   **Maximum Speed:** 90 mph.
Seating Layout: 2+2 unidirectional/facing.
Multiple Working: Within class only.

DMS(A). Stadler Bussnang 2021–22. –/40(+12). 39.5 t.
TS(A). Stadler Bussnang 2021–22. –/52(+10). 24.4 t.
PP. Stadler Bussnang 2021–22. 28.5 t.
TS(B). Stadler Bussnang 2021–22. –/38(+5) 1TD 2W. 25.4 t.
DMS(B). Stadler Bussnang 2021–22. –/40(+12). 39.9 t.

231 001	**TW** SM *TW*	CF	381001	381201	381401	381301	381101
231 002	**TW** SM *TW*	CF	381002	381202	381402	381302	381102
231 003	**TW** SM *TW*	CF	381003	381203	381403	381303	381103
231 004	**TW** SM *TW*	CF	381004	381204	381404	381304	381104
231 005	**TW** SM *TW*	CF	381005	381205	381405	381305	381105
231 006	**TW** SM *TW*	CF	381006	381206	381406	381306	381106
231 007	**TW** SM *TW*	CF	381007	381207	381407	381307	381107

231 008	**TW**	SM	*TW*	CF	381008	381208	381408	381308	381108
231 009	**TW**	SM	*TW*	CF	381009	381209	381409	381309	381109
231 010	**TW**	SM	*TW*	CF	381010	381210	381410	381310	381110
231 011	**TW**	SM	*TW*	CF	381011	381211	381411	381311	381111

Name (carried on both driving cars): 231 001   Sultan

3.3. DMU VEHICLES IN INDUSTRIAL SERVICE

This list comprises DMU vehicles that have been withdrawn from active service but continue to be used in industrial service (such as for use in education establishments or for emergency training).

142 033	55574	55624	South Wales Police RFC Ground, Waterton Cross, Bridgend
142 043	55584	55634	Sussex Police Training Centre, Kingstanding, near Crowborough
142 045	55586	55636	Kirk Merrington Primary School, Co. Durham
144 002	55802	55825	The Dales School Blyth
144 010	55810	55833	East Lancashire Railway (reserved for Greater Manchester Fire & Rescue)

55801	(ex-144 001)	Airedale Hospital, Keighley
55808	(ex-144 008)	Fagley Primary School, Bradford
55824	(ex-144 001)	Platform 1, Huddersfield Station

4. ELECTRIC MULTIPLE UNITS

INTRODUCTION

This section contains details of all Electric Multiple Units, usually referred to as EMUs, which can run on Britain's national railway network.

The number of EMUs in operation has been steadily increasing in recent years as both more lines have been opened or have been electrified and as the number of passengers travelling on the network has increased. EMUs work a wide variety of services, from long distance Intercity (such as the Class 390 Pendolinos) to inter-urban and suburban duties.

LAYOUT OF INFORMATION

25 kV AC 50 Hz overhead EMUs and dual voltage EMUs are listed in numerical order of set numbers. Individual "loose" vehicles are listed in numerical order after vehicles formed into fixed formations.

750 V DC third rail EMUs are listed in numerical order of class number, then in numerical order of set number. Some of these use the former Southern Region four-digit set numbers. These are derived from theoretical six digit set numbers which are the four-digit set number prefixed by the first two numbers of the class.

Where sets or vehicles have been renumbered in recent years, former numbering detail is shown alongside current detail. Each entry is laid out as in the following example:

Set No.	Detail	Livery	Owner	Operator	Allocation	Formation
377120	s	**SN**	P	*SN*	SU	78520 77120 78920 78720

Codes: Codes are used to denote the livery, owner, operator and depot allocation of each Electric Multiple Unit. Details of these can be found in section 6 of this book. Where a unit or spare car is off-lease, the operator column is left blank.

Detail Differences: Detail differences which currently affect the areas and types of train which vehicles may work are shown, plus differences in interior layout. Where such differences occur within a class, these are shown either in the heading information or alongside the individual set or vehicle number.

Set Formations: Regular set formations are shown where these are normally maintained. Readers should note set formations might be temporarily varied from time to time to suit maintenance and/or operational requirements. Vehicles shown as "Spare" are not formed in any regular set formation.

Names: Only names carried with official sanction are listed. Names are shown in UPPER/lower case characters as actually shown on the name carried on the vehicle(s). Unless otherwise shown, complete units are regarded as named rather than just the individual car(s) which carry the name.

GENERAL INFORMATION

CLASSIFICATION AND NUMBERING

25kV AC 50Hz overhead and "Versatile" EMUs are classified in the series 300–399. 750 V DC third rail EMUs are classified in the series 400–599. More recently dual-voltage units have been numbered in the 700+ series and Hitachi IEP design units in the 800+ series. Most of the Class 8xx units are bi-mode units which can operate under both diesel or electric power. The hydrogen demonstrator unit (ex-Class 314) has been reserved Class 614 and the new units for the Tyne & Wear Metro, which shares Network Rail tracks in places, have been allocated Class 555.

Until 2014 EMU individual cars were numbered in the series 61000–78999, except for vehicles used on the Isle of Wight – which are numbered in a separate series, and the Class 378s, 380s and 395s, which took up the 38xxx and 39xxx series'.

For all new vehicles allocated by the Rolling Stock Library since 2014 6-digit vehicle numbers have been used.

Any vehicle constructed or converted to replace another vehicle following accident damage and carrying the same number as the original vehicle is denoted by the suffix[II] in this publication

WHEEL ARRANGEMENT

A system whereby the number of powered axles on a bogie or frame is denoted by a letter (A = 1, B = 2, C= 3 etc) and the number of unpowered axles is denoted by a number is used in this publication. The letter "o" after a letter indicates that each axle is individually powered.

UNITS OF MEASUREMENT

Principal details and dimensions are quoted for each class in metric and/or imperial units as considered appropriate bearing in mind common UK usage.

All dimensions and weights are quoted for vehicles in an "as new" condition with all necessary supplies (eg oil, water, sand) on board. Dimensions are quoted in the order Length – Width. All lengths quoted are over buffers or couplers as appropriate. Where two lengths are quoted, the first refers to outer vehicles in a set and the second to inner vehicles. All width dimensions quoted are maxima. All weights are shown as metric tonnes (t = tonnes).

Bogie Types are quoted in the format motored/non-motored (eg BP20/BT13 denotes BP20 motored bogies and BT non-motored bogies).

Unless noted to the contrary, all vehicles listed have bar couplers at non-driving ends.

Unless stated, traction motors power details refer to each motored car per unit.

Vehicles ordered under the auspices of BR were allocated a Lot (batch) number when ordered and these are quoted in class headings and sub-headings. Vehicles ordered since 1995 have no Lot Numbers, but the manufacturer and location that they were built is given.

OPERATING CODES

These codes are used by train operating company staff to describe the various different types of vehicles and normally appear on data panels on the inner (ie non driving) ends of vehicles.

A "B" prefix indicates a battery vehicle.
A "P" prefix indicates a trailer vehicle on which is mounted the pantograph, instead of the default case where the pantograph is mounted on a motor vehicle.

The first part of the code describes whether or not the car has a motor or a driving cab as follows:

DM Driving motor   DT Driving trailer   M Motor   T Trailer

The next letter is a "B" for cars with a brake compartment.
This is followed by the saloon details:

F   First   S Standard   C Composite   V Van

The next letter denotes the style of accommodation, which is "O" for Open for all EMU vehicles still in service.

Finally, vehicles with a buffet or kitchen area are suffixed RB or RMB for a miniature buffet counter.

Where two vehicles of the same type are formed within the same unit, the above codes may be suffixed by (A) and (B) to differentiate between vehicles.

A composite is a vehicle containing both First and Standard Class accommodation, whilst a brake vehicle is a vehicle containing separate specific accommodation for the conductor.

ACCOMMODATION

The information given in class headings and sub-headings is in the form F/S nT (or TD) nW. For example, 12/54 1T 1W denotes 12 First Class and 54 Standard Class seats, one toilet and one space for a wheelchair. A number in brackets (ie (+2)) denotes tip-up seats (in addition to the fixed seats). The seating layout of open saloons is indicated as 2+1, 2+2 or 3+2. Where units have First Class accommodation as well as Standard Class and the layout is different for each class then these are shown separately prefixed by "1:" and "2:".

TD denotes a universal access toilet suitable for use by people with disabilities. By law all trains should have been fitted with such facilities by the start of 2020. All EMUs still in service are now fitted, or have been retrofitted, with a universal access toilet (this is not applicable for those suburban units that do not have toilet facilities).

4.1. 25 kV AC 50 Hz OVERHEAD & DUAL VOLTAGE UNITS

Except where otherwise stated, all units in this section operate on 25 kV AC 50 Hz overhead only.

CLASS 318   BREL YORK

Outer suburban units.

Formation: DTS–MS–DTS.
Construction: Steel.
Traction Motors: Four Brush TM 2141 of 268 kW.
Wheel Arrangement: 2-2 + Bo-Bo + 2-2.
Braking: Disc.   **Dimensions:** 19.83/19.92 x 2.82 m.
Bogies: BP20 (MS), BT13 (others).   **Couplers:** Tightlock.
Gangways: Within unit.   **Control System:** Thyristor.
Doors: Sliding.   **Maximum Speed:** 90 mph.
Seating Layout: 3+2 facing.
Multiple Working: Within class & with Classes 317, 319, 320, 321 and 323.

77240–259. DTS. Lot No. 30999 1985–86. –/55 1TD 2W. 32.0 t.
77288. DTS. Lot No. 31020 1987. –/55 1TD 2W. 32.0 t.
62866–885. MS. Lot No. 30998 1985–86. –/79. 53.0 t.
62890. MS. Lot No. 31019 1987. –/79. 53.0 t.
77260–279. DTS. Lot No. 31000 1985–86. –/69(+2). 31.6 t.
77289. DTS. Lot No. 31021 1987. –/69(+2). 31.6 t.

318 250	**SR**	E	*SR*	GW	77240	62866	77260
318 251	**SR**	E	*SR*	GW	77241	62867	77261
318 252	**SR**	E	*SR*	GW	77242	62868	77262
318 253	**SR**	E	*SR*	GW	77243	62869	77263
318 254	**SR**	E	*SR*	GW	77244	62870	77264
318 255	**SR**	E	*SR*	GW	77245	62871	77265
318 256	**SR**	E	*SR*	GW	77246	62872	77266
318 257	**SR**	E	*SR*	GW	77247	62873	77267
318 258	**SR**	E	*SR*	GW	77248	62874	77268
318 259	**SR**	E	*SR*	GW	77249	62875	77269
318 260	**SR**	E	*SR*	GW	77250	62876	77270
318 261	**SR**	E	*SR*	GW	77251	62877	77271
318 262	**SR**	E	*SR*	GW	77252	62878	77272
318 263	**SR**	E	*SR*	GW	77253	62879	77273
318 264	**SR**	E	*SR*	GW	77254	62880	77274
318 265	**SR**	E	*SR*	GW	77255	62881	77275
318 266	**SR**	E	*SR*	GW	77256	62882	77276
318 267	**SR**	E	*SR*	GW	77257	62883	77277
318 268	**SR**	E	*SR*	GW	77258	62884	77278
318 269	**SR**	E	*SR*	GW	77259	62885	77279
318 270	**SR**	E	*SR*	GW	77288	62890	77289

CLASS 319   BREL YORK

Express and outer suburban units. Units shown * or † have a universal access toilet. All Class 319s had been withdrawn from passenger service by early 2024, but some units have been rebuilt as bi-modes (see Class 769 and Class 799) or converted to parcels units for Orion (see Class 768).

Formation: Various, see sub-class headings.
Systems: 25 kV AC overhead/750 V DC third rail.
Construction: Steel.
Traction Motors: Four GEC G315BZ of 268 kW.
Wheel Arrangement: 2-2 + Bo-Bo + 2-2 + 2-2.
Braking: Disc.   **Dimensions:** 20.17/20.16 x 2.82 m.
Bogies: P7-4 (MS), T3-7 (others).   **Couplers:** Tightlock.
Gangways: Within unit + end doors. **Control System:** GTO chopper.
Doors: Sliding.   **Maximum Speed:** 100 mph.
Seating Layout: Various, see sub-class headings.
Multiple Working: Within class & with Classes 317, 318, 320, 321 and 323.

Class 319/0. DTS–MS–TS–DTS.

Seating Layout: 3+2 facing.

DTS(A). Lot No. 31022 (odd nos.) 1987–88. –/82. 28.2 t.
MS. Lot No. 31023 1987–88. –/82. 49.2 t.
TS. Lot No. 31024 1987–88. –/77 2T. 31.0 t.
DTS(B). Lot No. 31025 (even nos.) 1987–88. –/78. 28.1 t.

319011		**TL**	P		ZG		77311	62901	71782	77310

Class 319/2. DTS–MS–TS–DTC. Units converted from Class 319/0.

Seating Layout: 1: 2+1 facing, 2: 2+2/3+2 facing.

DTS. Lot No. 31022 (odd nos.) 1987–88. –/64. 30.0 t.
MS. Lot No. 31023 1987–88. –/73. 51.0 t.
TS. Lot No. 31024 1987–88. –/52 1TD 1T. 31.0 t.
DTC. Lot No. 31025 (even nos.) 1987–88. 18/36. 30.0 t.

319214	*	**TL**	P		NN		77317	62904	71785	77316

Class 319/3. DTS–MS–TS–DTS. Converted from Class 319/1.

Refurbished with a new universal access toilet except 319373, which has been converted for carrying parcels and roller-cages for Orion (it was originally due to be renumbered 326001).
Seating Layout: 3+2 facing.

DTS(A). Lot No. 31063 1990. –/79. 29.0 t.
MS. Lot No. 31064 1990. –/81. 50.6 t.
TS. Lot No. 31065 1990. –/64 1TD 2W. 31.0 t.
DTS(B). Lot No. 31066 1990. –/79. 29.7 t.

319363	*	**NR**	P	LM	77463	63045	71931	77462
319369	*	**NR**	P	AN	77475	63051	71937	77474
319371	*	**NR**	P	LM	77479	63053	71939	77478
319373		**ON**	P	CN	77483	63055	71941	77482
319377	*	**NR**	P	ZG	77491	63059	71945	77490
319379	*	**NR**	P	AN	77495	63061	71947	77494
319380	*	**NR**	P	ZG	77497	63062	71948	77496
319386	*	**NR**	P	AN	77983	63098	71984	77984

Class 319/4. DTC–MS–TS–DTS. Converted from Class 319/0. Refurbished with carpets. DTS(A) converted to composite.

319424/431/434/442/448/450/456/458 were converted to Class 769 bi-mode units for Northern.

319421/445/452 were converted to Class 769 bi-mode units for Transport for Wales. 319426 was rejected from this programme.

319422/423/425/427/428/430/432/435–440/443/444/446/447/449/459 were converted to Class 769 tri-mode units for Great Western Railway.

Non-standard livery: 319454 Porterbrook Innovation Hub (blue).

Seating Layout: 1: 2+1 facing 2: 2+2/3+2 facing.

77331–381. DTC. Lot No. 31022 (odd nos.) 1987–88. 12/51 (* 12/50). 30.0t (* 31.0 t).
77431–457. DTC. Lot No. 31038 (odd nos.) 1988. 12/51 (* 12/50). 30.0t (* 31.0 t).
62911–936. MS. Lot No. 31023 1987–88. –/74 (* –/75). 49.2 t (* 52.4 t).
62961–974. MS. Lot No. 31039 1988. –/74 (* –/75). 49.2 t (* 52.4 t).
71792–817. TS. Lot No. 31024 1987–88. –/67 2T (* –/58 1TD 2W). 31.0 t (* 33.7 t).
71866–879. TS. Lot No. 31040 1988. –/67 2T (* –/58 1TD 2W). 31.0 t (* 33.7 t).
77330–380. DTS. Lot No. 31025 (even nos.) 1987–88. –/71 1W (* –/73). 28.1t (* 30.7 t).
77430–456. DTS. Lot No. 31041 (even nos.) 1988. –/71 1W (* –/73). 28.1t (* 30.7 t).

319426	*	**NR**	P	ZN	77341	62916	71797	77290
319433	*	**LM**	P	NN	77355	62923	71804	77354
319441	*	**LM**	P	CN	77371	62931	71812	77370
319454		**O**	P	LM	77445	62968	71873	77444
319457	*	**LM**	P	NN	77451	62971	71876	77450

CLASS 320   BREL YORK

Suburban units. In 2016–19 ScotRail received 320 401/403/404/411–418/420 (ex-Class 321s) which were refurbished and reformed as 3-cars.

Formation: DTS–MS–DTS.
Construction: Steel
Traction Motors: Four Brush TM2141B of 268 kW.
Wheel Arrangement: 2-2 + Bo-Bo + 2-2.

Braking: Disc.	**Dimensions:** 19.95 x 2.82 m.
Bogies: P7-4 (MS), T3-7 (others).	**Couplers:** Tightlock.
Gangways: Within unit.	**Control System:** Thyristor.
Doors: Sliding.	**Maximum Speed:** 90 mph.

Seating Layout: 3+2 facing.
Multiple Working: Within class & with Classes 317, 318, 319, 321 and 323.

Class 320/3. Original build.

DTS(A). Lot No. 31060 1990. –/51(+4) 1TD 2W. 31.7 t.
MS. Lot No. 31062 1990. –/78. 52.6 t.
DTS(B). Lot No. 31061 1990. –/73(+2). 31.6 t.

320301	**SR**	E	*SR*	GW	77899	63021	77921
320302	**SR**	E	*SR*	GW	77900	63022	77922
320303	**SR**	E	*SR*	GW	77901	63023	77923
320304	**SR**	E	*SR*	GW	77902	63024	77924
320305	**SR**	E	*SR*	GW	77903	63025	77925
320306	**SR**	E	*SR*	GW	77904	63026	77926
320307	**SR**	E	*SR*	GW	77905	63027	77927
320308	**SR**	E	*SR*	GW	77906	63028	77928
320309	**SR**	E	*SR*	GW	77907	63029	77929
320310	**SR**	E	*SR*	GW	77908	63030	77930
320311	**SR**	E	*SR*	GW	77909	63031	77931
320312	**SR**	E	*SR*	GW	77910	63032	77932
320313	**SR**	E	*SR*	GW	77911	63033	77933
320314	**SR**	E	*SR*	GW	77912	63034	77934
320315	**SR**	E	*SR*	GW	77913	63035	77935
320316	**SR**	E	*SR*	GW	77914	63036	77936
320317	**SR**	E	*SR*	GW	77915	63037	77937
320318	**SR**	E	*SR*	GW	77916	63038	77938
320319	**SR**	E	*SR*	GW	77917	63039	77939
320320	**SR**	E	*SR*	GW	77918	63040	77940
320321	**SR**	E	*SR*	GW	77919	63041	77941
320322	**SR**	E	*SR*	GW	77920	63042	77942

Class 320/4. Former London Midland Class 321s reduced to 3-car formation and refurbished as Class 320/4s by Wabtec Doncaster/Kilmarnock 2015–19.

The original vehicles 71966 and 77960 from 321 418 (now 320 418) and 78114 and 63082 from 321 420 (now 320 420) were written off after the Watford Junction accident in 1996. The undamaged vehicles were formed together as 321 418 whilst four new vehicles were built in 1997, taking the same numbers as the scrapped vehicles, and these became the second 321 420.

DTS(A). Lot No. 31060 1990. –/54(+4) 1TD 2W. 32.0 t.
MS. Lot No. 31062 1990. –/79. 52.2 t.
DTS(B). Lot No. 31061 1990. –/74(+2). 32.0 t.

320401	(321401)	**SR**	E	*SR*	GW	78095	63063	77943
320403	(321403)	**SR**	E	*SR*	GW	78097	63065	77945
320404	(321404)	**SR**	E	*SR*	GW	78098	63066	77946
320411	(321411)	**SR**	E	*SR*	GW	78105	63073	77953
320412	(321412)	**SR**	E	*SR*	GW	78106	63074	77954
320413	(321413)	**SR**	E	*SR*	GW	78107	63075	77955
320414	(321414)	**SR**	E	*SR*	GW	78108	63076	77956
320415	(321415)	**SR**	E	*SR*	GW	78109	63077	77957
320416	(321416)	**SR**	E	*SR*	GW	78110	63078	77958
320417	(321417)	**SR**	E	*SR*	GW	78111	63079	77959
320418	(321418)	**SR**	E	*SR*	GW	78112	63080	77962
320420	(321420)	**SR**	E	*SR*	GW	78114[II]	63082[II]	77960[II]

CLASS 321   BREL YORK

Outer suburban units. All Class 321s have now been withdrawn from passenger service, but a number of units have been converted to carry parcels.

Formation: DTC (DTS on Class 321/9)–MS–TS–DTS.
Construction: Steel.
Traction Motors: Four Brush TM2141C of 268 kW (* Four TSA010163 AC motors of 300 kW).
Wheel Arrangement: 2-2 + Bo-Bo + 2-2 + 2-2.
Braking: Disc (* and regenerative).   **Dimensions:** 19.95 x 2.82 m.
Bogies: P7-4 (MS), T3-7 (others).   **Couplers:** Tightlock.
Gangways: Within unit.
Control System: Thyristor (* IGBT Inverter).
Doors: Sliding.   **Maximum Speed:** 100 mph.
Seating Layout: 1: 2+2 facing, 2: 3+2 facing.
Multiple Working: Within class & with Classes 317, 318, 319, 320, and 323.

† Converted to a freight carrying unit with all seats removed.

Class 321/3.

* "Renatus" rebuilt units with completely new interiors, air conditioning and Quantum seating, still arranged to a 3+2 layout in Standard Class. Fitted with new TSA AC traction motors.

Non-standard livery: 321 334 Swift Express Freight (dark blue).

DTC. Lot No. 31053 1988–90. 16/57 (* 16/31(+4) 1TD 2W. 29.7 t (* 34.1 t).
MS. Lot No. 31054 1988–90. –/82 (* –/80). 51.5 t (* 53.8 t).
TS. Lot No. 31055 1988–90. –/75 2T (* –/78 1T). 29.1 t (* 31.7 t).
DTS. Lot No. 31056 1988–90. –/78 (* –/76). 29.7 t (* 32.8 t.)

321301	*	**GR**	E		WB	78049	62975	71880	77853
321302	*	**GR**	E		WA	78050	62976	71881	77854
321303	*	**GR**	E		WB	78051	62977	71882	77855
321304	*	**GR**	E		WB	78052	62978	71883	77856
321305	*	**GR**	E		IL	78053	62979	71884	77857
321306	*	**GR**	E		WA	78054	62980	71885	77858
321307	*	**GR**	E		WA	78055	62981	71886	77859
321308	*	**GR**	E		WA	78056	62982	71887	77860
321309	*	**GR**	E		WB	78057	62983	71888	77861
321310	*	**GR**	E		WB	78058	62984	71889	77862
321311	*	**GR**	E		WA	78059	62985	71890	77863
321312	*	**GR**	E		WA	78060	62986	71891	77864
321313	*	**GR**	E		WB	78061	62987	71892	77865
321314	*	**GR**	E		WA	78062	62988	71893	77866
321315	*	**GR**	E		WB	78063	62989	71894	77867
321316	*	**GR**	E		WB	78064	62990	71895	77868
321317	*	**GR**	E		WB	78065	62991	71896	77869
321318	*	**GR**	E		WB	78066	62992	71897	77870
321319	*	**GR**	E		WA	78067	62993	71898	77871
321320	*	**GR**	E		WA	78068	62994	71899	77872
321321	*	**GR**	E		IL	78069	62995	71900	77873
321322	*	**GR**	E		WB	78070	62996	71901	77874
321323	*	**GR**	E		WB	78071	62997	71902	77875
321324	*	**GR**	E		WB	78072	62998	71903	77876
321325	*	**GR**	E		WB	78073	62999	71904	77877
321326	*	**GR**	E		WA	78074	63000	71905	77878
321327	*	**GR**	E		WB	78075	63001	71906	77879
321328	*	**GR**	E		WB	78076	63002	71907	77880
321329	*	**GR**	E		WB	78077	63003	71908	77881
321330	*	**GR**	E		WB	78078	63004	71909	77882
321332		**NC**	E		ZN	78080	63006	71911	77884
321334	†	**O**	E	VA	GW	78082	63008	71913	77886
321337		**NC**	E		WS	78085	63011	71916	77889
321338		**NC**	E		ZN	78086	63012	71917	77890
321339		**NC**	E		ZN	78087	63013	71918	77891
321341		**NC**	E		ZN	78089	63015	71920	77893
321342		**NC**	E		ZN	78090	63016	71921	77894

Class 321/4.

DTC. Lot No. 31067 1989–90. 28/40 (321 421–436 16/52, 321 439–444 16/56). 29.8 t.
MS. Lot No. 31068 1989–90. –/79 (321 439–444 –/82). 51.6 t.
TS. Lot No. 31069 1989–90. –/74 2T (321 439–444 –/75 2T). 29.2 t.
DTS. Lot No. 31070 1989–90. –/78. 29.8 t.

321407	†	**FB**	E	*VA*	GW	78101	63069	71955	77949
321419	†	**FB**	E	*VA*	GW	78113	63081	71967	77961
321428		**NX**	E		ZN	78122	63090	71976	77970
321429		**NX**	E		ZN	78123	63091	71977	77971
321434		**NC**	ER		YA	78154	63128	72014	78303
321440		**GA**	E		WS	78160	63134	72020	78309
321443		**GA**	E		GA	78125	63099	71985	78274

CLASS 323 HUNSLET TRANSPORTATION PROJECTS

Suburban units.

Formation: DMS–PTS–DMS.
Construction: Welded aluminium alloy.
Traction Motors: Four Holec DMKT 52/24 asynchronous of 146 kW.
Wheel Arrangement: Bo-Bo + 2-2 + Bo-Bo.
Braking: Disc & regenerative.   **Dimensions:** 23.37/23.44 x 2.80 m.
Bogies: SRP BP62 (DMS), BT52 (PTS). **Couplers:** Tightlock.
Gangways: Within unit.   **Control System:** IGBT Inverter.
Doors: Sliding plug.   **Maximum Speed:** 90 mph.
Seating Layout: 3+2 facing/unidirectional.
Multiple Working: Within class & with Classes 317, 318, 319, 320 and 321.

DMS(B) vehicles 65003 and 65005 in 323 203/205 and 65019 and 65021 in 323 219/221 switched between units following accident damage and were not returned to their original sets, instead swapping numbers.

DMS(A). Lot No. 31112 Hunslet 1992–93. –/97. 41.0 t.
TS. Lot No. 31113 Hunslet 1992–93. –/81(+3) 1TD 2W. 39.3t.
DMS(B). Lot No. 31114 Hunslet 1992–93. –/97. 41.0 t.

323201	**WI**	P	*WM*	SO	64001	72201	65001
323202	**WI**	P	*WM*	SO	64002	72202	65002
323203	**WI**	P	*WM*	SO	64003	72203	65003
323204	**WI**	P	*WM*	SO	64004	72204	65004
323205	**WI**	P	*WM*	SO	64005	72205	65005
323206	**WI**	P	*WM*	SO	64006	72206	65006
323207	**WI**	P	*WM*	SO	64007	72207	65007
323208	**WI**	P	*NO*	AN	64008	72208	65008
323209	**WI**	P	*WM*	SO	64009	72209	65009
323210	**WI**	P	*WM*	SO	64010	72210	65010
323211	**WI**	P	*WM*	SO	64011	72211	65011
323212	**WI**	P	*WM*	SO	64012	72212	65012
323213	**WI**	P	*WM*	SO	64013	72213	65013
323214	**WI**	P	*WM*	SO	64014	72214	65014

323215	**WI**	P	*WM*	SO	64015	72215	65015
323216	**WI**	P	*WM*	SO	64016	72216	65016
323217	**WI**	P	*WM*	SO	64017	72217	65017
323218	**WI**	P	*WM*	SO	64018	72218	65018
323219	**WI**	P	*WM*	SO	64019	72219	65019
323220	**WI**	P	*WM*	SO	64020	72220	65020
323221	**CO**	P	*WM*	SO	64021	72221	65021
323222	**WI**	P	*WM*	SO	64022	72222	65022
323223	**NR**	P	*NO*	AN	64023	72223	65023
323224	**NR**	P	*NO*	AN	64024	72224	65024
323225	**NR**	P	*NO*	AN	64025	72225	65025
323226	**NR**	P	*NO*	AN	64026	72226	65026
323227	**NR**	P	*NO*	AN	64027	72227	65027
323228	**NR**	P	*NO*	AN	64028	72228	65028
323229	**NR**	P	*NO*	AN	64029	72229	65029
323230	**NR**	P	*NO*	AN	64030	72230	65030
323231	**NR**	P	*NO*	AN	64031	72231	65031
323232	**NR**	P	*NO*	AN	64032	72232	65032
323233	**NR**	P	*NO*	AN	64033	72233	65033
323234	**NR**	P	*NO*	AN	64034	72234	65034
323235	**NR**	P	*NO*	AN	64035	72235	65035
323236	**NR**	P	*NO*	AN	64036	72236	65036
323237	**NR**	P	*NO*	AN	64037	72237	65037
323238	**NR**	P	*NO*	AN	64038	72238	65038
323239	**NR**	P	*NO*	AN	64039	72239	65039
323240	**WI**	P	*WM*	SO	64040	72340	65040
323241	**WI**	P	*WM*	SO	64041	72341	65041
323242	**WI**	P	*WM*	SO	64042	72342	65042
323243	**WI**	P	*WM*	SO	64043	72343	65043

Names (carried on one side of TS):

323201	Duddeston	323215	Gravelly Hill
323202	Butlers Lane	323216	University
323203	Aston	323217	Chester Road
323204	Selly Oak	323218	Lichfield City
323205	Blake Street	323219	Kings Norton
323206	Barnt Green	323220	Lichfield Trent Valley
323207	Bournville	323222	Redditch
323209	Birmingham New Street	323240	Erdington
323210	Shenstone	323241	Dave Pomroy 323 Fleet
323211	Four Oaks		Engineer 40 Years Service
323212	Bromsgrove	323242	Alvechurch
323213	Sutton Coldfield	323243	Longbridge
323214	Wylde Green		

CLASS 325   ABB DERBY

Postal units based on Class 319s. Compatible with diesel or electric locomotive haulage. Built for dual voltage use, but 750 V DC third rail shoe gear has been removed as it is not required on current duties.

Formation: DTPMV–MPMV–TPMV–DTPMV.
System: 25 kV AC overhead.
Construction: Steel.
Traction Motors: Four GEC G315BZ of 268 kW.
Wheel Arrangement: 2-2 + Bo-Bo + 2-2 + 2-2.
Braking: Disc.   **Dimensions:** 19.33 x 2.82 m.
Bogies: P7-4 (MPMV), T3-7 (others).   **Couplers:** Drop-head buckeye.
Gangways: None.   **Control System:** GTO Chopper.
Doors: Roller shutter.   **Maximum Speed:** 100 mph.
Multiple Working: Within class.

DTPMV. Lot No. 31144 1995. 29.1 t.
MPMV. Lot No. 31145 1995. 49.5 t.
TPMV. Lot No. 31146 1995. 30.7 t.

325001	**RM**	RM	*DB*	CE	68300	68340	68360	68301
325002	**RM**	RM	*DB*	CE	68302	68341	68361	68303
325003	**RM**	RM	*DB*	CE	68304	68342	68362	68305
325004	**RM**	RM	*DB*	CE	68306	68343	68363	68307
325005	**RM**	RM	*DB*	CE	68308	68344	68364	68309
325006	**RM**	RM	*DB*	CE	68310	68345	68365	68311
325007	**RM**	RM	*DB*	CE	68312	68346	68366	68313
325008	**RM**	RM	*DB*	CE	68314	68347	68367	68315
325009	**RM**	RM	*DB*	CE	68316	68349	68368	68317
325011	**RM**	RM	*DB*	CE	68320	68350	68370	68321
325012	**RM**	RM	*DB*	CE	68322	68351	68371	68323
325013	**RM**	RM	*DB*	CE	68324	68352	68372	68325
325014	**RM**	RM	*DB*	CE	68326	68353	68373	68327
325015	**RM**	RM	*DB*	CE	68328	68354	68374	68329
325016	**RM**	RM	*DB*	CE	68330	68355	68375	68331

Name (carried on one side of each DTPMV):

325008   Peter Howarth CBE

CLASS 331   CIVITY   CAF

New Northern outer suburban units.

Formation: DMS–PTS–DMS or DMS–PTS–TS–DMS.
Construction: Aluminium.
Traction Motors: Four TSA asynchronous of 220 kW.
Wheel Arrangement: Bo-Bo + 2-2 + Bo-Bo or Bo-Bo + 2-2 + 2-2 + Bo-Bo.
Braking: Disc & regenerative.   **Dimensions:** 24.03/23.35 x 2.55 m.
Bogies: CAF.   **Couplers:** Dellner.
Gangways: Within unit.   **Control System:** IGBT Inverter.
Doors: Sliding plug.   **Maximum Speed:** 100 mph.
Heating & ventilation: Air conditioning.
Seating: 2+2 facing/unidirectional.   **Multiple Working:** Within class.

Class 331/0. DMS–PTS–DMS. 3-car units.

DMS. CAF Zaragoza/Newport 2017–20. –/45(+8) 1TD 2W. 40.8 t.
PTS. CAF Zaragoza/Newport 2017–20. –/76(+4). 34.9 t.
DMS. CAF Zaragoza/Newport 2017–20. –/63(+7), 39.8 t.

331001	**NR**	E	NO	NL	463001	464001	466001
331002	**NR**	E	NO	NL	463002	464002	466002
331003	**NR**	E	NO	NL	463003	464003	466003
331004	**NR**	E	NO	NL	463004	464004	466004
331005	**NR**	E	NO	NL	463005	464005	466005
331006	**NR**	E	NO	NL	463006	464006	466006
331007	**NR**	E	NO	NL	463007	464007	466007
331008	**NR**	E	NO	NL	463008	464008	466008
331009	**NR**	E	NO	NL	463009	464009	466009
331010	**NR**	E	NO	AN	463010	464010	466010
331011	**NR**	E	NO	AN	463011	464011	466011
331012	**NR**	E	NO	AN	463012	464012	466012
331013	**NR**	E	NO	AN	463013	464013	466013
331014	**NR**	E	NO	AN	463014	464014	466014
331015	**NR**	E	NO	AN	463015	464015	466015
331016	**NR**	E	NO	AN	463016	464016	466016
331017	**NR**	E	NO	AN	463017	464017	466017
331018	**NR**	E	NO	AN	463018	464018	466018
331019	**NR**	E	NO	AN	463019	464019	466019
331020	**NR**	E	NO	AN	463020	464020	466020
331021	**NR**	E	NO	AN	463021	464021	466021
331022	**NR**	E	NO	AN	463022	464022	466022
331023	**NR**	E	NO	AN	463023	464023	466023
331024	**NR**	E	NO	AN	463024	464024	466024
331025	**NR**	E	NO	AN	463025	464025	466025
331026	**NR**	E	NO	AN	463026	464026	466026
331027	**NR**	E	NO	AN	463027	464027	466027
331028	**NR**	E	NO	AN	463028	464028	466028
331029	**NR**	E	NO	AN	463029	464029	466029
331030	**NR**	E	NO	AN	463030	464030	466030
331031	**NR**	E	NO	AN	463031	464031	466031

Class 331/1. DMS–PTS–TS–DMS. 4-car units.

DMS. CAF Zaragoza/Newport 2017–19. –/45(+8) 1TD 2W. 40.8 t.
PTS. CAF Zaragoza/Newport 2017–19. –/76(+4). 34.9 t.
TS. CAF Zaragoza/Newport 2017–19. –/76(+4). 30.1 t.
DMS. CAF Zaragoza/Newport 2017–19. –/63(+7). 39.8 t.

331 101	**NR**	E	*NO*	AN	463101	464101	465101	466101
331 102	**NR**	E	*NO*	AN	463102	464102	465102	466102
331 103	**NR**	E	*NO*	AN	463103	464103	465103	466103
331 104	**NR**	E	*NO*	AN	463104	464104	465104	466104
331 105	**NR**	E	*NO*	AN	463105	464105	465105	466105
331 106	**NR**	E	*NO*	AN	463106	464106	465106	466106
331 107	**NR**	E	*NO*	AN	463107	464107	465107	466107
331 108	**NR**	E	*NO*	AN	463108	464108	465108	466108
331 109	**NR**	E	*NO*	AN	463109	464109	465109	466109
331 110	**NR**	E	*NO*	AN	463110	464110	465110	466110
331 111	**NR**	E	*NO*	AN	463111	464111	465111	466111
331 112	**NR**	E	*NO*	AN	463112	464112	465112	466112

Names (carried on driving cars):

331 106	Proud to be Northern	331 110	Proud to be Northern

CLASS 333   CAF/SIEMENS

West Yorkshire area suburban units.

Formation: DMS–PTS–TS–DMS.
Construction: Steel.
Traction Motors: Two Siemens monomotors asynchronous of 350 kW.
Wheel Arrangement: B-B + 2-2 + 2-2 + B-B.
Braking: Disc.   **Dimensions:** 23.74/23.35 x 2.75 m.
Bogies: CAF.   **Couplers:** Dellner 10L.
Gangways: Within unit.   **Control System:** IGBT Inverter.
Doors: Sliding plug.   **Maximum Speed:** 100 mph.
Heating & ventilation: Air conditioning. **Multiple Working:** Within class.
Seating Layout: 3+2 facing/unidirectional.

333001–008 were made up to 4-car units from 3-car units in 2002.

333009–016 were made up to 4-car units from 3-car units in 2003.

DMS(A). (odd Nos.) CAF Zaragoza 2001. –/90. 50.0 t.
PTS. CAF Zaragoza 2001. –/73(+7) 1TD 2W. 46.0 t.
TS. CAF Zaragoza 2002–03. –/100. 38.5 t.
DMS(B). (even Nos.) CAF Zaragoza 2001. –/90. 50.0 t.

333001	**NR**	A	*NO*	NL	78451	74461	74477	78452
333002	**NR**	A	*NO*	NL	78453	74462	74478	78454
333003	**NR**	A	*NO*	NL	78455	74463	74479	78456
333004	**NR**	A	*NO*	NL	78457	74464	74480	78458
333005	**NR**	A	*NO*	NL	78459	74465	74481	78460
333006	**NR**	A	*NO*	NL	78461	74466	74482	78462
333007	**NR**	A	*NO*	NL	78463	74467	74483	78464

333008	**NR**	A	*NO*	NL	78465	74468	74484	78466
333009	**NR**	A	*NO*	NL	78467	74469	74485	78468
333010	**NR**	A	*NO*	NL	78469	74470	74486	78470
333011	**NR**	A	*NO*	NL	78471	74471	74487	78472
333012	**NR**	A	*NO*	NL	78473	74472	74488	78474
333013	**NR**	A	*NO*	NL	78475	74473	74489	78476
333014	**NR**	A	*NO*	NL	78477	74474	74490	78478
333015	**NR**	A	*NO*	NL	78479	74475	74491	78480
333016	**NR**	A	*NO*	NL	78481	74476	74492	78482

CLASS 334   JUNIPER   ALSTOM BIRMINGHAM

Outer suburban units.

Formation: DMS–PTS–DMS.
Construction: Steel.
Traction Motors: Two Alstom ONIX 800 asynchronous of 270 kW.
Wheel Arrangement: 2-Bo + 2-2 + Bo-2.

Braking: Disc.	**Dimensions:** 21.01/19.94 x 2.80 m.
Bogies: Alstom LTB3/TBP3.	**Couplers:** Dellner.
Gangways: Within unit.	**Control System:** IGBT Inverter.
Doors: Sliding plug.	**Maximum Speed:** 90 mph.

Heating & ventilation: Air conditioning.
Seating Layout: 2+2 facing/unidirectional (3+2 in PTS).
Multiple Working: Within class.

Non-standard livery: 334006 Pride celebration colours (vehicle 64106).

DMS(A). Alstom Birmingham 1999–2001. –/64. 42.6 t.
PTS. Alstom Birmingham 1999–2001. –/55 1TD 1W. 39.4 t.
DMS(B). Alstom Birmingham 1999–2001. –/59(+3). 42.6 t.

334001	**SR**	E	*SR*	GW	64101	74301	65101
334002	**SR**	E	*SR*	GW	64102	74302	65102
334003	**SR**	E	*SR*	GW	64103	74303	65103
334004	**SR**	E	*SR*	GW	64104	74304	65104
334005	**SR**	E	*SR*	GW	64105	74305	65105
334006	**0**	E	*SR*	GW	64106	74306	65106
334007	**SR**	E	*SR*	GW	64107	74307	65107
334008	**SR**	E	*SR*	GW	64108	74308	65108
334009	**SR**	E	*SR*	GW	64109	74309	65109
334010	**SR**	E	*SR*	GW	64110	74310	65110
334011	**SR**	E	*SR*	GW	64111	74311	65111
334012	**SR**	E	*SR*	GW	64112	74312	65112
334013	**SR**	E	*SR*	GW	64113	74313	65113
334014	**SR**	E	*SR*	GW	64114	74314	65114
334015	**SR**	E	*SR*	GW	64115	74315	65115
334016	**SR**	E	*SR*	GW	64116	74316	65116
334017	**SR**	E	*SR*	GW	64117	74317	65117
334018	**SR**	E	*SR*	GW	64118	74318	65118
334019	**SR**	E	*SR*	GW	64119	74319	65119
334020	**SR**	E	*SR*	GW	64120	74320	65120

334 021	**SR**	E	*SR*	GW	64121	74321	65121
334 022	**SR**	E	*SR*	GW	64122	74322	65122
334 023	**SR**	E	*SR*	GW	64123	74323	65123
334 024	**SR**	E	*SR*	GW	64124	74324	65124
334 025	**SR**	E	*SR*	GW	64125	74325	65125
334 026	**SR**	E	*SR*	GW	64126	74326	65126
334 027	**SR**	E	*SR*	GW	64127	74327	65127
334 028	**SR**	E	*SR*	GW	64128	74328	65128
334 029	**SR**	E	*SR*	GW	64129	74329	65129
334 030	**SR**	E	*SR*	GW	64130	74330	65130
334 031	**SR**	E	*SR*	GW	64131	74331	65131
334 032	**SR**	E	*SR*	GW	64132	74332	65132
334 033	**SR**	E	*SR*	GW	64133	74333	65133
334 034	**SR**	E	*SR*	GW	64134	74334	65134
334 035	**SR**	E	*SR*	GW	64135	74335	65135
334 036	**SR**	E	*SR*	GW	64136	74336	65136
334 037	**SR**	E	*SR*	GW	64137	74337	65137
334 038	**SR**	E	*SR*	GW	64138	74338	65138
334 039	**SR**	E	*SR*	GW	64139	74339	65139
334 040	**SR**	E	*SR*	GW	64140	74340	65140

CLASS 345   AVENTRA   BOMBARDIER DERBY

These 9-car units are used on London's Crossrail (now branded as the Elizabeth Line), the core section of which opened in 2022. The design was marketed as "Aventra" by Bombardier and is a development of the successful Electrostar design. Some units initially operated as 7-car sets.

Formation: DMS–PMS–MS–MS–TS–MS–MS–PMS–DMS.
System: 25 kV AC overhead.
Construction: Aluminium.
Traction Motors: Two Bombardier asynchronous of 265 kW.
Wheel Arrangement: 2-Bo + Bo-2 + Bo-Bo + Bo-2 + 2-2 + 2-Bo + Bo-Bo + 2-Bo + Bo-2.
Braking: Disc & regenerative.   **Dimensions:** 23.62/22.50 m x 2.78 m.
Bogies: FLEXX B5000 inside-frame.   **Couplers:** Dellner.
Gangways: Within unit.   **Control System:** IGBT Inverter.
Doors: Sliding plug (three per vehicle). **Maximum Speed:** 90 mph.
Heating & ventilation: Air conditioning.
Seating Layout: Mostly longitudinal, with some 2+2 facing.
Multiple Working: Within class.

Non-standard livery: 345 055 Pride celebration colours (driving cars).

DMS(A). Bombardier Derby 2015–19. –/46. 39.0 t.
PMS(A). Bombardier Derby 2015–19. –/46(+6). 37.1 t.
MS(A). Bombardier Derby 2015–19. –/46(+6). 36.5 t.
MS(B). Bombardier Derby 2015–19. –/49(+3). 31.4 t.
TS. Bombardier Derby 2015–19. –/38(+12). 29.7 t.
MS(C). Bombardier Derby 2015–19. –/49(+3). 31.4 t.
MS(D). Bombardier Derby 2015–19. –/46(+6). 37.2 t.

PMS(B). Bombardier Derby 2015–19. –/46(+6). 37.1 t.
DMS(B). Bombardier Derby 2015–19. –/46. 39.0 t.

345001	**XR**	RF	*EL*	OC	340101	340201	340301	340401	340501
					340601	340701	340801	340901	
345002	**XR**	RF	*EL*	OC	340102	340202	340302	340402	340502
					340602	340702	340802	340902	
345003	**XR**	RF	*EL*	OC	340103	340203	340303	340403	340503
					340603	340703	340803	340903	
345004	**XR**	RF	*EL*	OC	340104	340204	340304	340404	340504
					340604	340704	340804	340904	
345005	**XR**	RF	*EL*	OC	340105	340205	340305	340405	340505
					340605	340705	340805	340905	
345006	**XR**	RF	*EL*	OC	340106	340206	340306	340406	340506
					340606	340706	340806	340906	
345007	**XR**	RF	*EL*	OC	340107	340207	340307	340407	340507
					340607	340707	340807	340907	
345008	**XR**	RF	*EL*	OC	340108	340208	340308	340408	340508
					340608	340708	340808	340908	
345009	**XR**	RF	*EL*	OC	340109	340209	340309	340409	340509
					340609	340709	340809	340909	
345010	**XR**	RF	*EL*	OC	340110	340210	340310	340410	340510
					340610	340710	340810	340910	
345011	**XR**	RF	*EL*	OC	340111	340211	340311	340411	340511
					340611	340711	340811	340911	
345012	**XR**	RF	*EL*	OC	340112	340212	340312	340412	340512
					340612	340712	340812	340912	
345013	**XR**	RF	*EL*	OC	340113	340213	340313	340413	340513
					340613	340713	340813	340913	
345014	**XR**	RF	*EL*	OC	340114	340214	340314	340414	340514
					340614	340714	340814	340914	
345015	**XR**	RF	*EL*	OC	340115	340215	340315	340415	340515
					340615	340715	340815	340915	
345016	**XR**	RF	*EL*	OC	340116	340216	340316	340416	340516
					340616	340716	340816	340916	
345017	**XR**	RF	*EL*	OC	340117	340217	340317	340417	340517
					340617	340717	340817	340917	
345018	**XR**	RF	*EL*	OC	340118	340218	340318	340418	340518
					340618	340718	340818	340918	
345019	**XR**	RF	*EL*	OC	340119	340219	340319	340419	340519
					340619	340719	340819	340919	
345020	**XR**	RF	*EL*	OC	340120	340220	340320	340420	340520
					340620	340720	340820	340920	
345021	**XR**	RF	*EL*	OC	340121	340221	340321	340421	340521
					340621	340721	340821	340921	
345022	**XR**	RF	*EL*	OC	340122	340222	340322	340422	340522
					340622	340722	340822	340922	
345023	**XR**	RF	*EL*	OC	340123	340223	340323	340423	340523
					340623	340723	340823	340923	
345024	**XR**	RF	*EL*	OC	340124	340224	340324	340424	340524
					340624	340724	340824	340924	

345 025	**XR**	RF	*EL*	OC	340125	340225	340325	340425	340525
					340625	340725	340825	340925	
345 026	**XR**	RF	*EL*	OC	340126	340226	340326	340426	340526
					340626	340726	340826	340926	
345 027	**XR**	RF	*EL*	OC	340127	340227	340327	340427	340527
					340627	340727	340827	340927	
345 028	**XR**	RF	*EL*	OC	340128	340228	340328	340428	340528
					340628	340728	340828	340928	
345 029	**XR**	RF	*EL*	OC	340129	340229	340329	340429	340529
					340629	340729	340829	340929	
345 030	**XR**	RF	*EL*	OC	340130	340230	340330	340430	340530
					340630	340730	340830	340930	
345 031	**XR**	RF	*EL*	OC	340131	340231	340331	340431	340531
					340631	340731	340831	340931	
345 032	**XR**	RF	*EL*	OC	340132	340232	340332	340432	340532
					340632	340732	340832	340932	
345 033	**XR**	RF	*EL*	OC	340133	340233	340333	340433	340533
					340633	340733	340833	340933	
345 034	**XR**	RF	*EL*	OC	340134	340234	340334	340434	340534
					340634	340734	340834	340934	
345 035	**XR**	RF	*EL*	OC	340135	340235	340335	340435	340535
					340635	340735	340835	340935	
345 036	**XR**	RF	*EL*	OC	340136	340236	340336	340436	340536
					340636	340736	340836	340936	
345 037	**XR**	RF	*EL*	OC	340137	340237	340337	340437	340537
					340637	340737	340837	340937	
345 038	**XR**	RF	*EL*	OC	340138	340238	340338	340438	340538
					340638	340738	340838	340938	
345 039	**XR**	RF	*EL*	OC	340139	340239	340339	340439	340539
					340639	340739	340839	340939	
345 040	**XR**	RF	*EL*	OC	340140	340240	340340	340440	340540
					340640	340740	340840	340940	
345 041	**XR**	RF	*EL*	OC	340141	340241	340341	340441	340541
					340641	340741	340841	340941	
345 042	**XR**	RF	*EL*	OC	340142	340242	340342	340442	340542
					340642	340742	340842	340942	
345 043	**XR**	RF	*EL*	OC	340143	340243	340343	340443	340543
					340643	340743	340843	340943	
345 044	**XR**	RF	*EL*	OC	340144	340244	340344	340444	340544
					340644	340744	340844	340944	
345 045	**XR**	RF	*EL*	OC	340145	340245	340345	340445	340545
					340645	340745	340845	340945	
345 046	**XR**	RF	*EL*	OC	340146	340246	340346	340446	340546
					340646	340746	340846	340946	
345 047	**XR**	RF	*EL*	OC	340147	340247	340347	340447	340547
					340647	340747	340847	340947	
345 048	**XR**	RF	*EL*	OC	340148	340248	340348	340448	340548
					340648	340748	340848	340948	
345 049	**XR**	RF	*EL*	OC	340149	340249	340349	340449	340549
					340649	340749	340849	340949	

345050	**XR**	RF	*EL*	OC	340150	340250	340350	340450	340550
					340650	340750	340850	340950	
345051	**XR**	RF	*EL*	OC	340151	340251	340351	340451	340551
					340651	340751	340851	340951	
345052	**XR**	RF	*EL*	OC	340152	340252	340352	340452	340552
					340652	340752	340852	340952	
345053	**XR**	RF	*EL*	OC	340153	340253	340353	340453	340553
					340653	340753	340853	340953	
345054	**XR**	RF	*EL*	OC	340154	340254	340354	340454	340554
					340654	340754	340854	340954	
345055	**0**	RF	*EL*	OC	340155	340255	340355	340455	340555
					340655	340755	340855	340955	
345056	**XR**	RF	*EL*	OC	340156	340256	340356	340456	340556
					340656	340756	340856	340956	
345057	**XR**	RF	*EL*	OC	340157	340257	340357	340457	340557
					340657	340757	340857	340957	
345058	**XR**	RF	*EL*	OC	340158	340258	340358	340458	340558
					340658	340758	340858	340958	
345059	**XR**	RF	*EL*	OC	340159	340259	340359	340459	340559
					340659	340759	340859	340959	
345060	**XR**	RF	*EL*	OC	340160	340260	340360	340460	340560
					340660	340760	340860	340960	
345061	**XR**	RF	*EL*	OC	340161	340261	340361	340461	340561
					340661	340761	340861	340961	
345062	**XR**	RF	*EL*	OC	340162	340262	340362	340462	340562
					340662	340762	340862	340962	
345063	**XR**	RF	*EL*	OC	340163	340263	340363	340463	340563
					340663	340763	340863	340963	
345064	**XR**	RF	*EL*	OC	340164	340264	340364	340464	340564
					340664	340764	340864	340964	
345065	**XR**	RF	*EL*	OC	340165	340265	340365	340465	340565
					340665	340765	340865	340965	
345066	**XR**	RF	*EL*	OC	340166	340266	340366	340466	340566
					340666	340766	340866	340966	
345067	**XR**	RF	*EL*	OC	340167	340267	340367	340467	340567
					340667	340767	340867	340967	
345068	**XR**	RF	*EL*	OC	340168	340268	340368	340468	340568
					340668	340768	340868	340968	
345069	**XR**	RF	*EL*	OC	340169	340269	340369	340469	340569
					340669	340769	340869	340969	
345070	**XR**	RF	*EL*	OC	340170	340270	340370	340470	340570
					340670	340770	340870	340970	

Names:

345004	Andy Byford
345024	Heidi Alexander

CLASS 350   DESIRO UK   SIEMENS

Outer suburban and long distance units. All now Standard Class only.

Formation: DMC–TC–PTS–DMC.
Systems: 25 kV AC overhead (350/1s built with 750 V DC, but equipment currently decommissioned).
Construction: Welded aluminium.
Traction Motors: 4 Siemens 1TB2016-0GB02 asynchronous of 250 kW.
Wheel Arrangement: Bo-Bo + 2-2 + 2-2 + Bo-Bo.

Braking: Disc & regenerative.	**Dimensions:** 20.34 x 2.79 m.
Bogies: SGP SF5000.	**Couplers:** Dellner 12.
Gangways: Throughout.	**Control System:** IGBT Inverter.
Doors: Sliding plug.	**Maximum Speed:** 110 mph.

Heating & ventilation: Air conditioning.
Seating Layout: Various, see sub-class headings.
Multiple Working: Within class.

Class 350/1. Original-build units owned by Angel Trains. Formerly part of an aborted South West Trains 5-car Class 450/2 order. 2+2 seating.

Seating Layout: 2+2 facing/unidirectional.

Advertising liveries:

350 104 Eurovision (various colours).
350 108 Anti-trespass rail safety (pink/blue – vehicle 63768).

DMS(A). Siemens Krefeld 2004–05. –/60. 48.7 t.
TS. Siemens Krefeld/Prague 2004–05. –/56 1T. 36.2 t.
PTS. Siemens Krefeld/Prague 2004–05. –/50(+9) 1TD 2W. 45.2 t.
DMS(B). Siemens Krefeld 2004–05. –/60. 49.2 t.

350 101	**LN**	A	*WM*	NN	63761	66811	66861	63711
350 102	**LN**	A	*WM*	NN	63762	66812	66862	63712
350 103	**LN**	A	*WM*	NN	63765	66813	66863	63713
350 104	**AL**	A	*WM*	NN	63764	66814	66864	63714
350 105	**LN**	A	*WM*	NN	63763	66815	66868	63715
350 106	**LN**	A	*WM*	NN	63766	66816	66866	63716
350 107	**LN**	A	*WM*	NN	63767	66817	66867	63717
350 108	**AL**	A	*WM*	NN	63768	66818	66865	63718
350 109	**LN**	A	*WM*	NN	63769	66819	66869	63719
350 110	**LN**	A	*WM*	NN	63770	66820	66870	63720
350 111	**LN**	A	*WM*	NN	63771	66821	66871	63721
350 112	**LN**	A	*WM*	NN	63772	66822	66872	63722
350 113	**LN**	A	*WM*	NN	63773	66823	66873	63723
350 114	**LN**	A	*WM*	NN	63774	66824	66874	63724
350 115	**LN**	A	*WM*	NN	63775	66825	66875	63725
350 116	**LN**	A	*WM*	NN	63776	66826	66876	63726
350 117	**LN**	A	*WM*	NN	63777	66827	66877	63727
350 118	**LN**	A	*WM*	NN	63778	66828	66878	63728
350 119	**LN**	A	*WM*	NN	63779	66829	66879	63729
350 120	**LN**	A	*WM*	NN	63780	66830	66880	63730
350 121	**LN**	A	*WM*	NN	63781	66831	66881	63731

350 122	**LN**	A	*WM*	NN	63782	66832	66882	63732
350 123	**LN**	A	*WM*	NN	63783	66833	66883	63733
350 124	**LN**	A	*WM*	NN	63784	66834	66884	63734
350 125	**LN**	A	*WM*	NN	63785	66835	66885	63735
350 126	**LN**	A	*WM*	NN	63786	66836	66886	63736
350 127	**LN**	A	*WM*	NN	63787	66837	66887	63737
350 128	**LN**	A	*WM*	NN	63788	66838	66888	63738
350 129	**LN**	A	*WM*	NN	63789	66839	66889	63739
350 130	**LN**	A	*WM*	NN	63790	66840	66890	63740

Class 350/2. Owned by Porterbrook Leasing.

Seating Layout: 3+2 facing/unidirectional (former First Class area 2+2).

350 233/246/264 are running with misformed formations, as shown.

DMS(A). Siemens Krefeld 2008–09. –/70. 43.7 t.
TS. Siemens Prague 2008–09. /66 1T. 35.3 t.
PTS. Siemens Prague 2008–09. –/61(+9) 1TD 2W. 42.9 t.
DMS(B). Siemens Krefeld 2008–09. –/70. 44.2 t.

350 231	**LI**	P	*WM*	NN	61431	65231	67531	61531
350 232	**LI**	P	*WM*	NN	61432	65232	67532	61532
350 233	**LM**	P	*WM*	NN	61433	65233	67533	61546
350 234	**LI**	P	*WM*	NN	61434	65234	67534	61534
350 235	**LM**	P	*WM*	NN	61435	65235	67535	61535
350 236	**LM**	P	*WM*	NN	61436	65236	67536	61536
350 237	**LM**	P	*WM*	NN	61437	65237	67537	61537
350 238	**LM**	P	*WM*	NN	61438	65238	67538	61538
350 239	**LI**	P	*WM*	NN	61439	65239	67539	61539
350 240	**LI**	P	*WM*	NN	61440	65240	67540	61540
350 241	**LM**	P	*WM*	NN	61441	65241	67541	61541
350 242	**LM**	P	*WM*	NN	61442	65242	67542	61542
350 243	**LM**	P	*WM*	NN	61443	65243	67543	61543
350 244	**LI**	P	*WM*	NN	61444	65244	67544	61544
350 245	**LI**	P	*WM*	NN	61445	65245	67545	61545
350 246	**LM**	P	*WM*	NN	61446	65246	67546	61564
350 247	**LM**	P	*WM*	NN	61447	65247	67547	61547
350 248	**LM**	P	*WM*	NN	61448	65248	67548	61548
350 249	**LM**	P	*WM*	NN	61449	65249	67549	61549
350 250	**LM**	P	*WM*	NN	61450	65250	67550	61550
350 251	**LM**	P	*WM*	NN	61451	65251	67551	61551
350 252	**LI**	P	*WM*	NN	61452	65252	67552	61552
350 253	**LI**	P	*WM*	NN	61453	65253	67553	61553
350 254	**LI**	P	*WM*	NN	61454	65254	67554	61554
350 255	**LM**	P	*WM*	NN	61455	65255	67555	61555
350 256	**LM**	P	*WM*	NN	61456	65256	67556	61556
350 257	**LI**	P	*WM*	NN	61457	65257	67557	61557
350 258	**LI**	P	*WM*	NN	61458	65258	67558	61558
350 259	**LI**	P	*WM*	NN	61459	65259	67559	61559
350 260	**LM**	P	*WM*	NN	61460	65260	67560	61560
350 261	**LM**	P	*WM*	NN	61461	65261	67561	61561
350 262	**LI**	P	*WM*	NN	61462	65262	67562	61562

350263	LI	P	WM	NN	61463	65263	67563	61563
350264	LM	P	WM	NN	61464	65264	67564	61533
350265	LM	P	WM	NN	61465	65265	67565	61565
350266	LM	P	WM	NN	61466	65266	67566	61566
350267	LI	P	WM	NN	61467	65267	67567	61567

Class 350/3. Owned by Angel Trains.

Seating Layout: 2+2 facing/unidirectional.

DMS(A). Siemens Krefeld 2014. –/60. 44.2 t.
TS. Siemens Krefeld 2014. –/60 1T. 36.3 t.
PTS. Siemens Krefeld 2014. –/50(+9) 1TD 2W. 44.0 t.
DMS(B). Siemens Krefeld 2014. –/60. 45.0 t.

350368	LN	A	WM	NN	60141	60511	60651	60151
350369	LN	A	WM	NN	60142	60512	60652	60152
350370	LN	A	WM	NN	60143	60513	60653	60153
350371	LN	A	WM	NN	60144	60514	60654	60154
350372	LN	A	WM	NN	60145	60515	60655	60155
350373	LN	A	WM	NN	60146	60516	60656	60156
350374	LN	A	WM	NN	60147	60517	60657	60157
350375	LN	A	WM	NN	60148	60518	60658	60158
350376	LN	A	WM	NN	60149	60519	60659	60159
350377	LN	A	WM	NN	60150	60520	60660	60160

Names (carried on one side of PTS):

| 350375 | Vic Hall | | 350377 | Graham Taylor OBE |

Class 350/4. Owned by Angel Trains. Previously operated by TransPennine Express before transfer to West Midlands Trains in 2019–20.

Seating Layout: 2+2 facing/unidirectional.

DMS(A). Siemens Krefeld 2013–14. –/56. 44.2 t.
TS. Siemens Krefeld 2013–14. –/48 1T. 36.2 t.
PTS. Siemens Krefeld 2013–14. –/42 1TD 1T. 44.6 t.
DMS(B). Siemens Krefeld 2013–14. –/56. 45.0 t.

350401	LN	A	WM	NN	60691	60901	60941	60671
350402	LN	A	WM	NN	60692	60902	60942	60672
350403	LN	A	WM	NN	60693	60903	60943	60673
350404	LN	A	WM	NN	60694	60904	60944	60674
350405	LN	A	WM	NN	60695	60905	60945	60675
350406	LN	A	WM	NN	60696	60906	60946	60676
350407	LN	A	WM	NN	60697	60907	60947	60677
350408	LN	A	WM	NN	60698	60908	60948	60678
350409	LN	A	WM	NN	60699	60909	60949	60679
350410	LN	A	WM	NN	60700	60910	60950	60680

CLASS 357 ELECTROSTAR
ADTRANZ/BOMBARDIER DERBY

Provision for 750 V DC supply if required.

Formation: DMS–MS–PTS–DMS.
Construction: Welded aluminium alloy underframe, sides and roof with steel ends. All sections bolted together.
Traction Motors: Two Adtranz asynchronous of 250 kW.
Wheel Arrangement: 2-Bo + 2-Bo + 2-2 + Bo-2.
Braking: Disc & regenerative. **Dimensions:** 20.40/19.99 x 2.80 m.
Bogies: Adtranz P3-25/T3-25. **Couplers:** Tightlock.
Gangways: Within unit. **Control System:** IGBT Inverter.
Doors: Sliding plug. **Maximum Speed:** 100 mph.
Heating & ventilation: Air conditioning.
Seating Layout: 3+2 facing/unidirectional.
Multiple Working: Within class.

Class 357/0. Owned by Porterbrook Leasing.

Advertising liveries:

357 008 Gold Geese (yellow).
357 016 British Transport Police Guardian app (dark blue).

DMS(A). Adtranz Derby 1999–2001. –/71. 40.7 t.
MS. Adtranz Derby 1999–2001. –/78. 36.7 t.
PTS. Adtranz Derby 1999–2001. –/58(+4) 1TD 2W. 39.5 t.
DMS(B). Adtranz Derby 1999–2001. –/71. 40.7 t.

357 001	**C2**	P	*C2*	EM	67651	74151	74051	67751
357 002	**C2**	P	*C2*	EM	67652	74152	74052	67752
357 003	**C2**	P	*C2*	EM	67653	74153	74053	67753
357 004	**C2**	P	*C2*	EM	67654	74154	74054	67754
357 005	**C2**	P	*C2*	EM	67655	74155	74055	67755
357 006	**C2**	P	*C2*	EM	67656	74156	74056	67756
357 007	**C2**	P	*C2*	EM	67657	74157	74057	67757
357 008	**AL**	P	*C2*	EM	67658	74158	74058	67758
357 009	**C2**	P	*C2*	EM	67659	74159	74059	67759
357 010	**C2**	P	*C2*	EM	67660	74160	74060	67760
357 011	**C2**	P	*C2*	EM	67661	74161	74061	67761
357 012	**C2**	P	*C2*	EM	67662	74162	74062	67762
357 013	**C2**	P	*C2*	EM	67663	74163	74063	67763
357 014	**C2**	P	*C2*	EM	67664	74164	74064	67764
357 015	**C2**	P	*C2*	EM	67665	74165	74065	67765
357 016	**AL**	P	*C2*	EM	67666	74166	74066	67766
357 017	**C2**	P	*C2*	EM	67667	74167	74067	67767
357 018	**C2**	P	*C2*	EM	67668	74168	74068	67768
357 019	**C2**	P	*C2*	EM	67669	74169	74069	67769
357 020	**C2**	P	*C2*	EM	67670	74170	74070	67770
357 021	**C2**	P	*C2*	EM	67671	74171	74071	67771
357 022	**C2**	P	*C2*	EM	67672	74172	74072	67772

357 023	**C2**	P	*C2*	EM	67673	74173	74073	67773
357 024	**C2**	P	*C2*	EM	67674	74174	74074	67774
357 025	**C2**	P	*C2*	EM	67675	74175	74075	67775
357 026	**C2**	P	*C2*	EM	67676	74176	74076	67776
357 027	**C2**	P	*C2*	EM	67677	74177	74077	67777
357 028	**C2**	P	*C2*	EM	67678	74178	74078	67778
357 029	**C2**	P	*C2*	EM	67679	74179	74079	67779
357 030	**C2**	P	*C2*	EM	67680	74180	74080	67780
357 031	**C2**	P	*C2*	EM	67681	74181	74081	67781
357 032	**C2**	P	*C2*	EM	67682	74182	74082	67782
357 033	**C2**	P	*C2*	EM	67683	74183	74083	67783
357 034	**C2**	P	*C2*	EM	67684	74184	74084	67784
357 035	**C2**	P	*C2*	EM	67685	74185	74085	67785
357 036	**C2**	P	*C2*	EM	67686	74186	74086	67786
357 037	**C2**	P	*C2*	EM	67687	74187	74087	67787
357 038	**C2**	P	*C2*	EM	67688	74188	74088	67788
357 039	**C2**	P	*C2*	EM	67689	74189	74089	67789
357 040	**C2**	P	*C2*	EM	67690	74190	74090	67790
357 041	**C2**	P	*C2*	EM	67691	74191	74091	67791
357 042	**C2**	P	*C2*	EM	67692	74192	74092	67792
357 043	**C2**	P	*C2*	EM	67693	74193	74093	67793
357 044	**C2**	P	*C2*	EM	67694	74194	74094	67794
357 045	**C2**	P	*C2*	EM	67695	74195	74095	67795
357 046	**C2**	P	*C2*	EM	67696	74196	74096	67796

Names (carried on DMS(A) and DMS(B) (one plate on each)):

357 001 BARRY FLAXMAN
357 002 ARTHUR LEWIS STRIDE 1841–1922
357 003 SOUTHEND city.on.sea
357 004 TONY AMOS
357 005 SOUTHEND: 2017 Alternative City of Culture
357 006 DIAMOND JUBILEE 1952–2012
357 007 Sir Andrew Foster
357 011 JOHN LOWING
357 018 Remembering our Fallen 88 1914–1918
357 028 London, Tilbury & Southend Railway 1854–2004
357 029 THOMAS WHITELEGG 1840–1922
357 030 ROBERT HARBEN WHITELEGG 1871–1957

Class 357/2. Owned by Angel Trains.

DMS(A). Bombardier Derby 2001–02. –/71. 40.7 t.
MS. Bombardier Derby 2001–02. –/78. 36.7 t.
PTS. Bombardier Derby 2001–02. –/58(+4) 1TD 2W. 39.5 t.
DMS(B). Bombardier Derby 2001–02. –/71. 40.7 t.

357 201	**C2**	A	*C2*	EM	68601	74701	74601	68701
357 202	**C2**	A	*C2*	EM	68602	74702	74602	68702
357 203	**C2**	A	*C2*	EM	68603	74703	74603	68703
357 204	**C2**	A	*C2*	EM	68604	74704	74604	68704
357 205	**C2**	A	*C2*	EM	68605	74705	74605	68705
357 206	**C2**	A	*C2*	EM	68606	74706	74606	68706

357 207	**C2**	A	*C2*	EM	68607	74707	74607	68707
357 208	**C2**	A	*C2*	EM	68608	74708	74608	68708
357 209	**C2**	A	*C2*	EM	68609	74709	74609	68709
357 210	**C2**	A	*C2*	EM	68610	74710	74610	68710
357 211	**C2**	A	*C2*	EM	68611	74711	74611	68711

Names (carried on DMS(A) and DMS(B) (one plate on each)):

357 201	KEN BIRD	357 206	MARTIN AUNGIER
357 202	KENNY MITCHELL	357 207	JOHN PAGE
357 203	HENRY PUMFRETT	357 208	DAVE DAVIS
357 204	DEREK FOWERS	357 209	JAMES SNELLING
357 205	JOHN D'SILVA		

Class 357/3. Owned by Angel Trains. In 2015–16 17 Class 357/2s (357 212–228) were reconfigured as "high density" units 357 312–328 with fewer seats and more standing room for shorter distance workings.

Seating Layout: 2+2 facing/unidirectional.

DMS(A). Bombardier Derby 2001–02. –/56. 40.7 t.
MS. Bombardier Derby 2001–02. –/60. 36.7 t.
PTS. Bombardier Derby 2001–02. –/50 1TD 2W. 39.5 t.
DMS(B). Bombardier Derby 2001–02. –/56. 40.7 t.

357 312	(357 212)	**C2**	A	*C2*	EM	68612	74712	74612	68712
357 313	(357 213)	**C2**	A	*C2*	EM	68613	74713	74613	68713
357 314	(357 214)	**C2**	A	*C2*	EM	68614	74714	74614	68714
357 315	(357 215)	**C2**	A	*C2*	EM	68615	74715	74615	68715
357 316	(357 216)	**C2**	A	*C2*	EM	68616	74716	74616	68716
357 317	(357 217)	**C2**	A	*C2*	EM	68617	74717	74617	68717
357 318	(357 218)	**C2**	A	*C2*	EM	68618	74718	74618	68718
357 319	(357 219)	**C2**	A	*C2*	EM	68619	74719	74619	68719
357 320	(357 220)	**C2**	A	*C2*	EM	68620	74720	74620	68720
357 321	(357 221)	**C2**	A	*C2*	EM	68621	74721	74621	68721
357 322	(357 222)	**C2**	A	*C2*	EM	68622	74722	74622	68722
357 323	(357 223)	**C2**	A	*C2*	EM	68623	74723	74623	68723
357 324	(357 224)	**C2**	A	*C2*	EM	68624	74724	74624	68724
357 325	(357 225)	**C2**	A	*C2*	EM	68625	74725	74625	68725
357 326	(357 226)	**C2**	A	*C2*	EM	68626	74726	74626	68726
357 327	(357 227)	**C2**	A	*C2*	EM	68627	74727	74627	68727
357 328	(357 228)	**C2**	A	*C2*	EM	68628	74728	74628	68728

Names (carried on DMS(A) and DMS(B) (one plate on each)):

357 313 UPMINSTER I.E.C.C.
357 317 ALLAN BURNELL
357 327 SOUTHEND UNITED

CLASS 360/0   DESIRO UK   SIEMENS

Outer suburban/express units. Originally operated by Greater Anglia, then transferred to East Midlands Railway to operate services between London St Pancras and Corby from May 2021.

Formation: DMC–PTS–TS–DMC.
Construction: Welded aluminium.
Traction Motors: Four Siemens 1TB2016-0GB02 asynchronous of 250 kW.
Wheel Arrangement: Bo-Bo + 2-2 + 2-2 + Bo-Bo.

Braking: Disc & regenerative.	**Dimensions:** 20.34 x 2.80 m.
Bogies: SGP SF5000.	**Couplers:** Dellner 12.
Gangways: Within unit.	**Control System:** IGBT Inverter.
Doors: Sliding plug.	**Maximum Speed:** 100 mph.

Heating & ventilation: Air conditioning.
Seating Layout: 1: 2+2 facing, 2: 3+2 facing/unidirectional.
Multiple Working: Within class.

DMC(A). Siemens Krefeld 2002–03. 8/59. 45.0 t.
PTS. Siemens Vienna 2002–03. –/60(+9) 1TD 2W. 43.6 t.
TS. Siemens Vienna 2002–03. –/78. 34.3 t.
DMC(B). Siemens Krefeld 2002–03. 8/59. 44.1 t.

360 101	**ER**	A	*EM*	BF	65551	72551	74551	68551
360 102	**ER**	A	*EM*	BF	65552	72552	74552	68552
360 103	**ER**	A	*EM*	BF	65553	72553	74553	68553
360 104	**ER**	A	*EM*	BF	65554	72554	74554	68554
360 105	**ER**	A	*EM*	BF	65555	72555	74555	68555
360 106	**ER**	A	*EM*	BF	65556	72556	74556	68556
360 107	**ER**	A	*EM*	BF	65557	72557	74557	68557
360 108	**ER**	A	*EM*	BF	65558	72558	74558	68558
360 109	**ER**	A	*EM*	BF	65559	72559	74559	68559
360 110	**ER**	A	*EM*	BF	65560	72560	74560	68560
360 111	**ER**	A	*EM*	BF	65561	72561	74561	68561
360 112	**ER**	A	*EM*	BF	65562	72562	74562	68562
360 113	**ER**	A	*EM*	BF	65563	72563	74563	68563
360 114	**ER**	A	*EM*	BF	65564	72564	74564	68564
360 115	**ER**	A	*EM*	BF	65565	72565	74565	68565
360 116	**ER**	A	*EM*	BF	65566	72566	74566	68566
360 117	**ER**	A	*EM*	BF	65567	72567	74567	68567
360 118	**ER**	A	*EM*	BF	65568	72568	74568	68568
360 119	**ER**	A	*EM*	BF	65569	72569	74569	68569
360 120	**ER**	A	*EM*	BF	65570	72570	74570	68570
360 121	**ER**	A	*EM*	BF	65571	72571	74571	68571

CLASS 360/2   DESIRO UK   SIEMENS

4-car Class 350 testbed units rebuilt for use by Heathrow Express on "Heathrow Connect" stopping services. The five Class 360/2s were stored in 2020, their duties having been taken over by Class 345s. 360 204/205 were scrapped in 2022 and 360 201–203 were sold to the Global Centre of Rail Excellence (GCRE) for use as test train units at the new test centre now under construction in South Wales.

Formation: DMS–PTS–TS–TS–DMS.
Construction: Welded aluminium.
Traction Motors: Four Siemens 1TB2016-0GB02 asynchronous of 250 kW.
Wheel Arrangement: Bo-Bo + 2-2 + 2-2 + 2-2 + Bo-Bo.
Braking: Disc & regenerative.   **Dimensions:** 20.34 x 2.80 m.
Bogies: SGP SF5000.   **Couplers:** Dellner 12.
Gangways: Within unit.   **Control System:** IGBT Inverter.
Doors: Sliding plug.   **Maximum Speed:** 100 mph.
Heating & ventilation: Air conditioning.
Seating Layout: 3 | 2 facing/unidirectional.
Multiple Working: Within class.

DMS(A). Siemens Krefeld 2002–06. –/63). 44.8 t.
PTS. Siemens Krefeld 2002–06. –/57(+9) 1TD 2W. 44.2 t.
TS(A). Siemens Krefeld 2005–06. –/74. 35.3 t.
TS(B). Siemens Krefeld 2002–06. –/74. 34.1 t.
DMS(B). Siemens Krefeld 2002–06. –/63. 44.4 t.

360 201	**HC**	GR	BR	78431	63421	72431	72421	78441
360 202	**HC**	GR	BR	78432	63422	72432	72422	78442
360 203	**HC**	GR	BR	78433	63423	72433	72423	78443

CLASS 375 ELECTROSTAR
ADTRANZ/BOMBARDIER DERBY

Express and outer suburban units. Southeastern declassified all First Class in its Class 375 units in 2022.

Formation: Various, see sub-class headings.
Systems: 25 kV AC overhead/750 V DC third rail (some third rail only with provision for retro-fitting of AC equipment).
Construction: Welded aluminium alloy underframe, sides and roof with steel ends. All sections bolted together.
Traction Motors: Two Adtranz asynchronous of 250 kW.
Wheel Arrangement: 2-Bo (+ 2-Bo) + 2-2 + Bo-2.
Braking: Disc & regenerative.   **Dimensions:** 20.40/19.99 x 2.80 m.
Bogies: Adtranz P3-25/T3-25.   **Couplers:** Dellner 12.
Gangways: Throughout.   **Control System:** IGBT Inverter.
Doors: Sliding plug.   **Maximum Speed:** 100 mph.
Heating & ventilation: Air conditioning.
Seating Layout: 2+2 facing/unidirectional (375/9: 3+2 facing/unidirectional).
Multiple Working: Within class and with Classes 376, 377, 378 and 379.

Class 375/3. Express units. 750 V DC only. DMS–TS–DMS.

DMS(A). Bombardier Derby 2001–02. –/60. 43.8 t.
TS. Bombardier Derby 2001–02. –/56 1TD 2W. 35.5 t.
DMS(B). Bombardier Derby 2001–02. –/60. 43.8 t.

375 301	**SB**	E	*SE*	RM	67921	74351	67931
375 302	**SB**	E	*SE*	RM	67922	74352	67932
375 303	**SB**	E	*SE*	RM	67923	74353	67933
375 304	**SB**	E	*SE*	RM	67924	74354	67934
375 305	**SB**	E	*SE*	RM	67925	74355	67935
375 306	**SB**	E	*SE*	RM	67926	74356	67936
375 307	**SB**	E	*SE*	RM	67927	74357	67937
375 308	**SB**	E	*SE*	RM	67928	74358	67938
375 309	**SB**	E	*SE*	RM	67929	74359	67939
375 310	**SB**	E	*SE*	RM	67930	74360	67940

Class 375/6. Express units. 25 kV AC/750 V DC. DMS–MS–PTS–DMS.

DMS(A). Adtranz Derby 1999–2001. –/60. 46.2 t.
MS. Adtranz Derby 1999–2001. –/66 1T. 40.5 t.
PTS. Adtranz Derby 1999–2001. –/56 1TD 2W. 40.7 t.
DMS(B). Adtranz Derby 1999–2001. –/60. 46.2 t.

375 601	**SB**	E	*SE*	RM	67801	74251	74201	67851
375 602	**SB**	E	*SE*	RM	67802	74252	74202	67852
375 603	**SB**	E	*SE*	RM	67803	74253	74203	67853
375 604	**SB**	E	*SE*	RM	67804	74254	74204	67854
375 605	**SB**	E	*SE*	RM	67805	74255	74205	67855
375 606	**SB**	E	*SE*	RM	67806	74256	74206	67856
375 607	**SB**	E	*SE*	RM	67807	74257	74207	67857
375 608	**SB**	E	*SE*	RM	67808	74258	74208	67858
375 609	**SB**	E	*SE*	RM	67809	74259	74209	67859
375 610	**SB**	E	*SE*	RM	67810	74260	74210	67860
375 611	**SB**	E	*SE*	RM	67811	74261	74211	67861
375 612	**SB**	E	*SE*	RM	67812	74262	74212	67862
375 613	**SB**	E	*SE*	RM	67813	74263	74213	67863
375 614	**SB**	E	*SE*	RM	67814	74264	74214	67864
375 615	**SB**	E	*SE*	RM	67815	74265	74215	67865
375 616	**SB**	E	*SE*	RM	67816	74266	74216	67866
375 617	**SB**	E	*SE*	RM	67817	74267	74217	67867
375 618	**SB**	E	*SE*	RM	67818	74268	74218	67868
375 619	**SB**	E	*SE*	RM	67819	74269	74219	67869
375 620	**SB**	E	*SE*	RM	67820	74270	74220	67870
375 621	**SB**	E	*SE*	RM	67821	74271	74221	67871
375 622	**SB**	E	*SE*	RM	67822	74272	74222	67872
375 623	**SB**	E	*SE*	RM	67823	74273	74223	67873
375 624	**SB**	E	*SE*	RM	67824	74274	74224	67874
375 625	**SB**	E	*SE*	RM	67825	74275	74225	67875
375 626	**SB**	E	*SE*	RM	67826	74276	74226	67876
375 627	**SB**	E	*SE*	RM	67827	74277	74227	67877
375 628	**SB**	E	*SE*	RM	67828	74278	74228	67878
375 629	**SB**	E	*SE*	RM	67829	74279	74229	67879
375 630	**SB**	E	*SE*	RM	67830	74280	74230	67880

Names (carried on one side of each MS or TS):

375 619 Driver John Neve | 375 623 Hospice in the Weald

Class 375/7. Express units. 750 V DC only. DMS–MS–TS–DMS.

DMS(A). Bombardier Derby 2001–02. –/60. 43.8 t.
MS. Bombardier Derby 2001–02. –/66 1T. 36.4 t.
TS. Bombardier Derby 2001–02. –/56 1TD 2W. 34.1 t.
DMS(B). Bombardier Derby 2001–02. –/60. 43.8 t.

375 701	**SB**	E	*SE*	RM	67831	74281	74231	67881
375 702	**SB**	E	*SE*	RM	67832	74282	74232	67882
375 703	**SB**	E	*SE*	RM	67833	74283	74233	67883
375 704	**SB**	E	*SE*	RM	67834	74284	74234	67884
375 705	**SB**	E	*SE*	RM	67835	74285	74235	67885
375 706	**SB**	E	*SE*	RM	67836	74286	74236	67886
375 707	**SB**	E	*SE*	RM	67837	74287	74237	67887
375 708	**SB**	E	*SE*	RM	67838	74288	74238	67888
375 709	**SB**	E	*SE*	RM	67839	74289	74239	67889
375 710	**SB**	E	*SE*	RM	67840	74290	74240	67890
375 711	**SB**	E	*SE*	RM	67841	74291	74241	67891
375 712	**SB**	E	*SE*	RM	67842	74292	74242	67892
375 713	**SB**	E	*SE*	RM	67843	74293	74243	67893
375 714	**SB**	E	*SE*	RM	67844	74294	74244	67894
375 715	**SB**	E	*SE*	RM	67845	74295	74245	67895

Names (carried on one side of each MS or TS):

375 701 Kent Air Ambulance Explorer | 375 714   Rochester Cathedral
375 710 Rochester Castle

Class 375/8. Express units. 750 V DC only. DMS–MS–TS–DMS.

375 801–820 are fitted with de-icing equipment. TS weighs 36.5 t.

DMS(A). Bombardier Derby 2004. –/60. 43.3 t.
MS. Bombardier Derby 2004. –/66 1T. 39.8 t.
TS. Bombardier Derby 2004. –/52 1TD 2W. 35.9 t.
DMS(B). Bombardier Derby 2004. –/64. 43.3 t.

375 801	**SB**	E	*SE*	RM	73301	79001	78201	73701
375 802	**SB**	E	*SE*	RM	73302	79002	78202	73702
375 803	**SB**	E	*SE*	RM	73303	79003	78203	73703
375 804	**SB**	E	*SE*	RM	73304	79004	78204	73704
375 805	**SB**	E	*SE*	RM	73305	79005	78205	73705
375 806	**SB**	E	*SE*	RM	73306	79006	78206	73706
375 807	**SB**	E	*SE*	RM	73307	79007	78207	73707
375 808	**SB**	E	*SE*	RM	73308	79008	78208	73708
375 809	**SB**	E	*SE*	RM	73309	79009	78209	73709
375 810	**SB**	E	*SE*	RM	73310	79010	78210	73710
375 811	**SB**	E	*SE*	RM	73311	79011	78211	73711
375 812	**SB**	E	*SE*	RM	73312	79012	78212	73712
375 813	**SB**	E	*SE*	RM	73313	79013	78213	73713
375 814	**SB**	E	*SE*	RM	73314	79014	78214	73714
375 815	**SB**	E	*SE*	RM	73315	79015	78215	73715

375816	**SB**	E	*SE*	RM	73316	79016	78216	73716
375817	**SB**	E	*SE*	RM	73317	79017	78217	73717
375818	**SB**	E	*SE*	RM	73318	79018	78218	73718
375819	**SB**	E	*SE*	RM	73319	79019	78219	73719
375820	**SB**	E	*SE*	RM	73320	79020	78220	73720
375821	**SB**	E	*SE*	RM	73321	79021	78221	73721
375822	**SB**	E	*SE*	RM	73322	79022	78222	73722
375823	**SB**	E	*SE*	RM	73323	79023	78223	73723
375824	**SB**	E	*SE*	RM	73324	79024	78224	73724
375825	**SB**	E	*SE*	RM	73325	79025	78225	73725
375826	**SB**	E	*SE*	RM	73326	79026	78226	73726
375827	**SB**	E	*SE*	RM	73327	79027	78227	73727
375828	**SB**	E	*SE*	RM	73328	79028	78228	73728
375829	**SB**	E	*SE*	RM	73329	79029	78229	73729
375830	**SB**	E	*SE*	RM	73330	79030	78230	73730

Names (carried on one side of each MS or TS):

375823 Ashford Proudly served by rail since 1842
375829 Verera Holmes (1889–1964) Women in Engineering

Class 375/9. Outer suburban units. 750 V DC only. DMS–MS–TS–DMS.

DMS(A). Bombardier Derby 2003–04. –/71. 43.4 t.
MS. Bombardier Derby 2003–04. –/73 1T. 39.3 t.
TS. Bombardier Derby 2003–04. –/62 1TD 2W. 35.6 t.
DMS(B). Bombardier Derby 2003–04. –/71. 43.4 t.

375901	**SB**	E	*SE*	RM	73331	79031	79061	73731
375902	**SB**	E	*SE*	RM	73332	79032	79062	73732
375903	**SB**	E	*SE*	RM	73333	79033	79063	73733
375904	**SB**	E	*SE*	RM	73334	79034	79064	73734
375905	**SB**	E	*SE*	RM	73335	79035	79065	73735
375906	**SB**	E	*SE*	RM	73336	79036	79066	73736
375907	**SB**	E	*SE*	RM	73337	79037	79067	73737
375908	**SB**	E	*SE*	RM	73338	79038	79068	73738
375909	**SB**	E	*SE*	RM	73339	79039	79069	73739
375910	**SB**	E	*SE*	RM	73340	79040	79070	73740
375911	**SB**	E	*SE*	RM	73341	79041	79071	73741
375912	**SB**	E	*SE*	RM	73342	79042	79072	73742
375913	**SB**	E	*SE*	RM	73343	79043	79073	73743
375914	**SB**	E	*SE*	RM	73344	79044	79074	73744
375915	**SB**	E	*SE*	RM	73345	79045	79075	73745
375916	**SB**	E	*SE*	RM	73346	79046	79076	73746
375917	**SB**	E	*SE*	RM	73347	79047	79077	73747
375918	**SB**	E	*SE*	RM	73348	79048	79078	73748
375919	**SB**	E	*SE*	RM	73349	79049	79079	73749
375920	**SB**	E	*SE*	RM	73350	79050	79080	73750
375921	**SB**	E	*SE*	RM	73351	79051	79081	73751
375922	**SB**	E	*SE*	RM	73352	79052	79082	73752
375923	**SB**	E	*SE*	RM	73353	79053	79083	73753
375924	**SB**	E	*SE*	RM	73354	79054	79084	73754
375925	**SB**	E	*SE*	RM	73355	79055	79085	73755

| 375926 | **SB** | E | *SE* | RM | 73356 79056 79086 73756 |
| 375927 | **SB** | E | *SE* | RM | 73357 79057 79087 73757 |

CLASS 376   ELECTROSTAR   BOMBARDIER DERBY

Inner suburban units.

Formation: DMS–MS–TS–MS–DMS.
System: 750 V DC third rail.
Construction: Welded aluminium alloy underframe, sides and roof with steel ends. All sections bolted together.
Traction Motors: Two Bombardier asynchronous of 200 kW.
Wheel Arrangement: 2-Bo + 2-Bo + 2-2 + Bo-2 + Bo-2.
Braking: Disc & regenerative.   **Dimensions**: 20.40/19.99 x 2.80 m.
Bogies: Bombardier P3-25/T3-25.   **Couplers**: Dellner 12.
Gangways: Within unit.   **Control System**: IGBT Inverter.
Doors: Sliding.   **Maximum Speed**: 75 mph.
Heating & ventilation: Pressure heating and ventilation.
Seating Layout: 2+2 low density facing.
Multiple Working: Within class and with Classes 375, 377, 378 and 379.

DMS(A). Bombardier Derby 2004–05. –/36(+6) 1W. 42.1 t.
MS. Bombardier Derby 2004–05. –/48. 36.2 t.
TS. Bombardier Derby 2004–05. –/48. 36.3 t.
DMS(B). Bombardier Derby 2004–05. –/36(+6) 1W. 42.1 t.

376001	**CN**	E	*SE*	SG	61101 63301 64301 63501 61601
376002	**CN**	E	*SE*	SG	61102 63302 64302 63502 61602
376003	**CN**	E	*SE*	SG	61103 63303 64303 63503 61603
376004	**CN**	E	*SE*	SG	61104 63304 64304 63504 61604
376005	**CN**	E	*SE*	SG	61105 63305 64305 63505 61605
376006	**CN**	E	*SE*	SG	61106 63306 64306 63506 61606
376007	**CN**	E	*SE*	SG	61107 63307 64307 63507 61607
376008	**CN**	E	*SE*	SG	61108 63308 64308 63508 61608
376009	**CN**	E	*SE*	SG	61109 63309 64309 63509 61609
376010	**CN**	E	*SE*	SG	61110 63310 64310 63510 61610
376011	**CN**	E	*SE*	SG	61111 63311 64311 63511 61611
376012	**CN**	E	*SE*	SG	61112 63312 64312 63512 61612
376013	**CN**	E	*SE*	SG	61113 63313 64313 63513 61613
376014	**CN**	E	*SE*	SG	61114 63314 64314 63514 61614
376015	**CN**	E	*SE*	SG	61115 63315 64315 63515 61615
376016	**CN**	E	*SE*	SG	61116 63316 64316 63516 61616
376017	**CN**	E	*SE*	SG	61117 63317 64317 63517 61617
376018	**CN**	E	*SE*	SG	61118 63318 64318 63518 61618
376019	**CN**	E	*SE*	SG	61119 63319 64319 63519 61619
376020	**CN**	E	*SE*	SG	61120 63320 64320 63520 61620
376021	**CN**	E	*SE*	SG	61121 63321 64321 63521 61621
376022	**CN**	E	*SE*	SG	61122 63322 64322 63522 61622
376023	**CN**	E	*SE*	SG	61123 63323 64323 63523 61623
376024	**CN**	E	*SE*	SG	61124 63324 64324 63524 61624
376025	**CN**	E	*SE*	SG	61125 63325 64325 63525 61625
376026	**CN**	E	*SE*	SG	61126 63326 64326 63526 61626

376027	**CN**	E	*SE*	SG	61127	63327	64327	63527	61627
376028	**CN**	E	*SE*	SG	61128	63328	64328	63528	61628
376029	**CN**	E	*SE*	SG	61129	63329	64329	63529	61629
376030	**CN**	E	*SE*	SG	61130	63330	64330	63530	61630
376031	**CN**	E	*SE*	SG	61131	63331	64331	63531	61631
376032	**CN**	E	*SE*	SG	61132	63332	64332	63532	61632
376033	**CN**	E	*SE*	SG	61133	63333	64333	63533	61633
376034	**CN**	E	*SE*	SG	61134	63334	64334	63534	61634
376035	**CN**	E	*SE*	SG	61135	63335	64335	63535	61635
376036	**CN**	E	*SE*	SG	61136	63336	64336	63536	61636

Name (carried on TSO): 376001   Alan Doggett

CLASS 377   ELECTROSTAR   BOMBARDIER DERBY

Express and outer suburban units.

Formation: Various, see sub-class headings.
Systems: 25 kV AC overhead/750 V DC third rail or third rail only with provision for retro-fitting of AC equipment.
Construction: Welded aluminium alloy underframe, sides and roof with steel ends. All sections bolted together.
Traction Motors: Two Bombardier asynchronous of 250 kW.
Wheel Arrangement: 2-Bo + 2-2 + Bo-2 or 2-Bo + 2-Bo + 2-2 + Bo-2 or 2-Bo + 2-Bo + 2-2 + Bo-2.

Braking: Disc & regenerative.	**Dimensions:** 20.39/20.00 x 2.80 m.
Bogies: Bombardier P3-25/T3-25.	**Couplers:** Dellner 12.
Gangways: Throughout.	**Control System:** IGBT Inverter.
Doors: Sliding plug.	**Maximum Speed:** 100 mph.

Heating & ventilation: Air conditioning.
Seating Layout: Various, see sub-class headings.
Multiple Working: Within class and with Classes 375, 376, 378, 379 and 387.

Class 377/1. 750 V DC only. DMC–MS–TS–DMC.
Seating layout: 1: 2+2 facing/unidirectional, 2: 2+2 facing/unidirectional (377101–119), 3+2/2+2 facing/unidirectional (377120–139), 3+2 (middle cars and 2+2 (end cars) facing/unidirectional (377140–164).

DMC(A). Bombardier Derby 2002–03. 12/48 (s 12/56). 44.8 t.
MS. Bombardier Derby 2002–03. –/62 (s –/70, t –/69). 1T. 39.0 t.
TS. Bombardier Derby 2002–03. –/52 (s –/60, t –/57). 1TD 2W. 35.4 t.
DMC(B). Bombardier Derby 2002–03. 12/48 (s 12/56). 43.4 t.

377101	**SN**	P	*SN*	SU	78501	77101	78901	78701
377102	**SN**	P	*SN*	SU	78502	77102	78902	78702
377103	**SN**	P	*SN*	SU	78503	77103	78903	78703
377104	**SN**	P	*SN*	SU	78504	77104	78904	78704
377105	**SN**	P	*SN*	SU	78505	77105	78905	78705
377106	**SN**	P	*SN*	SU	78506	77106	78906	78706
377107	**SN**	P	*SN*	SU	78507	77107	78907	78707
377108	**SN**	P	*SN*	SU	78508	77108	78908	78708
377109	**SN**	P	*SN*	SU	78509	77109	78909	78709
377110	**SN**	P	*SN*	SU	78510	77110	78910	78710

377 111		**SN**	P	*SN*	SU	78511	77111	78911	78711
377 112		**SN**	P	*SN*	SU	78512	77112	78912	78712
377 113		**SN**	P	*SN*	SU	78513	77113	78913	78713
377 114		**SN**	P	*SN*	SU	78514	77114	78914	78714
377 115		**SN**	P	*SN*	SU	78515	77115	78915	78715
377 116		**SN**	P	*SN*	SU	78516	77116	78916	78716
377 117		**SN**	P	*SN*	SU	78517	77117	78917	78717
377 118		**SN**	P	*SN*	SU	78518	77118	78918	78718
377 119		**SN**	P	*SN*	SU	78519	77119	78919	78719
377 120	s	**SN**	P	*SN*	SU	78520	77120	78920	78720
377 121	s	**SN**	P	*SN*	SU	78521	77121	78921	78721
377 122	s	**SN**	P	*SN*	SU	78522	77122	78922	78722
377 123	s	**SN**	P	*SN*	SU	78523	77123	78923	78723
377 124	s	**SN**	P	*SN*	SU	78524	77124	78924	78724
377 125	s	**SN**	P	*SN*	SU	78525	77125	78925	78725
377 126	s	**SN**	P	*SN*	SU	78526	77126	78926	78726
377 127	s	**SN**	P	*SN*	SU	78527	77127	78927	78727
377 128	s	**SN**	P	*SN*	SU	78528	77128	78928	78728
377 129	s	**SN**	P	*SN*	SU	78529	77129	78929	78729
377 130	s	**SN**	P	*SN*	SU	78530	77130	78930	78730
377 131	s	**SN**	P	*SN*	SU	78531	77131	78931	78731
377 132	s	**SN**	P	*SN*	SU	78532	77132	78932	78732
377 133	s	**SN**	P	*SN*	SU	78533	77133	78933	78733
377 134	s	**SN**	P	*SN*	SU	78534	77134	78934	78734
377 135	s	**SN**	P	*SN*	SU	78535	77135	78935	78735
377 136	s	**SN**	P	*SN*	SU	78536	77136	78936	78736
377 137	s	**SN**	P	*SN*	SU	78537	77137	78937	78737
377 138	s	**SN**	P	*SN*	SU	78538	77138	78938	78738
377 139	s	**SN**	P	*SN*	SU	78539	77139	78939	78739
377 140	t	**SN**	P	*SN*	SU	78540	77140	78940	78740
377 141	t	**SN**	P	*SN*	SU	78541	77141	78941	78741
377 142	t	**SN**	P	*SN*	SU	78542	77142	78942	78742
377 143	t	**SN**	P	*SN*	SU	78543	77143	78943	78743
377 144	t	**SN**	P	*SN*	SU	78544	77144	78944	78744
377 145	t	**SN**	P	*SN*	SU	78545	77145	78945	78745
377 146	t	**SN**	P	*SN*	SU	78546	77146	78946	78746
377 147	t	**SN**	P	*SN*	SU	78547	77147	78947	78747
377 148	t	**SN**	P	*SN*	SU	78548	77148	78948	78748
377 149	t	**SN**	P	*SN*	SU	78549	77149	78949	78749
377 150	t	**SN**	P	*SN*	SU	78550	77150	78950	78750
377 151	t	**SN**	P	*SN*	SU	78551	77151	78951	78751
377 152	t	**SN**	P	*SN*	SU	78552	77152	78952	78752
377 153	t	**SN**	P	*SN*	SU	78553	77153	78953	78753
377 154	t	**SN**	P	*SN*	SU	78554	77154	78954	78754
377 155	t	**SN**	P	*SN*	SU	78555	77155	78955	78755
377 156	t	**SN**	P	*SN*	SU	78556	77156	78956	78756
377 157	t	**SN**	P	*SN*	SU	78557	77157	78957	78757
377 158	t	**SN**	P	*SN*	SU	78558	77158	78958	78758
377 159	t	**SN**	P	*SN*	SU	78559	77159	78959	78759
377 160	t	**SN**	P	*SN*	SU	78560	77160	78960	78760
377 161	t	**SN**	P	*SN*	SU	78561	77161	78961	78761

377 162	t	**SN**	P	*SN*	SU	78562	77162	78962	78762
377 163	t	**SN**	P	*SN*	SU	78563	77163	78963	78763
377 164	t	**SN**	P	*SN*	SU	78564	77164	78964	78764

Class 377/2. 25 kV AC/750 V DC. DMC–MS–PTS–DMC. Dual-voltage units.
Seating layout: 1: 2+2 facing/unidirectional, 2: 2+2 and 3+2 facing/unidirectional (3+2 seating in middle cars only).

DMC(A). Bombardier Derby 2003–04. 12/48. 44.2 t.
MS. Bombardier Derby 2003–04. –/69 1T. 39.8 t.
PTS. Bombardier Derby 2003–04. –/57 1TD 2W. 40.1 t.
DMC(B). Bombardier Derby 2003–04. 12/48. 44.2 t.

377 201	**SN**	P	*SN*	SU	78571	77171	78971	78771
377 202	**SN**	P	*SN*	SU	78572	77172	78972	78772
377 203	**SN**	P	*SN*	SU	78573	77173	78973	78773
377 204	**SN**	P	*SN*	SU	78574	77174	78974	78774
377 205	**SN**	P	*SN*	SU	78575	77175	78975	78775
377 206	**SN**	P	*SN*	SU	78576	77176	78976	78776
377 207	**SN**	P	*SN*	SU	78577	77177	78977	78777
377 208	**SN**	P	*SN*	SU	78578	77178	78978	78778
377 209	**SN**	P	*SN*	SU	78579	77179	78979	78779
377 210	**SN**	P	*SN*	SU	78580	77180	78980	78780
377 211	**SN**	P	*SN*	SU	78581	77181	78981	78781
377 212	**SN**	P	*SN*	SU	78582	77182	78982	78782
377 213	**SN**	P	*SN*	SU	78583	77183	78983	78783
377 214	**SN**	P	*SN*	SU	78584	77184	78984	78784
377 215	**SN**	P	*SN*	SU	78585	77185	78985	78785

Class 377/3. 750 V DC only. DMC–TS–DMC.
Seating Layout: 1: 2+2 facing/unidirectional, 2: 2+2 facing/unidirectional.

Units built as Class 375, but renumbered in the Class 377/3 range when fitted with Dellner couplers.

DMC(A). Bombardier Derby 2001–02. 12/48. 43.5 t.
TS. Bombardier Derby 2001–02. –/56 1TD 2W. 35.4 t.
DMC(B). Bombardier Derby 2001–02. 12/48. 43.5 t.

377 301	(375 311)	**SN**	P	*SN*	SU	68201	74801	68401
377 302	(375 312)	**SN**	P	*SN*	SU	68202	74802	68402
377 303	(375 313)	**SN**	P	*SN*	SU	68203	74803	68403
377 304	(375 314)	**SN**	P	*SN*	SU	68204	74804	68404
377 305	(375 315)	**SN**	P	*SN*	SU	68205	74805	68405
377 306	(375 316)	**SN**	P	*SN*	SU	68206	74806	68406
377 307	(375 317)	**SN**	P	*SN*	SU	68207	74807	68407
377 308	(375 318)	**SN**	P	*SN*	SU	68208	74808	68408
377 309	(375 319)	**SN**	P	*SN*	SU	68209	74809	68409
377 310	(375 320)	**SN**	P	*SN*	SU	68210	74810	68410
377 311	(375 321)	**SN**	P	*SN*	SU	68211	74811	68411
377 312	(375 322)	**SN**	P	*SN*	SU	68212	74812	68412
377 313	(375 323)	**SN**	P	*SN*	SU	68213	74813	68413
377 314	(375 324)	**SN**	P	*SN*	SU	68214	74814	68414
377 315	(375 325)	**SN**	P	*SN*	SU	68215	74815	68415

377316	(375326)	**SN**	P	*SN*	SU	68216	74816	68416
377317	(375327)	**SN**	P	*SN*	SU	68217	74817	68417
377318	(375328)	**SN**	P	*SN*	SU	68218	74818	68418
377319	(375329)	**SN**	P	*SN*	SU	68219	74819	68419
377320	(375330)	**SN**	P	*SN*	SU	68220	74820	68420
377321	(375331)	**SN**	P	*SN*	SU	68221	74821	68421
377322	(375332)	**SN**	P	*SN*	SU	68222	74822	68422
377323	(375333)	**SN**	P	*SN*	SU	68223	74823	68423
377324	(375334)	**SN**	P	*SN*	SU	68224	74824	68424
377325	(375335)	**SN**	P	*SN*	SU	68225	74825	68425
377326	(375336)	**SN**	P	*SN*	SU	68226	74826	68426
377327	(375337)	**SN**	P	*SN*	SU	68227	74827	68427
377328	(375338)	**SN**	P	*SN*	SU	68228	74828	68428

Class 377/4. 750 V DC only. DMC–MS–TS–DMC.
Seating Layout: 1: 2+2 facing/two seats longitudinal, 2: 2+2 and 3+2 facing/unidirectional (3+2 seating in middle cars only).

377442 operated as 3-car 377342 between 2016 and 2021 after fire damage to MS vehicle 78842 in 2016.

DMC(A). Bombardier Derby 2004–05. 10/48. 43.1 t.
MS. Bombardier Derby 2004–05. –/69 1T. 39.3 t.
TS. Bombardier Derby 2004–05. –/56 1TD 2W. 35.3 t.
DMC(B). Bombardier Derby 2004–05. 10/48. 43.2 t.

377401	**SN**	P	*SN*	SU	73401	78801	78601	73801
377402	**SN**	P	*SN*	SU	73402	78802	78602	73802
377403	**SN**	P	*SN*	SU	73403	78803	78603	73803
377404	**SN**	P	*SN*	SU	73404	78804	78604	73804
377405	**SN**	P	*SN*	SU	73405	78805	78605	73805
377406	**SN**	P	*SN*	SU	73406	78806	78606	73806
377407	**SN**	P	*SN*	SU	73407	78807	78607	73807
377408	**SN**	P	*SN*	SU	73408	78808	78608	73808
377409	**SN**	P	*SN*	SU	73409	78809	78609	73809
377410	**SN**	P	*SN*	SU	73410	78810	78610	73810
377411	**SN**	P	*SN*	SU	73411	78811	78611	73811
377412	**SN**	P	*SN*	SU	73412	78812	78612	73812
377413	**SN**	P	*SN*	SU	73413	78813	78613	73813
377414	**SN**	P	*SN*	SU	73414	78814	78614	73814
377415	**SN**	P	*SN*	SU	73415	78815	78615	73815
377416	**SN**	P	*SN*	SU	73416	78816	78616	73816
377417	**SN**	P	*SN*	SU	73417	78817	78617	73817
377418	**SN**	P	*SN*	SU	73418	78818	78618	73818
377419	**SN**	P	*SN*	SU	73419	78819	78619	73819
377420	**SN**	P	*SN*	SU	73420	78820	78620	73820
377421	**SN**	P	*SN*	SU	73421	78821	78621	73821
377422	**SN**	P	*SN*	SU	73422	78822	78622	73822
377423	**SN**	P	*SN*	SU	73423	78823	78623	73823
377424	**SN**	P	*SN*	SU	73424	78824	78624	73824
377425	**SN**	P	*SN*	SU	73425	78825	78625	73825
377426	**SN**	P	*SN*	SU	73426	78826	78626	73826
377427	**SN**	P	*SN*	SU	73427	78827	78627	73827

377 428	**SN**	P	*SN*	SU	73428	78828	78628	73828
377 429	**SN**	P	*SN*	SU	73429	78829	78629	73829
377 430	**SN**	P	*SN*	SU	73430	78830	78630	73830
377 431	**SN**	P	*SN*	SU	73431	78831	78631	73831
377 432	**SN**	P	*SN*	SU	73432	78832	78632	73832
377 433	**SN**	P	*SN*	SU	73433	78833	78633	73833
377 434	**SN**	P	*SN*	SU	73434	78834	78634	73834
377 435	**SN**	P	*SN*	SU	73435	78835	78635	73835
377 436	**SN**	P	*SN*	SU	73436	78836	78636	73836
377 437	**SN**	P	*SN*	SU	73437	78837	78637	73837
377 438	**SN**	P	*SN*	SU	73438	78838	78638	73838
377 439	**SN**	P	*SN*	SU	73439	78839	78639	73839
377 440	**SN**	P	*SN*	SU	73440	78840	78640	73840
377 441	**SN**	P	*SN*	SU	73441	78841	78641	73841
377 442	**SN**	P	*SN*	SU	73442	78842	78642	73842
377 443	**SN**	P	*SN*	SU	73443	78843	78643	73843
377 444	**SN**	P	*SN*	SU	73444	78844	78644	73844
377 445	**SN**	P	*SN*	SU	73445	78845	78645	73845
377 446	**SN**	P	*SN*	SU	73446	78846	78646	73846
377 447	**SN**	P	*SN*	SU	73447	78847	78647	73847
377 448	**SN**	P	*SN*	SU	73448	78848	78648	73848
377 449	**SN**	P	*SN*	SU	73449	78849	78649	73849
377 450	**SN**	P	*SN*	SU	73450	78850	78650	73850
377 451	**SN**	P	*SN*	SU	73451	78851	78651	73851
377 452	**SN**	P	*SN*	SU	73452	78852	78652	73852
377 453	**SN**	P	*SN*	SU	73453	78853	78653	73853
377 454	**SN**	P	*SN*	SU	73454	78854	78654	73854
377 455	**SN**	P	*SN*	SU	73455	78855	78655	73855
377 456	**SN**	P	*SN*	SU	73456	78856	78656	73856
377 457	**SN**	P	*SN*	SU	73457	78857	78657	73857
377 458	**SN**	P	*SN*	SU	73458	78858	78658	73858
377 459	**SN**	P	*SN*	SU	73459	78859	78659	73859
377 460	**SN**	P	*SN*	SU	73460	78860	78660	73860
377 461	**SN**	P	*SN*	SU	73461	78861	78661	73861
377 462	**SN**	P	*SN*	SU	73462	78862	78662	73862
377 463	**SN**	P	*SN*	SU	73463	78863	78663	73863
377 464	**SN**	P	*SN*	SU	73464	78864	78664	73864
377 465	**SN**	P	*SN*	SU	73465	78865	78665	73865
377 466	**SN**	P	*SN*	SU	73466	78866	78666	73866
377 467	**SN**	P	*SN*	SU	73467	78867	78667	73867
377 468	**SN**	P	*SN*	SU	73468	78868	78668	73868
377 469	**SN**	P	*SN*	SU	73469	78869	78669	73869
377 470	**SN**	P	*SN*	SU	73470	78870	78670	73870
377 471	**SN**	P	*SN*	SU	73471	78871	78671	73871
377 472	**SN**	P	*SN*	SU	73472	78872	78672	73872
377 473	**SN**	P	*SN*	SU	73473	78873	78673	73873
377 474	**SN**	P	*SN*	SU	73474	78874	78674	73874
377 475	**SN**	P	*SN*	SU	73475	78875	78675	73875

Class 377/5. 25kV AC/750V DC. DMC–MS–PTS–DMS. Dual-voltage units sub-leased from Southern. Details as Class 377/2 unless stated.

DMC. Bombardier Derby 2008–09. 10/48. 43.1t.
MS. Bombardier Derby 2008–09. –/69 1T. 40.3t.
PTS. Bombardier Derby 2008–09. –/56 1TD 2W. 40.6 t.
DMS. Bombardier Derby 2008–09. –/58. 44.9t.

377501	**FB**	P	*SE*	RM	73501	75901	74901	73601
377502	**FB**	P	*SE*	RM	73502	75902	74902	73602
377503	**FB**	P	*SE*	RM	73503	75903	74903	73603
377504	**FB**	P	*SE*	RM	73504	75904	74904	73604
377505	**FB**	P	*SE*	RM	73505	75905	74905	73605
377506	**FB**	P	*SE*	RM	73506	75906	74906	73606
377507	**FB**	P	*SE*	RM	73507	75907	74907	73607
377508	**FB**	P	*SE*	RM	73508	75908	74908	73608
377509	**FB**	P	*SE*	RM	73509	75909	74909	73609
377510	**FB**	P	*SE*	RM	73510	75910	74910	73610
377511	**FB**	P	*SE*	RM	73511	75911	74911	73611
377512	**FB**	P	*SE*	RM	73512	75912	74912	73612
377513	**FB**	P	*SE*	RM	73513	75913	74913	73613
377514	**FB**	P	*SE*	RM	73514	75914	74914	73614
377515	**FB**	P	*SE*	RM	73515	75915	74915	73615
377516	**FB**	P	*SE*	RM	73516	75916	74916	73616
377517	**FB**	P	*SE*	RM	73517	75917	74917	73617
377518	**FB**	P	*SE*	RM	73518	75918	74918	73618
377519	**FB**	P	*SE*	RM	73519	75919	74919	73619
377520	**FB**	P	*SE*	RM	73520	75920	74920	73620
377521	**FB**	P	*SE*	RM	73521	75921	74921	73621
377522	**FB**	P	*SE*	RM	73522	75922	74922	73622
377523	**FB**	P	*SE*	RM	73523	75923	74923	73623

Class 377/6. 750V DC. DMS–MS–TS–MS–DMS. 5-car suburban units fitted with Fainsa seating. Technically the same as the 377/5s but using the slightly modified Class 379-style bodyshell.

Seating Layout: 2+2 facing/unidirectional.

DMS. Bombardier Derby 2012–13. 24/36. 44.7 t.
MS. Bombardier Derby 2012–13. –/64 1T. 38.8 t.
TS. Bombardier Derby 2012–13. –/46(+2) 1TD 2W. 37.8 t.
MS. Bombardier Derby 2012–13. –/66. 38.3 t.
DMS. Bombardier Derby 2012–13. –/62. 44.7 t.

377601	**SN**	P	*SN*	SU	70101	70201	70301	70401	70501
377602	**SN**	P	*SN*	SU	70102	70202	70302	70402	70502
377603	**SN**	P	*SN*	SU	70103	70203	70303	70403	70503
377604	**SN**	P	*SN*	SU	70104	70204	70304	70404	70504
377605	**SN**	P	*SN*	SU	70105	70205	70305	70405	70505
377606	**SN**	P	*SN*	SU	70106	70206	70306	70406	70506
377607	**SN**	P	*SN*	SU	70107	70207	70307	70407	70507
377608	**SN**	P	*SN*	SU	70108	70208	70308	70408	70508
377609	**SN**	P	*SN*	SU	70109	70209	70309	70409	70509
377610	**SN**	P	*SN*	SU	70110	70210	70310	70410	70510

377611	**SN**	P	*SN*	SU	70111 70211 70311 70411 70511
377612	**SN**	P	*SN*	SU	70112 70212 70312 70412 70512
377613	**SN**	P	*SN*	SU	70113 70213 70313 70413 70513
377614	**SN**	P	*SN*	SU	70114 70214 70314 70414 70514
377615	**SN**	P	*SN*	SU	70115 70215 70315 70415 70515
377616	**SN**	P	*SN*	SU	70116 70216 70316 70416 70516
377617	**SN**	P	*SN*	SU	70117 70217 70317 70417 70517
377618	**SN**	P	*SN*	SU	70118 70218 70318 70418 70518
377619	**SN**	P	*SN*	SU	70119 70219 70319 70419 70519
377620	**SN**	P	*SN*	SU	70120 70220 70320 70420 70520
377621	**SN**	P	*SN*	SU	70121 70221 70321 70421 70521
377622	**SN**	P	*SN*	SU	70122 70222 70322 70422 70522
377623	**SN**	P	*SN*	SU	70123 70223 70323 70423 70523
377624	**SN**	P	*SN*	SU	70124 70224 70324 70424 70524
377625	**SN**	P	*SN*	SU	70125 70225 70325 70425 70525
377626	**SN**	P	*SN*	SU	70126 70226 70326 70426 70526

Class 377/7. 25kV AC/750 V DC. DMS–MS–TS–MS–DMS. Dual-voltage units.

DMS. Bombardier Derby 2013–14. 24/36. 45.6 t.
MS. Bombardier Derby 2013–14. –/64 1T. 41.0 t.
PTS. Bombardier Derby 2013–14. –/46(+2) 1TD 2W. 40.9 t.
MS. Bombardier Derby 2013–14. –/66. 39.6 t.
DMS. Bombardier Derby 2013–14. –/62. 45.2 t.

377701	**SN**	P	*SN*	SU	65201 70601 65601 70701 65401
377702	**SN**	P	*SN*	SU	65202 70602 65602 70702 65402
377703	**SN**	P	*SN*	SU	65203 70603 65603 70703 65403
377704	**SN**	P	*SN*	SU	65204 70604 65604 70704 65404
377705	**SN**	P	*SN*	SU	65205 70605 65605 70705 65405
377706	**SN**	P	*SN*	SU	65206 70606 65606 70706 65406
377707	**SN**	P	*SN*	SU	65207 70607 65607 70707 65407
377708	**SN**	P	*SN*	SU	65208 70608 65608 70708 65408

CLASS 378   CAPITALSTAR   BOMBARDIER DERBY

These suburban Electrostars are designated "Capitalstars" by TfL.

Formation: DMS–MS–TS–MS–DMS or DMS–MS–PTS–MS–DMS.
System: Class 378/1 750 V DC third rail only. Class 378/2 25 kV AC overhead and 750 V DC third rail.
Construction: Welded aluminium alloy underframe, sides and roof with steel ends. All sections bolted together.
Traction Motors: Three Bombardier asynchronous of 200 kW.
Wheel Arrangement: 1A-Bo + 1A-Bo + 2-2 + Bo-1A + Bo-1A.
Braking: Disc & regenerative.   **Dimensions:** 20.46/20.14 x 2.80 m.
Bogies: Bombardier P3-25/T3-25.   **Couplers:** Dellner 12.
Gangways: Within unit + end doors. **Control System:** IGBT Inverter.
Doors: Sliding.   **Maximum Speed:** 75 mph.
Heating & ventilation: Air conditioning.
Seating Layout: Longitudinal ("tube style") low density.

Multiple Working: Within class and with Classes 375, 376, 377 and 379.

57 extra MSs (in the 384xx number series) were delivered 2014–15 to make all units up to 5-cars.

Class 378/1. 750V DC. DMS–MS–TS–MS–DMS. Third rail only units used on the East London Line. Provision for retro-fitting as dual voltage.

378 150–154 are fitted with de-icing equipment.

DMS(A). Bombardier Derby 2009–10. –/36. 43.1 t.
MS(A). Bombardier Derby 2009–10. –/40. 39.3 t.
TS. Bombardier Derby 2009–10. –/34(+6) 2W. 34.3 t.
MS(B). Bombardier Derby 2014–15. –/40. 40.2 t.
DMS(B). Bombardier Derby 2009–10. –/36. 42.7 t.

378 135	LD	QW	LO	NG	38035	38235	38335	38435	38135
378 136	LD	QW	LO	NG	38036	38236	38336	38436	38136
378 137	LO	QW	LO	NG	38037	38237	38337	38437	38137
378 138	LO	QW	LO	NG	38038	38238	38338	38438	38138
378 139	LO	QW	LO	NG	38039	38239	38339	38439	38139
378 140	LO	QW	LO	NG	38040	38240	38340	38440	38140
378 141	LO	QW	LO	NG	38041	38241	38341	38441	38141
378 142	LO	QW	LO	NG	38042	38242	38342	38442	38142
378 143	LO	QW	LO	NG	38043	38243	38343	38443	38143
378 144	LO	QW	LO	NG	38044	38244	38344	38444	38144
378 145	LO	QW	LO	NG	38045	38245	38345	38445	38145
378 146	LO	QW	LO	NG	38046	38246	38346	38446	38146
378 147	LD	QW	LO	NG	38047	38247	38347	38447	38147
378 148	LO	QW	LO	NG	38048	38248	38348	38448	38148
378 149	LO	QW	LO	NG	38049	38249	38349	38449	38149
378 150	LD	QW	LO	NG	38050	38250	38350	38450	38150
378 151	LO	QW	LO	NG	38051	38251	38351	38451	38151
378 152	LO	QW	LO	NG	38052	38252	38352	38452	38152
378 153	LO	QW	LO	NG	38053	38253	38353	38453	38153
378 154	LO	QW	LO	NG	38054	38254	38354	38454	38154

Names (carried on DMS(A)):

378 135 Daks Hamilton | 378 136   Transport for London

Class 378/2. 25kV AC/750V DC. DMS–MS–PTS–MS–DMS. Dual-voltage units mainly used on North London Railway services. 378 201–224 were built as 3-car units 378 001–024, extended to 4-car units in 2010 and then extended to 5-cars in 2014–15.

Fitted with tripcocks for operation on the tracks shared with London Underground between Queens Park and Harrow & Wealdstone.

378 216–220 are fitted with de-icing equipment.

Non-standard livery: 378 205 Pride celebration colours.

DMS(A). Bombardier Derby 2008–11. –/36. 43.4 t.
MS(A). Bombardier Derby 2008–11. –/40. 39.6 t.
PTS. Bombardier Derby 2008–11. –/34(+6) 2W. 39.2 t.

MS(B). Bombardier Derby 2014–15. –/40. 40.4 t.
DMS(B). Bombardier Derby 2008–11. –/36. 43.1 t.

378 201	**L0**	QW	*LO*	NG	38001	38201	38301	38401	38101
378 202	**L0**	QW	*LO*	NG	38002	38202	38302	38402	38102
378 203	**L0**	QW	*LO*	NG	38003	38203	38303	38403	38103
378 204	**LD**	QW	*LO*	NG	38004	38204	38304	38404	38104
378 205	**0**	QW	*LO*	NG	38005	38205	38305	38405	38105
378 206	**LD**	QW	*LO*	NG	38006	38206	38306	38406	38106
378 207	**L0**	QW	*LO*	NG	38007	38207	38307	38407	38107
378 208	**L0**	QW	*LO*	NG	38008	38208	38308	38408	38108
378 209	**L0**	QW	*LO*	NG	38009	38209	38309	38409	38109
378 210	**L0**	QW	*LO*	NG	38010	38210	38310	38410	38110
378 211	**LD**	QW	*LO*	NG	38011	38211	38311	38411	38111
378 212	**L0**	QW	*LO*	NG	38012	38212	38312	38412	38112
378 213	**L0**	QW	*LO*	NG	38013	38213	38313	38413	38113
378 214	**L0**	QW	*LO*	NG	38014	38214	38314	38414	38114
378 215	**L0**	QW	*LO*	NG	38015	38215	38315	38415	38115
378 216	**L0**	QW	*LO*	NG	38016	38216	38316	38416	38116
378 217	**L0**	QW	*LO*	NG	38017	38217	38317	38417	38117
378 218	**L0**	QW	*LO*	NG	38018	38218	38318	38418	38118
378 219	**L0**	QW	*LO*	NG	38019	38219	38319	38419	38119
378 220	**L0**	QW	*LO*	NG	38020	38220	38320	38420	38120
378 221	**L0**	QW	*LO*	NG	38021	38221	38321	38421	38121
378 222	**L0**	QW	*LO*	NG	38022	38222	38322	38422	38122
378 223	**L0**	QW	*LO*	NG	38023	38223	38323	38423	38123
378 224	**L0**	QW	*LO*	NG	38024	38224	38324	38424	38124
378 225	**L0**	QW	*LO*	NG	38025	38225	38325	38425	38125
378 226	**L0**	QW	*LO*	NG	38026	38226	38326	38426	38126
378 227	**L0**	QW	*LO*	NG	38027	38227	38327	38427	38127
378 228	**L0**	QW	*LO*	NG	38028	38228	38328	38428	38128
378 229	**L0**	QW	*LO*	NG	38029	38229	38329	38429	38129
378 230	**L0**	QW	*LO*	NG	38030	38230	38330	38430	38130
378 231	**L0**	QW	*LO*	NG	38031	38231	38331	38431	38131
378 232	**LD**	QW	*LO*	NG	38032	38232	38332	38432	38132
378 233	**L0**	QW	*LO*	NG	38033	38233	38333	38433	38133
378 234	**L0**	QW	*LO*	NG	38034	38234	38334	38434	38134
378 255	**L0**	QW	*LO*	NG	38055	38255	38355	38455	38155
378 256	**L0**	QW	*LO*	NG	38056	38256	38356	38456	38156
378 257	**L0**	QW	*LO*	NG	38057	38257	38357	38457	38157

Names (carried on DMS(A)):

378 204	Professor Sir Peter Hall	378 232	Jeff Langston
378 211	Gary Hunter	378 233	Ian Brown CBE

CLASS 379   ELECTROSTAR   BOMBARDIER DERBY

Express Electrostars built for Liverpool Street–Stansted Airport and Liverpool Street–Cambridge services. The whole fleet was stored in 2022 after being replaced on Greater Anglia by Class 720s.

Formation: DMS–MS–PTS–DMC.
System: 25 kV AC overhead.
Construction: Welded aluminium alloy underframe, sides and roof with steel ends. All sections bolted together.
Traction Motors: Two Bombardier asynchronous of 200 kW.
Wheel Arrangement: 2-Bo + 2-Bo + 2-2 + Bo-2.
Braking: Disc & regenerative.   **Dimensions:** 20.00 x 2.80 m.
Bogies: Bombardier P3-25/T3-25.   **Couplers:** Dellner 12.
Gangways: Throughout.   **Control System:** IGBT Inverter.
Doors: Sliding plug.   **Maximum Speed:** 100 mph.
Heating & ventilation: Air conditioning.
Seating Layout: 1: 2+1 facing. 2: 2+2 facing/unidirectional.
Multiple Working: Within class and with Classes 375, 376, 377 and 378.

DMS. Bombardier Derby 2010–11. –/60. 42.1 t.
MS. Bombardier Derby 2010–11. –/62 1T. 38.6 t.
PTS. Bombardier Derby 2010–11. –/43(+2) 1TD 2W. 40.9 t.
DMC. Bombardier Derby 2010–11. 20/24. 42.3 t.

379001	**NC**	AK	WS	61201	61701	61901	62101
379002	**NC**	AK	WS	61202	61702	61902	62102
379003	**NC**	AK	WS	61203	61703	61903	62103
379004	**NC**	AK	WS	61204	61704	61904	62104
379005	**NC**	AK	WS	61205	61705	61905	62105
379006	**NC**	AK	WS	61206	61706	61906	62106
379007	**NC**	AK	WS	61207	61707	61907	62107
379008	**NC**	AK	WS	61208	61708	61908	62108
379009	**NC**	AK	WS	61209	61709	61909	62109
379010	**NC**	AK	WS	61210	61710	61910	62110
379011	**NC**	AK	WS	61211	61711	61911	62111
379012	**NC**	AK	WS	61212	61712	61912	62112
379013	**NC**	AK	WS	61213	61713	61913	62113
379014	**NC**	AK	WS	61214	61714	61914	62114
379015	**NC**	AK	WS	61215	61715	61915	62115
379016	**NC**	AK	WS	61216	61716	61916	62116
379017	**NC**	AK	WS	61217	61717	61917	62117
379018	**NC**	AK	WS	61218	61718	61918	62118
379019	**NC**	AK	WS	61219	61719	61919	62119
379020	**NC**	AK	WS	61220	61720	61920	62120
379021	**NC**	AK	WS	61221	61721	61921	62121
379022	**NC**	AK	WS	61222	61722	61922	62122
379023	**NC**	AK	WS	61223	61723	61923	62123
379024	**NC**	AK	WS	61224	61724	61924	62124
379025	**NC**	AK	WS	61225	61725	61925	62125
379026	**NC**	AK	WS	61226	61726	61926	62126
379027	**NC**	AK	WS	61227	61727	61927	62127

379028	**NC**	AK		WS	61228	61728	61928	62128
379029	**NC**	AK		WS	61229	61729	61929	62129
379030	**NC**	AK		WS	61230	61730	61930	62130

CLASS 380   DESIRO UK   SIEMENS

ScotRail units mainly used on Strathclyde area services.

Formation: DMS–PTS–DMS or DMS–PTS–TS–DMS.
System: 25 kV AC overhead.
Construction: Welded aluminium with steel ends.
Traction Motors: Four Siemens ITB2016-0GB02 asynchronous of 250 kW.
Wheel Arrangement: Bo-Bo + 2-2 (+2-2) + Bo-Bo

Braking: Disc & regenerative.	**Dimensions:** 23.78/23.57 x 2.80 m.
Bogies: SGP SF5000.	**Couplers:** Voith.
Gangways: Throughout.	**Control System:** IGBT Inverter.
Doors: Sliding plug.	**Maximum Speed:** 100 mph.
Heating & ventilation: Air conditioning.	**Seating Layout:** 2+2 facing/unidirectional.
Multiple Working: Within class.	

DMS(A). Siemens Krefeld 2009–10. –/70. 45.0 t.
PTS. Siemens Krefeld 2009–10. –/57(+12) 1TD 2W. 42.7 t.
TS. Siemens Krefeld 2009–10. –/74 1T. 34.8 t.
DMS(B). Siemens Krefeld 2009–10. –/64(+5). 44.9 t.

Class 380/0. 3-car units. **Formation:** DMS–PTS–DMS.

380001	**SR**	E	*SR*	GW	38501	38601	38701
380002	**SR**	E	*SR*	GW	38502	38602	38702
380003	**SR**	E	*SR*	GW	38503	38603	38703
380004	**SR**	E	*SR*	GW	38504	38604	38704
380005	**SR**	E	*SR*	GW	38505	38605	38705
380006	**SR**	E	*SR*	GW	38506	38606	38706
380007	**SR**	E	*SR*	GW	38507	38607	38707
380008	**SR**	E	*SR*	GW	38508	38608	38708
380009	**SR**	E	*SR*	GW	38509	38609	38709
380010	**SR**	E	*SR*	GW	38510	38610	38710
380011	**SR**	E	*SR*	GW	38511	38611	38711
380012	**SR**	E	*SR*	GW	38512	38612	38712
380013	**SR**	E	*SR*	GW	38513	38613	38713
380014	**SR**	E	*SR*	GW	38514	38614	38714
380015	**SR**	E	*SR*	GW	38515	38615	38715
380016	**SR**	E	*SR*	GW	38516	38616	38716
380017	**SR**	E	*SR*	GW	38517	38617	38717
380018	**SR**	E	*SR*	GW	38518	38618	38718
380019	**SR**	E	*SR*	GW	38519	38619	38719
380020	**SR**	E	*SR*	GW	38520	38620	38720
380021	**SR**	E	*SR*	GW	38521	38621	38721
380022	**SR**	E	*SR*	GW	38522	38622	38722

Class 380/1. 4-car units. **Formation:** DMS–PTS–TS–DMS.

380 101	**SR**	E	*SR*	GW	38551	38651	38851	38751
380 102	**SR**	E	*SR*	GW	38552	38652	38852	38752
380 103	**SR**	E	*SR*	GW	38553	38653	38853	38753
380 104	**SR**	E	*SR*	GW	38554	38654	38854	38754
380 105	**SR**	E	*SR*	GW	38555	38655	38855	38755
380 106	**SR**	E	*SR*	GW	38556	38656	38856	38756
380 107	**SR**	E	*SR*	GW	38557	38657	38857	38757
380 108	**SR**	E	*SR*	GW	38558	38658	38858	38758
380 109	**SR**	E	*SR*	GW	38559	38659	38859	38759
380 110	**SR**	E	*SR*	GW	38560	38660	38860	38760
380 111	**SR**	E	*SR*	GW	38561	38661	38861	38761
380 112	**SR**	E	*SR*	GW	38562	38662	38862	38762
380 113	**SR**	E	*SR*	GW	38563	38663	38863	38763
380 114	**SR**	E	*SR*	GW	38564	38664	38864	38764
380 115	**SR**	E	*SR*	GW	38565	38665	38865	38765
380 116	**SR**	E	*SR*	GW	38566	38666	38866	38766

CLASS 385   AT200   HITACHI

3- and 4-car ScotRail units, financed by Caledonian Rail Leasing.

Formation: DMS–PTS–DMS or DMC–PTS–TS–DMS.
System: 25 kV AC overhead.
Construction: Aluminium.
Traction Motors: Four Hitachi asynchronous of 250 kW.
Wheel Arrangement: Bo-Bo + 2-2 + Bo-2 or Bo-Bo + 2-2 + 2-2 + Bo-Bo.
Braking: Disc & regenerative.
Dimensions: 23.18/22.08 x 2.74 m.   **Couplers:** Dellner.
Bogies: Hitachi.   **Control System:** IGBT Inverter.
Gangways: Throughout.   **Maximum Speed:** 100 mph.
Doors: Sliding plug.   **Multiple Working:** Within class only.
Heating & ventilation: Air conditioning.
Seating Layout: 1: 2+1 facing. 2: 2+2 facing/unidirectional.

Class 385/0. 3-car units. Standard Class only. **Formation:** DMS–PTS–DMS.

DMS(A): Hitachi Newton Aycliffe/Kasado 2016–18. –/48(+9) 1TD 2W. 44.6 t.
PTS: Hitachi Newton Aycliffe/Kasado 2016–18. –/80. 38.4 t.
DMS(B): Hitachi Newton Aycliffe/Kasado 2016–18. –62(+5) 1T. 42.0 t.

385 001	**SR**	CL	*SR*	EC	441001	442001	444001
385 002	**SR**	CL	*SR*	EC	441002	442002	444002
385 003	**SR**	CL	*SR*	EC	441003	442003	444003
385 004	**SR**	CL	*SR*	EC	441004	442004	444004
385 005	**SR**	CL	*SR*	EC	441005	442005	444005
385 006	**SR**	CL	*SR*	EC	441006	442006	444006
385 007	**SR**	CL	*SR*	EC	441007	442007	444007
385 008	**SR**	CL	*SR*	EC	441008	442008	444008
385 009	**SR**	CL	*SR*	EC	441009	442009	444009
385 010	**SR**	CL	*SR*	EC	441010	442010	444010
385 011	**SR**	CL	*SR*	EC	441011	442011	444011

385 012	**SR**	CL	*SR*	EC	441012	442012	444012	
385 013	**SR**	CL	*SR*	EC	441013	442013	444013	
385 014	**SR**	CL	*SR*	EC	441014	442014	444014	
385 015	**SR**	CL	*SR*	EC	441015	442015	444015	
385 016	**SR**	CL	*SR*	EC	441016	442016	444016	
385 017	**SR**	CL	*SR*	EC	441017	442017	444017	
385 018	**SR**	CL	*SR*	EC	441018	442018	444018	
385 019	**SR**	CL	*SR*	EC	441019	442019	444019	
385 020	**SR**	CL	*SR*	EC	441020	442020	444020	
385 021	**SR**	CL	*SR*	EC	441021	442021	444021	
385 022	**SR**	CL	*SR*	EC	441022	442022	444022	
385 023	**SR**	CL	*SR*	EC	441023	442023	444023	
385 024	**SR**	CL	*SR*	EC	441024	442024	444024	
385 025	**SR**	CL	*SR*	EC	441025	442025	444025	
385 026	**SR**	CL	*SR*	EC	441026	442026	444026	
385 027	**SR**	CL	*SR*	EC	441027	442027	444027	
385 028	**SR**	CL	*SR*	EC	441028	442028	444028	
385 029	**SR**	CL	*SR*	EC	441029	442029	444029	
385 030	**SR**	CL	*SR*	EC	441030	442030	444030	
385 031	**SR**	CL	*SR*	EC	441031	442031	444031	
385 032	**SR**	CL	*SR*	EC	441032	442032	444032	
385 033	**SR**	CL	*SR*	EC	441033	442033	444033	
385 034	**SR**	CL	*SR*	EC	441034	442034	444034	
385 035	**SR**	CL	*SR*	EC	441035	442035	444035	
385 036	**SR**	CL	*SR*	EC	441036	442036	444036	
385 037	**SR**	CL	*SR*	EC	441037	442037	444037	
385 038	**SR**	CL	*SR*	EC	441038	442038	444038	
385 039	**SR**	CL	*SR*	EC	441039	442039	444039	
385 040	**SR**	CL	*SR*	EC	441040	442040	444040	
385 041	**SR**	CL	*SR*	EC	441041	442041	444041	
385 042	**SR**	CL	*SR*	EC	441042	442042	444042	
385 043	**SR**	CL	*SR*	EC	441043	442043	444043	
385 044	**SR**	CL	*SR*	EC	441044	442044	444044	
385 045	**SR**	CL	*SR*	EC	441045	442045	444045	
385 046	**SR**	CL	*SR*	EC	441046	442046	444046	

Class 385/1. 4-car units. Standard Class and First Class seating.
Formation: DMC–PTS–TS–DMS.

DMC: Hitachi Newton Aycliffe/Kasado 2016–18. 20/15(+9) 1TD 2W. 44.7 t.
PTS: Hitachi Newton Aycliffe/Kasado 2016–18. –/80. 38.4 t.
TS: Hitachi Newton Aycliffe/Kasado 2016–18. –/80. 31.5 t.
DMS: Hitachi Newton Aycliffe/Kasado 2016–18. –62(+5) 1T. 44.5 t.

385 101	**SR**	CL	*SR*	EC	441101	442101	443101	444101
385 102	**SR**	CL	*SR*	EC	441102	442102	443102	444102
385 103	**SR**	CL	*SR*	EC	441103	442103	443103	444103
385 104	**SR**	CL	*SR*	EC	441104	442104	443104	444104
385 105	**SR**	CL	*SR*	EC	441105	442105	443105	444105
385 106	**SR**	CL	*SR*	EC	441106	442106	443106	444106
385 107	**SR**	CL	*SR*	EC	441107	442107	443107	444107
385 108	**SR**	CL	*SR*	EC	441108	442108	443108	444108

385 109	**SR**	CL	*SR*	EC	441109	442109	443109	444109
385 110	**SR**	CL	*SR*	EC	441110	442110	443110	444110
385 111	**SR**	CL	*SR*	EC	441111	442111	443111	444111
385 112	**SR**	CL	*SR*	EC	441112	442112	443112	444112
385 113	**SR**	CL	*SR*	EC	441113	442113	443113	444113
385 114	**SR**	CL	*SR*	EC	441114	442114	443114	444114
385 115	**SR**	CL	*SR*	EC	441115	442115	443115	444115
385 116	**SR**	CL	*SR*	EC	441116	442116	443116	444116
385 117	**SR**	CL	*SR*	EC	441117	442117	443117	444117
385 118	**SR**	CL	*SR*	EC	441118	442118	443118	444118
385 119	**SR**	CL	*SR*	EC	441119	442119	443119	444119
385 120	**SR**	CL	*SR*	EC	441120	442120	443120	444120
385 121	**SR**	CL	*SR*	EC	441121	442121	443121	444121
385 122	**SR**	CL	*SR*	EC	441122	442122	443122	444122
385 123	**SR**	CL	*SR*	EC	441123	442123	443123	444123
385 124	**SR**	CL	*SR*	EC	441124	442124	443124	444124

CLASS 387   ELECTROSTAR   BOMBARDIER DERBY

The first 29 110 mph Class 387/1s were delivered in 2014–15 for Thameslink. In 2016–17 these transferred to Great Northern for services from King's Cross to Cambridge/King's Lynn and Peterborough.

A further 27 Class 387/2 units were delivered to Southern for Gatwick Express services in 2016 but one is now used by Great Northern.

Great Western Railway took 45 Class 387/1s for services between London Paddington and Reading, Didcot Parkway and Newbury and these now also operate a small number of services to Cardiff Central. 387 130–141 have been fitted with ETCS and are dedicated to the Heathrow Express service.

Part of a speculative order by Porterbrook Leasing, c2c had six Class 387/3s on lease but these are now used by Great Northern.

Formation: DMC/DMS–MS–PTS–DMS.
System: 25 kV AC overhead and 750 V DC third rail.
Construction: Welded aluminium alloy underframe, sides and roof with steel ends. All sections bolted together.
Traction Motors: Two Bombardier asynchronous of 250 kW.
Wheel Arrangement: 2-Bo + 2-Bo + 2-2 + Bo-2.
Braking: Disc & regenerative.   **Dimensions:** 20.39/20.00 x 2.80 m.
Bogies: Bombardier P3-25/T3-25.   **Couplers:** Dellner 12.
Gangways: Throughout.   **Control System:** IGBT Inverter.
Doors: Sliding plug.   **Maximum Speed:** 110 mph.
Heating & ventilation: Air conditioning.
Seating Layout: 2+2 facing/unidirectional.
Multiple Working: Within class and with Class 377.

Class 387/1. Units built for Thameslink, now used by Great Northern.

DMC. Bombardier Derby 2014–15. 22/34. 46.0 t.
MS. Bombardier Derby 2014–15. –/62 1T. 41.3 t.
PTS. Bombardier Derby 2014–15. –/45(+2) 1TD 2W. 41.6 t.
DMS. Bombardier Derby 2014–15. –/60. 45.9 t.

387 101	**TG**	P	*GN*	HE	421101	422101	423101	424101
387 102	**TG**	P	*GN*	HE	421102	422102	423102	424102
387 103	**TG**	P	*GN*	HE	421103	422103	423103	424103
387 104	**TG**	P	*GN*	HE	421104	422104	423104	424104
387 105	**TG**	P	*GN*	HE	421105	422105	423105	424105
387 106	**TG**	P	*GN*	HE	421106	422106	423106	424106
387 107	**TG**	P	*GN*	HE	421107	422107	423107	424107
387 108	**TG**	P	*GN*	HE	421108	422108	423108	424108
387 109	**TG**	P	*GN*	HE	421109	422109	423109	424109
387 110	**TG**	P	*GN*	HE	421110	422110	423110	424110
387 111	**TG**	P	*GN*	HE	421111	422111	423111	424111
387 112	**TG**	P	*GN*	HE	421112	422112	423112	424112
387 113	**TG**	P	*GN*	HE	421113	422113	423113	424113
387 114	**TG**	P	*GN*	HE	421114	422114	423114	424114
387 115	**TG**	P	*GN*	HE	421115	422115	423115	424115
387 116	**TG**	P	*GN*	HE	421116	422116	423116	424116
387 117	**TG**	P	*GN*	HE	421117	422117	423117	424117
387 118	**TG**	P	*GN*	HE	421118	422118	423118	424118
387 119	**TG**	P	*GN*	HE	421119	422119	423119	424119
387 120	**TG**	P	*GN*	HE	421120	422120	423120	424120
387 121	**TG**	P	*GN*	HE	421121	422121	423121	424121
387 122	**TG**	P	*GN*	HE	421122	422122	423122	424122
387 123	**TG**	P	*GN*	HE	421123	422123	423123	424123
387 124	**TG**	P	*GN*	HE	421124	422124	423124	424124
387 125	**TG**	P	*GN*	HE	421125	422125	423125	424125
387 126	**TG**	P	*GN*	HE	421126	422126	423126	424126
387 127	**TG**	P	*GN*	HE	421127	422127	423127	424127
387 128	**TG**	P	*GN*	HE	421128	422128	423128	424128
387 129	**TG**	P	*GN*	HE	421129	422129	423129	424129

Name (carried on DMC): 387 124   Paul McCann

Class 387/1. Heathrow Express units. Fitted with First Class and a modified seating layout with more luggage space and fewer seats for use on Paddington–Heathrow Airport Heathrow Express services. ETCS fitted.

DMC. Bombardier Derby 2016–17. 22/20. 46.0 t.
MS. Bombardier Derby 2016–17. –/54 1T. 41.3 t.
PTS. Bombardier Derby 2016–17. –/39(+2) 1TD 2W. 41.6 t.
DMS. Bombardier Derby 2016–17. –/52. 45.9 t.

387 130	**HX**	P	*HE*	RG	421130	422130	423130	424130
387 131	**HX**	P	*HE*	RG	421131	422131	423131	424131
387 132	**HX**	P	*HE*	RG	421132	422132	423132	424132
387 133	**HX**	P	*HE*	RG	421133	422133	423133	424133
387 134	**HX**	P	*HE*	RG	421134	422134	423134	424134
387 135	**HX**	P	*HE*	RG	421135	422135	423135	424135

387 136	**HX**	P	*HE*	RG	421136	422136	423136	424136
387 137	**HX**	P	*HE*	RG	421137	422137	423137	424137
387 138	**HX**	P	*HE*	RG	421138	422138	423138	424138
387 139	**HX**	P	*HE*	RG	421139	422139	423139	424139
387 140	**HX**	P	*HE*	RG	421140	422140	423140	424140
387 141	**HX**	P	*HE*	RG	421141	422141	423141	424141

Names (carried on end cars):

387 130	SAN FRANCISCO	387 136	PARIS
387 131	SYDNEY	387 137	AMSTERDAM
387 132	NEW YORK	387 138	LAS VEGAS
387 133	TOKYO	387 139	DUBLIN
387 134	BARCELONA	387 140	LONDON
387 135	ROME	387 141	PRAGUE

Class 387/1. Great Western Railway or Great Northern units.

DMS(A). Bombardier Derby 2016–17. –/56. 46.0 t.
MS. Bombardier Derby 2016–17. –/62 1T. 41.3 t.
PTS. Bombardier Derby 2016–17. –/45(+2) 1TD 2W. 41.6 t.
DMS(B). Bombardier Derby 2016–17. –/60. 45.9 t.

387 142	**GW**	P	*GW*	RG	421142	422142	423142	424142
387 143	**GW**	P	*GW*	RG	421143	422143	423143	424143
387 144	**GW**	P	*GW*	RG	421144	422144	423144	424144
387 145	**GW**	P	*GW*	RG	421145	422145	423145	424145
387 146	**GW**	P	*GW*	RG	421146	422146	423146	424146
387 147	**GW**	P	*GW*	RG	421147	422147	423147	424147
387 148	**GW**	P	*GW*	RG	421148	422148	423148	424148
387 149	**GW**	P	*GW*	RG	421149	422149	423149	424149
387 150	**GW**	P	*GW*	RG	421150	422150	423150	424150
387 151	**GW**	P	*GW*	RG	421151	422151	423151	424151
387 152	**GW**	P	*GW*	RG	421152	422152	423152	424152
387 153	**GW**	P	*GW*	RG	421153	422153	423153	424153
387 154	**GW**	P	*GW*	RG	421154	422154	423154	424154
387 155	**GW**	P	*GW*	RG	421155	422155	423155	424155
387 156	**GW**	P	*GW*	RG	421156	422156	423156	424156
387 157	**GW**	P	*GW*	RG	421157	422157	423157	424157
387 158	**GW**	P	*GW*	RG	421158	422158	423158	424158
387 159	**GW**	P	*GW*	RG	421159	422159	423159	424159
387 160	**GW**	P	*GW*	RG	421160	422160	423160	424160
387 161	**GW**	P	*GW*	RG	421161	422161	423161	424161
387 162	**GW**	P	*GW*	RG	421162	422162	423162	424162
387 163	**GW**	P	*GW*	RG	421163	422163	423163	424163
387 164	**GW**	P	*GW*	RG	421164	422164	423164	424164
387 165	**GW**	P	*GW*	RG	421165	422165	423165	424165
387 166	**GW**	P	*GW*	RG	421166	422166	423166	424166
387 167	**GW**	P	*GW*	RG	421167	422167	423167	424167
387 168	**GW**	P	*GW*	RG	421168	422168	423168	424168
387 169	**GW**	P	*GW*	RG	421169	422169	423169	424169
387 170	**GW**	P	*GW*	RG	421170	422170	423170	424170
387 171	**GW**	P	*GW*	RG	421171	422171	423171	424171

387 172	**GW**	P	*GN*	HE	421172	422172	423172	424172
387 173	**GW**	P	*GN*	HE	421173	422173	423173	424173
387 174	**GW**	P	*GN*	HE	421174	422174	423174	424174

Class 387/2. Southern units built for use Gatwick Express-branded services on the London Victoria–Gatwick Airport–Brighton route, but also used on other Southern routes.

DMC. Bombardier Derby 2015–16. 22/34. 46.0 t.
MS. Bombardier Derby 2015–16. –/60 1T. 41.3 t.
PTS. Bombardier Derby 2015–16. –/45(+2) 1TD 2W. 41.6 t.
DMS. Bombardier Derby 2015–16. –/60. 45.9 t.

387 201	**GX**	P	*GN*	HE	421201	422201	423201	424201
387 202	**GX**	P	*SN*	SL	421202	422202	423202	424202
387 203	**GX**	P	*SN*	SL	421203	422203	423203	424203
387 204	**GX**	P	*SN*	SL	421204	422204	423204	424204
387 205	**GX**	P	*SN*	SL	421205	422205	423205	424205
387 206	**GX**	P	*SN*	SL	421206	422206	423206	424206
387 207	**GX**	P	*SN*	SL	421207	422207	423207	424207
387 208	**GX**	P	*SN*	SL	421208	422208	423208	424208
387 209	**GX**	P	*SN*	SL	421209	422209	423209	424209
387 210	**GX**	P	*SN*	SL	421210	422210	423210	424210
387 211	**GX**	P	*SN*	SL	421211	422211	423211	424211
387 212	**GX**	P	*SN*	SL	421212	422212	423212	424212
387 213	**GX**	P	*SN*	SL	421213	422213	423213	424213
387 214	**GX**	P	*SN*	SL	421214	422214	423214	424214
387 215	**GX**	P	*SN*	SL	421215	422215	423215	424215
387 216	**GX**	P	*SN*	SL	421216	422216	423216	424216
387 217	**GX**	P	*SN*	SL	421217	422217	423217	424217
387 218	**GX**	P	*SN*	SL	421218	422218	423218	424218
387 219	**GX**	P	*SN*	SL	421219	422219	423219	424219
387 220	**GX**	P	*SN*	SL	421220	422220	423220	424220
387 221	**GX**	P	*SN*	SL	421221	422221	423221	424221
387 222	**GX**	P	*SN*	SL	421222	422222	423222	424222
387 223	**GX**	P	*SN*	SL	421223	422223	423223	424223
387 224	**GX**	P	*SN*	SL	421224	422224	423224	424224
387 225	**GX**	P	*SN*	SL	421225	422225	423225	424225
387 226	**GX**	P	*SN*	SL	421226	422226	423226	424226
387 227	**GX**	P	*SN*	SL	421227	422227	423227	424227

Class 387/3. Former c2c units now used by Great Northern.

DMS(A). Bombardier Derby 2016. –/56. 46.0 t.
MS. Bombardier Derby 2016. –/62 1T. 41.3 t.
PTS. Bombardier Derby 2016. –/45(+2) 1TD 2W. 41.6 t.
DMS(B). Bombardier Derby 2016. –/60. 45.9 t.

387 301	**C2**	P	*GN*	HE	421301	422301	423301	424301
387 302	**C2**	P	*GN*	HE	421302	422302	423302	424302
387 303	**C2**	P	*GN*	HE	421303	422303	423303	424303
387 304	**C2**	P	*GN*	HE	421304	422304	423304	424304
387 305	**C2**	P	*GN*	HE	421305	422305	423305	424305
387 306	**C2**	P	*GN*	HE	421306	422306	423306	424306

CLASS 390   PENDOLINO   ALSTOM

Tilting units used on the West Coast Main Line.

Formation: As listed below.   **Construction:** Welded aluminium alloy.
Traction Motors: Two Alstom ONIX 800 of 425 kW.
Wheel Arrangement: 1A-A1 + 1A-A1 + 2-2 + 1A-A1 (+ 2-2 + 1A-A1) + 2-2 +
1A-A1 + 2-2 + 1A-A1 + 1A-A1.   **Braking:** Disc, rheostatic & regenerative.
Dimensions: 24.80/23.90 x 2.73 m.   **Couplers:** Dellner 12.
Bogies: Fiat-SIG.   **Control System:** IGBT Inverter.
Gangways: Within unit.   **Maximum Speed:** 125 mph.
Doors: Sliding plug.   **Heating & ventilation:** Air conditioning.
Seating Layout: 1: 2+1 facing/unidirectional, 2: 2+2 facing/unidirectional.
Multiple Working: Within class. Can also be controlled from Class 57/3 locos.

Units up to 390034 were delivered as 8-car sets, without the TS (688xx).
During 2004–05 these units were increased to 9-cars.

62 extra vehicles were built 2010–12 to lengthen 31 sets to 11-cars. On
renumbering units were renumbered by adding 100 to the set number. Four new
complete 11-car units were also delivered. All these extra vehicles were built
at Savigliano, Italy (all original Pendolino vehicles were built at Birmingham).

The 9-car units had their MF(B) converted to an MS in 2015 to give them a
better balance of Standard to First Class seating.

390033 was written off in the Lambrigg accident of February 2007.

Non-standard liveries:

390 119 Pride celebration colours.
390 121 Race Against Climate Change (various colours).

Class 390/0. Original build 9-car units.

* Refurbished units.

Formation: DMRF–MF–PTF–MS–TS–MS–PTSRMB–MS–DMS.

DMRBF: Alstom Birmingham/Savigliano 2001–05. 18/–. 56.3 t.
MF: Alstom Birmingham/Savigliano 2001–05. 37/–(+2) 1TD 1W. 52.3 t.
PTF: Alstom Birmingham/Savigliano 2001–05. 44/– 1T. 51.2 t.
MS: Alstom Birmingham/Savigliano 2001–05. –/76 1T. 52.3 t.
TS: Alstom Birmingham/Savigliano 2001–05. –/76 1T. 45.5 t.
MS: Alstom Birmingham/Savigliano 2001–05. –/62(+4) 1TD 1W. 52.0 t.
PTSRMB: Alstom Birmingham/Savigliano 2001–05. –/48. 53.2 t.
MS: Alstom Birmingham/Savigliano 2001–05. –/62(+2) 1TD 1W. 52.5 t.
DMS: Alstom Birmingham/Savigliano 2001–05. –/46 1T. 54.5 t.

390 001	*	**AT**	A	*AW* MA	69101	69401	69501	69601	68801
					69701	69801	69901	69201	
390 002		**AT**	A	*AW* MA	69102	69402	69502	69602	68802
					69702	69802	69902	69202	
390 005	*	**AT**	A	*AW* MA	69105	69405	69505	69605	68805
					69705	69805	69905	69205	

390 006	*	AT	A	AW MA	69106 69406 69506 69606 68806
					69706 69806 69906 69206
390 008		AT	A	AW MA	69108 69408 69508 69608 68808
					69708 69808 69908 69208
390 009	*	AT	A	AW MA	69109 69409 69509 69609 68809
					69709 69809 69909 69209
390 010		AT	A	AW MA	69110 69410 69510 69610 68810
					69710 69810 69910 69210
390 011		AT	A	AW MA	69111 69411 69511 69611 68811
					69711 69811 69911 69211
390 013		AT	A	AW MA	69113 69413 69513 69613 68813
					69713 69813 69913 69213
390 016	*	AT	A	AW MA	69116 69416 69516 69616 68816
					69716 69816 69916 69216
390 020		AT	A	AW MA	69120 69420 69520 69620 68820
					69720 69820 69920 69220
390 039	*	AT	A	AW MA	69139 69439 69539 69639 68839
					69739 69839 69939 69239
390 040	*	AT	A	AW MA	69140 69440 69540 69640 68840
					69740 69840 69940 69240
390 042		AT	A	AW MA	69142 69442 69542 69642 68842
					69742 69842 69942 69242
390 043		AT	A	AW MA	69143 69443 69543 69643 68843
					69743 69843 69943 69243
390 044	*	AT	A	AW MA	69144 69444 69544 69644 68844
					69744 69844 69944 69244
390 045	*	AT	A	AW MA	69145 69445 69545 69645 68845
					69745 69845 69945 69245
390 046		AT	A	AW MA	69146 69446 69546 69646 68846
					69746 69846 69946 69246
390 047		AT	A	AW MA	69147 69447 69547 69647 68847
					69747 69847 69947 69247
390 049		AT	A	AW MA	69149 69449 69549 69649 68849
					69749 69849 69949 69249
390 050	*	AT	A	AW MA	69150 69450 69550 69650 68850
					69750 69850 69950 69250

Class 390/1. Original build 9-car units later extended to 11-cars, except 390 154–157 which were built new (in Italy) as 11-cars. All units have been refurbished at Alstom Widnes which included converting an MF coach to an MS and removing a number of Standard Class seats to provide additional luggage space.

Formation: DMRF–MF–PTF–MS–TS–MS–TS–MS–PTSRMB–MS–DMS.

DMRBF: Alstom Birmingham/Savigliano 2001–05/2010–12. 18/–. 56.3 t.
MF: Alstom Birmingham/Savigliano 2001–05/2010–12. 37/–(+2) 1TD 1W. 52.3 t.
PTF: Alstom Birmingham/Savigliano 2001–05/2010–12. 44/– 1T. 51.2 t.
MS: Alstom Birmingham/Savigliano 2001–05/2010–12. –/74 1T. 52.3 t.
TS: Alstom Savigliano 2010–12. –/72 1T. 49.2 t.
MS: Alstom Savigliano 2010–12. –/74 1T. 52.2 t.
TS: Alstom Birmingham/Savigliano 2001–05/2010–12. –/74 1T. 45.5 t.

MS: Alstom Birmingham/Savigliano 2001–05/2010–12. –/60(+4) 1TD 1W. 52.0 t.
PTSRMB: Alstom Birmingham/Savigliano 2001–05/2010–12. –/48. 53.2 t.
MS: Alstom Birmingham/Savigliano 2001–05/2010–12. –/60(+2) 1TD 1W. 52.5 t.
DMS: Alstom Birmingham/Savigliano 2001–05/2010–12. –/46 1T. 54.5 t.

390 103	**AT**	A	*AW* MA	69103 69403 69503 69603 65303 68903
				68803 69703 69803 69903 69203
390 104	**AT**	A	*AW* MA	69104 69404 69504 69604 65304 68904
				68804 69704 69804 69904 69204
390 107	**AT**	A	*AW* MA	69107 69407 69507 69607 65307 68907
				68807 69707 69807 69907 69207
390 112	**AT**	A	*AW* MA	69112 69412 69512 69612 65312 68912
				68812 69712 69812 69912 69212
390 114	**AT**	A	*AW* MA	69114 69414 69514 69614 65314 68914
				68814 69714 69814 69914 69214
390 115	**AT**	A	*AW* MA	69115 69415 69515 69615 65315 68915
				68815 69715 69815 69915 69215
390 117	**AT**	A	*AW* MA	69117 69417 69517 69617 65317 68917
				68817 69717 69817 69917 69217
390 118	**AT**	A	*AW* MA	69118 69418 69518 69618 65318 68918
				68818 69718 69818 69918 69218
390 119	**0**	A	*AW* MA	69119 69419 69519 69619 65319 68919
				68819 69719 69819 69919 69219
390 121	**0**	A	*AW* MA	69121 69421 69521 69621 65321 68921
				68821 69721 69821 69921 69221
390 122	**AT**	A	*AW* MA	69122 69422 69522 69622 65322 68922
				68822 69722 69822 69922 69222
390 123	**AT**	A	*AW* MA	69123 69423 69523 69623 65323 68923
				68823 69723 69823 69923 69223
390 124	**AT**	A	*AW* MA	69124 69424 69524 69624 65324 68924
				68824 69724 69824 69924 69224
390 125	**AT**	A	*AW* MA	69125 69425 69525 69625 65325 68925
				68825 69725 69825 69925 69225
390 126	**AT**	A	*AW* MA	69126 69426 69526 69626 65326 68926
				68826 69726 69826 69926 69226
390 127	**AT**	A	*AW* MA	69127 69427 69527 69627 65327 68927
				68827 69727 69827 69927 69227
390 128	**AT**	A	*AW* MA	69128 69428 69528 69628 65328 68928
				68828 69728 69828 69928 69228
390 129	**AT**	A	*AW* MA	69129 69429 69529 69629 65329 68929
				68829 69729 69829 69929 69229
390 130	**AT**	A	*AW* MA	69130 69430 69530 69630 65330 68930
				68830 69730 69830 69930 69230
390 131	**AT**	A	*AW* MA	69131 69431 69531 69631 65331 68931
				68831 69731 69831 69931 69231
390 132	**AT**	A	*AW* MA	69132 69432 69532 69632 65332 68932
				68832 69732 69832 69932 69232
390 134	**AT**	A	*AW* MA	69134 69434 69534 69634 65334 68934
				68834 69734 69834 69934 69234
390 135	**AT**	A	*AW* MA	69135 69435 69535 69635 65335 68935
				68835 69735 69835 69935 69235

390 136	**AT**	A	*AW* MA	69136	69436	69536	69636	65336	68936
				68836	69736	69836	69936	69236	
390 137	**AT**	A	*AW* MA	69137	69437	69537	69637	65337	68937
				68837	69737	69837	69937	69237	
390 138	**AT**	A	*AW* MA	69138	69438	69538	69638	65338	68938
				68838	69738	69838	69938	69238	
390 141	**AT**	A	*AW* MA	69141	69441	69541	69641	65341	68941
				68841	69741	69841	69941	69241	
390 148	**AT**	A	*AW* MA	69148	69448	69548	69648	65348	68948
				68848	69748	69848	69948	69248	
390 151	**AT**	A	*AW* MA	69151	69451	69551	69651	65351	68951
				68851	69751	69851	69951	69251	
390 152	**AT**	A	*AW* MA	69152	69452	69552	69652	65352	68952
				68852	69752	69852	69952	69252	
390 153	**AT**	A	*AW* MA	69153	69453	69553	69653	65353	68953
				68853	69753	69853	69953	69253	
390 154	**AT**	A	*AW* MA	69154	69454	69554	69654	65354	68954
				68854	69754	69854	69954	69254	
390 155	**AT**	A	*AW* MA	69155	69455	69555	69655	65355	68955
				68855	69755	69855	69955	69255	
390 156	**AT**	A	*AW* MA	69156	69456	69556	69656	65356	68956
				68856	69756	69856	69956	69256	
390 157	**AT**	A	*AW* MA	69157	69457	69557	69657	65357	68957
				68857	69757	69857	69957	69257	

Names (carried on MF No. 696xx):

390 001 Bee Together	390 119 PROGRESS
390 002 Stephen Sutton	390 121 OPPORTUNITY
390 005 City of Wolverhampton	390 122 Penny the Pendolino
390 006 Rethink Mental Illness	390 128 City of Preston
390 008 CHARLES RENNIE MACKINTOSH	390 129 City of Stoke-on-Trent
390 009 Treaty of Union	390 130 City of Edinburgh
390 010 Cumbrian Spirit	390 131 City of Liverpool
390 011 City of Lichfield	390 132 City of Birmingham
390 013 Blackpool Belle	390 134 City of Carlisle
390 039 Lady Godiva	390 135 City of Lancaster
390 044 Royal Scot	390 136 City of Coventry
390 045 BIRMINGHAM PRIDE	390 138 City of London
390 103 ASQUITH XAVIER	390 148 Flying Scouseman
390 104 Alstom Pendolino	390 151 Unknown Soldier
390 114 City of Manchester	390 155 RAILWAY BENEFIT FUND
390 115 Crewe – All Change	390 156 Pride and Prosperity
390 117 Blue Peter	390 157 Chad Varah

CLASS 395   JAVELIN   HITACHI JAPAN

6-car dual-voltage units used on Southeastern High Speed trains from London St Pancras.

Formation: PDTS–MS–MS–MS–MS–PDTS.
Systems: 25 kV AC overhead/750 V DC third rail.
Construction: Aluminium.
Traction Motors: Four Hitachi asynchronous of 210 kW.
Wheel Arrangement: 2-2 + Bo-Bo + Bo-Bo + Bo-Bo + Bo-Bo + 2-2.
Braking: Disc, rheostatic & regenerative.
Dimensions: 20.88/20.0 x 2.81 m.   **Couplers:** Scharfenberg.
Bogies: Hitachi.   **Control System:** IGBT Inverter.
Gangways: Within unit.   **Maximum Speed:** 140 mph.
Doors: Single-leaf sliding.   **Multiple Working:** Within class only.
Heating & ventilation: Air conditioning.
Seating Layout: 2+2 facing/unidirectional (mainly unidirectional).

PDTS(A): Hitachi Kasado, Japan 2006–09. –/28(+12) 1TD 2W. 46.7 t.
MS: Hitachi Kasado, Japan 2006–09. –/66. 45.0t–45.7 t.
PDTS(B): Hitachi Kasado, Japan 2006–09. –/48 1T. 46.7 t.

395001	**SB**	E	*SE*	AD	39011	39012	39013	39014	39015	39016
395002	**SB**	E	*SE*	AD	39021	39022	39023	39024	39025	39026
395003	**SB**	E	*SE*	AD	39031	39032	39033	39034	39035	39036
395004	**SB**	E	*SE*	AD	39041	39042	39043	39044	39045	39046
395005	**SB**	E	*SE*	AD	39051	39052	39053	39054	39055	39056
395006	**SB**	E	*SE*	AD	39061	39062	39063	39064	39065	39066
395007	**SB**	E	*SE*	AD	39071	39072	39073	39074	39075	39076
395008	**SB**	E	*SE*	AD	39081	39082	39083	39084	39085	39086
395009	**SB**	E	*SE*	AD	39091	39092	39093	39094	39095	39096
395010	**SB**	E	*SE*	AD	39101	39102	39103	39104	39105	39106
395011	**SB**	E	*SE*	AD	39111	39112	39113	39114	39115	39116
395012	**SB**	E	*SE*	AD	39121	39122	39123	39124	39125	39126
395013	**SB**	E	*SE*	AD	39131	39132	39133	39134	39135	39136
395014	**SB**	E	*SE*	AD	39141	39142	39143	39144	39145	39146
395015	**SB**	E	*SE*	AD	39151	39152	39153	39154	39155	39156
395016	**SB**	E	*SE*	AD	39161	39162	39163	39164	39165	39166
395017	**SB**	E	*SE*	AD	39171	39172	39173	39174	39175	39176
395018	**SB**	E	*SE*	AD	39181	39182	39183	39184	39185	39186
395019	**SB**	E	*SE*	AD	39191	39192	39193	39194	39195	39196
395020	**SB**	E	*SE*	AD	39201	39202	39203	39204	39205	39206
395021	**SB**	E	*SE*	AD	39211	39212	39213	39214	39215	39216
395022	**SB**	E	*SE*	AD	39221	39222	39223	39224	39225	39226
395023	**SB**	E	*SE*	AD	39231	39232	39233	39234	39235	39236
395024	**SB**	E	*SE*	AD	39241	39242	39243	39244	39245	39246
395025	**SB**	E	*SE*	AD	39251	39252	39253	39254	39255	39256
395026	**SB**	E	*SE*	AD	39261	39262	39263	39264	39265	39266
395027	**SB**	E	*SE*	AD	39271	39272	39273	39274	39275	39276
395028	**SB**	E	*SE*	AD	39281	39282	39283	39284	39285	39286
395029	**SB**	E	*SE*	AD	39291	39292	39293	39294	39295	39296

Names (carried on end cars):

395001	Dame Kelly Holmes	395018	THE VICTORY Javelin
395002	Sebastian Coe	395019	Jessica Ennis
395003	Sir Steve Redgrave	395020	Jason Kenny
395004	Sir Chris Hoy	395021	Ed Clancy MBE
395005	Dame Tanni Grey-Thompson	395022	Alistair Brownlee
395006	Daley Thompson	395023	Ellie Simmonds
395007	Steve Backley	395024	Jonnie Peacock
395008	Ben Ainslie	395025	Victoria Pendleton
395009	Rebecca Adlington	395026	Marc Woods
395010	Duncan Goodhew	395027	Hannah Cockroft
395011	Katherine Grainger	395028	Laura Trott
395013	HORNBY Visitor Centre Margate, Kent	395029	David Weir
395014	Dina Asher-Smith		

CLASS 397 CIVITY CAF

TransPennine Express units used on the West Coast Main Line Manchester Airport–Edinburgh/Glasgow services, plus Liverpool–Glasgow.

Formation: DMF–PTS–MS–PTS–DMS.
Construction: Aluminium.
Traction Motors: Four TSA of 220 kW.
Wheel Arrangement:

Braking: Disc and regenerative.	**Dimensions:** 24.03/23.35 x 2.71 m.
Bogies: CAF.	**Couplers:** Dellner.
Gangways: Within unit.	**Control System:** IGBT Inverter.
Doors: Sliding plug.	**Maximum Speed:** 125 mph.

Heating & ventilation: Air conditioning.
Seating: 1: 2+1 facing/unidirectional; 2: 2+2 facing/unidirectional.
Multiple Working: Within class.

DMF. CAF Beasain 2017–19. 24/– 1TD 2W. 41.4 t.
PTS(A). CAF Beasain 2017–19. –/76. 34.5 t.
MS. CAF Beasain 2017–19. –/68 2T. 36.6 t.
PTS(B). CAF Beasain 2017–19. –/76. 34.9 t.
DMS. CAF Beasain 2017–19. –/44(+8) 1T. 39.2 t.

397001	**TP**	E	*TP*	MA	471001	472001	473001	474001	475001
397002	**TP**	E	*TP*	MA	471002	472002	473002	474002	475002
397003	**TP**	E	*TP*	MA	471003	472003	473003	474003	475003
397004	**TP**	E	*TP*	MA	471004	472004	473004	474004	475004
397005	**TP**	E	*TP*	MA	471005	472005	473005	474005	475005
397006	**TP**	E	*TP*	MA	471006	472006	473006	474006	475006
397007	**TP**	E	*TP*	MA	471007	472007	473007	474007	475007
397008	**TP**	E	*TP*	MA	471008	472008	473008	474008	475008
397009	**TP**	E	*TP*	MA	471009	472009	473009	474009	475009
397010	**TP**	E	*TP*	MA	471010	472010	473010	474010	475010
397011	**TP**	E	*TP*	MA	471011	472011	473011	474011	475011
397012	**TP**	E	*TP*	MA	471012	472012	473012	474012	475012

CLASS 398   CITYLINK   STADLER

New 3-car Citylink bi-mode electric/battery metro tram-train units currently being delivered for Transport for Wales for use on the Cardiff Valley Lines (Aberdare, Merthyr Tydfil, Treherbert and the Cardiff City Line). Due to enter service from late 2024 working from the new depot at Taff's Well.

Formation: DMS–TS–DMS.
Systems: 25 kV AC overhead/battery.
Construction: Steel.
Traction Motors: 4 x 140 kW (per unit).
Wheel Arrangement: Bo-2-2-Bo.   **Weight:** 76.8 t.
Braking: Disc, regenerative & emergency track.
Dimensions: 40.00 x 2.65 m (full set). **Couplers:**
Bogies: Stadler.   **Control System:** IGBT Inverter.
Gangways: Within unit.   **Maximum Speed:** 60 mph.
Doors: Sliding plug.   **Multiple Working:** Within class only.
Seating Layout: 2+2 unidirectional/facing.

DMS(A): Stadler, Valencia 2020–24. –/34(+7).
MS: Stadler, Valencia 2020–24. –/36(+14).
DMS(B): Stadler, Valencia 2020–24. –/34(+7).

398001	**TW**	SM		999051	999151	999251
398002	**TW**	SM		999052	999152	999252
398003	**TW**	SM		999053	999153	999253
398004	**TW**	SM		999054	999154	999254
398005	**TW**	SM		999055	999155	999255
398006	**TW**	SM		999056	999156	999256
398007	**TW**	SM		999057	999157	999257
398008	**TW**	SM		999058	999158	999258
398009	**TW**	SM		999059	999159	999259
398010	**TW**	SM		999060	999160	999260
398011	**TW**	SM		999061	999161	999261
398012	**TW**	SM		999062	999162	999262
398013	**TW**	SM		999063	999163	999263
398014	**TW**	SM		999064	999164	999264
398015	**TW**	SM		999065	999165	999265
398016	**TW**	SM		999066	999166	999266
398017	**TW**	SM		999067	999167	999267
398018	**TW**	SM		999068	999168	999268
398019	**TW**	SM		999069	999169	999269
398020	**TW**	SM		999070	999170	999270
398021	**TW**	SM		999071	999171	999271
398022	**TW**	SM		999072	999172	999272
398023	**TW**	SM		999073	999173	999273
398024	**TW**	SM		999074	999174	999274
398025	**TW**	SM		999075	999175	999275
398026	**TW**	SM		999076	999176	999276
398027	**TW**	SM		999077	999177	999277
398028	**TW**	SM		999078	999178	999278
398029	**TW**	SM		999079	999179	999279

398 030	**TW**	SM	999080	999180	999280
398 031	**TW**	SM	999081	999181	999281
398 032	**TW**	SM	999082	999182	999282
398 033	**TW**	SM	999083	999183	999283
398 034	**TW**	SM	999084	999184	999284
398 035	**TW**	SM	999085	999185	999285
398 036	**TW**	SM	999086	999186	999286

CLASS 399   CITYLINK   VOSSLOH/STADLER

The Class 399s are tram-trains used on the pilot Sheffield–Rotherham Parkgate tram-train service. This launched in 2018, operated by Stagecoach Supertram. They are dual-voltage 750 V DC/25 kV AC (although currently only operating on 750 V DC). For operation on Network Rail lines EMU running numbers 399 201–207 are carried (as well as vehicle numbers in the 999xxx series), in addition to the Stagecoach Supertram fleet numbers 201–207.

Following two separate accidents in autumn 2018 units 399 202 and 399 204 are operating in mixed formations, as shown.

At the time of writing units 399 201–205 have tram-train wheel profiles for operating on the National Rail network to Rotherham Parkgate. 399 206/207 can only operate on the tramway network, but could be modified to operate to Rotherham if required, 399 206 having been modified to operate to Rotherham in 2018–20 to cover for the accident-damaged 399 204.

Formation: DMS–MS–DMS.
Systems: 750 V DC/25 kV AC overhead.
Construction: Steel.
Traction Motors: Six VEM of 145 kW (per unit).
Wheel Arrangement: Bo-2-Bo-Bo.   **Weight:** 64 t.
Braking: Disc, regenerative & emergency brake.
Dimensions: 37.20 x 2.65 m (full set). **Couplers:** Albert (emergency use).
Bogies: Vossloh.   **Control System:** IGBT Inverter.
Gangways: Within unit.   **Maximum Speed:** 60 mph.
Doors: Sliding plug.   **Multiple Working:** Within class only.
Seating Layout: 2+2 facing/unidirectional.

DMS(A): Vossloh, Valencia 2014–15. –/22(+4) 1W.
MS: Vossloh, Valencia 2014–15. –/44.
DMS(B): Vossloh, Valencia 2014–15. –/22(+4) 1W.

399 201	**SD**	SY	*SY*	NU	999001	999101	999201
399 202	**SD**	SY	*SY*	NU	999002	999102	999204
399 203	**SD**	SY	*SY*	NU	999003	999103	999203
399 204	**SD**	SY	*SY*	NU	999004	999104	999202
399 205	**SD**	SY	*SY*	NU	999005	999105	999205
399 206	**SD**	SY	*SY*	NU	999006	999106	999206
399 207	**SD**	SY	*SY*	NU	999007	999107	999207

Name (carried on cars 999002 and 999204):

399 202   Theo – The Children's Hospital Charity

4.2. 750 V DC THIRD RAIL EMUs

These classes use the third rail system at 750 V DC (unless stated). Outer couplers are buckeyes on units built before 1982 with bar couplers within the units. Newer units generally have Dellner outer couplers.

CLASS 444   DESIRO UK   SIEMENS

Express units.

Formation: DMS–TS–TS–TS–DMC.
Construction: Aluminium.
Traction Motors: Four Siemens 1TB2016-0GB02 asynchronous of 250 kW.
Wheel Arrangement: Bo-Bo + 2-2 + 2-2 + 2-2 + Bo-Bo.
Braking: Disc, rheostatic & regenerative. **Dimensions:** 23.57 x 2.69 m.
Bogies: SGP SF5000.   **Couplers:** Dellner 12.
Gangways: Throughout.   **Control System:** IGBT Inverter.
Doors: Single-leaf sliding plug.   **Maximum Speed:** 100 mph.
Heating & Ventilation: Air conditioning.
Seating Layout: 1: 2+2 facing/unidirectional, 2: 2+2 facing/unidirectional.
Multiple Working: Within class and with Class 450.

DMS. Siemens Vienna/Krefeld 2003–04. –/76. 51.0t.
TS 67101–145. Siemens Vienna/Krefeld 2003–04. –/76 1T. 40.3t.
TS 67151–195. Siemens Vienna/Krefeld 2003–04. –/76 1T. 36.8t.
TS. Siemens Vienna/Krefeld 2003–04. –/59 1TD 1T 2W. 42.1t.
DMC. Siemens Vienna/Krefeld 2003–04. 32/40. 51.3t.

444 001	**SW**	A	*SW*	NT	63801	67101	67151	67201	63851
444 002	**SW**	A	*SW*	NT	63802	67102	67152	67202	63852
444 003	**SW**	A	*SW*	NT	63803	67103	67153	67203	63853
444 004	**SW**	A	*SW*	NT	63804	67104	67154	67204	63854
444 005	**SW**	A	*SW*	NT	63805	67105	67155	67205	63855
444 006	**SW**	A	*SW*	NT	63806	67106	67156	67206	63856
444 007	**SW**	A	*SW*	NT	63807	67107	67157	67207	63857
444 008	**SW**	A	*SW*	NT	63808	67108	67158	67208	63858
444 009	**SW**	A	*SW*	NT	63809	67109	67159	67209	63859
444 010	**SW**	A	*SW*	NT	63810	67110	67160	67210	63860
444 011	**SW**	A	*SW*	NT	63811	67111	67161	67211	63861
444 012	**SW**	A	*SW*	NT	63812	67112	67162	67212	63862
444 013	**SW**	A	*SW*	NT	63813	67113	67163	67213	63863
444 014	**SW**	A	*SW*	NT	63814	67114	67164	67214	63864
444 015	**SW**	A	*SW*	NT	63815	67115	67165	67215	63865
444 016	**SW**	A	*SW*	NT	63816	67116	67166	67216	63866
444 017	**SW**	A	*SW*	NT	63817	67117	67167	67217	63867
444 018	**SW**	A	*SW*	NT	63818	67118	67168	67218	63868
444 019	**SW**	A	*SW*	NT	63819	67119	67169	67219	63869
444 020	**SW**	A	*SW*	NT	63820	67120	67170	67220	63870
444 021	**SW**	A	*SW*	NT	63821	67121	67171	67221	63871
444 022	**SW**	A	*SW*	NT	63822	67122	67172	67222	63872
444 023	**SW**	A	*SW*	NT	63823	67123	67173	67223	63873

444024	**SW**	A	*SW*	NT	63824	67124	67174	67224	63874
444025	**SW**	A	*SW*	NT	63825	67125	67175	67225	63875
444026	**SW**	A	*SW*	NT	63826	67126	67176	67226	63876
444027	**SW**	A	*SW*	NT	63827	67127	67177	67227	63877
444028	**SW**	A	*SW*	NT	63828	67128	67178	67228	63878
444029	**SW**	A	*SW*	NT	63829	67129	67179	67229	63879
444030	**SW**	A	*SW*	NT	63830	67130	67180	67230	63880
444031	**SW**	A	*SW*	NT	63831	67131	67181	67231	63881
444032	**SW**	A	*SW*	NT	63832	67132	67182	67232	63882
444033	**SW**	A	*SW*	NT	63833	67133	67183	67233	63883
444034	**SW**	A	*SW*	NT	63834	67134	67184	67234	63884
444035	**SW**	A	*SW*	NT	63835	67135	67185	67235	63885
444036	**SW**	A	*SW*	NT	63836	67136	67186	67236	63886
444037	**SW**	A	*SW*	NT	63837	67137	67187	67237	63887
444038	**SW**	A	*SW*	NT	63838	67138	67188	67238	63888
444039	**SW**	A	*SW*	NT	63839	67139	67189	67239	63889
444040	**SW**	A	*SW*	NT	63840	67140	67190	67240	63890
444041	**SW**	A	*SW*	NT	63841	67141	67191	67241	63891
444042	**SW**	A	*SW*	NT	63842	67142	67192	67242	63892
444043	**SW**	A	*SW*	NT	63843	67143	67193	67243	63893
444044	**SW**	A	*SW*	NT	63844	67144	67194	67244	63894
444045	**SW**	A	*SW*	NT	63845	67145	67195	67245	63895

Names (carried on TSRMB):

444001	NAOMI HOUSE	444023	The Alex Wardle Foundation
444012	DESTINATION WEYMOUTH	444038	SOUTH WESTERN RAILWAY
444018	THE FAB 444	444040	THE D-DAY STORY PORTSMOUTH

CLASS 450   DESIRO UK   SIEMENS

Outer suburban units.

Formation: DMC–TS–TS–DMC.
Construction: Aluminium.
Traction Motors: Four Siemens 1TB2016-0GB02 asynchronous of 250 kW.
Wheel Arrangement: Bo-Bo + 2-2 + 2-2 + Bo-Bo.
Braking: Disc, rheostatic & regenerative. **Dimensions:** 20.34 x 2.79 m.
Bogies: SGP SF5000.   **Couplers:** Dellner 12.
Gangways: Throughout.   **Control System:** IGBT Inverter.
Doors: Sliding plug.   **Maximum Speed:** 100 mph.
Heating & Ventilation: Air conditioning.
Seating Layout: 1: 2+2 facing/unidirectional, 2: 3+2 facing/unidirectional.
Multiple Working: Within class and with Class 444.

Advertising livery: 450067 Keyworkers (blue on driving cars).

450043–070 were numbered 450543–570 between 2007/08 and 2019. They were renumbered back into the 450/0 series in 2019.

DMC(A). Siemens Krefeld/Vienna 2002–06. 8/62. 48.0 t.
TS(A). Siemens Krefeld/Vienna 2002–06. –/70(+4) 1T. 35.8 t.
TS(B). Siemens Krefeld/Vienna 2002–06. –/61(+9) 1TD 2W. 39.8 t.
DMC(B). Siemens Krefeld/Vienna 2002–06. 8/62. 48.6 t.

450001	**SW**	A	*SW*	NT	63201	64201	68101	63601
450002	**SW**	A	*SW*	NT	63202	64202	68102	63602
450003	**SW**	A	*SW*	NT	63203	64203	68103	63603
450004	**SW**	A	*SW*	NT	63204	64204	68104	63604
450005	**SW**	A	*SW*	NT	63205	64205	68105	63605
450006	**SW**	A	*SW*	NT	63206	64206	68106	63606
450007	**SW**	A	*SW*	NT	63207	64207	68107	63607
450008	**SW**	A	*SW*	NT	63208	64208	68108	63608
450009	**SW**	A	*SW*	NT	63209	64209	68109	63609
450010	**SW**	A	*SW*	NT	63210	64210	68110	63610
450011	**SW**	A	*SW*	NT	63211	64211	68111	63611
450012	**SW**	A	*SW*	NT	63212	64212	68112	63612
450013	**SW**	A	*SW*	NT	63213	64213	68113	63613
450014	**SW**	A	*SW*	NT	63214	64214	68114	63614
450015	**SW**	A	*SW*	NT	63215	64215	68115	63615
450016	**SW**	A	*SW*	NT	63216	64216	68116	63616
450017	**SW**	A	*SW*	NT	63217	64217	68117	63617
450018	**SW**	A	*SW*	NT	63218	64218	68118	63618
450019	**SW**	A	*SW*	NT	63219	64219	68119	63619
450020	**SW**	A	*SW*	NT	63220	64220	68120	63620
450021	**SW**	A	*SW*	NT	63221	64221	68121	63621
450022	**SW**	A	*SW*	NT	63222	64222	68122	63622
450023	**SW**	A	*SW*	NT	63223	64223	68123	63623
450024	**SW**	A	*SW*	NT	63224	64224	68124	63624
450025	**SW**	A	*SW*	NT	63225	64225	68125	63625
450026	**SW**	A	*SW*	NT	63226	64226	68126	63626
450027	**SW**	A	*SW*	NT	63227	64227	68127	63627
450028	**SW**	A	*SW*	NT	63228	64228	68128	63628
450029	**SW**	A	*SW*	NT	63229	64229	68129	63629
450030	**SW**	A	*SW*	NT	63230	64230	68130	63630
450031	**SD**	A	*SW*	NT	63231	64231	68131	63631
450032	**SW**	A	*SW*	NT	63232	64232	68132	63632
450033	**SW**	A	*SW*	NT	63233	64233	68133	63633
450034	**SW**	A	*SW*	NT	63234	64234	68134	63634
450035	**SW**	A	*SW*	NT	63235	64235	68135	63635
450036	**SW**	A	*SW*	NT	63236	64236	68136	63636
450037	**SW**	A	*SW*	NT	63237	64237	68137	63637
450038	**SW**	A	*SW*	NT	63238	64238	68138	63638
450039	**SW**	A	*SW*	NT	63239	64239	68139	63639
450040	**SW**	A	*SW*	NT	63240	64240	68140	63640
450041	**SW**	A	*SW*	NT	63241	64241	68141	63641
450042	**SW**	A	*SW*	NT	63242	64242	68142	63642
450043	**SW**	A	*SW*	NT	63243	64243	68143	63643
450044	**SW**	A	*SW*	NT	63244	64244	68144	63644
450045	**SW**	A	*SW*	NT	63245	64245	68145	63645
450046	**SW**	A	*SW*	NT	63246	64246	68146	63646
450047	**SW**	A	*SW*	NT	63247	64247	68147	63647
450048	**SW**	A	*SW*	NT	63248	64248	68148	63648
450049	**SW**	A	*SW*	NT	63249	64249	68149	63649
450050	**SW**	A	*SW*	NT	63250	64250	68150	63650
450051	**SW**	A	*SW*	NT	63251	64251	68151	63651

450 052	SW	A	SW	NT	63252	64252	68152	63652
450 053	SW	A	SW	NT	63253	64253	68153	63653
450 054	SW	A	SW	NT	63254	64254	68154	63654
450 055	SW	A	SW	NT	63255	64255	68155	63655
450 056	SW	A	SW	NT	63256	64256	68156	63656
450 057	SW	A	SW	NT	63257	64257	68157	63657
450 058	SW	A	SW	NT	63258	64258	68158	63658
450 059	SW	A	SW	NT	63259	64259	68159	63659
450 060	SW	A	SW	NT	63260	64260	68160	63660
450 061	SW	A	SW	NT	63261	64261	68161	63661
450 062	SW	A	SW	NT	63262	64262	68162	63662
450 063	SW	A	SW	NT	63263	64263	68163	63663
450 064	SW	A	SW	NT	63264	64264	68164	63664
450 065	SW	A	SW	NT	63265	64265	68165	63665
450 066	SW	A	SW	NT	63266	64266	68166	63666
450 067	AL	A	SW	NT	63267	64267	68167	63667
450 068	SW	A	SW	NT	63268	64268	68168	63668
450 069	SW	A	SW	NT	63269	64269	68169	63669
450 070	SW	A	SW	NT	63270	64270	68170	63670
450 071	SW	A	SW	NT	63271	64271	68171	63671
450 072	SW	A	SW	NT	63272	64272	68172	63672
450 073	SW	A	SW	NT	63273	64273	68173	63673
450 074	SW	A	SW	NT	63274	64274	68174	63674
450 075	SW	A	SW	NT	63275	64275	68175	63675
450 076	SW	A	SW	NT	63276	64276	68176	63676
450 077	SW	A	SW	NT	63277	64277	68177	63677
450 078	SW	A	SW	NT	63278	64278	68178	63678
450 079	SW	A	SW	NT	63279	64279	68179	63679
450 080	SW	A	SW	NT	63280	64280	68180	63680
450 081	SW	A	SW	NT	63281	64281	68181	63681
450 082	SW	A	SW	NT	63282	64282	68182	63682
450 083	SW	A	SW	NT	63283	64283	68183	63683
450 084	SW	A	SW	NT	63284	64284	68184	63684
450 085	SW	A	SW	NT	63285	64285	68185	63685
450 086	SW	A	SW	NT	63286	64286	68186	63686
450 087	SW	A	SW	NT	63287	64287	68187	63687
450 088	SW	A	SW	NT	63288	64288	68188	63688
450 089	SW	A	SW	NT	63289	64289	68189	63689
450 090	SW	A	SW	NT	63290	64290	68190	63690
450 091	SW	A	SW	NT	63291	64291	68191	63691
450 092	SW	A	SW	NT	63292	64292	68192	63692
450 093	SW	A	SW	NT	63293	64293	68193	63693
450 094	SW	A	SW	NT	63294	64294	68194	63694
450 095	SW	A	SW	NT	63295	64295	68195	63695
450 096	SW	A	SW	NT	63296	64296	68196	63696
450 097	SW	A	SW	NT	63297	64297	68197	63697
450 098	SW	A	SW	NT	63298	64298	68198	63698
450 099	SD	A	SW	NT	63299	64299	68199	63699
450 100	SW	A	SW	NT	63300	64300	68200	63700
450 101	SW	A	SW	NT	63701	66851	66801	63751
450 102	SW	A	SW	NT	63702	66852	66802	63752

450 103	**SW**	A	*SW*	NT	63703	66853	66803	63753
450 104	**SW**	A	*SW*	NT	63704	66854	66804	63754
450 105	**SW**	A	*SW*	NT	63705	66855	66805	63755
450 106	**SW**	A	*SW*	NT	63706	66856	66806	63756
450 107	**SW**	A	*SW*	NT	63707	66857	66807	63757
450 108	**SW**	A	*SW*	NT	63708	66858	66808	63758
450 109	**SW**	A	*SW*	NT	63709	66859	66809	63759
450 110	**SW**	A	*SW*	NT	63710	66860	66810	63760
450 111	**SW**	A	*SW*	NT	63921	66901	66921	63901
450 112	**SW**	A	*SW*	NT	63922	66902	66922	63902
450 113	**SW**	A	*SW*	NT	63923	66903	66923	63903
450 114	**SW**	A	*SW*	NT	63924	66904	66924	63904
450 115	**SW**	A	*SW*	NT	63925	66905	66925	63905
450 116	**SD**	A	*SW*	NT	63926	66906	66926	63906
450 117	**SW**	A	*SW*	NT	63927	66907	66927	63907
450 118	**SD**	A	*SW*	NT	63928	66908	66928	63908
450 119	**SW**	A	*SW*	NT	63929	66909	66929	63909
450 120	**SW**	A	*SW*	NT	63930	66910	66930	63910
450 121	**SW**	Λ	*SW*	NT	63931	66911	66931	63911
450 122	**SW**	A	*SW*	NT	63932	66912	66932	63912
450 123	**SW**	A	*SW*	NT	63933	66913	66933	63913
450 124	**SW**	A	*SW*	NT	63934	66914	66934	63914
450 125	**SW**	A	*SW*	NT	63935	66915	66935	63915
450 126	**SW**	A	*SW*	NT	63936	66916	66936	63916
450 127	**SW**	A	*SW*	NT	63937	66917	66937	63917

Names (carried on DMSO(B)):

450015 DESIRO
450042 TRELOAR COLLEGE
450100 Transport Benevolent Fund CIO 1923–2023
450114 FAIRBRIDGE investing in the future
450127 DAVE GUNSON

CLASS 455   BREL YORK

Inner suburban units. During 2016–17 the South Western Railway fleet was fitted with new AC traction motors by Vossloh Kiepe. During 2022 the whole Southern fleet of Class 455/8 units was withdrawn and scrapped.

Formation: DTS–MS–TS–DTS.
Construction: Steel. Class 455/7 TS have a steel underframe and an aluminium alloy body and roof.
Traction Motors: Four TSA010163 AC motors of 240 kW.
Wheel Arrangement: 2-2 + Bo-Bo + 2-2 + 2-2.
Braking: Disc and regenerative).   **Dimensions:** 19.92/19.83 x 2.82 m.
Bogies: P7 (motor) and T3 (455/8 & 455/9) BX1 (455/7) trailer.
Gangways: Within unit + end doors.
Couplers: Tightlock.   **Maximum Speed:** 75 mph.
Control System: IGBT Inverter.
Doors: Sliding.   **Heating & Ventilation:** Various.

Seating Layout: 2+2 high-back unidirectional/facing seating.
Multiple Working: Within class.

Class 455/7. Second series with TSs originally in Class 508s. Pressure heating & ventilation.

DTS. Lot No. 30976 1984–85. –/50(+4) 1W. 30.8t.
MS. Lot No. 30975 1984–85. –/68. 45.7t.
TS. Lot No. 30944 1979–80. –/68. 26.1t.

5701	**SS**	P	*SW*	WD	77727	62783	71545	77728
5702	**SS**	P	*SW*	WD	77729	62784	71547	77730
5703	**SS**	P	*SW*	WD	77731	62785	71540	77732
5705	**SS**	P	*SW*	WD	77735	62787	71565	77736
5706	**SS**	P	*SW*	WD	77737	62788	71534	77738
5707	**SS**	P	*SW*	WD	77739	62789	71536	77740
5708	**SS**	P	*SW*	WD	77741	62790	71560	77742
5709	**SS**	P	*SW*	WD	77743	62791	71532	77744
5710	**SS**	P	*SW*	WD	77745	62792	71566	77746
5711	**SS**	P	*SW*	WD	77747	62793	71542	77748
5712	**SS**	P	*SW*	WD	77749	62794	71546	77750
5713	**SS**	P	*SW*	WD	77751	62795	71567	77752
5714	**SS**	P	*SW*	WD	77753	62796	71539	77754
5715	**SS**	P	*SW*	WD	77755	62797	71535	77756
5716	**SS**	P	*SW*	WD	77757	62798	71564	77758
5717	**SS**	P	*SW*	WD	77759	62799	71528	77760
5718	**SS**	P	*SW*	WD	77761	62800	71557	77762
5719	**SS**	P	*SW*	WD	77763	62801	71558	77764
5720	**SS**	P	*SW*	WD	77765	62802	71568	77766
5721	**SS**	P	*SW*	WD	77767	62803	71553	77768
5723	**SS**	P	*SW*	WD	77771	62805	71526	77772
5724	**SS**	P	*SW*	WD	77773	62806	71561	77774
5725	**SS**	P	*SW*	WD	77775	62807	71541	77776
5727	**SS**	P	*SW*	WD	77779	62809	71562	77780
5728	**SS**	P	*SW*	WD	77781	62810	71527	77782
5729	**SS**	P	*SW*	WD	77783	62811	71550	77784
5730	**SS**	P	*SW*	WD	77785	62812	71551	77786
5731	**SS**	P	*SW*	WD	77787	62813	71555	77788
5732	**SS**	P	*SW*	WD	77789	62814	71552	77790
5733	**SS**	P	*SW*	WD	77791	62815	71549	77792
5734	**SS**	P	*SW*	WD	77793	62816	71531	77794
5735	**SS**	P	*SW*	WD	77795	62817	71563	77796
5737	**SS**	P	*SW*	WD	77799	62819	71544	77800
5738	**SS**	P	*SW*	WD	77801	62820	71529	77802
5739	**SS**	P	*SW*	WD	77803	62821	71537	77804
5741	**SS**	P	*SW*	WD	77807	62823	71559	77808
5742	**SS**	P	*SW*	WD	77809	62824	71543	77810
5750	**SS**	P	*SW*	WD	77811	62825	71538	77812

Class 455/8. First series. Pressure heating & ventilation.

DTS. Lot No. 30972 York 1982–84. –50(+4) 1W. 29.5 t.
MS. Lot No. 30973 York 1982–84. –/68. 45.6 t.
TS. Lot No. 30974 York 1982–84. –/68. 27.1 t.

5848	**SS**	P	*SW*	WD	77673	62756	71684	77674
5849	**SS**	P	*SW*	WD	77675	62757	71685	77676
5850	**SS**	P	*SW*	WD	77677	62758	71686	77678
5851	**SS**	P	*SW*	WD	77679	62759	71687	77680
5852	**SS**	P	*SW*	WD	77681	62760	71688	77682
5853	**SS**	P	*SW*	WD	77683	62761	71689	77684
5854	**SS**	P	*SW*	WD	77685	62762	71690	77686
5856	**SS**	P	*SW*	WD	77689	62764	71692	77690
5857	**SS**	P	*SW*	WD	77691	62765	71693	77692
5858	**SS**	P	*SW*	WD	77693	62766	71694	77694
5859	**SS**	P	*SW*	WD	77695	62767	71695	77696
5860	**SS**	P	*SW*	WD	77697	62768	71696	77698
5861	**SS**	P	*SW*	WD	77699	62769	71697	77700
5862	**SS**	P	*SW*	WD	77701	62770	71698	77702
5863	**SS**	P	*SW*	WD	77703	62771	71699	77704
5864	**SS**	P	*SW*	WD	77705	62772	71700	77706
5865	**SS**	P	*SW*	WD	77707	62773	71701	77708
5866	**SS**	P	*SW*	WD	77709	62774	71702	77710
5867	**SS**	P	*SW*	WD	77711	62775	71703	77712
5868	**SS**	P	*SW*	WD	77713	62776	71704	77714
5869	**SS**	P	*SW*	WD	77715	62777	71705	77716
5870	**SS**	P	*SW*	WD	77717	62778	71706	77718
5871	**SS**	P	*SW*	WD	77719	62779	71707	77720
5872	**SS**	P	*SW*	WD	77721	62780	71708	77722
5873	**SS**	P	*SW*	WD	77723	62781	71709	77724
5874	**SS**	P	*SW*	WD	77725	62782	71710	77726

Class 455/9. Third series. Convection heating.
Dimensions: 19.96/20.18 x 2.82 m.

67301 and 67400 were converted from Class 210 DEMU vehicles to replace accident damaged cars.

DTS. Lot No. 30991 York 1985. –/50(+4) 1W. 30.7 t.
MS. Lot No. 30992 York 1985. –/68. 46.3 t.
MS 67301. Lot No. 30932 Derby 1981. –/68.   t.
TS. Lot No. 30993 York 1985. –/68. 28.3 t.
TS 67400. Lot No. 30932 Derby 1981. –/68. 28.3 t.

5901	**SS**	P	*SW*	WD	77813	62826	71714	77814
5902	**SS**	P	*SW*	WD	77815	62827	71715	77816
5903	**SS**	P	*SW*	WD	77817	62828	71716	77818
5904	**SS**	P	*SW*	WD	77819	62829	71717	77820
5905	**SS**	P	*SW*	WD	77821	62830	71725	77822
5906	**SS**	P	*SW*	WD	77823	62831	71719	77824
5908	**SS**	P	*SW*	WD	77827	62833	71721	77828
5909	**SS**	P	*SW*	WD	77829	62834	71722	77830
5910	**SS**	P	*SW*	WD	77831	62835	71723	77832

5911	**SS**	P	*SW*	WD	77833	62836	71724	77834
5912	**SS**	P	*SW*	WD	77835	62837	67400	77836
5913	**SS**	P	*SW*	WD	77837	67301	71726	77838
5914	**SS**	P	*SW*	WD	77839	62839	71727	77840
5915	**SS**	P	*SW*	WD	77841	62840	71728	77842
5916	**SS**	P	*SW*	WD	77843	62841	71729	77844
5917	**SS**	P	*SW*	WD	77845	62842	71730	77846
5919	**SS**	P	*SW*	WD	77849	62844	71718	77850
5920	**SS**	P	*SW*	WD	77851	62845	71733	77852

CLASS 458   JUNIPER   ALSTOM BIRMINGHAM

Outer suburban units. In 2013–16 the fleet of 30 4-car Class 458 units and the former Gatwick Express eight 8-car Class 460 units was combined to form a fleet of 36 5-car Standard Class only Class 458/5s. Former Class 460 driving cars 67901/903/907/908 were not included in this programme and were scrapped. After lengthening each unit was renumbered into the 458 5xx series. All individual vehicles retained their original numbers.

In the longer-term South Western Railway is retaining 28 units (458501–528) which are currently being reformed back as 4-car sets numbered 458401–428. The work to refurbish these units is being carried out at Alstom, Widnes and also includes a change in maximum speed to 100 mph for longer-distance work.

Formation: See class sub-headings.
Construction: Steel.   **Dimensions:** 21.16 or 21.06 x 2.80 m.
Traction Motors: Two Alstom ONIX 800 asynchronous of 270 kW.
Wheel Arrangement: 2-Bo (+ 2-2) + 2-2 + Bo-2 + Bo-2.
Braking: Disc & regenerative.   **Control System:** IGBT Inverter.
Bogies: ACR.   **Doors:** Sliding plug.
Gangways: Throughout.   **Couplers:** Voith 136.
Maximum Speed: 458/4: 100 mph; 458/5: 75 mph.
Heating & Ventilation: Air conditioning. **Multiple Working:** Within class.
Seating Layout: 2+2 facing/unidirectional.

Class 458/4. 4-car units. Following refurbishment these units are being returned to their original formation for longer-distance duties. Full details awaited. **Formation:** DMC–TS–MS–DMC.

DMC(A). Alstom 1998–2000. 12/52.
TS. Alstom 1998–2000. –/42 1TD 2W.
MS. Alstom 1998–2000. –/64 1T.
DMC(B). Alstom 1998–2000. 12/52.

458 401							
458 402							
458 403							
458 404	**SW**	P		WI	67604	74004	74104	67704
458 405	**SW**	P		BM	67605	74005	74105	67705
458 406							

458 407	**SW**	P	*SW*	BM	67607	74007	74107	67707
458 408								
458 409								
458 410								
458 411								
458 412								
458 413								
458 414								
458 415								
458 416	**SW**	P		WI	67616	74016	74116	67716
458 417	**SW**	P	*SW*	BM	67617	74017	74117	67717
458 418								
458 419								
458 420	**SW**	P		WI	67620	74020	74120	67720
458 421								
458 422								
458 423	**SW**	P	*SW*	BM	67623	74023	74123	67723
458 424	**SW**	P		BM	67624	74024	74124	67724
458 425	**SW**	P		BM	67625	74025	74125	67725
458 426								
458 427								
458 428	**SW**	P		BM	67628	74028	74128	67728

Class 458/5. 5-car units. **Formation:** DMS–TS*–TS–MS–DMS (* ex-Class 460 in 458 501–530).

DMS(A). Alstom 1998–2000. –/60. 45.7 t.
TS. Alstom 1998–2000. 458 501–530 –/56; 458 531–536 –/52 1T. 34.4 t.
TS. Alstom 1998–2000. –/42 1TD 2W. 34.1 t.
MS. Alstom 1998–2000. 458 501–530 –/56 1T; 458 531–536 –/56. 40.1 t.
DMS(B). Alstom 1998–2000. –/60. 44.9 t.

458 501	**SD**	P	*SW*	WD	67601	74431	74001	74101	67701
458 502	**SD**	P	*SW*	WD	67602	74421	74002	74102	67702
458 503	**SD**	P	*SW*	WD	67603	74441	74003	74103	67703
458 506	**SD**	P	*SW*	WD	67606	74436	74006	74106	67706
458 508	**SD**	P	*SW*	WD	67608	74433	74008	74108	67708
458 509	**SD**	P	*SW*	WD	67609	74452	74009	74109	67709
458 510	**SD**	P	*SW*	WD	67610	74405	74010	74110	67710
458 511	**SD**	P	*SW*	WD	67611	74435	74011	74111	67711
458 512	**SD**	P	*SW*	WD	67612	74427	74012	74112	67712
458 513	**SD**	P	*SW*	WD	67613	74437	74013	74113	67713
458 514	**SD**	P	*SW*	WD	67614	74407	74014	74114	67714
458 515	**SD**	P	*SW*	WD	67615	74404	74015	74115	67715
458 518	**SD**	P	*SW*	WD	67618	74432	74018	74118	67718
458 519	**SD**	P	*SW*	WD	67619	74403	74019	74119	67719
458 521	**SD**	P	*SW*	WD	67621	74438	74021	74121	67721
458 522	**SD**	P	*SW*	WD	67622	74424	74022	74122	67722
458 526	**SD**	P	*SW*	WD	67626	74442	74026	74126	67726
458 527	**SD**	P	*SW*	WD	67627	74412	74027	74127	67727
458 529	**SD**	P	*SW*	WD	67629	74423	74029	74129	67729
458 530	**SD**	P	*SW*	WD	67630	74411	74030	74130	67730

| Spares | **SD** | P | | LM | 74401 74402 74406 74408 74422 |
| | | | | | 74425 74426 74428 74434 74451 |

The following units were converted entirely from Class 460s.

458531	**SD**	P	*SW*	WD	67913 74418 74446 74458 67912
458532	**SD**	P	*SW*	WD	67904 74417 74447 74457 67905
458533	**SD**	P	*SW*	WD	67917 74413 74443 74453 67916
458534	**SD**	P	*SW*	WD	67914 74414 74444 74454 67918
458535	**SD**	P	*SW*	WD	67915 74415 74445 74455 67911
458536	**SD**	P	*SW*	WD	67906 74416 74448 74456 67902

CLASS 465   NETWORKER

Inner and outer suburban units.

Formation: DMS–TS–TS–DMS.
Construction: Welded aluminium alloy.
Traction Motors: Four Hitachi asynchronous of 280 kW (Classes 465/0 and 465/1) or Four GEC-Alsthom G352BY of 280 kW (Classes 465/2 and 465/9).
Wheel Arrangement: Bo-Bo + 2-2 + 2-2 + Bo-Bo.
Braking: Disc & rheostatic and regenerative (Classes 465/0 and 465/1 only).
Bogies: BREL P3/T3 (465/0 and 465/1), SRP BP62/BT52 (465/2 and 465/9).
Dimensions: 20.89/20.06 x 2.81 m.
Control System: IGBT Inverter (465/0 and 465/1) or 1992-type GTO Inverter.
Gangways: Within unit.   **Couplers:** Tightlock.
Doors: Sliding plug.   **Maximum Speed:** 75 mph.
Seating Layout: 3+2 facing/unidirectional.
Multiple Working: Within class and with Class 466.

64759–808. DMS(A). Lot No. 31100 BREL York 1991–93. –/86. 39.2t.
64809–858. DMS(B). Lot No. 31100 BREL York 1991–93. –/86. 39.2t.
65734–749. DMS(A). Lot No. 31103 Metro-Cammell 1991–93. –/86. 39.2t.
65784–799. DMS(B). Lot No. 31103 Metro-Cammell 1991–93. –/86. 39.2t.
65800–846. DMS(A). Lot No. 31130 ABB York 1993–94. –/86. 39.2t.
65847–893. DMS(B). Lot No. 31130 ABB York 1993–94. –/86. 39.2t.
72028–126 (even nos.) TS. Lot No. 31102 BREL York 1991–93. –/90. 27.2t.
72029–127 (odd nos.) TS. Lot No. 31101 BREL York 1991–93. –/65(+7) 1TD 2W. 29.6 t.
72787–817 (odd nos.) TS. Lot No. 31104 Metro-Cammell 1991–92. –/65(+7) 1TD 2W. 30.2 t.
72788–818 (even nos.) TS. Lot No. 31105 Metro-Cammell 1991–92. –/90. 29.4t.
72900–992 (even nos.) TS. Lot No. 31102 ABB York 1993–94. –/90. 27.2t.
72901–993 (odd nos.) TS. Lot No. 31101 ABB York 1993–94. –/65(+7) 1TD 2W. 29.6 t.

Class 465/0. Built by BREL/ABB.

465001	**SE**	E	*SE*	SG	64759	72028	72029	64809
465002	**SE**	E	*SE*	SG	64760	72030	72031	64810
465003	**SE**	E	*SE*	SG	64761	72032	72033	64811
465004	**SE**	E	*SE*	SG	64762	72034	72035	64812
465005	**SE**	E	*SE*	SG	64763	72036	72037	64813
465006	**SE**	E	*SE*	SG	64764	72038	72039	64814
465007	**SE**	E	*SE*	SG	64765	72040	72041	64815

465 008	**SE**	E	*SE*	SG	64766	72042	72043	64816
465 009	**SE**	E	*SE*	SG	64767	72044	72045	64817
465 010	**SE**	E	*SE*	SG	64768	72046	72047	64818
465 011	**SE**	E	*SE*	SG	64769	72048	72049	64819
465 012	**SE**	E	*SE*	SG	64770	72050	72051	64820
465 013	**SE**	E	*SE*	SG	64771	72052	72053	64821
465 014	**SE**	E	*SE*	SG	64772	72054	72055	64822
465 015	**SE**	E	*SE*	SG	64773	72056	72057	64823
465 016	**SE**	E	*SE*	SG	64774	72058	72059	64824
465 017	**SE**	E	*SE*	SG	64775	72060	72061	64825
465 018	**SE**	E	*SE*	SG	64776	72062	72063	64826
465 019	**SE**	E	*SE*	SG	64777	72064	72065	64827
465 020	**SE**	E	*SE*	SG	64778	72066	72067	64828
465 021	**SE**	E	*SE*	SG	64779	72068	72069	64829
465 022	**SE**	E	*SE*	SG	64780	72070	72071	64830
465 023	**SE**	E	*SE*	SG	64781	72072	72073	64831
465 024	**SE**	E	*SE*	SG	64782	72074	72075	64832
465 025	**SE**	E	*SE*	SG	64783	72076	72077	64833
465 026	**SE**	E	*SE*	SG	64784	72078	72079	64834
465 027	**SE**	E	*SE*	SG	64785	72080	72081	64835
465 028	**SE**	E	*SE*	SG	64786	72082	72083	64836
465 029	**SE**	E	*SE*	SG	64787	72084	72085	64837
465 030	**SE**	E	*SE*	SG	64788	72086	72087	64838
465 031	**SE**	E	*SE*	SG	64789	72088	72089	64839
465 032	**SE**	E	*SE*	SG	64790	72090	72091	64840
465 033	**SE**	E	*SE*	SG	64791	72092	72093	64841
465 034	**SE**	E	*SE*	SG	64792	72094	72095	64842
465 035	**SE**	E	*SE*	SG	64793	72096	72097	64843
465 036	**SE**	E	*SE*	SG	64794	72098	72099	64844
465 037	**SE**	E	*SE*	SG	64795	72100	72101	64845
465 038	**SE**	E	*SE*	SG	64796	72102	72103	64846
465 039	**SE**	E	*SE*	SG	64797	72104	72105	64847
465 040	**SE**	E	*SE*	SG	64798	72106	72107	64848
465 041	**SE**	E	*SE*	SG	64799	72108	72109	64849
465 042	**SE**	E	*SE*	SG	64800	72110	72111	64850
465 043	**SE**	E	*SE*	SG	64801	72112	72113	64851
465 044	**SE**	E	*SE*	SG	64802	72114	72115	64852
465 045	**SE**	E	*SE*	SG	64803	72116	72117	64853
465 046	**SE**	E	*SE*	SG	64804	72118	72119	64854
465 047	**SE**	E	*SE*	SG	64805	72120	72121	64855
465 048	**SE**	E	*SE*	SG	64806	72122	72123	64856
465 049	**SE**	E	*SE*	SG	64807	72124	72125	64857
465 050	**SE**	E	*SE*	SG	64808	72126	72127	64858

Class 465/1. Built by BREL/ABB. Similar to Class 465/0 but with detail differences.

465 151	**SE**	E	*SE*	SG	65800	72900	72901	65847
465 152	**SE**	E	*SE*	SG	65801	72902	72903	65848
465 153	**SE**	E	*SE*	SG	65802	72904	72905	65849
465 154	**SE**	E	*SE*	SG	65803	72906	72907	65850
465 155	**SE**	E	*SE*	SG	65804	72908	72909	65851
465 156	**SE**	E	*SE*	SG	65805	72910	72911	65852

465 157	**SE**	E	*SE*	SG	65806	72912	72913	65853
465 158	**SE**	E	*SE*	SG	65807	72914	72915	65854
465 159	**SE**	E	*SE*	SG	65808	72916	72917	65855
465 160	**SE**	E	*SE*	SG	65809	72918	72919	65856
465 161	**SE**	E	*SE*	SG	65810	72920	72921	65857
465 162	**SE**	E	*SE*	SG	65811	72922	72923	65858
465 163	**SE**	E	*SE*	SG	65812	72924	72925	65859
465 164	**SE**	E	*SE*	SG	65813	72926	72927	65860
465 165	**SE**	E	*SE*	SG	65814	72928	72929	65861
465 166	**SE**	E	*SE*	SG	65815	72930	72931	65862
465 167	**SE**	E	*SE*	SG	65816	72932	72933	65863
465 168	**SE**	E	*SE*	SG	65817	72934	72935	65864
465 169	**SE**	E	*SE*	SG	65818	72936	72937	65865
465 170	**SE**	E	*SE*	SG	65819	72938	72939	65866
465 171	**SE**	E	*SE*	SG	65820	72940	72941	65867
465 172	**SE**	E	*SE*	SG	65821	72942	72943	65868
465 173	**SE**	E	*SE*	SG	65822	72944	72945	65869
465 174	**SE**	E	*SE*	SG	65823	72946	72947	65870
465 175	**SE**	E	*SE*	SG	65824	72948	72949	65871
465 176	**SE**	E	*SE*	SG	65825	72950	72951	65872
465 177	**SE**	E	*SE*	SG	65826	72952	72953	65873
465 178	**SE**	E	*SE*	SG	65827	72954	72955	65874
465 179	**SE**	E	*SE*	SG	65828	72956	72957	65875
465 180	**SE**	E	*SE*	SG	65829	72958	72959	65876
465 181	**SE**	E	*SE*	SG	65830	72960	72961	65877
465 182	**SE**	E	*SE*	SG	65831	72962	72963	65878
465 183	**SE**	E	*SE*	SG	65832	72964	72965	65879
465 184	**SE**	E	*SE*	SG	65833	72966	72967	65880
465 185	**SE**	E	*SE*	SG	65834	72968	72969	65881
465 186	**SE**	E	*SE*	SG	65835	72970	72971	65882
465 187	**SE**	E	*SE*	SG	65836	72972	72973	65883
465 188	**SE**	E	*SE*	SG	65837	72974	72975	65884
465 189	**SE**	E	*SE*	SG	65838	72976	72977	65885
465 190	**SE**	E	*SE*	SG	65839	72978	72979	65886
465 191	**SE**	E	*SE*	SG	65840	72980	72981	65887
465 192	**SE**	E	*SE*	SG	65841	72982	72983	65888
465 193	**SE**	E	*SE*	SG	65842	72984	72985	65889
465 194	**SE**	E	*SE*	SG	65843	72986	72987	65890
465 195	**SE**	E	*SE*	SG	65844	72988	72989	65891
465 196	**SE**	E	*SE*	SG	65845	72990	72991	65892
465 197	**SE**	E	*SE*	SG	65846	72992	72993	65893

Class 465/2. Built by Metro-Cammell. **Dimensions:** 20.80/20.15 x 2.81 m.

465 235	**SE**	A		ZB	65734	72787	72788	65784
465 236	**SE**	A		EP	65735	72789	72790	65785
465 237	**SE**	A		EP	65736	72791	72792	65786
465 238	**SE**	A		EP	65737	72793	72794	65787
465 239	**SE**	A		EP	65738	72795	72796	65788
465 240	**SE**	A		EP	65739	72797	72798	65789
465 241	**SE**	A		WS	65740	72799	72800	65790
465 242	**SE**	A		WS	65741	72801	72802	65791

465 243	**SE**	A		EP	65742	72803	72804	65792
465 244	**SE**	A		EP	65743	72805	72806	65793
465 245	**SE**	A		EP	65744	72807	72808	65794
465 246	**SE**	A		EP	65745	72809	72810	65795
465 247	**SE**	A		WS	65746	72811	72812	65796
465 248	**SE**	A		EP	65747	72813	72814	65797
465 249	**SE**	A		EP	65748	72815	72816	65798
465 250	**SE**	A		EP	65749	72817	72818	65799

Class 465/9. Built by Metro-Cammell. Refurbished 2005 for longer distance services, with the addition of First Class (now declassified). Details as Class 465/0 unless stated.

Formation: DMC–TS–TS–DMC.
Seating Layout: 1: 2+2 facing/unidirectional, 2: 3+2 facing/unidirectional.

65700–733. DMC(A). Lot No. 31103 Metro-Cammell 1991–93. –/80. 39.2t.
72719–785 (odd nos.) TS(A). Lot No. 31104 Metro-Cammell 1991–92. –/65(+7) 1TD 2W. 30.3t.
72720–786 (even nos.) TS(B). Lot No. 31105 Metro-Cammell 1991–92. –/90. 29.5t.
65750–783. DMC(B). Lot No. 31103 Metro-Cammell 1991–93. –/80. 39.2t.

465 901	(465 201)	**SE**	A	*SE*	SG	65700	72719 72720	65750
465 902	(465 202)	**SE**	A	*SE*	SG	65701	72721 72722	65751
465 903	(465 203)	**SE**	A	*SE*	SG	65702	72723 72724	65752
465 904	(465 204)	**SE**	A	*SE*	SG	65703	72725 72726	65753
465 905	(465 205)	**SE**	A		WS	65704	72727 72728	65754
465 906	(465 206)	**SE**	A	*SE*	SG	65705	72729 72730	65755
465 907	(465 207)	**SE**	A	*SE*	SG	65706	72731 72732	65756
465 908	(465 208)	**SE**	A	*SE*	SG	65707	72733 72734	65757
465 909	(465 209)	**SE**	A	*SE*	SG	65708	72735 72736	65758
465 910	(465 210)	**SE**	A	*SE*	SG	65709	72737 72738	65759
465 911	(465 211)	**SE**	A	*SE*	SG	65710	72739 72740	65760
465 912	(465 212)	**SE**	A	*SE*	SG	65711	72741 72742	65761
465 913	(465 213)	**SE**	A	*SE*	SG	65712	72743 72744	65762
465 914	(465 214)	**SE**	A	*SE*	SG	65713	72745 72746	65763
465 915	(465 215)	**SE**	A		WS	65714	72747 72748	65764
465 916	(465 216)	**SE**	A	*SE*	SG	65715	72749 72750	65765
465 917	(465 217)	**SE**	A		WS	65716	72751 72752	65766
465 918	(465 218)	**SE**	A		WS	65717	72753 72754	65767
465 919	(465 219)	**SE**	A	*SE*	SG	65718	72755 72756	65768
465 920	(465 220)	**SE**	A		WS	65719	72757 72758	65769
465 921	(465 221)	**SE**	A		WS	65720	72759 72760	65770
465 922	(465 222)	**SE**	A	*SE*	SG	65721	72761 72762	65771
465 923	(465 223)	**SE**	A	*SE*	SG	65722	72763 72764	65772
465 924	(465 224)	**SE**	A	*SE*	SG	65723	72765 72766	65773
465 925	(465 225)	**SE**	A	*SE*	SG	65724	72767 72768	65774
465 926	(465 226)	**SE**	A	*SE*	SG	65725	72769 72770	65775
465 927	(465 227)	**SE**	A	*SE*	SG	65726	72771 72772	65776
465 928	(465 228)	**SE**	A	*SE*	SG	65727	72773 72774	65777
465 929	(465 229)	**SE**	A	*SE*	SG	65728	72775 72776	65778
465 930	(465 230)	**SE**	A		WS	65729	72777 72778	65779
465 931	(465 231)	**SE**	A		WS	65730	72779 72780	65780

465932	(465232)	**SE**	A	*SE*	SG	65731 72781 72782 65781
465933	(465233)	**SE**	A		WS	65732 72783 72784 65782
465934	(465234)	**SE**	A		WS	65733 72785 72786 65783

CLASS 466   NETWORKER   GEC-ALSTHOM

Inner and outer suburban units.

Formation: DMS–DTS.
Construction: Welded aluminium alloy.
Traction Motors: Two GEC-Alsthom G352AY asynchronous of 280 kW.
Wheel Arrangement: Bo-Bo + 2-2.   **Couplers:** Tightlock.
Braking: Disc, rheostatic & regen.   **Control System:** 1992-type GTO Inverter.
Dimensions: 20.80 x 2.80 m.   **Maximum Speed:** 75 mph.
Bogies: BREL P3/T3.   **Doors:** Sliding plug.
Gangways: Within unit.
Seating Layout: 3+2 facing/unidirectional.
Multiple Working: Within class and with Class 465.

DMS. Lot No. 31128 Birmingham 1993–94. –/86. 40.6t.
DTS. Lot No. 31129 Birmingham 1993–94. –/82 1T. 31.4t.

466001	**SE**	A		WS	64860 78312
466002	**SE**	A	*SE*	SG	64861 78313
466003	**SE**	A	*SE*	SG	64862 78314
466004	**SE**	A	*SE*	SG	64863 78315
466005	**SE**	A		WS	64864 78316
466006	**SE**	A	*SE*	SG	64865 78317
466007	**SE**	A	*SE*	SG	64866 78318
466008	**SE**	A	*SE*	SG	64867 78319
466009	**SE**	A		WS	64868 78320
466010	**SE**	A		WS	64869 78321
466011	**SE**	A	*SE*	SG	64870 78322
466012	**SE**	A	*SE*	SG	64871 78323
466013	**SE**	A		WS	64872 78324
466014	**SE**	A	*SE*	SG	64873 78325
466015	**SE**	A	*SE*	SG	64874 78326
466016	**SE**	A		ZB	64875 78327
466017	**SE**	A		WS	64876 78328
466018	**SE**	A	*SE*	SG	64877 78329
466019	**SE**	A	*SE*	SG	64878 78330
466020	**SE**	A	*SE*	SG	64879 78331
466021	**SE**	A	*SE*	SG	64880 78332
466022	**SE**	A	*SE*	SG	64881 78333
466023	**SE**	A	*SE*	SG	64882 78334
466024	**SE**	A		WS	64883 78335
466025	**SE**	A	*SE*	SG	64884 78336
466026	**SE**	A	*SE*	SG	64885 78337
466027	**SE**	A		WS	64886 78338
466028	**SE**	A	*SE*	SG	64887 78339
466029	**SE**	A	*SE*	SG	64888 78340

466030	**SE**	A		WS	64889	78341
466031	**SE**	A	*SE*	SG	64890	78342
466032	**SE**	A		WS	64891	78343
466033	**SE**	A		WS	64892	78344
466034	**SE**	A	*SE*	SG	64893	78345
466035	**SE**	A	*SE*	SG	64894	78346
466036	**SE**	A	*SE*	SG	64895	78347
466037	**SE**	A	*SE*	SG	64896	78348
466038	**SE**	A	*SE*	SG	64897	78349
466039	**SE**	A	*SE*	SG	64898	78350
466040	**SE**	A	*SE*	SG	64899	78351
466041	**SE**	A	*SE*	SG	64900	78352
466042	**SE**	A	*SE*	SG	64901	78353
466043	**SE**	A		WS	64902	78354

CLASS 484 D-TRAIN METRO-CAMMELL/VIVARAIL

Rebuilt from former London Underground D78 stock for use by South Western Railway on the Isle of Wight "Island Line". Similar to the converted Class 230 DMUs or diesel-battery units, the Class 484s are straight third-rail EMUs.

Formation: DMS–DMS.
Construction: Aluminium.
Traction motors: TSA AC motors.
Braking: Rheostatic & Dynamic.
Bogies: Bombardier FLEXX1000 flexible-frame.
Gangways: Within unit only.
Doors: Sliding.
Seating Layout: Longitudinal or 2+2 facing.
Multiple Working: Within class.

System: 750 V DC third rail.
Wheel Arrangement:
Couplers: LUL automatic wedgelock.
Dimensions: 18.37 x 2.84 m.
Control System: IGBT Inverter.
Maximum Speed: 60 mph.

DMS(A). Metro-Cammell Birmingham 1979–83. –/40(+2). 32.5 t.
DMS(B). Metro-Cammell Birmingham 1979–83. –/40(+2). 30.4 t.

484001	**SW**	LF	*SW*	RY	131	(7086)	231	(7011)
484002	**SW**	LF	*SW*	RY	132	(7068)	232	(7002)
484003	**SW**	LF	*SW*	RY	133	(7059)	233	(7083)
484004	**SW**	LF	*SW*	RY	134	(7074)	234	(7111)
484005	**SW**	LF	*SW*	RY	135	(7124)	235	(7093)

▲ ScotRail-liveried 318261 and 320315 arrive at Partick with the 12.47 Dalmuir–Larkhall on 09/06/23. **Robert Pritchard**

▼ Swift Express Freight-liveried 321334, operated by Varamis Rail, passes Symington with 1M04 17.34 Mossend Down Yard–Birmingham International parcels service on 04/09/23. **Robin Ralston**

▲ Northern-liveried 323 236 is seen at Mauldeth Road with the 15.36 Manchester Piccadilly–Crewe on 29/05/23.   **Robert Pritchard**

▼ Northern-liveried 331 023 and 331 027 (nearest camera) are seen between Manchester Oxford Road and Piccadilly stations with the 10.26 Blackpool North–Manchester Airport on 29/05/23.   **Robert Pritchard**

▲ ScotRail-liveried 334025 and 334028 arrive at Hyndland with the 13.24 Helensburgh Central–Edinburgh on 09/06/23. **Robert Pritchard**

▼ Elizabeth Line-liveried 345066 passes West Ealing with the 13.57 Reading–London Paddington on 17/10/22. **Robert Pritchard**

▲ London Northwestern Railway-liveried 350 107 leaves Wolverhampton with the 11.52 Crewe–Birmingham New Street on 14/10/22. **Robert Pritchard**

▼ c2c-liveried 357 322 and 357 022 pass Shadwell DLR station with the 11.53 London Fenchurch Street–Grays on 04/05/23. **Robert Pritchard**

▲ Southeastern-liveried 375310 leaves Maidstone Barracks with the 10.00 Paddock Wood–Strood on 07/04/23. **Robert Pritchard**

▼ Still in their original Connex livery, 376004 and 376018 leave Abbey Wood with the 12.23 London Cannon Street–Cannon Street loop service on 24/05/22. **Robert Pritchard**

▲ ScotRail-liveried 380 020 leaves Glasgow Central with the 17.10 to Cathcart on 09/06/23. **Robert Pritchard**

▼ ScotRail-liveried 385 006 pauses at Bishopbriggs with the 08.49 Glasgow Queen Street–Alloa on 09/06/23. **Robert Pritchard**

▲ Great Western Railway-liveried 387 152 and 387 166 pass Langley with the 11.08 Didcot Parkway–London Paddington on 18/10/22.   **Robert Pritchard**

▼ Avanti West Coast-liveried 390 152 passes South Kenton with the 13.43 Liverpool Lime Street–London Euston on 04/05/23.   **Robert Pritchard**

▲ Southeastern blue-liveried 395 014 exits the North Downs Tunnel on HS1 with the 12.37 London St Pancras–Margate on 07/04/23. **Robert Pritchard**

▼ TransPennine Express-liveried 397 006 passes Wandel with the 18.11 Edinburgh–Manchester Airport on 02/08/22. **Robin Ralston**

▲ Four of the new Transport for Wales Class 398 tram-trains are seen at the new Taffs Wells depot on 18/07/23, with 398006 and 398007 in the foreground.
Courtesy Transport for Wales

▼ South Western Railway-liveried 450090 leads old South West Trains blue-liveried 450121 through Ashford (Surrey) with the 14.20 London Waterloo–Reading on 18/10/22. **Robert Pritchard**

▲ Southeastern suburban-liveried 465 159 arrives at Rochester with the 16.42 London Victoria–Gillingham on 08/04/23. **Robert Pritchard**

▼ South Western Railway-liveried 484 003 calls at Sandown with the 12.44 Ryde Pier Head–Shanklin on 15/11/21. **Robert Pritchard**

▲ Thameslink-liveried 700154 arrives at Luton Airport Parkway with the 11.34 Bedford–Three Bridges on 25/03/23. **Robert Pritchard**

▼ South Western Railway-liveried new Aventra 701017 passes Putney with a 5Q22 11.15 London Waterloo–Waterloo mileage accumulation run on 10/11/22. **Alex Ayre**

▲ London Overground-liveried 710102 arrives at Hackney Downs with the 14.10 Chingford–London Liverpool Street on 13/08/23. **Robert Pritchard**

▼ Govia Thameslink-liveried 717010 is seen at London King's Cross with a service to Stevenage on 29/07/23. **Ian Beardsley**

▲ Greater Anglia-liveried 720 129 and 720 522 arrive at Stratford with the 11.50 Southend Victoria–London Liverpool Street on 17/06/23.　　**Robert Pritchard**

▼ West Midlands Railway-liveried 730 018 is seen at Milton Keynes Central whilst on display to the press on 30/06/23.　　**Robert Pritchard**

▲ Greater Anglia-liveried 745006 arrives at Colchester with the 13.41 Ipswich–London Liverpool Street on 16/10/22. **Robert Pritchard**

▼ HydroFlex prototype unit 799201 (converted from 319382) is seen at Besford, being hauled from Gloucester Yard to Long Marston via Worcester on 05/09/23. **Dave Gommersall**

▲ Great Western Railway-liveried 800008 (with Pride stripes) and 800032 pass Slough with the 11.30 Bristol Temple Meads–London Paddington on 18/10/22.
Robert Pritchard

▼ LNER Azuma-liveried 801210 passes East Linton with the 11.00 Edinburgh–London King's Cross on 19/04/23.
Robin Ralston

▲ Lumo-liveried 803 002 passes Sunderland Bridge with the 10.45 London King's Cross–Edinburgh on 22/06/22. **Alex Ayre**

▼ Class 374 Eurostar 4005/06 is seen on HS1 near Harrietsham with the 14.43 Paris Nord–London St Pancras on 09/04/23. **Robert Pritchard**

CLASS 507   BREL YORK

Formation: BDMS–TS–DMS.
Construction: Steel underframe, aluminium alloy body and roof.
Traction Motors: Four GEC G310AZ of 82.125 kW.
Wheel Arrangement: Bo-Bo + 2-2 + Bo-Bo.
Braking: Disc & rheostatic.   **Dimensions:** 20.18 x 2.82 m.
Bogies: BX1.   **Couplers:** Tightlock.
Gangways: Within unit + end doors. **Control System:** Camshaft.
Doors: Sliding.   **Maximum Speed:** 75 mph.
Seating Layout: All refurbished with 2+2 high-back facing seating.
Multiple Working: Within class and with Class 508.

Fitted with tripcocks for operating on the Merseyrail Wirral Lines.

Advertising livery: 507 002 Liverpool Hope University (white).

BDMS. Lot No. 30906 1978–80. –/56(+3) 1W. 37.0 t.
TS. Lot No. 30907 1978–80. –/74. 25.5 t.
DMS. Lot No. 30908 1978–80. –/56(+3) 1W. 35.5 t.

507 001	**BG**	A	*ME*	BD	64367	71342	64405
507 002	**AL**	A	*ME*	BD	64368	71343	64406
507 003	**MY**	A	*ME*	BD	64369	71344	64407
507 004	**MY**	A	*ME*	BD	64388	71345	64408
507 007	**MY**	A	*ME*	BD	64373	71348	64411
507 010	**MY**	A	*ME*	BD	64376	71351	64414
507 011	**MY**	A	*ME*	BD	64377	71352	64415
507 013	**MY**	A	*ME*	BD	64379	71354	64417
507 014	**MY**	A	*ME*	BD	64380	71355	64418
507 015	**MY**	A	*ME*	BD	64381	71356	64419
507 016	**MY**	A	*ME*	BD	64382	71357	64420
507 017	**MY**	A	*ME*	BD	64383	71358	64421
507 018	**MY**	A	*ME*	BD	64384	71359	64422
507 020	**MY**	A	*ME*	BD	64386	71361	64424
507 021	**MY**	A	*ME*	BD	64387	71362	64425
507 023	**MY**	A	*ME*	BD	64389	71364	64427
507 028	**MY**	A	*ME*	BD	64394	71369	64432
507 029	**MY**	A	*ME*	BD	64395	71370	64433
507 030	**MY**	A	*ME*	BD	64396	71371	64434
507 031	**MY**	A	*ME*	BD	64397	71372	64435
507 032	**MY**	A	*ME*	BD	64398	71373	64436
507 033	**MY**	A	*ME*	BD	64399	71374	64437

Names:

507 004 Bob Paisley	507 021 Red Rum
507 016 Merseyrail – celebrating the first ten years 2003–2013	507 023 Operations Inspector Stuart Mason
507 020 John Peel	507 033 Councillor Jack Spriggs

CLASS 508   BREL YORK

Formation: DMS–TS–BDMS.
Construction: Steel underframe, aluminium alloy body and roof.
Traction Motors: Four GEC G310AZ of 82.125 kW.
Wheel Arrangement: Bo-Bo + 2-2 + Bo-Bo.
Braking: Disc & rheostatic.   **Dimensions:** 20.18 x 2.82 m.
Bogies: BX1.   **Couplers:** Tightlock.
Gangways: Within unit + end doors.   **Control System:** Camshaft.
Doors: Sliding.   **Maximum Speed:** 75 mph.
Seating Layout: All refurbished with 2+2 high-back facing seating.
Multiple Working: Within class and with Class 507.

Fitted with tripcocks for operating on the Merseyrail Wirral Lines.

DMS. Lot No. 30979 1979–80. –/56(+3) 1W. 36.0 t.
TS. Lot No. 30980 1979–80. –/74. 26.5 t.
BDMS. Lot No. 30981 1979–80. –/56(+3) 1W. 36.5 t.

508 104	**MY**	A	*ME*	BD	64652	71486	64695
508 108	**MY**	A		BD	64656	71490	64699
508 114	**MY**	A		BD	64662	71496	64705

CLASS 555   STADLER

This fleet of articulated 5-car units was ordered from Stadler in 2020 by
Nexus for the Tyne & Wear Metro, which shares Network Rail tracks between
Heworth and Sunderland. They will replace the original Tyne & Wear Metro
light rail stock which dates from 1975–81. The first of the new units were
delivered in spring 2023, and the fleet is due to enter service from early
2024. The trains are also fitted with batteries for use in an emergency
situation.

Formation: DMS–MS–MS–MS–DMS.
System: 1500 V DC overhead + batteries.
Construction: Aluminium.
Traction Motors: Eight TSA air-cooled TMF 41-17-4 of 120 kW (161 hp).
Wheel Arrangement: 2-Bo-Bo-Bo-Bo-2.
Dimensions: 59.90 x 2.65 m (full unit).
Braking: Disc, regenerative & magnetic track brakes.
Couplers: Dellner.
Bogies: Jacobs.   **Control System:** IGBT Inverter.
Gangways: Within unit.   **Maximum Speed:** 50 mph.
Doors: Sliding plug.   **Heating & ventilation:** Air conditioning.
Seating Layout: Longitudinal.
Multiple Working: Within class.

DMS(A). Stadler Szolnok/St Margrethen 2021–24. –/18(+6).
MS(A). Stadler Szolnok/St Margrethen 2021–24. –/24 2W.
MS(B). Stadler Szolnok/St Margrethen 2021–24. –/20.
MS(C). Stadler Szolnok/St Margrethen 2021–24. –/24 2W.
DMS(B). Stadler Szolnok/St Margrethen 2021–24. –/18(+6).

555001	**TY**	990101	990201	990301	990401	990501
555002	**TY**	990102	990202	990302	990402	990502
555003	**TY**	990103	990203	990303	990403	990503
555004	**TY**	990104	990204	990304	990404	990504
555005	**TY**	990105	990205	990305	990405	990505
555006	**TY**	990106	990206	990306	990406	990506
555007	**TY**	990107	990207	990307	990407	990507
555008	**TY**	990108	990208	990308	990408	990508
555009	**TY**	990109	990209	990309	990409	990509
555010	**TY**	990110	990210	990310	990410	990510
555011	**TY**	990111	990211	990311	990411	990511
555012	**TY**	990112	990212	990312	990412	990512
555013	**TY**	990113	990213	990313	990413	990513
555014	**TY**	990114	990214	990314	990414	990514
555015	**TY**	990115	990215	990315	990415	990515
555016	**TY**	990116	990216	990316	990416	990516
555017	**TY**	990117	990217	990317	990417	990517
555018	**TY**	990118	990218	990318	990418	990518
555019	**TY**	990119	990219	990319	990419	990519
555020	**TY**	990120	990220	990320	990420	990520
555021	**TY**	990121	990221	990321	990421	990521
555022	**TY**	990122	990222	990322	990422	990522
555023	**TY**	990123	990223	990323	990423	990523
555024	**TY**	990124	990224	990324	990424	990524
555025	**TY**	990125	990225	990325	990425	990525
555026	**TY**	990126	990226	990326	990426	990526
555027	**TY**	990127	990227	990327	990427	990527
555028	**TY**	990128	990228	990328	990428	990528
555029	**TY**	990129	990229	990329	990429	990529
555030	**TY**	990130	990230	990330	990430	990530
555031	**TY**	990131	990231	990331	990431	990531
555032	**TY**	990132	990232	990332	990432	990532
555033	**TY**	990133	990233	990333	990433	990533
555034	**TY**	990134	990234	990334	990434	990534
555035	**TY**	990135	990235	990335	990435	990535
555036	**TY**	990136	990236	990336	990436	990536
555037	**TY**	990137	990237	990337	990437	990537
555038	**TY**	990138	990238	990338	990438	990538
555039	**TY**	990139	990239	990339	990439	990539
555040	**TY**	990140	990240	990340	990440	990540
555041	**TY**	990141	990241	990341	990441	990541
555042	**TY**	990142	990242	990342	990442	990542
555043	**TY**	990143	990243	990343	990443	990543
555044	**TY**	990144	990244	990344	990444	990544
555045	**TY**	990145	990245	990345	990445	990545
555046	**TY**	990146	990246	990346	990446	990546

4.3. PROTOTYPE HYDROGEN UNIT

During 2021–22 Arcola Energy converted the sole remaining former ScotRail Class 314 EMU into a testbed hydrogen train at Bo'ness on the Bo'ness & Kinneil Railway, as part of the Scottish Hydrogen Train Project sponsored by the Scottish Government to demonstrate how existing trains can be converted to operate using hydrogen power. To reflect its new identity the unit has been renumbered in the Class 614 series. It has been tested on the Bo'ness & Kinneil Railway.

All hydrogen equipment has been fitted to the vehicle underframes rather than taking up room in the passenger areas. A fuel cell raft is located in each driving car, comprising a 70kW Ballard fuel cell and hydrogen cylinders. The DC traction motors have be replaced by magnet motors powered by three-phase AC. The centre car houses Toshiba lithium-titanate batteries. The interior of the centre car has also been refurbished, using former Pendolino seats.

CLASS 614   BREL YORK

Formation: DMS–PTS–DMS.
Construction: Steel underframe, aluminium alloy body and roof.
Traction Motors: Dana AC traction motors.
Wheel Arrangement: Bo-Bo + 2-2 + Bo-Bo.
Braking: Disc & rheostatic.   **Dimensions:** 20.33/20.18 x 2.82 m.
Bogies: BX1.   **Couplers:** Tightlock.
Gangways: Within unit + end doors. **Control System:**
Doors: Sliding.   **Maximum Speed:** 70 mph.
Seating Layout: Originally 3+2 low-back facing, PTS reseated as 2+2 facing.
Multiple Working: Within class.

DMS. Lot No. 30912 1979.
PTS. Lot No. 30913 1979.
DMS. Lot No. 30912 1979.

614 209	(314 209)	**SR**	SR		BO	64599	71458	64600

4.4. DUAL VOLTAGE OR 25 kV AC OVERHEAD UNITS

The Class 7xx series is being used for some new-build EMUs built from 2014 onwards as freight wagons take up many of the remaining potential Class 3xx series'. Rebuilt Class 319s as either Class 768, 769 or 799 also take up this number series.

CLASS 700   DESIRO CITY   SIEMENS

The Class 700s are the large new fleet of EMUs for Govia Thameslink, entering service between 2016 and 2018. The units are financed by Cross London Trains (a consortium of Siemens Project Ventures, Innisfree Ltd and 3i Infrastructure Ltd).

Formation (8-car): DMC–PTS–MS–TS–TS–MS–PTS–DMC or
(12-car): DMC–PTS–MS–MS–TS–TS–TS–TS–MS–MS–PTS–DMC.
Systems: 25 kV AC overhead/750 V DC third rail.
Construction: Aluminium.
Traction Motors: Four Siemens asynchronous of 200 kW.
Wheel Arrangement (8-car): Bo-Bo + 2-2 + Bo-Bo + 2-2 + 2-2 + Bo-Bo + 2-2 + Bo-Bo. **(12-car):** Bo-Bo + 2-2 + Bo-Bo + Bo-Bo + 2-2 + 2-2 + 2-2 + 2-2 + Bo-Bo + Bo-Bo + 2-2 + Bo-Bo.
Braking: Disc, tread & regenerative.   **Dimensions:** 20.52/20.16 m x 2.80 m.
Bogies: Siemens SF7000 inside-frame. **Couplers:** Dellner 12.
Gangways: Within unit.   **Control System:** IGBT Inverter.
Doors: Sliding plug.   **Maximum Speed:** 100 mph.
Heating & ventilation: Air conditioning.
Seating Layout: 2+2 facing/unidirectional.
Multiple Working: Within class and with Classes 707 and 717.

Class 700/0. 8-car units.

DMC(A). Siemens Krefeld 2014–18. 26/16(+3). 38.5 t.
PTS. Siemens Krefeld 2014–18. –/54 1T. 33.1 t.
MS. Siemens Krefeld 2014–18. –/64. 36.2 t.
TS. Siemens Krefeld 2014–18. –/56(+3). 28.7 t.
TS(W). Siemens Krefeld 2014–18. –/40(+8) 1TD 2W. 29.1 t.
MS. Siemens Krefeld 2014–18. –/64. 36.2 t.
PTS. Siemens Krefeld 2014–18. –/54 1T. 33.2 t.
DMC(B). Siemens Krefeld 2014–18. 26/16(+3). 38.5 t.

700001	**TL**	CT	*TL*	TB	401001	402001	403001	406001
					407001	410001	411001	412001
700002	**TL**	CT	*TL*	TB	401002	402002	403002	406002
					407002	410002	411002	412002
700003	**TL**	CT	*TL*	TB	401003	402003	403003	406003
					407003	410003	411003	412003
700004	**TL**	CT	*TL*	TB	401004	402004	403004	406004
					407004	410004	411004	412004

700 005	**TL**	CT	*TL*	TB	401005	402005	403005	406005
					407005	410005	411005	412005
700 006	**TL**	CT	*TL*	TB	401006	402006	403006	406006
					407006	410006	411006	412006
700 007	**TL**	CT	*TL*	TB	401007	402007	403007	406007
					407007	410007	411007	412007
700 008	**TL**	CT	*TL*	TB	401008	402008	403008	406008
					407008	410008	411008	412008
700 009	**TL**	CT	*TL*	TB	401009	402009	403009	406009
					407009	410009	411009	412009
700 010	**TL**	CT	*TL*	TB	401010	402010	403010	406010
					407010	410010	411010	412010
700 011	**TL**	CT	*TL*	TB	401011	402011	403011	406011
					407011	410011	411011	412011
700 012	**TL**	CT	*TL*	TB	401012	402012	403012	406012
					407012	410012	411012	412012
700 013	**TL**	CT	*TL*	TB	401013	402013	403013	406013
					407013	410013	411013	412013
700 014	**TL**	CT	*TL*	TB	401014	402014	403014	406014
					407014	410014	411014	412014
700 015	**TL**	CT	*TL*	TB	401015	402015	403015	406015
					407015	410015	411015	412015
700 016	**TL**	CT	*TL*	TB	401016	402016	403016	406016
					407016	410016	411016	412016
700 017	**TL**	CT	*TL*	TB	401017	402017	403017	406017
					407017	410017	411017	412017
700 018	**TL**	CT	*TL*	TB	401018	402018	403018	406018
					407018	410018	411018	412018
700 019	**TL**	CT	*TL*	TB	401019	402019	403019	406019
					407019	410019	411019	412019
700 020	**TL**	CT	*TL*	TB	401020	402020	403020	406020
					407020	410020	411020	412020
700 021	**TL**	CT	*TL*	TB	401021	402021	403021	406021
					407021	410021	411021	412021
700 022	**TL**	CT	*TL*	TB	401022	402022	403022	406022
					407022	410022	411022	412022
700 023	**TL**	CT	*TL*	TB	401023	402023	403023	406023
					407023	410023	411023	412023
700 024	**TL**	CT	*TL*	TB	401024	402024	403024	406024
					407024	410024	411024	412024
700 025	**TL**	CT	*TL*	TB	401025	402025	403025	406025
					407025	410025	411025	412025
700 026	**TL**	CT	*TL*	TB	401026	402026	403026	406026
					407026	410026	411026	412026
700 027	**TL**	CT	*TL*	TB	401027	402027	403027	406027
					407027	410027	411027	412027
700 028	**TL**	CT	*TL*	TB	401028	402028	403028	406028
					407028	410028	411028	412028
700 029	**TL**	CT	*TL*	TB	401029	402029	403029	406029
					407029	410029	411029	412029

700 030	**TL**	CT	*TL*	TB	401030	402030	403030	406030
					407030	410030	411030	412030
700 031	**TL**	CT	*TL*	TB	401031	402031	403031	406031
					407031	410031	411031	412031
700 032	**TL**	CT	*TL*	TB	401032	402032	403032	406032
					407032	410032	411032	412032
700 033	**TL**	CT	*TL*	TB	401033	402033	403033	406033
					407033	410033	411033	412033
700 034	**TL**	CT	*TL*	TB	401034	402034	403034	406034
					407034	410034	411034	412034
700 035	**TL**	CT	*TL*	TB	401035	402035	403035	406035
					407035	410035	411035	412035
700 036	**TL**	CT	*TL*	TB	401036	402036	403036	406036
					407036	410036	411036	412036
700 037	**TL**	CT	*TL*	TB	401037	402037	403037	406037
					407037	410037	411037	412037
700 038	**TL**	CT	*TL*	TB	401038	402038	403038	406038
					407038	410038	411038	412038
700 039	**TL**	CT	*TL*	TB	401039	402039	403039	406039
					407039	410039	411039	412039
700 040	**TL**	CT	*TL*	TB	401040	402040	403040	406040
					407040	410040	411040	412040
700 041	**TL**	CT	*TL*	TB	401041	402041	403041	406041
					407041	410041	411041	412041
700 042	**TL**	CT	*TL*	TB	401042	402042	403042	406042
					407042	410042	411042	412042
700 043	**TL**	CT	*TL*	TB	401043	402043	403043	406043
					407043	410043	411043	412043
700 044	**TL**	CT	*TL*	TB	401044	402044	403044	406044
					407044	410044	411044	412044
700 045	**TL**	CT	*TL*	TB	401045	402045	403045	406045
					407045	410045	411045	412045
700 046	**TL**	CT	*TL*	TB	401046	402046	403046	406046
					407046	410046	411046	412046
700 047	**TL**	CT	*TL*	TB	401047	402047	403047	406047
					407047	410047	411047	412047
700 048	**TL**	CT	*TL*	TB	401048	402048	403048	406048
					407048	410048	411048	412048
700 049	**TL**	CT	*TL*	TB	401049	402049	403049	406049
					407049	410049	411049	412049
700 050	**TL**	CT	*TL*	TB	401050	402050	403050	406050
					407050	410050	411050	412050
700 051	**TL**	CT	*TL*	TB	401051	402051	403051	406051
					407051	410051	411051	412051
700 052	**TL**	CT	*TL*	TB	401052	402052	403052	406052
					407052	410052	411052	412052
700 053	**TL**	CT	*TL*	TB	401053	402053	403053	406053
					407053	410053	411053	412053
700 054	**TL**	CT	*TL*	TB	401054	402054	403054	406054
					407054	410054	411054	412054

700055	**TL** CT *TL*	TB	401055	402055	403055	406055		
			407055	410055	411055	412055		
700056	**TL** CT *TL*	TB	401056	402056	403056	406056		
			407056	410056	411056	412056		
700057	**TL** CT *TL*	TB	401057	402057	403057	406057		
			407057	410057	411057	412057		
700058	**TL** CT *TL*	TB	401058	402058	403058	406058		
			407058	410058	411058	412058		
700059	**TL** CT *TL*	TB	401059	402059	403059	406059		
			407059	410059	411059	412059		
700060	**TL** CT *TL*	TB	401060	402060	403060	406060		
			407060	410060	411060	412060		

Class 700/1. 12-car units.

Additions to the standard livery: 700155 Pride stripes on driving cars.

DMC(A). Siemens Krefeld 2013–18. 26/20. 38.2 t.
PTS. Siemens Krefeld 2013–18. –/54 1T. 34.4 t.
MS. Siemens Krefeld 2013–18. –/60(+3). 36.0 l.
MS. Siemens Krefeld 2013–18. –/56 1T. 35.8 t.
TS. Siemens Krefeld 2013–18. –/64. 26.8 t.
TS. Siemens Krefeld 2013–18. –/56(+3). 28.3 t.
TS(W). Siemens Krefeld 2013–18. –/38(+9) 1TD 2W. 28.7 t.
TS. Siemens Krefeld 2013–18. –/64. 27.9 t.
MS. Siemens Krefeld 2013–18. –/56 1T. 35.6 t.
MS. Siemens Krefeld 2013–18. –/60(+3). 35.3 t.
PTS. Siemens Krefeld 2013–18. –/54 1T. 34.4 t.
DMC(B). Siemens Krefeld 2013–18. 26/20. 38.2 t.

700101	**TL** CT *TL*	TB	401101 402101 403101 404101 405101 406101					
			407101 408101 409101 410101 411101 412101					
700102	**TL** CT *TL*	TB	401102 402102 403102 404102 405102 406102					
			407102 408102 409102 410102 411102 412102					
700103	**TL** CT *TL*	TB	401103 402103 403103 404103 405103 406103					
			407103 408103 409103 410103 411103 412103					
700104	**TL** CT *TL*	TB	401104 402104 403104 404104 405104 406104					
			407104 408104 409104 410104 411104 412104					
700105	**TL** CT *TL*	TB	401105 402105 403105 404105 405105 406105					
			407105 408105 409105 410105 411105 412105					
700106	**TL** CT *TL*	TB	401106 402106 403106 404106 405106 406106					
			407106 408106 409106 410106 411106 412106					
700107	**TL** CT *TL*	TB	401107 402107 403107 404107 405107 406107					
			407107 408107 409107 410107 411107 412107					
700108	**TL** CT *TL*	TB	401108 402108 403108 404108 405108 406108					
			407108 408108 409108 410108 411108 412108					
700109	**TL** CT *TL*	TB	401109 402109 403109 404109 405109 406109					
			407109 408109 409109 410109 411109 412109					
700110	**TL** CT *TL*	TB	401110 402110 403110 404110 405110 406110					
			407110 408110 409110 410110 411110 412110					
700111	**TL** CT *TL*	TB	401111 402111 403111 404111 405111 406111					
			407111 408111 409111 410111 411111 412111					

700 112	**TL** CT *TL*	TB	401112	402112	403112	404112	405112	406112		
			407112	408112	409112	410112	411112	412112		
700 113	**TL** CT *TL*	TB	401113	402113	403113	404113	405113	406113		
			407113	408113	409113	410113	411113	412113		
700 114	**TL** CT *TL*	TB	401114	402114	403114	404114	405114	406114		
			407114	408114	409114	410114	411114	412114		
700 115	**TL** CT *TL*	TB	401115	402115	403115	404115	405115	406115		
			407115	408115	409115	410115	411115	412115		
700 116	**TL** CT *TL*	TB	401116	402116	403116	404116	405116	406116		
			407116	408116	409116	410116	411116	412116		
700 117	**TL** CT *TL*	TB	401117	402117	403117	404117	405117	406117		
			407117	408117	409117	410117	411117	412117		
700 118	**TL** CT *TL*	TB	401118	402118	403118	404118	405118	406118		
			407118	408118	409118	410118	411118	412118		
700 119	**TL** CT *TL*	TB	401119	402119	403119	404119	405119	406119		
			407119	408119	409119	410119	411119	412119		
700 120	**TL** CT *TL*	TB	401120	402120	403120	404120	405120	406120		
			407120	408120	409120	410120	411120	412120		
700 121	**TL** CT *TL*	TB	401121	402121	403121	404121	405121	406121		
			407121	408121	409121	410121	411121	412121		
700 122	**TL** CT *TL*	TB	401122	402122	403122	404122	405122	406122		
			407122	408122	409122	410122	411122	412122		
700 123	**TL** CT *TL*	TB	401123	402123	403123	404123	405123	406123		
			407123	408123	409123	410123	411123	412123		
700 124	**TL** CT *TL*	TB	401124	402124	403124	404124	405124	406124		
			407124	408124	409124	410124	411124	412124		
700 125	**TL** CT *TL*	TB	401125	402125	403125	404125	405125	406125		
			407125	408125	409125	410125	411125	412125		
700 126	**TL** CT *TL*	TB	401126	402126	403126	404126	405126	406126		
			407126	408126	409126	410126	411126	412126		
700 127	**TL** CT *TL*	TB	401127	402127	403127	404127	405127	406127		
			407127	408127	409127	410127	411127	412127		
700 128	**TL** CT *TL*	TB	401128	402128	403128	404128	405128	406128		
			407128	408128	409128	410128	411128	412128		
700 129	**TL** CT *TL*	TB	401129	402129	403129	404129	405129	406129		
			407129	408129	409129	410129	411129	412129		
700 130	**TL** CT *TL*	TB	401130	402130	403130	404130	405130	406130		
			407130	408130	409130	410130	411130	412130		
700 131	**TL** CT *TL*	TB	401131	402131	403131	404131	405131	406131		
			407131	408131	409131	410131	411131	412131		
700 132	**TL** CT *TL*	TB	401132	402132	403132	404132	405132	406132		
			407132	408132	409132	410132	411132	412132		
700 133	**TL** CT *TL*	TB	401133	402133	403133	404133	405133	406133		
			407133	408133	409133	410133	411133	412133		
700 134	**TL** CT *TL*	TB	401134	402134	403134	404134	405134	406134		
			407134	408134	409134	410134	411134	412134		
700 135	**TL** CT *TL*	TB	401135	402135	403135	404135	405135	406135		
			407135	408135	409135	410135	411135	412135		
700 136	**TL** CT *TL*	TB	401136	402136	403136	404136	405136	406136		
			407136	408136	409136	410136	411136	412136		

700 137	**TL** CT *TL*	TB	401137	402137	403137	404137	405137	406137		
			407137	408137	409137	410137	411137	412137		
700 138	**TL** CT *TL*	TB	401138	402138	403138	404138	405138	406138		
			407138	408138	409138	410138	411138	412138		
700 139	**TL** CT *TL*	TB	401139	402139	403139	404139	405139	406139		
			407139	408139	409139	410139	411139	412139		
700 140	**TL** CT *TL*	TB	401140	402140	403140	404140	405140	406140		
			407140	408140	409140	410140	411140	412140		
700 141	**TL** CT *TL*	TB	401141	402141	403141	404141	405141	406141		
			407141	408141	409141	410141	411141	412141		
700 142	**TL** CT *TL*	TB	401142	402142	403142	404142	405142	406142		
			407142	408142	409142	410142	411142	412142		
700 143	**TL** CT *TL*	TB	401143	402143	403143	404143	405143	406143		
			407143	408143	409143	410143	411143	412143		
700 144	**TL** CT *TL*	TB	401144	402144	403144	404144	405144	406144		
			407144	408144	409144	410144	411144	412144		
700 145	**TL** CT *TL*	TB	401145	402145	403145	404145	405145	406145		
			407145	408145	409145	410145	411145	412145		
700 146	**TL** CT *TL*	TB	401146	402146	403146	404146	405146	406146		
			407146	408146	409146	410146	411146	412146		
700 147	**TL** CT *TL*	TB	401147	402147	403147	404147	405147	406147		
			407147	408147	409147	410147	411147	412147		
700 148	**TL** CT *TL*	TB	401148	402148	403148	404148	405148	406148		
			407148	408148	409148	410148	411148	412148		
700 149	**TL** CT *TL*	TB	401149	402149	403149	404149	405149	406149		
			407149	408149	409149	410149	411149	412149		
700 150	**TL** CT *TL*	TB	401150	402150	403150	404150	405150	406150		
			407150	408150	409150	410150	411150	412150		
700 151	**TL** CT *TL*	TB	401151	402151	403151	404151	405151	406151		
			407151	408151	409151	410151	411151	412151		
700 152	**TL** CT *TL*	TB	401152	402152	403152	404152	405152	406152		
			407152	408152	409152	410152	411152	412152		
700 153	**TL** CT *TL*	TB	401153	402153	403153	404153	405153	406153		
			407153	408153	409153	410153	411153	412153		
700 154	**TL** CT *TL*	TB	401154	402154	403154	404154	405154	406154		
			407154	408154	409154	410154	411154	412154		
700 155	**TL** CT *TL*	TB	401155	402155	403155	404155	405155	406155		
			407155	408155	409155	410155	411155	412155		

CLASS 701 AVENTRA BOMBARDIER/ALSTOM DERBY

South Western Railway has 60 10-car and 30 5-car Aventra EMUs on order from Alstom (previously Bombardier), financed by Rock Rail. The first units were completed in late 2019 but a number of design problems and industrial relations issues delayed service introduction until the start of 2024. The units have been branded "Arterio" by SWR and will be used on inner and outer suburban duties.

Formation (10-car): DMS–MS–TS–MS–MS–MS–MS–TS–MS–DMS or **(5-car):** DMS–MS–TS–MS–DMS.
Systems: 750 V DC third rail.
Construction: Aluminium.
Traction Motors: Two Bombardier asynchronous of 250 kW.
Wheel Arrangement (10-car): 2-Bo + Bo-2 + 2-2 + 2-Bo + Bo-2 + 2-Bo + Bo-2 + 2-2 + 2-Bo + Bo-2 or (5-car): 2-Bo + Bo-2 + 2-2 + 2-Bo + Bo-2.
Braking: Disc, rheostatic & regenerative.
Dimensions: 20.89/20.70/19.99 m x 2.77 m.
Bogies: FLEXX B5000 inside-frame.   **Couplers:** Dellner 12.
Gangways: Within unit.   **Control System:** IGBT Inverter.
Doors: Sliding plug.   **Maximum Speed:** 100 mph.
Heating & ventilation: Air conditioning.
Seating Layout: 2+2 unidirectional/facing.
Multiple Working: Within class.

Class 701/0. 10-car units.

DMS(A). Alstom Derby 2019–24. –/56. 42.1 t.
MS. Alstom Derby 2019–24. –/60. 32.7 t.
TS. Alstom Derby 2019–24. –/34(+10) 1TD 2W. 29.4 t.
MS. Alstom Derby 2019–24. –/60. 31.5 t.
MS. Alstom Derby 2019–24. –/60. 37.9 t.
MS. Alstom Derby 2019–24. –/60. 37.9 t.
MS. Alstom Derby 2019–24. –/60. 31.5 t.
TS. Alstom Derby 2019–24. –/34(+10) 1TD 2W. 29.4 t.
MS. Alstom Derby 2019–24. –/60. 32.7 t.
DMS(B). Alstom Derby 2019–24. –/56. 42.1 t.

701 001	**SW**	RR	480001	481001	482001	483001	484001
			485001	486001	487001	488001	489001
701 002	**SW**	RR	480002	481002	482002	483002	484002
			485002	486002	487002	488002	489002
701 003	**SW**	RR	480003	481003	482003	483003	484003
			485003	486003	487003	488003	489003
701 004	**SW**	RR	480004	481004	482004	483004	484004
			485004	486004	487004	488004	489004
701 005	**SW**	RR	480005	481005	482005	483005	484005
			485005	486005	487005	488005	489005
701 006	**SW**	RR	480006	481006	482006	483006	484006
			485006	486006	487006	488006	489006
701 007	**SW**	RR	480007	481007	482007	483007	484007
			485007	486007	487007	488007	489007

701 008	**SW** RR	480008	481008	482008	483008	484008	
		485008	486008	487008	488008	489008	
701 009	**SW** RR	480009	481009	482009	483009	484009	
		485009	486009	487009	488009	489009	
701 010	**SW** RR	480010	481010	482010	483010	484010	
		485010	486010	487010	488010	489010	
701 011	**SW** RR	480011	481011	482011	483011	484011	
		485011	486011	487011	488011	489011	
701 012	**SW** RR	480012	481012	482012	483012	484012	
		485012	486012	487012	488012	489012	
701 013	**SW** RR	480013	481013	482013	483013	484013	
		485013	486013	487013	488013	489013	
701 014	**SW** RR	480014	481014	482014	483014	484014	
		485014	486014	487014	488014	489014	
701 015	**SW** RR	480015	481015	482015	483015	484015	
		485015	486015	487015	488015	489015	
701 016	**SW** RR	480016	481016	482016	483016	484016	
		485016	486016	487016	488016	489016	
701 017	**SW** RR	480017	481017	482017	483017	484017	
		485017	486017	487017	488017	489017	
701 018	**SW** RR	480018	481018	482018	483018	484018	
		485018	486018	487018	488018	489018	
701 019	**SW** RR	480019	481019	482019	483019	484019	
		485019	486019	487019	488019	489019	
701 020	**SW** RR	480020	481020	482020	483020	484020	
		485020	486020	487020	488020	489020	
701 021	**SW** RR	480021	481021	482021	483021	484021	
		485021	486021	487021	488021	489021	
701 022	**SW** RR	480022	481022	482022	483022	484022	
		485022	486022	487022	488022	489022	
701 023	**SW** RR	480023	481023	482023	483023	484023	
		485023	486023	487023	488023	489023	
701 024	**SW** RR	480024	481024	482024	483024	484024	
		485024	486024	487024	488024	489024	
701 025	**SW** RR	480025	481025	482025	483025	484025	
		485025	486025	487025	488025	489025	
701 026	**SW** RR	480026	481026	482026	483026	484026	
		485026	486026	487026	488026	489026	
701 027	**SW** RR	480027	481027	482027	483027	484027	
		485027	486027	487027	488027	489027	
701 028	**SW** RR	480028	481028	482028	483028	484028	
		485028	486028	487028	488028	489028	
701 029	**SW** RR	480029	481029	482029	483029	484029	
		485029	486029	487029	488029	489029	
701 030	**SW** RR	480030	481030	482030	483030	484030	
		485030	486030	487030	488030	489030	
701 031	**SW** RR	480031	481031	482031	483031	484031	
		485031	486031	487031	488031	489031	
701 032	**SW** RR	480032	481032	482032	483032	484032	
		485032	486032	487032	488032	489032	

701 033	**SW**	RR			480033	481033	482033	483033	484033
					485033	486033	487033	488033	489033
701 034	**SW**	RR			480034	481034	482034	483034	484034
					485034	486034	487034	488034	489034
701 035	**SW**	RR			480035	481035	482035	483035	484035
					485035	486035	487035	488035	489035
701 036	**SW**	RR			480036	481036	482036	483036	484036
					485036	486036	487036	488036	489036
701 037	**SW**	RR	*SW*	WD	480037	481037	482037	483037	484037
					485037	486037	487037	488037	489037
701 038	**SW**	RR			480038	481038	482038	483038	484038
					485038	486038	487038	488038	489038
701 039	**SW**	RR	*SW*	WD	480039	481039	482039	483039	484039
					485039	486039	487039	488039	489039
701 040	**SW**	RR			480040	481040	482040	483040	484040
					485040	486040	487040	488040	489040
701 041	**SW**	RR			480041	481041	482041	483041	484041
					485041	486041	487041	488041	489041
701 042	**SW**	RR			480042	481042	482042	483042	484042
					485042	486042	487042	488042	489042
701 043	**SW**	RR			480043	481043	482043	483043	484043
					485043	486043	487043	488043	489043
701 044	**SW**	RR			480044	481044	482044	483044	484044
					485044	486044	487044	488044	489044
701 045	**SW**	RR			480045	481045	482045	483045	484045
					485045	486045	487045	488045	489045
701 046	**SW**	RR			480046	481046	482046	483046	484046
					485046	486046	487046	488046	489046
701 047	**SW**	RR			480047	481047	482047	483047	484047
					485047	486047	487047	488047	489047
701 048	**SW**	RR			480048	481048	482048	483048	484048
					485048	486048	487048	488048	489048
701 049	**SW**	RR			480049	481049	482049	483049	484049
					485049	486049	487049	488049	489049
701 050	**SW**	RR			480050	481050	482050	483050	484050
					485050	486050	487050	488050	489050
701 051	**SW**	RR			480051	481051	482051	483051	484051
					485051	486051	487051	488051	489051
701 052	**SW**	RR			480052	481052	482052	483052	484052
					485052	486052	487052	488052	489052
701 053	**SW**	RR			480053	481053	482053	483053	484053
					485053	486053	487053	488053	489053
701 054	**SW**	RR			480054	481054	482054	483054	484054
					485054	486054	487054	488054	489054
701 055	**SW**	RR			480055	481055	482055	483055	484055
					485055	486055	487055	488055	489055
701 056	**SW**	RR			480056	481056	482056	483056	484056
					485056	486056	487056	488056	489056
701 057	**SW**	RR			480057	481057	482057	483057	484057
					485057	486057	487057	488057	489057

701058	**SW** RR	480058	481058	482058	483058	484058
		485058	486058	487058	488058	489058
701059	**SW** RR	480059	481059	482059	483059	484059
		485059	486059	487059	488059	489059
701060	**SW** RR	480060	481060	482060	483060	484060
		485060	486060	487060	488060	489060

Class 701/5. 5-car units.

DMS(A). Alstom Derby 2019–24. –/56.   t.
MS. Alstom Derby 2019–24. –/60.   t.
TS. Alstom Derby 2019–24. –/34(+10) 1TD 2W.   t.
MS. Alstom Derby 2019–24. –/60.   t.
DMS(B). Alstom Derby 2019–24. –/56.   t.

701501	**SW** RR	480101	481101	482101	483101	484101
701502	**SW** RR	480102	481102	482102	483102	484102
701503	**SW** RR	480103	481103	482103	483103	484103
701504	**SW** RR	480104	481104	482104	483104	484104
701505	**SW** RR	480105	481105	482105	483105	484105
701506	**SW** RR	480106	481106	482106	483106	484106
701507	**SW** RR	480107	481107	482107	483107	484107
701508	**SW** RR	480108	481108	482108	483108	484108
701509	**SW** RR	480109	481109	482109	483109	484109
701510	**SW** RR	480110	481110	482110	483110	484110
701511	**SW** RR	480111	481111	482111	483111	484111
701512	**SW** RR	480112	481112	482112	483112	484112
701513	**SW** RR	480113	481113	482113	483113	484113
701514	**SW** RR	480114	481114	482114	483114	484114
701515	**SW** RR	480115	481115	482115	483115	484115
701516	**SW** RR	480116	481116	482116	483116	484116
701517	**SW** RR	480117	481117	482117	483117	484117
701518	**SW** RR	480118	481118	482118	483118	484118
701519	**SW** RR	480119	481119	482119	483119	484119
701520	**SW** RR	480120	481120	482120	483120	484120
701521	**SW** RR	480121	481121	482121	483121	484121
701522	**SW** RR	480122	481122	482122	483122	484122
701523	**SW** RR	480123	481123	482123	483123	484123
701524	**SW** RR	480124	481124	482124	483124	484124
701525	**SW** RR	480125	481125	482125	483125	484125
701526	**SW** RR	480126	481126	482126	483126	484126
701527	**SW** RR	480127	481127	482127	483127	484127
701528	**SW** RR	480128	481128	482128	483128	484128
701529	**SW** RR	480129	481129	482129	483129	484129
701530	**SW** RR	480130	481130	482130	483130	484130

CLASS 707   DESIRO CITY   SIEMENS

Suburban units. Built with the capability to be easily converted to dual-voltage units. Operated by South West Trains/South Western Railway until 2021–23 when all but two units were transferred to Southeastern. Southeastern markets the units as "City Beam" units.

Formation: DMS–TS–TS–TS–DMS.
Systems: 750 V DC third rail but with 25 kV AC overhead capability.
Construction: Aluminium.
Traction Motors: Four Siemens asynchronous of 200 kW.
Wheel Arrangement: Bo-Bo + 2-2 + 2-2 + 2-2 + Bo-Bo.
Braking: Disc, tread & regenerative. **Dimensions:** 20.00/20.16 m x 2.80 m.
Bogies: Siemens SF7000 inside-frame. **Couplers:** Dellner 12.
Gangways: Within unit.   **Control System:** IGBT Inverter.
Doors: Sliding plug.   **Maximum Speed:** 100 mph.
Heating & ventilation: Air conditioning.
Seating Layout: 2+2/2+1 facing/unidirectional.
Multiple Working: Within class and with Classes 700 and 717.

DMS(A). Siemens Krefeld 2015–17. –/46. 37.9 t.
TS. Siemens Krefeld 2015–17. –/64. 28.3 t.
TS. Siemens Krefeld 2015–17. –/53(+4) 2W. 28.5 t.
TS. Siemens Krefeld 2015–17. –/62. 27.7 t.
DMS(B). Siemens Krefeld 2015–17. –/46. 37.9 t.

707 001	**SB**	A	*SE*	SG	421001	422001	423001	424001	425001
707 002	**SB**	A	*SE*	SG	421002	422002	423002	424002	425002
707 003	**SB**	A	*SE*	SG	421003	422003	423003	424003	425003
707 004	**SB**	A	*SE*	SG	421004	422004	423004	424004	425004
707 005	**SB**	A	*SE*	SG	421005	422005	423005	424005	425005
707 006	**SB**	A	*SE*	SG	421006	422006	423006	424006	425006
707 007	**SB**	A	*SE*	SG	421007	422007	423007	424007	425007
707 008	**SB**	A	*SE*	SG	421008	422008	423008	424008	425008
707 009	**SB**	A	*SE*	SG	421009	422009	423009	424009	425009
707 010	**SB**	A	*SE*	SG	421010	422010	423010	424010	425010
707 011	**SB**	A	*SE*	SG	421011	422011	423011	424011	425011
707 012	**SB**	A	*SE*	SG	421012	422012	423012	424012	425012
707 013	**SB**	A	*SE*	SG	421013	422013	423013	424013	425013
707 014	**SB**	A	*SE*	SG	421014	422014	423014	424014	425014
707 015	**SB**	A	*SE*	SG	421015	422015	423015	424015	425015
707 016	**SB**	A	*SE*	SG	421016	422016	423016	424016	425016
707 017	**SB**	A	*SE*	SG	421017	422017	423017	424017	425017
707 018	**SB**	A	*SE*	SG	421018	422018	423018	424018	425018
707 019	**SB**	A	*SE*	SG	421019	422019	423019	424019	425019
707 020	**SB**	A	*SE*	SG	421020	422020	423020	424020	425020
707 021	**SB**	A	*SE*	SG	421021	422021	423021	424021	425021
707 022	**SB**	A	*SE*	SG	421022	422022	423022	424022	425022
707 023	**SB**	A	*SE*	SG	421023	422023	423023	424023	425023
707 024	**SS**	A	*SW*	WD	421024	422024	423024	424024	425024
707 025	**SB**	A	*SE*	SG	421025	422025	423025	424025	425025
707 026	**SB**	A	*SE*	SG	421026	422026	423026	424026	425026

707027	**SB**	A	*SE*	SG	421027	422027	423027	424027	425027
707028	**SB**	A	*SE*	SG	421028	422028	423028	424028	425028
707029	**SB**	A	*SE*	SG	421029	422029	423029	424029	425029
707030	**SS**	A	*SW*	WD	421030	422030	423030	424030	425030

Names:

707001 Spirit of Ukraine
707005 Rt Hon James Brokenshire MP Old Bexley and Sidcup

CLASS 710 AVENTRA BOMBARDIER/ALSTOM DERBY

These suburban 4-car Aventras are used by London Overground on Gospel Oak–Barking, London Euston–Watford Junction and Liverpool Street local services. There are a mix of AC only and dual-voltage units.

Originally 45 4-car units were ordered. In 2018 an extra three 4-cars and six 5-cars were ordered.

Formation: DMS–MS–PMS DMS or DMS MS PMS–MS–DMS.
Systems: Class 710/1 25 kV AC overhead only. Class 710/2 and 710/3 25 kV AC overhead and 750 V DC third rail.
Construction: Aluminium.
Traction Motors: Two Bombardier asynchronous of 265 kW.
Wheel Arrangement: Bo-2 + 2-Bo + Bo-2 (+ 2-Bo) + 2-Bo.
Braking: Disc & regenerative. **Dimensions:** 21.45/19.99 m x 2.78 m.
Bogies: FLEXX B5000 inside-frame. **Couplers:** Dellner 12.
Gangways: Within unit. **Control System:** IGBT Inverter.
Doors: Sliding plug. **Maximum Speed:** 75 mph.
Heating & ventilation: Air conditioning.
Seating Layout: Longitudinal ("tube style") low density.
Multiple Working: Within class.

Class 710/1. 25 kV AC only 4-car units.

DMS(A). Alstom Derby 2017–19. –/40(+6). 41.1 t.
MS. Alstom Derby 2017–19. –/52. 32.2 t.
PMS. Alstom Derby 2017–19. –/45(+6) 2W. 38.5 t.
DMS(B). Alstom Derby 2017–19. –/40(+6). 41.1 t.

710101	**LD**	RF	*LO*	WN	431101	431201	431301	431501
710102	**LD**	RF	*LO*	WN	431102	431202	431302	431502
710103	**LD**	RF	*LO*	WN	431103	431203	431303	431503
710104	**LD**	RF	*LO*	WN	431104	431204	431304	431504
710105	**LD**	RF	*LO*	WN	431105	431205	431305	431505
710106	**LD**	RF	*LO*	WN	431106	431206	431306	431506
710107	**LD**	RF	*LO*	WN	431107	431207	431307	431507
710108	**LD**	RF	*LO*	WN	431108	431208	431308	431508
710109	**LD**	RF	*LO*	WN	431109	431209	431309	431509
710110	**LD**	RF	*LO*	WN	431110	431210	431310	431510
710111	**LD**	RF	*LO*	WN	431111	431211	431311	431511
710112	**LD**	RF	*LO*	WN	431112	431212	431312	431512
710113	**LD**	RF	*LO*	WN	431113	431213	431313	431513
710114	**LD**	RF	*LO*	WN	431114	431214	431314	431514

710115	**LD**	RF	*LO*	WN	431115	431215	431315	431515
710116	**LD**	RF	*LO*	WN	431116	431216	431316	431516
710117	**LD**	RF	*LO*	WN	431117	431217	431317	431517
710118	**LD**	RF	*LO*	WN	431118	431218	431318	431518
710119	**LD**	RF	*LO*	WN	431119	431219	431319	431519
710120	**LD**	RF	*LO*	WN	431120	431220	431320	431520
710121	**LD**	RF	*LO*	WN	431121	431221	431321	431521
710122	**LD**	RF	*LO*	WN	431122	431222	431322	431522
710123	**LD**	RF	*LO*	WN	431123	431223	431323	431523
710124	**LD**	RF	*LO*	WN	431124	431224	431324	431524
710125	**LD**	RF	*LO*	WN	431125	431225	431325	431525
710126	**LD**	RF	*LO*	WN	431126	431226	431326	431526
710127	**LD**	RF	*LO*	WN	431127	431227	431327	431527
710128	**LD**	RF	*LO*	WN	431128	431228	431328	431528
710129	**LD**	RF	*LO*	WN	431129	431229	431329	431529
710130	**LD**	RF	*LO*	WN	431130	431230	431330	431530

Class 710/2. 25 kV AC/750 V DC 4-car units.

DMS(A). Alstom Derby 2017–19. –/40(+6). 43.5 t.
MS. Alstom Derby 2017–19. –/52. 32.3 t.
PMS. Alstom Derby 2017–19. –/45(+6) 2W. 38.5 t.
DMS(B). Alstom Derby 2017–19. –/40(+6).43.5 t.

710256	**LD**	RF	*LO*	WN	432156	432256	432356	432556
710257	**LD**	RF	*LO*	WN	432157	432257	432357	432557
710258	**LD**	RF	*LO*	WN	432158	432258	432358	432558
710259	**LD**	RF	*LO*	WN	432159	432259	432359	432559
710260	**LD**	RF	*LO*	WN	432160	432260	432360	432560
710261	**LD**	RF	*LO*	WN	432161	432261	432361	432561
710262	**LD**	RF	*LO*	WN	432162	432262	432362	432562
710263	**LD**	RF	*LO*	WN	432163	432263	432363	432563
710264	**LD**	RF	*LO*	WN	432164	432264	432364	432564
710265	**LD**	RF	*LO*	WN	432165	432265	432365	432565
710266	**LD**	RF	*LO*	WN	432166	432266	432366	432566
710267	**LD**	RF	*LO*	WN	432167	432267	432367	432567
710268	**LD**	RF	*LO*	WN	432168	432268	432368	432568
710269	**LD**	RF	*LO*	WN	432169	432269	432369	432569
710270	**LD**	RF			432170	432270	432370	432570
710271	**LD**	RF	*LO*	WN	432171	432271	432371	432571
710272	**LD**	RF	*LO*	WN	432172	432272	432372	432572
710273	**LD**	RF	*LO*	WN	432173	432273	432373	432573

Class 710/3. 25 kV AC/750 V DC 5-car units. Originally numbered 710274–279 as-built, but renumbered in the 7103xx series before entering service.

DMS(A). Alstom Derby 2019–20. –/40(+6). 43.5 t.
MS. Alstom Derby 2019–20. –/52. 32.3 t.
PMS. Alstom Derby 2019–20. –/45(+6) 2W. 38.5 t.
MS. Alstom Derby 2019–20. –/52. 33.1 t.
DMS(B). Alstom Derby 2019–20. –/40(+6). 43.5 t.

710374	**LD**	RF			432174	432274	432374	432474	432574
710375	**LD**	RF	*LO*	WN	432175	432275	432375	432475	432575

710376	**LD**	RF	*LO*	WN	432176	432276	432376	432476	432576
710377	**LD**	RF	*LO*	WN	432177	432277	432377	432477	432577
710378	**LD**	RF	*LO*	WN	432178	432278	432378	432478	432578
710379	**LD**	RF	*LO*	WN	432179	432279	432379	432479	432579

CLASS 717　　　　　　　DESIRO CITY　　　　　　　SIEMENS

Dual-voltage 6-car units used on Great Northern services from London Moorgate. The design is based on Classes 700/707, but has emergency end doors for tunnel operation.

Formation: DMS–TS–TS–MS–PTS–DMS.
Systems: 25 kV AC overhead and 750 V DC third rail.
Construction: Aluminium.
Traction Motors: Four Siemens asynchronous of 200 kW.
Wheel Arrangement: Bo-Bo + 2-2 + 2-2 + Bo-Bo + 2-2 + Bo-Bo.
Braking: Disc, tread & regenerative. **Dimensions:** 20.00 x 2.80 m.
Bogies: Siemens SF7000 inside-frame. **Couplers:** Dellner 12.
Gangways: Within unit + end doors. **Control System:** IGBT Inverter.
Doors: Sliding plug. **Maximum Speed:** 85 mph.
Heating & ventilation: Air conditioning.
Seating Layout: 2+2 facing/unidirectional.
Multiple Working: Within class and with Classes 700 and 707.

DMS(A). Siemens Krefeld 2017–18. –/52(+4). 38.8 t.
TS. Siemens Krefeld 2017–18. –/68. 28.8 t.
TS. Siemens Krefeld 2017–18. –/61(+4) 2W. 28.7 t.
MS. Siemens Krefeld 2017–18. –/68. 35.5 t.
PTS. Siemens Krefeld 2017–18. –/61(+3). 33.9 t.
DMS(B). Siemens Krefeld 2017–18. –/52(+4). 38.8 t.

717001	**TL**	RR	*GN*	HE	451001	452001	453001	454001	455001	456001
717002	**TL**	RR	*GN*	HE	451002	452002	453002	454002	455002	456002
717003	**TL**	RR	*GN*	HE	451003	452003	453003	454003	455003	456003
717004	**TL**	RR	*GN*	HE	451004	452004	453004	454004	455004	456004
717005	**TL**	RR	*GN*	HE	451005	452005	453005	454005	455005	456005
717006	**TL**	RR	*GN*	HE	451006	452006	453006	454006	455006	456006
717007	**TL**	RR	*GN*	HE	451007	452007	453007	454007	455007	456007
717008	**TL**	RR	*GN*	HE	451008	452008	453008	454008	455008	456008
717009	**TL**	RR	*GN*	HE	451009	452009	453009	454009	455009	456009
717010	**TL**	RR	*GN*	HE	451010	452010	453010	454010	455010	456010
717011	**TL**	RR	*GN*	HE	451011	452011	453011	454011	455011	456011
717012	**TL**	RR	*GN*	HE	451012	452012	453012	454012	455012	456012
717013	**TL**	RR	*GN*	HE	451013	452013	453013	454013	455013	456013
717014	**TL**	RR	*GN*	HE	451014	452014	453014	454014	455014	456014
717015	**TL**	RR	*GN*	HE	451015	452015	453015	454015	455015	456015
717016	**TL**	RR	*GN*	HE	451016	452016	453016	454016	455016	456016
717017	**TL**	RR	*GN*	HE	451017	452017	453017	454017	455017	456017
717018	**TL**	RR	*GN*	HE	451018	452018	453018	454018	455018	456018
717019	**TL**	RR	*GN*	HE	451019	452019	453019	454019	455019	456019
717020	**TL**	RR	*GN*	HE	451020	452020	453020	454020	455020	456020
717021	**TL**	RR	*GN*	HE	451021	452021	453021	454021	455021	456021

717022	**TL**	RR	*GN*	HE	451022	452022	453022	454022	455022 456022
717023	**TL**	RR	*GN*	HE	451023	452023	453023	454023	455023 456023
717024	**TL**	RR	*GN*	HE	451024	452024	453024	454024	455024 456024
717025	**TL**	RR	*GN*	HE	451025	452025	453025	454025	455025 456025

CLASS 720 AVENTRA BOMBARDIER/ALSTOM DERBY

This large fleet of Standard Class only Aventra EMUs was ordered by Greater Anglia in 2016 to replace its entire Class 317, 321, 360 and 379 fleets on outer suburban and medium-distance services. In 2020 the order was amended – originally it was to be for 89 5-car units and 22 10-car units, but it was changed so that the whole order consists of 5-car units (133 5-cars in total). The additional 5-car units are still numbered in the 720/1 series.

After many delays the units were finally introduced in autumn 2020.

The Class 720/6 units are 5-car sets on order for c2c (originally these were also to be formed as six 10-car units but the order was later amended to 12 5-car units).

Formation: DMS–PMS–MS–MS–DTS.
Systems: 25 kV AC overhead.
Construction: Aluminium.
Traction Motors: Two Bombardier asynchronous of 265 kW.
Wheel Arrangement:

Braking: Disc & regenerative	**Dimensions:** 24.54/24.21 x 2.77 m.
Bogies: FLEXX B5000 inside-frame.	**Couplers:** Dellner 12.
Gangways: Within unit.	**Control System:** IGBT Inverter.
Doors: Sliding plug.	**Maximum Speed:** 100 mph.

Heating & ventilation: Air conditioning.
Seating Layout: 3+2 facing/unidirectional.
Multiple Working: Within class.

Class 720/1. Greater Anglia units.

Additions to the standard livery: 720506 Pride stripes on driving cars.

DMS. Alstom Derby 2018–23. –/91(+4). 42.5 t.
PMS. Alstom Derby 2018–23. –/93(+8) 1T. 39.8 t.
MS(A). Alstom Derby 2018–23. –/109(+4). 39.6 t.
MS(B). Alstom Derby 2018–23. –/109(+4). 34.1 t.
DTS. Alstom Derby 2018–23. –/59(+9) 1TD 2W. 37.7 t.

720101	**GR**	A			450101	451101	452101	453101	459101
720102	**GR**	A			450102	451102	452102	453102	459102
720103	**GR**	A	*GA*	IL	450103	451103	452103	453103	459103
720104	**GR**	A			450104	451104	452104	453104	459104
720105	**GR**	A	*GA*	IL	450105	451105	452105	453105	459105
720106	**GR**	A	*GA*	IL	450106	451106	452106	453106	459106
720107	**GR**	A	*GA*	IL	450107	451107	452107	453107	459107
720108	**GR**	A	*GA*	IL	450108	451108	452108	453108	459108
720109	**GR**	A	*GA*	IL	450109	451109	452109	453109	459109
720110	**GR**	A	*GA*	IL	450110	451110	452110	453110	459110
720111	**GR**	A	*GA*	IL	450111	451111	452111	453111	459111

720 112	**GR**	A	*GA*	IL	450112	451112	452112	453112	459112
720 113	**GR**	A	*GA*	IL	450113	451113	452113	453113	459113
720 114	**GR**	A	*GA*	IL	450114	451114	452114	453114	459114
720 115	**GR**	A	*GA*	IL	450115	451115	452115	453115	459115
720 116	**GR**	A	*GA*	IL	450116	451116	452116	453116	459116
720 117	**GR**	A	*GA*	IL	450117	451117	452117	453117	459117
720 118	**GR**	A	*GA*	IL	450118	451118	452118	453118	459118
720 119	**GR**	A	*GA*	IL	450119	451119	452119	453119	459119
720 120	**GR**	A	*GA*	IL	450120	451120	452120	453120	459120
720 121	**GR**	A	*GA*	IL	450121	451121	452121	453121	459121
720 122	**GR**	A	*GA*	IL	450122	451122	452122	453122	459122
720 123	**GR**	A	*GA*	IL	450123	451123	452123	453123	459123
720 124	**GR**	A	*GA*	IL	450124	451124	452124	453124	459124
720 125	**GR**	A	*GA*	IL	450125	451125	452125	453125	459125
720 126	**GR**	A	*GA*	IL	450126	451126	452126	453126	459126
720 127	**GR**	A	*GA*	IL	450127	451127	452127	453127	459127
720 128	**GR**	A	*GA*	IL	450128	451128	452128	453128	459128
720 129	**GR**	A	*GA*	IL	450129	451129	452129	453129	459129
720 130	**GR**	A	*GA*	IL	450130	451130	452130	453130	459130
720 131	**GR**	A	*GA*	IL	450131	451131	452131	453131	459131
720 132	**GR**	A	*GA*	IL	450132	451132	452132	453132	459132
720 133	**GR**	A	*GA*	IL	450133	451133	452133	453133	459133
720 134	**GR**	A	*GA*	IL	450134	451134	452134	453134	459134
720 135	**GR**	A	*GA*	IL	450135	451135	452135	453135	459135
720 136	**GR**	A	*GA*	IL	450136	451136	452136	453136	459136
720 137	**GR**	A			450137	451137	452137	453137	459137
720 138	**GR**	A			450138	451138	452138	453138	459138
720 139	**GR**	A			450139	451139	452139	453139	459139
720 140	**GR**	A			450140	451140	452140	453140	459140
720 141	**GR**	A			450141	451141	452141	453141	459141
720 142	**GR**	A			450142	451142	452142	453142	459142
720 143	**GR**	A			450143	451143	452143	453143	459143
720 144	**GR**	A			450144	451144	452144	453144	459144
720 501	**GR**	A	*GA*	IL	450501	451501	452501	453501	459501
720 502	**GR**	A			450502	451502	452502	453502	459502
720 503	**GR**	A			450503	451503	452503	453503	459503
720 504	**GR**	A			450504	451504	452504	453504	459504
720 505	**GR**	A			450505	451505	452505	453505	459505
720 506	**GR**	A	*GA*	IL	450506	451506	452506	453506	459506
720 507	**GR**	A	*GA*	IL	450507	451507	452507	453507	459507
720 508	**GR**	A	*GA*	IL	450508	451508	452508	453508	459508
720 509	**GR**	A	*GA*	IL	450509	451509	452509	453509	459509
720 510	**GR**	A			450510	451510	452510	453510	459510
720 511	**GR**	A	*GA*	IL	450511	451511	452511	453511	459511
720 512	**GR**	A	*GA*	IL	450512	451512	452512	453512	459512
720 513	**GR**	A	*GA*	IL	450513	451513	452513	453513	459513
720 514	**GR**	A	*GA*	IL	450514	451514	452514	453514	459514
720 515	**GR**	A	*GA*	IL	450515	451515	452515	453515	459515
720 516	**GR**	A			450516	451516	452516	453516	459516
720 517	**GR**	A	*GA*	IL	450517	451517	452517	453517	459517

720518	GR	A	GA	IL	450518	451518	452518	453518	459518
720519	GR	A			450519	451519	452519	453519	459519
720520	GR	A	GA	IL	450520	451520	452520	453520	459520
720521	GR	A	GA	IL	450521	451521	452521	453521	459521
720522	GR	A	GA	IL	450522	451522	452522	453522	459522
720523	GR	A	GA	IL	450523	451523	452523	453523	459523
720524	GR	A	GA	IL	450524	451524	452524	453524	459524
720525	GR	A	GA	IL	450525	451525	452525	453525	459525
720526	GR	A	GA	IL	450526	451526	452526	453526	459526
720527	GR	A	GA	IL	450527	451527	452527	453527	459527
720528	GR	A	GA	IL	450528	451528	452528	453528	459528
720529	GR	A	GA	IL	450529	451529	452529	453529	459529
720530	GR	A	GA	IL	450530	451530	452530	453530	459530
720531	GR	A	GA	IL	450531	451531	452531	453531	459531
720532	GR	A	GA	IL	450532	451532	452532	453532	459532
720533	GR	A	GA	IL	450533	451533	452533	453533	459533
720534	GR	A			450534	451534	452534	453534	459534
720535	GR	A	GA	IL	450535	451535	452535	453535	459535
720536	GR	A	GA	IL	450536	451536	452536	453536	459536
720537	GR	A	GA	IL	450537	451537	452537	453537	459537
720538	GR	A	GA	IL	450538	451538	452538	453538	459538
720539	GR	A	GA	IL	450539	451539	452539	453539	459539
720540	GR	A	GA	IL	450540	451540	452540	453540	459540
720541	GR	A	GA	IL	450541	451541	452541	453541	459541
720542	GR	A	GA	IL	450542	451542	452542	453542	459542
720543	GR	A	GA	IL	450543	451543	452543	453543	459543
720544	GR	A	GA	IL	450544	451544	452544	453544	459544
720545	GR	A	GA	IL	450545	451545	452545	453545	459545
720546	GR	A	GA	IL	450546	451546	452546	453546	459546
720547	GR	A	GA	IL	450547	451547	452547	453547	459547
720548	GR	A	GA	IL	450548	451548	452548	453548	459548
720549	GR	A	GA	IL	450549	451549	452549	453549	459549
720550	GR	A	GA	IL	450550	451550	452550	453550	459550
720551	GR	A	GA	IL	450551	451551	452551	453551	459551
720552	GR	A	GA	IL	450552	451552	452552	453552	459552
720553	GR	A	GA	IL	450553	451553	452553	453553	459553
720554	GR	A	GA	IL	450554	451554	452554	453554	459554
720555	GR	A	GA	IL	450555	451555	452555	453555	459555
720556	GR	A	GA	IL	450556	451556	452556	453556	459556
720557	GR	A	GA	IL	450557	451557	452557	453557	459557
720558	GR	A	GA	IL	450558	451558	452558	453558	459558
720559	GR	A	GA	IL	450559	451559	452559	453559	459559
720560	GR	A	GA	IL	450560	451560	452560	453560	459560
720561	GR	A	GA	IL	450561	451561	452561	453561	459561
720562	GR	A	GA	IL	450562	451562	452562	453562	459562
720563	GR	A	GA	IL	450563	451563	452563	453563	459563
720564	GR	A	GA	IL	450564	451564	452564	453564	459564
720565	GR	A	GA	IL	450565	451565	452565	453565	459565
720566	GR	A	GA	IL	450566	451566	452566	453566	459566
720567	GR	A	GA	IL	450567	451567	452567	453567	459567
720568	GR	A	GA	IL	450568	451568	452568	453568	459568

720569	**GR**	A	*GA*	IL	450569	451569	452569	453569	459569
720570	**GR**	A	*GA*	IL	450570	451570	452570	453570	459570
720571	**GR**	A	*GA*	IL	450571	451571	452571	453571	459571
720572	**GR**	A	*GA*	IL	450572	451572	452572	453572	459572
720573	**GR**	A	*GA*	IL	450573	451573	452573	453573	459573
720574	**GR**	A	*GA*	IL	450574	451574	452574	453574	459574
720575	**GR**	A	*GA*	IL	450575	451575	452575	453575	459575
720576	**GR**	A	*GA*	IL	450576	451576	452576	453576	459576
720577	**GR**	A	*GA*	IL	450577	451577	452577	453577	459577
720578	**GR**	A	*GA*	IL	450578	451578	452578	453578	459578
720579	**GR**	A	*GA*	IL	450579	451579	452579	453579	459579
720580	**GR**	A	*GA*	IL	450580	451580	452580	453580	459580
720581	**GR**	A	*GA*	IL	450581	451581	452581	453581	459581
720582	**GR**	A	*GA*	IL	450582	451582	452582	453582	459582
720583	**GR**	A	*GA*	IL	450583	451583	452583	453583	459583
720584	**GR**	A	*GA*	IL	450584	451584	452584	453584	459584
720585	**GR**	A	*GA*	IL	450585	451585	452585	453585	459585
720586	**GR**	A	*GA*	IL	450586	451586	452586	453586	459586
720587	**GR**	A	*GA*	IL	450587	451587	452587	453587	459587
720588	**GR**	A	*GA*	IL	450588	451588	452588	453588	459588
720589	**GR**	A	*GA*	IL	450589	451589	452589	453589	459589

Class 720/6. c2c units.

DMS. Alstom Derby 2021–22. –/89. 42.5 t.
PMS. Alstom Derby 2021–22. –/90(+6) 1T. 39.8 t.
MS(A). Alstom Derby 2021–22. –/103. 40.1 t.
MS(B). Alstom Derby 2021–22. –/103. 34.1 t.
DTS. Alstom Derby 2021–22. –/58(+12) 1TD 2W. 37.7 t.

720601	**C2C**	P	*C2*	EM	450601	451601	452601	453601	459601
720602	**C2C**	P	*C2*	EM	450602	451602	452602	453602	459602
720603	**C2C**	P	*C2*	EM	450603	451603	452603	453603	459603
720604	**C2C**	P	*C2*	EM	450604	451604	452604	453604	459604
720605	**C2C**	P	*C2*	EM	450605	451605	452605	453605	459605
720606	**C2C**	P	*C2*	EM	450606	451606	452606	453606	459606
720607	**C2C**	P	*C2*	EM	450607	451607	452607	453607	459607
720608	**C2C**	P	*C2*	EM	450608	451608	452608	453608	459608
720609	**C2C**	P	*C2*	EM	450609	451609	452609	453609	459609
720610	**C2C**	P	*C2*	EM	450610	451610	452610	453610	459610
720611	**C2C**	P	*C2*	EM	450611	451611	452611	453611	459611
720612	**C2C**	P	*C2*	EM	450612	451612	452612	453612	459612

Name: 720601 Julian Drury c2c Managing Director 2008–2020

CLASS 730 AVENTRA BOMBARDIER/ALSTOM DERBY

West Midlands Trains has a mixed fleet of 3- and 5-car Aventra EMUs on order from Alstom (previously Bombardier). The 3-car units will be used on suburban services around Birmingham, mainly on the Cross City line, while the 5-car units will be used on outer suburban and inter urban services from London Euston and in the West Midlands. The 3-car units entered service initially on selected services from London Euston in autumn 2023.

The order was amended in 2022, originally it was for 36 x 3-cars and 45 x 5-cars split into Class 730/1 and 730/2 but this was changed to 48 x 3-cars and 36 x 5-cars each with the same interior specification.

Formation: DMS–PMS–DMS or DMS–MS–PMS–MS–DMS.
Systems: 25 kV AC overhead.
Construction: Aluminium.
Traction Motors: Two Bombardier asynchronous of 250 kW.
Wheel Arrangement:
Braking: Disc & regenerative. **Dimensions:** 23.91/24.21 x 2.77 m.
Bogies: FLEXX B5000 inside-frame. **Couplers:** Dellner 12.
Gangways: End gangways. **Control System:** IGBT Inverter.
Doors: Sliding plug.
Maximum Speed: 730/0: 90 mph; 730/2: 110 mph.
Heating & ventilation: Air conditioning.
Seating Layout: 2+2 facing/unidirectional.
Multiple Working: Within class.

Class 730/0. 3-car units. Principally for West Midlands area suburban services but some units initially in traffic on services from London Euston.

DMS(A). Alstom Derby 2020–23. –/67. 41.7 t.
PMS. Alstom Derby 2020–23. –/57(+12) 1TD 2W. 39.8 t.
DMS(B). Alstom Derby 2020–23. –/67. 41.7 t.

730001	**WM** CO			490001	492001	494001
730002	**WM** CO			490002	492002	494002
730003	**WM** CO			490003	492003	494003
730004	**WM** CO			490004	492004	494004
730005	**WM** CO			490005	492005	494005
730006	**WM** CO	*WM*	BY	490006	492006	494006
730007	**WM** CO	*WM*	BY	490007	492007	494007
730008	**WM** CO			490008	492008	494008
730009	**WM** CO			490009	492009	494009
730010	**WM** CO	*WM*	BY	490010	492010	494010
730011	**WM** CO	*WM*	BY	490011	492011	494011
730012	**WM** CO	*WM*	BY	490012	492012	494012
730013	**WM** CO	*WM*	BY	490013	492013	494013
730014	**WM** CO	*WM*	BY	490014	492014	494014
730015	**WM** CO	*WM*	BY	490015	492015	494015
730016	**WM** CO	*WM*	BY	490016	492016	494016
730017	**WM** CO			490017	492017	494017
730018	**WM** CO	*WM*	BY	490018	492018	494018
730019	**WM** CO	*WM*	BY	490019	492019	494019

730020	**WM**	CO	*WM*	BY	490020	492020	494020
730021	**WM**	CO	*WM*	BY	490021	492021	494021
730022	**WM**	CO			490022	492022	494022
730023	**WM**	CO			490023	492023	494023
730024	**WM**	CO			490024	492024	494024
730025	**WM**	CO			490025	492025	494025
730026	**WM**	CO			490026	492026	494026
730027	**WM**	CO			490027	492027	494027
730028	**WM**	CO			490028	492028	494028
730029	**WM**	CO			490029	492029	494029
730030	**WM**	CO			490030	492030	494030
730031	**WM**	CO			490031	492031	494031
730032	**WM**	CO			490032	492032	494032
730033	**WM**	CO			490033	492033	494033
730034	**WM**	CO			490034	492034	494034
730035	**WM**	CO			490035	492035	494035
730036	**WM**	CO			490036	492036	494036
730037	**WM**	CO			490037	492037	494037
730038	**WM**	CO			490038	492038	494038
730039	**WM**	CO			490039	492039	494039
730040	**WM**	CO			490040	492040	494040
730041	**WM**	CO			490041	492041	494041
730042	**WM**	CO			490042	492042	494042
730043	**WM**	CO			490043	492043	494043
730044	**WM**	CO			490044	492044	494044
730045	**WM**	CO			490045	492045	494045
730046	**WM**	CO			490046	492046	494046
730047	**WM**	CO			490047	492047	494047
730048	**WM**	CO			490048	492048	494048

Class 730/2. 5-car units. Pre-series units 730 201–203 were originally built as 730 101–103. Full details awaited.

DMS(A). Alstom Derby 2020–24.   t.
MS(A). Alstom Derby 2020–24.   t.
PMS. Alstom Derby 2020–24.   t.
MS(B). Alstom Derby 2020–24.   t.
DMS(B). Alstom Derby 2020–24.   t.

730201	**LN**	CO	490201	491201	492201	493201	494201
730202	**LN**	CO	490202	491202	492202	493202	494202
730203	**LN**	CO	490203	491203	492203	493203	494203
730204	**LN**	CO	490204	491204	492204	493204	494204
730205	**LN**	CO	490205	491205	492205	493205	494205
730206	**LN**	CO	490206	491206	492206	493206	494206
730207	**LN**	CO	490207	491207	492207	493207	494207
730208	**LN**	CO	490208	491208	492208	493208	494208
730209	**LN**	CO	490209	491209	492209	493209	494209
730210	**LN**	CO	490210	491210	492210	493210	494210
730211	**LN**	CO	490211	491211	492211	493211	494211
730212	**LN**	CO	490212	491212	492212	493212	494212
730213	**LN**	CO	490213	491213	492213	493213	494213

730 214	**LN**	CO	490214	491214	492214	493214	494214
730 215	**LN**	CO	490215	491215	492215	493215	494215
730 216	**LN**	CO	490216	491216	492216	493216	494216
730 217	**LN**	CO	490217	491217	492217	493217	494217
730 218	**LN**	CO	490218	491218	492218	493218	494218
730 219	**LN**	CO	490219	491219	492219	493219	494219
730 220	**LN**	CO	490220	491220	492220	493220	494220
730 221	**LN**	CO	490221	491221	492221	493221	494221
730 222	**LN**	CO	490222	491222	492222	493222	494222
730 223	**LN**	CO	490223	491223	492223	493223	494223
730 224	**LN**	CO	490224	491224	492224	493224	494224
730 225	**LN**	CO	490225	491225	492225	493225	494225
730 226	**LN**	CO	490226	491226	492226	493226	494226
730 227	**LN**	CO	490227	491227	492227	493227	494227
730 228	**LN**	CO	490228	491228	492228	493228	494228
730 229	**LN**	CO	490229	491229	492229	493229	494229
730 230	**LN**	CO	490230	491230	492230	493230	494230
730 231	**LN**	CO	490231	491231	492231	493231	494231
730 232	**LN**	CO	490232	491232	492232	493232	494232
730 233	**LN**	CO	490233	491233	492233	493233	494233
730 234	**LN**	CO	490234	491234	492234	493234	494234
730 235	**LN**	CO	490235	491235	492235	493235	494235
730 236	**LN**	CO	490236	491236	492236	493236	494236

CLASS 745   FLIRT ELECTRIC   STADLER

These 20 12-car articulated Stadler EMUs were ordered by Greater Anglia in 2016 to replace its locomotive-hauled sets on Liverpool Street–Norwich services and Class 379s on the Stansted Express services. The 12-car units are formed of two 6-car half units formed of three coupled articulated pairs.

Formations (745/0): DMF–PTF–TS–TS–TS–MS–MS–TS–TS–TS–PTS–DMS or **(745/1):** DMS–PTS–TS–TS–TS–MS–MS–TS–TS–TS–PTS–DMS.
Systems: 25 kV AC overhead.
Construction: Aluminium.
Traction Motors: Four TSA of 325 kW.
Wheel Arrangement: Bo-2-2 + 2-2-2 + 2-2-Bo + Bo-2-2 + 2-2-2 + 2-2-Bo.
Braking: Disc & regenerative   **Dimensions:** 21.05/19.45 x 2.72 m.
Bogies: Stadler/Jacobs.   **Couplers:** Dellner 10.
Gangways: Within unit.   **Control System:** IGBT Inverter.
Doors: Sliding plug (one per vehicle). **Maximum Speed:** 100 mph.
Heating & ventilation: Air conditioning.
Seating Layout: 1: 2+1 facing/unidirectional, 2: 2+2 unidirectional/facing.
Multiple Working: Within class.

Class 745/0. Fitted with First Class and café bar and built for use on the London Liverpool Street–Norwich route.

DMF. Stadler Bussnang/Szolnok 2018–19. 36/–. 41.3 t.
PTF. Stadler Bussnang/Szolnok 2018–19. 44/– 1T. 28.4 t.
TSMB. Stadler Bussnang/Szolnok 2018–19. –/26(+9) 1TD 2W. 26.8 t.

TS. Stadler Bussnang/Szolnok 2018–19. –/66(+12). 26.7 t.
TS. Stadler Bussnang/Szolnok 2018–19. –/70(+4) 1T. 28.0 t.
MS. Stadler Bussnang/Szolnok 2018–19. –/58(+4). 37.4 t.
MS. Stadler Bussnang/Szolnok 2018–19. –/58(+4). 37.4 t.
TS. Stadler Bussnang/Szolnok 2018–19. –/70(+4) 1T. 28.0 t.
TS. Stadler Bussnang/Szolnok 2018–19. –/74(+4). 25.9 t.
TS. Stadler Bussnang/Szolnok 2018–19. –/74(+4). 25.9 t.
PTS. Stadler Bussnang/Szolnok 2018–19. –/70(+4) 1T. 28.7 t.
DMS. Stadler Bussnang/Szolnok 2018–19. –/58(+4). 41.3 t.

745001	**GR**	RR	*GA*	NC	413001 426001 332001 343001 341001 301001
					302001 342001 344001 346001 322001 312001
745002	**GR**	RR	*GA*	NC	413002 426002 332002 343002 341002 301002
					302002 342002 344002 346002 322002 312002
745003	**GR**	RR	*GA*	NC	413003 426003 332003 343003 341003 301003
					302003 342003 344003 346003 322003 312003
745004	**GR**	RR	*GA*	NC	413004 426004 332004 343004 341004 301004
					302004 342004 344004 346004 322004 312004
745005	**GR**	RR	*GA*	NC	413005 426005 332005 343005 341005 301005
					302005 342005 344005 346005 322005 312005
745006	**GR**	RR	*GA*	NC	413006 426006 332006 343006 341006 301006
					302006 342006 344006 346006 322006 312006
745007	**GR**	RR	*GA*	NC	413007 426007 332007 343007 341007 301007
					302007 342007 344007 346007 322007 312007
745008	**GR**	RR	*GA*	NC	413008 426008 332008 343008 341008 301008
					302008 342008 344008 346008 322008 312008
745009	**GR**	RR	*GA*	NC	413009 426009 332009 343009 341009 301009
					302009 342009 344009 346009 322009 312009
745010	**GR**	RR	*GA*	NC	413010 426010 332010 343010 341010 301010
					302010 342010 344010 346010 322010 312010

Class 745/1. Standard Class only units mainly for use between London Liverpool Street and Stansted Airport and for selected services to/from Norwich for maintenance purposes.

DMS. Stadler Bussnang/Szolnok 2018–19. –/48(+6). 41.3 t.
PTS. Stadler Bussnang/Szolnok 2018–19. –/68 1T. 28.4 t.
TS(A). Stadler Bussnang/Szolnok 2018–19. –/50(+9) 1TD 2W. 26.8 t.
TS(B). Stadler Bussnang/Szolnok 2018–19. –/64(+8). 26.7 t.
TS(C). Stadler Bussnang/Szolnok 2018–19. –/68 1T. 28.0 t.
MS(A). Stadler Bussnang/Szolnok 2018–19. –/56. 37.4 t.
MS(B). Stadler Bussnang/Szolnok 2018–19. –/56. 37.4 t.
TS(D). Stadler Bussnang/Szolnok 2018–19. –/68 1T. 28.0 t.
TS(E). Stadler Bussnang/Szolnok 2018–19. –/64(+8). 25.9 t.
TS(F). Stadler Bussnang/Szolnok 2018–19. –/64(+8). 25.9 t.
PTS. Stadler Bussnang/Szolnok 2018–19. –/68 1T. 28.7 t.
DMS. Stadler Bussnang/Szolnok 2018–19. –/48(+6). 41.3 t.

745101	**GR**	RR	*GA*	NC	313101 326101 332101 343101 341101 301101
					302101 342101 344101 346101 322101 312101
745102	**GR**	RR	*GA*	NC	313102 326102 332102 343102 341102 301102
					302102 342102 344102 346102 322102 312102

745 103	**GR**	RR	*GA*	NC	313103 326103 332103 343103 341103 301103
					302103 342103 344103 346103 322103 312103
745 104	**GR**	RR	*GA*	NC	313104 326104 332104 343104 341104 301104
					302104 342104 344104 346104 322104 312104
745 105	**GR**	RR	*GA*	NC	313105 326105 332105 343105 341105 301105
					302105 342105 344105 346105 322105 312105
745 106	**GR**	RR	*GA*	NC	313106 326106 332106 343106 341106 301106
					302106 342106 344106 346106 322106 312106
745 107	**GR**	RR	*GA*	NC	313107 326107 332107 343107 341107 301107
					302107 342107 344107 346107 322107 312107
745 108	**GR**	RR	*GA*	NC	313108 326108 332108 343108 341108 301108
					302108 342108 344108 346108 322108 312108
745 109	**GR**	RR	*GA*	NC	313109 326109 332109 343109 341109 301109
					302109 342109 344109 346109 322109 312109
745 110	**GR**	RR	*GA*	NC	313110 326110 332110 343110 341110 301110
					302110 342110 344110 346110 322110 312110

CLASS 755   FLIRT BI-MODE   STADLER

This fleet of 3- and 4-car articulated Stadler bi-mode units was ordered by Greater Anglia in 2016 to replace all of its older DMU fleets. The first units entered service in summer 2019. The design features a "power pack" in the middle that houses two diesel engines for the 3-car units and four diesel engines for the 4-car units. This has been given its own number, effectively making the units 4- and 5-car, although there is no passenger accommodation in the power pack car.

Formation: DMS–PP–PTS–DMS or DMS–PTS–PP–PTS–DMS.
Systems: Diesel/25 kV AC overhead.
Construction: Aluminium.
Engines: (4-car): Four Deutz V8 of 480 kW (645 hp), (3-car): Two Four Deutz V8 of 480 kW (645 hp).
Traction Motors: 4 x TSA of 325 kW.
Wheel Arrangement: Bo-2-2-2-Bo or Bo-2-2-2-2-Bo.
Braking: Disc & regenerative.
Dimensions: 20.81/15.22/6.69 (PP) m x 2.72/2.82 (PP) m.
Bogies: Stadler/Jacobs.   **Couplers:** Dellner 10.
Gangways: Within unit.   **Control System:** IGBT Inverter.
Doors: Sliding plug (one per vehicle).**Maximum Speed:** 100 mph.
Heating & ventilation: Air conditioning.
Seating Layout: 2+2 unidirectional/facing.
Multiple Working: Within class.

Class 755/3. 3-car (plus power pack) units.

DMS(A). Stadler Szolnok/Siedlce/Bussnang/Valencia 2018–19. –/60(+4). 43.4 t.
PP. Stadler Bussnang/Valencia 2018–19. 25.4 t.
PTS. Stadler Szolnok/Siedlce/Bussnang/Valencia 2018–19. –/32(+7) 1TD 1T 2W. 24.2 t.
DMS(B). Stadler Szolnok/Siedlce/Bussnang/Valencia 2018–19. –/52(+12). 42.1 t.

755 325	**GR**	RR	*GA*	NC	911325	971325	981325	912325
755 326	**GR**	RR	*GA*	NC	911326	971326	981326	912326
755 327	**GR**	RR	*GA*	NC	911327	971327	981327	912327
755 328	**GR**	RR	*GA*	NC	911328	971328	981328	912328
755 329	**GR**	RR	*GA*	NC	911329	971329	981329	912329
755 330	**GR**	RR	*GA*	NC	911330	971330	981330	912330
755 331	**GR**	RR	*GA*	NC	911331	971331	981331	912331
755 332	**GR**	RR	*GA*	NC	911332	971332	981332	912332
755 333	**GR**	RR	*GA*	NC	911333	971333	981333	912333
755 334	**GR**	RR	*GA*	NC	911334	971334	981334	912334
755 335	**GR**	RR	*GA*	NC	911335	971335	981335	912335
755 336	**GR**	RR	*GA*	NC	911336	971336	981336	912336
755 337	**GR**	RR	*GA*	NC	911337	971337	981337	912337
755 338	**GR**	RR	*GA*	NC	911338	971338	981338	912338

Class 755/4. 4-car (plus power pack) units.

DMS(A). Stadler Szolnok/Siedlce/Bussnang/Valencia 2018–19. –/60(+4). 41.4 t.
PTS(A). Stadler Szolnok/Siedlce/Bussnang/Valencia 2018–19. –/58(+4). 25.0 t.
PP. Stadler Bussnang/Valencia 2018–19. 28.5 t.
PTS(B). Stadler Szolnok/Siedlce/Bussnang/Valencia 2018–19. –/32(+7). 1TD 1T 2W. 26.4 t.
DMS(B). Stadler Szolnok/Siedlce/Bussnang/Valencia 2018–19. –/52(+12). 42.2 t.

755 401	**GR**	RR	*GA*	NC	911401	961401	971401	981401	912401
755 402	**GR**	RR	*GA*	NC	911402	961402	971402	981402	912402
755 403	**GR**	RR	*GA*	NC	911403	961403	971403	981403	912403
755 404	**GR**	RR	*GA*	NC	911404	961404	971404	981404	912404
755 405	**GR**	RR	*GA*	NC	911405	961405	971405	981405	912405
755 406	**GR**	RR	*GA*	NC	911406	961406	971406	981406	912406
755 407	**GR**	RR	*GA*	NC	911407	961407	971407	981407	912407
755 408	**GR**	RR	*GA*	NC	911408	961408	971408	981408	912408
755 409	**GR**	RR	*GA*	NC	911409	961409	971409	981409	912409
755 410	**GR**	RR	*GA*	NC	911410	961410	971410	981410	912410
755 411	**GR**	RR	*GA*	NC	911411	961411	971411	981411	912411
755 412	**GR**	RR	*GA*	NC	911412	961412	971412	981412	912412
755 413	**GR**	RR	*GA*	NC	911413	961413	971413	981413	912413
755 414	**GR**	RR	*GA*	NC	911414	961414	971414	981414	912414
755 415	**GR**	RR	*GA*	NC	911415	961415	971415	981415	912415
755 416	**GR**	RR	*GA*	NC	911416	961416	971416	981416	912416
755 417	**GR**	RR	*GA*	NC	911417	961417	971417	981417	912417
755 418	**GR**	RR	*GA*	NC	911418	961418	971418	981418	912418
755 419	**GR**	RR	*GA*	NC	911419	961419	971419	981419	912419
755 420	**GR**	RR	*GA*	NC	911420	961420	971420	981420	912420
755 421	**GR**	RR	*GA*	NC	911421	961421	971421	981421	912421
755 422	**GR**	RR	*GA*	NC	911422	961422	971422	981422	912422
755 423	**GR**	RR	*GA*	NC	911423	961423	971423	981423	912423
755 424	**GR**	RR	*GA*	NC	911424	961424	971424	981424	912424

CLASS 756   FLIRT TRI-MODE   STADLER

This fleet of articulated FLIRT tri-mode diesel/electric/battery units is on order for Transport for Wales for use on the Cardiff Valley Lines (Rhymney, Coryton, Vale of Glamorgan, Penarth and Barry Island) from 2024–25. The units look similar to Greater Anglia's Class 755s.

Formation: DMS–PP–PTS–DMS or DMS–PP–PTS–PP–PTS–DMS.
Systems: Diesel/25 kV AC overhead/battery.
Construction: Aluminium.
Engines: Deutz V8 of 480 kW (645 hp) + three battery modules.
Traction Motors: 4 x TSA of 325 kW.
Battery: 1300 kW.
Wheel Arrangement: Bo-2-2-2-Bo or Bo-2-2-2-2-Bo.
Braking: Disc & regenerative.
Dimensions: 21.05/15.70/7.20 (PP) m x 2.72/2.82 (PP) m.
Bogies: Stadler/Jacobs.   **Couplers:** Dellner 10.
Gangways: Within unit.   **Control System:** IGBT Inverter.
Doors: Sliding plug.   **Maximum Speed:** 75 mph.
Heating & ventilation: Air conditioning.
Seating Layout: 2+2 unidirectional/facing.
Multiple Working: Within class.

Class 756/0. 3-car (plus power pack) units.

DMS(A). Stadler Bussnang 2021–23. –/40(+12).
PP. Stadler Bussnang 2021–23.
PTS. Stadler Bussnang 2021–23. –/38(+5) 1TD 2W.
DMS(B). Stadler Bussnang 2021–23. –/40(+12).

756 001	**TW**	SM	911001	971001	981001	912001
756 002	**TW**	SM	911002	971002	981002	912002
756 003	**TW**	SM	911003	971003	981003	912003
756 004	**TW**	SM	911004	971004	981004	912004
756 005	**TW**	SM	911005	971005	981005	912005
756 006	**TW**	SM	911006	971006	981006	912006
756 007	**TW**	SM	911007	971007	981007	912007

Class 756/1. 4-car (plus power pack) units.

DMS(A). Stadler Bussnang 2021–23. –/40(+12). 42.3 t.
PTS(A). Stadler Bussnang 2021–23. –/40(+8). 25.9 t.
PP. Stadler Bussnang 2021–23. 28.7 t.
PTS(B). Stadler Bussnang 2021–23. –/38(+5) 1TD 2W. 26.6 t.
DMS(B). Stadler Bussnang 2021–23. –/40(+12). 42.7 t.

756 101	**TW**	SM	911101	961101	971101	981101	912101
756 102	**TW**	SM	911102	961102	971102	981102	912102
756 103	**TW**	SM	911103	961103	971103	981103	912103
756 104	**TW**	SM	911104	961104	971104	981104	912104
756 105	**TW**	SM	911105	961105	971105	981105	912105
756 106	**TW**	SM	911106	961106	971106	981106	912106
756 107	**TW**	SM	911107	961107	971107	981107	912107
756 108	**TW**	SM	911108	961108	971108	981108	912108

756109	**TW**	SM	911109	961109	971109	981109	912109
756110	**TW**	SM	911110	961110	971110	981110	912110
756111	**TW**	SM	911111	961111	971111	981111	912111
756112	**TW**	SM	911112	961112	971112	981112	912112
756113	**TW**	SM	911113	961113	971113	981113	912113
756114	**TW**	SM	911114	961114	971114	981114	912114
756115	**TW**	SM	911115	961115	971115	981115	912115
756116	**TW**	SM	911116	961116	971116	981116	912116
756117	**TW**	SM	911117	961117	971117	981117	912117

CLASS 768   FLEX   BREL YORK/BRUSH

Two Class 319/0 and 319/4 units were converted for Rail Operations Group's subsidiary Orion as bi-mode parcels/freight units and renumbered in the Class 768 series but have since been stored.

Formation: DTV–PMV–TV–DTV.
Systems: Diesel/25 kV AC overhead/750 V DC third rail.
Construction: Steel.
Engines: Two MAN D2876 of 390 kW (523 hp).
Traction Motors: Four GEC G315BZ of 268 kW.
Wheel Arrangement: 2-2 + Bo-Bo + 2-2 + 2-2.
Braking: Disc.   **Dimensions:** 20.17/20.16 x 2.82 m.
Bogies: P7-4 (MS), T3-7 (others). **Couplers:** Tightlock.
Gangways: Within unit + end doors. **Control System:** GTO chopper.
Doors: Sliding.
Maximum Speed: 100 mph (electric); 85 mph (diesel).
Seating Layout: No seats (removed to allow space for parcels and freight).
Multiple Working: Within class & with Classes 319 and 769.

DTV. Lot No. 31022 (odd nos.) 1987–88.
PMV. Lot No. 31023 1987–88.
TV. Lot No. 31024 1987–88.
DTV. Lot No. 31025 (even nos.) 1987–88.

| 768001 | (319010) | **ON** | P | CN | 77309 62900 71781 77308 |
| 768002 | (319009) | **ON** | P | CN | 77307 62899 71780 77306 |

CLASS 769   FLEX   BREL YORK/BRUSH

In 2016 it was announced that Porterbrook would be converting eight Class 319s into bi-mode "Flex" units for Northern, with two new diesel engines being fitted (one under each of the driving trailer cars) to drive ABB alternators. After a series of problems and delays the units finally entered service with Northern in 2021. Subsequently orders were placed by Transport for Wales for nine units (later reduced to eight, which entered service in 2020–21) and Great Western Railway for 19 units. The units for GWR were "tri-mode", with both AC overhead and DC third rail capability. Unfortunately, owing to continued unreliability of the units on test and changing passenger growth forecasts, in 2022 GWR decided that it would not be leasing its Class 769/9s and the units would be returned to

Porterbrook Leasing. The Transport for Wales units were withdrawn from service in 2022–23.

Work on the conversions took place at Brush Loughborough. All conversions were from Class 319/0 or 319/4 Phase 1 units.

Formation: DTC–MS–TS–DTS.
Systems: Diesel/25 kV AC overhead/750 V DC third rail (GWR units only).
Construction: Steel.
Engines: Two MAN D2876 of 390 kW (523 hp).
Traction Motors: Four GEC G315BZ of 268 kW.
Wheel Arrangement: 2-2 + Bo-Bo + 2-2 + 2-2.
Braking: Disc.   **Dimensions:** 20.17/20.16 x 2.82 m.
Bogies: P7-4 (MS), T3-7 (others).   **Couplers:** Tightlock.
Gangways: Within unit + end doors. **Control System:** GTO chopper.
Doors: Sliding.
Maximum Speed: 100 mph (electric); 85 mph (diesel).
Seating Layout: 1: 2+1 facing (declassified); 2: 2+2/3+2 facing.
Multiple Working: Within class and with Classes 319, 326 and 768.

Class 769/0. Former Transport for Wales bi-mode units converted from Class 319/0.

DTS(A). Lot No. 31022 (odd nos.) 1987–88.–/79. 37.5 t.
MS. Lot No. 31023 1987–88. –/79. 51.0 t.
TS. Lot No. 31024 1987–88. –/64 1TD 2W. 34.0 t.
DTS(B). Lot No. 31025 (even nos.) 1987–88. –/79. 37.2 t.

769002	(319002)	**TW**	P		LM	77293 62892 71773 77292
769003	(319003)	**TW**	P		LM	77295 62893 71774 77294
769006	(319006)	**TW**	P		LM	77301 62896 71777 77300
769007	(319007)	**TW**	P		LM	77303 62897 71778 77302
769008	(319008)	**TW**	P		LM	77305 62898 71779 77304

Class 769/4. Northern and former Transport for Wales bi-mode units converted from Class 319/4.

77331–381. DTC. Lot No. 31022 (odd nos.) 1987–88. 12/50. 37.3 t.
77431–457. DTC. Lot No. 31038 (odd nos.) 1988. 12/50. 37.3 t.
62911–936. MS. Lot No. 31023 1987–88. –/75. 51.0 t.
62961–974. MS. Lot No. 31039 1988. –/75. 51.0 t.
71792–817. TS. Lot No. 31024 1987–88. –/58 1TD 2W. 34.0 t.
71866–879. TS. Lot No. 31040 1988. –/58 1TD 2W. 34.0 t.
77330–380. DTS. Lot No. 31025 (even nos.) 1987–88. –/73. 37.2 t.
77430–456. DTS. Lot No. 31041 (even nos.) 1988. –/73. 37.2 t.

769421	(319421)	**TW**	P		LM	77331 62911 71792 77330
769424	(319424)	**NR**	P	NO	AN	77337 62914 71795 77336
769431	(319431)	**NR**	P	NO	AN	77351 62921 71802 77350
769434	(319434)	**NR**	P	NO	AN	77357 62924 71805 77356
769442	(319442)	**NR**	P	NO	AN	77373 62932 71813 77372
769445	(319445)	**TW**	P		LM	77379 62935 71816 77378
769448	(319448)	**NR**	P	NO	AN	77433 62962 71867 77432
769450	(319450)	**NR**	P	NO	AN	77437 62964 71869 77436
769452	(319452)	**TW**	P		LM	77441 62966 71871 77440

769 456	(319 456)	**NR**	P	*NO*	AN	77449	62970	71875	77448
769 458	(319 458)	**NR**	P	*NO*	AN	77453	62972	71877	77452

Class 769/9. Units rebuilt for Great Western Railway as tri-mode units converted from Class 319/4. Now stored awaiting a decision on their future.

77331–381. DTC. Lot No. 31022 (odd nos.) 1987–88. 12/52.
77431–457. DTC. Lot No. 31038 (odd nos.) 1988. 12/52.
62911–936. MS. Lot No. 31023 1987–88. –/77.
62961–974. MS. Lot No. 31039 1988. –/77.
71792–817. TS. Lot No. 31024 1987–88. –/60 1TD 2W.
71866–879. TS. Lot No. 31040 1988. –/60 1TD 2W.
77330–380. DTS. Lot No. 31025 (even nos.) 1987–88. –/75.
77430–456. DTS. Lot No. 31041 (even nos.) 1988. –/75.

769 922	(319 422)	**GW**	P		ZK	77333	62912	71793	77332
769 923	(319 423)	**GW**	P		LM	77335	62913	71794	77334
769 925	(319 425)	**GW**	P		LM	77339	62915	71796	77338
769 927	(319 427)	**GW**	P		LM	77343	62917	71798	77342
769 928	(319 428)	**GW**	P		LM	77345	62918	71799	77344
769 930	(319 430)	**GW**	P		LM	77349	62920	71801	77348
769 932	(319 432)	**GW**	P		LM	77353	62922	71803	77352
769 935	(319 435)	**GW**	P		LM	77359	62925	71806	77358
769 936	(319 436)	**GW**	P		LM	77361	62926	71807	77360
769 937	(319 437)	**GW**	P		LM	77363	62927	71808	77362
769 938	(319 438)	**GW**	P		LM	77365	62928	71809	77364
769 939	(319 439)	**GW**	P		LM	77367	62929	71810	77366
769 940	(319 440)	**GW**	P		LM	77369	62930	71811	77368
769 943	(319 443)	**GW**	P		LM	77375	62933	71814	77374
769 944	(319 444)	**GW**	P		LM	77377	62934	71815	77376
769 946	(319 446)	**GW**	P		LM	77381	62936	71817	77380
769 947	(319 447)	**GW**	P		LM	77431	62961	71866	77430
769 949	(319 449)	**GW**	P		LM	77435	62963	71868	77434
769 959	(319 459)	**GW**	P		ZK	77455	62973	71878	77454

CLASS 777   STADLER

This fleet of articulated 4-car units was ordered from Stadler in 2017 by Merseytravel for the DC third rail Merseyrail suburban network. An option exists for up to a further 59 units. Seven units at the end of the build have been equipped with batteries and numbered in the Class 777/1 series.

Formation: DMS–MS–MS–DMS.
System: 750 V DC third rail.
Construction: Aluminium.
Traction Motors: Six TSA of 350 kW (470 hp) per unit.
Wheel Arrangement: 2-Bo-Bo-Bo-2. **Dimensions:** 18.10/14.40 x 2.82 m.
Braking: Tread & regenerative. **Couplers:** Dellner 12.
Bogies: Jacobs. **Control System:** IGBT Inverter.
Gangways: Within unit. **Maximum Speed:** 75 mph.
Doors: Sliding plug. **Heating & ventilation:** Air conditioning.
Seating Layout: 2+2 facing/unidirectional.
Multiple Working: Within class.

Class 777/0. Original series, third rail 750 V DC only.

DMS(A). Stadler Szolnok/Siedlce/Altenrhein 2018–22. –/53.   t.
MS(A). Stadler Szolnok/Siedlce/Altenrhein 2018–22. –/38(+1) 1W.   t.
MS(B). Stadler Szolnok/Siedlce/Altenrhein 2018–22. –/38(+1) 1W.   t.
DMS(B). Stadler Szolnok/Siedlce/Altenrhein 2018–22. –/53.   t.

777001	**ME**	MT	*ME*	KK	427001	428001	429001	430001
777002	**ME**	MT	*ME*	KK	427002	428002	429002	430002
777003	**ME**	MT	*ME*	KK	427003	428003	429003	430003
777004	**ME**	MT	*ME*	KK	427004	428004	429004	430004
777005	**ME**	MT	*ME*	KK	427005	428005	429005	430005
777006	**ME**	MT	*ME*	KK	427006	428006	429006	430006
777007	**ME**	MT	*ME*	KK	427007	428007	429007	430007
777008	**ME**	MT	*ME*	KK	427008	428008	429008	430008
777009	**ME**	MT	*ME*	KK	427009	428009	429009	430009
777010	**ME**	MT	*ME*	KK	427010	428010	429010	430010
777011	**ME**	MT	*ME*	KK	427011	428011	429011	430011
777012	**ME**	MT	*ME*	KK	427012	428012	429012	430012
777013	**ME**	MT	*ME*	KK	427013	428013	429013	430013
777014	**ME**	MT	*ME*	KK	427014	428014	429014	430014
777015	**ME**	MT	*ME*	KK	427015	428015	429015	430015
777016	**ME**	MT	*ME*	KK	427016	428016	429016	430016
777017	**ME**	MT	*ME*	KK	427017	428017	429017	430017
777018	**ME**	MT	*ME*	KK	427018	428018	429018	430018
777019	**ME**	MT	*ME*	KK	427019	428019	429019	430019
777020	**ME**	MT	*ME*	KK	427020	428020	429020	430020
777021	**ME**	MT			427021	428021	429021	430021
777022	**ME**	MT			427022	428022	429022	430022
777023	**ME**	MT	*ME*	KK	427023	428023	429023	430023
777024	**ME**	MT	*ME*	KK	427024	428024	429024	430024
777025	**ME**	MT			427025	428025	429025	430025
777026	**ME**	MT	*ME*	KK	427026	428026	429026	430026
777027	**ME**	MT			427027	428027	429027	430027
777028	**ME**	MT	*ME*	KK	427028	428028	429028	430028
777029	**ME**	MT			427029	428029	429029	430029
777030	**ME**	MT	*ME*	KK	427030	428030	429030	430030
777031	**ME**	MT	*ME*	KK	427031	428031	429031	430031
777032	**ME**	MT			427032	428032	429032	430032
777033	**ME**	MT			427033	428033	429033	430033
777034	**ME**	MT			427034	428034	429034	430034
777035	**ME**	MT			427035	428035	429035	430035
777036	**ME**	MT	*ME*	KK	427036	428036	429036	430036
777037	**ME**	MT			427037	428037	429037	430037
777038	**ME**	MT			427038	428038	429038	430038
777039	**ME**	MT			427039	428039	429039	430039
777041	**ME**	MT			427041	428041	429041	430041
777043	**ME**	MT			427043	428043	429043	430043
777045	**ME**	MT			427045	428045	429045	430045
777047	**ME**	MT			427047	428047	429047	430047
777049	**ME**	MT	*ME*	KK	427049	428049	429049	430049
777051	**ME**	MT			427051	428051	429051	430051

777 053	**ME**	MT			427053	428053	429053	430053

Class 777/1. Fitted with 360 kWh Lithium Titanate Oxide traction batteries for operation away from the 750 V DC third rail network, initially between Kirkby and Headbolt Lane.

777 140	**ME**	MT	*ME*	KK	427140	428140	429140	430140
777 142	**ME**	MT	*ME*	KK	427142	428142	429142	430142
777 144	**ME**	MT	*ME*	KK	427144	428144	429144	430144
777 146	**ME**	MT	*ME*	KK	427146	428146	429146	430146
777 148	**ME**	MT	*ME*	KK	427148	428148	429148	430148
777 150	**ME**	MT	*ME*	KK	427150	428150	429150	430150
777 152	**ME**	MT	*ME*	KK	427152	428152	429152	430152

CLASS 799   HYDROFLEX   BREL YORK/BRUSH

Porterbrook rebuilt two Class 319s as hydrogen demonstrator units, although the first conversion in 2019 (799001) has now been scrapped. In 2021 a second demonstrator was converted. One of the driving cars was converted to a hydrogen chamber housing 36 high pressure 150 kg aluminium tanks to store hydrogen. The chamber feeds a 400 kW fuel cell system supported by a lithium-ion battery.

Formation: DMC–MS–TS–DMS.
Systems: Hydrogen/25 kV AC overhead/750 V DC third rail.
Construction: Steel.
Traction Motors: Four GEC G315BZ of 268 kW.
Wheel Arrangement: 2-2 + Bo-Bo + 2-2 + 2-2.
Braking: Disc.   **Dimensions:** 20.17/20.16 x 2.82 m.
Bogies: P7-4 (MS), T3-7 (others).   **Couplers:** Tightlock.
Gangways: Within unit + end doors. **Doors:** Sliding.
Maximum Speed: 75 mph.
Seating Layout: 1: 2+1 facing (declassified); 2: 2+2/3+2 facing unless stated.

Class 799/2. Second Prototype unit converted 2021. Currently used only for testing or demonstration purposes.

Non-standard livery: HydroFlex (dark blue & green).

77975. DMC. Lot No. 31063. 1990. No seats (hydrogen chamber). 49.2 t.
63094. MS. Lot No. 31064. 1990. –/57. 50.6 t.
71980. TS. Lot No. 31065. 1990. Converted to boardroom. –/26 1TD 2W. 31.0 t.
77976. DMS. Lot No. 31066. 1990. –/79. 29.7 t.

799 201	(319 382)	**0**	P		LM	77975	63094	71980	77976

4.5. HITACHI IEP UNITS

CLASS 800 INTERCITY EXPRESS PROGRAMME
BI-MODE   HITACHI

In 2012 Agility Trains, a consortium of Hitachi and John Laing, signed a deal with the DfT to design, build, finance and maintain the next generation of InterCity rolling stock for the Great Western and East Coast Main Lines, principally to replace ageing High Speed Trains on these routes. A follow-on order in 2013 was placed for 30 9-car trains to replace the Class 91 and Mark 4 carriages on the ECML. This brought the total number of vehicles ordered to 866. Both GWR and LNER were originally planned to have a mix of 5-car and 9-car units which will be bi-mode and straight electric trains (although the EMUs also have one diesel engine fitted to each set). However, owing to delays with electrification works on the GWML, in 2016 it was announced that the 21 9-car electric Class 801 units for GWR would be built as 21 9-car bi-mode units, numbered instead in the Class 800/3 series.

The initial units were broadly based on the Southeastern Class 395s, but have 25–25.35m length bodyshells. These are numbered in the Class 800 (bi-mode) and Class 801 (EMU) number series'. 12 trains (76 vehicles) were fully manufactured at Kasado in Japan before the new Hitachi factory at Newton Aycliffe, County Durham was up and running. The remaining trains were assembled at either Newton Aycliffe or Kasado. New maintenance depots for the trains have been built at Stoke Gifford (Bristol), Swansea and North Pole (London, the former Eurostar depot) for the GWR sets and at Doncaster for the LNER units.

The first trains arrived for testing in 2015. 5-car units entered service on the Great Western Main Line in autumn 2017 and the fleet of Class 800s and 801s entered service on the East Coast Main Line in 2019–20.

In 2015 GWR ordered a further similar 22 5-car and seven 9-car IEPs, designated Class 802/0 (5-car) and Class 802/1 (9-car). These are mainly used on Paddington–West of England services.

In 2016 GWR ordered a further seven 9-car Class 802s, TransPennine Express ordered 19 5-car Class 802s and Hull Trains ordered five 5-car Class 802s, for delivery 2019–20. The majority of the Class 802s were constructed at Pistoia in Italy, with some at Kasado.

Subsequent orders for similar derivatives of this type of train have come from First Group for its ECML open access service (Lumo – the electric-only Class 803), Avanti West Coast (Classes 805 and 807) and East Midlands Railway (Class 810).

Formation: Various, see class headings for details.
Systems: Diesel/25 kV AC overhead electric.
Construction: Aluminium.
Diesel engines: In the 5-car sets diesel engines are located in cars 2, 3 and 4. In the 9-car sets diesel engines are located in cars 2, 3, 5, 7 and 8.

Engines: MTU 12V 1600 R80L of 700 kW (940 hp).
Traction Motors: Four Hitachi asynchronous of 226 kW.
Wheel Arrangement: 2-2 + Bo-Bo + Bo-Bo + Bo-Bo + 2-2 or
2-2 + Bo-Bo + Bo-Bo + 2-2 + Bo-Bo + 2-2 + Bo-Bo + Bo-Bo + 2-2.
Braking: Disc & regenerative.   **Dimensions:** 25.35/25.00 m x 2.74 m.
Bogies: Hitachi.   **Couplers:** Dellner 10.
Gangways: Within unit.   **Control System:** IGBT Inverter.
Doors: Single-leaf sliding.   **Maximum Speed:** 125 mph.
Heating & ventilation: Air conditioning.
Seating Layout: 1: 2+1 facing/unidirectional; 2+2 facing/unidirectional.
Multiple Working: Within class and with all Classes 8xx.

Class 800/0. 5-car Great Western Railway units.
Formation: PDTS–MS–MS–MC–PDTRBF.

Additions to the standard livery: 800008 Pride stripes on driving cars.

PDTS. Hitachi Newton Aycliffe/Kasado 2013–17. –/56 1TD. 47.8 t.
MS. Hitachi Newton Aycliffe/Kasado 2013–17. –/88. 50.1 t.
MS. Hitachi Newton Aycliffe/Kasado 2013–17. –/88 2T. 50.3 t.
MC. Hitachi Newton Aycliffe/Kasado 2013–17. 18/58 1T. 50.6 t.
PDTRBF. Hitachi Newton Aycliffe/Kasado 2013–17. 18/– 1TD 2W. 51.7 t.

800001	**GW**	AT	*GW*	NP	811001	812001	813001	814001	815001
800002	**GW**	AT	*GW*	NP	811002	812002	813002	814002	815002
800003	**GW**	AT	*GW*	NP	811003	812003	813003	814003	815003
800004	**GW**	AT	*GW*	NP	811004	812004	813004	814004	815004
800005	**GW**	AT	*GW*	NP	811005	812005	813005	814005	815005
800006	**GW**	AT	*GW*	NP	811006	812006	813006	814006	815006
800007	**GW**	AT	*GW*	NP	811007	812007	813007	814007	815007
800008	**GW**	AT	*GW*	NP	811008	812008	813008	814008	815008
800009	**GW**	AT	*GW*	NP	811009	812009	813009	814009	815009
800010	**GW**	AT	*GW*	NP	811010	812010	813010	814010	815010
800011	**GW**	AT	*GW*	NP	811011	812011	813011	814011	815011
800012	**GW**	AT	*GW*	NP	811012	812012	813012	814012	815012
800013	**GW**	AT	*GW*	NP	811013	812013	813013	814013	815013
800014	**GW**	AT	*GW*	NP	811014	812014	813014	814014	815014
800015	**GW**	AT	*GW*	NP	811015	812015	813015	814015	815015
800016	**GW**	AT	*GW*	NP	811016	812016	813016	814016	815016
800017	**GW**	AT	*GW*	NP	811017	812017	813017	814017	815017
800018	**GW**	AT	*GW*	NP	811018	812018	813018	814018	815018
800019	**GW**	AT	*GW*	NP	811019	812019	813019	814019	815019
800020	**GW**	AT	*GW*	NP	811020	812020	813020	814020	815020
800021	**GW**	AT	*GW*	NP	811021	812021	813021	814021	815021
800022	**GW**	AT	*GW*	NP	811022	812022	813022	814022	815022
800023	**GW**	AT	*GW*	NP	811023	812023	813023	814023	815023
800024	**GW**	AT	*GW*	NP	811024	812024	813024	814024	815024
800025	**GW**	AT	*GW*	NP	811025	812025	813025	814025	815025
800026	**GW**	AT	*GW*	NP	811026	812026	813026	814026	815026
800027	**GW**	AT	*GW*	NP	811027	812027	813027	814027	815027
800028	**GW**	AT	*GW*	NP	811028	812028	813028	814028	815028
800029	**GW**	AT	*GW*	NP	811029	812029	813029	814029	815029
800030	**GW**	AT	*GW*	NP	811030	812030	813030	814030	815030

800031	**GW**	AT	*GW*	NP	811031	812031	813031	814031	815031
800032	**GW**	AT	*GW*	NP	811032	812032	813032	814032	815032
800033	**GW**	AT	*GW*	NP	811033	812033	813033	814033	815033
800034	**GW**	AT	*GW*	NP	811034	812034	813034	814034	815034
800035	**GW**	AT	*GW*	NP	811035	812035	813035	814035	815035
800036	**GW**	AT	*GW*	NP	811036	812036	813036	814036	815036

Names (one on each driving car unless shown):

800003	Queen Victoria/Queen Elizabeth II
800005	Aneurin Bevan NHS 1948–2023 *(vehicle 815005)*
800008	Alan Turing OBE FRS *(vehicle 815008)*
800009	Sir Gareth Edwards/John Charles
800010	Michael Bond/Paddington Bear
800014	Megan Lloyd George CH/Edith New
800016	WHITE RIBBON *(carried on both driving cars)*
800019	Joy Lofthouse/Johnny Johnson MBE DFM
800020	Bob Woodward/Elizabeth Ralph
800022	Tulbahadur Pun VC *(vehicle 815022)*
800023	Firefighter Fleur Lombard QGM/Kathryn Osmond
800025	Captain Sir Tom Moore *(vehicle 815025)*
800026	Don Cameron *(vehicle 815026)*
800028	Sir Peter Parker/Oliver Lovell
800029	Evette Wakely/Christopher Dando
800030	Henry Cleary/Lincoln Callaghan
800031	Charlotte Marsland/Mazen Salmou
800032	Iain Bugler/Sarah Williams-Martin
800033	Emma Hurrell/Martin Heath
800034	Tracy Devlin/Jo Prosser
800035	Naomi Betts/Liz Gallagher
800036	Dr Paul Stephenson OBE *(carried on both driving cars)*

Class 800/1. 9-car LNER units.

Additions to the standard livery:

800104	Scottish Saltire flag on driving car 819104.
800106	"You Belong" branding (green/purple on alternate sides of driving car 819106)

Formation: PDTS–MS–MS–TSRB–MS–TS–MC–MF–PDTRBF.

PDTS. Hitachi Kasado/Newton Aycliffe 2013–18. –/48 1TD 2W. 47.7 t.
MS. Hitachi Kasado/Newton Aycliffe 2013–18. –/84 1T. 50.5 t.
MS. Hitachi Kasado/Newton Aycliffe 2013–18. –/84 2T. 50.3 t.
TSRB. Hitachi Kasado/Newton Aycliffe 2013–18. –/70. 41.0 t.
MS. Hitachi Kasado/Newton Aycliffe 2013–18. –/84 2T. 50.3 t.
TS. Hitachi Kasado/Newton Aycliffe 2013–18. –/84 2T. 38.3 t.
MC. Hitachi Kasado/Newton Aycliffe 2013–18. 30/36. 49.1 t.
MF. Hitachi Kasado/Newton Aycliffe 2013–18. 55/– 1T. 50.6 t.
PDTRBF. Hitachi Kasado/Newton Aycliffe 2013–18. 15/– 1TD 2W. 51.7 t.

800101	**LZ**	AT	*LN*	DN	811101	812101	813101	814101	815101
					816101	817101	818101	819101	

800 102	**LZ**	AT	*LN*	DN	811102	812102	813102	814102	815102
					816102	817102	818102	819102	
800 103	**LZ**	AT	*LN*	DN	811103	812103	813103	814103	815103
					816103	817103	818103	819103	
800 104	**LZ**	AT	*LN*	DN	811104	812104	813104	814104	815104
					816104	817104	818104	819104	
800 105	**LZ**	AT	*LN*	DN	811105	812105	813105	814105	815105
					816105	817105	818105	819105	
800 106	**LZ**	AT	*LN*	DN	811106	812106	813106	814106	815106
					816106	817106	818106	819106	
800 107	**LZ**	AT	*LN*	DN	811107	812107	813107	814107	815107
					816107	817107	818107	819107	
800 108	**LZ**	AT	*LN*	DN	811108	812108	813108	814108	815108
					816108	817108	818108	819108	
800 109	**LZ**	AT	*LN*	DN	811109	812109	813109	814109	815109
					816109	817109	818109	819109	
800 110	**LZ**	AT	*LN*	DN	811110	812110	813110	814110	815110
					816110	817110	818110	819110	
800 111	**LZ**	AT	*LN*	DN	811111	812111	813111	814111	815111
					816111	817111	818111	819111	
800 112	**LZ**	AT	*LN*	DN	811112	812112	813112	814112	815112
					816112	817112	818112	819112	
800 113	**LZ**	AT	*LN*	DN	811113	812113	813113	814113	815113
					816113	817113	818113	819113	

Name (carried on PDTRBF):

800 106   YOU BELONG

Class 800/2. 5-car LNER units.
Formation: PDTS–MSRB–MS–MC–PDTRBF.

PDTS. Hitachi Newton Aycliffe/Kasado 2018–19. –/56 1TD. 47.8 t.
MSRB. Hitachi Newton Aycliffe/Kasado 2018–19. –/72. 50.1 t.
MS. Hitachi Newton Aycliffe/Kasado 2018–19. –/88 2T. 50.3 t.
MC. Hitachi Newton Aycliffe/Kasado 2018–19. 30/38 1T. 50.6 t.
PDTRBF. Hitachi Newton Aycliffe/Kasado 2018–19. 18/– 1TD 2W. 51.7 t.

800 201	**LZ**	AT	*LN*	DN	811201	812201	813201	814201	815201
800 202	**LZ**	AT	*LN*	DN	811202	812202	813202	814202	815202
800 203	**LZ**	AT	*LN*	DN	811203	812203	813203	814203	815203
800 204	**LZ**	AT	*LN*	DN	811204	812204	813204	814204	815204
800 205	**LZ**	AT	*LN*	DN	811205	812205	813205	814205	815205
800 206	**LZ**	AT	*LN*	DN	811206	812206	813206	814206	815206
800 207	**LZ**	AT	*LN*	DN	811207	812207	813207	814207	815207
800 208	**LZ**	AT	*LN*	DN	811208	812208	813208	814208	815208
800 209	**LZ**	AT	*LN*	DN	811209	812209	813209	814209	815209
800 210	**LZ**	AT	*LN*	DN	811210	812210	813210	814210	815210

Class 800/3. 9-car Great Western Railway units. Originally to be built as electric trains and numbered in the Class 801/0 series.
Formation: PDTS–MS–MS–TS–MS–TS–MS–MF–PDTRBF.

PDTS. Hitachi Newton Aycliffe/Kasado 2017–18. –/48 1TD 2W. 47.8 t.

MS. Hitachi Newton Aycliffe/Kasado 2017–18. –/88 1T. 50.1 t.
MS. Hitachi Newton Aycliffe/Kasado 2017–18. –/88 2T. 50.3 t.
TS. Hitachi Newton Aycliffe/Kasado 2017–18. –/88. 41.0 t.
MS. Hitachi Newton Aycliffe/Kasado 2017–18. –/88 2T. 50.3 t.
TS. Hitachi Newton Aycliffe/Kasado 2017–18. –/88 2T. 38.3 t.
MS. Hitachi Newton Aycliffe/Kasado 2017–18. –/88. 49.1 t.
MF. Hitachi Newton Aycliffe/Kasado 2017–18. 56/– 1T. 50.6 t.
PDTRBF. Hitachi Newton Aycliffe/Kasado 2017–18. 15/– 1TD 2W. 51.7 t.

800 301	**GW**	AT	*GW*	NP	821001	822001	823001 824001 825001
					826001	827001	828001 829001
800 302	**GW**	AT	*GW*	NP	821002	822002	823002 824002 825002
					826002	827002	828002 829002
800 303	**GW**	AT	*GW*	NP	821003	822003	823003 824003 825003
					826003	827003	828003 829003
800 304	**GW**	AT	*GW*	NP	821004	822004	823004 824004 825004
					826004	827004	828004 829004
800 305	**GW**	AT	*GW*	NP	821005	822005	823005 824005 825005
					826005	827005	828005 829005
800 306	**GW**	AT	*GW*	NP	821006	822006	823006 824006 825006
					826006	827006	828006 829006
800 307	**GW**	AT	*GW*	NP	821007	822007	823007 824007 825007
					826007	827007	828007 829007
800 308	**GW**	AT	*GW*	NP	821008	822008	823008 824008 825008
					826008	827008	828008 829008
800 309	**GW**	AT	*GW*	NP	821009	822009	823009 824009 825009
					826009	827009	828009 829009
800 310	**GW**	AT	*GW*	NP	821010	822010	823010 824010 825010
					826010	827010	828010 829010
800 311	**GW**	AT	*GW*	NP	821011	822011	823011 824011 825011
					826011	827011	828011 829011
800 312	**GW**	AT	*GW*	NP	821012	822012	823012 824012 825012
					826012	827012	828012 829012
800 313	**GW**	AT	*GW*	NP	821013	822013	823013 824013 825013
					826013	827013	828013 829013
800 314	**GW**	AT	*GW*	NP	821014	822014	823014 824014 825014
					826014	827014	828014 829014
800 315	**GW**	AT	*GW*	NP	821015	822015	823015 824015 825015
					826015	827015	828015 829015
800 316	**GW**	AT	*GW*	NP	821016	822016	823016 824016 825016
					826016	827016	828016 829016
800 317	**GW**	AT	*GW*	NP	821017	822017	823017 824017 825017
					826017	827017	828017 829017
800 318	**GW**	AT	*GW*	NP	821018	822018	823018 824018 825018
					826018	827018	828018 829018
800 319	**GW**	AT	*GW*	NP	821019	822019	823019 824019 825019
					826019	827019	828019 829019
800 320	**GW**	AT	*GW*	NP	821020	822020	823020 824020 825020
					826020	827020	828020 829020
800 321	**GW**	AT	*GW*	NP	821021	822021	823021 824021 825021
					826021	827021	828021 829021

Names (one on each driving car unless shown):

800 306	Allan Leonard Lewis VC/Harold Day DSC
800 310	Wing Commander Ken Rees *(vehicle 821010)*
800 314	Odette Hallowes GC MBE LdH *(vehicle 829014)*
800 317	Freya Bevan *(vehicle 829017)*

CLASS 801 INTERCITY EXPRESS PROGRAMME
ELECTRIC   HITACHI

The Class 801s are electric units, but still have one diesel engine fitted per unit for emergency use or for use on diversionary routes when coupled to a Class 800.

Formation: Various, see class headings for details.
Systems: 25 kV AC overhead electric, plus one diesel engine per set.
Construction: Aluminium.
Diesel engines: In the 5-car sets the single diesel engine is located in car 2 and in the 9-car sets the diesel engine is located in car 8.
Engines: MTU 12V 1600 R80L of 700 kW (940 hp).
Traction Motors: Four Hitachi asynchronous of 226 kW.
Wheel Arrangement: 2-2 + Bo-Bo + Bo-Bo + Bo-Bo + 2-2 or
2-2 + Bo-Bo + Bo-Bo + 2-2 + Bo-Bo + 2-2 + Bo-Bo + Bo-Bo + 2-2.

Braking: Disc & regenerative.	**Dimensions:** 25.35/25.00 m x 2.74 m.
Bogies: Hitachi.	**Couplers:** Dellner 10.
Gangways: Within unit.	**Control System:** IGBT Inverter.
Doors: Single-leaf sliding.	**Maximum Speed:** 125 mph.

Heating & ventilation: Air conditioning.
Seating Layout: 1: 2+1 facing/unidirectional; 2+2 facing/unidirectional.
Multiple Working: Within class and with all Classes 8xx.

Class 801/1. 5-car LNER units.
Formation: PDTS–MSRB–MS–MC–PDTRBF.

PDTS. Hitachi Newton Aycliffe/Kasado 2016–19. –/56 1TD. 47.8 t.
MSRB. Hitachi Newton Aycliffe/Kasado 2016–19. –/72. 52.1 t.
MS. Hitachi Newton Aycliffe/Kasado 2016–19. –/88 2T. 43.5 t.
MC. Hitachi Newton Aycliffe/Kasado 2016–19. 30/38 1T. 44.1 t.
PDTRBF. Hitachi Newton Aycliffe/Kasado 2016–19. 18/– 1TD 2W. 51.2 t.

801 101	**LZ**	AT	*LN*	DN	821101	822101	823101	824101	825101
801 102	**LZ**	AT	*LN*	DN	821102	822102	823102	824102	825102
801 103	**LZ**	AT	*LN*	DN	821103	822103	823103	824103	825103
801 104	**LZ**	AT	*LN*	DN	821104	822104	823104	824104	825104
801 105	**LZ**	AT	*LN*	DN	821105	822105	823105	824105	825105
801 106	**LZ**	AT	*LN*	DN	821106	822106	823106	824106	825106
801 107	**LZ**	AT	*LN*	DN	821107	822107	823107	824107	825107
801 108	**LZ**	AT	*LN*	DN	821108	822108	823108	824108	825108
801 109	**LZ**	AT	*LN*	DN	821109	822109	823109	824109	825109
801 110	**LZ**	AT	*LN*	DN	821110	822110	823110	824110	825110
801 111	**LZ**	AT	*LN*	DN	821111	822111	823111	824111	825111
801 112	**LZ**	AT	*LN*	DN	821112	822112	823112	824112	825112

Class 801/2. 9-car LNER units.

Additions to the standard livery:

801226   Pride celebration colours around the windows.

Formation: PDTS–MS–MS–TSRB–MS–TS–MC–MF–PDTRBF.

PDTS. Hitachi Newton Aycliffe/Kasado 2018–20. –/48 1TD 2W. 47.7 t.
MS. Hitachi Newton Aycliffe/Kasado 2018–20. –/84 1T. 50.5 t.
MS. Hitachi Newton Aycliffe/Kasado 2018–20. –/84 2T. 43.5 t.
TSRB. Hitachi Newton Aycliffe/Kasado 2018–20. –/70. 43.0 t.
MS. Hitachi Newton Aycliffe/Kasado 2018–20. –/84 2T. 43.5 t.
TS. Hitachi Newton Aycliffe/Kasado 2018–20. –/84 2T. 38.3 t.
MC. Hitachi Newton Aycliffe/Kasado 2018–20. 30/36. 42.6 t.
MF. Hitachi Newton Aycliffe/Kasado 2018–20. 15/– 1TD 2W. 51.7 t.
PDTRBF. Hitachi Newton Aycliffe/Kasado 2018–20. 55/– 1T. 43.8 t.

801201	**LZ**	AT	*LN*	BN	821201	822201	823201	824201	825201
					826201	827201	828201	829201	
801202	**LZ**	AT	*LN*	BN	821202	822202	823202	824202	825202
					826202	827202	828202	829202	
801203	**LZ**	AT	*LN*	BN	821203	822203	823203	824203	825203
					826203	827203	828203	829203	
801204	**LZ**	AT	*LN*	BN	821204	822204	823204	824204	825204
					826204	827204	828204	829204	
801205	**LZ**	AT	*LN*	BN	821205	822205	823205	824205	825205
					826205	827205	828205	829205	
801206	**LZ**	AT	*LN*	BN	821206	822206	823206	824206	825206
					826206	827206	828206	829206	
801207	**LZ**	AT	*LN*	BN	821207	822207	823207	824207	825207
					826207	827207	828207	829207	
801208	**LZ**	AT	*LN*	BN	821208	822208	823208	824208	825208
					826208	827208	828208	829208	
801209	**LZ**	AT	*LN*	BN	821209	822209	823209	824209	825209
					826209	827209	828209	829209	
801210	**LZ**	AT	*LN*	BN	821210	822210	823210	824210	825210
					826210	827210	828210	829210	
801211	**LZ**	AT	*LN*	BN	821211	822211	823211	824211	825211
					826211	827211	828211	829211	
801212	**LZ**	AT	*LN*	BN	821212	822212	823212	824212	825212
					826212	827212	828212	829212	
801213	**LZ**	AT	*LN*	BN	821213	822213	823213	824213	825213
					826213	827213	828213	829213	
801214	**LZ**	AT	*LN*	BN	821214	822214	823214	824214	825214
					826214	827214	828214	829214	
801215	**LZ**	AT	*LN*	BN	821215	822215	823215	824215	825215
					826215	827215	828215	829215	
801216	**LZ**	AT	*LN*	BN	821216	822216	823216	824216	825216
					826216	827216	828216	829216	
801217	**LZ**	AT	*LN*	BN	821217	822217	823217	824217	825217
					826217	827217	828217	829217	
801218	**LZ**	AT	*LN*	BN	821218	822218	823218	824218	825218
					826218	827218	828218	829218	

801 219	LZ	AT	LN	BN	821219	822219	823219	824219	825219
					826219	827219	828219	829219	
801 220	LZ	AT	LN	BN	821220	822220	823220	824220	825220
					826220	827220	828220	829220	
801 221	LZ	AT	LN	BN	821221	822221	823221	824221	825221
					826221	827221	828221	829221	
801 222	LZ	AT	LN	BN	821222	822222	823222	824222	825222
					826222	827222	828222	829222	
801 223	LZ	AT	LN	BN	821223	822223	823223	824223	825223
					826223	827223	828223	829223	
801 224	LZ	AT	LN	BN	821224	822224	823224	824224	825224
					826224	827224	828224	829224	
801 225	LZ	AT	LN	BN	821225	822225	823225	824225	825225
					826225	827225	828225	829225	
801 226	LZ	AT	LN	BN	821226	822226	823226	824226	825226
					826226	827226	828226	829226	
801 227	LZ	AT	LN	BN	821227	822227	823227	824227	825227
					826227	827227	828227	829227	
801 228	LZ	AT	LN	BN	821228	822228	823228	824228	825228
					826228	827228	828228	829228	
801 229	LZ	AT	LN	BN	821229	822229	823229	824229	825229
					826229	827229	828229	829229	
801 230	LZ	AT	LN	BN	821230	822230	823230	824230	825230
					826230	827230	828230	829230	

Names (carried on PDTRBF):

801 226   TOGETHER
801 228   CENTURY

CLASS 802   AT300   HITACHI

These units are technically very similar to the Class 800s. The GWR units have modifications to the roof-mounted brake resistors for frequent operation along the Dawlish seawall.

Formation: Various, full details awaited.
Systems: Diesel/25 kV AC overhead electric.
Construction: Aluminium.
Diesel engines: In the 5-car sets diesel engines are located in cars 2, 3 and 4. In the 9-car sets diesel engines are located in cars 2, 3, 5, 7 and 8.
Engines: MTU 12V 1600 R80L of 700 kW (940 hp).
Traction Motors: Four Hitachi asynchronous of 226 kW.
Wheel Arrangement: 2-2 + Bo-Bo + Bo-Bo + Bo-Bo + 2-2 or
2-2 + Bo-Bo + Bo-Bo + 2-2 + Bo-Bo + 2-2 + Bo-Bo + Bo-Bo + 2-2.

Braking: Disc & regenerative.	**Dimensions:** 25.35/25.00 m x 2.74 m.
Bogies: Hitachi.	**Couplers:** Dellner 10.
Gangways: Within unit.	**Control System:** IGBT Inverter.
Doors: Single-leaf sliding.	**Maximum Speed:** 125 mph.

Heating & ventilation: Air conditioning.
Seating Layout: 1: 2+1 facing/unidirectional; 2+2 facing/unidirectional.
Multiple Working: Within class and with all Classes 8xx.

Class 802/0. 5-car Great Western Railway units. Pre-series units 802 001/002 were built at Kasado and the remainder at Pistoia.
Formation: PDTS–MS–MS–MC–PDTRBF.

PDTS. Hitachi Pistoia/Kasado 2017–18. –/56 1TD. 48.0 t.
MS. Hitachi Pistoia/Kasado 2017–18. –/88. 50.9 t.
MS. Hitachi Pistoia/Kasado 2017–18. –/88 2T 51.1 t.
MC. Hitachi Pistoia/Kasado 2017–18. 18/58 1T. 51.5 t.
PDTRBF. Hitachi Pistoia/Kasado 2017–18. 18/– 1TD 2W. 51.3 t.

802 001	**GW**	E	*GW*	NP	831001	832001	833001	834001	835001
802 002	**GW**	E	*GW*	NP	831002	832002	833002	834002	835002
802 003	**GW**	E	*GW*	NP	831003	832003	833003	834003	835003
802 004	**GW**	E	*GW*	NP	831004	832004	833004	834004	835004
802 005	**GW**	E	*GW*	NP	831005	832005	833005	834005	835005
802 006	**GW**	E	*GW*	NP	831006	832006	833006	834006	835006
802 007	**GW**	E	*GW*	NP	831007	832007	833007	834007	835007
802 008	**GW**	E	*GW*	NP	831008	832008	833008	834008	835008
802 009	**GW**	E	*GW*	NP	831009	832009	833009	834009	835009
802 010	**GW**	E	*GW*	NP	831010	832010	833010	834010	835010
802 011	**GW**	E	*GW*	NP	831011	832011	833011	834011	835011
802 012	**GW**	E	*GW*	NP	831012	832012	833012	834012	835012
802 013	**GW**	E	*GW*	NP	831013	832013	833013	834013	835013
802 014	**GW**	E	*GW*	NP	831014	832014	833014	834014	835014
802 015	**GW**	E	*GW*	NP	831015	832015	833015	834015	835015
802 016	**GW**	E	*GW*	NP	831016	832016	833016	834016	835016
802 017	**GW**	E	*GW*	NP	831017	832017	833017	834017	835017
802 018	**GW**	E	*GW*	NP	831018	832018	833018	834018	835018
802 019	**GW**	E	*GW*	NP	831019	832019	833019	834019	835019
802 020	**GW**	E	*GW*	NP	831020	832020	833020	834020	835020
802 021	**GW**	E	*GW*	NP	831021	832021	833021	834021	835021
802 022	**GW**	E	*GW*	NP	831022	832022	833022	834022	835022

Names (one on each driving car unless shown):

802 002	Steve Whiteway *(vehicle 831002)*
802 006	Harry Billinge MBE LdH *(vehicle 835006)*
802 008	Rick Rescorla/RNLB Solomon Browne
802 010	Kieron Griffin/Corporal George Sheard
802 011	Sir Joshua Reynolds PRA/Capt. Robert Falcon Scott RN CVO
802 013	Michael Eavis CBE *(vehicle 835013)*
802 018	Preston de Mendonça/Jeremy Doyle

Class 802/1. 9-car Great Western Railway units. Pre-series unit 802 101 was built at Kasado and the remainder at Pistoia.
Formation: PDTS–MS–MS–TS–MS–TS–MC–MF–PDTRBF.

PDTS. Hitachi Pistoia/Kasado 2017–18. –/48 1TD 2W. 47.7 t.
MS. Hitachi Pistoia/Kasado 2017–18. –/88 1T. 50.1 t.
MS. Hitachi Pistoia/Kasado 2017–18. –/88 2T. 50.3 t.
TS. Hitachi Pistoia/Kasado 2017–18. –/88. 41.0 t.
MS. Hitachi Pistoia/Kasado 2017–18. –/88 2T. 50.3 t.
TS. Hitachi Pistoia/Kasado 2017–18. –/88 2T. 38.3 t.

MS. Hitachi Pistoia/Kasado 2017–18. –/88. 50.3 t.
MF. Hitachi Pistoia/Kasado 2017–18. 56/– 1T. 50.6 t.
PDTRBF. Hitachi Pistoia/Kasado 2017–18. 15/– 1TD 2W. 51.7 t.

802 101	**GW**	E	*GW*	NP	831101	832101	833101	834101	835101
					836101	837101	838101	839101	
802 102	**GW**	E	*GW*	NP	831102	832102	833102	834102	835102
					836102	837102	838102	839102	
802 103	**GW**	E	*GW*	NP	831103	832103	833103	834103	835103
					836103	837103	838103	839103	
802 104	**GW**	E	*GW*	NP	831104	832104	833104	834104	835104
					836104	837104	838104	839104	
802 105	**GW**	E	*GW*	NP	831105	832105	833105	834105	835105
					836105	837105	838105	839105	
802 106	**GW**	E	*GW*	NP	831106	832106	833106	834106	835106
					836106	837106	838106	839106	
802 107	**GW**	E	*GW*	NP	831107	832107	833107	834107	835107
					836107	837107	838107	839107	
802 108	**GW**	E	*GW*	NP	831108	832108	833108	834108	835108
					836108	837108	838108	839108	
802 109	**GW**	E	*GW*	NP	831109	832109	833109	834109	835109
					836109	837109	838109	839109	
802 110	**GW**	E	*GW*	NP	831110	832110	833110	834110	835110
					836110	837110	838110	839110	
802 111	**GW**	E	*GW*	NP	831111	832111	833111	834111	835111
					836111	837111	838111	839111	
802 112	**GW**	E	*GW*	NP	831112	832112	833112	834112	835112
					836112	837112	838112	839112	
802 113	**GW**	E	*GW*	NP	831113	832113	833113	834113	835113
					836113	837113	838113	839113	
802 114	**GW**	E	*GW*	NP	831114	832114	833114	834114	835114
					836114	837114	838114	839114	

Names:

802 101	Nancy Astor CH *(vehicle 839101)*
802 103	FLYING CAROLEAN/Y CAROLEAN HEDEGOG *(alternate sides of vehicle 839103)*
802 110	DAME AGATHA CHRISTIE

Class 802/2. TransPennine Express units.
Formation: PDTS–MS–MS–MS–PDTF.

PDTS. Hitachi Pistoia/Kasado 2018–19. –/56 1TD. 48.0 t.
MS. Hitachi Pistoia/Kasado 2018–19. –/86. 50.9 t.
MS. Hitachi Pistoia/Kasado 2018–19. –/88 2T 51.1 t.
MS. Hitachi Pistoia/Kasado 2018–19. –/88 1T 51.3 t.
PDTRBF. Hitachi Pistoia/Kasado 2018–19. 24/– 1TD 2W. 50.2 t.

802 201	**TP**	A	*TP*	EC	831201	832201	833201	834201	835201
802 202	**TP**	A	*TP*	EC	831202	832202	833202	834202	835202
802 203	**TP**	A	*TP*	EC	831203	832203	833203	834203	835203
802 204	**TP**	A	*TP*	EC	831204	832204	833204	834204	835204

802 205	**TP**	A	*TP*	EC	831205	832205	833205	834205	835205
802 206	**TP**	A	*TP*	EC	831206	832206	833206	834206	835206
802 207	**TP**	A	*TP*	EC	831207	832207	833207	834207	835207
802 208	**TP**	A	*TP*	EC	831208	832208	833208	834208	835208
802 209	**TP**	A	*TP*	EC	831209	832209	833209	834209	835209
802 210	**TP**	A	*TP*	EC	831210	832210	833210	834210	835210
802 211	**TP**	A	*TP*	EC	831211	832211	833211	834211	835211
802 212	**TP**	A	*TP*	EC	831212	832212	833212	834212	835212
802 213	**TP**	A	*TP*	EC	831213	832213	833213	834213	835213
802 214	**TP**	A	*TP*	EC	831214	832214	833214	834214	835214
802 215	**TP**	A	*TP*	EC	831215	832215	833215	834215	835215
802 216	**TP**	A	*TP*	EC	831216	832216	833216	834216	835216
802 217	**TP**	A	*TP*	EC	831217	832217	833217	834217	835217
802 218	**TP**	A	*TP*	EC	831218	832218	833218	834218	835218
802 219	**TP**	A	*TP*	EC	831219	832219	833219	834219	835219

Names (carried on driving cars):

802 208	Diligence Robert Stephenson & Co
802 210	Hailes Castle
802 212	St Abb's Head
802 215	Palace of Holyroodhouse

Class 802/3. Hull Trains units.
Formation: PDTS–MS–MS–MS–PDTF.

PDTS. Hitachi Pistoia 2018–19. –/50 1TD 1W. 48.0 t.
MS. Hitachi Pistoia 2018–19. –/88. 49.6 t.
MS. Hitachi Pistoia 2018–19. –/88 2T 50.4 t.
MC. Hitachi Pistoia 2018–19. 18/58 1T 50.4 t.
PDTRBF. Hitachi Pistoia 2018–19. 25/– 1TD 2W. 49.6 t.

802 301	**HT**	A	*HT*	BN	831301	832301	833301	834301	835301
802 302	**HT**	A	*HT*	BN	831302	832302	833302	834302	835302
802 303	**HT**	A	*HT*	BN	831303	832303	833303	834303	835303
802 304	**HT**	A	*HT*	BN	831304	832304	833304	834304	835304
802 305	**HT**	A	*HT*	BN	831305	832305	833305	834305	835305

Names (carried on driving cars):

802 301	Amy Johnson	802 304	William Wilberforce
802 302	Jean Bishop (The Bee Lady)	802 305	The Humber Bridge
802 303	Land of Green Ginger		

CLASS 803   HITACHI

Five 5-car electric-only, single-class units that entered service in October 2021 with new East Coast Main Line open access operator Lumo, running between London King's Cross and Edinburgh.

Formation: PDTS–MS–MS–MS–PDTS.
Systems: 25 kV AC overhead electric.
Construction: Aluminium.
Traction Motors: Four Hitachi asynchronous of 226 kW.
Wheel Arrangement: 2-2 + Bo-Bo + Bo-Bo + Bo-Bo + 2-2.
Braking: Disc & regenerative.   **Dimensions:** 25.35/25.00 m x 2.74 m.
Bogies: Hitachi.   **Couplers:** Dellner 10.
Gangways: Within unit.   **Control System:** IGBT Inverter.
Doors: Single-leaf sliding.   **Maximum Speed:** 125 mph.
Heating & ventilation: Air conditioning.
Seating Layout: 2+2 mostly unidirectional.
Multiple Working: Within class and with all Classes 8xx.

PDTS. Hitachi Kasado/Newton Aycliffe 2020–21. –/52(+2) 1TD 2W. 47.7 t.
MS. Hitachi Kasado/Newton Aycliffe 2020–21. –/94 1T. 45.0 t.
MS. Hitachi Kasado/Newton Aycliffe 2020–21. –/94. 44.2 t.
MS. Hitachi Kasado/Newton Aycliffe 2020–21. –/94 1T 45.0 t.
PDTS. Hitachi Kasado/Newton Aycliffe 2020–21. –/60(+2) 1TD. 47.8 t.

803001	LU	BN	*LU*	EC	841001	842001	843001	844001	845001
803002	LU	BN	*LU*	EC	841002	842002	843002	844002	845002
803003	LU	BN	*LU*	EC	841003	842003	843003	844003	845003
803004	LU	BN	*LU*	EC	841004	842004	843004	844004	845004
803005	LU	BN	*LU*	EC	841005	842005	843005	844005	845005

Name (carried on driving cars):

803005   PROUDLY FROM NEWCASTLE – THE HOME OF STEPHENSON'S
          WORKS BICENTENARY 1823–2023

CLASS 805   HITACHI

13 5-car bi-mode units currently being delivered to Avanti West Coast to replace the Class 221 Voyagers during 2024 and operate services such as Euston–Chester–Holyhead, allowing the elimination of long-distance diesel passenger operation on the West Coast Main Line. Full details awaited.

Formation: PDTS–MS–MS–MS–PDTF.
Systems: Diesel/25 kV AC overhead electric.
Construction: Aluminium.
Engines:
Construction: Aluminium.
Traction Motors:
Wheel Arrangement: 2-2 + Bo-Bo + Bo-Bo + Bo-Bo + 2-2.
Braking: Disc & regenerative.   **Dimensions:**
Bogies: Hitachi.   **Couplers:** Dellner 10.
Gangways: Within unit.   **Control System:** IGBT Inverter.

Doors: Single-leaf sliding.   **Maximum Speed:** 125 mph.
Heating & ventilation: Air conditioning.
Seating Layout: 1: 2+1 facing/unidirectional; 2+2 facing/unidirectional.
Multiple Working: Within class and with all Classes 8xx.

PDTS. Hitachi Kasado/Newton Aycliffe 2020–23.
MS. Hitachi Kasado/Newton Aycliffe 2020–23.
MS. Hitachi Kasado/Newton Aycliffe 2020–23.
MS. Hitachi Kasado/Newton Aycliffe 2020–23.
PDTF. Hitachi Kasado/Newton Aycliffe 2020–23.

805 001	**AT**	RR	861001	862001	863001	864001	865001
805 002	**AT**	RR	861002	862002	863002	864002	865002
805 003	**AT**	RR	861003	862003	863003	864003	865003
805 004	**AT**	RR	861004	862004	863004	864004	865004
805 005	**AT**	RR	861005	862005	863005	864005	865005
805 006	**AT**	RR	861006	862006	863006	864006	865006
805 007	**AT**	RR	861007	862007	863007	864007	865007
805 008	**AT**	RR	861008	862008	863008	864008	865008
805 009	**AT**	RR	861009	862009	863009	864009	865009
805 010	**AT**	RR	861010	862010	863010	864010	865010
805 011	**AT**	RR	861011	862011	863011	864011	865011
805 012	**AT**	RR	861012	862012	863012	864012	865012
805 013	**AT**	RR	861013	862013	863013	864013	865013

CLASS 807   HITACHI

7-car electric units for Avanti West Coast which will be similar to Class 801s, in that they will have one diesel engine. They are planned to be used on services between Euston, the Midlands and Liverpool from 2024. Full details awaited.

Formation: PDTS–MS–MS–TS–MS–MC–PDTF.
Systems: 25 kV AC overhead electric, plus one diesel engine per set.
Construction: Aluminium.
Engines:
Construction: Aluminium.
Traction Motors:
Wheel Arrangement:
Braking: Disc & regenerative.   **Dimensions:**
Bogies: Hitachi.   **Couplers:** Dellner 10.
Gangways: Within unit.   **Control System:** IGBT Inverter.
Doors: Single-leaf sliding.   **Maximum Speed:** 125 mph.
Heating & ventilation: Air conditioning.
Seating Layout: 1: 2+1 facing/unidirectional; 2+2 facing/unidirectional.
Multiple Working: Within class and with all Classes 8xx.

PDTS. Hitachi Kasado/Newton Aycliffe 2021–24.
MS. Hitachi Kasado/Newton Aycliffe 22021–24.
MS. Hitachi Kasado/Newton Aycliffe 2021–24.
TS. Hitachi Kasado/Newton Aycliffe 22021–24.
MS. Hitachi Kasado/Newton Aycliffe 2021–24.
MC. Hitachi Kasado/Newton Aycliffe 2021–24.
PDTF. Hitachi Kasado/Newton Aycliffe 2021–24.

807001	**AT**	RR	871001 872001	873001 874001 875001
			876001 877001	
807002	**AT**	RR	871002 872002	873002 874002 875002
			876002 877002	
807003	**AT**	RR	871003 872003	873003 874003 875003
			876003 877003	
807004	**AT**	RR	871004 872004	873004 874004 875004
			876004 877004	
807005	**AT**	RR	871005 872005	873005 874005 875005
			876005 877005	
807006	**AT**	RR	871006 872006	873006 874006 875006
			876006 877006	
807007	**AT**	RR	871007 872007	873007 874007 875007
			876007 877007	
807008	**AT**	RR	871008 872008	873008 874008 875008
			876008 877008	
807009	**AT**	RR	871009 872009	873009 874009 875009
			876009 877009	
807010	**AT**	RR	871010 872010	873010 874010 875010
			876010 877010	

CLASS 810   AT300 SXR   HITACHI

East Midlands Railway has ordered this fleet of 33 5-car bi-mode units for use on the Midland Main Line, principally between St Pancras and Sheffield/ Nottingham, from 2024. They are technically different from other Class 8xx trains, with more powerful engines and also have shorter 24m bodies to better match platforms on the route. Full details awaited.

Formation: PDTRBF–MC–TS–MS–DPTS.
Systems: Diesel/25 kV AC overhead electric.
Construction: Aluminium.
Diesel engines: Diesel engines are located in cars 1, 2, 4 and 5.
Engines: MTU of 735 kW (985 hp).
Construction: Aluminium.
Traction Motors: Four Hitachi asynchronous of 290 kW.
Wheel Arrangement:
Braking: Disc & regenerative.   **Dimensions:**
Bogies: Hitachi.   **Couplers:** Dellner 10.
Gangways: Within unit.   **Control System:** IGBT Inverter.
Doors: Single-leaf sliding.   **Maximum Speed:** 125 mph.
Heating & ventilation: Air conditioning.
Seating Layout: 1: 2+1 facing/unidirectional; 2+2 facing/unidirectional.
Multiple Working: Within class and with all Classes 8xx.

PDTRBF. Hitachi Newton Aycliffe/Pistoia 2021–24.
MC. Hitachi Newton Aycliffe/Pistoia 2021–24.
TS. Hitachi Newton Aycliffe/Pistoia 2021–24.
MS. Hitachi Newton Aycliffe/Pistoia 2021–24.
DPTS. Hitachi Newton Aycliffe/Pistoia 2021–24.

810001	ER	RR	851001	852001	853001	854001	855001
810002	ER	RR	851002	852002	853002	854002	855002
810003	ER	RR	851003	852003	853003	854003	855003
810004	ER	RR	851004	852004	853004	854004	855004
810005	ER	RR	851005	852005	853005	854005	855005
810006	ER	RR	851006	852006	853006	854006	855006
810007	ER	RR	851007	852007	853007	854007	855007
810008	ER	RR	851008	852008	853008	854008	855008
810009	ER	RR	851009	852009	853009	854009	855009
810010	ER	RR	851010	852010	853010	854010	855010
810011	ER	RR	851011	852011	853011	854011	855011
810012	ER	RR	851012	852012	853012	854012	855012
810013	ER	RR	851013	852013	853013	854013	855013
810014	ER	RR	851014	852014	853014	854014	855014
810015	ER	RR	851015	852015	853015	854015	855015
810016	ER	RR	851016	852016	853016	854016	855016
810017	ER	RR	851017	852017	853017	854017	855017
810018	ER	RR	851018	852018	853018	854018	855018
810019	ER	RR	851019	852019	853019	854019	855019
810020	ER	RR	851020	852020	853020	854020	855020
810021	ER	RR	851021	852021	853021	854021	855021
810022	ER	RR	851022	852022	853022	854022	855022
810023	ER	RR	851023	852023	853023	854023	855023
810024	ER	RR	851024	852024	853024	854024	855024
810025	ER	RR	851025	852025	853025	854025	855025
810026	ER	RR	851026	852026	853026	854026	855026
810027	ER	RR	851027	852027	853027	854027	855027
810028	ER	RR	851028	852028	853028	854028	855028
810029	ER	RR	851029	852029	853029	854029	855029
810030	ER	RR	851030	852030	853030	854030	855030
810031	ER	RR	851031	852031	853031	854031	855031
810032	ER	RR	851032	852032	853032	854032	855032
810033	ER	RR	851033	852033	853033	854033	855033

4.6. EUROSTAR UNITS

The original Eurostar Class 373 units were built for and are normally used on services between Britain and continental Europe via the Channel Tunnel.

The trailers from SNCF set 3203/04 were refurbished and renumbered to run with power cars 3211/12 (original power cars 3203/04 have been scrapped, as have the trailers from 3211/12).

Each Class 373 train consists of two 10-car units coupled, with a motor car at each driving end. All units are articulated with an extra motor bogie on the coach adjacent to the motor car.

All Class 373 sets can be used between London St Pancras and Paris, Brussels and Disneyland Paris. Certain sets (shown *) were equipped for 1500 V DC operation for the winter service to Bourg Saint Maurice and the summer service to Avignon. All eight refurbished units are fitted for operation on 1500 V DC.

Seven 8-car Class 373 sets were built for Regional Eurostar services, but apart from power cars 3304 and 3308 which have been preserved, the rest have been scrapped.

The second generation Eurostar trains, the Siemens Class 374s, have replaced most of the Class 373s. Eight Class 373s have been fully refurbished and will be retained as part of Eurostar's long-term fleet – 3007/08, 3015/16, 3205/06, 3209/10, 3211/12, 3219/20, 3221/22 and 3229/30.

CLASS 373   "THREE CAPITALS" EUROSTARS

10-car half-sets. Built for services starting from or terminating in London Waterloo (now St Pancras). Individual vehicles in each set are allocated numbers 373xxx0 + 373xxx1 + 373xxx2 + 373xxx3 + 373xxx4 + 373xxx5 + 373xxx6 + 373xxx7 + 373xxx8 + 373xxx9, where 3xxx denotes the set number.

Formation: DM–MS–4TS–RB–2TF–TBF. Gangwayed within pair of units. Air conditioned.
Construction: Steel.
Supply Systems: 25 kV AC 50 Hz overhead or 3000 V DC overhead (* also equipped for 1500 V DC overhead operation).
Control System: GTO–GTO Inverter on UK 750 V DC and 25 kV AC, GTO Chopper on SNCB 3000 V DC.
Continuous rating: 12 x 240 kW (25 kV AC); 5700 kW (1500 and 3000 V DC).
Wheel Arrangement: Bo-Bo + Bo–2–2–2–2–2–2–2–2.
Lengths: 22.15 m (DM), 21.85 m (MS & TBF), 18.70 m (other cars).
Couplers: Schaku 10S at outer ends, Schaku 10L at inner end of each DM and outer ends of each sub set.
Maximum Speed: 186 mph (300 km/h).
Built: 1992–93 by GEC-Alsthom/Brush/ANF/De Dietrich/BN Construction/ACEC.

DM vehicles carry the set numbers indicated below.

Non-standard livery: 3213 and 3224 – Izy (green, white & purple).

† Refurbished.

At the time of writing the following sets were misformed: 3213 with 3224 and 3214 with 3223.

373xxx0 series. DM. Lot No. 31118 1992–95. 68.5 t.
373xxx1 series. MS. Lot No. 31119 1992–95. –/48 2T. 44.6 t.
373xxx2 series. TS. Lot No. 31120 1992–95. –/56 1T. 28.1 t.
373xxx3 series. TS. Lot No. 31121 1992–95. –/56 2T. 29.7 t.
373xxx4 series. TS. Lot No. 31122 1992–95. –/56 1T. 28.3 t.
373xxx5 series. TS. Lot No. 31123 1992–95. –/56 2T. 29.2 t.
373xxx6 series. RB. Lot No. 31124 1992–95. 31.1 t.
373xxx7 series. TF. Lot No. 31125 1992–95. 39/– 1T. 29.6 t.
373xxx8 series. TF. Lot No. 31126 1992–95. 39/– 1T. 32.2 t.
373xxx9 series. TBF. Lot No. 31127 1992–95. 25/– 1TD. 39.4 t.

3007	†* **ES**	EU	*EU*	LY	
3008	†* **ES**	EU	*EU*	LY	
3015	†* **ES**	EU	*EU*	LY	
3016	†* **ES**	EU	*EU*	LY	
3205	†* **ES**	SF	*EU*	LY	
3206	†* **ES**	SF	*EU*	LY	
3209	†* **ES**	SF	*EU*	LY	
3210	†* **ES**	SF	*EU*	LY	
3211	†* **ES**	SF	*EU*	LY	
3212	†* **ES**	SF	*EU*	LY	
3213	* **0**	SF		Le Havre	
3214	* **EU**	SF		Le Havre	
3215	* **EU**	SF		TI	
3216	* **EU**	SF		TI	
3217	**EU**	SF		TI	
3218	**EU**	SF		TI	
3219	†* **ES**	SF	*EU*	LY	
3220	†* **ES**	SF	*EU*	LY	
3221	†* **ES**	SF	*EU*	LY	
3222	†* **ES**	SF	*EU*	LY	
3223	* **EU**	SF		Le Havre	
3224	* **0**	SF		Le Havre	
3229	†* **ES**	SF	*EU*	LY	
3230	†* **ES**	SF	*EU*	LY	

Spare DM:

3999	**ES**	EU	*EU*	TI

CLASS 374   SIEMENS VELARO e320

8-car half-sets. These units are similar to the DB Class 407 ICE sets, with distributed power rather than a power car at either end like the Class 373s. The first sets entered service in November 2015, operating initially on the St Pancras–Paris route. They have also been used on the new St Pancras–Amsterdam service from 2018.

The initial order was for ten units (4001–20) and this was then increased by another seven (4021–34) in 2014.

Formation: DMF–TBF–MS–TS–TS–MS–TS–MSRB.
Gangwayed within pair of units. Air conditioned.
Construction: Aluminium.   **Control System:** IGBT Inverter.
Supply Systems: 25 kV AC 50 Hz overhead, 1500 V DC overhead and 3000 V DC overhead.
Continuous rating: 8000 kW (25 kV AC), 4200 kW (1500 and 3000 V DC).
Wheel Arrangement: Bo-Bo + 2-2 + Bo-Bo + 2-2 + 2-2 + Bo-Bo + 2-2 + Bo-Bo.
Lengths: 26.035 m (DMF), 24.775 m (other cars).
Couplers: Dellner 12.   **Maximum Speed:** 200 mph (320 km/h).
Built: 2012–17 by Siemens, Krefeld, Germany.

DM vehicles carry the full 12-digit EVNs as indicated below. For example, set 4001/02 carries the numbers 93 70 3740 011-9 + 93 70 3740 012-7 + 93 70 3740 013-5 + 93 70 3740 014-3 + 93 70 3740 015-0 + 93 70 3740 016-8 + 93 70 3740 017-6 + 93 70 3740 018-4 + 93 70 3740 028-3 + 93 70 3740 027-5 + 93 70 3740 026-7 + 93 70 3740 025-9 + 93 70 3740 024-2 + 93 70 3740 023-4 + 93 70 3740 022-6 + 93 70 3740 021-8.

93 70 3740 xx1-c series. DMF. Siemens Krefeld 2012–17. 40/–. 58.0 t.
93 70 3740 xx2-c series. TBF. Siemens Krefeld 2012–17. 36/– 2T. 59.0 t.
93 70 3740 xx3-c series. MF. Siemens Krefeld 2012–17. 34/–(+2) 1TD 2W. 59.0 t.
93 70 3740 xx4-c series. TS. Siemens Krefeld 2012–17. –/76 2T. 53.0 t.
93 70 3740 xx5-c series. TS. Siemens Krefeld 2012–17. –/76 2T. 53.0 t.
93 70 3740 xx6-c series. MS. Siemens Krefeld 2012–17. –/76 2T. 58.0 t.
93 70 3740 xx7-c series. TS. Siemens Krefeld 2012–17. –/76 2T. 57.0 t.
93 70 3740 xx8-c series. MSRB. Siemens Krefeld 2012–17. –/32 2T. 58.0 t.

4001	**ES**	EU	*EU*	TI	4018	**ES**	EU	*EU*	TI
4002	**ES**	EU	*EU*	TI	4019	**ES**	EU	*EU*	TI
4003	**ES**	EU	*EU*	TI	4020	**ES**	EU	*EU*	TI
4004	**ES**	EU	*EU*	TI	4021	**ES**	EU	*EU*	TI
4005	**ES**	EU	*EU*	TI	4022	**ES**	EU	*EU*	TI
4006	**ES**	EU	*EU*	TI	4023	**ES**	EU	*EU*	TI
4007	**ES**	EU	*EU*	TI	4024	**ES**	EU	*EU*	TI
4008	**ES**	EU	*EU*	TI	4025	**ES**	EU	*EU*	TI
4009	**ES**	EU	*EU*	TI	4026	**ES**	EU	*EU*	TI
4010	**ES**	EU	*EU*	TI	4027	**ES**	EU	*EU*	TI
4011	**ES**	EU	*EU*	TI	4028	**ES**	EU	*EU*	TI
4012	**ES**	EU	*EU*	TI	4029	**ES**	EU	*EU*	TI
4013	**ES**	EU	*EU*	TI	4030	**ES**	EU	*EU*	TI
4014	**ES**	EU	*EU*	TI	4031	**ES**	EU	*EU*	TI
4015	**ES**	EU	*EU*	TI	4032	**ES**	EU	*EU*	TI
4016	**ES**	EU	*EU*	TI	4033	**ES**	EU	*EU*	TI
4017	**ES**	EU	*EU*	TI	4034	**ES**	EU	*EU*	TI

4.7. EMU VEHICLES IN INDUSTRIAL SERVICE

This list comprises EMU vehicles that have been withdrawn from active service but continue to be used in industrial service or for emergency training.

Cl. 317	71621			Oracle UK, Thames Valley Park, Reading (ex-unit 317345)
Cl. 332	63400	72412	78400	Siemens, Goole (ex-unit 332001)
Cl. 390	69133	69833		Avanti West Coast Training Centre, Westmere Drive, Crewe, Cheshire (ex-unit 390033)
Cl. 390	69933			Safety & Accident Investigation Centre, Cranfield University, Cranfield, Bedfordshire (ex-unit 390033)
Cl. 508	64649	64712		Emergency Services Training Centre, Seacombe, Merseyside (ex-units 508201/209)
Cl. 508	64681	71511	64724	The Fire Service College, Moreton-in-Marsh, Gloucestershire (unit 508212)

4.8. EMUS AWAITING DISPOSAL

This list comprises EMU vehicles which are awaiting disposal.

The majority of the Class 442s were disposed of during 2021 and only 13 vehicles are left awaiting disposal at either Eastleigh Works or Wolverton Works.

Cl. 309	RR	WC	CS	71758				(ex-309623)
Cl. 317	GA	A	EP	77024	62661	71577	77048	(unit 317501)
Cl. 321	FB	E	MH	63064	78096			(ex-321402)
Cl. 365	N	X	ZN	65919				(ex-365526)
Cl. 442	GV	SW	ZG	71822	71846			(ex-442405)
Cl. 442	GV	SW	ZG	71824	71848	77388		(ex-442407)
Cl. 442	GV	SW	ZG	77393	71829	71853	77417	(ex-442412)
Cl. 442	GV	SW	ZG	62954				(ex-442418)
Cl. 442	GV	SW	ZN	77400				(ex-442419)
Cl. 442	GV	SW	ZG	71841	71865			(ex-442424)

5. ON-TRACK MACHINES

These machines are used for maintaining, renewing and enhancing the infrastructure of the national railway network. With the exception of snowploughs all can be self-propelled, controlled either from a cab mounted on the machine or remotely. They are permitted to operate either under their own power or in train formations throughout the network both within and outside engineering possessions. Machines only permitted to be used within engineering possessions, referred to as On-Track Plant, are not included. Also not included are wagons included in OTM consists and overseas based machines that might make occasional short visits.

For each machine its GB operational number, owner or responsible custodian and type is given, plus its name if carried. In addition, for snow clearance equipment the berthing location is given. Actual operation of each machine is undertaken by either the owner/responsible custodian or a contracted responsible custodian.

Machines were numbered by British Rail with either six-digit wagon series numbers or in the CEPS (Civil Engineers Plant System) series with five prefixed digits. Machines delivered from 2013 onwards carry 12-digit EVN series numbers, most additionally carrying a shorter GB operational number. In most cases the later resemble CEPS numbers. Machines are listed here by GB operational number, which in some cases is also the EVN number. Anomalies in such numbering mean this is not strictly numeric, but the order they would have been if allocated CEPS numbers correctly. Machines that carry additional identifying numbers have these shown "xxxx".

(S) after the registered number designates a machine that is currently stored (the storage location of each is given at the end of this section).

DYNAMIC TRACK STABILISERS

DR 72211	BB	Plasser & Theurer DGS 62-N
DR 72213	BB	Plasser & Theurer DGS 62-N

TAMPERS

Plasser & Theurer 09 Series

DR 73109	SK	Plasser & Theurer 09-3X-RT	
DR 73111	SK	Plasser & Theurer 09-3X-Dynamic	
DR 73113	SK	Plasser & Theurer 09-3X-Dynamic	
DR 73114	NR	Plasser & Theurer 09-3X-Dynamic	Ron Henderson
DR 73115	NR	Plasser & Theurer 09-3X-Dynamic	
DR 73116	NR	Plasser & Theurer 09-3X Dynamic	
DR 73117	NR	Plasser & Theurer 09-3X Dynamic	
DR 73118	NR	Plasser & Theurer 09-3X Dynamic	
DR 73120	NR	Plasser & Theurer 09-3X Dynamic	"99 70 9123 120-6"

| DR 73121 | NR | Plasser & Theurer 09-2X Dynamic | "99 70 9123 121-4" |
| DR 73122 | NR | Plasser & Theurer 09-2X Dynamic | "99 70 9123 122-2" |

| 928001 | SK | Plasser & Theurer Unimat 09-4x4/4S Dynamic | "99 70 9128 001-3" |
| DR 74002 | SK | Plasser & Theurer Unimat 09-4x4/4S Dynamic | "99 70 9128 002-1" |

DR 75008	CS	Plasser & Theurer 09-4x4/4S Dynamic	"99 70 9123 008-3"
DR 75009	CS	Plasser & Theurer 09-4x4/4S Dynamic	"99 70 9123 009-1"
DR 75010	CS	Plasser & Theurer 09-4x4/4S Dynamic	"99 70 9123 010-9"
DR 75011	CS	Plasser & Theurer 09-4x4/4S Dynamic	"99 70 9123 011-7"
DR 75012	SK	Plasser & Theurer 09-4x4/4S Dynamic	"99 70 9123 012-5"
DR 75013	SK	Plasser & Theurer 09-4x4/4S Dynamic	"99 70 9123 013-3"
DR 75014	SK	Plasser & Theurer 09-4x4/4S Dynamic	"99 70 9123 014-1"
DR 75015	SK	Plasser & Theurer 09-4x4/4S Dynamic	"99 70 9123 015-8"

Names:

DR 75010 Roger Nicholas | DR 75011   Andrew Smith

Plasser & Theurer 08 Series and 08 Series (compact)

DR 73803	SK	Plasser & Theurer 08-32U-RT	Alexander Graham Bell
DR 73806	CS	Plasser & Theurer 08-16/32U-RT	Karine
DR 73904	SK	Plasser & Theurer 08-4x4/4S-RT	Thomas Telford
DR 73905	CS	Plasser & Theurer 08-4x4/4S-RT	
DR 73906	CS	Plasser & Theurer 08-4x4/4S-RT	Panther
DR 73907	CS	Plasser & Theurer 08-4x4/4S-RT	
DR 73908	CS	Plasser & Theurer 08-4x4/4S-RT	
DR 73909	CS	Plasser & Theurer 08-4x4/4S-RT	Saturn
DR 73910	CS	Plasser & Theurer 08-4x4/4S-RT	Jupiter
DR 73913	CS	Plasser & Theurer 08-12/4x4C-RT	
DR 73914	SK	Plasser & Theurer 08-4x4/4S-RT	Robert McAlpine
DR 73915	SK	Plasser & Theurer 08-16/4x4C-RT	William Arrol
DR 73916	SK	Plasser & Theurer 08-16/4x4C-RT	First Engineering
DR 73917	BB	Plasser & Theurer 08-4x4/4S-RT	
DR 73918	BB	Plasser & Theurer 08-4x4/4S-RT	
DR 73919	CS	Plasser & Theurer 08-16/4x4C100-RT (with trailer)	
DR 73920	CS	Plasser & Theurer 08-16/4x4C80-RT	
DR 73921	CS	Plasser & Theurer 08-16/4x4C80-RT	
DR 73922	CS	Plasser & Theurer 08-16/4x4C80-RT	John Snowdon
DR 73923	CS	Plasser & Theurer 08-4x4/4S-RT	
DR 73924	CS	Plasser & Theurer 08-16/4x4C100-RT	
DR 73925	CS	Plasser & Theurer 08-16/4x4C100-RT	Europa
DR 73926	BB	Plasser & Theurer 08-16/4x4C100-RT	Stephen Keith Blanchard
DR 73927 (S)	BB	Plasser & Theurer 08-16/4x4C100-RT	
DR 73929	CS	Plasser & Theurer 08-4x4/4S-RT	
DR 73930	CS	Plasser & Theurer 08-4x4/4S-RT	
DR 73931	CS	Plasser & Theurer 08-16/4x4C100-RT	
DR 73932	SK	Plasser & Theurer 08-4x4/4S-RT	
DR 73933	SK	Plasser & Theurer 08-16/4x4/C100-RT (with trailer)	
DR 73934	SK	Plasser & Theurer 08-16/4x4/C100-RT (with trailer)	
DR 73935	CS	Plasser & Theurer 08-4x4/4S-RT	
DR 73936	CS	Plasser & Theurer 08-4x4/4S-RT	
DR 73937	BB	Plasser & Theurer 08-16/4x4C100-RT	

DR 73938	BB	Plasser & Theurer 08-16/4x4C100-RT		
DR 73939	BB	Plasser & Theurer 08-16/4x4C100-RT	Pat Best	
DR 73940	SK	Plasser & Theurer 08-4x4/4S-RT		
DR 73941	SK	Plasser & Theurer 08-4x4/4S-RT		
DR 73942	CS	Plasser & Theurer 08-4x4/4S-RT		
DR 73943	BB	Plasser & Theurer 08-16/4x4C100-RT		
DR 73944	BB	Plasser & Theurer 08-16/4x4C100-RT		
DR 73945	BB	Plasser & Theurer 08-16/4x4C100-RT		
DR 73946	VO	Plasser & Theurer Euromat 08-4x4/4S		
DR 73947	CS	Plasser & Theurer 08-4x4/4S-RT		
DR 73948	CS	Plasser & Theurer 08-4x4/4S-RT		
DR 73949	BB	Plasser & Theurer 08-4x4/4S-RT		"99 70 9123 016-6"
DR 73950	BB	Plasser & Theurer 08-4x4/4S-RT		"99 70 9123 017-4"

Matisa

DR 75301	VO	Matisa B 45 UE		
DR 75302	VO	Matisa B 45 UE		
DR 75303	VO	Matisa B 45 UE	Gary Wright	
DR 75401	VO	Matisa B 41 UE		
DR 75402	VO	Matisa B 41 UE		
DR 75404	VO	Matisa B 41 UE		
DR 75405	VO	Matisa B 41 UE		
DR 75406	CS	Matisa B 41 UE	Eric Machell	
DR 75407	CS	Matisa B 41 UE	Gerry Taylor	
DR 75408	BB	Matisa B 41 UE		
DR 75409	BB	Matisa B 41 UE		
DR 75411	BB	Matisa B 41 UE		
DR 75501	BB	Matisa B 66 UC		
DR 75502	BB	Matisa B 66 UC		
DR 75503	VO	Matisa B 66 UC	"Gill Cowling"	"99 70 9124 001-7"
DR 75504	VO	Matisa B 66 UC		"99 70 9124 002-5"
DR 75505	VO	Matisa B 66 UC		"99 70 9124 003-3"
DR 75506	VO	Matisa B 66 UC		"99 70 9124 004-1"

BALLAST CLEANERS

DR 76501	NR	Plasser & Theurer RM-900-RT	
DR 76502	NR	Plasser & Theurer RM-900-RT	
DR 76503	NR	Plasser & Theurer RM-900-RT	
DR 76504	NR	Plasser & Theurer RM-900	"99 70 9314 504-0"

VACUUM PREPARATION MACHINES

| DR 76701 | NR | Plasser & Theurer VM80-NR |
| DR 76703 | NR | Plasser & Theurer VM80-NR |

RAIL VACUUM MACHINES

99 70 9515 002-2	RC	Railcare 16000-480-UK RailVac OTM
99 70 9515 003-0	RC	Railcare 16000-480-UK RailVac OTM
99 70 9515 004-8	RC	Railcare 16000-480-UK RailVac OTM
99 70 9515 005-5	RC	Railcare 16000-480-UK RailVac OTM

BALLAST FEEDER MACHINE

99 70 9552 020-8	RC	Railcare Ballast Feeder UK

BALLAST TRANSFER MACHINES

DR 76750	NR	Matisa D75	*(works with DR 78802/DR 78812/DR 78822/DR 78832)*
DR 76751	NR	Matisa D75	*(works with DR 78801/DR 78811/DR 78821/DR 78831)*

CONSOLIDATION MACHINES

DR 76801	NR	Plasser & Theurer 09-CM-NR
DR 76802	NR	Plasser & Theurer 09-2X-CM "99 70 9320 802-0"

FINISHING MACHINES & BALLAST REGULATORS

DR 77001	SK	Plasser & Theurer AFM 2000-RT Finishing Machine	Anthony Lou Phillips
DR 77002	SK	Plasser & Theurer AFM 2000-RT Finishing Machine	
DR 77010	NR	Plasser & Theurer USP 6000 Regulator "99 70 9125 010-7"	
DR 77322 (S)	BB	Plasser & Theurer USP 5000C Regulator	
DR 77327	CS	Plasser & Theurer USP 5000C Regulator	
DR 77801	VO	Matisa R 24 S Regulator	
DR 77802	VO	Matisa R 24 S Regulator	
DR 77901	CS	Plasser & Theurer USP 5000-RT Regulator	
DR 77903	SK	Plasser & Theurer USP 5000-RT Regulator	
DR 77904	NR	Plasser & Theurer USP 5000-RT Regulator	
DR 77905	NR	Plasser & Theurer USP 5000-RT Regulator	
DR 77906	NR	Plasser & Theurer USP 5000-RT Regulator	
DR 77907	NR	Plasser & Theurer USP 5000-RT Regulator	
DR 77909	NR	Plasser & Theurer USP 5000 Regulator "99 70 9125 909-0"	
DR 77910	CS	Plasser & Theurer USP 5000 Regulator "99 70 9125 008-1"	

TWIN JIB TRACK RELAYERS

DRP 78213	VO	Plasser & Theurer Self-Propelled Heavy Duty
DRP 78215	BB	Plasser & Theurer Self-Propelled Heavy Duty
DRP 78216	BB	Plasser & Theurer Self-Propelled Heavy Duty
DRP 78217 (S)	SK	Plasser & Theurer Self-Propelled Heavy Duty

DRP 78219   BB   Plasser & Theurer Self-Propelled Heavy Duty
DRP 78221   BB   Plasser & Theurer Self-Propelled Heavy Duty
DRP 78222   BB   Plasser & Theurer Self-Propelled Heavy Duty
DRC 78226   CS   Cowans Sheldon Self-Propelled Heavy Duty
DRC 78229 (S) NR   Cowans Sheldon Self-Propelled Heavy Duty
DRC 78231 (S) NR   Cowans Sheldon Self-Propelled Heavy Duty
DRC 78234 (S) NR   Cowans Sheldon Self-Propelled Heavy Duty
DRC 78235   CS   Cowans Sheldon Self-Propelled Heavy Duty

NEW TRACK CONSTRUCTION
TRAIN PROPULSION MACHINES

DR 78701   BB   Harsco Track Technologies NTC-PW
DR 78702   BB   Harsco Track Technologies NTC-PW

TRACK RENEWAL MACHINES

Matisa P95 Track Renewals Trains
DR 78801+DR 78811+DR 78821+DR 78831 NR *(works with DR 76751)*
DR 78802+DR 78812+DR 78822+DR 78832 NR *(works with DR 76750)*

RAIL GRINDING TRAINS

Loram C21
DR 79231 + DR 79232 + DR 79233 + DR 79236 + DR 79237   NR
DR 79241 + DR 79242 + DR 79243 + DR 79244 + DR 79245 + DR 79246 + DR 79247   NR
DR 79251 + DR 79252 + DR 79253 + DR 79254 + DR 79255 + DR 79256 + DR 79257   NR
DR 79234 + DR 79235 (S)   NR

Names: DR 79231/237   Pete Erwin *(one plate on opposite sides of each)*
          DR 79241/247   Roger South *(one plate on opposite sides of each)*
          DR 79251/257   Martin Elwood *(one plate on opposite sides of each)*

Harsco Track Technologies RGH20C
DR 79261 + DR 79271   NR
DR 79262 + DR 79272   NR   Chris Gibb (on DR 79262)
DR 79263 + DR 79273   NR
DR 79265 + DR 79264 +DR 79274 NR
DR 79267 + DR 79277   NR   Bridget Rosewell CBE (on DR 79267)

Loram C44
DR 79301 + DR 79302 +   NR   99 70 9427 038-3 + 99 70 9427 039-1+
DR 79303 + DR 79304 +   99 70 9427 040-9 + 99 70 9427 041-7
DR 79401 + DR 79402 +   NR   99 70 9427 042-5 + 99 70 9427 043-3+
DR 79403 + DR 79404 +   99 70 9427 044-1 + 99 70 9427 045-8
DR 79501 + DR 79502 +   NR   99 70 9427 046-6 + 99 70 9427 047-4 +
DR 79503 + DR 79504 +   99 70 9427 048-2 + 99 70 9427 049-0+
DR 79505 + DR 79506 +   99 70 9427 050-8 + 99 70 9427 051-6 +
DR 79507   99 70 9427 052-4

Name: DR 79501   Guy Babbs

RAIL MILLING MACHINES

DR 79101	XR	Linsinger MG31-UK Milling Machine	"99 70 9127 006-3"
DR 79102	NR	Linsinger SF06-UK Milling Machine + trailer DR 79103	"99 70 9127 007-1"
DR 79104	NR	Linsinger SF06-UK Milling Machine + trailer DR 79105	"99 70 9127 008-9"

DR 79601 + DR 79602 +	SC	99 70 9427 063-1 + 99 70 9427 064-9
DR 79603 + DR 79604		99 70 9427 065-6 + 99 70 9527 005-1
	Schweerbau High Speed Milling Machine	

STONEBLOWERS

DR 80200 (S)	HR	Pandrol Jackson Plain Line	
DR 80201	NR	Pandrol Jackson Plain Line	
DR 80202 (S)	HR	Pandrol Jackson Plain Line	
DR 80203 (S)	HR	Pandrol Jackson Plain Line	
DR 80204 (S)	HR	Pandrol Jackson Plain Line	
DR 80205	NR	Pandrol Jackson Plain Line	
DR 80206	NR	Pandrol Jackson Plain Line	
DR 80207	HR	Pandrol Jackson Plain Line	99 70 9426 020-2
DR 80208	NR	Pandrol Jackson Plain Line	
DR 80209	NR	Pandrol Jackson Plain Line	
DR 80210	NR	Pandrol Jackson Plain Line	
DR 80211	NR	Pandrol Jackson Plain Line	
DR 80213	NR	Harsco Track Technologies Plain Line	
DR 80214	NR	Harsco Track Technologies Plain Line	
DR 80215	NR	Harsco Track Technologies Plain Line	
DR 80216	NR	Harsco Track Technologies Plain Line	
DR 80217	NR	Harsco Track Technologies Plain Line	
DR 80301	NR	Harsco Track Technologies Multi-purpose	Stephen Cornish
DR 80302	NR	Harsco Track Technologies Multi-purpose	
DR 80303	NR	Harsco Track Technologies Multi-purpose	

CRANES

DRP 81505	BB	Plasser & Theurer 12 tonne Heavy Duty Diesel Hydraulic
DRP 81508	BB	Plasser & Theurer 12 tonne Heavy Duty Diesel Hydraulic
DRP 81513	BB	Plasser & Theurer 12 tonne Heavy Duty Diesel Hydraulic
DRP 81517	BB	Plasser & Theurer 12 tonne Heavy Duty Diesel Hydraulic
DRP 81525	BB	Plasser & Theurer 12 tonne Heavy Duty Diesel Hydraulic
DRP 81532	BB	Plasser & Theurer 12 tonne Heavy Duty Diesel Hydraulic

DRK 81601	VO	Kirow KRC 810UK 100 tonne Heavy Duty Diesel Hydraulic
DRK 81602	BB	Kirow KRC 810UK 100 tonne Heavy Duty Diesel Hydraulic
DRK 81611	BB	Kirow KRC 1200UK 125 tonne Heavy Duty Diesel Hydraulic
DRK 81612	CS	Kirow KRC 1200UK 125 tonne Heavy Duty Diesel Hydraulic

DRK 81613	VO	Kirow KRC 1200UK 125 tonne Heavy Duty Diesel Hydraulic
DRK 81621	VO	Kirow KRC 250UK 25 tonne Diesel Hydraulic
DRK 81622	VO	Kirow KRC 250UK 25 tonne Diesel Hydraulic
DRK 81623	SK	Kirow KRC 250UK 25 tonne Diesel Hydraulic
DRK 81624	SK	Kirow KRC 250UK 25 tonne Diesel Hydraulic
DRK 81625	SK	Kirow KRC 250UK 25 tonne Diesel Hydraulic
DRK 81626	SK	Kirow KRC 250S 25 tonne Diesel Hydraulic "99 70 9319 012-9"

99 70 9319 013-7 NR Kirow KRC 1200UK 125 tonne Heavy Duty Diesel Hydraulic

Names:

| DRK 81601 | Nigel Chester | | DRK 81611 | Malcolm L. Pearce |

LONG WELDED RAIL TRAIN PROPULSION MACHINES

DR 89005	NR	Cowans Boyd PW
DR 89007	NR	Cowans Boyd PW
DR 89008	NR	Cowans Boyd PW

BALLAST SYSTEM PROPULSION MACHINES

DR 92285	NR	Plasser & Theurer PW-RT	
DR 92286	NR	Plasser & Theurer NPW-RT	
DR 92331	NR	Plasser & Theurer PW-RT	
DR 92332	NR	Plasser & Theurer NPW-RT	
DR 92431	NR	Plasser & Theurer PW-RT	
DR 92432	NR	Plasser & Theurer NPW-RT	
DR 92477	NR	Plasser & Theurer PW	"99 70 9310 477-3"
DR 92478	NR	Plasser & Theurer NPW	"99 70 9310 478-1"

BREAKDOWN CRANES

ADRC 96715 (S)　NR　Cowans Sheldon 75 tonne Diesel Hydraulic

HIGH SPEED 1 MAINTENANCE TRAIN VEHICLES

DR 97001	H1	Eiv de Brieve DU94BA TRAMM with Crane	"DU 94 B 001 URS"
DR 97011	H1	Windhoff MPV (Modular)	
DR 97012	H1	Windhoff MPV (Modular)	Geoff Bell
DR 97013	H1	Windhoff MPV (Modular)	
DR 97014	H1	Windhoff MPV (Modular)	

MOBILE MAINTENANCE TRAINS

Robel Type 69.70 Mobile Maintenance System
DR 97501/601/801 NR "99 70 9481 001-4 + 99 70 9559 001-1 + 99 70 9580 001-4"
DR 97502/602/802 NR "99 70 9481 002-2 + 99 70 9559 002-9 + 99 70 9580 002-2"
DR 97503/603/803 NR "99 70 9481 003-0 + 99 70 9559 003-7 + 99 70 9580 003-0"
DR 97504/604/804 NR "99 70 9481 004-8 + 99 70 9559 004-5 + 99 70 9580 004-8"
DR 97505/605/805 NR "99 70 9481 005-5 + 99 70 9559 005-2 + 99 70 9580 005-5"
DR 97506/606/806 NR "99 70 9481 006-3 + 99 70 9559 006-0 + 99 70 9580 006-3"
DR 97507/607/807 NR "99 70 9481 007-1 + 99 70 9559 007-8 + 99 70 9580 007-1"
DR 97508/608/808 NR "99 70 9481 008-9 + 99 70 9559 008-6 + 99 70 9580 008-9"

ELIZABETH LINE MAINTENANCE TRAIN VEHICLES

DR 97509	XR	Robel Power Car A	"99 70 9481 009-7"
DR 97510	XR	Robel Power Car B	"99 70 9481 010-5"
DR 97511	XR	Robel Power Car B	"99 70 9481 011-3"
DR 97512	XR	Robel Power Car E	"99 70 9481 012-1"

ELECTRIFICATION VEHICLES

DR 76901	NR	Windhoff MPV with Piling Equipment	"99 70 9131 001-8"
DR 76903	NR	Windhoff MPV with Piling Equipment	"99 70 9131 003-4"
DR 76905	NR	Windhoff MPV with Piling Equipment	"99 70 9131 005-9"
DR 76906	NR	Windhoff MPV with Concrete Equipment	"99 70 9131 006-7"
DR 76910	NR	Windhoff MPV with Concrete Equipment	"99 70 9131 010-9"
DR 76911	NR	Windhoff MPV with Structure Equipment	"99 70 9131 011-7"
DR 76913	NR	Windhoff MPV with Structure Equipment	"99 70 9131 013-3"
DR 76914	NR	Windhoff MPV with Overhead Line Equipment	"99 70 9131 014-1"
DR 76915	NR	Windhoff MPV with Overhead Line Equipment	"99 70 9131 015-8"
DR 76918	NR	Windhoff MPV with Overhead Line Equipment	"99 70 9131 018-2"
DR 76920	NR	Windhoff MPV with Overhead Line Equipment	"99 70 9131 020-8"
DR 76921	NR	Windhoff MPV with Overhead Line Equipment	"99 70 9131 021-6"
DR 76922	NR	Windhoff MPV with Final Works Equipment	"99 70 9131 022-4"
DR 76923	NR	Windhoff MPV with Final Works Equipment	"99 70 9131 023-2"

DR 98001	NR	Windhoff MPV with Piling Equipment
DR 98002	NR	Windhoff MPV with Overhead Line Renewal Equipment
DR 98003	NR	Windhoff MPV with Overhead Line Renewal Equipment
DR 98004	NR	Windhoff MPV with Overhead Line Renewal Equipment
DR 98005	NR	Windhoff MPV with Overhead Line Renewal Equipment
DR 98006	NR	Windhoff MPV with Overhead Line Renewal Equipment
DR 98007	NR	Windhoff MPV with Piling Equipment
DR 98009	NR	Windhoff MPV with Overhead Line Renewal Equipment
DR 98010	NR	Windhoff MPV with Overhead Line Renewal Equipment
DR 98011	NR	Windhoff MPV with Overhead Line Renewal Equipment
DR 98012	NR	Windhoff MPV with Overhead Line Renewal Equipment
DR 98013	NR	Windhoff MPV with Overhead Line Renewal Equipment
DR 98014	NR	Windhoff MPV with Overhead Line Renewal Equipment

99 70 9231 001-7 AM SVI RT250 with crane & access platform
99 70 9231 004-1 AM SVI PT500 with wire manipulator & access platform
99 70 9231 005-8 AM SVI RSM9 with access platform
99 70 9231 006-6 AM SVI RSM9 with access platform
99 70 9231 007-4 AM APV250 with access platform

Names:

DR 76901   BRUNEL
DR 76923   GAVIN ROBERTS
DR 98003   ANTHONY WRIGHTON 1944–2011
DR 98004   PHILIP CATTRELL 1961–2011
DR 98006   JASON MCDONNELL 1970–2016
DR 98009   MELVYN SMITH 1953–2011
DR 98010   BENJAMIN GAUTREY 1992–2011
DR 98012   TERENCE HAND 1962–2016
DR 98013   DAVID WOOD 1951–2015
DR 98014   WAYNE IMLACH 1955–2015

GENERAL PURPOSE VEHICLES

DR 98215A + DR 98215B   BB Plasser & Theurer GP-TRAMM with Trailer
DR 98216A + DR 98216B   BB Plasser & Theurer GP-TRAMM with Trailer
DR 98217A + DR 98217B   BB Plasser & Theurer GP-TRAMM with Trailer
DR 98218A + DR 98218B   BB Plasser & Theurer GP-TRAMM with Trailer
DR 98219A + DR 98219B   BB Plasser & Theurer GP-TRAMM with Trailer
DR 98220A + DR 98220B   BB Plasser & Theurer GP-TRAMM with Trailer

DR 98307A (S)   CS Geismar GP-TRAMM VMT 860 PL/UM
DR 98307B*   CS Geismar GP-TRAMM Trailer
DR 98308A + DR 98308B (S) CS Geismar GP-TRAMM VMT 860 PL/UM with Trailer

* In use as a propelling control vehicle at Baglan Bay Yard.

DR 98901 + DR 98951   NR   Windhoff MPV Master & Slave
DR 98902 + DR 98952   NR   Windhoff MPV Master & Slave
DR 98903 + DR 98953   NR   Windhoff MPV Master & Slave
DR 98904 + DR 98954   NR   Windhoff MPV Master & Slave
DR 98905 + DR 98955   NR   Windhoff MPV Master & Slave
DR 98906 + DR 98956   NR   Windhoff MPV Master & Slave
DR 98907 + DR 98957   NR   Windhoff MPV Master & Slave
DR 98908 + DR 98958   NR   Windhoff MPV Master & Slave
DR 98909 + DR 98959   NR   Windhoff MPV Master & Slave
DR 98910 + DR 98960   NR   Windhoff MPV Master & Slave
DR 98911 + DR 98961   NR   Windhoff MPV Master & Slave
DR 98912 + DR 98962   NR   Windhoff MPV Master & Slave
DR 98913 + DR 98963   NR   Windhoff MPV Master & Slave
DR 98914 + DR 98964   NR   Windhoff MPV Master & Slave
DR 98915 + DR 98965   NR   Windhoff MPV Master & Slave
DR 98916 + DR 98966   NR   Windhoff MPV Master & Slave
DR 98917 + DR 98967   NR   Windhoff MPV Master & Slave
DR 98918 + DR 98968   NR   Windhoff MPV Master & Slave
DR 98919 + DR 98969   NR   Windhoff MPV Master & Slave

DR 98920 + DR 98970	NR	Windhoff MPV Master & Slave
DR 98921 + DR 98971	NR	Windhoff MPV Master & Slave
DR 98922 + DR 98972	NR	Windhoff MPV Master & Slave
DR 98923 + DR 98973	NR	Windhoff MPV Master & Slave
DR 98924 + DR 98974	NR	Windhoff MPV Master & Slave
DR 98925 + DR 98975	NR	Windhoff MPV Master & Slave
DR 98926 + DR 98976	NR	Windhoff MPV Master & Powered Slave
DR 98927 + DR 98977	NR	Windhoff MPV Master & Powered Slave
DR 98928 + DR 98978	NR	Windhoff MPV Master & Powered Slave
DR 98929 + DR 98979	NR	Windhoff MPV Master & Powered Slave
DR 98930 + DR 98980	NR	Windhoff MPV Master & Powered Slave
DR 98931 + DR 98981	NR	Windhoff MPV Master & Powered Slave
DR 98932 + DR 98982	NR	Windhoff MPV Master & Powered Slave

Names:

DR 98914+DR 98964 Dick Preston	DR 98923+DR 98973 Chris Lemon
DR 98915+DR 98965 Nigel Cummins	DR 98926+DR 98976 John Denyer

INFRASTRUCTURE MONITORING VEHICLES

"950 001" is a purpose-built Track Assessment Unit based on the BREL Class 150/1 design.

DR 98008	NR	Windhoff MPV Twin-cab with surveying equipment
999600+999601	NR	BREL York Track Assessment Unit "950 001"
999800	NR	Plasser & Theurer EM-SAT 100/RT Track Survey Car
999801	NR	Plasser & Theurer EM-SAT 100/RT Track Survey Car

Name: 999800 Richard Spoors

SNOWPLOUGHS

ADB 965203	NR	Independent Drift Plough	Carlisle Kingmoor Yard
ADB 965206	NR	Independent Drift Plough	Crewe Gresty Bridge
ADB 965208	NR	Independent Drift Plough	Norwich Thorpe Yard
ADB 965209	NR	Independent Drift Plough	Motherwell Depot
ADB 965210	NR	Independent Drift Plough	Carlisle Kingmoor Yard
ADB 965211	NR	Independent Drift Plough	Tonbridge West Yard
ADB 965217	NR	Independent Drift Plough	York Leeman Road Sidings
ADB 965219	NR	Independent Drift Plough	Norwich Thorpe Yard
ADB 965223	NR	Independent Drift Plough	Taunton Fairwater Yard
ADB 965224	NR	Independent Drift Plough	Inverness Millburn Yard
ADB 965230	NR	Independent Drift Plough	Inverness Millburn Yard
ADB 965231	NR	Independent Drift Plough	Motherwell Depot
ADB 965234	NR	Independent Drift Plough	Motherwell Depot
ADB 965235	NR	Independent Drift Plough	Taunton Fairwater Yard
ADB 965236	NR	Independent Drift Plough	Motherwell Depot
ADB 965237	NR	Independent Drift Plough	Tonbridge West Yard
ADB 965240	NR	Independent Drift Plough	York North Yard Sidings
ADB 965241	NR	Independent Drift Plough	Crewe Gresty Bridge

ADB 965242	NR	Independent Drift Plough	Carlisle Kingmoor Yard
ADB 965243	NR	Independent Drift Plough	Carlisle Kingmoor Yard
ADB 965576	NR	Beilhack Type PB600 Plough	Crewe Basford Hall Yard
ADB 965577	NR	Beilhack Type PB600 Plough	Crewe Basford Hall Yard
ADB 965578	NR	Beilhack Type PB600 Plough	Doncaster West Yard
ADB 965579	NR	Beilhack Type PB600 Plough	Doncaster West Yard
ADB 965580	NR	Beilhack Type PB600 Plough	Doncaster West Yard
ADB 965581	NR	Beilhack Type PB600 Plough	Doncaster West Yard
ADB 966098	NR	Beilhack Type PB600 Plough	Doncaster West Yard
ADB 966099	NR	Beilhack Type PB600 Plough	Doncaster West Yard

SNOWBLOWERS

ADB 968500	NR	Beilhack Self-Propelled Rotary	Rutherglen OTP Depot
ADB 968501	NR	Beilhack Self-Propelled Rotary	Rutherglen OTP Depot

ON-TRACK MACHINES AWAITING DISPOSAL

Twin Jib track relayer
DRB 78123 British Hoist & Crane Non-Self-Propelled   Polmadie Down
                                                       Holding Sidings

LOCATIONS OF STORED ON-TRACK MACHINES

The locations of machines shown above as stored (S) are shown here.

DR 73927	West Ealing OTM Depot	DR 80202	HNRC, Worksop Depot
DR 77322	West Ealing OTM Depot	DR 80203	HNRC, Worksop Depot
DRP 78217	Glasgow Rutherglen Depot	DR 80204	Dereham, Mid Norfolk Railway
DRC 78229	Land Recovery, Radway Green	ARDC 96715	Nemesis Rail, Burton-upon-Trent
DRC 78231	Land Recovery, Radway Green		
DRC 78234	Land Recovery, Radway Green	DR 98307A	Darley Dale
DR 79234+	LORAM, Derby	DR 98308A+	
DR 79235	LORAM, Derby	DR 98308B	Barry Rail Centre
DR 80200	Dereham, Mid Norfolk Railway		

6. CODES

6.1. LIVERY CODES

Livery codes are used to denote the various liveries carried. It is impossible to list every livery variation which currently exists. In particular items ignored for this publication include:

- Minor colour variations.
- Omission of logos.
- All numbering, lettering and brandings.

Descriptions quoted are thus a general guide only. Logos as appropriate for each livery are normally deemed to be carried. The colour of the lower half of the bodyside is generally stated first.

Code Description

AB	Arriva Trains Wales/Welsh Government sponsored all over dark blue.
AG	Arlington Fleet Services (green).
AI	Aggregate Industries (green, light grey & blue).
AL	Advertising/promotional livery (see class heading for details).
AM	Avanti West Coast Voyager {interim}. Dark green ends on **VT** silver livery.
AR	Anglia Railways (turquoise blue with a white stripe).
AT	Avanti West Coast (dark green, dark grey, white, cream & orange).
AV	Arriva Trains (turquoise blue with white doors & a cream "swish").
AW	Arriva Trains Wales or Arriva TrainCare dark & light blue.
AZ	Advenza Freight (deep blue with green Advenza brandings).
B	BR blue.
BG	BR blue & grey lined out in white.
BL	BR Revised blue with yellow cabs, grey roof, large numbers & logo.
BN	Beacon Rail (blue).
C2	c2c (white with dark blue doors).
C2C	New c2c Class 720 (white with pink doors and end flashes).
CA	Caledonian Sleeper (dark blue).
CC	BR Carmine & Cream.
CD	Cotswold Rail (silver with blue & red logo).
CE	BR Civil Engineers (yellow & grey with black cab doors & window surrounds).
CH	BR Western Region/GWR (chocolate & cream lined out in gold).
CL	Chiltern Railways Mainline Class 168 (white & silver).
CM	Chiltern Railways Mainline loco-hauled (two-tone grey/white & silver with blue stripes).
CN	Connex/Southeastern (white with black window surrounds & grey lower band).
CO	Centro (grey & light green with light blue, white & yellow stripes).
CR	Chiltern Railways (blue & white with a red stripe).
CS	Colas Rail (yellow, orange & black).
CT	Colas Rail HST (orange with broad black & yellow vertical stripes).
CU	Corus (silver with red logos).
DB	DB Cargo (Deutsche Bahn red with grey roof & solebar).
DC	Devon & Cornwall Railways (metallic silver).
DG	BR Departmental (dark grey with black cab doors & window surrounds).

DI   DRS {Class 68 style} (deep blue & aquamarine with large compass logo).
DR   Direct Rail Services (dark blue with light blue or dark grey roof).
DS   Revised DRS (dark blue, light blue & green. "Compass" logo).
E   English Welsh & Scottish Railway (maroon bodyside & roof with a broad gold bodyside band).
EA   East Midlands Trains revised HST (dark blue, orange & red).
EB   Eurotunnel (two-tone grey with a broad blue stripe).
ECR Euro Cargo Rail (light grey).
EG   "EWS grey" (as **F** but with large yellow & red EWS logo).
EI   East Midlands Railway {interim} (white with deep purple swish at unit ends).
EP   European Passenger Services (two-tone grey with dark blue roof).
EM   East Midlands Trains {Connect} (blue with red & orange swish at unit ends).
ER   East Midlands Railway (purple with white or grey lower bodyside lining and doors).
ES   Revised Eurostar (deep blue & two-tone grey).
EU   Eurostar (white with dark blue & yellow stripes).
EX   Europhoenix (silver, blue & red).
F   BR Trainload Freight (two-tone grey with black cab doors & window surrounds. Various logos).
FA   Fastline Freight (grey & black with white & orange stripes).
FB   First Group dark blue.
FD   First Great Western "Dynamic Lines" (dark blue with thin multi-coloured lines on the lower bodyside).
FE   Railfreight Distribution International (two tone-grey with black cab doors & dark blue roof).
FF   Freightliner grey (two-tone grey with black cab doors & window surrounds. Freightliner logo).
FG   New Freightliner Genesee & Wyoming style (orange with black & yellow lower bodyside stripes).
FH   Revised Freightliner {PowerHaul} (dark green with yellow cab ends & grey stripe/buffer beam).
FL   Freightliner (dark green with yellow cabs).
FO   BR Railfreight (grey bodysides, yellow cabs & red lower bodyside stripe, large BR logo).
FR   Fragonset Railways (black with silver roof & a red bodyside band lined out in white).
FS   First Group (indigo blue with pink & white stripes).
G¹   BR Green (plain green, with white stripe on main line locomotives).
G²   BR Southern Region/SR or BR DMU green.
GA   Greater Anglia (white with red doors & black window surrounds).
GB   GB Railfreight (blue with orange cantrail & solebar stripes, orange cabs).
GC   Grand Central (all over black with an orange stripe).
GG   BR two-tone green.
GL   First Great Western locomotives (green with a gold stripe).
GR   New Greater Anglia (white/grey with black window surrounds & red & dark grey on the lower bodyside).
GV   Gatwick Express Class 442 (red, white & indigo blue with mauve & blue doors).
GW   Great Western Railway (TOC) dark green.
GY   Eurotunnel (grey & yellow).
GX   Gatwick Express Class 387 (red with white lining and grey doors).
HA   Hanson Quarry Products (dark blue/silver with oxide red roof).

HB	HSBC Rail (Oxford blue & white).
HC	Heathrow Connect (grey with a broad deep blue bodyside band & orange doors).
HH	Hanson & Hall (dark grey with green branding).
HM	Heidelberg Materials (green).
HN	Harry Needle Railroad Company (orange with a black roof and solebar).
HT	Hull Trains (First Group dark blue with a multi-coloured band on lower bodyside depicting images from the route).
HU	Hunslet Engine Company (dark blue & orange).
HX	Heathrow Express (silver, grey & purple).
IC	BR InterCity (dark grey/white/red/white).
IE	BR InterCity Executive (yellow/light grey/dark grey with a red stripe).
IS	BR ScotRail InterCity (as **IC** but with a blue stripe).
K	Black.
KB	Knorr-Bremse Rail UK (blue, white & light green).
LC	New LNER Class 91+Mark 4 (oxblood, white & light grey with a red stripe).
LD	New London Overground (black upper bodyside with white, orange & blue lower bodyside stripes & orange doors).
LH	BR Loadhaul (black with orange cabsides).
LI	London Northwestern Railway {interim} (dark green at unit ends and doors applied on **LM** light grey/black livery).
LM	London Midland (light grey & green with black stripe around the windows).
LN	London Northwestern Railway (light grey, dark green & light green).
LO	London Overground (all over white with a blue solebar & black window surrounds and orange doors).
LR	LORAM (red, white & grey).
LT	London Transport maroon & cream.
LU	Lumo (blue).
LZ	LNER Azuma (white with red window surrounds).
M	BR maroon (maroon lined out in straw & black).
ME	New Merseyrail (grey and yellow with black window surrounds).
MG	Meridian Generic Rail (blue & grey with white lining).
ML	BR Mainline Freight (aircraft blue with a silver stripe).
MP	Midland Pullman (nanking blue & white).
MT	Maritime (blue with white lettering).
MY	Merseyrail (all over yellow or all over grey (alternate sides)).
N	BR Network SouthEast (white & blue with red lower bodyside stripe, grey solebar & cab ends).
NC	National Express white (white with blue doors).
NO	Northern (deep blue, purple & white).
NR	New Northern (white & purple).
NX	National Express (white with grey ends).
O	Non-standard (see class heading for details).
ON	Orion (dark blue with light blue doors).
PB	Porterbrook Leasing Company (blue).
PC	Pullman Car Company (umber & cream with gold lettering lined out in gold).
RA	Rail Adventure (dark grey with light grey cabs and green lettering).
RB	Riviera Trains Oxford blue.
RC	Rail Charter Services (green with a broad silver bodyside stripe).
RG	Rail Operations Group dark green.
RL	RMS Locotec (dark blue with light grey or green cabsides).

RM   Royal Mail (all over red).
RO   Rail Operations Group (dark blue).
RP   Royal Train (claret, lined out in red & black).
RR   Regional Railways (dark blue & grey with light blue & white stripes, three narrow dark blue stripes at vehicle ends).
RS   Railway Support Services (grey with a red solebar).
RX   Rail Express Systems (dark grey & red with or without blue markings).
RZ   Royal Train revised (plain claret, no lining).
SB   Southeastern blue (all over blue with black window surrounds).
SD   Stagecoach/South West Trains outer suburban {Class 450 style} (deep blue with red doors & orange & red cab sides).
SE   Southeastern suburban (all over white with black window surrounds, light blue doors and (on some units) dark blue lower bodyside stripe).
SI   ScotRail InterCity HST (light grey & dark blue with INTER7CITY branding).
SL   Silverlink (indigo blue with white stripe, green lower body & yellow doors).
SN   Southern (white & dark green with light green semi-circles at one end of each vehicle. Light grey band at solebar level).
SR   ScotRail – Scotland's Railways (dark blue with Scottish Saltire flag & white/light blue flashes).
SS   South West Trains inner suburban {Class 455 style} (red with blue & orange flashes at unit ends).
ST   Stagecoach {long-distance stock} (white & dark blue with dark blue window surrounds and red & orange swishes at unit ends).
SW   South Western Railway (two-tone grey with a yellow lower bodyside stripe).
TB   Transport for Wales all over black with a red logo.
TG   Govia Thameslink interim {Class 387} (white with dark green doors).
TL   Govia Thameslink Railway (light grey & white with blue doors).
TP   TransPennine Express (silver, grey, blue & purple).
TT   Transmart Trains (all over green).
TW   Transport for Wales (white with a broad red stripe at cantrail level & red doors).
TY   Tyne & Wear Metro (light grey, black & yellow).
U   Plain white or grey undercoat.
V   Virgin Trains (red with black doors extending into bodysides, three white lower bodysides stripes).
VE   Virgin Trains East Coast (red & white with black window surrounds).
VP   Virgin Trains shunters (black with a large black & white chequered flag on the bodyside).
VN   Northern Belle (crimson lake & cream lined out in gold).
VT   Virgin Trains silver (silver, with black window surrounds, white cantrail stripe & red roof. Red swept down at unit ends).
VW   New Virgin Trains (all over white with Avanti logos).
WA   Wabtec Rail (black).
WC   West Coast Railway Company maroon.
WI   West Midlands Railway {interim} (gold at unit ends & gold doors applied on **LM** light grey/black livery).
WM   West Midlands Railway (gold & metallic purple).
XC   CrossCountry (two-tone silver with deep crimson ends & pink doors).
XR   Elizabeth Line (white with black window surrounds and a purple lower bodyside).
Y   Network Rail yellow.

6.2. OWNER CODES

The following codes are used to define the ownership details of the locomotives or rolling stock listed in this book. Codes shown indicate either the legal owner or "responsible custodian" of each vehicle.

125	125 Group
20	Class 20189
37	Scottish Thirty-Seven Group
40	Class 40 Preservation Society
47	Stratford 47 Group
50	Class 50 Alliance
56	Class 56 Locomotives
70	7029 Clun Castle
71	71A Locomotives
2L	Class 20 Locomotives
A	Angel Trains
AD	AV Dawson
AF	Arlington Fleet Services
AK	Akiem
AM	Alstom UK
AN	Andania Engineering
AT	Agility Trains
AV	Arriva UK Trains
BA	Babcock Rail
BB	Balfour Beatty Rail Infrastructure Services
BD	Bardon Aggregates
BE	Belmond (UK)
BN	Beacon Rail
BR	Brodie Leasing
CD	Crewe Diesel Preservation Group
CL	Caledonian Rail Leasing
CO	Corelink Rail Infrastructure
CT	Cross London Trains
CS	Colas Rail
D0	D05 Preservation Group
DB	DB Cargo (UK)
DC	DC Rail
DE	Diesel and Electric Preservation Group
DP	Deltic Preservation Society
DR	Direct Rail Services
DT	The Diesel Traction Group
E	Eversholt Rail (UK)
ED	Ed Murray & Sons
EE	English Electric Preservation
EL	Electric Traction Limited
EM	East Midlands Railway
EO	ElectroMotive Diesel Services
EP	Europhoenix
ER	Eastern Rail Services
ET	Eurotunnel

EU   Eurostar International
EY   European Metal Recycling
FG   First Group
FL   Freightliner
GB   GB Railfreight
GR   Global Centre of Rail Excellence
GW   Great Western Railway
H1   Network Rail (High Speed)
HD   Hastings Diesels
HH   Hanson & Hall Rail Services
HN   Harry Needle Railroad Company
HR   Harsco Track Technologies
HU   Hunslet Engine Company
HX   Halifax Bank of Scotland
LF   Lombard North Central
LN   London Overground
LO   Loram (UK)
LS   Locomotive Services
LU   London Underground
ME   Meteor Power
MG   Meridian Generic Rail
MR   Mendip Rail
MT   Merseytravel
NB   Boden Rail Engineering
NM   National Museum of Science & Industry
NN   North Norfolk Railway
NR   Network Rail
NS   Nemesis Rail
NY   North Yorkshire Moors Railway Enterprises
P   Porterbrook Leasing Company
PG   Progress Rail UK Leasing
PO   Other private owner
PP   Peter Pan Locomotive Company
PR   The Princess Royal Class Locomotive Trust
PT   Positive Traction
QW   QW Rail Leasing
RA   Rail Adventure
RC   RailCare UK
RF   Rail for London (Transport for London)
RL   Rail Management Services (trading as RMS Locotec)
RM   Royal Mail
RO   Rail Operations Group
RR   Rock Rail
RS   Railway Support Services
RU   Russell Logistics
RV   Riviera Trains
SB   Steve Beniston
SC   Schweerbau (UK)
SF   SNCF (Société Nationale des Chemins de fer Français)
SG   Swanage Railway
SI   Speno International

SK   Swietelsky Babcock Rail
SM   SMBC Leasing/Equitix
SP   The Scottish Railway Preservation Society
SR   ScotRail
ST   Shaun Wright
SU   SembCorp Utilities UK
SW   South Western Railway
SY   South Yorkshire Passenger Transport Executive
TW   Transport for Wales
UR   UK Rail Leasing
VG   Victoria Group
VO   VolkerRail
VT   Vintage Trains
WA   Wabtec Rail Group
WC   West Coast Railway Company
WM   West Midlands Trains
X   Sold for scrap/further use and awaiting collection

6.3. LOCOMOTIVE POOL CODES

Locomotives are split into operational groups ("pools") for diagramming and maintenance purposes. The codes used to denote these pools are shown in this publication.

AWCA   West Coast Railway Company operational locomotives.
AWCX   West Coast Railway Company stored locomotives.
CFOL   Class 50 Operations locomotives.
CFSL   Class 40 Preservation Society Locomotives.
COFS   Colas Rail Classes 37 & 56.
COLO   Colas Rail Classes 66 & 70.
COLS   Colas Rail stored locomotives.
COTS   Colas Rail Classes 37 & 43.
DCRO   DC Rail operational locomotives.
DCRS   DC Rail stored locomotives.
DFGI   Freightliner Class 70.
DFHG   Freightliner Class 59.
DFHH   Freightliner Class 66/6.
DFIM   Freightliner Class 66/5.
DFIN   Freightliner low emission Class 66.
DFLC   Freightliner Class 90.
DFLH   Freightliner Class 47.
DHLT   Freightliner locomotives awaiting maintenance/repair/disposal.
EFOO   Great Western Railway Class 57.
EFPC   Great Western Railway Class 43.
EPEX   Europhoenix UK stored locomotives.
EPUK   Europhoenix UK locomotives.
ERSL   Eastern Rail Services locomotives.
GBBS   GB Railfreight Class 57.
GBBT   GB Railfreight Class 66. Large fuel tanks.
GBCS   GB Railfreight Class 73/9. Caledonian Sleeper.
GBCT   GB Railfreight Class 92. Channel Tunnel traffic.

GBDF	GB Railfreight Class 47.
GBEB	GB Railfreight Class 66. Ex-European, large fuel tanks.
GBED	GB Railfreight Class 73.
GBEL	GB Railfreight Class 66. New build, small fuel tanks.
GBFM	GB Railfreight Class 66. RETB fitted.
GBGD	GB Railfreight Class 56. Operational locomotives.
GBHH	GB Railfreight Class 66. Regeared locomotives.
GBLT	GB Railfreight Class 66. Small fuel tanks.
GBNB	GB Railfreight Class 66. New build.
GBNR	GB Railfreight Class 73/9. Network Rail contracts.
GBOB	GB Railfreight Class 66. Former DB Cargo locomotives; large fuel tanks and buckeye couplers.
GBRG	GB Railfreight Class 69.
GBSD	GB Railfreight. Stored locomotives.
GBSL	GB Railfreight Class 92. Caledonian Sleeper.
GBST	GB Railfreight Class 92. Caledonian Sleeper & Channel Tunnel.
GBTG	GB Railfreight Class 60.
GBYH	GB Railfreight Class 59.
GBZZ	GB Railfreight locomotives for disposal.
GROG	Rail Operations Group diesel locomotives.
HAPC	ScotRail Class 43.
HHPC	Rail Adventure Class 43.
HNRL	Harry Needle Railroad Company hire locomotives.
HNRS	Harry Needle Railroad Company stored locomotives.
HTLX	Hanson & Hall Rail Services locomotives.
HVAC	Hanson & Hall Rail Services Class 50.
HYWD	South Western Railway Class 73.
ICHP	125 Group Class 43.
IECA	London North Eastern Railway Class 91.
IECP	London North Eastern Railway Class 43 (stored).
LRLO	Loram locomotives.
LSLO	Locomotive Services operational locomotives.
LSLS	Locomotive Services stored locomotives.
MBDL	Non TOC-owned diesel locomotives.
MBED	Non TOC-owned electro-diesel locomotives.
MBEL	Non TOC-owned electric locomotives.
MOLO	Class 20189 Ltd Class 20.
NRLO	Nemesis Rail locomotives.
QADD	Network Rail locomotives.
QCAR	Network Rail New Measurement Train Class 43.
QETS	Network Rail Class 37.
RAJV	Scottish Railway Preservation Society Class 37.
SAXL	Eversholt Rail off-lease locomotives.
SBXL	Porterbrook Leasing Company stored locomotives.
SCEL	Angel Trains stored locomotives.
SROG	Rail Operations Group stored locomotives
TPEX	TransPennine Express Class 68 locomotives.
UKRL	UK Rail Leasing. Operational locomotives.
UKRM	UK Rail Leasing. Locomotives for overhaul.
UKRS	UK Rail Leasing. Stored locomotives.
WAAC	DB Cargo Class 67.

WAEC	DB Cargo Class 67. Fitted with ETCS.
WAWC	DB Cargo Class 67 for hire to Transport for Wales.
WBAE	DB Cargo Class 66. Locomotives fitted with "stop-start" technology.
WBAI	DB Cargo Class 66. Locomotives returned from DB Cargo Rail France.
WBAK	DB Cargo Class 66. ETCS fitted.
WBAR	DB Cargo Class 66. Fitted with remote monitoring equipment.
WBAT	DB Cargo Class 66.
WBBE	DB Cargo Class 66. RETB fitted and fitted with "stop-start" technology.
WBBT	DB Cargo Class 66. RETB fitted.
WBET	DB Cargo Class 66. Fitted with ETCS.
WBLE	DB Cargo Class 66. Dedicated locomotives for Lickey Incline banking duties. Fitted with "stop-start" technology.
WBHT	DB Cargo Class 66. Locos regeared or planned to be regeared.
WBRT	DB Cargo Class 66. Locomotives dedicated to autumn RHTT trains.
WBVT	DB Cargo Class 66. For hire to Victa Railfreight.
WCAT	DB Cargo Class 60.
WCBT	DB Cargo Class 60. Extended-range fuel tanks.
WEAC	DB Cargo Class 90.
WEDC	DB Cargo Class 90. Modified for operation with Mark 4s.
WFAC	DB Cargo Class 92.
WFBC	DB Cargo Class 92 with TVM430 cab signalling equipment for use on High Speed 1.
WQAA	DB Cargo stored locomotives Group 1A (short-term maintenance).
WQAB	DB Cargo stored locomotives Group 1B.
WQBA	DB Cargo stored locomotives Group 2 (unserviceable).
WQCA	DB Cargo stored locomotives Group 3 (unserviceable).
WQDA	DB Cargo stored locomotives Group 4 (awaiting disposal or for sale).
XHAC	Direct Rail Services Class 57/3.
XHCE	Direct Rail Services Class 68 for hire to Chiltern Railways.
XHCS	Direct Rail Services Class 68 for hire to Chiltern Railways (spare locomotives).
XHIM	Direct Rail Services locomotives – Intermodal traffic.
XHSO	Direct Rail Services Supply Chain Operations locomotives.
XHTP	Direct Rail Services Class 68 for hire to TransPennine Express (spare locomotives).
XHVE	Direct Rail Services Classes 68 & 88.
XHVT	Direct Rail Services Class 57/3 for hire to Avanti West Coast.
XSDP	Direct Rail Services locomotives for disposal.
XWSS	Direct Rail Services stored locomotives.

6.4. OPERATOR CODES

Operator codes are used to denote the organisation that facilitates the use of that vehicle, and may not be the actual Train Operating Company which runs the train. Where no operator code is shown, vehicles are currently not in use.

AW	Avanti West Coast
BP	Belmond British Pullman
C2	c2c
CA	Caledonian Sleeper
CR	Chiltern Railways

CS	Colas Rail
DB	DB Cargo (UK)
DR	Direct Rail Services
EL	Elizabeth Line
EM	East Midlands Railway
EU	Eurostar (UK)
GA	Greater Anglia
GB	GB Railfreight
GC	Grand Central
GN	Great Northern (part of Govia Thameslink Railway)
GW	Great Western Railway
HD	Hastings Diesels
HE	Heathrow Express
HT	Hull Trains
LN	London North Eastern Railway
LO	London Overground
LS	Locomotive Services
LU	Lumo
ME	Merseyrail
NO	Northern
NY	North Yorkshire Moors Railway
PR	The Princess Royal Class Locomotive Trust
RA	Rail Adventure
RO	Rail Operations Group
RS	The Royal Scotsman (Belmond)
RT	Royal Train
RV	Riviera Trains
SE	Southeastern
SG	Swanage Railway
SN	Southern (part of Govia Thameslink Railway)
SP	The Scottish Railway Preservation Society
SR	ScotRail
SW	South Western Railway
SY	Stagecoach Supertram
TL	Thameslink (part of Govia Thameslink Railway)
TP	TransPennine Express
TW	Transport for Wales
VA	Varamis Rail
VT	Vintage Trains
WC	West Coast Railway Company
WM	West Midlands Trains
XC	CrossCountry

6.5. ALLOCATION & LOCATION CODES

Allocation codes are used in this publication to denote the normal maintenance base ("depots") of each operational locomotive, multiple unit or coach. However, maintenance may be carried out at other locations and may also be carried out by mobile maintenance teams. Location codes are used to denote common storage locations whilst the full place name is used for other locations. The designation (S) denotes stored.

Code	Depot	Depot Operator
AD	Ashford (Kent)	Hitachi
AK	Ardwick (Manchester)	Siemens
AL	Aylesbury	Chiltern Railways
AN	Allerton (Liverpool)	Northern
BD	Birkenhead North	Stadler Rail Service UK
BF	Bedford Cauldwell Walk	Siemens
BG	Hull Botanic Gardens	Northern
BH	Barrow Hill (Chesterfield)	Barrow Hill Engine Shed Society
BI	Brighton Lovers Walk	Govia Thameslink Railway
BK	Bristol Barton Hill	Arriva TrainCare
BL	Shackerstone, Battlefield Line	*Storage location only*
BM	Bournemouth	South Western Railway
BN	Bounds Green (London)	Hitachi
BO	Bo'ness (West Lothian)	The Bo'ness & Kinneil Railway
BQ	Bury (Greater Manchester)	East Lancashire Railway Trust
BR	MoD Bicester	*Storage location only*
BU	Burton-on-Trent	Nemesis Rail
BY	Bletchley	West Midlands Trains
CB	Crewe Basford Hall	Freightliner Engineering
CE	Crewe International	DB Cargo (UK)
CF	Cardiff Canton	Transport for Wales
CH	Chester	CAF
CK	Corkerhill (Glasgow)	ScotRail
CL	Crewe LNWR Heritage	LNWR Heritage Company
CN	Castle Donington RFT	*Storage location only*
CO	Coquelles (France)	Eurotunnel
CP	Crewe Carriage Shed	Arriva TrainCare
CQ	Crewe Heritage Centre	Crewe Heritage Trust
CR	Crewe Gresty Bridge	Direct Rail Services
CS	Carnforth	West Coast Railway Company
CT	Cheriton (Folkestone)	Eurotunnel
CW	Colwick (Rectory Junction)	Boden Rail Engineering
CY	Crewe South Yard/Gresty Green	*Storage locations only*
CZ	Central Rivers (Barton-under-Needwood)	Bombardier Transportation
DC	Derby Chaddesden Sidings	*Storage location only*
DE	East Dereham (Norfolk)	Mid Norfolk Railway
DN	Doncaster Carr	Hitachi
DY	Derby Etches Park	East Midlands Railway
EC	Edinburgh Craigentinny	Hitachi
EH	Eastleigh	Arriva TrainCare
EM	East Ham (London)	c2c
EP	Ely Papworth Sidings	*Storage location only*
EX	Exeter	Great Western Railway
FA	Fawley (Hampshire)	*Storage location only*
GA	Gascoigne Wood Sidings (South Milford)	*Storage location only*
GCR	Great Central Railway	Great Central Railway
GW	Glasgow Shields Road	ScotRail
HA	Haymarket (Edinburgh)	ScotRail
HD	Holyhead	*Storage location only*
HE	Hornsey (London)	Govia Thameslink Railway

HJ	Hoo Junction (Kent)	Colas Rail
HL	Hellifield	*Storage location only*
HM	Healey Mills (Wakefield)	*Storage location only*
HN	Hamilton (Glasgow)	Assenta Rail
HO	Hope Cement Works	Breedon Hope Cement
HT	Heaton (Newcastle-upon-Tyne)	Northern
IL	Ilford (London)	Greater Anglia/Elizabeth Line
IS	Inverness	ScotRail
KK	Kirkdale (Liverpool)	Stadler Rail Service UK
KM	Carlisle Kingmoor	Direct Rail Services
KR	Kidderminster	Severn Valley Railway
KY	Knottingley	DB Cargo (UK)
LA	Laira (Plymouth)	Great Western Railway
LB	Loughborough Works	UK Rail Leasing
LD	Leeds Midland Road	Freightliner Engineering
LE	Landore (Swansea)	Chrysalis Rail
LM	Long Marston Rail Innovation Centre	Porterbrook Leasing
LR	Leicester	UK Rail Leasing
LT	Longport (Stoke-on-Trent)	ElectroMotive Diesel Services
LW	MoD Longtown (Cumbria)	*Storage location only*
LY	Le Landy (Paris)	SNCF
MA	Longsight (Manchester)	Alstom UK
MD	Merehead	Mendip Rail
ME	Mossend Yard (Glasgow)	*Storage location only*
MG	Margate One:One Collection	Locomotive Services
MH	Millerhill (Edinburgh)	*Storage location only*
ML	Motherwell	Direct Rail Services
MN	Machynlleth	Transport for Wales
NC	Norwich Crown Point	Greater Anglia
NG	New Cross Gate (London)	London Overground
NH	Newton Heath (Manchester)	Northern
NL	Neville Hill (Leeds)	Northern
NM	Nottingham Eastcroft	East Midlands Railway
NN	Northampton King's Heath	Siemens
NO	Weybourne (Norfolk)	North Norfolk Railway
NP	North Pole (London)	Hitachi
NT	Northam (Southampton)	Siemens
NU	Sheffield Nunnery	Stagecoach Supertram
NY	Grosmont (North Yorkshire)	North Yorkshire Moors Railway Enterprises
OC	Old Oak Common (London)	Elizabeth Line
PG	Peterborough	GB Railfreight
PM	St Philip's Marsh (Bristol)	Great Western Railway
PO	Polmadie (Glasgow)	Alstom UK
PZ	Penzance Long Rock	Great Western Railway
RD	Ruddington (Nottingham Heritage Railway)	125 Group
RG	Reading	Great Western Railway
RM	Ramsgate	Southeastern
RO	Rowsley (Derbyshire)	Peak Rail
RR	Doncaster Robert's Road	ElectroMotive Diesel Services
RS	Ruislip (London)	London Underground
RU	Rugby	Colas Rail

RY	Ryde (Isle of Wight)	South Western Railway
SA	Salisbury	South Western Railway
SC	Scunthorpe Steelworks	British Steel
SE	St Leonards (Hastings)	St Leonards Railway Engineering
SG	Slade Green (London)	Southeastern
SH	Southall (London)	West Coast Rly Co/Locomotive Services
SJ	Stourbridge Junction	Parry People Movers
SK	Swanwick West (Derbyshire)	Princess Royal Loco Trust/125 Group
SL	Stewarts Lane (London)	Govia Thameslink Railway/Belmond
SO	Soho (Birmingham)	West Midlands Trains
SP	Springs Branch (Wigan)	DB Cargo (UK)
SU	Selhurst (Croydon)	Govia Thameslink Railway
SW	Swanage	Swanage Railway
TB	Three Bridges (Crawley)	Siemens
TI	Temple Mills (London)	Eurostar International
TJ	Tavistock Junction Yard (Plymouth)	*Storage location only*
TN	Tonbridge	GB Railfreight
TM	Tyseley Locomotive Works	Vintage Trains
TO	Toton (Nottinghamshire)	DB Cargo (UK)
TS	Tyseley (Birmingham)	West Midlands Trains
TY	Tyne Yard (Newcastle)	*Storage location only*
WA	Warrington Walton Old Jn Sidings	*Storage location only*
WB	Wembley (London)	Alstom UK
WD	Wimbledon (London)	South Western Railway
WE	Willesden Brent sidings	*Storage location only*
WI	Widnes (Cheshire)	Alstom UK
WN	Willesden (London)	Alstom UK
WO	Wolsingham, Weardale Railway	RMS Locotec
WS	Worksop (Nottinghamshire)	Harry Needle Railroad Company
YA	Great Yarmouth	Eastern Rail Services
YK	National Railway Museum (York)	National Museum of Science & Industry
XW	Crofton (Wakefield)	Alstom (UK)
ZA	RTC Business Park (Derby)	Loram (UK)
ZB	Doncaster Works	Wabtec Rail
ZD	Derby Works	Alstom UK
ZG	Eastleigh Works	Arlington Fleet Services
ZI	Ilford Works	Alstom UK
ZK	Kilmarnock Works	Brodie Engineering
ZN	Wolverton Works	Gemini Rail Group

6.6. ABBREVIATIONS

The following general abbreviations are used in this book:

AC	Alternating Current (ie Overhead supply)	DC	Direct Current (ie Third Rail)
AFD	Air Force Department	DEMU	Diesel Electric Multiple Unit
BAA	British Airports Authority		
BR	British Railways	DERA	Defence Evaluation & Research Agency
BSI	Bergische Stahl Industrie		
C&W	Carriage & Wagon	DfT	Department for Transport

Dia	Diagram number	mph	Miles per hour
DMU	Diesel Multiple Unit	NPCCS	Non Passenger Carrying
DSDC	Defence Storage &		Coaching Stock
	Distribution Centre	PTE	Passenger Transport
DRS	Direct Rail Services		Executive
ETS	Electric Train Supply	RCH	Railway Clearing House
EMU	Electric Multiple Unit	RMT	Royal Mail Terminal
GWR	Great Western Railway	rpm	Revolutions per minute
FLT	Freightliner Terminal	RR	Rolls Royce
HB	Hunslet-Barclay	RSL	Rolling Stock Library
hp	Horsepower	SR	BR Southern Region and
HNRC	Harry Needle Railroad		Southern Railway
	Company	t	Tonnes
Hz	Hertz	T	Toilet
kN	Kilonewtons	TD	Toilet suitable for use by
km/h	Kilometres per hour		people with disabilities
kW	Kilowatts	TDM	Time Division Multiplex
lbf	Pounds force	TOPS	Total Operations
LT	London Transport		Processing System
LUL	London Underground Ltd	V	Volts
m	Metres	W	Wheelchair space
mm	Millimetres		

6.7 BUILDERS

Builders are shown in the class headings. The workshops of British Railways and the pre-nationalisation and pre-grouping companies were first transferred to a wholly owned subsidiary called British Rail Engineering Ltd (BREL). These workshops were later privatised, BREL then becoming BREL Ltd. Some of the works were then taken over by ABB, which was later merged with Daimler-Benz Transportation to become Adtranz. This was later taken over by Bombardier Transportation, which itself was taken over by Alstom in 2021: Alstom now operates the Derby Litchurch Lane works. Bombardier also built vehicles for the British market in Brugge, Belgium.

Other workshops were the subject of separate sales, Springburn, Glasgow and Wolverton becoming "Railcare" and Eastleigh becoming "Wessex Traincare". All three were sold to GEC-Alsthom (now Alstom) but Eastleigh closed in 2006, although the site is now used as a storage and refurbishment location, now operated by Arlington Fleet Services.

Part of Doncaster Works was sold to RFS Engineering, which became insolvent and was bought out and renamed RFS Industries. Doncaster Works now forms part of Wabtec Rail Group.

A number of companies still manufacture or assemble trains in Great Britain, with others planning to open new plants. Alstom builds trains at its Derby Works and Hitachi at Newton Aycliffe, County Durham. In 2018 CAF opened a new manufacturing and assembly plant at Llanwern, near Newport, and Siemens is constructing a new plant at Goole, which will initially manufacture trains for London Underground.

The builder details in the class headings show the owner at the time of vehicle construction followed by details of the works as follows:

Ashford	Ashford Works (now Ashford Rail Plant depot, not the same location as the Ashford Chart Leacon Works).
Birmingham	The former Metro-Cammell works at Saltley, Birmingham, later operated by Alstom.
Cowlairs	Cowlairs Works, Glasgow.
Derby	Derby Carriage Works (also known as Litchurch Lane).
Doncaster	Doncaster Works.
Eastleigh	Eastleigh Works
Swindon	Swindon Works.
Wolverton	Wolverton Works.
York	York Carriage Works.

Other builders are:

Alexander	Walter Alexander, Falkirk.
Alstom	Valencia, Spain (later sold to Vossloh and then Stadler) and Savigliano (Italy). Alstom now operates the former Bombardier works at Derby and has its own site in Widnes
Barclay	Andrew Barclay, Caledonia Works, Kilmarnock (now Brodies).
BRCW	Birmingham Railway Carriage & Wagon, Smethwick.
CAF	Construcciones y Auxiliar de Ferrocarriles (works in Newport, UK and Zaragoza, Beasain, Castejon and Irun in Spain).
Cravens	Cravens, Sheffield.
Gloucester	Gloucester Railway Carriage & Wagon, Gloucester.
Hitachi	Hitachi Rail Europe (Newton Aycliffe, UK, Kasado, Japan and Pistoia, Italy).
Hunslet-Barclay	Hunslet-Barclay, Caledonia Works, Kilmarnock (later Wabtec, now Brodie Engineering).
Hunslet TPL	Hunslet Transportation Projects, Leeds.
Lancing	SR, Lancing Works.
Leyland Bus	Leyland Bus, Workington.
Metro-Cammell	Metropolitan-Cammell, Saltley, Birmingham
Pressed Steel	Pressed Steel, Linwood.
Charles Roberts	Charles Roberts, Horbury Junction, Wakefield (later Bombardier).
SGP	Simmering-Graz-Pauker, Austria (now owned by Siemens).
Siemens	Siemens Transportation Systems (principal works is in Krefeld (Germany) with others in Vienna (Austria) and Prague (Czech Republic, now closed). A new plant is under construction in Goole, UK.
SRP	Specialist Rail Products Ltd (A subsidiary of RFS).
Stadler	Stadler Rail Group. Principal works building rolling stock for the UK market at Altenrhein, Bussnang and St Margrethen (Switzerland), Siedlce (Poland), Szolnok (Hungary) and Valencia, Spain (the former Alstom plant).
Vossloh	Vossloh Rail Vehicles, Valencia, Spain (sold to Stadler in 2015).